Art in a State of Siege

Art in a State of Siege

Joseph Leo Koerner

PRINCETON UNIVERSITY PRESS

Princeton & Oxford

Published by Princeton University Press, 41 William Street, Princeton, New Jersey 08540
In the United Kingdom: Princeton University Press, 99 Banbury Road, Oxford OX2 6JX

GPSR Authorized Representative: Easy Access System Europe - Mustamäe tee 50, 10621 Tallinn, Estonia, gpsr.requests@easproject.com

press.princeton.edu

Jacket image: Hieronymus Bosch, *The Garden of Earthly Delights* (detail), c. 1490–1500. Oil on oak panel, 205.5 × 384.9 cm. Museo Nacional del Prado, Madrid

Library of Congress Cataloging-in-Publication Data

Names: Koerner, Joseph Leo, author.
Title: Art in a state of siege / Joseph Leo Koerner.
Description: Princeton : Princeton University Press, [2025] |
    Includes bibliographical references and index.
Identifiers: LCCN 2024018746 (print) | LCCN 2024018747 (ebook) |
    ISBN 9780691267210 (hardcover) | ISBN 9780691267241 (ebook)
Subjects: LCSH: Artists—Psychology. | Crises (Philosophy) | Creation
    (Literary, artistic, etc.) | Bosch, Hieronymus, –1516—Criticism and
    interpretation. | Beckmann, Max, 1884–1950—Criticism and interpretation. |
    Kentridge, William, 1955- —Criticism and interpretation.
Classification: LCC N71 .K63 2025 (print) | LCC N71 (ebook) |
    DDC 701/.15—dc23/eng/20240702
LC record available at https://lccn.loc.gov/2024018746
LC ebook record available at https://lccn.loc.gov/2024018747

British Library Cataloging-in-Publication Data is available

Editorial: Michelle Komie and Annie Miller
Production Editorial: Terri O'Prey
Text Design: Heather Hansen
Jacket Design: Heather Hansen
Production: Steven Sears
Publicity: Jodi Price and Kathryn Stevens

This book is published as part of the E. H. Gombrich lecture series, cosponsored by the Warburg Institute and Princeton University Press. The lectures upon which this book is based were delivered in March 2016.

This book has been composed in Signifier with Söhne

Printed in the United States of America

10 9 8 7 6 5 4 3 2 1

For Ben, Sigi, Leo, and Lulu

Contents

Color plates follow pages 110 and 302.

Art in a State of Siege

5 Aug 23!

11 Aug 23

Reise - Erinnerungen

aus dem Gebiet der

Pueblos

(Fragmente zur Psychologie des primitiven Menschen)

10. April 923.

Kreuzlingen, 1923

We recognize the thing even if we cannot read it, the dog-eared draft of a title page (fig. 1).[1] Typed in *Sperrsatz*, with a space between letters, stands the title: "Travel Recollections from the Region of the Pueblos." A more ambitious subtitle follows, in parentheses: "Fragments toward the Psychology of Primitive Man." Re-reading these typed words, their author clarifies, "the Pueblo *Indians of North America*." Then he changes "primitive man" to "art practices of the primitive," and tries out new formulations: "The survival of primitive humanity in the culture of the Pueblo Indians," with an alternative, the "civilization" of the Pueblo Indians, and below those, "Documents from the culture of primitive man, towards the problem of symbolic relations." "Symbolic relations" adds a new idea, as does a next try, scribbled small: "Evolution and decline of thought-space."

Between "travel recollections" and whatever these are meant by their author now to represent there erupts that huge, sick-making uncertainty with which all writers will be familiar. What is this activity going to be about? When I begin to write, I need some inkling of where I am headed, but that goal comes by way of writing. Beginning in the dark, writing often ends up somewhere else, its goal missed, changed, or forgotten, hence the headache of a proper title. The author of this one tests out the capacious idea that his recollections will be about thought itself, about what he calls "thought-space," whatever that means. His recollections will even be about the "creation" and "destruction" of thought-space, about how thought proceeds thanks to protective walls that thought itself constructs, if only for a moment. Like cities, or like "civilizations" that flourish thanks to fortressed cities (Latin *civitates*), the walls will eventually fail, although not yet. Our author seems to enjoy one of those expansive instants in the writing process when every-

FIG. 1. Aby Warburg, draft title page for *Images from the Region of the Pueblo Indians of North America* (1923). The Warburg Institute, London

thing is, as the line above puts it, "symbolically" related to everything else; when, late at night, perhaps, as the words "opium treatment" written above the typed title affirm, buoyed by psycho-pharmaceuticals, the writer imagines his text to be the answer to everything with a capital "E". The mood suddenly passes. The walls of thought-space are breached, chaos rushes in, and the author pushes his writing away in disgust. "Dusty material," he scribbles later, "drafts that ought never to be printed." "Don't even look at this mess!" he wants to say, even as he has added at the upper part of the sheet, just where a reader will ordinarily begin, a panic cry, "Help!"

Dated (upper left) August 8, 1923, towards the end of the seven-month period indicated by dates found elsewhere in the manuscripts to which the title page belongs, this cry to everyone and to no one resounds from *writing in a state of siege*. The opposite of thought-space, symbolic relations, and survival, it is a primal scream of art historical scholarship. The uncanny thing about this draft title page is that many in my profession have been there both in a general sense, as writers grappling with their material, and in a concrete sense, as persons seated in the very workspace where these panicked thoughts originally took place. For the author of all these typed and handwritten sentences was Aby Warburg, whose great library and archives, smuggled from Germany to England in 1933, form the core of the institute in London that bears its creator's name.

Like countless scholars before me, I did some of my most productive work in that library. And like other users, I didn't only read books and articles gathered there. In the physical arrangements and adjacencies of its material—periodicals in the basement, up through books dealing with "Image" (First Floor), "Word" (Second Floor), "Orientation" (Third Floor), up to "Action" (Fourth), the thought-space of the Warburg Library *used me*, inscribing my writing into a struggle begun a century ago. For as any user of the library will attest, it is by wandering those open stacks, sometimes with a book targeted for retrieval, sometimes just browsing books by subject, that the most surprising thoughts flash suddenly up. Allow me therefore to return to the founder's desk and pick up the sheet of paper he left behind.

At the bottom of the page, Warburg noted that "the delivered lecture is on lined paper and is in a large gray envelope." This lecture was presented to prove its author was sane. Warburg gave his talk on April 21, 1923, before an audience of inmates, doctors, and guests at the sanatorium Bellevue, in Kreuzlingen, Switzerland. The town is named right on the page. Warburg had been confined there since 1921. Prior to that he had languished for three years in psychiatric clinics in Lienau, near his native Hamburg, and Jena. For late in 1918, in the days just following Germany's defeat in World War I, Warburg, a fervent German nationalist and a Jew, became convinced that he and his family would be arrested by nameless persecutors and taken to secret prisons to be tortured and murdered, which fate he sought to avoid by actually trying to shoot his family before they fell into enemy hands.

Sometimes Warburg took these enemies to be Bolsheviks bent on murdering capitalists and intellectuals. Sometimes he believed his foes to be preternatural furies conjured by his scholarship and avenging his own lapse from Judaism. Raised in a worldly but Orthodox home, Warburg matriculated in 1886 at the University of Bonn in the then-gentile (and often anti-Semitic) field of the history of art. This choice of subject provoked opposition from his religiously observant parents because they expected a career in the practical professions, and perhaps because attachment to the visual arts ran counter to the Jewish law against images.[2] Within days of arriving in Bonn, Warburg defied his family's wish that he remain kosher: "Since I do not arrange my courses of study according to the quality of ritual restaurants but according to the quality of my teachers," he wrote his father Moritz, "I do not eat ritually."[3] And in 1892, against Moritz's passionate objections, he married a Christian art student, Mary Hertz, and he refused to raise his children as Jews or circumcise his sons. Balking at compromise, he explained that Jewish intellectual culture was not superior to German culture. He did not attend his father's funeral and refused to say Kaddish for him. He referred to himself as a person under a ban, owing to his mixed marriage and non-Jewish children. And when he took his children to his mother's house on Passover, he substituted for the Hebrew Seder songs German nursery rhymes.[4]

Warburg's repudiation of his religion haunted him during his collapse. In the days after Germany's surrender, he pulled a friend into a corner and whispered that once he had declared to a gentile professor, "At the bottom of my soul I am a Christian."[5] After swearing his friend to secrecy about his confession, Warburg screamed the sentence again through the open windows. He wanted the neighbors to hear it. Sometimes in his madness, Warburg believed his pursuers to be Germany's anti-Semites who were now plotting to kill influential Jews. Even as his doctors worked to cure Warburg of these delusions, his younger brother Max Moritz, who had assumed leadership of the great merchant bank M. M. Warburg & Co., was actually targeted for assassination by right-wing terrorists. The policeman guarding him round the clock turned out to be a Nazi spy.[6] On June 24, 1922, these same conspirators murdered Walter Rathenau, Germany's first and last Jewish foreign minister and the Warburgs' close associate.

The Bellevue records of his medical history register Warburg's diagnosis as "Schizophrenia," later put into parentheses and followed by a penciled note, based on an alternative opinion of Emil Kraepelin: "manic-depressive mixed condition."[7] He had been violent already at his arrival (he believed he had been brought to prison), and remained dangerous to the end: he attacked his caregivers with "colossal strength" (so the case history records), once almost strangling a nurse.[8] Isolated for his own and others' safety in the clinic's closed wing, he came under the care of Bellevue's distinguished director, Ludwig Binswanger. In 1906 Binswanger had been the first to introduce Freudian psychoanalysis into a clinical setting. Sigmund Freud himself took an interest in Warburg's illness. In a letter of 1921 to Binswanger, Freud enquired about the patient's prognosis, asking whether he would ever work again—he noted that he knew Warburg both because of his prominent family and through "his penetrating work."[9] Binswanger replied that in his view no "resumption of scholarly activities will be possible."

Freud had just published a seminal account of nervous breakdown. Written after Austria and Germany's defeat in World War I, *Beyond the Pleasure Principle* (1920) responded in part to an epidemic of "shellshock" among soldiers returning from battle. By December 1914, just four months into the war, almost 10 percent of officers and 4 percent of enlisted men in the British Expeditionary Force in Europe had to be sent home because of "nervous and mental shock."[10] Sufferers displayed maladies resembling the effects of damage to the brain, such as debilitating tremors, confusion, and impaired vision, yet no physical injuries could be found. Some medical professionals theorized that the shock caused by machine-gun fire, grenades, and heavy artillery harmed the nervous system invisibly at the cellular or molecular level. Others theorized that sheer cowardice caused these symptoms. "The World War," wrote Franz Kafka in 1916 in an attempt to establish a *Nervenklinik* in Prague, "is a war of nerves, more so than any previous war."[11]

Somatic symptoms with no apparent physical cause intrigued Freud. These obtained in hysteria, the study of which stood at the foundation of psychoanalysis. But symptoms of shellshock contradicted what Freud had taken to be the mind's governing principle of procuring pleasure while avoiding pain. Rather than forgetting distressful experiences, victims compulsively repeated their pain. In their dreams, maladies, and behavior, they experienced shock as perpetually real and new. Theirs were wounds suffered "on the organ of the mind" and produced by a "breach in the shield against stimuli."[12] "Mechanical violence," the shock arising subjectively during mechanized warfare's "storm of steel" (to use Ernst Jünger's metaphor coined in 1920), was so sudden and extreme that no defense sufficed save repetition. The "primitive" defense of last resort, repetition mastered violent stimulus retrospectively, by developing the anxiety whose omission caused the trauma.[13]

Trauma made siege permanent. This conclusion occasioned some of the strangest pages in all of Freud's writings. Forced to venture "beyond the pleasure principle" (in other words, outside the assumption that living creatures seek to live painlessly) he postulated a new, antithetical set of drives: the death instincts, biological urges aimed at bringing the living being back to the inorganic state. In a passage he himself admitted was "far-fetched," Freud reduced organic life to "this little fragment of living substances [...] suspended in the middle of an external world charged with the most powerful energies."[14] Such an organism would be instantly killed "were it not provided with a protective shield against stimuli." Life acquires its first defense by its boundary dying. Living matter becomes a dead barrier resistant to bombarding stimuli: "By its death, the outer layer has saved all the deeper ones from a similar fate—unless [...] stimuli reach it which are so strong that they break through the protective shield." Trauma arises when the psyche's protective and receptive walls fail to prevent a hostile intrusion. Freud's earliest model of the human mind, sketched out in 1897, already had the character of a besieged fortress. Inspired—perhaps—by a visit to Nuremberg, where picturesque medieval walls remained intact, he drew a diagram of the "architecture of hysteria" with triangles, like spiky towers, representing neurotic symptoms, and dangerous memories kept out of mind by "psychic outworks" (*Vorbauten*) and "defensive structures" (*Schutzbauten*).[15] Drawn from siegecraft, these terms would have been familiar to anyone living (as Freud did) near Vienna's Ringstrasse, that wide boulevard built on the footprint of the city's ancient walls. On this model, the mind had to defend itself against stimuli both from the outside world and from painful (usually childhood) memories that had penetrated the weak defenses of the developing mind, there to remain unprocessed and restless.

At the time of his psychic siege, Aby Warburg had not yet achieved his legendary status as inventor of modern art history's dominant procedure, the method called "iconology." Iconology decodes images for their messages, which may then themselves be decoded for the cultural attitudes they communicate. The artwork becomes a meaningful symptom of its time. Part I of this book explores an object that has invited and eluded Warburg's influential approach. Although iconology had not been established by 1923, Warburg's work on the afterlife of pagan antiquity in the Christian Renaissance had already paved the way towards a new history of art and earned him an international reputation.

At Binswanger's clinic, Warburg's brilliance and wealth were nothing exceptional. Beautifully situated on Lake Constance and relatively humane, Bellevue was the asylum of choice for Europe's disturbed elite, a place, in the words of the novelist Joseph Roth, where "spoiled wealthy madmen underwent careful and cautious treatment, and the attendants were as nurturing as midwives."[16] Inmates included the dancer Nijinsky, the Expressionist artist Ernst Ludwig Kirchner (who suffered a nervous breakdown in World War I), and the feminist Bertha Pappenheim (famous as Freud's first patient, "Anna O."). Warburg delivered his 1923 lecture before an audience remarkably fit to receive it.

Even after the lecture had secured his release, Warburg referred to Bellevue as his "inferno" and termed himself *revenant*—a ghost back from the grave.[17] In April 1923, Fritz Saxl, his academic assistant, wrote that with Warburg's release the "different, more difficult" challenge begins: "permanently living together with him."[18] Clinical records indicate that the patient left Kreuzlingen still haunted by delusions and prone to fits of rage. During his confinement he had been certain that his family was secretly jailed in the clinic awaiting slaughter, that the cries in the hallway were his wife's under torture, that the meat served at supper was his children's flesh, and that Binswanger had been their butcher. Again, delusions mingle with fact and foresight. While at Bellevue, Aby had in fact been joined by his son Max Adolph, whose nervous breakdown (triggered by his father's) was treated by confinement and tepid baths. During these "calming" measures, Max Adolph heard his father's animal screams resounding through the clinic.[19] And with hindsight Aby's fantasies of arrest, transport, imprisonment, torture, and extermination turned out to be terrifyingly prophetic. Members of the Warburg family who did not manage to flee Germany, or who emigrated to Holland, perished in Nazi camps.

Warburg's therapy consisted of bed rest, opium, and analysis. But his was less a talking cure than a working one. It was the labor, performed by writing the 1923 lecture itself, of changing fear into thought. With Saxl's help, Warburg convinced his doctors to pledge his release if he could successfully compose and deliver a scholarly talk on a subject of his choosing. Rather than select an impersonal theme to foster detachment, he chose a topic eerily close to his obsessions: the serpent, primal wellspring of fear, whose threat is inborn in the mind, and whose cult Warburg had encountered among the Pueblo peoples, during an American journey that had helped at once to found and up-end his thought. From a practical perspective, the choice was shrewd, and not only because of the diversion that a slide lecture about travel would offer its captive audience. Reporting to Freud, Binswanger had despaired that, while his logic and memory remained sound, Warburg was distracted by fears and had lost the power "to fix on scholarly themes." By choosing terror as his topic, by writing on his distraction from writing itself, Warburg achieved that attention required for scholarly prose.

And yet Warburg's choice accomplished more than simply productive mania. By his account, the Hopi peoples had themselves turned objects of terror into means of control. Through sympathetic magic, they modeled how fear could indeed be transmuted into thought. Specifically, the Hopi, in their rain dances, carried the poison serpent—the rattlesnake—in their mouths. They did this because, in their world view as Warburg imagined it, the snake *was* the lightning that produced storms. Subduing the snake meant mastering rain. The serpent performed the work of culture, which consisted principally in referring amorphous fears to specific causes—whether divine or natural. At once poison and medicine, the serpent exemplified how fear occasioned images and images occasioned thought, and how thought, in its turn, enabled the composure that Warburg and his doctors understood as mental health.

The lecture fascinates because of how Warburg identifies with his theme. He could explain irrational images because he himself had lost his reason. Conversely, these irrational images, explained, could save Warburg, since they were themselves mechanisms of self-control. He makes this doubling explicit by asking, using the medical label applied to him, whether the Pueblo Indians are "schizoid," and what it means to be in a "mixed condition" between fantasy and reason. To the original audience in the sanatorium, many of whom were steeped in contemporary interest in the so-called "primitive" or "savage" mind, the likeness between the snake dance and Warburg's lecture about it must have seemed like sympathetic magic in action. By 1923, many artists, including (as we will see) German Expressionists such as Kirchner, Erich Heckel, and Max Beckmann, had appropriated the practices of what they took to be "tribal" art. In this understanding, such art included religious images made by pre-Reformation "Germanic" artists like Matthias Grünewald and Hieronymus Bosch. Warburg, however, was the first *historian* of art to give this impulse scholarly form.

Where the Hopi bit the serpent without themselves being bitten, Warburg spoke his terror without himself sounding afraid. How did Warburg pass his test, when just a few months before he had ended dinner with a visiting colleague by remarking that the meat they had eaten was human? Certainly, the lecture makes sense. By the period's standards a coherent piece of scholarly prose, it evidenced its author's sanity. And where Warburg names his malady ("schizoid"), he distances it as a symptom of civilization's discontents. Yet his argument also depends on a kind of circularity usually avoided in scholarship, because compromising to its objectivity. The facts he reports are also images of his own delusion; scholarly writing resembles the rituals it portrays. Instead of thwarting Warburg's release, though, this mixed condition deflected negative judgment on his condition as such. A decade after declaring his patient "furloughed to normalcy," and five years after Warburg's fatal heart attack in 1929, Binswanger still pondered the affinity, observed in his patient, between insanity and scholarship. In a letter to Max Warburg, he mused that a psychiatrist ought to write about Aby's sickness, for "in your brother's case very interesting passages can be indicated between his scholarly views and specific delusions."[20]

Binswanger later theorized the obscure passage connecting writer to writing. Reflecting on Henrik Ibsen's *The Master Builder*, in which an architect falls from a tower he designed, Binswanger argued that creativity happens when the mind departs from its ordinary paths. Writers "realize themselves" in their works through an extravagance similar to madness. They leap an abyss between their flesh-and-blood "empirical self" and an "ontological self," the persona constructed by writing.[21] Writing's cause may be a real individual's thoughts and feelings, but writing speaks another voice. Warburg felt the strong impulse of an extravagant subjectivity. In a note jotted down the week before his death, he wrote, "Sometimes it seems to me that, as a psycho-historian, I attempt to derive the schizophrenia of the West from its visual culture as if in an autobiographical reflex: on one hand the ecstatic Nymph, on the other the mourning river-god; manic on the one hand, depressive on the other."[22]

Warburg published no memoirs and revealed his personhood in the guise of scholarship. But he did live an exceptional life, one in which war, ethnicity, nation, colonialism, wealth, reason, and unreason constitute a fable about European identity. Musing on the image he would project to posterity, Warburg boasted, "I'm just cut out for a beautiful story."[23] In his Kreuzlingen lecture, he recounted his youthful westward journey as a tale of civilization told in reverse.[24] Each step forward in his travels among the Pueblo peoples of Arizona and New Mexico seemed to his eyes one step backwards from culture to nature, and from art through masked ritual to blood sacrifice. The tale begins in the village of Acoma in the east, where, in the decoration of pottery and architecture, Warburg discovers the image of the serpent, symbol of lightning and harbinger of life-giving rain. Further west, he visits San Ildefonso and witnesses an antelope dance in which the animal imagery encountered in ornament appears performed in the identification of dancer and mask. At his journey's end, he arrives at Oraibi, in the far west, where he personally observes the seasonal Katsina festivities. In these elaborate rites performed (he believed) to ensure a successful corn crop, Warburg discerns a yet more elemental cultural form: if at San Ildefonso the dancers merge with their masks, at Oraibi they seek magically to influence nature itself.

Warburg did not travel the distance spanned by his lecture. Leaving Oraibi after the dances, he missed the serpent ritual itself and had to rely on photographs—some by the Mennonite missionary, Henry R. Voth, who accompanied

Warburg part-way on his journey. In this rite where dancers manipulate live animals, Warburg detected a crucial turning point to culture: after their ritual use the serpents are set free. This proved (to him) that blood sacrifice has been sublimated into symbolism, and that animalistic "fetishism" was on the way "to the pure religion of redemption."[25] At this point Warburg returns to Europe in a loop captured in the lecture's motto: "It is an old story: Athens and Oraibi, all cousins."[26] Greek and Jewish serpent cults had originally been sacrificial. Like the more westerly Puebloans, the Christian West transitioned through the snake from sacrifice to symbolism. To bring his point home to his audience, Warburg pointed to an artwork nearby. Ceiling frescoes in Kreuzlingen's parish church featured a scene of *Moses with the Brazen Serpent*, proving that snake symbolism survived just around the corner.

For Warburg this movement is never final, but must be constantly defended. When he visited them, the cultural achievements of the Pueblo peoples were threatened by the encroaching barbarism of modern America, which killed the serpent and imprisons lightning in wire: "It now faces extermination," writes Warburg of the rattlesnake, but also hinting at the genocidal efforts of settler colonialism. Warburg darkly concludes, "Telegram and telephone destroy the cosmos. Mythical and symbolic thinking strive to form spiritual bonds between humanity and the surrounding world, shaping distance into the space required for devotion and reflection: the distance undone by the instantaneous electric connection."[27] The snake dance that he yearned to witness drew hordes of tourists with modern snapshot cameras to northern New Mexico. Warburg purchased a simple Buckeye camera in Santa Fe and photographed extensively during his travels, and intrusively. Although he obtained permission from leaders of the indigenous community to photograph some of the rites he attended, he admitted to sometimes violating his subjects' cultural code, a practice he blithely termed "photography with obstacles."[28] During a break in their dance he grabbed the arm of one of the Katsina and had his picture taken with the unmasked man, knowing full well that "whoever sees a dancer without his mask, will die."[29]

Warburg drew a distinction between "grasping" (*greifen*) as primitive reflex akin to shock and grasping by means of a concept (*Begriff*). And there he was, the putative *Begriffsmensch*, unable to grasp the violence of his incursion. By the 1920s, after a long and divisive struggle, Hopi villages succeeded in prohibiting cameras at their ceremonies.[30] In the decades between Warburg's travels and his lecture, the influx of tourists divided Hopi communities. Some argued that the snake dance projected to outsiders an image of cultural fortitude. Others vehemently resisted the incursion into their way of life, recognizing it as a threat to their survival—or their survivance, to use Gerald Vizenor's term.[31] When Warburg visited their communities, the Hopi stood threatened externally by land seizure, missionaries, tourism, and the forced separation of children from their families, and internally by political division. Their state of siege reached back four centuries and continues today.

Warburg never intended the lecture for publication. In a letter attached to the original typescript, he instructed Saxl not to show the piece to anyone without his approval: "This lecture is so formless, and rests on such poor philological foundations, that its only value (and a questionable one it is) lies in bringing together some documents towards a history of symbolic behavior. [...] This gruesome twitching of a decapitated frog should absolutely not find its way to print."[32] Warburg's published work got its energy from obscure documents and artifacts of a specific culture, rather than from speculation about culture in general—"God is in the details," was his scholarly motto. His writing obeyed the rules of academic prose, even if it intimated, in hermetic turns of phrase, a time bomb underneath. By these standards, the serpent lecture lacked "philological foundations." Warburg admits ignorance of the Hopi language and culture. In a page attached to a revised typescript, he scorns Binswanger's praise of the lecture's "findings." The images and words "are the confessions of an incurable schizoid, deposited in the archives of mental healers."[33] A few months earlier Warburg had spotted Hans Prinzhorn's picture-book *Art of the Mentally Ill* in Binswanger's office and flew into a rage.[34] He ranted that the book had been placed there to torment him and was about him. His madness involved the mutually reinforcing fantasies that the world conspired against him and did so by treating him as a pathological case. Warburg meant to turn the tables on his observers. By appearing to define his own "schizoid" condition, he performed, in the lecture that he would come to call "the beginning of [his] Renaissance," a rite of passage from object to subject.[35] To complete this ritual, he himself defined its script retrospectively as case material.

Warburg encountered European art as an outsider, as a non-observant, cosmopolitan Jew exposing the ruptures in Christian religious art, as when in Ghirlandaio's *Birth of John the Baptist* a beautiful woman in a windblown, diaphanous garb rushes into a static scene of Christian domestic life, like a character from a different movie (fig. 2).[36] Warburg called the rushing maiden Nympha and obsessed about her all his life.[37] "I lost my reason," he remembers of first glimpsing her in Florence's Santa Maria Novella. The "embodiment of movement," she was "unpleasant to her lover." "Who is she?" her image asks, and "Where does she come from?"[38] Warburg traced her lineage back to the frenzied serpent-bearing attendants of Dionysus. Mobile and erotic, Nympha breached more than merely bourgeois decorum and

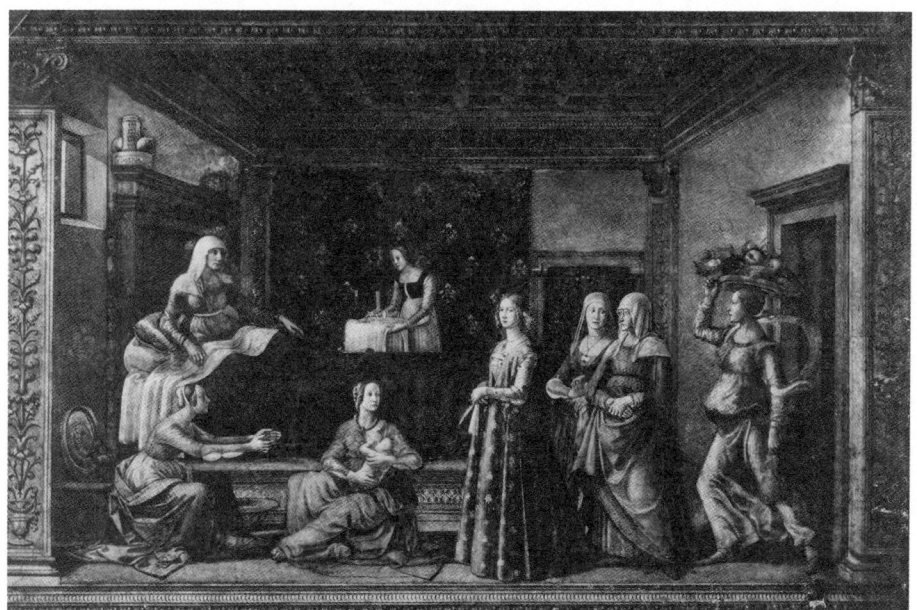

FIG. 2. Domenico Ghirlandaio, *The Birth of John the Baptist*, c. 1490, fresco, Santa Maria Novella, Tornabuoni Chapel, Florence. Photo c. 1907, detail from Panel 46 of Aby Warburg's *Mnemosyne Atlas*, last version of October 1929, Warburg Library, Hamburg

the consistency of Ghirlandaio's style. Her presence a clash of cultures, pagan versus Christian, she violated the harmony and balance believed, in Warburg's day, to be constitutive of art. He made his trip to America partly out of "an honest disgust of aestheticizing art history."[39] Against an inherited aesthetics of the closed and stable whole, Warburg located art's deeper powers in restless contradiction. Images like Nympha besieged the viewer, but fictively, giving space to thought: "You live yet you do me no harm."[40]

In his serpent lecture, Warburg imagined an insider's perspective on the history of art. In the "contaminated" and "schizoid" state of the Puebloans, Warburg thought he recognized his own identity. His motto (coined in Italian) expresses this openly: "Born in Hamburg, Hebrew by blood, in soul a Florentine."[41] In a map he sketched of his personal geography, he put one point at Oraibi, adding another star to his imaginary constellation. His travel documents introduce him as a "German scientist" and "man of means."[42] And in a note penned at Bellevue he remembers wanting to "escape to the natural object and to science."[43] Arriving in New York to attend the 1895 society wedding of his brother Paul, he sickened of the "emptiness of civilization." Inspired by ethnographers at the Smithsonian he decided to visit the Puebloans of the Southwest. Other notes from Bellevue make his motives less detached: redress for his army failure; a need to be manly after abandoning his wife and children to a cholera epidemic; a "will to the Romantic." And his goal evoked mixed memories. When he was seven, his mother fell gravely ill. Oppressed by the Hebrew prayers at her sickbed, and disgusted by "an inferior Jewish-Austrian student, who was supposed to be a tutor," he snuck off to eat pork sausages and "consume" tales about American Indians, delectable for their "romantic cruelty."[44]

Warburg did not cross the Pueblo people's path perpendicularly, as us against them, for he did not belong to the missionizing Catholics, Mormons, and Mennonites who accompanied him. When he observes how the Puebloans "are not easily led inside the church," his irony recalls that in Germany he too was not easily thus led. Refusing once to attend a church wedding, he remarked, "It's better that people wonder why we're not there than why we're there."[45] He may have been born in Hamburg and felt Florentine in his soul, but non-Jewish Europeans would deem him Hebrew no matter what. During World War I, in the years leading to his madness, Warburg began to gather and collate all information about the war that came his way. From newspapers, books, letters, and postcards, he endeavored to establish, through the weapons of scholarship, who started the great conflict. Warburg called this labor *Verzettelung*, playing on the German word *Zettel* ("note card") and *verzetteln* ("to fritter away"). Enlisting his wife and children in this manic labor, he assembled some twenty-five thousand excerpts of wartime news, filling his library with clippings and notes. With the approach of Germany's defeat, he came to believe that he was himself the war's hidden cause. He fancied his scholarship on Nympha had reawakened the ancient pagan demons, who now plunged Europe into chaos. This is the historian's ultimate madness: to be the cause, rather than the diagnostician, of history. Even the material residue of Warburg's research came to resemble the thing it purported to investigate. A family friend reported that Warburg's library looked like a "battlefield" with Aby as the grim commander.[46] When the war ended in November 1918, watching the demons swarm around him, Warburg turned (in his mind) into a werewolf and tried to murder his family with a pistol—hence his five-year confinement.

It would be wrong to attribute Warburg's breakdown to scholarship too vigorously pursued. Whilst finding symbolic relations among the bits of wartime news engendered a paranoid logic, it was also this labor that cured him. In Kreuzlingen, he began to arrange photographs in suggestive groups. These he pinned to big panels, each almost two meters wide (fig. 3).[47] From such montages the serpent lecture was born. Returned to Hamburg, he used large bulletin boards to create a constellation of image-constellations—he made some seventy-seven of them—which he would number, photograph, and file away to be combined with other

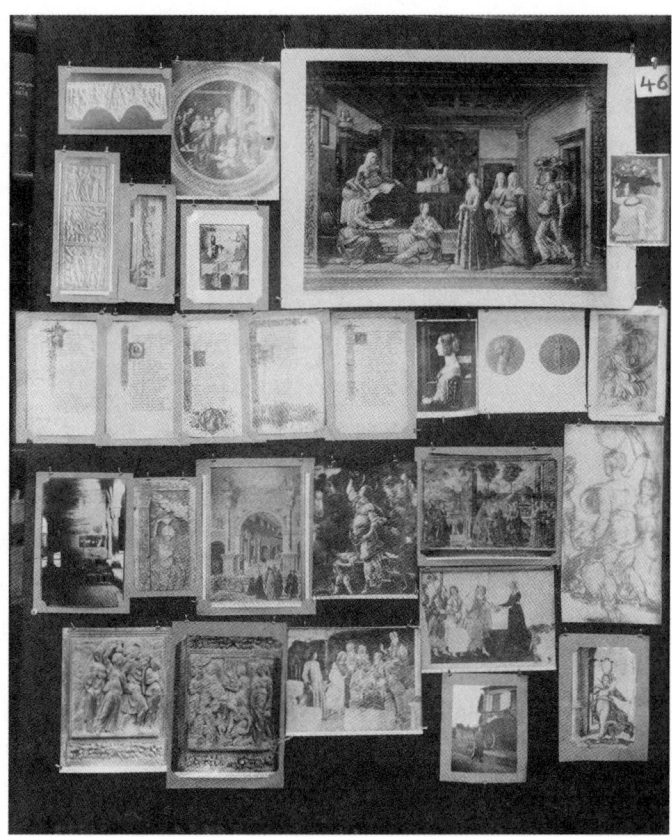

FIG. 3. Panel 46 of Aby Warburg's *Mnemosyne Atlas*, last version of October 1929, Warburg Library, Hamburg

image-constellations. Symbolic relations among images remain open-ended, like the collages of Surrealist and Dada artists of this period, or like Walter Benjamin's "thought-images" (*Denkbilder*) which flash forth "in a moment of danger." Warburg intended his arrangements to be published in a vast picture-book of culture titled *Mnemosyne*, Greek for "memory." He had other titles, too, such as "On the Surviving Patterning-Power of Antique Expressive Values in the European Spiritual Economy," "Image-Atlas towards the Critique of Unreason," and "Ghost-Stories for True Grown-Ups." One draft proposed this gargantuan heading:

> Unity of Imaginative Finding of Causes (Orientation) Traced on (through) the between (through) (from) iconic and (to) sign-like (cyclically) back-and-forth commuting polar (symbolic form of the) function of antiquizing expressions in the form-world of the European Renaissance ... 2 September 1928, Heilwigstrasse 116, on the edge of the bed at 4:45 a.m. ... imagistically pregnant descriptive form and symbolic, futuristic determination/relation ... Where is Bing? Want to speak to Einstein.

This is scholarship in panic mode, swelling until it collapses. Warburg called himself "a seismograph" of the European soul. His writing registers a sort of earthquake, a modern breaking point where, as Ludwig Wittgenstein put it in his *Tractatus* of 1921, speech must give way to silence. Warburg's image-atlas represents scholarship freed from writing. It imagines art history's holy grail of arguments based solely on the evidence of images.

After Warburg's death, Saxl planned to publish the atlas, but got bogged down and in 1936 enlisted the young Ernst Gombrich to finish the work. Of a different temperament and generation from Warburg, Gombrich had witnessed art history under Hitler descend into an irrational and racialist discipline. He declared the project to be incompletable and filed the material away. In 1982, on a bench in the gardens of Clare College, while finishing the English Tripos at Cambridge, I devoured Gombrich's description of *Mnemosyne*. It seemed to me—the thought is now commonplace—that Warburg's collages were analogous in scope, method, and incompletion to Benjamin's *Arcades Project*, which had just appeared in its first German edition. That summer J. B. Trapp allowed me to shuffle through Warburg's old photos, index cards, and draft manuscript notes with the intention of writing a doctoral dissertation comparing Warburg to Benjamin. That is when I first came upon the title page discussed above. But writing on the inability to write seemed dodgy, so I changed fields and moved to Berkeley, there to dissertate on German Renaissance art. Three years into the Ph.D. I returned to the Warburg Institute as reader, not as a diagnostician, and I have used the library many times since. In 2016 I had the honor of delivering the Gombrich Lectures at the Warburg. Those talks form the basis of the present book.

It chanced that I finished *Art in a State of Siege* in April 2023, exactly one century after Warburg's Kreuzlingen talk. In the course of my work other relevant centennials came and went: the fifth centenary of Bosch's death, also the fifth of the Reformation, and the first centenary of World War I. Dates organize this book, not in chronological order, but to capture the synchronicities, ruptures, flashbacks, and predictions that—I hope—tell the story of volatile objects that managed to endure. The dates of sieges punctuate history jaggedly. The attack by an enemy acting on their initiative, they violently interrupt the smooth unfolding of ordinary collective life, often changing it forever. The siege and destruction of Jerusalem in 70 CE (3830 by the Hebrew calendar) remains a singular wound in Jewish memory, but scores of other sieges scatter the city's history, some when the walls stood strong, others when they fell, and death and ruin followed. When civilizations have their origin and center in cities, which require walls to protect them and allow them to endure (in Chinese the words for city and wall are the same), then the dates of incursions resisted or suffered will organize time into irregular singularities: Constantinople in 1204 and 1453, Vienna in 1529 and 1683, Magdeburg in 1631, Turin in 1640 (a rare "triple siege" when one army surrounded another, which surrounded a third that was laying siege to the city). Vienna, originally (when it was Vindobona) the eastern outpost of the Roman Empire against the "barbarian" invasions, confirmed its identity as Europe's fortress city, Christian bulwark against the Moslem infidel, in twice withstanding the Ottoman armies, then becoming, after 1683, the bastion of Catholic rule against Protestantism, revolution, and industrialization. When Emperor Franz Joseph finally removed the medieval walls and glacis of his imperial capital and allowed them to be turned into wide modern boulevard, he meant the new Ring Street (built with military arsenals at regular turns of its path) still to function as barrier against rebellious workers from the suburbs. And when Hitler, once a resident in the city and steeped in its symbolism, marched unopposed into Vienna in March 1938, he knew to parade around the Ring Street before entering the city center in triumph.

Sieges mark history suddenly and irreversibly, and as they unfold, they suspend the ordinary pace of time. Sieges are states of temporal exception, with delay as the essential strategy of the besieged.[48] Beginning suddenly, siege intensifies the days, weeks, and sometimes years of its duration, dependent as endurance is on the strength of walls, the availability of food and water, the unity of the besieged, and the might, exposure, and determination of the besiegers. With these and countless other variables in play, time no longer flows smoothly, breaking under the threat of approaching catastrophe as the walls give way, wells dry up, storehouses empty, and epidemics rage. During the ten-month siege of Sancerre, when in 1572–73 the Huguenot populace held out—unsuccessfully—against the Catholic armies of King Charles IX, the besieged swiftly consumed all stockpiled food and edible livestock, then turned to the horses, cats, dogs, rats, moles, and mice for sustenance. "Necessity, the mistress of the arts" led people to find nourishment in scraped, washed, soaked, and boiled animal skins, and when these leathers had all been eaten, "the more subtle and ingenious" among the citizenry turned to vellum, "and not only blank parchment, but also letters, legal titles, printed books and manuscript, not hesitating to eat the most ancient of them, some as old as 160 years."[49]

A Protestant minister and New World traveler, Jean de Léry endured thirst and starvation at sea and reported cannibalism among the Tupinamba. He also survived the siege of Sancerre to write a book about it. His *Memorable History of the Town of Sancerre* details how exactly to turn libraries into food: "one fricasseed" the soaked and boiled parchment "like tripe, or cooked them with herbs and spice in the manner of a hochepot," adding: "I could still see the printed or written letters, and you could read what was written on the pieces that were flattened out and ready to eat."[50] Even horses' hooves could be made palatable, and bread could be baked of straw and slate. Some looked elsewhere for nourishment. A couple was discovered to have eaten the brain, liver, and viscera of their three-year-old daughter, who (they claimed) had died of hunger. When they were caught, "the tongue, as thick as a finger cooked, was ready to eat. Two thighs, legs, and feet stood in a cauldron with vinegar, spices, and salt, to be cooked and placed on the fire."[51] The culprits were executed to set an example; otherwise cannibalism might have spread, reducing Sancerre to an even more terrible state.

During siege life becomes bare survival, and not only for the besieged. Besiegers risk counter-siege, poor morale, and disruptions to their supply chain. Bertolt Brecht wrote *Mother Courage* in exile in 1939, in response to Hitler's invasion of Poland. Set during the Thirty Years' War, the play follows the titular heroine's journeys through the Polish countryside in the baggage train of the Swedish army. In a quarrel with a cook, to whom she wants to sell a sorry capon, Mother Courage explains that prices have to be high "in a siege." To which the cook replies, "But we're not 'in a siege,' we're doing the besieging, it's the other side that's 'in a siege,' when will you get this into your head?"[52] Siege is the extreme state of collective historical experience. The Greek literary canon centers on the sieges of Troy and Thebes, and in the Hebrew Bible, in the direst passages of Deuteronomy and the darkest warnings of the prophets, siege represents the ultimate human calamity: "a distant nation [...] whose language you do not understand" will sweep in to enslave and "exterminate you," warns the Deuteronomist. Not only will the enemy be wholly alien, piercing the protective enclave, but you will become enemies to yourselves, friends against friends, parents against their offspring: you will "eat your own children" (Deuteronomy 28:49, 53). Sieges are commonplace. Wikipedia posts thousands of articles on individual sieges, several hundred for the seventeenth-century alone, when the increasing power of gunpowder artillery prompted reciprocal advances in the architecture of protective walls. Visited on countless peoples for at least five millennia, sieges have etched themselves into human memory, encompassing a range of extreme states both real and metaphorical: Israel besieged by enemies and by God, the pious Christian besieged by temptations, lovers besieging their beloved, the state of nature as perpetual siege, the mind besieged by sense impressions. Some metaphorical extensions of siege have epochal consequences. In Napoleonic law, and in modern polities ever since, civil unrest can be termed, and treated militarily, as a "fictive" state of siege.[53] Opponents inside the city walls can be treated like external foes.

If in Judaism exile became the object of ceaseless ritual remembrance, this was perhaps because siege, like extreme physical pain, is better forgotten. The verse in Deuteronomy describing how a mother will begrudge her husband and children "the afterbirth of her womb," intending to eat the placenta and fetal membranes—and her offspring too—secretly herself, is read swiftly and silently during the annual Torah cycle. Siege brings warfare home, and potentially undoes even that enclave. "No one today has the faintest idea of the boundless amount of theoretical writings on the building of fortifications," notes W. G. Sebald's Austerlitz, "no one now understands its simplest terms, *escarpe* and *courtine*, *faussebraie*, *réduit*, and *glacis*." Useless for defense, the old walls survive as one of literature's powerful "time-spaces"—spaces "charged and responsive to the movements of time, plot, and history."[54]

Works of the visual arts do not *happen* in the way texts do. True, their creation takes time. A painting—as that verbal noun suggests—comes into being through a sequential process of applying pigments in layers to prepared or unprepared ground, and (in most Old Master techniques) of waiting for these layers slowly to dry. Some painters expose process itself by allowing the layers to appear as such, or by making the event of the brushstroke stand forth. Max Beckmann painted his *Self-Portrait in Tuxedo* over many weeks in 1927, and when the canvas left his studio it was meant to look in crucial passages unfinished (plate 18). That way the viewer could imagine the struggle that brought it about. And that way the viewer had to "take part in the construction of the painting," as William Kentridge put it, commenting on Beckmann.[55] The *Self-Portrait* becomes a puzzle about layers—black and white, shiny and matte—and which has the upper hand. Hieronymus Bosch distinguished himself from his contemporaries by impulsively executing certain parts of his paintings. He drew with his brush sometimes wet on wet, in one go, the hellish hybrids that made him famous. Bosch also made the first finished and collectable drawings in the Netherlandish tradition, because in drawings, much more than in paintings, the time of making shows. Kentridge made process and procession his central theme. He became an artist through a rigorous commitment to the medium of drawing, and in his animated drawings he tells a story about drawing itself.

Taking time to create, artworks are also experienced in time. Artists work in this condition, and the artists explored in this book work actively with this condition. Like most painters of his day, Bosch made winged altarpieces that opened and closed, and therefore displayed or hid, at the tempo of liturgical time, their shutters closed except on Sundays and saints' days. When Bosch worked for noble collectors he also made his paintings in triptych form: even in a palace, where framed paintings hung static on the wall (as they do in museums today), Bosch triptychs required opening of their shutters (plates 1 and 2). Seeing their climax became a dramatic event. Beckmann began painting triptychs in 1932, on the eve of Hitler's coming to power. Though not movable, the three-canvas structure endowed his ensembles—Beckmann made nine of them—with restless energy, their imagery jumping fitfully from frame to frame (plate 20). Through the triptych form, Beckmann reached back before the modern gallery picture— that beautiful whole set apart from the world—to images like Bosch's that stood embedded in religious mysteries. Several of Kentridge's breakthrough drawings and prints form triptychs, too, including his Beckmann-inspired *Dreams of Europe* and his silkscreen *Art in a State of Siege*—our titular work (fig. 74, plate 25). Dividing the visual field exposed viewing as an active process. Kentridge called this "meeting the object halfway" and understood it as the ethical condition: the observer morally implicated in the observed.[56] In his "Drawings for Projection," Kentridge found a novel way of making his images—often about time—happen in time. We explore this through one of the artist's core motifs, the body of a victim of state violence disappearing in the landscape.

In his *Laokoön* (1766), Gotthold Ephraim Lessing distinguished painting from poetry by painting's use of "figures and colors in space rather than articulated sounds in time." If painting aspires to depict human bodies engaged in significant action (as ambitious artists of Lessing's time tried in their history paintings to do), and if bodies "do not exist in space only, but also in time," each "moment of their duration" being the result of a prior moment and the cause of a subsequent one, then painting must seek "the center of the action," the "single moment" that is "most suggestive and from which the preceding and succeeding actions are most easily comprehensible."[57] Lessing called this moment (in German, this *Augenblick*: "blink of an eye") the "fruitful" or "pregnant" one. And we will see what he means, for example in Bosch's unprecedented portrayal of Adam's very first glimpse of Eve: the painter makes that *Augenblick* a nanosecond preceded by the whole of divine creation and succeeded, perhaps instantly, by hell (plate 2).

The focus here is less on the fruitful moment than on the dangerous one: paradise lost before our own eyes thanks to a cleverly timed portrayal. In Bosch the dangerous moment collapses time. The Fall occurs both "back then" in Eden and here and now, when with our inborn culpability we repeat Adam's ocular trespass. Modernist and contemporary artists, in this study Beckmann and Kentridge, rely on different stories, but their focus remains on the fleeting, perilous, and decisive present moment. This book is itself organized as a triptych. Each of its three parts tells the story of a single image through splintered moments in that image's career. The first concerns perhaps the most elusive painting ever painted. Created around 1500, Bosch's triptych refuses even being named, though today it goes by the provisional title *The Garden of Earthly Delights* (plate 2). The story I tell is largely that of the work's reception. I begin and end around 1945, with Germans reflecting on their different situations by way of Bosch's masterpiece. The second story fast-forwards to Beckmann's *Self-Portrait in Tuxedo* and its remarkable after-life, one that morphs even as I write (plate 18). But the *Self-Portrait*'s creation in 1927 picks up threads of the story about Bosch. Point-of-view characters through whose eyes we see the *Garden of Delights* reappear to shed light on Beckmann. William Kentridge makes an appearance among Beckmann's beholders, and for good reason: he launched his artistic career partly through a retrospective glance at Beckmann, and it was Beckmann who exemplified what Kentridge called "art in a state of siege." The image I explore in Kentridge's oeuvre—the "body in the veld"—flashes up suddenly, and disappears, thanks to the artist's unique method of animation. In Kentridge, as in this book, siege "is not necessarily the subject" but, rather, "the starting point and the area of [the] work."[58]

Kentridge's phrase "art in a state of siege" named what was the case for South African artists working under apartheid. Siege also described how past art was perceived in emergencies. Beckmann's art looked different in Johannesburg in 1986 than it had previously, just as it looked different in Germany in 1927 than it did in 1933 under Hitler. In this sense, "art in a state of siege" is not primarily the work produced during, or addressing, the dangerous moment. It is rather a perspective on art arising in that moment—what Bosch's triptych looked like to the Duke of Alba subduing rebellion in the Netherlands, or to Carl Schmitt in prison in Nuremberg, or to Erwin Panofsky lecturing at Harvard. Or to us today, with some 200 million people around the world living in declared states of emergency, democratically elected officials contesting the rule of law, and the capital of the United States besieged and stormed. "The danger affects both the content of the tradition and its receivers," observed Walter Benjamin, himself besieged in Nazi-occupied Paris in 1940. Danger affects "content" because of what happens to a tradition, whether it is celebrated, destroyed, or rewritten; danger does this to each reception, especially when the stakes are high.

I have borrowed Kentridge's phrase and applied it retroactively to Bosch's *Garden* and Beckmann's *Self-Portrait*. Both these paintings were produced under emergency conditions. Yet countless artworks have been created in extreme states, so why my triptych? Bosch, Beckmann, and Kentridge all responded to siege with the "military irony" particular to satire.[59] The vices or human frailties that each artist's humor attacks may differ, but the polemical edge of their humor is similar.

All three are also compulsive self-portraitists, Bosch obliquely, Beckmann and Kentridge directly. Reflecting on their own activity, these artists foreground process and accident in the creation of images. Walking a tightrope between the base and the exalted, they direct a militant irony against themselves. Originally, I meant the triptych to represent three different scales of distance from the present: the premodern, the modern, and the contemporary. Each also involves distinct forms of engagement with the past: historical for Bosch, pedagogical for Beckmann, and living and interpersonal for Kentridge. Despite connections among the parts, I admit the triptych remains an idiosyncratic collage—like Warburg's collages, more symptom than symbol. I study in three parts what art looks like in a state of siege, when images "flash up," as Warburg's Nympha did, singling each of us out in history. For as Benjamin wrote during the siege he did not escape, "*even the dead* will not be safe from the enemy if he wins. And this enemy has not ceased to be victorious."[60]

Hieronymus Bosch

Cambridge, Massachusetts, 1947

The signs of war lingered even in the ivory tower. At Harvard, returning US military veterans supported by the G.I. Bill doubled the incoming class, crowding the lecture halls and forcing the College to turn its gymnasia into temporary dorms. Speaking at the graduation ceremonies of the Class of 1947, Secretary of State George Marshall warned of the challenges ahead: "I need not tell you that the world situation is very serious." For his service as a general and chief of staff of the US Army, Marshall had received an honorary doctorate already in 1946, but work kept him from traveling to Cambridge to claim his degree. In his Commencement address, delivered without flourish and sometimes inaudibly, in just twelve minutes, Marshall urged America to rebuild and stabilize Western Europe—the allied nations as well as defeated Germany and Italy—through economic aid. Enacted in 1948, his proposal would be called the Marshall Plan. Arguably the most successful structural adjustment program in history, it normalized relations between former foes while countering Soviet influence in Europe.

In 1947 Harvard resumed holding the Charles Eliot Norton Lectures, the university's most prestigious academic event, held annually in the huge Sanders Theater. These had been suspended during the war. A faculty committee put forward a ranked list of candidates for the year-long professorship. Originally in first place, the composer Francesco Malipiero was ultimately rejected due to his ties with Mussolini's fascist regime. Kenneth Clark, until 1945 the director of the National Gallery in London, was invited but regretfully declined: he had just been appointed the Slade Professor of Fine Art at Oxford, though he would soon impress an American audience with his lectures on "the Nude," delivered at Washington's National Gallery in 1953. The committee's third choice was the German-Jewish émigré art historian Erwin Panofsky, by then a professor at the Institute for Advanced Study in Princeton. Receiving the invitation on January 23, 1947, Panofsky gladly accepted, confiding in a letter to his children that the honor was "the nearest thing to a Nobel Prize in our field in this country."[1]

Endowed in 1925, the Norton Lectures are intended to treat "poetry in the widest sense." As Panofsky understood their brief, the talks—each lecturer gives six over as many weeks—could embrace "every creative expression of the human mind, be it by language, color, sound, or form."[2] Poetry in this expanded sense means *poiesis*, defined by Aristotle as the human capacity to bring forth something into being that did not exist before.[3] Poets and writers from T. S. Eliot and Jorge Luis Borges to Czesław Miłosz and Toni Morrison have held the professorship, but the committees overseeing the Nortons typically rotate their purview annually from literature to the visual arts and film to music and performance. By 1947 Panofsky was already a towering figure in the field of art history. Born in Hanover in 1892 to a wealthy Jewish mining family from Silesia, he received his *Abitur* from Berlin's princely Joachimsthal Gymnasium, where Latin and Greek were treated practically as mother tongues. After studying law, philosophy, philology, and art history at the universities of Berlin, Munich, and Freiburg, he dissertated with a thesis on Albrecht Dürer's theories of art. Steeped in classical languages and learning, philosophically ambitious, and wildly prolific, Panofsky elaborated—in theoretical texts and through numerous meticulous cases studies—a distinctive method for interpreting images. Termed "iconology," defined most succinctly as "an iconography turned interpretive," this method had been inaugurated by Aby Warburg and developed by scholars at the library of "cultural sciences" that bore Warburg's name.[4]

In 1920, Panofsky joined the faculty of the newly founded University of Hamburg, supported in that decision by a fellow Warburg admirer, Ernst Cassirer, who had been elected to Hamburg's first philosophy chair in 1919. Trained in the neo-Kantian tradition, Cassirer studied the worldmaking functions of myth, language, religion, art, and science—he did this chiefly in the Warburg Library in Hamburg. Capacious without being systematic, objective but focused on human creativity, rational (compared to Friedrich Nietzsche and Martin Heidegger) but not rationalist (like Rudolf Carnap and Moritz Schlick), Cassirer's "philosophy of symbolic forms," like Panofsky's iconology, supported the beleaguered cause of liberal humanism in Germany between the wars.[5] In 1928, in a speech celebrating the tenth anniversary of the Weimar Constitution, Cassirer affirmed the enlightened German roots of parliamentary democracy against the legion of academics who deemed the elected government to be un-German and illegitimate.[6]

After Hitler came to power in 1933, the Nazi leadership promptly dismissed all Jewish professors from their posts, forcing Panofsky (and Cassirer, by then rector of Hamburg University) to flee Germany, while the Warburg's library and staff escaped from Hamburg to London. In 1934, on the strength of his scholarship and art historical range, which extended from Gothic cathedrals to contemporary cinema, New York University gave Panofsky an "emergency professorship" in its new graduate department in art history, soon named the Institute of Fine Arts. Established in the Upper East Side, adjacent to the Metropolitan Museum of Art, the Institute filled its ranks with German and German-Jewish émigrés.[7] In 1935, Princeton's new Institute for Advanced Study—another foundation started by hiring exiled Europeans—offered Panofsky a permanent professorship. He accepted, joining a stellar faculty that included J. Robert Oppenheimer and Albert Einstein.

Panofsky was well known at Harvard University, as well. He delivered two lectures there in 1934: one on Dürer, the other titled "Principles of Iconographical Interpretation Illustrated by some Van Eyck Pictures."[8] But the Norton Lectures offered him the chance to present on a larger canvas, and to a lay audience, those "principles" announced in his earlier talk.

For his topic, Panofsky chose early Netherlandish painting. This might have seemed narrow, as previous Norton Lectures had been on broad themes and familiar material. Panofsky trusted he could engage his audience in the remarkable artistic flowering that occurred in the Low Countries—roughly today's Benelux—around the time of the better-known Renaissance occurring in Italy. He wagered that, projected from good black-and-white glass lantern slides (Harvard introduced repurposed high-tech military projectors into its lecture rooms), a panel painting like Jan van Eyck's portrayal of a wealthy patron in dialogue with the Virgin and Christ could captivate viewers five centuries later in the darkened basement of a Harvard auditorium (fig. 4). Panofsky endeavored to explain this remarkable *poiesis*, "this Eyckian miracle,"[9] as he put it, that caused pigments suspended in oil and deposited in glazed layers on a prepared wooden support to resemble a slice of the visible world.

Panofsky explored the origins of Van Eyck's achievement in the incremental feats of illusionism performed by book illuminators at the noble courts of France and Burgundy. And he considered the Netherlandish breakthrough in the medium of panel painting, leaving out contemporary developments in sculpture and in the—at the time—more prestigious luxury arts of embroidery, tapestry, enamel, and goldsmith work. Panofsky pursued painting's flourishing only to a point. His story ends around 1500, when powerful influences from Italy transformed the Northern tradition. The field understood early Netherlandish painting to stretch from Van Eyck to Pieter Bruegel the Elder. Panofsky's Norton Lectures focused on the founders, Van Eyck, Rogier van der Weyden, and the anonymous Master of Flémalle, followed by a survey of painters working under their influence, with Hieronymus Bosch as bookend. Narrowing his scope down to the medial transformation through which painting seemed to disappear into the persons, things, and spaces it represented, Panofsky puzzled especially over one effect of this artistic revolution. Divine miracles could be shown physically to take place, but this caused trouble for a picture's symbolism.

The Virgin's appearance within the lifeworld of the painting's patron, Chancellor Nicolas Rolin, looks natural, like events unfolding on our side—the mundane side—of the picture plane. The artist understood the momentous status of his departure. Not just the convex mirror at the back of the *Arnolfini Double*

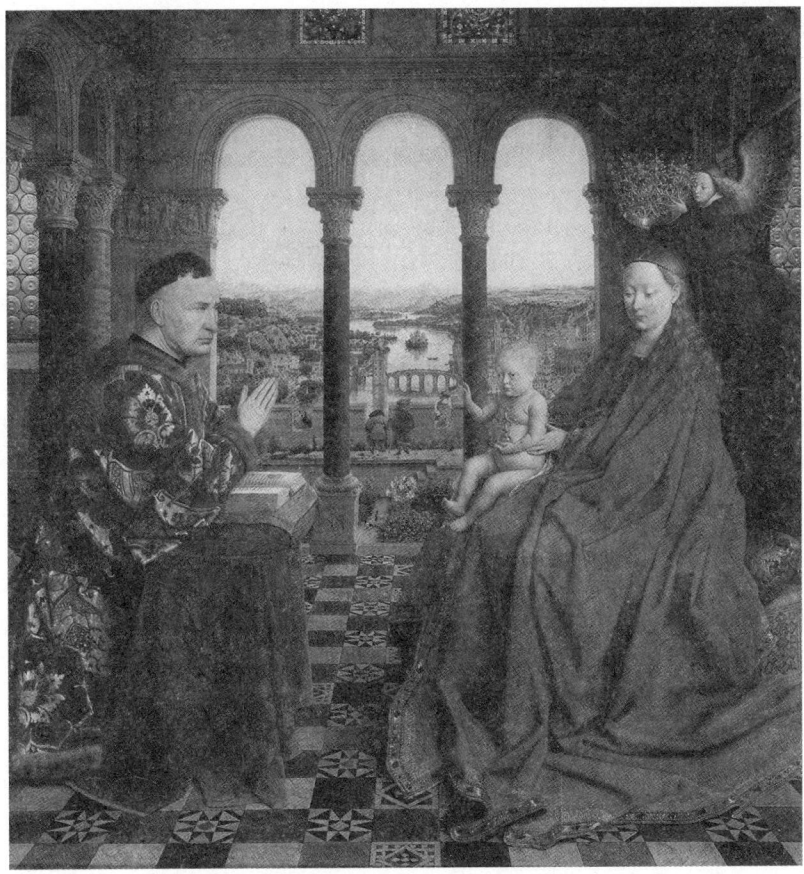

FIG. 4. Jan van Eyck, *Rolin Madonna*, c. 1435. Oil on panel, 66 × 62 cm. Musée du Louvre, Paris

Portrait, but also the countless reflections that bring into the painting what stands in front of it, affirm that images occurring in nature, rather than any painting or artifacts, however well made, are the Eyckian image's real-world equivalent. Like nature, such paintings celebrate the natural. Two men occupy the exact geometric center of the *Rolin Madonna*. One bends over the parapet to gaze into the vast river landscape. The other is red-turbaned, as Van Eyck is in a *Self-Portrait* of 1433. Bearing a courtly staff—Duke Philip the Good made the painter his *valet de chambre* and sent him to foreign lands on secret missions—this figure stands to the side as if showing off the vista to his companion. The former a beholder, the latter (probably) a maker, this eye-catching duo elevates visual appearance to a pictorial theme. They enact and sanction the ocular curiosity aroused by the painting itself in all its lustrous details, including the sacred apparition appearing to Rolin. Yet while Van Eyck made visions look natural and concrete, his approach caused a dilemma. Symbols had been the lifeblood of Christian art. According to a powerful narrative that Panofsky partly sketched at his lectures' beginning, Christian art was more otherworldly than worldly. Conflicted over images due to their Jewish inheritance, early Christians countered the embodied deities of antique statuary with spiritualizing styles and media. Picturing a god who died miserably and unrecognized on the cross, Christian image-makers also had to transport viewers beyond appearances to invisible truths, since in the Crucifixion vision had been deceived. Artists did this by means of symbols. Greek *symbolon* means a token, watchword, or sign referring inferentially to something else. More literally, a *symbolon* is each half of a divided thing. Unapologetically schematic, medieval art placed such tokens front and center.

Early Netherlandish painting sought to incorporate symbols into the naturalistically consistent whole of the represented world. Christian doctrine held that Christ's incarnation and death on the cross atoned for Adam and Eve's sin. Van Eyck therefore smuggled in the symbol of original human trespass in the guise of a tiny material part of the room's actual décor. He depicts the Expulsion of Eve and Adam as a carved stone capital stationed above and just behind Nicolas Rolin's head (fig. 5). This arrangement suggests that the, as it were, "found" Old Testament program sculpted in the loggia contains the Fall, but in a carving accidentally blocked by the two capitals closer to our eye. Each decorated by vegetal motifs, those intervening capitals have been carved in a manner that any well-trained art historian can date. They look to be early twelfth-century French, four centuries older than Van Eyck's painting. Important examples of limestone capitals with interlacing vegetation occur in the Cathedral of Saint Lazarus in Autun, the city of Rolin's birth. That the painted details can be dated so precisely, indeed that everything in Rolin's fabulous loggia, as well as the churches, castles, houses, walls, roads, and bridges in the landscape beyond, evidences a legible period style, is because the painting itself, the artifact crafted in the 1440s by Van Eyck, seems to have no historical style of its own. Even the vineyards visible in the landscape right above Rolin's praying hands capture the planting patterns of Burgundian viniculture. Like his brushwork, Van Eyck's style disappears into whatever it depicts. Styles become facts of the represented world, as do symbols. This resulted, Panofsky writes, "in what may be termed concealed or disguised symbolism as opposed to open or obvious symbolism."[10] The bulk of the Norton Lectures consisted in discovering the symbols and interpreting them. In his most elaborate reading, Panofsky proposes that historical styles were themselves symbolic. The twelfth-century French Romanesque, by Van Eyck's time an archaic artisanal manner, signified the Old Testament, while the later Gothic style signified the new dispensation of Christ.

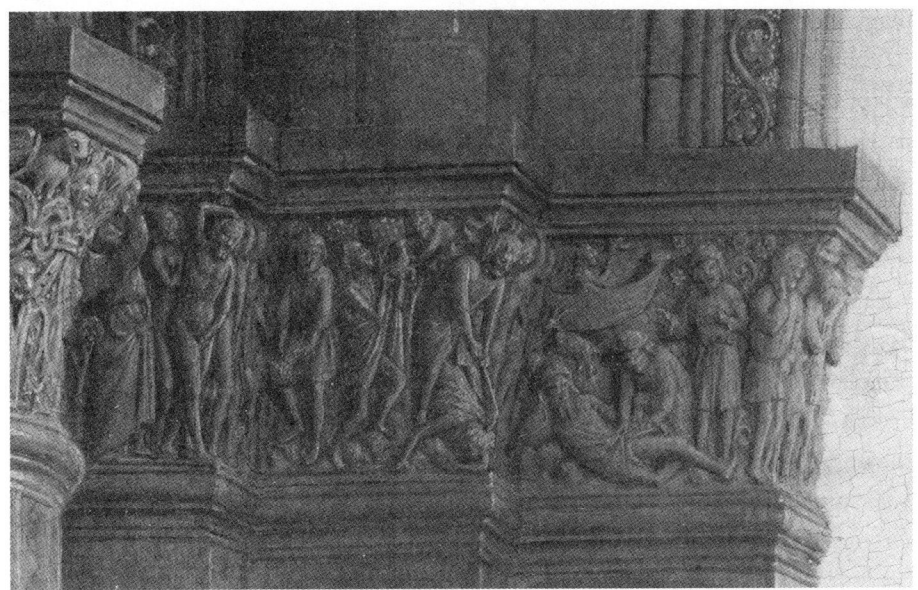

FIG. 5. Detail from Jan van Eyck, *Rolin Madonna*, c. 1435. Oil on panel, 66 × 62 cm. Musée du Louvre, Paris

If nothing is openly symbolic, then every object might be a symbol in disguise. Four shiny brass beasts decorating the armrests of the Virgin's throne in a Van Eyck now in Frankfurt refer to the lions decorating King Solomon's throne; the Virgin nursing the Christ Child on her lap thus becomes the "Throne of Wisdom." Oranges placed on a windowsill to the Virgin's right stand for paradise regained through Christ, as does the flowering foliage of the Virgin's embroidered balda-chin. And a niche to her left, resembling recessed piscinas where Communion vessels are washed, makes Mary into the symbol of an altar, with Christ, resting on a white linen cloth (or liturgical corporal, from Latin *corpus*, "body"), as the flesh and blood Eucharist. Brimming with visual elements, Van Eyck's pictures were destined to become, in the work of Panofsky's epigones, interpretive bonanzas. Because "all meaning has assumed the shape of reality," Panofsky writes, "all reality is saturated with meaning."[11] Van Eyck's symbolism, the form iconography itself takes in his pictures, receives an iconographic or—more precisely—an iconolog-ical interpretation. According to Panofsky, such symbolism represents a novel approach to the venerable Christian idea that physical objects are, in Thomas Aquinas's words, "spiritualia sub metaphoris corporalium" (corporeal metaphors of things spiritual).[12]

Panofsky has been criticized above all on one point: the idea that symbols in early Netherlandish painting are "concealed or disguised [...] as opposed to open or obvious."[13] Those terms beg awkward questions. If a symbol were truly disguised, how can we discover it, or prove it to be a symbol? And are the symbols that an art historian finds ones simply that have been inadequately disguised; in which case, why call them hidden? The Expulsion may be small in Van Eyck's composition, and its being a mere artifact, a carving of the biblical event, may soft-pedal its presence; but there they are: Adam, Eve, and the cherub "with a flaming sword" (Gen. 3:24), bathed in daylight. Panofsky acknowledged the imprecise nature of the concept, introducing the wavering "concealed or disguised" with the hypothetical "might be termed." And disguise for this art historian never meant deceit, nor did it ever imply anything occult—no mystery, like the ones that fascinated Warburg. Howsoever "cloaked" under "real things" they might be, Van Eyck's symbols (by Panofsky's account) are consistently exoteric. They convey meanings of a doctrinal kind, with no reading between the lines. And they are consistent with divine revelation, where "the whole visible world is a book written by the finger of God," and where, at the end of time, that world-book shall be brought forth "in which all is contained, from which the world shall be judged"[14]

In a text published in German in 1932 and revised in lectures delivered at Bryn Mawr College in 1937, Panofsky sketched the outlines of his historical method.[15] "Iconography," he explains, "is that branch of the history of art which concerns itself with the subject matter or meaning of works of art, as opposed to their form."[16] In his original German exposition, he exemplified this difference through a work of art: Matthias Grünewald's *Resurrection* panel from the *Isenheim Altarpiece*. He also expressed the difference between visual forms and verbal meanings in agonistic terms, citing Heidegger's verdict that every interpretation "must use violence to wrestle out of what the words say what they want to say."[17] At Bryn Mawr, perhaps because of Grünewald's Germanic connotations and Heidegger's politics, he reached for a friendlier example:

> When an acquaintance greets me in the street by lifting his hat, what I see from a *formal* point of view is nothing but the change of certain details within a configuration forming part of a general pattern of color, lines, and volumes which constitute my world of vision.[18]

No one beholds things in this way naturally. Panofsky wants us to perform the mental exercise of beholding the phenomenon afresh, free of any prior knowledge. In the philosophical practice of the time, this exercise would have been understood as phenomenological reduction. By beholding the world as if one were a stranger to it, one restored philosophy's starting point in wonder. Neither a formalist nor a phenomenologist, Panofsky proceeds swiftly to his vantage point:

When I identify, as I automatically do, this configuration as an *object* (a gentleman), and the change of detail as an *event* (hat-removing), I have already overstepped the limits of purely *formal* perception and entered a first sphere of *subject matter* or *meaning*.[19]

Facts and meanings overstep formal perception involuntarily. In real life, they will have preceded formal perception, since apprehending "color, lines, and volumes" is not a prior moment of experience but a willful suspension—an *epoché*—of judgments instinctively applied. Our relation to reality, this suspension makes clear, is not natural, but the product of the beholder's consciousness. This suggests that although form comes first, iconography, which seems to follow form, has already arrived and is thus primary.

But because of the example Panofsky chose to explore, the "sphere of *subject matter* or *meaning*" becomes suddenly volatile.

> Now the objects and events thus identified will naturally produce a certain reaction within myself. From the way my acquaintance performs his action I may be able to sense whether he is in a good or bad humor, and whether his feelings towards me are indifferent, friendly, or hostile.[20]

In Panofsky, iconographies are rarely hostile. In contrast to Warburg, who imagined beholding as a state of siege, with images as wavering allies that "live and do me no harm," iconology as practiced in postwar Europe and America emphasized peaceful accord. Fruits of paradise, thrones of wisdom, the Virgin as altar table: these were friendly communications, however unfamiliar they might have become. Correctly identified symbols could be left where they lie, their purpose settled. Hat-tipping, on the other hand, signals amity but need not be amicable. Considered historically, it even presumes hostility:

> my realization that the lifting of the hat stands for a greeting belongs in an altogether different realm of interpretation. This form of salute is peculiar to the Western world and is a residue of mediaeval chivalry: armed men used to remove their helmets to make clear their peaceful intentions and their confidence in the peaceful intentions of others.

The friendly greeting proves to be dangerous. First come the raw, senseless visual forms, the world as it looks to an outsider. Then forms are synthesized into facts, though ones that need to be judged for their "feelings towards me." And these become an amiable communication only to people who share "the more-than-practical world of customs and cultural traditions peculiar to a certain civilization."[21]

Panofsky assumed his audience was acquainted with the greeting. These days few wear hats for elegance, but hat-lifting has not been forgotten. The surprise of the example therefore remains—how, traced to its historical origins, a friendly gesture thrusts us out of a peaceable kingdom. Familiar encounters depend on there being common ground, and such ground is won dangerously, by ceasefire. "Friendship," observed Aristotle, "would seem to hold cities together."[22] Civilization hangs on peace reached between persons who temporarily lower their guard. Violence presses up against concord. Inside each person swirl unstable patterns of color, lines, and volumes. Outside, the war of all against all remains a possibility. In the history of hat-lifting, ceasefire occurred in the waning Middle Ages when men exposed their heads to their potential foes. Today's greeting gets its iconography from a state of siege.

Panofsky published his Bryn Mawr lectures in 1939, at the start of World War II. Escaped to America with his life, he knew the dangers and safety of acquaintances and the importance of reading correctly, whether their feelings towards him were "indifferent, friendly, or hostile." Was it by accident that talks given at an originally Quaker college in suburban Philadelphia, "city of brotherly love," took a peaceful greeting as a model for art? Panofsky's iconology assumes that its objects issue friendly communications. Circulating in past cultures, these may be hard today to recover. Aimed at a circle of elites, they may have been deliberately opaque. But the communiqués themselves had good intentions. To their intended beholder they spoke peacefully, and iconology recovers that accord.

The association of art with friendship is old and powerful. Forged during the Renaissance and celebrated by the Romantics, it has shaped basic assumptions about historical interpretation. In this view artists are singular creatures. Set apart by their genius, they express themselves in autonomous creations mirroring their singularity. Ideally the artist's solitude is only temporary, however. They endure it hoping to find, if not presently then in some future, an audience that understands. The utopia of maker and audience as friends finds literal expression in the friendship painting. Friendship portraits cement the bonds between persons who may be separated by distance, destiny, or death. According to Leon Battista Alberti, painting had the "divine power" to make "the absent present (as they say of friendship)."[23] Desiderius Erasmus and Pieter Gillis (town clerk of Antwerp) sent a diptych portrait of themselves to Thomas More in London. Letters between the three discuss the painter's progress, making the virtual visit among them a collaborative project.[24] Gifted to friends, the friendship portraits make amity their purpose and theme. Economic mobility, political change, and religious conflict encouraged people to imagine that the social order might change, as well. Meanwhile, though, family still determined a person's estate. One exception was friendship. Friends formed a historically vanguard society of equals. And within that society the best thing to communicate freely *about*, the objects that exemplified elective affinities, were works of art. Loved passionately, art objects spoke lovingly to a community of friends. A new aristocracy of culture sought to replace an aristocracy of birth. The modern cult of friendship arose among Renaissance humanists, who defined themselves through a shared intimacy with literature and art.

Humanists argued that human beings, unique among creatures, freely shaped their nature. Humanists also prized friendship as the social bond chosen and maintained without restrictions. And they cherished art, understood as *poiesis*, because it manifested the human capacity freely to create. Panofsky was a historian of humanism and one of humanism's modern avatars: the Bryn Mawr lectures were titled "Humanistic Themes in the Art of the Renaissance." That humanism could survive to have an avatar was a feature Panofsky especially studied. Following in Warburg's footsteps, he explored how a humanism arising in classical antiquity was periodically reborn. Renaissance humanism, and later the humanistic *Bildung* that Panofsky received and transmitted, were revivals of ancient Greece and Rome on which Europe's shared culture rested. By surviving, humanism validated its claim that humanity has a common ground. When Petrarch discovered unknown letters of Cicero, he heard a voice so intimate that he wrote letters back. Panofsky dreamt of a similar intimacy. Past cultures speak differently, using artifacts, symbols, and myths distinct to them. But crack their iconography and they greet you as friends.

This conviction faced an enemy. Hitler fueled his war against the Jews through the belief that identity derived primarily from race, that races sought each other's extinction, and that humanity shared its common ground in hatred. As the Third Reich's Association of Legal Professionals put it in arguing that the term "man" should be eliminated from the German Civil Code:

> The legal concept of 'man' [...] conceals and falsifies the differences between a citizen of the Reich, a foreigner, a Jew, and so on. Replacing scientific abstraction as something removed from reality, thinking in concrete terms, seeing equal as equal and above all unequal as unequal, and emphasizing the difference among different races, nations, and occupational estates in the sense of God-given realities—that is the goal of National Socialist academic jurists, not just of those who are organizationally led by Carl Schmitt.[25]

To such thinking, Panofsky would have been a double adversary: an assimilated Jew espousing humanism, the concealed enemy preaching there are no enemies.

And as we will soon see, Carl Schmitt, who probably wrote this diatribe, directed his anti-Semitism expressly at Panofsky.

The history of art abounds in images of the enemy. The Northern European painters Panofsky studied excelled in portraying Christ's adversaries, and the earliest woodcuts and engravings broadcast in printed form the villainy of foes concrete and phantasmagorical: from Jews, Turks, lepers, vagabonds, and beggars to witches, werewolves, demons, and Antichrist. Such pictures pose no special challenge to iconography. They show the enemy as a friend does to a friend. Not only enemies *in* pictures, but also enemies *of* pictures remain transparent to iconography. Protestant iconoclasts who broke the arms and gouged out the eyes of sacred effigies punished the image in targeted ways. To them the paintings and sculptures were enemy pictures. They deserved being punished like criminals, through blinding, amputation, and decapitation. Iconoclasts sometimes relished the monster their hammers made, exposing the ruin for mockery or archiving it in "idol chambers" (*Götzenkammern*), ancestors of some local German museums.[26] Defacement conveys a message against the image, but for the image-breakers. It has a legible iconography: idols ought to be broken. But what about images that treat their intended viewers as foes, approaching them with bad intent? What happens to meaning in the visual arts when, instead of friendship paintings, we encounter their antithesis: not enemies depicted in painting, not enemies of painting as an art, but *enemy paintings* as such?

Panofsky's iconology wins many battles in *Early Netherlandish Painting*. These spill over into the 150 double-column pages of references, some endnotes expanding into short essays complete with illustrations, diagrams, and bibliography. Even disproven readings remain obligatory reference points for future scholarship. Van Eyck's double portrait of Giovanni de Nicolao Arnolfini and his wife Costanza Trenta does not depict a clandestine marriage ceremony, as Panofsky argued.[27] The panel probably started off as a celebration of Constanza's pregnancy but ended up, almost certainly, as a memorial portrait after her death (perhaps in childbirth).[28] But the picture remains in the imagination of many "the Arnolfini Marriage." With all his triumphs, one might imagine that Panofsky would end with a victory lap, but he does not. What defeats him has been necessarily included. "No survey of Early Netherlandish Painting can be complete without a discussion of Jerome Bosch," Panofsky explains, only to demur: "Such a discussion, however, is not only beyond the scope of this volume, but also, I am afraid, beyond the capacity of its author." Bosch is an "island" in the stream of tradition, an "archaist" in an era of artistic progress, a strange growth rooted in "the subsoil of popular and semipopular art," a maker of "crass" physiognomic overstatements and visual-verbal puns in the epoch of naturalism, beauty, and elegance. Panofsky knows Bosch well. He knows the artist's iconographical reference points: "[e]difying—and horrifying—religious literature," popular science, folklore, "Rabbinical legend," and straightforward Christian theology.[29] He has read and rejected new theories of Bosch as a heretic, citing as counterproof the artist's solid social status, religious respectability, and princely patronage. But for Panofsky, this painter, alone among the artists of his tradition, was alien and better left untouched.

Already at his death in 1516, five centuries ago, the painter Hieronymus van Aken, who called himself "Bosch" after his hometown of 's-Hertogenbosch, was famously inscrutable, the maker, in the words of an Italian traveler, "of things fantastical and bizarre."[30] This painter's masterpiece, the large, winged triptych which goes by the provisional title *Garden of Delights*, has especially eluded iconology (plate 2). Its format, a triptych with hinged wings, is standard in Netherlandish art. When shut its wings show, in shades of gray, the newly created world. Many Netherlandish triptychs have gray, or *grisaille*, depictions on their outer wings, both to save on the cost of pigments and to make the burst of color at the ensemble's festive opening more dramatic. Outer wings sometimes feature a preamble to the imagery they conceal. Accordingly, Bosch's wings depict a cosmic "In the beginning" and open to what seem to be three next chapters. In the left panel, human history starts in Eden, with Adam beholding the newly formed Eve, and in the right panel, hell conjures the apocalyptic End of Time. It is only the center that confuses. Its scene of naked multitudes cavorting on a vast verdant plane is neither described in the Bible nor does it conform to any familiar history or fable. It poses a fundamental question: is it positive or negative, good or evil, friendly or hostile?

To say no consensus has been reached about what the triptych shows belies the animus that fuels the question. For one erudite, it celebrates carnal pleasures; for his esteemed colleague in the audience, it utterly damns the flesh. One recognizes a false utopia; the next, an alchemical tract; a third, a Jewish marriage canopy and Aztec calendar combined. Amity finds no toehold in Bosch's hostile carousel of love. For Panofsky, this incomprehensibility had one cause: "We have bored a few holes through the door of the locked room; but somehow we do not seem to have discovered the key."[31] Hoping that a key would eventually come to light, Panofsky closed his Norton lectures with a last gasp of resigned erudition—a rhymed couplet penned in 1505 by Johannes Adelphus, an obscure German translator stumped by an arcane philosophical text:

This, too high for my wit
I prefer to omit.[32]

Brandenburg on the Havel, 1947

In the year Panofsky declared the key missing, an art historian in occupied Germany announced he had found it. Devised by a cunning locksmith, this scholar's theory went, the key was intricate and singular. It unlocked not just the so-called *Garden of Delights*, but every painting and drawing Hieronymus Bosch created. For behind this artist's oeuvre lay a vast and strange secret involving entire communities outside mainstream Christian society, their existence under the radar of chronicles and written documents. In its full exposition, developed in books and articles published from 1947 until 1964, the author of this thesis conjured a colorful cast of characters entangled in a mesmerizing plot, with Bosch himself playing a mere supporting role.[33] At the story's center stood the artist's mentor and patron, a "Grand Master" of a heretical sect dedicated to recovering innocent sexuality by practicing it. It was this individual, as remarkable in his way as Erasmus, who commissioned Bosch to paint symbols of his creed.

The key's discoverer occupies a dubious position in the scholarship on Bosch. In the opinion of most art historians, Wilhelm Fraenger did not merely err in his theses about the painter. Dangerously wrong, his name should go unmentioned lest it lead scholarship astray. Whole books have been written to refute him, and when his heresies do get mentioned, in the weeds of a footnote or in a mocking aside, it is to admonish against them.[34] Fraenger is the iconologist gone rogue. His scandalous reputation among Bosch specialists contrasts with the esteem he enjoyed among German artists and intellectuals of his time. Even today, a flourishing institute for politics and culture in Berlin bears his name.[35] When in 1947, Fraenger first made his findings public, he had behind him successful careers as a folklorist, radio presenter, publisher, library director, progressive dramaturge, and historian and critic of art. A precocious researcher, he won in 1913—in only his second year at university—Heidelberg's annual Gold Medal for scholarship. Submitted to the Philosophical Faculty, his essay treated art criticism in seventeenth-century Holland. Fraenger garnered praise for the depth of his sources, yet he read the historical material against the grain. Art theory, he argued, categorically failed to understand the art of its time. Rembrandt stood beyond the reach of his contemporaries because Dutch writers, using academic standards set by Italian and French theorists, applied the wrong concepts to him.

To create a sociable context for his gentle subversion he founded in 1919 an association called "Die Gemeinschaft" (The Community). Led by a distinguished board of directors—including Hans Prinzhorn, whose *Art of the Mentally Ill* enraged Warburg at Kreuzlingen—the Gemeinschaft stood opposed to academic elitism and to Right-leaning "folkish" tendencies in German culture. It pitted the free association of a community (hence *Gemeinschaft*) against human groupings based on race or nation, and it championed German and Austrian representatives of the literary and artistic avant-garde. Fraenger became a leading writer on contemporary art in the Weimar era. In 1922 Max Beckmann urged his publisher, Reinhard Piper, to engage Fraenger as contributor to the first major Beckmann monograph.[36] Published in 1924, Fraenger's essay on Beckmann's *The Dream* (1921) remains a seminal text on Expressionism (see fig. 53). It argued that the violent subjects of Beckmann's art, its focus on war, cruelty, and suffering, necessitates distorting the old aesthetic forms. States of emergency (*Notzustände*) make pictorial extremes a necessity: "That word, expressive form's 'necessity' [*Not-wendigkeit*] as understood in its basic meaning, is what we explore."[37] Previously banished by academic criticism, ugliness now reigns, extending its sovereignty from the caricatures in Beckmann's pictures to his entire artistic style, which renders a just judgment on the modern world.

Fraenger championed artistic rebels. In Frankfurt in 1920 he staged matinee performances of Oskar Kokoschka's radical one-act plays. Kokoschka was the self-styled bad boy of the art world. "Our God," wrote Carl Zuckmayer of his days as a struggling playwright in Frankfurt, "was Oskar Kokoschka, and Fraenger was his zealous prophet."[38] Already in 1909, Kokoschka's *Self-Portrait as Warrior* had scandalized the Viennese public at its first exhibition. Created as if impulsively out of unfired clay, the war this "warrior" bust fought was of self against itself. "[My] room became 'the Chamber of Horrors,' and my work a laughingstock," recalls Kokoschka. "Every day I found bits of chocolate and other debris in the mouth of my bust."[39] Fraenger's matinees caused a similar uproar. To play a woman personifying "Life" in Kokoschka's play *Job*, indicated in the script as appearing nude, Fraenger had to employ a prostitute. Standing naked before the public, she had trouble reading her lines. People heckled her and catcalled the production, and when the play ended people stormed the stage. "We battled for Kokoschka and for the theater against outraged men who wanted to beat up the actors," remembers Zuckmayer with pride.[40] Dubbed a lion-tamer by collaborators, Fraenger had tried to avert outrage by explaining the plays before their performance.[41] Speaking in a preacherly voice from the back of the theater, with a spotlight on him, he looked to his friends like a mad scholar from one of E.T.A. Hoffmann's gothic tales.

In his scholarship, Fraenger favored eccentrics: not Van Eyck, but Bosch; not Rubens, but Hercules Seghers; not Dürer, but the obscure "Petrarch Master," Hans Weiditz. After Bosch, Fraenger's passion was the minor German Renaissance master Jörg Ratgeb.[42] Probably born in Schwäbish Gmünd and forced to move from place to place due to his marriage to a bondswoman of the ruling duke, Ratgeb is best-known for his *Herrenberg Altarpiece*, a polyptych dated 1519 that looks like it could have been painted by an Expressionist circa 1919. This painter took the peasants' side in their disastrous 1525 rebellion; convicted of treason, he was quartered by four horses attached to his limbs. Fascinated by the artist's biography and attracted to his modern-looking art, Fraenger interpreted Ratgeb's oeuvre as a political manifesto—personalized with cameo portraits of Ratgeb and his wife—and including paintings of martyrdoms that prophesied his death. Even canonical artists became radicals in Fraenger's eyes. Writing on Dürer, he focused on that artist's woodcut *Memorial for a Victory over the Rebellious Peasants* (1525), deciphering it as a defense of revolution.[43] Not all Fraenger's work was as speculative. In *Peasant Bruegel and the German Proverb* (1922), he pioneered a folkloristic reading of Bruegel, skillfully identifying ninety-two of the artist's painted proverbs.[44] Reaching beyond famous artists, he studied the mass-produced imagery of woodcuts and broadsheets, treating these as windows onto the otherwise obscure "folk."

In his later years in East Germany as a member of Academy of Sciences of the GDR, Fraenger helped shape the discipline of ethnology (German *Volkskunde*) in the Communist bloc, purging it of its racialist and nationalist inheritances. In his understanding, the *Volk* stood apart from biological and geopolitical divisions. Invented or imposed from above, such artificial groupings encountered resistance from below, as the people organized itself in its own different ways, often surreptitiously. Entered freely, by voluntary association rather than naturally or by force, communities posed a threat to state rule, hence their drift towards secrecy. Fraenger tried to dig beneath written history to the generally unrecorded lives of ordinary people.[45] Their voices could be faintly heard in popular media such as print and in hidden forms of subversion, such as humor and heresy. Having explored Bruegel's humor, he turned his attention to Bosch's heresy. In 1934, he announced to a friend that he was working on studies of Bosch's "paradise of lust." The subtitle, "A Dionysian Scenario," telegraphed an antithetical reading of Bosch as celebrant of sensual pleasure.[46]

Perceived subversion had speeded Fraenger's dismissal in 1933 from his directorship of the Mannheim Palace Library. The Nazi leadership censured him for acquiring the Great Soviet Encyclopedia and for giving a lecture on Rembrandt and the Synagogue. But under Hitler, radical theories could also rehabilitate a scholar. In 1938, the Gestapo forgave Fraenger's socialist leanings and associations with "Jewish circles," allowing him to serve as artistic advisor at the Schiller Theater in Berlin. Working under Heinrich Georg (a former Communist who starred in Nazi propaganda films, including the anti-Semitic *Jud Süß*), he spent the early years of World War II organizing literary and musical matinees. But it was not until 1943, during a hospital stay in Spandau, that he resumed his scholarly work. His Berlin residence burnt to the ground, the Schiller Theater destroyed by air raids, Fraenger buried himself in "Bosch apocalyptica."[47] In a letter written from his sickroom to the jurist and Nazi Party member Carl Schmitt, he describes how, while his "range of movements" was "confined to the space between elbows, ink, and paper," bombs turned Berlin into "a real infernal crater."[48] Released from hospital, he moved to Päwesin, a town hidden among the lakes formed by the Havel River. In a room in an abandoned brick factory, with German tanks rolling out and Soviet "thunderboxes" rolling in, he had his eureka moment.

It had often been observed that, with its triptych format and outer shutters painted in shades of gray, Bosch's masterpiece resembled a Christian altarpiece— Max J. Friedländer's standard corpus of early Netherlandish painting terms the triptych an "altarpiece."[49] Scholars struggled to understand this likeness, since the central panel's show of nudity made the work's display behind an altar hard to imagine. Fraenger's solution was simple. The triptych was an altarpiece, but not a Christian one. Instead, it stood in a completely different space than a church: a hidden interior, perhaps a chamber underground, where it functioned as the cult object of a clandestine community of Adamites. Members of an obscure sect that waxed and waned since its emergence in the second or third century after Christ, the Adamites believed that since God created humans—men and women equally—in his image and likeness (Gen. 1:26), whatever is natural to humans must be good in their creator's eyes; therefore humans, though fallen from their original perfection and shackled by laws that punish and kill, can return to their innocent state by throwing off their garments and fulfilling their desires freely, shamelessly, and pleasurably, and with people other than their spouse. Made for such believers covertly flourishing in 's-Hertogenbosch, Bosch's triptych shows paradise regained through sexual intercourse. Across its several panels, it displays, in Adamite terms, where we were and whither we are bound. From the world's creation on the outer shutters, through our first home in Eden, on the right inner wing, it takes us right to paradise, imagined as the here and now of pleasurable sex pictured at the triptych's center. The work thus functioned for its community as a symbol "with the original double sense of the word," as both sign and confession of faith—in Greek, "symbol" originally meant a certification mark between friends, contractual partners, or messengers and then was applied to statements, or "confessions," setting out the essential doctrines.[50]

Fraenger never portrays what exactly these Adamites did before their putative altar. His intricate reading of tiny details suggests cult members beheld the painting intently, learning from it what to believe and how to behave. But whether they held their sacred orgies right there in front of the triptych, with its open wings embracing their rite, Fraenger does not say. His reticence derives neither from prudery nor scholarly caution, but follows instead from the nature of the key that he discovered. On the one hand, the key opens up secrets. God appears on the outer panels because the reign of the Old Testament creator-god has waned. Seeds spilling from a thorn-pierced fruit condemn masturbation as a form of gratification born of shame. The abundant fruits and waters signal how coitus with multiple partners is as natural as eating and drinking; the inferno at the right punishes the very idea of divine punishment. On the other hand, secrets remain secret to everybody but an inner circle of initiates. Fraenger and the Grand Master alike turn things into their opposites. Fraenger flips a painting against lust over into a celebration of lust; the Grand Master makes ascetic "thou shalt not" into an ecstatic "thou shalt." Both prodigiously inventive, the scholar and the mystagogue possess *gnosis* (knowledge)—but of a kind that the earliest heresy hunters qualified as "falsely so-called."[51]

The sect that Fraenger discovered in Bosch's pictures never existed. And the so-called *Garden of Delights* turns out to have served a different purpose than either an Adamite or a Christian liturgical one. As we will see, documents brought to bear on the triptych in 1967 (after Fraenger's death) pinpoint its original place of display in a room in a noble palace in Brussels.[52] Proven to be erroneous, Fraenger's arguments seem maddeningly circular, like the *Garden of Delight*'s ceaseless parade: persecuted, the Adamites communicated among themselves cryptically, using pictures instead of words. Made for that purpose, the pictures Bosch painted are the sole surviving evidence of the heresy. They alone reveal Adamite practices and beliefs, allowing Fraenger to turn back to the triptych and interpret its every detail, via evidence found only in it. True, he produces proof of an Adamite sect purported to have flourished in Brussels around 1400: a record of twenty articles submitted for retraction by a certain Willem of Hildernissen to Henry of Selles, inquisitor of the episcopal court of Cambrai. Dated June 12, 1411, the protocol lists egregious acts Willem admits to having carried out for a group calling itself "Homines intelligentiae" (people of intelligence).[53] By then the group's leader—an unlettered layperson named Giles the Cantor—had died, so Willem passes the blame on Giles, reporting that "this lay seducer" repeated many times "I am the savior of humanity,"[54] and that anyone saying "magnificent Lucifer" would be saved. The statements wrung from Willem echo earlier ones obtained from persons accused of membership in the so-called Brethren of the Free Spirit. These confessions include refusing prayer and penance, fabricating a private language to conceal the sect's doings, women fornicating with multiple men, and sexual intercourse performed (thus Willem's confession) in the "particular way" that "Adam did in Paradise."[55]

Whatever happened in Brussels around 1400, however, is nowhere documented in 's-Hertogenbosch a century later, and the heresy confessed may itself be an artifact of the inquisitor's imaginings. As Hugh Trevor-Roper wrote of the putative practices and beliefs of accused witches extracted under torture, "The similarity of answers can be explained by a combination of identical questions and intolerable pain."[56] Distrust of lay religious orders, hostility between secular and regular clergy, misunderstandings of ecstatic mysticism, remembered doctrines of older heresies, a long tradition of sexual slander, the use of judicial torture: these and more may have created the fiction of the Adamites. But if his sources are dubious and his arguments false, why bring up Fraenger at all? Is his thesis a mere historical curiosity—what the triptych looked like to an eccentric besieged in a brickworks? Despite his errors, Fraenger has had defenders. In the postwar period, champions of sexual liberation took Bosch to be a precursor. Herbert Read, who gave the 1953 Norton Lectures, thought the West would have been better if Bosch's Adamites, and not Luther and Calvin, had won the day. Henry Miller, with Fraenger in hand, likened the oranges in Bosch's painting to the hallucinatory beauty of the Big Sur, a "dreamlike reality which constantly eludes us and which is the very substance of life." Norman O. Brown hung a print of Bosch's *Garden* on his office wall and used it to explain his bestseller, *Love's Body* (1966).[57] Scholars continue to take direction from Fraenger, projecting alternative heresies—Manichean, Cathar, Rosicrucian, Gnostic—on the artist.

But Fraenger's legacy runs deeper than this. His vision of a paradise of lust cannot be unseen. Rare is the reader who does not think, if just for one worrisome moment, "Maybe Fraenger is right!" For this reason, no account of Bosch that takes the triptych to damn the revelry it shows can proceed without some shadow of doubt. Fraenger begins with the evidence of the images. He starts by shedding biases about medieval people as terrified moralists and by looking at the painted panels for what they actually show. He notes correctly that in Eden the Fall has not yet occurred. No law has been broken, no fruit has been plucked, and the serpent has not yet appeared. He notes, too, that the landscape of unfallen paradise passes seamlessly into the central panel's lush terrain. Whatever happens in these two panels does so among similar woods, meadows, and waterways and under the same horizon punctuated by mineral-vegetal outcroppings, and all painted in the same greens, blues, and pinks. The central scene of sexual revelry follows naturally from the innocent one in Eden. Naked, and therefore innocent because unashamed, humans have simply been fruitful and multiplied, according to God's plan.

What one reveler wants another will perform. No one says "No" in this garden. Granted, the fires, war, and torture in the right panel threaten the peaceable scenes to the left, and they share the same horizon. To this total negation, Fraenger responds that hell is an inferno for the cynics. Here all who say "No" to what the triptych affirms—the fear-mongering clerics, petty legalists, and (especially) the egoists who set themselves against nature and community—all receive their just deserts. To these nay-sayers, modern ones included, who doubt his hypothesis, Fraenger responds that, just as Christian altarpieces dedicated to the Virgin Mary celebrate her purity, so too Bosch's Adamitic triptych affirms pleasurable sex. And as with ordinary altarpieces, redemption is the goal; only the path there takes a different turn. The way depicted at the triptych's center shows what might have been had our first parents not sinned, and it does this in the guise, so Fraenger, of a "chiliastic state when humanity, after expiating its fall, is allowed to return to Paradise and to the peaceable well-being of all creation." Salvation through sex, liberation from the law, return to Eden, and perpetual peace: "All this," concludes Fraenger, "stares one in the face."[58]

Freud observed that the unconscious mind can only affirm: "There is no such thing as an unconscious 'No.'" If a patient insists about someone in his dream, "It's *not* my mother," the analyst amends it: "So it *is* his mother."[59] Fraenger reads the triptych oppositely to how others do, and sends nay-sayers to hell. This connects him to a wider tendency of his own time. Heresy was an intellectual obsession in Germany after World War I. The carnage of mechanized combat, Germany's defeat, crippling hyperinflation, widespread bankruptcy, and armed clashes among radical political factions cast doubt on the old liberal ideals of human progress, rationality, and perfectibility. Frequent and prolonged states of emergency marred the country's brief experiment with parliamentary democracy. Created and adopted in Weimar in 1919, the constitution failed to withstand its political opponents, and in 1933, through the Enabling Act that gave him emergency powers, Hitler effectively repealed it. Under siege conditions, the old forms of consolation seemed dubious. Serious artists agitated instead, as Fraenger's text about Beckmann explained. Germany's official religious confessions—Protestant and Catholic—seemed more like symptoms than solutions. Neutralized politically and represented in parliament as mere constituencies, they pertained to the inner person and thus to a bourgeois social order that, thanks to its obliviousness, had reached its end.

As in art and politics, so too in religion extremes flourished. "Crisis Theology" rejected the private emphasis of liberal Protestantism and disputed divinity's progressive unfolding in history. Post-liberal thinkers such as Karl Barth extracted God from entanglement in a world proven to be corrupt. They also equated faith with a radical decision. Friedrich Nietzsche's dictum, "God remains dead. And we have killed him," provoked them, and Søren Kierkegaard's notion of faith as a leap into the unknown inspired them, but they also reached back still further to the ancient Gnostic idea of the absent God. In Adolf von Harnack's 1921 monograph on Marcion of Sinope they found a deity opposed to just about everything orthodox religion affirmed.[60] In Marcion's eyes the god of Jewish scripture was a belligerent tribal deity opposed to Christ. Where in the Old Testament the demiurge rules vengefully by laying down a law and punishing sinners, Christ prevails through unrestricted love. Marcion's "gospel of the alien God" was just one of many heresies that captured the German imagination.[61] Some of these interwar engagements helped to shape modern thought: for example, Hans Jonas's reconstruction of late-antique Gnosticism, Leo Strauss's study of Spinoza and pantheism, and Gershom Scholem's work on Kabbalah. Other thinkers, such as Rudolf Steiner, who dabbled in Gnosticism and convinced the young Fraenger to meditate on a mandrake root, drifted into the margins. In any case, the idea of Bosch as a heretic would have seemed plausible.

In 1947, Fraenger published his solution in the book *Das tausendjährige Reich* (The thousand-year realm).[62] His publishers—Winkler Verlag in Coburg—balked at Fraenger's title. "This Nazi catchphrase easily could lead to errors," they wrote, "especially here in the American Zone."[63] *Reich* can mean both "realm" and "empire." Germany still called itself a *Reich* after the German Empire's collapse and even after 1918. Mystical ideas of *Reich* pre-date Hitler's rise to power. Written in opposition to the post-World War I settlement, Arthur Moeller van den Bruck's 1923 *Das dritte Reich* (*Germany's Third Empire* [1934]) imagined a future Germany not as a republic or nation, but as a territory where German *Volk*, divided and scattered, would gather and flourish. Borrowing van den Bruck's phrase, Hitler called his regime a "Third Reich" and predicted it would last a thousand years. This end of history would arrive not peacefully, but after Armageddon. Hitler aimed his war of aggression at establishing a "Greater Germanic Reich" stretching westward into France to pre-1500 borders, north through all the Scandinavian lands, and eastward deep into Russia.

In 1945, Fraenger spent several weeks in Russian prisoner-of-war camps near Päwesin. On his release he joined the Communist Party of Germany and served briefly as Päwesin's mayor. Moving to Brandenburg, he became in 1946 director of the city's *Volkshochschule*, a public community college that Fraenger dubbed an "Academy for Everyman." In 1947 the Social Unity Party of Germany (SED)—a forced merger, by the Soviet occupiers, of Germany's Communist and Social Democrat parties—initiated an inquiry into Fraenger's wartime activities, including his collaboration with Heinrich Georg (who died of starvation in a Soviet prison camp in 1946), his publications of his works "under the swastika banner," and his wife's membership in the National Socialist Women's league.[64] Despite this ongoing investigation, which lasted into 1948, and with US censors scrutinizing the book, Fraenger stuck to his guns. "Bosch is 450 years older than Adolf Hitler," he explained, "[and] consequently even with the best intentions his cannot be mistaken for [Hitler's] twelve-year *Reich*."[65] Also unsettlingly for a German under suspicion in 1947, Fraenger proposed that the painting's secret mastermind, the putative Grand Master of the Adamites in 's-Hertogenbosch, was a Jew, probably an antinomian one, perhaps also a backsliding erstwhile convert to Christianity. It turns out that Fraenger had arrived at this theory some time around February 1944, and that he first tested it out in letter and manuscript forms on only one person.

Nuremberg, 1947

That man was Carl Schmitt, and in 1947 he sat in prison in Nuremberg awaiting possible prosecution for war crimes. He had been Germany's most original and controversial jurist, the inventor—among other things—of the idea of politics as a struggle between friend and foe. Ordinarily politics are pursued by individuals or groups through discussion, debate, negotiation, and elections, all encompassed by the state and safeguarded by some rule of law. For Schmitt, politics exceed these bounds. Not simply a struggle of one candidate or party against, politics rest on the life-and-death struggle against an enemy: "The specific political distinction to which political actions and motives can be reduced is that between friend and enemy."[66] The political is the most volatile and foundational human domain. Whereas morality distinguishes between good and evil, aesthetics between beauty and ugliness, and economics between profit and loss, the political separates friend from enemy, a distinction that "denotes the utmost degree of intensity of a union or separation."[67]

Friend and enemy concepts "receive their real meaning precisely when they refer to the real possibility of physical killing."[68] Where Fraenger's solution to Bosch's triptych was lovemaking, Schmitt's key to a bigger mystery was enmity. Humans are by nature dangerous, risky, and dynamic animals, as "every political thinker in the proper sense" knows. The political stands above the moral, aesthetic, and economic realms. Logically and historically, it precedes the sovereign state and will outlast it: "The concept of the state presupposes the concept of the political."[69] Indeed—and this is Schmitt's other key idea—a state's legal order does not contain the political, but is created out of it as if *ex nihil*. "Looked at normatively, the decision [about the enemy] emanates from nothingness."[70] It may seem that laws are passed through legislation and tested by the courts under the umbrella of an a priori legal order—as enshrined, say, in a constitution. But the law itself says otherwise, because every legal order contains some provision for the dire condition, in German a "state of exception" (*Ausnahmezustand*), when the law can be legally suspended, freeing the executive from any legal restraints on its power. Written into constitutions in "emergency powers" clauses, the exception is, to Schmitt, "a borderline concept."[71] An element internal to law, it lies outside the law and prior to it, since every legal order has historically some violent, extra-juridical beginning in conquest and the seizure of land.

Emergency states can come about by natural and medical catastrophe—floods, fires, pandemics, and so on. But these are not juridically salient, because (the maxim holds) "necessity knows no law." The *Ausnahmezustand* is exceptional in and to the law. It pertains to political and economic disturbances, most obviously war, when a people is willing to kill in order "to preserve [their] own form of existence," but also during periods of civil strife, when the enemy is an internal one.[72] Deciding that someone is an enemy, and deciding the exception: these can be done neither by a previously determined legal norm nor by judgment of a neutral third party. Only the combatants themselves, the friends and the foes, understand, judge, and settle the extreme case of conflict. And the one who finally decides on the extreme case is sovereign: "Sovereign is he who decides on the exception."[73]

These twin ideas—politics as the friend–foe distinction and the sovereign as decider—made Schmitt famous, and useful too, because the situation in Germany in the 1920s, when Schmitt published his seminal books, was riven by political violence and by uncertainty as to who decides.[74] Rejecting centuries of autocratic princely rule, the legal experts who framed Germany's constitution in 1918 wanted a state founded on popular consent: a constitutional democracy roughly like Britain and the United States, who had won the war. These jurists enshrined personal liberties, such as free speech, equality before the law, and universal suffrage—in Germany women could vote a year before the United States granted that right. Predicting attacks against the state by armed right-wing and left-wing militias, its framers built into the constitution a powerful emergency powers provision. If the state did not fulfill the duties imposed upon it by the constitution, or if "public security and order" were "seriously disturbed or endangered," then the president of the Reich could "make use of the armed forces" to compel the state to fulfill its duties and to restore law and order. In theory a last resort, these provisions, contained in Article 48 of the Weimar constitution, became in practice the normal form of governance: during certain years of Germany's short experiment in parliamentary democracy, Article 48 was invoked sixty times or more.

Schmitt became the expert on governance by emergency powers.[75] Jurists of all persuasions knew that Article 48 could be the republic's Achilles heel, but most sought ways of establishing uninterrupted parliamentary rule. Schmitt thought otherwise. Surveying in 1921 the forms that dictatorship had historically taken—including in the United States under Abraham Lincoln—he observed that emergencies declared merely to restore an indecisive norm make the state vulnerable to enemies.[76] Accepting states of exception as the norm, he favored ones restoring the "noble" dictatorship of the saber over the insurrectionist dictatorship of the dagger. In March 1933 he supported the Enabling Act allowing Hitler to make and enforce the law. Though formed by a power-sharing coalition, Hitler's cabinet—Schmitt argued—was a new government. No longer fettered by the "false neutrality" and "empty legalism" of the "Weimar system," now "the Führer defends the law."[77]

In Schmitt's view, the Third Reich was entirely constitutional, a twelve-year-long *Ausnahmezustand* based on Article 48. And after the war, he would defend his defense of the Nazi regime on the grounds that, as a mere jurist, he did not write the law but only interpreted it—he "made a diagnosis" is how he put it to his American interrogators.[78] His actions, however, suggest otherwise. Joining the Nazi Party on April 27, 1933 (three days before Martin Heidegger), he applauded the burning of books by Jewish authors and demanded that texts influenced by Jews should be destroyed as well.[79] Zealous in his attacks on former Jewish colleagues, he personally orchestrated the dismissal of his rival Erich Kaufmann from his professorship in Berlin. A Protestant convert from Judaism, Kaufmann—in Schmitt's diatribe—was an "especially pronounced form of the Jewish assimilated type" who, "aimed solely at concealing origins and at disguise," could confuse and "damage" German students.[80] Schmitt's theories changed under Hitler. In the original 1927 formulation of *The Concept of the Political*, the enemy "is simply the other, the stranger; and it is sufficient for his nature that he is, in a specially intense way, existentially something different and alien."[81] The 1933 edition racializes the friend–foe distinction: "the other" (*der Andere*) becomes "another kind" (*der Andersgeartete*).[82] Friends become a biologically homogeneous *Volk*, while enemies are no longer paradigmatically foreigners, invaders, barbarians. Instead, they may be—are more perilously—strangers *within* the state. Turning such outsiders into citizens, liberal constitutions allow these foes to operate unseen. And they operate in a particularly dangerous way: by preaching to the *Volk*, whose territory they—the "other kind"—have infiltrated, that there are no enemies. To people close to Schmitt this had already been implied earlier. "The Jews are the immediate enemy," wrote the virulently anti-Semitic jurist Günther Krauss to Schmitt, his *Doktorvater*, in 1932. "Their place in the passage about the *métoikos* in your *Concept of the Political* is to be noted."[83] Indeed, of all his hatreds, enmity towards "the Jews" was that which would bind Schmitt to National Socialism the longest.[84]

In the summer of 1933 Schmitt received competing offers from the universities of Heidelberg, Munich, and Cologne, but at the urging of Hans Frank (later the genocidal governor-general of occupied Poland), Berlin offered Schmitt a professorship, which he accepted, calling the appointment "the highest distinction" of his profession. Within weeks Hermann Göring himself named Schmitt Prussian state councillor.[85] Schmitt proposed a new Führer Council inside that council, headed by him as juridical Führer of the Führer. This never happened. Hitler cared little for the law, and in 1936 Schmitt's enemies in the Nazi regime denounced him as a craven opportunist and cynic. His years as "crown jurist" of the Third Reich were over. Protected by Göring and Frank, Schmitt retreated into scholarship and turned his attention to Thomas Hobbes. After the war, Schmitt would hint that his interpretation of Leviathan—Hobbes's symbol of total state power swallowing the rights and dignity of its subjects—was really a surreptitious parable of the Nazi regime, like Ernst Jünger's novella *On Marble Cliffs* (1939) had been. But when *The Leviathan in the State Theory of Thomas Hobbes* first appeared in 1938, readers recognized a completely different subtext.[86]

A sea monster referred to in the Book of Job, Leviathan was Hobbes's name for commonwealth. Although invested with terrifying powers, sovereign rule by mutual covenant was preferable to the state of nature, "where every man is Enemy to every man," and life was "solitary, poore, nasty, brutish and short"—England in Hobbes's time had returned to that extreme state through religiously motivated civil war.[87] Schmitt accepted that Hobbes's peace in the modern era required a religiously and morally neutral state, but he was hostile to the English philosopher's "neutralization of every truth," which turned the state into a machine.[88] So Schmitt dug into Leviathan's symbolism and claimed he had discovered its hidden core. According to certain esoteric "Jewish-cabbalistic interpretations" (where he read these Schmitt never explains) Leviathan signified heathen sea powers. It would fight Behemoth, representing heathen land powers. Meanwhile the Jews "stand by and watch" this mutual slaughter.[89] Afterwards, in a thousand years of sweet revenge, the Jews will then feast on the two monsters' "kosher" flesh. Stateless and neither of land nor sea, the Jews revel in the self-destruction of the heathen, which is to say, the gentiles. And thus today, in the era of the secular commonwealth, the Jews secretly undermine sovereignty through the empty legalism of the liberal constitutions that they, erstwhile people of the law and now scheming professorial jurists, created, rendering states indecisive and vulnerable to enemies.[90]

Schmitt's lurid fantasy hardly protests against National Socialism. It reaches back to medieval accusations of Jewish blood cannibalism and forward to the Nazis' special loathing of kosher slaughtering. And it affirms Hitler's Big Lie of an international Jewish conspiracy that schemed World War I and Germany's defeat, and their doing this for profit and revenge. The modern assimilated Jew, Schmitt writes, has an "unerring instinct for the undermining of state power that served to paralyze the alien and to emancipate his own Jewish folk."[91] The vision of an apocalyptic battle between powers of the land and the sea would inspire Schmitt's own elaborate *Großraum* (great space) theories supporting, among other things, the German Reich's expansion through military conquest. Schmitt's *Leviathan* also inspired Wilhelm Fraenger while he worked on Bosch in his sickbed—the hospital chaplain, who had heard Schmitt lecture, spotted Fraenger's copy of Schmitt's book and engaged him in a debate.[92] After the war, Schmitt's writings, and particularly his thoughts about *Großraum* and violent "land appropriation," caught the attention of the US Military Government in Germany and led to the jurist's arrest.[93]

Schmitt spent the first postwar months in freedom, drafting legal memoranda in defense of industrialists charged with aiding Germany's war of aggression. He argued that international law contained no statutes against such a war. On the maxim "no crime without a law," the charges should be dropped. He would observe that in the sixteenth and seventeenth centuries European states created a new international order in response to catastrophic wars of religion. And through this new order—the *ius publicum Europaeum*—enemies came to be regarded not as criminals or heretics, but as political antagonists of equal moral standing. Charges of "aggressive war" and "war crimes," made in the name of humanity, reintroduced vengeance into the modern rules of interstate warfare. On August 25, 1945, Schmitt directed his book-length memorandum "The International Crime of the War of Aggression and the Principle 'nullum crimen, nulla poena sine lege'" to the American judges at Nuremberg.[94] A month later, on September 26, the Americans arrested Schmitt at his home in Berlin-Schlachtensee on the charge of war crimes.[95]

The warrant for his arrest had been drafted by Karl Loewenstein. A Jewish-German law professor who had been forced into exile in 1933, Loewenstein knew Schmitt's writings and career intimately, so when he returned to Germany as legal advisor to the Military Government in charge of "de-Nazifying" German justice, Schmitt was high on his list of potential felons. Either the Americans dropped the ball or German authorities took charge of the case and dismissed it as trivial, but after twelve months of internment Schmitt was released without trial. On March 19, 1947 the Americans rearrested Schmitt, this time rushing him by train to the International Military Tribunal (IMT) in Nuremberg. Now the charges were vague and provisional. Officially listed as a "potential defendant," Schmitt asked the American questioners directly, "Why am I here?" To which the chief interrogator, Robert Kempner, answered, "That remains to be seen."[96]

Kempner had been a successful lawyer in Berlin and served as chief legal advisor to the Prussian police until the Nazis forced him to emigrate. Because of his knowledge of the German legal system he was made head of IMT's Defense Rebuttal Section, a unit tasked with predicting legal strategies of the accused. In interrogating Schmitt, Kempner seemed more interested in hearing the brilliant jurist's arguments than in prosecuting him for his involvement in the Nazi regime. In his published memoirs, Kempner recalls asking Schmitt to draft two briefs, one explaining "Why I am a war criminal," the other, "Why I am not a war criminal." The latter turned out to be the better argument, so Kempner set the prisoner free. "Herr Professor Schmitt, go home," Kempner remembers saying, then asking: "What will you do now?"[97] "I will take safety in silence," was Schmitt's answer, though he would continue to publish, including his self-exculpating reflections written between 1945 and 1947 and published under the title *Ex Captivitate Salus*. And before he released him, Kempner asked Schmitt to draft four legal opinions that would be useful to the prosecution. The boastful "last knowing representative of the *ius publicum Europaeum*" outlined why the Nuremberg trials were not legal from the perspective of existent public law in the international sphere.[98] Personal questions were more difficult to answer. The first one, heading a questionnaire presented to Schmitt in 1945, asked simply, "Who are you?" To which Schmitt gave a tortuous answer—dated April 1947—called "The Wisdom of the Cell."[99]

Alone in his prison cell and reflecting on his "real condition," Schmitt feels himself naked and vulnerable: "it becomes clear to me that the human being is naked," he writes, dressed in prisoner's garb. And "most naked" is he who stands unclothed "before someone clothed, disarmed before someone armed, powerless before someone in power. Adam and Eve already knew this upon their eviction from the Garden of Eden."[100] Cast out as an enemy of humanity, Schmitt returned to the resources of his thought. He translated the questioners' intrusive "Who are you?" into its Schmittian a priori: "Who is my enemy?" To which the authoritarian jurist replies: ego is the enemy. It seeks a new paradise in and through the self. And it is here in the jurist's personal state of siege, with Adam as alter ego, that Bosch's triptych rises up as foe:

> This is the true yearning of the egomaniac. This is the new paradise. This is nature and natural law, suspension of self-alienation and self-externalization in a problem-free corporeality: the Adamitic happiness of the garden of earthly delights, that Hieronymus Bosch cast in white nakedness upon a panel.[101]

The Bosch that haunts Schmitt's prison cell is Fraenger's creation. In 1946, Fraenger had sent Schmitt *Das tausendjährige Reich* in page-proof form. Schmitt called the work "a great triumph over the misers of the day," and on reading its arguments "again" (he had read earlier drafts), he marveled at how far it transcended the usual art historical literature.[102] On the eve of his detainment, Schmitt was still reading the galleys and sending Fraenger corrections. But "the whole is superb and opens a new horizon," and Fraenger was wise to break his argument off where he did and pick it up again in a future volume, because "the fate of the Grand Master has to be revealed in one blow, with overwhelming argumentation."[103]

Schmitt knew Fraenger's reveal in 1947, two years before the latter published it. The mystagogue behind Bosch's masterpiece was Jacob van Almaengien, a Jew baptized in 's-Hertogenbosch on December 15, 1496, at the climax of the city's homage to Philip the Fair, future duke of Burgundy and Habsburg king of Castile.[104] Philip was one of several illustrious godfathers to the convert, who had the title of "Magister" and received the Christian name of Philips van St. John's, after the Habsburg duke and the Cathedral of St. John where baptism took place. For once Fraenger had a historical source to back him up. Albertus Cuperinus's *Chronicles of the Renowned and Pious Town of 's-Hertogenbosch* (1558) recorded the events, including a coda: "this Jew did not remain steadfast but lapsed from Christendom and became again a Jew."[105] Where Almaengien came from the records do not say. Some scholars take his name to be Spanish, suggesting he arrived in northern Europe after the Catholic monarchs expelled the Jews from Spain in 1492. But 's-Hertogenbosch had the oldest documented Jewish community in the northern Netherlands. In the eleventh century, under the duke of Brabant's protection, they sheltered in the forest where 's-Hertogenbosch would be built. According to a contemporary chronicle, in 1164 a "crowd of Jews" was found there engaged in "false trade" and holding "ugly beliefs." A few years later, 186 men and women were burned alive near the place where the city would build its gallows field. Children would either have been killed or baptized as orphans—the largest recorded Netherlandish massacre of Jews.[106]

The mystery of Jacob van Almaengien's origins allowed Fraenger to make up a biography on evidence drawn from Bosch's paintings. In the art historian's telling, Jacob did not convert to Christianity from Judaism, because he had not been an observant Jew. Instead, he was a Jewish-Christian Ebionite. Another of Fraenger's undocumented survivals, the Ebionites—known only through early Christian heresy hunters condemning them—believed that Christ was Mary and Joseph's human son who, because of his obedience to Jewish law, God chose as a prophet. A latter-day Ebionite, Jacob abandoned his sect, repulsed by its ritual castrations and worship of a frog goddess and her "swamp-like" promiscuity (this explains Bosch's nefarious toads). Then a terrible debacle occurred that would haunt him ever after. Meeting a demonically possessed Ebionite girl, Jacob exorcises, converts, and marries her, only to watch her die in a fiery disaster caused by sectarian enemies. Banished he spends years wandering—Bosch portrays him as a vagabond and peddler. He finds his way to 's-Hertogenbosch where he becomes Grand Master of the Adamites, backsliding Christian convert, and Bosch's patron before "dropping out of sight again into the no-man's-land between *ecclesia* and *synagoga*."[107]

It is possible that Schmitt brought Fraenger's page proofs with him to prison. After his release in May 1947, Schmitt was showing off the published volume to friends. But the book's strange findings had been long known to the jurist, since Fraenger had outlined them already in 1944 in personal letters to Schmitt. A long missive dated February 26, 1944 (during massive Allied offensives) gives a feverish account of the Grand Master's "tragic fate" based on details of paintings by Bosch. In a Boschian *Wedding at Cana*—now known to be a work made after the artist's death—Fraenger sees antinomian Jews feasting on swan meat and pork, the unkosher delicacies of a Satan-synagogue. The art historian admits that his account, "appears to go wild, like a romance," but he assures Schmitt that he has kept himself "strictly to the pure visible facts."[108] Although they diverged in their politics, Fraenger and Schmitt were similar in their love for conceptual extremes. Bosch was an Adamite, self is the enemy, sovereign is he who decides on the exception, and so forth. And Schmitt's most telling statement under interrogation was, "I am an intellectual adventurer." To which Kempner swiftly responded, what happens if the adventure ends "in the murder of millions of people?"[109]

One pursuing Leviathan, the other Bosch, the adventures of Schmitt and Fraenger intersect at Judaism. In 1944 Fraenger enlisted one of the jurist's doctoral students, Emil Ross, to trawl Dutch archives for Jews in Bosch's milieu. He wanted his theory to be "rock solid." The timing is perverse. Starting in 1942, the Nazi occupiers deported some hundred thousand Jews from the Netherlands. Only about five thousand escaped extermination. Fraenger admitted to Schmitt that the search for Bosch's Jewish patron was "untimely" and "not exactly uncomfortable" (nicht gerade bequem), but he assured the Prussian state councillor that this sleuthing would bring astounding results.[110] Fraenger went on to ask Schmitt to be his eyes for him when, in 1943, the jurist, lecturing in Franco's Spain, might visit the Prado Museum and stare into the "concentration point" in Bosch.[111] He wanted the jurist to behold and be beheld by the artist's *The Seven Deadly Sins*, a dizzying picture in roundel form representing terrible God's all-seeing eye (plate 3).

Schmitt did go to the Prado, though what he thought while beholding the originals he did not say. But Bosch's imagery would flash forth in dangerous moments when the jurist felt besieged. The most immediate of these flashes appears in a letter to Ernst Jünger dated August 4, 1943, shortly after Schmitt returned from Spain. Schmitt and Jünger—political reactionaries and champions of the extreme—pursued a lively correspondence from 1930 until Schmitt's death in 1985 (Schmitt lived to ninety-six, Jünger to a hundred and two). In 1943, at Schmitt's urging, the two immersed themselves in Léon Bloy. "It's just getting bigger and truer," reports Schmitt in his August 4 letter on rereading Bloy.[112] Published in 1892, Bloy's *Salvation through the Jews* responded to the racial anti-Semitism rampant in France on the eve of the Dreyfus Affair. Beginning with the seeming paradox that the Jews murdered Christ, but the gospel preaches "salvation is from the Jews" (John 4:22), Bloy explores, in chapter after hate-filled chapter, Jewish depravity and endurance. Everyone loathes the Jews, even the Arabs, who "make a disgusting ointment out of them, which they smear on mangy goats." Yet no matter how often and how justly the nations try to exterminate them, this "damned people" remains. Then, in the Jewish market in Hamburg, among the "filthy groveling misers," Bloy observes a trio of miserable old Jews and has a revelation. They are Abraham, Isaac, and Jacob, their blood relatives "descended into this calamitous sphere!: Their wretched flesh, for so many centuries resisting intermixing, shows us abundantly their prodigious state of exception within humanity."[113] Bloy builds the argument that Jewish depravity stemmed from their idolatry of gold, but at the end of time, this abject people will convert and reveal themselves to be their opposite: the least member of the Trinity, the Holy Spirit, whose age replaces the era of the suffering Son.

This, roughly, is what seemed to Schmitt in 1943 to be "getting bigger and truer." After the Red Army besieged and crushed the Germans at Stalingrad, the

Nazi leadership recognized that the war could not be won, not against the Allies and not against the Jews. Their dreams of German *Großraum* dashed, Schmitt and others began to contemplate, more urgently than before, Jewish survival. And Jewish vengeance. At Nuremberg the jurist felt besieged by vindictive Jewish émigrés, Loewenstein and Kempner. This "prodigious state of exception" was the "situation" that Bloy illuminated and that brought Bosch to mind. "About Hieronymus Bosch," wrote Schmitt to Jünger, "I have learned much that is new through the appearance of the pictures in the Prado and through a specialist, Wilhelm Fraenger. These insights, too, keep step with the situation" (Schmitt used that English loan word). Schmitt never reported what the "concentration point" felt like, but the letter traces a train of thought from Bloy's fantasies about Jewish infamy and redemption, through Fraenger's fantasy of a crypto-Jewish millennium, to the current "situation" that, in Schmitt's eyes, is swiftly moving towards a catastrophe. These thoughts will erupt again in his prison cell in 1947, with Fraenger's texts in his head, and Bosch looking more dangerous than ever. What exactly Schmitt, besieged, thinks he sees in that painting, and why he sees it: these will be clearer once we have traveled the winding history of Bosch's triptych.

Schmitt's letter ends with a final paragraph that returns us to where we began. Out of nowhere, the jurist tells this anecdote:

> In Hamburg there was a Jewish art historian, Panofsky, who in 1933, during a street march with shouts of "*Juda verrecke*" [Perish Jews!], made the statement: "*eher werden die Recken verjuden*" [Sooner will the warriors be judaized!]. Whereupon he was arrested, rightly. I remembered this upon reading L. Bloy. Always your old and true Carl Schmitt.[114]

What reminded Schmitt of this story? Bloy's visit to Hamburg's Jewish market? The three "horrible" Jews "personifying the whole indestructible people who, for almost two millennia, have succeeded in surviving their exterminators" (Bloy)? In Schmitt's account, which seems to be apocryphal, Panofsky turns Nazi slogans against themselves—*verrecken* into *verjuden*. This accords with Bloy's story of obstinate survival. But it is Panofsky's cleverness with the German tongue, in which alone the wordplay makes sense, that provokes Schmitt's murderous aside: "Whereupon he [Panofsky] was promptly arrested, rightly." *Mit recht*. Legally, and against Jews as people of the Law, who believe that they will be redeemed through the Law. Schmitt's phrase lashes out angrily, like Bosch's cruel and unexpected painting of hell.

Two weeks after receiving Schmitt's letter Jünger writes back that he told the "Hamburg story about the warriors [*Recken*]" to an art historian seated beside him on the train. "That can only have been Panofsky," the anonymous traveler said in response.[115] Who else in the profession but Panofsky, now safely in Princeton, had such wit? In 1947, all three persons represented in the letter—Panofsky, Fraenger, and Schmitt—would respond to Bosch in their own fashion. For Panofsky, the evidence was missing and the art "too high for his wit"; therefore Bosch was better left untouched, for now. For Fraenger, the painting *was* the evidence, and it showed an antinomian utopia of sex and amity: "the thing in itself actually *is* the idea."[116] For Schmitt, too, the painting was evidence, but what it manifested was the enemy, Schmitt's personal enemy, who, preaching human rights, was now destroying his entire way of life.

Schmitt was right about one thing. "Bosch's devils," he noted in his *Leviathan* book, "are ontological reality."[117] That was how Schmitt understood Bosch before he read Fraenger: the artist was an avatar of enmity. Hatred was—so to speak—the painter's professional specialty. At the beginning of a stage in European art when, due to an expanding art market, painters' shops narrowed their production to pictures of discrete saleable types (landscape, portrait, still-life, etc.), Bosch made portraying enemies his trademark skill. The devil's hatred of people, people's hatred of other people, the Jews' hatred of Christ and Christians, the hatred of Christians for their enemies, the hatred directed towards an 'us' by an invisible 'them,' and the wrath of God that consumes just about everyone: this global economy of loathing stands not just portrayed in Bosch's pictures. It is performed in them, as if his brush were enmity's instrument. Hatred contaminates. The aversion these images depict and enact defiles how we react to them. Uncertain whether they are for us or against us, we turn against each other. Bosch built his masterpiece to act like a time bomb set to detonate in every dangerous here and now. The explosions in 1947, occurring in the wake of World War II, are but episodes in the story of the triptych's afterlife.

Brussels, 1517

The story begins with the earliest surviving written description of the work: one sentence in a travel journal dated July 30, 1517, a year after Bosch's decease. Its author, Antonio de Beatis, hailed from the tiny harbor town Molfetta, near Bari, and served as chaplain and secretary in the splendid entourage of Cardinal Luigi of Aragon.[118] His travels with the cardinal, begun in Ferrara and undertaken on horseback with some thirty-five mounts—French musicians and players joined them on their return journey, bringing that number to forty-five—wound its way north through Germany to the Netherlands, then circled back to Italy by way of Paris, Nantes, and Marseille. Covering around 3,400 miles, and with scores of festive stops along the way, the trip took only nine months to complete, testament to the period of relative calm between the Wars of Italy and the conflicts ignited by the Reformation. Why the wealthy and eccentric cardinal—by blood the grandson of the King of Naples—undertook the journey remains unclear. Upon his departure a group of Venetian senators conferred among themselves about this matter. Some reported that he wanted to secure support from King Charles I of Spain (the future Emperor Charles V) while others hinted that Francis I's favor was his goal. But Antonio explained the trip as an adventure: having seen Italy and Spain, the cardinal set forth also "to know Germany, France and all those regions bordering the northern and western oceans and make himself known to so great a variety of people." To visit these reaches safely he traveled incognito, dressed as his courtiers were, in "pink silk with sashes of black velvet"—the servants dressed the same, but without the sashes. Only in the courts of kings did he don his cardinal's robes.[119]

Happily, for readers of the journal, which comes down to us in transcriptions by his hand, Antonio is himself eager "to know" whatever he encounters, recording vividly new impressions and finding explanations when confused. On the last day of their passage through Germany (June 29) he reflects on what struck him about that land, aside from its obviously warlike nature. Since leaving Trent on the Alps' southern slopes, large crucifixes marked the roads inducing "no less fear than devotion." Everywhere they "came upon an infinite number of wheels and gibbets," with whole fields planted with such torture instruments, "each with its body on the top."[120] Antonio's curiosity is well matched by the cardinal's—the journal is a collaboration between the two. In Amboise a group goes off to the suburbs to see the elderly Leonardo da Vinci and admire paintings still underway. Luigi seems not the leader but a follower: he "went with the rest of us." But when they visit the workshop in Brussels where the tapestry series for the Sistine Chapel is being woven in silk and gold and admire the one completed weaving—*Christ's Charge to Peter*, alone worth two thousand ducats—it is the cardinal who gives "his opinion" that the tapestries will be "among the finest in Christendom."[121]

It was in Brussels earlier that same day that Antonio saw them, displayed in a room in the palace of the counts of Nassau: "some panel paintings of various bizarre themes [de diverse bizzerrie]." The diarist does not name the painter, but neither does he Raphael, who made the full-scale cartoons for those tapestries, nor Pieter Coecke van Aelst, whose shop did the intricate weaving. More frustrating, and causing the sentence to go unnoticed by historians, Antonio gives the panels no title and lists but a few details:

seas, skies, woods, the countryside are simulated, together with figures who emerge from a mussel shell, others who defecate cranes; and men and women, white and black, with different postures and expressions, birds, animals of all kinds rendered with great naturalness, things so pleasing and so fantastic that they could not be properly described in any way to those who do not know them.[122]

Two scholars published the same discovery in the same year. In 1967, in a "Note" in the *Journal of the Warburg and Courtauld Institutes*, Ernst Gombrich connected Antonio's words to Bosch and briefly sketched the triptych's provenance after 1517. Also in 1967, in a volume of essays accompanying an important Bosch exhibition in 's-Hertogenbosch, Jan Karel Steppe did the same, in greater detail, and having also already publicized his findings in a lecture in Utrecht and a 1962 report to Royal Flemish Academy in Brussels.[123] Whoever gets credit for the discovery, the trouble previous scholars had of linking Antonio's words to an object was a problem evident to Antonio himself. Bosch offers too much to identify, and too little. Spread loosely across its three panels, the triptych's countless details—mostly hybrid anomalies—cannot be succinctly named, described, or even verbally located. And this information overload extends from the parts to the whole. Over the centuries, the triptych has received many names, but no title has ever satisfied. In 1967 Gombrich suggested impermanence or fortune as Bosch's theme, but he admitted these were clues and not a solution. He would later argue that the triptych depicted the world before the Flood, but few were convinced.[124] The trouble lies in the work's center, in the circular revelry revolving around a watery middle that resembles no nameable event; indeed, that perpetual counterclockwise rotation refuses the temporality that would make what we see into an event. And this non-event unfolds in a non-place. Although, as Fraenger noted, all the panels share the same horizon, nowhere on this earth—in this world where we "eat our bread" by the sweat of our brow—have the doings at the center ever occurred. No event, no story, no there there.

Antonio names a painting's subject when he knows it. "In the palace there are many beautiful paintings, among others a Hercules and Deianeira, naked figures of considerable size, and the story of Paris, with the three goddesses most perfectly done." The *Judgment of Paris*, probably by Lucas Cranach, who painted many pictures of this subject, would have been easy to recognize, and the club-bearing Hercules, almost certainly by the Netherlander Jan Gossaert, would have been obvious, too (fig. 6). "Dehyanira," as Antonio spells her name, takes erudition to identify. The well-educated cardinal could have supplied the name, but the

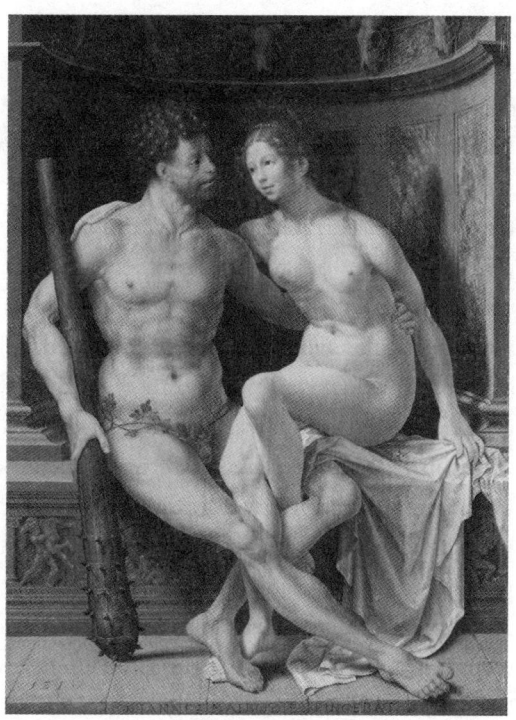

FIG. 6. Jan Gossaert, *Hercules and Deia-neira*, c. 1517. Oil on panel, 36.8 × 26.6 cm. Barber Institute of Fine Arts, University of Birmingham

entourage did not walk through the Brussels palace alone. "We gathered," Antonio writes of a bed "34 spans *di canna*" wide, "that the Count made it because he liked to hold frequent banquets and to see his guests get drunk, and when they could no longer stand on their feet, he had them thrown on this bed."[125] The guests learned this because someone told them. It may even be that the bed's size was ceremoniously demonstrated with a measuring rod one Roman *canna* long. When Dürer visited the same palace in 1520 he too was made to admire the giant bed, along with a big meteorite that "the storm hurled down in a field right next to the Count."[126] In the lively journal he kept of his travels in the Netherlands, Dürer made no mention of Bosch's triptych. When visitors strolled through this palace and beheld its curiosities a guide accompanied them. But with Bosch, it seems, they had to puzzle it out on their own.

The place where the triptych stood offered visitors clues about how to understand it. Antonio experiences neither "fear" nor "devotion"—the emotions elicited by German wayside shrines—but rather amusement and confusion. Which makes sense in a princely palace. Although "bizarre" in its themes, the work fit in with objects displayed nearby. Visitors moved through a cabinet of "curiosities," those singular products of art and nature that elicited the special and, in the early modern period, desirable feelings of fascination and wonder. Assembled mostly by princes, who could afford such costly assemblies, curiosity cabinets brought under one roof exquisite artifacts and natural rarities. A curiosity like the meteorite that almost struck the count was understood as a precious instance of nature "playing with herself," dangerously and humorously, because against her own rules. The crafted curiosities included "beautiful paintings." These were playful too, for in their ingenious *poiesis* they imitated not created nature, but creative nature. *Natura naturans* was an unruly force capable of producing novelties at will. Of all curiosities the most valuable were those that confused art and nature, as in the case of shells and figured marble (which resemble perfect artifacts), and automata (which resemble living creatures). Such marvels eluded all categories but one: exceptions to the norm, they violated the bedrock order of the nameable species. Accordingly, they made beholders speechless. When he beheld the gold and silver artifacts arrived from Mexico, Dürer fell silent: "I cannot find words to describe all those things I found there."[127] And thus Antonio, beholding Bosch's panels could not describe them "in any way to those who do not know them."

Early modern curiosity cabinets confused the categories, but certain sorts of things prevailed. Paris and the naked goddesses, Hercules and his naked wife, the guests tossed into the gigantic bed: all are erotically charged. And all are also disastrous, the bed for the hangover, the paintings for something far worse. Helen—Aphrodite's dangerous gift to Paris—brings about the Trojan War. Deianeira dooms Hercules. Gossaert's painting in Brussels is lost, but a smaller version, dated 1517, survives.[128] In it the ill-fated couple gaze into each other's eyes, their libidinal entanglement mimicked by their knotted legs. The hero clamps his bride between his thighs, while Deianeira keeps her toes on the earth—unlike Antaeus, carved on the bench below Hercules. Antaeus, in Greek, means "opponent." Hercules kills this half-giant by lifting him clear off the earth from where he derives his power, as son of Gaia. Deianeira means "man-destroyer." With the poisoned tunic she grasps—her imprudent check on Hercules's infidelity—she will bring her husband low. Soaked in a magic potion of blood and semen, the cloth will burn the hero's flesh so painfully that he will throw himself on a funeral pyre. Enflamed, erotic desire become deadly. Women brings disaster to Hercules and Paris, and to Adam. This theme connects Gossaert's and Cranach's paintings to Bosch's triptych. Hung in the same or nearby rooms, these works all show men succumbing to the erotic allure of the naked female body. In Bosch, Adam appears ensnared, as are the multitude of men circling the women sporting in the pool. The trouble starts with the dangerous moment when Adam lays eyes on Eve and is, Troy-like, besieged.

The Nassau palace stood in sight of an older and greater palace on the Coudenberg where, since 1430, the Burgundian overlords exerted their sovereignty over the Duchy of Brabant and beyond. Rivaling the French kings, to whom they had been subordinate, the dukes of Burgundy had powerful support from the House of Nassau. Descending from an old aristocratic line, the Nassau counts served as supreme administrative officers in the Netherlands. Engelbert II, and after his death in 1504 his nephew and heir Henry III, built and outfitted their Brussels residence to rival the seat of Burgundian rule with which their destiny was emphatically linked.[129] At the time of the cardinal's visit to it, the Nassau palace was in Henry III's hands, but whether he or his uncle commissioned Bosch's triptych remains unknown. On the Coudenberg Antonio admired the tennis court, zoo, and hedge maze, but the Nassau palace impressed him more, as it did Dürer. Visiting both residences, the artist declared "the house of Nassau" to be "unequalled in all the German lands."[130]

Count Engelbert II's political detractors—and these were legion—charged that he built his palace using bribes, corruption, and plunder. Even his most fawning biographers portrayed him as a dangerous man. Time and time again he, and later his nephew, meted out violent justice against their foes. Engelbrecht's father, John IV, led the infamous slaughter by Burgundian troops of the entire citizenry of Dinant simply for mocking the duke and his wife in effigy. At fourteen, Engelbert entered the court of Charles the Bold and followed the duke into war against Liège, the Swiss, and the duke of Lorraine. On Charles's death in battle, Engelbert was captured and imprisoned in Switzerland. Ransomed, he became a trusted commander under Mary of Burgundy and Emperor Maximilian, leading armies against the French and besieging and crushing the rebellious cities of Flanders. During the siege of Bruges in 1490, a delegation of the starving citizenry came to Engelbert at his encampment to sue for peace. The count's response (after decapitating their leaders and displaying their heads on spikes): "You are all criminals due to your perjurious breaking of the Treaty of Tours!"[131] The charge was vicious and unfounded, since Bruges had a legal if practically useless right of resistance, and according to rules of war, enemies could be slaughtered in battle but were not criminals, neither during war nor after. This was the legal order that would become the *ius publicum Europaeum* celebrated by Schmitt. Dinant had been laid waste on the grounds that, because common law allowed the homes of outlaws to be destroyed, this rogue city—men, women, and children—could be annihilated. The dukes of Burgundy asserted their rule by festively riding into walled cities, or when such "joyous entries" were withheld, by siege.

Under Emperor Charles V an idea prevailed that God gave the emperor absolute power over the world, but in Bosch's time, imperial power was legally checked by local rights and privileges. Not royal and certainly not imperial, the Burgundian dukes had ruled by force and exception.[132] Nominally a fiefdom of France, Burgundy, the dukes' hereditary seat, was an agricultural region around Dijon. But through marriage, inheritance, and conquest the dukes extended their sovereignty over the burgeoning mercantile cities of Flanders, but not without fierce local resistance. After 1504, Henry III upheld his uncle's Burgundian allegiance. He rose to be captain-general of the Netherlands in Philip the Fair's bloody war against The Duchy of Guelders. The Burgundian dukes founded their sovereignty in the emergency state of a polity at war with its parts, which entitled rulers to destroy entire cities, as Rome did Carthage. Belated champions of reconquering the Holy Land, the dukes turned their crusade against internal foes. "These people," Philip the Good said of the citizenry of rebellious Liège, "are my Turks."[133] Such an approach made the Burgundian rule a model for future state formation by its direct heirs, as Charles V and Philip II laid claim to universal dominion over the Old World and the so-called New.

Violent men, the Nassau counts designed their palace as a place of dangerous delight. Antonio describes "a most ingenious secret device" contained in several rooms. In corner niches, oak planks "carved in wavy lines to look like camlet" concealed doors leading to other rooms: "if it were not pointed out you would never have guessed that there was door at all." Such passages gave insiders special dominion, as visitors moved from room to room, potentially shadowed by their hosts, and pranked. The giant bed was a curiosity and a trap. The count, Antonio reports, liked "to see" his guests get drunk and have them tossed into the bed, presumably to do with one another whatever they might still be capable of.[134] Their forced revelry was "for his noble pleasure"—to borrow a phrase from the one surviving document of a commission for Bosch's art.[135] In princely curiosity cabinets, artistry often made jokes at visitors' expense. Listed in inventories as "engines of fun" the automata created and maintained at great expense by the Burgundian dukes played tricks on guests at court. Lecterns with tempting books to read would suddenly spout soot and water.[136] Mirrors used for clean-up would then blast flour on the wet victims, caking their finery, while the delirious host expected them to laugh with him. One mechanism renovated in 1430 by Philip the Good at his chateau in Hesdin hinged on guests being at the ruler's beck and call. A wooden effigy would artificially summon guests "on behalf of *Monsieur le Duc*." Those duped into obeying would be beaten with sticks, while those who stayed put would be almost drowned with water. The sovereign—"he who decides on the exception" (Schmitt)—displayed his terrifying caprice. German political discourse of the early modern period defined princely power as *Willkür*, Latin *arbitium*: decision as unfettered willfulness.

At the 1481 meeting of the chivalric Order of the Golden Fleece, Count Engel-bert—a high-ranking member—was censured for immoral acts. Ten years later, he received the same reprimand and was threatened with fines if he did not cease surrendering himself to women.[137] Diseased, perhaps fatally, by syphilis, he fa-thered at least two children with mistresses, but none produced legitimate heirs. This may be why his nephew succeeded him. Engelbert also patronized the arts, and especially book illumination. He commissioned the most lavish surviving manuscript of *The Romance of the Rose*, with ninety-two miniatures of amorous pursuits. Bosch painted his triptych on wood with an earliest possible felling date of 1458. The work could thus pre-date Engelbert's death. Paul Vandenbroeck has proposed that Bosch made the triptych to celebrate one of Count Henry's first two marriages, probably his first, in 1503, to Françoise-Louise of Savoy.[138] Henry spent the period of 1501 to 1503 in Castile as companion of Duke Philip the Fair. He would have had little time to order the work from Bosch. It is tempting to speculate that the commission came from his uncle, who, still alive in 1503, might have intended the work as a mischievous wedding gift for his heir.

In my view, the simplest possible explanation for the triptych is this: either Engelbert or Henry enlisted Bosch to paint an allegory of lust. Famous for his triptychs of Last Judgments, this artist also produced a relatively straightforward allegory of avarice in Last Judgment form, with a hay cart symbolizing the greedy pursuit of earthly acquisitions rolling from Eden to hell (plate 9). Asked to create an allegory of lust—that most enigmatic of vices, with roots in the Eden, links to ocular pleasures, and powers virtually impossible to resist—he came up with his strange solution. Lust began with Adam's first glimpse of Eve. Enflamed, it pro-duces an infinitude of fantasies and vicissitudes, as the central panel shows. And it ends disastrously, in marriage or infidelity, with or without God's punishment, as it did for Paris and Hercules. This is where you came from and where you are going, the triptych said ironically to Henry at his wedding.

With no interdict to worry Eve and Adam, and no divinity in judgment above the pleasurable terrain, the ending seems arbitrary and cruel. But *Willkür* is God's prerogative, to destroy or create, curse or bless, punish or forgive capricious-ly. Decision is the worldly sovereign's right, as well, to go to war or bully one's guests. Bosch's triptych does not move mechanically. Its wings must be opened by hand, its pastel fountains and infernal soot cannot wet or dirty us, hell's rough music does not reach our ears. The machinery remains frozen, like the icy waters of hell. If the picture humiliates, it does so inwardly, in the thoughts it elicits in its beholder. Imagining Antonio passing through the Nassau palace, perhaps observed secretly by his host, it is no wonder that he says so little about what he saw or thought, since any observation could be dangerous or wrong. Did he really see people "who defecate cranes"? Beyond his one long sentence penned in 1517 we cannot go, not only because no earlier words about the work survive. Period descriptions of Netherlandish paintings are exceedingly rare; Antonio's vivid one is the exception. Yet the "wit" of art historical scholarship remains high enough for other masters of the tradition. Antonio stops himself, finds safety in silence even in his diary. Whatever went through his mind in Brussels in 1517 was better left unsaid.

Brussels, 1567

Objects of unspeakable delight, Bosch's panels enflamed an overwhelming desire to own them. Some twelve early copies survive, including a tapestry version nearly five meters wide (fig. 7).[139] Exquisitely crafted of silk, wool, and gilt-wrapped threads, it replicates the original roughly to scale, but with added borders and everything reversed. Woven from the back, with a painted cartoon attached to the loom, the finished tapestry puts hell on the left and Eden on the right, further confusing the triptych's puzzling conceit. Whoever commissioned this object, which took longer to weave than the panels did to paint, relished Boschian artistry. For this tapestry belongs to a series of four after paintings by, or imitating, Bosch. Considerably larger than the other three, the woven *Garden of Delights* magnifies the physical presence of the original. Fluted Corinthian columns embellish the triptych's hinged frames. Receding into shallow perspective, they, and the stepped moldings below and triumphal entablature above, give weight to Bosch's airy creation. The original's steeply sloped ground plan and high horizon made it suitable for translation into tapestry—from a distance the pictures resemble late-medieval millefleur weavings. The tapestry's classicizing framework updates Bosch's manner and turns his visions into vistas behind a triumphal portal.

The four tapestries were almost certainly products of a sophisticated Brussels workshop circa 1560, like the one Antonio de Beatis visited some fifty years earlier. The weavings the diarist had admired shared a common theme and purpose. They all depicted the Acts of the Apostles and would adorn the Sistine Chapel in the Vatican. That the series had Raphael as its designer made no impression on Antonio—he marveled at their workmanship and cost but said nothing about their maker. The Boschian tapestries, by contrast, have nothing in common except for the author of their designs. Together they create a solo exhibition, Bosch in woven form.

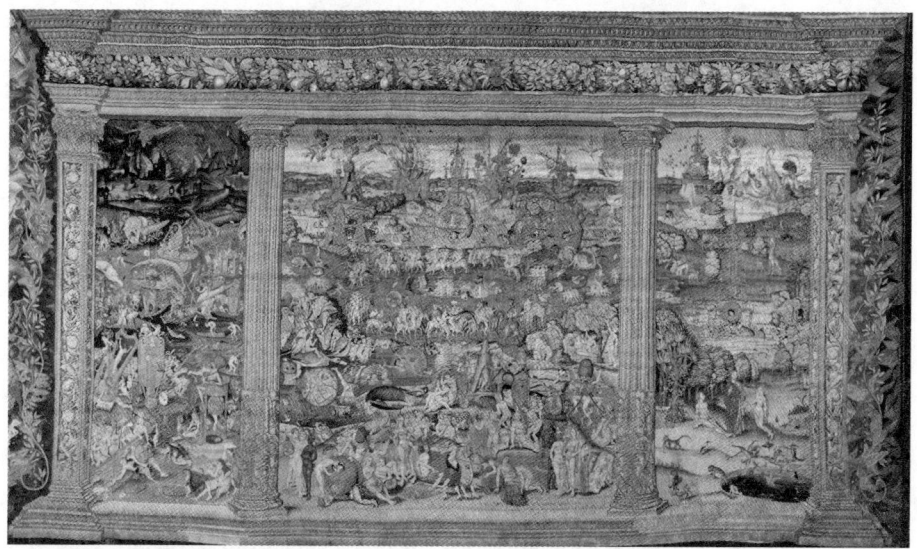

FIG. 7. Brussels Workshop after Hieronymus Bosch, *Garden of Delights*, 1550–70. Tapestry in gold, silver, silk, and wool, 288 × 490 cm. Palacio Real, Patrimonio Nacional, Madrid

The story behind these tapestries belongs to the bloodiest chapter in the triptych's career. That story begins in 1566, with the earliest report of tapestries made after works by Bosch. Writing from Brussels, an agent for Antoine Perrenot, cardinal of Granvelle, announced that "the new tapestries and the ones of Bosch" were ready to be sent to Granvelle's residence in Malines.[140] Also in 1566, just two months later, iconoclasm broke out in the Netherlands with unprecedented fury. Protestants had broken sacred images before: in Wittenberg in 1522, later in the Zwinglian and Calvinist towns of Switzerland, then in England under Edward VI. In the Low Countries, Protestants had been prohibited from practicing their religion. But in 1566, inspired by sermons given by "hedge" preachers in the countryside, they turned their hammers against the physical fabric of the Catholic church. "Idols," including paintings, sculpture, figured stained-glass, vestments, and gravestones, were their target. From Antwerp, where the violence began, iconoclasm spread south to Ghent and Valenciennes and north to Groningen, with gangs of image-breakers moving from village to village attacking parish churches and monasteries along the way. To iconoclasts, 1566 was the "wonder year" when centuries of idolatry were swept away, sometimes in a single night. After the rampage, a Welsh merchant reported, the Church of Our Lady in Antwerp "lokyd lyke a hell, where were above 10000 tourches burnyng, and syche a nowsse as yf heven and yerth had god togede , with fallyng of images and betyng downe of costyly works, syche sortt that the spowll [spoil] was so grett that a man collde nott well passe throo the chourche." He concluded, "I can nott wrytt you in X shettes of paper the strange syghtt I saw there, orgens and all dysstryyd."[141] This was mute wonder of a different kind from Antonio de Beatis's before Bosch's triptych; yet the Welsh eyewitness's ellipsis was framed, as that painting had been, by apocalyptic imaginings.

To the authorities, such destruction posed a dire threat, for they recognized—and the iconoclasts' humiliating rites of destruction made it explicit—that image-breaking contested the power of church and state. King Philip II of Spain understood this dual threat to Catholic orthodoxy and to his sovereignty in the Netherlands. Not trusting his half-sister Margaret of Parma, who as governor-general of the Netherlands had reached a disastrous compromise with Protestant nobility, Philip, on August 22, 1567, sent his best general to crush the Netherlandish revolt.[142] Conqueror of Ottoman Tunis, victor over the Lutheran princes at Mühlberg, and master at the arts of siege, Fernando Álvarez de Toledo, third duke of Alba, arrived in Brussels at the head of a powerful Spanish army. In Philip's name Alba declared the local nobility to be rebels and heretics. Suspending local rights and privileges, he imposed martial law and established a special tribunal—the Council of Troubles—swiftly to question, prosecute, and punish enemies. During his five years in power Alba oversaw more than five thousand executions. The Iron Duke and his Blood Council—as the Netherlanders called Alba and his regime—would become the dark paradigm of future legal states of exception in Europe.

Just weeks after establishing the Council of Troubles, Alba's eyes turned to Bosch. The duke's lust for this artist would have been sparked by the countless copies, pastiches, and prints after Bosch's work circulating throughout Europe by this time. Alba may have seen some originals. Philip II was swiftly becoming the world's most avid Bosch collector. Around this time a Spaniard close to Philip's court, Felipe de Guevara, wrote of works his father, Diego de Guevara, had acquired from the artist. Felipe also reported on the many fakes in circulation, which forgers "smoked" in fireplaces to make them look old and authentic.[143] By 1570, several works from Felipe's estate had been purchased by Philip II, including *The Seven Deadly Sins* and *The Hay Wain* (plates 3 and 9). Meanwhile, new reproductive technologies allowed Bosch's inventions to be appreciated anywhere. During the 1550s and 1560s, the Antwerp press of Hieronymus Cock specialized in Boschian engravings, publishing these sheets with the inscription "Hieronymus Bosch, Inventor." In 1567, the Italian writer and merchant Ludovico Guicciardini, in his widely read *Description of the Low Countries*, called Bosch "the most noble and admirable inventor of things fantastical and bizarre." Giorgio Vasari, in the second

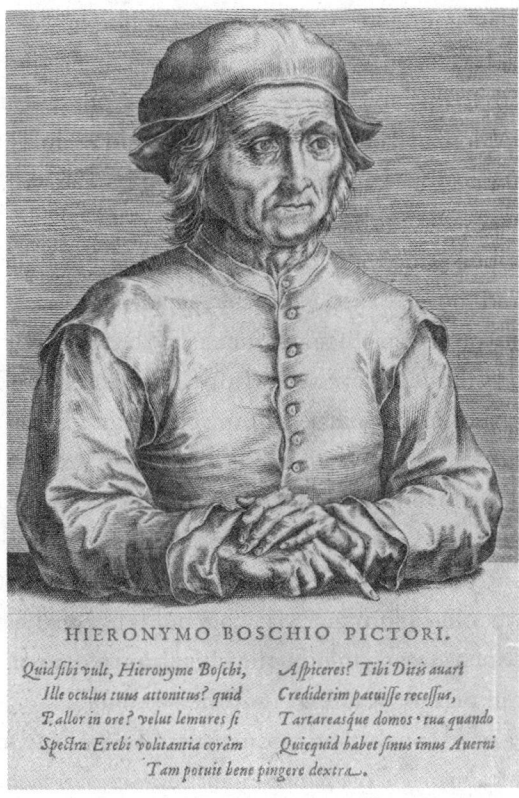

HIERONYMO BOSCHIO PICTORI.

Quid sibi vult, Hieronyme Boschi,
Ille oculus tuus attonitus? quid
Pallor in ore? velut lemures si
Spectra Erebi volitantia coràm
        Tam potuit bene pingere dextra.

Aspiceres? Tibi Ditis auari
Crediderim patuisse recessus,
Tartareasque domos · tua quando
Quicquid habet sinus imus Auerni

FIG. 8. Attributed to Cornelis Cort or Hieronymus Wierix, *Portrait of Hieronymus Bosch*, from Dominicus Lampsonius, *Pictorum aliquot celebrium Germaniae inferior effigies*, 1572. Engraving, 20.8 × 12.3 cm

edition of his *Lives* (1568), praised the painter's "fantastic and capricious inventions."[144] And by 1572 an engraved portrait of the artist would appear, placing him among the "famous painters" of the Netherlands—a verse inscription boasts he had glimpsed the specters of hell (fig. 8).[145]

Whatever it was that aroused his interest in Bosch, just weeks into his tyrannical rule Alba began to badger Granvelle's *maître des comptes*, Odet Viron, to have the set of Bosch tapestries brought back to Brussels so that he, Alba, could have copies of them made. "In order to rid myself of him," wrote Viron to Granvelle, "I let him know that the original is the property of the Prince of Orange, with which the pattern for the tapestry can be made more finely and faithfully." The Prince of Orange was William the Silent, leader of the Protestants, and no friend of Granvelle, having opposed the cardinal's harsh justice against his co-religionists. William had fled from Brussels to Nassau—his native home—upon hearing of Alba's departure to the Netherlands. The "original" he owned was Bosch's triptych. Focusing his efforts on that one Bosch, which Granvelle's "large tapestry" only copied, Alba soon received the cardinal's woven version, as Viron confirmed on December 14, 1567: "He has hung it in his residence, in order to contemplate it at his pleasure and have it woven on a larger scale."[146] Just two days later, with more pressing tasks requiring his attention, but the lust for Bosch's triptych burning in him, Alba decided to initiate proceedings against William. By December 20 the Palace of Nassau had been seized and its contents inventoried, including "a large tableau by Hieronymus Bosch" that hung in the Great Gallery, above or opposite the fireplace.[147]

Old enmities may have fueled Alba's desire. Foreordained by his parents to marry the wealthy and beautiful Spanish noblewoman Mencía de Mendoza, Alba was denied her by Charles V, who feared the combined power of the Toledo and Mendoza families. In 1524 Charles gave the bride instead to twice-widowed Henry III of Nassau, owner of the triptych when Antonio de Beatis glimpsed it in 1517. From Henry the triptych passed via his childless son to William the Silent, Alba's sworn foe. Moreover, in the decade prior to Alba's arrival, certain aspects of Bosch's art drew the attention of the Inquisition. In a letter of 1560, Granvelle successfully dissuaded Alba's cousin, García Álvarez de Toledo, from making copies of his (Granvelle's) Bosch tapestries. The cardinal writes that "little things" which seemed innocuous in the past no longer seem so in Spain.[148] By Christmas 1567 the triptych was finally in Alba's hands, but not without bloodshed. The duke's troops only seized it when William's concierge, under torture, revealed its hiding place. An anonymous memoir of the episode reports that "because [...] he had refused to surrender a painting by Hieronymus Bosch" William's concierge was dragged from the Nassau palace to a torture chamber on the Coudenberg hill:

> So they hoisted him on high with a weight of 100 pounds hanging from his feet until his hands touched the pulley, then they added a weight of 150 pounds. They scorched his body in several places. The torture he endured broke or dislocated every single limb of his body. He had no nails left on his feet or hands. He was no longer able to move, and could not even lift his hands to his mouth to eat, so that he had to forage for his food with teeth as best he could.[149]

Meanwhile, northern Europe was plunged into a war lasting eighty years, which permanently divided the Low Countries into a Catholic south and a Protestant north. But an initial spark of that great conflagration was Bosch's painting.

Alba declared a state of exception to seize a painted exception, Bosch's spectacle of lawless, godless, rebellious carnality punished without trial. The triptych, it turns out, appealed to dangerous men: Engelbert II, Henry III, Alba, and later Philip II. What did these urbicidal nobles relish in the work? The pleasure gardens? The lifelike portrait of a city besieged, its inhabitants tortured, its buildings and countryside torched? Or was it the combination they enjoyed: the lawless punished, chaos contained, diversity incinerated, a holy trinity of panels at war with itself? Beholding Bosch in the Prado, Carl Schmitt learned things about the "situation," Germany's situation after Stalingrad. Schmitt also traced the history of international public law back to the bloody sixteenth-century wars of religion. In his prison memoirs we read that the *ius publicum Europaeum* originated when, seeking to craft a settlement between belligerents who viewed each other as here-tics and "enemies of humanity," a new class of professional jurists drew the crucial distinction between criminals and foes. Wars will always seem just in the eyes of combatants, but from a neutral legal perspective the foe should be treated as just. This "restored awareness of the old distinction between enemy and criminal" was the "great achievement" of Bodin and Hobbes, Schmitt's two early modern friends. Both "entirely formed by civil war," they made an assertion foundational to the modern state: "Keep quiet, theologians, on matters outside your remit!"[150] No longer based on religious absolutes, law resulted from the mutual covenanting of subjects who bought protection with their obedience. Something of theology survived in the sphere of the political, the sphere that the state, however much it wanted to neutralize it, always presupposed. "The exception in jurisprudence," Schmitt wrote, "is analogous to the miracle in theology."[151] Schmitt drafted his reflections about the jurists' "Silence, theologians!" during what he imagined to be that principle's historical demise. At Nuremberg, he argued in his depositions to Kempner, the concept of "crimes against humanity" returned law to its medieval condition, but without any grounding in the divine. Now it was "the technicians of potentates and dogmatists [who] shout: 'Keep quiet, lawyers!'"[152]

Alba staged a terrifying spectacle of extralegal law. He could seize the Nassau palace and ship its contents to Spain, but William escaped his grasp, so he cap-tured the two next most prominent nobles in the Netherlands. Lamoral, count of Egmont, and Philip de Montmorency, count of Horn, had joined William in protesting at the inquisitorial justice that Granvelle, some years earlier, had es-tablished. Staunchly Catholic, however, and opposed to the image-breakers, they remained loyal to the king, hence their remaining after William fled. Their arrest on the charge of heresy drew protests from many European nobles, including Phil-ip II's cousin, Emperor Maximilian II. The Order of the Golden Fleece objected, too, as by its rules Egmont and Horn—both members—could only be tried by their peers. But on June 5, 1568, on the Grand Place with the citizens of Brussels watching, the two men were beheaded. Rarely had local estates and local laws suffered such a public blow.

A few blocks away from the scaffolds lived the most remarkable Netherlandish painter of the time. Creator in 1559 of the widely circulated engraving *Justitia*

(Justice; fig. 9), he would have marveled at the event, had he dared to show his face. For his prints and paintings vividly foreshadowed the events unfolding in his city. Pieter Bruegel the Elder began his career as the best of the many Bosch imitators that Felipe de Guevara wrote about. One of his earliest prints, published in Antwerp by Hieronymus Cock, bore Bosch's name as the image's "inventor." Faithfully following a drawing by Bruegel's hand, this engraving transforms its Boschian inheritance. Set in an everyday world, on the shabby banks of an ordinary Flemish harbor, the print makes a statement about everyday life: that in this world, "the big fish eat the little fish" (fig. 10). A father speaks this to his son before the spectacle that proves the point: "Behold" (*Ecce*), the father says, gesturing towards a beached behemoth disgorging fish-containing fish. Peculiarities abound: a larger colossus, wedged between boulders on an island offshore, has attracted gawkers armed with spears, and a fish-shaped bird in the sky and a man-shaped fish on land convey a world out of joint. But such *diverse bizzerrie* amuse more than they terrify. In Bruegel terror comes in inner-worldly form. The natural monstrosity seems to see us, but its eye is dead. That it ate all those fish illuminates the brute fact that, in nature as in human society, the strong devour the weak.

Carl Schmitt understood the essence of Bruegel's art and disapproved: "Between the demonology of Hieronymus Bosch and the hell of Bruegel the notion of worldly realism arose." Bosch still believed in hell—"his devils are ontological reality, not products of a fantasy of horror." Less than a century distant from Hobbes and close to him in spirit, Bruegel reduced hell to "an aesthetic and psychologically interesting place."[153] Few things are as objectionable to Schmitt as the merely "interesting." To treat urgent matters as interesting is to play with them rather than decide between them. Bruegel's worldliness represents one step towards the "age of naturalizations and politicizations," which "knows no other enemy than death" and which therefore "is no longer life but powerlessness and helplessness."[154]

Bruegel specialized in states of exception, not the divine ones of judgment and apocalypse, but the worldly ones of sovereign decision. His *Massacre of the Innocents* takes place not in Bethlehem but in the streets of a Flemish village circa 1567, when Bruegel painted the work (fig. 11). Soldiers in contemporary armor slaughter the children and a herald, surrounded by parents begging for mercy, wears the double-headed eagle of Habsburg rule. Emperor Rudolf II, when he acquired the picture, had the dead children and the heraldry overpainted. Similarly, Bruegel's *Census at Bethlehem*—dated 1566—shows the dangerous machinery of government at work, again in a Flemish village in winter. A Habsburg coat-of-arms affixed to the foreground makes the picture topical. The big fish of imperial power, in the Netherlands as in Judea, eat the little fish, the peasantry, who hardly

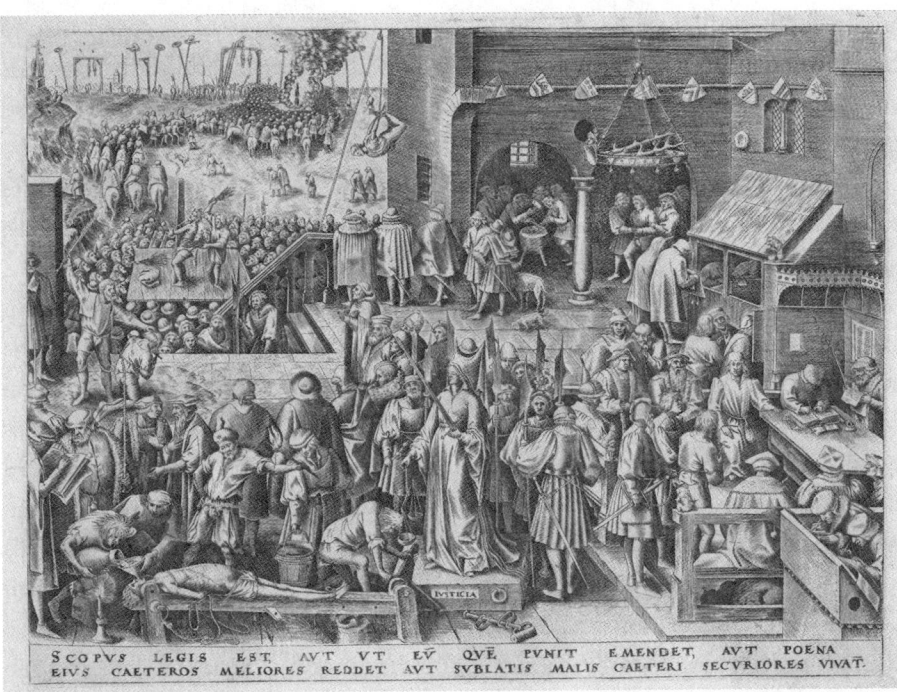

SCOPVS LEGIS EST, AVT VT EV QVE PVNIT EMENDET, AVT POENA
EIVS CAETEROS MELIORES REDDET AVT SVBLATIS MALIS CAETERI SECVRIORES VIVAT.

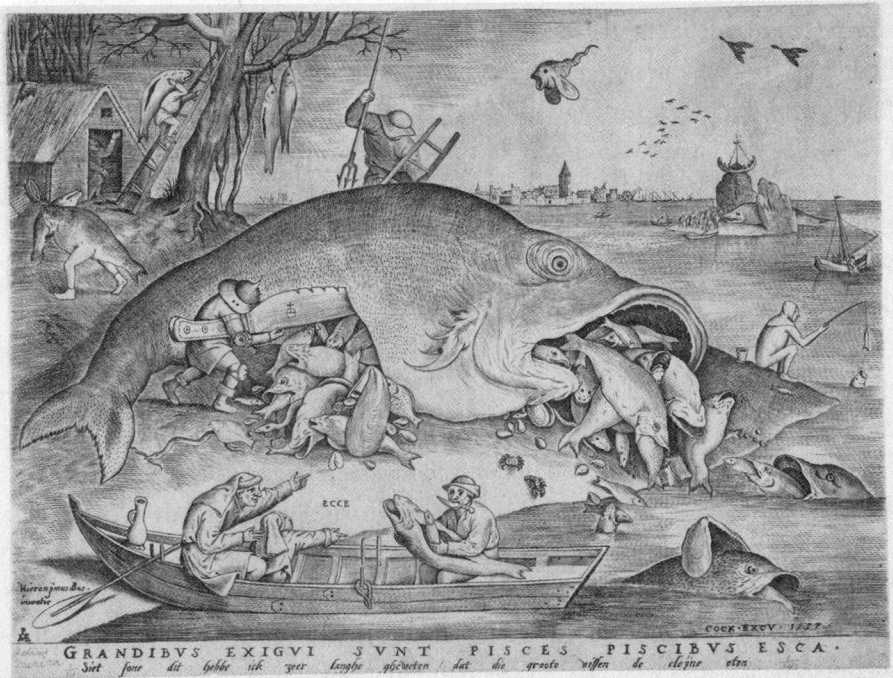

GRANDIBVS EXIGVI SVNT PISCES PISCIBVS ESCA.
Siet sone dit hebbe ick zeer langhe gheweten dat de groote visschen de cleine eten

TOP: FIG. 9. Philips Galle, after Pieter Bruegel the Elder, *Justitia* (*Justice*), from the *Virtues* series, c. 1559–60. Engraving (published by Hieronymus Cock, Antwerp), 22.5 × 29 cm

ABOVE: FIG. 10. Pieter van der Heyden after Pieter Bruegel the Elder, *Big Fish Eat Little Fish*, 1557. Engraving (published by Hieronymus Cock, Antwerp), 22.9 × 29.6 cm

need a costume change. At his most Boschian Bruegel refuses transcendence. In his *Triumph of Death*, an army of corpses conquers humanity, and all that ascends above the smoldering horizon are the bloated corpses of people hanged or broken on the wheel, and the raised arm of one cadaverous henchman (fig. 12).

The artist's first biographer reports that on his deathbed Bruegel had his wife burn some of his works "because they were too caustic or derisory, either because he was sorry or that he was afraid that on their account she would get into trouble or she might have to answer for them." The painter also left his wife a painting of a magpie on the gallows: "By the magpie he meant gossiping tongues, which he committed to the gallows."[155] Dated 1568, the year before his death, the picture survives (plate 15). On a wooden panel no larger than an open book, Bruegel has captured a rural enclave from a new planetary point of view. At the lower left a turned-away pair—onlookers like us—respond. One taps his foot to the near-by bagpiper's tune, the other gestures towards the vast world view. Perhaps this painting vilifies the damage wrought by gossips in dangerous times. Through its tiny scale it speaks softly and cloaked in riddles. An expert in local proverbs, Bruegel knew every saying the painting might suggest. The rustic defecating in the shadows at lower left conjures the adage "To shit on the gallows," meaning to ignore or to defy danger foolishly. And obviously the dancing trio enacts the variant, "To dance under the gallows."[156] This gallows rises where Antonio de Beatis observed them, at the village's edge to warn that the law is in force and trespassers will be punished.

The peasants know their proverbs better than we, better than Bruegel. They are his native informants—Bruegel was said to visit rustic villages disguised as a peasant "to observe the nature of the peasants—in eating, drinking, dancing, leaping, lovemaking and other amusements."[157] If they dance under the gallows they do so knowingly. In defiance of that castle on the hill but hidden by hedges, they play with the law. In Bruegel's rendering the gallows is bizarrely contorted. Its crosspiece and base are at different angles, and its feet striding vertiginously downhill. Built of beams whose wood the artist concretely portrays, the structure looks solid. It refuses optically to resolve into a stable whole, like a Penrose triangle.

Roger and Lionel Penrose called their triangle "impossibility in its purest form."[158] The gallows is the impossible made self-evident—Boschian drollery disenchanted. Bruegel constructs his visual puzzle to picture law in the state of siege.[159] The law might claim to contain its emergency suspension, but the events unfolding in Brussels in 1567 proved otherwise. Bruegel resided in that city from 1563 until his death in 1569. Lauded in his day as "Bosch once more returned to the world," he likely visited the Nassau palace and saw his precursor's most challenging

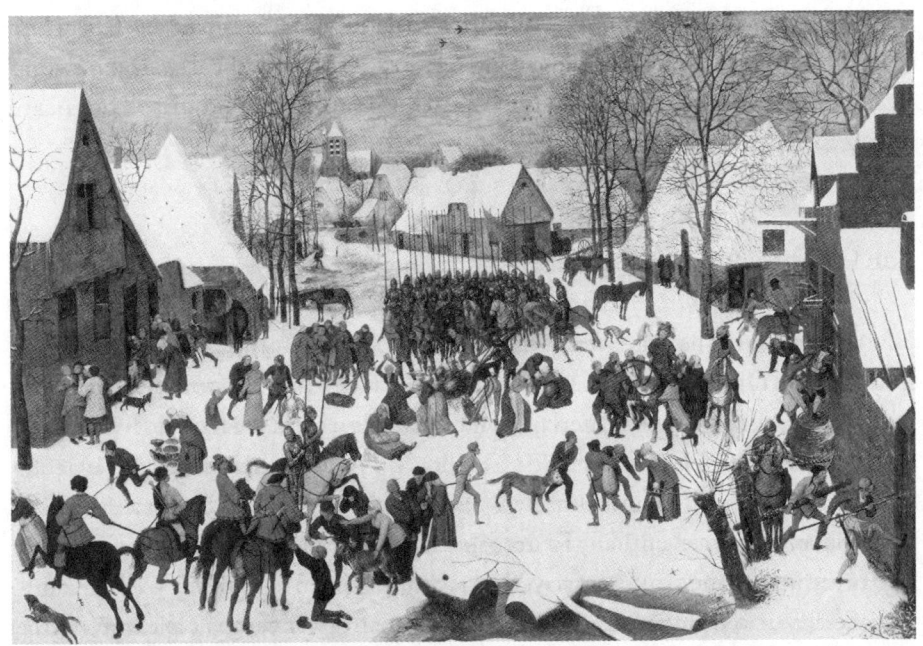

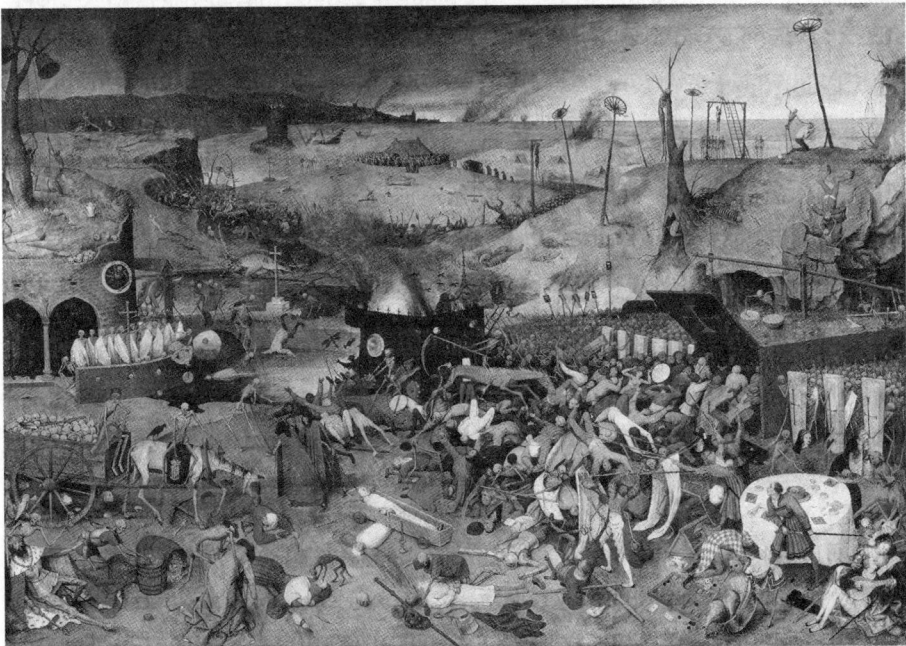

TOP: FIG. 11. Pieter Bruegel the Elder, *Massacre of the Innocents*, c. 1565–67. Oil on panel, 109.2 × 158.1 cm. Royal Collection Trust, UK

ABOVE: FIG. 12. Pieter Bruegel the Elder, *Triumph of Death*, c. 1562. Oil on panel, 117 × 162 cm. Museo Nacional del Prado, Madrid

creation. He may also have known of its seizure by Alba. It is tempting to think of the *Magpie on the Gallows* as a sequel to the confiscated triptych. Appareled in heavy rustic garb and reduced from Bosch's naked multitude to three, the peasants—Bruegel's innocents—dance deadly circles before the law.

San Lorenzo de El Escorial, 1593

The triptych must have arrived in Spain by 1573, brought back by Alba after Philip II relieved him of his offices. The Iron Duke's five years of governance had only widened rebellion in the Netherlands. At Alba's death in 1582 the triptych passed to his illegitimate son, Fernando de Toledo. In 1591 Philip II purchased it at the auction of Fernando's estate. For decades the Spanish king had been assembling a vast art collection eventually to decorate his palace San Lorenzo de El Escorial. It was there that the triptych arrived in 1593.[160]

Already as a young prince, Philip had been an adventurous collector. At the Imperial Diet of Augsburg in 1550, he engaged Titian (his father Charles V's favorite painter) to make a series of mythological paintings called the *poesie*. Based on Ovid's *Metamorphoses*, the six canvases depict the tragic loves between gods and humans: Actaeon's glimpse of Diana and her nymphs, Venus besotted with Adonis, Andromeda rescued by Perseus, and Jupiter inseminating Danaë, abducting Europa, and causing Callisto, pregnant by him, to be turned into a bear. In the chronology of their making, the series starts and finishes with Jupiter, king of the gods, "taking" a woman: Danaë at the beginning and Europa at the end. Heroes are born (Perseus) and continents claimed (Europe): fit themes for Philip's rule. The title *poesie*—Titian's own invention—boasts that these paintings will be "mute poems" adapted from poetical sources and rivaling them. The *poesie* also demonstrate *poiesis*, "the bringing forth of something new."

Titian tells epic tales through and about flesh. "Since the Danaë that I sent to your Majesty was seen from the front," he wrote to Philip, probably in 1554. about the first picture in the series, "in this other *poesia* I wanted to vary [the composition] and show the other side, so that the chamber where they are to be placed will be more beautiful."[161] Having aroused desire through one viewpoint (Danaë's body turned in our direction), the artist sparks new desires through an opposite viewing angle, as (in his second *poesia*) Venus twists away from us towards Adonis, who pulls away—to his doom. "The Venus has her back turned, not for any artistic deficiency but to double the art," wrote a Venetian humanist about Titian's painting in 1554. "One recognizes in the intimate parts here the creases of the flesh caused by her seated position," as well as the "evident signs of the fear that she was feeling in her heart, in view of the unhappy end that the young man met."[162] Titian's nudes spell disaster, most obviously for Actaeon, who because he looks illicitly at the naked nymphs is torn apart by his own raging hounds. Each painting orchestrates a dangerous moment, dangerous to the protagonists and the male beholder, who stands delighted and bewildered, like Actaeon.

Titian created the *poesie* over eleven years, dispatching the finished canvases to wherever Philip happened to be at the time, in London, the Netherlands, or Toledo. But the painter expected that, when complete, his suit of canvases would hang in a special room—a "chamber" (*camerino*) as mentioned in his letter quoted above. In 1520 he had painted two canvases for the Camerino d'Alabastro, a recreational chamber in the Ducal Palace in Ferrara. Such rooms were built for unembarrassed viewing of, and amical conversation about, paintings of an erotic kind. Doors could be closed, restricting access to a narrow circle of friends—Antonio de Beatis spotted Bosch's triptych in such an ocular playground. Viewers of Titian's *poesie* could contemplate how Danaë (hanging on one wall) would give birth to Perseus (hanging on another wall), and how Perseus would unknowingly slay Danaë's father, Acrisius, who, hearing this fate foretold, had imprisoned Danaë in the first place, causing her insemination (back on the first wall) by Jupiter. By trying to avoid fate both the gods and humans fulfill it. Hung around the room, the *poesie* form a magic circle, each end a beginning, and each beginning an end.

At the Escorial, dedicated in 1586, Philip encircled himself with paintings of a very different kind. As his chief librarian, Father José de Sigüenza, reported in 1605, the king had these paintings "in his house, his cloister, his apartment, the chapter house, and the sacristy; for all these places are adorned with them."[163] Of "great ingeniousness," these works were all "by a certain Geronimo Bosch." Neither were they "absurdities" (*disparates*), as people commonly thought, nor were they "tainted by heresy," since Philip, defender of Catholic orthodoxy, displayed them everywhere. Beside "a bookcase like those of the monks," in a special room for prayer, hung a most "excellent" piece (plate 3):

> In the center, in a circle of light and glory, [the artist] placed our Savior; around Him are seven circles in which are seen the Seven Deadly Sins, in which all the creatures that He redeemed offend Him without realizing that He is watching them and sees everything [.... A]nd because he painted it as a mirror in which the truth of Christianity is reflected, we might all see ourselves in it.[164]

The chamber where Philip contemplated Bosch's *Seven Deadly Sins* can still be visited. Attached to his bedroom, it looks out one way to a vista of the Herrería forest and Las Machotas. The other way, it looks towards the high altar of the Escorial's Basilica. Through one window, Philip's global empire stretching west to Lima on the South American coast and east to the Philippines; through the other window, liturgy ceaselessly affirming the Catholic Church; and between the two, looking at the ruler while he looked at it, Bosch's painted mirror.

This strange panel—signed at the lower center "Jheronimus bosch"—was probably sold to Philip by Felipe de Guevara, who inherited it from his father, Diego. A Spaniard in the service of the dukes of Burgundy, Diego de Guevara likely purchased the work directly from the artist. In his written commentary on the painting, Felipe seems to cast doubt on whether the work is by Bosch's hand, and its support—poplar—is unique among Netherlandish paintings. But whether by an assistant, a follower, or the master himself, *The Seven Deadly Sins* is the most perfect key I know of to the whole of Bosch's art. Felipe reports its being "a table" (*mesa*) while Sigüenza calls it as a "rectangular panel" (*tabla y quadro*).[165] Whether that means the work originally formed a tabletop, perhaps hinged so that it could be viewed in a vertical position, its detailed imagery can be best beheld by circling around it. The artist's signature, most of the Latin inscriptions, and four corner roundels orient the picture consistently, but the scenes of the deadly sins throw the beholder into confusion. Yet being topsy-turvy befits these seven scenes of everyday life. Among the first genre paintings in the history of European art, they repudiate ironically their own fascination: secular art begins with negation—how not to behave—and with viewers foolishly craning their necks. The mesmerizing circle of sins (also a seven-spoked wheel) wraps around the golden iris and deep blue pupil of a divine eye. Out of balance, we presently stand beheld by the picture, as a text written in red asserts: "Beware, beware, God sees!"

As features of an actual eye, the sins might be understood to be the world in front of the painting, as if reflected on the eye's moist sclera. Thus surrounded, the arrangement tells us, God's eye will see nothing but sin. Perverse, this world is upside down and inside out. The sinful walk as if on the inner surface of a globe, their legs like mice's on a treadmill, and with the golden rays of the sun, the divine eye's other valence, harshly illuminating everything. Hats, shoes, tables, chairs, a children's potty look tossed, as in a centrifuge. The painting turns us upside down, too, unless we stare steadfastly at its center. There inside the eye's pupil, Christ rises from his sarcophagus to display his wounds. Might he be what God sees, his only son cruelly tortured and killed by sinners like us? All-seeing, God can behold the center and the periphery simultaneously. He can hold Christ and "the creatures that he redeemed"—now caught in the act of "offend[ing] Him" (Sigüenza)—together in his gaze.[166] We do not have that power. Is the picture's hope that by ignoring the its dizzying temptations and looking solely at Christ, we glimpse the sparklet of God originally implanted in us?[167]

The image does not answer this question. And given what his eye sees—his son's body ruined by humans *and* the world corrupted by humans—God must be furious. This panel, like all of Bosch's paintings, shouts "Beware!" In the Middle Dutch of Bosch's time (as in German) the word for a sudden moment was *ogen-blik*, literally the blink, or glance, of the eye. The painting is a dangerous *ogenblik*. Below the genre scene of Anger, where opponents fight each other murderously before a disreputable inn, words on a banderole read, "I will hide my face from them. I will see what their end shall be." The line comes from the Song of Moses, at Deuteronomy 32:20. A pivotal Old Testament text about friends and enemies, it contrasts God's protection of an obedient Israel with his destruction of an idolatrous one. It follows one of the most gruesome passages in scripture, where Moses warns Israel of being attacked "by a nation whose tongue thou shalt not understand" (28:49). Surrounded by foes and starving inside their city's gates, the besieged resort to cannibalism. Besieging us in the present tense, Bosch's painting shows what, when God turns away in wrath, our end will be. The corner roundels depict a venerable eschatological summary: Death, Judgment, Heaven, and Earth, or Four Last Things. God decides on us in this *ogenblik*.

Fraenger envied Schmitt for the experiences he would have before this "concentration point," and how, visiting the Prado, he might "sink" into Bosch's painted eye. In Fraenger's view, Bosch "breaks the wall that normally separates subject from object, consciousness of self from consciousness of what is perceived." In this way "the self 'alien-ates' itself from the object it beholds; it identifies itself with the content of its vision so fully that it learns to live, think, and experience from within the nature and essence of the scene."[168] This vision of a return to nature will haunt Schmitt through the specter of Bosch's triptych. "Self-alienation" and "self-externalization in a problem-free corporality" are his enemy. Yet as *The Seven Deadly Sins* makes clear, Bosch's art hinges less on the shifting duality of self and world than on the distinction between, and decision on, friend and enemy. The painter should therefore be the jurist's friend, like Bodin and Hobbes. But to return to 1593: the decisionism of Bosch's tabletop would have appealed to the Spanish king as he undertook his daily devotions, flanked by church and state, with God's eye on him.

The Escorial was political theology in architectural form. Politically, it commemorated Philip's successful siege of St. Quentin and defeat of French forces on Saint Lawrence's Day (August 10) 1557. Theologically, as bastion of Catholicism against a world turned upside down by heresy, it tied Philip's rule to God. The church also had a dynastic function as burial place of the Spanish Habsburg family line. It affirmed the old political theology of the king's "two bodies," with the natural body being mortal but the political body immortal. "Each and every prince," wrote Philip's royal councillor, may be considered "in two distinct and different ways: as a man and as a sovereign."[169] Philip would not have distinguished between the two. At St. Quentin, seeing thousands dead, he made a solemn vow to build a great church because he believed victory depended on God's will. Philip drew up his "letter of foundation and endowment" for the Escorial on April 11, 1567, thinking he would march to the Netherlands himself to quell rebellion and unsure whether he would return alive.[170] It is said that the Escorial's gridiron plan recollects the grill on which Saint Lawrence (San Lorenzo in Spanish) was martyred, and on whose feast day Spain won in battle. While his enemies considered him a tyrant, and while his hunger for territory was violent and insatiable, Philip, melancholy, overworked, and sometimes indecisive, thought of himself as a martyr. On the one hand, his royal arms included a cartographic rendering of the earth as globe and the legend *Non Sufficit Orbis* (The world is not enough). On the other hand, while besieging peoples in Europe, Asia, and the Americas, Philip felt himself to be hopelessly besieged—by enemies and family woes (Don Carlos, his sole male heir, died while imprisoned by his father), and by paperwork. His courtiers complained that, though his brain "must be the largest in the world," the affairs he tried personally to manage were too multitudinous for any one person.[171] Torturing and burning heretics at the stake, prosecuting continual war against the Ottoman Turks, violently suppressing the Moriscos in Granada, crushing rebellion in the Netherlands, destroying the Incan Empire in Peru were, in his mind, defensive actions against a world out of joint and closing in on him. No person in history ever had a more global sovereignty than he. Spanning all twenty-four time zones, his was the first empire on which the sun never set. In prayer he could focus on Christ inside an inverted globe: Bosch's topsy-turvy world map, with enemies and distractions punished, and the sun never setting.

Bruegel's *The Magpie on the Gallows* fits the world into a tiny panel. A winding river carries boats, and the eye, out to sea (plate 15). Above the gallows, the convergence of meandering rivers and misty valleys makes the horizon seem curved, affirming that the earth is round, and that the waterways along which people travel empty into the oceans that encompass the globe. Born a half a century before Columbus's landfall, Bosch still pictured the world as a finite enclosure. In his art, waters do not circulate, as Bruegel's do, on the curved surface of a sphere, but instead seep downward into diabolical canals (plate 14; fig. 39). Water has its home in the sewer. Even Bosch's vast landscape vistas, which inspired Bruegel, sink into the entrapping hole of hell. But what appears claustrophobic to us looked different to Philip. In the era of colonial conquest, he ruled with Bosch's world picture, literally, in view.

Bosch's triptych arrived at the Escorial as part of the last of six shipments of artworks to the palace. The shipment inventory described the work as follows:

> A painting on panel in oil, with two wings, of the variety of the world, symbolized by diverse disparities by Hieronymus Bosch, which they call the Madrona, with gild frames; with closed wings it is 2½ ells high and 2⅓ wide; it was bought at the auction of Prior Don Fernando.[172]

The shippers measured and transported the triptych with its outer panels closed (plate 1). Unpacked, the work would have at first displayed the grisaille tableau of the newly formed world, with God tiny at the upper left and his creation a transparent globe hovering in the dark but reflecting light as if on a crystalline surface. Dry land, separated from the waters on this, the Third Day of Creation, is a disk bisecting the sphere. Already overgrown with grasses, this primordial terrain recedes into depth: at the limits of his perspectival rendering, Bosch sketches the distant mountains with his finest-tipped brush. But however vast it looks to human eyes, earth is encompassed spatially by the sphere, just as its whole history will be contained in the triptych's open state. Deposited on a divided plane—two panels of Baltic oak—the sphere presses forward to where the wings open. Its curvature emphasized by reflections on its surface, it asks to be opened.

The shipment inventory describes and interprets its open state. As published versions of the document usually have it, the painting is "of the variety [*bariedad*] of the world," which Bosch symbolized by means of "diverse disparities" (*diueros disparates*).[173] Whoever recorded the work liked that last word, *disparates*, as he applied it to all five works by Bosch itemized in the 1593 shipment: a *Last Judgment*, a *Temptation of Saint Anthony*, and a *Christ Crowned with Thorns* all contain "diverse disparities of Hieronymus Bosch," as does "another painting," described otherwise only as "dark."[174] The word derives from the Latin *disparitas* (not + equality). Applied to Bosch it suggests that his signature hybrid entities have parts that do not belong, that their pairing is impossible, and thus that they stand apart from the natural order. Artists before Bosch knew how to make disparities. The Roman poet Horace referred to painters joining a human head to a horse's body, or a fish's tail to a woman's waist and eliciting laughter from their audience; Saint Bernard of Clairvaux, in 1135, complained of the "deformed beauties and beautiful deformities"—centaurs, "half-men" and other "hybrid forms"—carved into stone and distracting monks from their devotions. Bosch uses diverse disparities to "cipher" (Spanish *cifrar*), in the sense of symbolizing in an encrypted way, the variety of the world. Variety was the cardinal virtue of the princely cabinets of wonder where, as we have seen, the panels originally stood. Such cabinets exemplified variety chiefly through anomalies. Accumulating since antiquity in great lists, anomalies multiplied through artistic experiment and global exploration. The triptych's portrayal of Eden contains an elephant, a giraffe, and a dragon tree, exotic species known through traveler's reports. The co-presence (in Antonio de Beatis's words) of "men and women, white and black," as well as their nakedness and paradisiacal habitat, might respond to tales arriving from the Americas about diverse peoples, shameless nudity, and fecund nature.[175]

Anomalies escaped all categories but one. Although they derived from nature's playful fecundity, they were themselves counter-natural, because they violated the separation between species. On Day Three of Creation, depicted in the triptych's closed state, God commanded living creatures to seed "according to their various kinds" (Gen. 1:11–12). The Christian tradition linked overabundant variety to vanity. Contrasted to God's oneness, extreme variation led to curiosity, and curiosity led to sin: Eve ate the apple at least partly because she was curious. The word in the 1593 shipment inventory usually transcribed as *bariedad* might better be construed as *banidad*, "vanity."[176] This would make the triptych's moral more explicit. It would also eliminate the redundance of "variety" being symbolized by "diverse disparities." It may be the world's vanity that Bosch's fantasies in 1593 were believed to encrypt. Whether as vanity or variety, the triptych's negative connotation is conveyed by the inventory's nickname for the ensemble: "the Madrona."[177] The madrone or "strawberry tree" is an evergreen with fruits resembling small strawberries. The fruit's bland taste allowed Pliny the Elder to derive the plant's Latin name, *Arbutus enedo*, from the phrase *unum edo*, "I eat one." Birds relish these fruits, as do bears: the ancient emblem of Madrid features a bear pawing madrone berries. Bosch scholars often mistranslate *madroño* as "strawberry," although strawberries (genus *fragaria*) also appear in the triptych.[178] Sigüenza explained the nickname succinctly: just as the madrona's berries look enticing but when eaten leave no flavor behind, so the pleasures enjoyed in Bosch's triptych are empty and fleeting. Vain, they are damnable, as the hell panel confirms. The librarian also "expounds" on the madrone metaphor through a reading of the triptych's left panel. In his eyes, the painting shows Adam as lord over the animals and birds, but tested "for his obedience and faith not to eat from the tree, and how later the devil deceived him in the form of a serpent." In other words, Adam and Eve are presently undergoing a trial—one involving the eating of fruit—the "later" outcome of which the painting also suggests. Presumably Sigüenza understands the snake wrapped around the tree in the right middle-ground as foreshadowing Eve and Adam's deception by the biblical serpent.

Sigüenza notes "this is more simply presented" in a painting called *The Hay Wain*, also at the Escorial.[179] Purchased from Felipe de Guevara's estate, that triptych portrays the history of evil in four scenes on its left inner wing (plate 9). In sequence from background to foreground, the Fall of the Rebel Angels, the Creation of Eve, the Fall, and the Expulsion form a tragic prequel to the allegorical central panel. Moving left to right between Eden and hell, the hay—a biblical and proverbial emblem of vanity here shaped like a misshapen globe—symbolizes the pleasurable "world" that humans seek to possess, disastrously, as the inferno in the right panel indicates. Meanwhile in the clouds above Christ appears showing his wounds, indicating that he sits in judgment. Wordlessly the picture warns: "Beware, God sees!" If the so-called *Madroña* shouts "Beware," it does so silently and cruelly. What happens in this triptych's Eden corresponds to no biblical episode. That God (looking out at us) is giving a command which Eve and Adam will disobey, and that one of the reptiles behind them will be involved: these are Sigüenza's inventions. With no warning label painted in red and no godhead ruling from above, the central panel makes beholding it a most dire *ogenblik*.

Sigüenza knew about hidden perils, for he himself had been touched by the "taint of heresy."[180] Erudite, multilingual, and trusted by the king, he oversaw the library's ten thousand volumes (including forbidden ones), invented allegories for the reading room's ceiling, and shaped the preaching practices at the Escorial—he replaced the florid and allusive sermonizing of his predecessors with a stricter, gospel-based preaching style. In 1586 he delivered the main sermon at the Escorial's dedication, when the corpse of Charles V was finally transferred to a crypt below the main altar. But in 1592, Philip II's confessor and prior of the Royal Monastery, Diego de Yepes, initiated an investigation into Sigüenza's teachings. Among the charges was that he preached the "naked gospel" and argued that Holy Scripture can be understood easily and on its own. *Sola scriptura* (scripture alone) had been Martin Luther's rallying cry.[181] In Catholic Spain, affirming this doctrine would have been heretical. Sigüenza appeared voluntarily before the inquisitorial tribunal in Toledo, and successfully defended himself against all accusations, arguing that his views had been absurdly misrepresented, probably by individuals envious of his access to the king. Acquitted but warned to keep clear of error, he returned to the Escorial circumspect.

Defending Bosch from the charge of heresy took courage. Already in 1560s the artist had come under scrutiny in Spain because of his anti-clerical imagery, Netherlandish heritage, and artistic afterlife in the visual polemics of Protestants.[182] Looking back on Bosch from the distance of a century, Sigüenza delivered a coherent account of the painter's entire oeuvre, from his straightforward biblical scenes, through his special focus on the hermit saints, to his cryptic works. This Sigüenza did to prove the artist's consistent orthodoxy, moral clarity, and realism. Bosch's works look strange only because he portrays human beings not from outside, but as they truly are, "from the inside."[183] Most scholars today agree with Sigüenza and evoke his testimony against the extravagances of Fraenger and his ilk. But in Spain after the librarian's death in 1606 a debate over Bosch raged. In 1649 the painter Francisco Pacheco faulted Sigüenza for turning Bosch's "fantasies into mysteries."[184] To the poet Francisco de Quevedo, Bosch's *disparates* were just that, "nothing but devils, buttocks and codpieces."[185]

A famed polemicist, Quevedo used Boschian fantasy as a weapon in his literary feud against his enemy, Luis de Góngora. Góngora's poetry, religion, and physical person, Quevedo charged, were grotesque, like Bosch's *disparates*. In "The Bedeviled Constable," the second of Quevedo's satirical *Dreams* written around 1607, Bosch appears among the damned. Answering questions about hell, the devil complains about how grotesquely humans portray his crew, giving them animal attributes when in fact they might pass for magistrates or hermits. A chief offender was Hieronymus Bosch, who "fetched up among us." The devil explains, "We asked him why he had dreamed so many fantastic recipes for us in his pictures, and he replied: 'Because I never believed devils really existed.' "[186] Already in 1568, a Netherlandish chronicler reported that Bosch "was called devil-maker, because he was never equaled in making devils."[187] In the literary wars that raged in Spain during its "Golden Age," Bosch became a cipher for disbelief. Meanwhile, his works fell into oblivion due to inaccessibility, changing tastes, and deteriorating physical condition. Rehabilitation came later for Bosch than for the other major Netherlandish painters, most of whom had been rediscovered and closely studied in the early nineteenth century, in the wake of Napoleon's secularization of church art. Bosch's revival began only in 1889, with Carl Justi's survey of his works in the Spanish royal collections. There we read of "the strangest and most obscure of Bosch's allegorical-moralizing productions," a picture "for which no one has been able to find a proper title."[188] For want of a title, Justi called the picture the *Lustgarten* ("Pleasure Garden"), and it is by some version of that name that the work still goes.

's-Hertogenbosch, 1516

From its rediscovery forward, the triptych's reception grows denser. An annotated bibliography could fill a big book. Thousands claim they have solved the work's riddle, but to no one else's satisfaction; for years I marched their circle. The way back frustrates, too. Before 1517, when the journal-keeping Italian glimpsed it in Brussels, the paper trail goes cold. In 2016 the fifth centenary of Bosch's death occasioned intense collective scrutiny of the facts. Archival research and technical analysis of the surviving artifacts have made our picture of the artist remarkably clear. Today we know more about Bosch than we do about most fifteenth-century painters.

A surviving record of payments for burial rites made in 1516 reveals much about the artist's person. "For the funeral of Jeronimus van Aken, painter, on the 19th of August," the entry begins.[189] The entry refers to the deceased by his given name, as do all but three of the nearly fifty contemporary documents that mention the artist. His surname, "van Aken," indicates that the painter's forebears hailed from Aachen, that ancient and imperial city where, since Charlemagne's burial there in 814 and until 1531, the Holy Roman emperors were crowned King of the Germans. The German toponym derives from *Aach*, meaning "river" or "stream," and translates the Latin *aquae* (waters), alluding to the warm mineral springs that since Roman times fed the city's healing baths. When the van Akens, probably painters in Aachen, moved to Nijmegen in Gelderland, and then to 's-Herto-genbosch in Brabant—probably to pursue their specialized craft in the boom economy of the Netherlands—they would have been proud to advertise their being "from Aachen."

The 1516 document spells the deceased's forename "Jeronimus." This lies be-tween the Dutch "Jeroen," "Jonen," or "Joen," as most other contemporary sources have it, and the Latin "Hieronymus," as it is written today, but by any spelling the name was unusual in 's-Hertogenbosch.[190] Given at the child's baptism around 1450, it honors the fourth-century ascetic and theologian Saint Jerome, whose translations of scripture from Hebrew, Aramaic, and Greek into Latin formed the basis of the Vulgate, the authoritative Holy Bible in the Christian West. Venerated as one of the four Great Fathers of the Catholic Church, Jerome became—in the decades before the artist's birth—the patron saint of the so-called *devotio moderna*. An important religious reform movement originating in the northern Nether-lands, this self-proclaimed new or "modern" devotion advocated simple, inward Christ-based piety and a humble Christ-like lifestyle. Some adherents withdrew into semi-monastic communities, calling themselves Brethren of the Common Life—Saint Jerome's years in ascetic seclusion were part of his biography. But the Brethren's writings and preaching influenced the worldly elite. In 's-Herto-genbosch, where they established a foundation in 1424, they were known as the Hieronymites. One of Bosch's three surviving portrayals of his namesake shows Jerome prostrate in the wilderness, with a crucifixion held awkwardly between his outstretched arms, parallel to the jagged diagonal of his body (plate 4). Stripped of his red cardinal's robes, the saint prays to Christ in abject humility in accordance with Modern Devotion's central teaching: to follow Christ is to imitate him, literally to become his likeness. "If you want to reign with Me," preaches Christ in the *Imitation of Christ* (the movement's literary monument), "bear the cross with Me."[191] To bear Christ's cross is to die to the world. Eyes closed, wrapped in shroud-like underclothes, and with a rock beside him to punish his body, Bosch's Jerome mortifies himself underground, as if in an early grave. The slab teetering above him resembles a toppled tombstone, his underground retreat, a ruined mausoleum. A portrait of self in the act of self-denial, this single panel would have made a fitting epitaph for Jheronimus van Aken, where death is not a departure but a homecoming, but analysis of the oak Bosch used place it early in his career.

Naming his son Jerome would have made special sense to Anthonius van Aken, the artist's painter-father, born circa 1420 in Nijmegen. Anthonius's own namesake, Saint Anthony the Great, was the legendary founder of monasticism and the early Christian prototype of ascetic piety. Born in Egypt around 250 CE—a century before Jerome—this Anthony cast aside worldly possessions and went into the Libyan desert, there to live for eighty years praying to Christ in pious and arduous seclusion. Bosch painted Saint Anthony often, and at least once together with Jerome on the same triptych. Literate in Latin, and friendly with learned theologians, scholars, and librarians, the painter knew intimately the legends of the saints. Fond of verbal-visual wordplay, he would have attended to the etymologies of his namesake, such as the one Jacobus de Voragine put forth in his compendium the *Golden Legend*: "Jerome (Hieronymus in Latin) comes from *gerar*, holy, and *nemus* a grove—hence a holy grove." That grove was holy, Jacobus speculates, digging back to the roots of Latin *sacer* (set apart), because it was "set apart for sacred use." And Jerome was called a grove "after the grove where he lived at times."[192]

When portraying his namesake Bosch set him in a wilderness apart from the world, with abbreviated woodlands framing his remove. With their painful thorns, sepulchral roots, and uncanny flowers and fruits pressing dangerously in on the saint, these groves seem more accursed than holy. After his brilliant career in Rome, Jerome withdrew into the Syrian desert to do penance for his sins. But vice haunted him even there. "All the company I had was scorpions and wild beasts," the saint reported in a letter cited by Voragine, "yet at times I felt myself surrounded by clusters of pretty girls, and the fires of lust were lighted in my frozen body and moribund flesh."[193] This is Bosch territory, where the self withdraws from the pleasures of the world only to be besieged by temptations from within. In the painting, reproductive organs of a plant arch luridly over the recumbent penitent. Gaudy red, like the robes Jerome cast off, and with a spent seedpod attached, this tuberous, parasitical extension is fecund in decay, like lust that flourishes most elaborately in denial. With plants like these, the bushy grove resonates less with "Jerome," the artist's Christian name, than with the alias he took to brand his works and set his artistic personality apart: the unforgettable monosyllabic "Bosch."

At least three documents from his lifetime and several afterward register his name in full. Two entries from 1509–10 have him as "Jheronimi van Aeken, painter, who signs himself Bosch," and a list of deceased members of a religious brotherhood in 's-Hertogenbosch includes "Hieronimus Aquens alias Bosch, renowned painter, deceased 1516."[194] The list dates from around 1577 but someone added the words "alias Bosch, renowned painter" later, perhaps after 1600. Before any of these archival sources, however, are the artist's paintings. Calligraphed in large letters in black, yellow, or gold at the lower edge of his panels, "Jheronimus Bosch" appears on works as early as 1490. Felipe de Guevara reported that copyists forged that signature, presumably also after 1516. As late as 1556 Hieronymus Cock signed engravings he published in Bosch's manner "Hieronimus Bos / inventor."[195] Only in his native city did the name "van Aken" remain attached to the artist, and there, only for a few generations. Short for " 's-Hertogenbosch," the alias "Bosch" was addressed mostly to *absent* admirers. To stamp it with a name assumes the artifact will travel beyond the place and time of its making. The name of Bosch's city also adds a story. A Dutch contraction of "des Hertogen bosch," the word " 's-Hertogenbosch" recollects that the city stands on what long ago—before the late twelfth century, when walls were built around a settled bit of wooded dunes—had been the rich and beloved "forest" (*bos* or *bosch*) belonging to the duke (*hertog*) of Brabant. Bois-le Duc is its French calque.

Local panegyrics played with the name. They celebrated how trees became buildings, errant paths broad roads and gates, and beasts and birds the town's diverse citizenry. Municipal coats-of-arms wrote the word in pictures. A heart or an antlered hart for "hert," a pair of eyes for "ogen," and trees for "bosch" add up to "hert-ogen-bosch."[196] In this period painters designed and fashioned heraldic shields. In Dutch the usual word for painter is *schilder* ("shield-maker") and a painting is *een schilderij*. Called *schilder* in most of the documents, Bosch's shop made armorial artifacts, including a parodic shield featuring a fool from whose head a quack extracts folly.[197] Bosch would have been familiar with the playful arms of his hometown. Expert in puns and proverbs—whole books have been written about Bosch's "picture language"—he would have delighted in devising contrivances for his name.[198] In the triptych's hell panel, the hybrid colossus with desiccated trees for limbs might allude to the maker. Looking backwards, as if to see its own story in retrospect, this "tree-man" is the artist's most remembered creation. In a spectacular drawing made perhaps for an admirer, he floats the monster on a marshy Brabantine inlet and adds trees, an owl, and a crescent-moon pennant to the mix (see fig. 28). Bosch's other two major pen and ink drawings also feature enigmatic trees, forests, and owls (see fig. 96). The artist is a tree-man. Creature of the forest, he is also a *bosvogel*, a Middle Dutch word for "owl," meaning literally "woods bird," and also possibly "bad bird" (*boze vogel*).[199] And so were all the burghers of that town. Alart du Hameel, the city's most distinguished architect and goldsmith, and an innovative creator of monster-filled engravings perhaps designed by our artist, signed his prints with a monogram and the calligraphed toponym "Bosche."

But our Bosch is sylvan in a special way. It must have occurred to him that his Christian name and his alias both have woods in them, but of two very different kinds. *Bosch* conjures a dangerous wilderness, the "dark wood" (*selva obscura*) where, at the opening of his *Divine Comedy*, Dante finds himself "midway in the journey of life," with "the straight way lost." *Bosch* in Latin is *silva*. Silva Ducis is the Latin name for 's-Hertogenbosch. Synonymous with *materia* ("matter"), *silva* translates the Greek word *hyle*, meaning "wood," which Aristotle used to denote the raw "stuff" out of which everything is made. English preserved that double meaning. In 1641, Ben Jonson titled his book of "discoveries made upon men and matter" *Timber*. Medieval cosmologists worried about *hyle*. They tried to reconcile antique pagan philosophy's ideas about primal matter with the biblical story of creation *ex nihil*, with God set apart from matter. Dürer's teacher, the painter and printmaker Michael Wolgemut, placed the Gothic letters "Yle" inside his woodcut roundel of the uncreated world (fig. 13). The whole left page of this, the first opening of the *World Chronicle*, is printed with a portrait of the Creator. God's right hand, gesturing his fiat, appears again on the facing page above "Yle." Published in Nuremberg 1493 and disseminated Europe-wide in Latin and German editions, the *World Chronicle* directly influenced Bosch. The closed state of Bosch's triptych, with its depiction of the newly formed earth, elaborated the *Chronicle*'s floating sphere. Bosch puts a scaled-down version of Wolgemut's portrait of God the Father at the upper left, in the spot where the woodcut places the disembodied hand, and he includes the same inscription as in the printed frontispiece: Psalm 33's abbreviation of God's creative act, "For he spoke and it was done."

The text of the *World Chronicle* begins with a refutation of Plato, Aristotle, and Epicurus. These pagan philosophers, the author explains, wrongly asserted that *hyle* pre-dates everything, since Moses affirmed that God created the world out

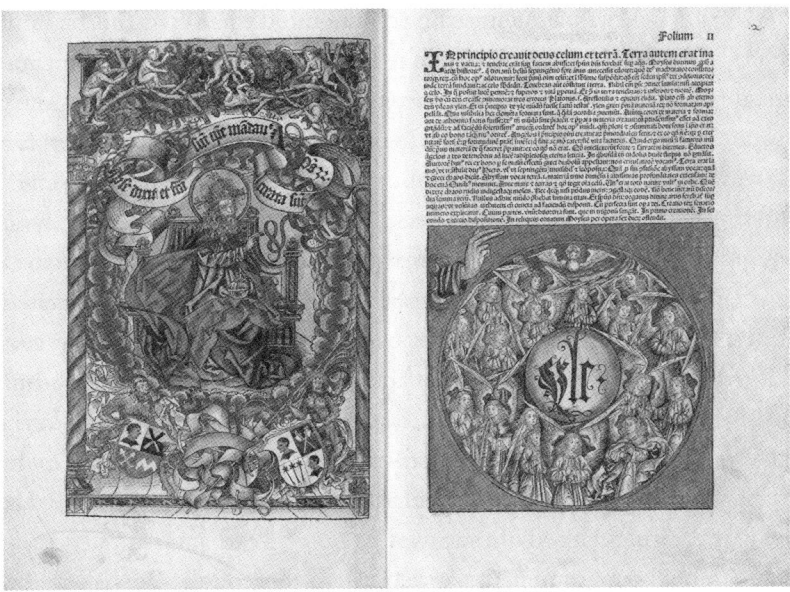

FIG. 13. Michael Wolgemut and Wilhelm Pleydenwurff, *God the Father and Yle*. Hand-colored woodcut frontispiece to Hartmann Schedel, *Liber Chronicarum* (Nuremberg: Anton Koberger, 1493). Bayerische Staatsbibliothek, Munich, Rar. 287, fol. 1r, 2v

of nothing. Not all Christian cosmologists were as certain. Bernardus Silvestris, the twelfth-century poet who took his own name from her, wrote that Silva—alias *hyle* alias *materia*—is "a formless pile." She existed restlessly at war with herself from "the first beginnings of things." An "unyielding, formless chaos, a hostile coalescence, a motley aspect of substance, a mass discordant with itself," Silva "longs in her turbulence for a tempering power."²⁰⁰ The "grove" conjured by the name Hieronymus stands in contrast to this. It is a sacred wood, "set apart" and unmingled, a haven rather than a hell. Voragine noted that the "-nemus" of Hieronymus might derive from "*noma*, a law," because the saint of that name "expounded and interpreted the sacred law."²⁰¹ Bosch and Hieronymus, wilderness and grove, chaos and law, enmity and amity, sanctuary and siege combine into the hybrid, or *disparates*, that is Hieronymus Bosch.

The 1516 accounting entry states that a "friend" financed the artist's funeral. The costs included payments to the priest to sing Mass and give a sermon and to a deacon and subdeacon to assist, and moneys to "all the other priests, singers, sacristans, pallbearers, gravediggers, bellringer, [and] organ-blower," as well as to choristers and "the poor": about twenty-four of the latter. Standing "before the chapel," these unfortunates made the rite charitable and pious.²⁰² Located inside the Church of St. John, that chapel belonged to the Illustrious Brotherhood of Our Blessed Lady of 's-Hertogenbosch. The Brotherhood's members included the friends making the payment, who remunerated their own confraternity for the funeral. Bosch had been an active member, as records of the Brotherhood document show. Founded in 1318 to promote devotion to the Virgin Mary, this lay confraternity boasted a distinguished membership. Its core consisted of about sixty "sworn members," all ordained but not necessarily as priests. The wider membership was large and international, and included notables from beyond the Netherlands. In Bosch's time the Brotherhood sent annually one candle to each of its thirteen thousand non-resident members—a massive effort to maintain distant affiliations. Performing the duties of a sworn brother was costly and time-consuming.[203] Bosch gained access to this inner circle by 1488, shortly after his admission as regular member—a rare feat. In 1489 he paid for one of the Brotherhood's lavish meals that sworn brothers periodically had to host.[204] Attended by friends and visiting dignitaries, these meals included roast swan, giving the confraternity the nickname "Brotherhood of the Swan."

Membership brought benefits, especially to someone of Bosch's profession. The Brotherhood's new chapel, created between 1479 and 1494 and known as the Chapel of the Sacraments, required a sumptuous display of images, ornaments, and furniture, including an elaborate altarpiece for performing the Eucharistic sacrament and for exhibiting—behind and above that performance—the Brotherhood's revered wooden statue of the Virgin (that object is lost). Carved by the Utrecht sculptor Adriaen van Wesel and overseen by Anthonius van Aken and his sons, this towering altarpiece would feature several wing panels painted by Bosch. Outside the confines of the chapel, the Church of St. John afforded ample opportunities for artists to pursue their craft. The most impressive Gothic edifice in the Netherlands, this collegiate and parish church (it became a cathedral in 1559) housed a further, miraculous, statue of the Virgin. Beginning with its first miracle in 1381, this wooden effigy dressed in costly textile garb drew tens of thousands of pilgrims to 's-Hertogenbosch each year. Votive offerings financed the church's adornment. Before Protestants destroyed most of them in 1566, the church boasted some fifty altars, each with a painted and sculpted retable. A chronicle composed in 1606–9 describing the church as it looked before the iconoclasm records at least three altarpieces by Bosch. These included a retable behind the high altar showing "the six-day creation of the world." An "Ode to the Church at 's-Hertogenbosch," composed around 1550, notes of this ensemble that "it was frequently permitted to view the marvelous colors applied to wood, which contains life-like, monstrous creatures from the underworld."[205]

One foreign visitor to the church may have been shown this wonder and commissioned something like it. Both Engelbert II and his nephew Henry II, either of whom may have commissioned the cosmic triptych for their palace, visited Bosch's town. Henry II belonged to the painter's Brotherhood, as did Philip the Fair, reigning duke of Burgundy and from 1504 to 1506 Habsburg king of Castile. Sworn membership afforded Bosch personal access to Europe's rich and powerful. Unusual for a craftsman, his admittance may have been helped by his marriage to Aleid van der Meervenne, daughter of a wealthy landowner who had been a sworn member himself. But the artist's talent, learning, and skill would have recommended him, as well. All sworn brothers had attended Latin school and many had university degrees. When Bosch dined on swan and other delicacies, he did so with famed musicians, architects, scholars, high-ranking clergy, nobles, ambassadors, and courtiers.[206] Supported by a network of illustrious friends, and independently wealthy through marriage, Bosch could pursue the craft of painting on his own terms, a freedom unique among other early Netherlandish painters.

Bosch's surviving oeuvre consists currently of about twenty-seven accepted works, several with parts held by different museums, and some works designated as only "workshop" productions. Recent studies of paint layers and underdrawings using infrared reflectography have revealed multiple hands at work in all of Bosch's productions and at various stages in the paintings' making. "Hieronymus Bosch" designated both a highly individual artistic personality and a recognizable brand. Of the accepted works, none is securely documented. Written records from before 1516 refer to works that have since been lost, and the paintings that have come down to us acquired their attribution posthumously, based on provenance, stylistic analysis, and scientific study, especially dendrochronology. But in 2001 two panels of different sizes and subjects and hitherto treated as separate creations were identified as wings of that altarpiece originally adorning the chapel of the artist's confraternity. Divided between Madrid and Berlin, these pictures probably formed the hinged upper shutters of a two-tiered retable, with the brotherhood's venerated statue of the Virgin permanently visible on top (plates 5, 6, and 7).[207]

The panels depict the two Johns of Christian history: John the Baptist, who recognizes Christ with the words "Behold the Lamb of God, which taketh away the sin of the world" (John 1:29), and John the Evangelist, who in the Book of Revelation traditionally attributed to him predicts Christ's final return. Often worshipped together—Jan van Eyck's *Ghent Altarpiece* is their most spectacular pairing—the two Johns bookend Christian history. The Baptist is the last Old Testament prophet. The Evangelist is Christ's youngest and favorite apostle. His is the last of the canonical four Gospels (after Matthew, Mark, and Luke) and his vision of the end of time concludes the New Testament. The Church of St. John and its city had the Evangelist as their patron saint and celebrated the Baptist with equal fervor. Bosch sets both personages in vast wilderness settings. The Baptist panel has been cut down on all four sides, changing its proportions. As originally displayed, it and the *John on Patmos* panel shared the same continuous horizon, and thus the same world. From that world, the Baptist points down to the Lamb in the painting's foreground and—further down and outside the picture's frame—to the Eucharist administered at the altar. The Evangelist gazes up to the "woman clothed with the sun" (Rev. 12:1) as he beheld her on Patmos and—further up in real space—to the carved Virgin Mary crowning the altarpiece. Though set apart in their own fictive wilderness, the saints interact with rituals and images located in the chapel.

The *John on Patmos* panel is painted on both sides. The verso, visible when the pendants closed, features concentric circles painted in semi-grisaille on a black ground (plate 7). Bosch used a compass to draw the circles—a needle mark is detectable at dead center. This arrangement anticipates the structure of the *Seven Deadly Sins*, only instead of that tabletop's topsy-turvy scenes, Bosch wraps a coherent world and a continuous narrative (plate 3). Beginning (as it were) at "three o'clock", eight episodes—six outdoors, two in dark interiors—tell the story of Christ's Passion from his prayer in the garden to his crucifixion and entombment. Time finds a double expression. The scenes have a clock dial arrangement and proceed in a right-handed direction. The Church of St. John boasted a gigantic "Judgment" clock, with moving tableaux of the end of time. One of the clockfaces was marked with the hours of the day, another with signs of the zodiac.[208] In 's-Hertogenbosch, dials had an eschatological charge. Bosch bathes the scenes in waxing and waning light. The panel's Lenten grays befit the sorrowful events depicted. They also conform to the cost-saving grisaille of altarpiece shutters. But Bosch naturalizes the convention. Darkness spreads across the sky, left to right, in reading direction, and measuring time. Of the moment of Christ's death the Gospels report, "It was about the sixth hour, and there was darkness over all the earth until the ninth hour" (Luke 23:44). As the sun's eclipse arrives and passes, the light would be too dim for human eyes to see color. Everything would look gray and drab.

This painted Passion encircles another view. Brighter (and more thinly painted), it shows a landscape dawning from the left. On a rock jutting from the sea a pelican feeds fledglings her own blood. Based on flawed observation—pelicans press their beaks against their chest to push mashed fish into the mouths of their young—this bit of medieval animal lore made the pelican an emblem for Christ, who redeems us with his blood. The concentric grisailles thus share the same symbolic structure as *Seven Deadly Sins*: vicious humanity surrounds and besieges God's self-sacrificing son. And as in the tabletop, the grisaille's sorrow-filled roundel forms the oculus of an angry god. The besieging enemies are thus besieged in a circle whose center is everywhere and circumference nowhere. The pendant panel of *Saint John the Baptist in the Wilderness* was originally painted on its verso, too. It probably featured concentric grisailles like the *Saint John on Patmos*, its companion. When closed, these shutters would thus have formed a pair of eyes peering dangerously at us from the gloom.

Bosch punctuates his grisaille with poisonous points of color. In the narrow chasm beside Gethsemane and above Judas's kiss, a torch—tiny dots of yellow, orange, and red—lights the enemy's path. And in a cavern at the base of the pelican's roost, blackening the rocks with soot, red flames belch forth from the gloom. In Bosch's depiction these infernal energies are everywhere, but one can hardly see them today, even with the *John on Patmos* panel displayed, both front and back, in Berlin's well-lit gallery. The sworn brothers would have been even harder pressed to glimpse these details high up on their altarpiece; but still, the black around the grisaille oculus swarms with colorful demons. At the upper right, painted in pale green, a leviathan opens its maw to gulp down a fleeing flock of birds; further up a monster outlined in red reaches up from its arrow-pierced pod; just below, an infernal harp, like the cruel one in the triptych's hell panel, thrusts forward in space. What seemed a blank abyss turns out to be a diabolical menagerie—including, at the bottom, a scene of antlered harts in a wooded grove. Together with the grisaille oculus, this forest scene perhaps yields "hert-ogen-bosch." Scores of miniscule green leaves and red and white blossoms scatter around the edges of darkness, as if flowers strewn at the carved Virgin's feet were sucked into the black hole below her.

What the "devil-maker" painted is less novel than how he painted. Bosch created these *disparates* in one go, wet on wet. The black of their hellish environs he applied with a broad brush over the pale creamy ground that covers the whole panel: delicate parallel marks of brush bristles can be observed in raking light. Before that black had dried, Bosch drew the demons swiftly, playfully, using a fine brush devoid of, or barely charged with, paint. These creatures thus began as undifferentiated black minutely perturbated. Once these scribbles dried, Bosch finished some with pale colors and tiny highlights, endowing them with volume and movement. Others he left as merest scratches in the smooth black ground. Masterfully drawn, like this artist's pen-and-ink monsters, these creatures became less visible as the paint aged. Some are evident only in infrared reflectography. Infrared radiation has a wavelength too long for the human eye to see. Such radiation can penetrate the paint layers. When photographed by special cameras, infrared imaging allows us to see what lies under: enemies that, everywhere and nowhere, swarm God's dangerous *Augenblick*.

The altarpiece from which these eyes stared out took half a century to complete. It began with Adriaen van Wesel's carvings, commissioned in 1475–76 and surviving only in two fragments, and it ended with the creation of a second set of outer wings for the lower register, commissioned in 1521–22. In 1488–89 the brotherhood commissioned "two doors" presumably for the upper register: almost certainly Bosch's two Saint Johns. With a total of eight wings decorated front and back, the altarpiece could be displayed in many ways, as a mid-sixteenth-century chronical reports: "A two-fold image can be seen there on the altar. For on working days, it displays one picture, so artistic. On feast days the golden legend is shown."[209] Thus the gray, demon-plagued "eyes" stared out at churchgoers on ordinary weekdays, reserving Bosch's full-color panels of the two Johns, based on stories from Voragine's *Golden Legend*, for festive occasions.

Bosch portrays the Evangelist writing his Apocalypse with a goose or swan feather pen. His portable inkpot and pencase lie at his feet. Patmos, the island where John had his revelations, has become an inland mount circled by rivers, with fields, woods, and cities beyond, all contemporary Netherlandish and not ancient Greek. In the distance, disaster has struck a sailing vessel. Flames and smoke punctuate the pale blue sea. On shore a corpse—its shroud a pinpoint of white—rots on a torture wheel. Terrible for those affected, these are mere workaday catastrophes. They may count as portents since calamities increase as the final day draws near. But that day has not yet arrived, neither on Patmos in the first century CE nor in 's-Hertogenbosch circa 1490, on the anxious eve of the half-millennium. What arrives is the portent recorded in John's book: "A great and wondrous sign appeared in heaven: a woman clothed with the sun, with the moon under her feet and a crown of twelve stars on her head" (Rev. 12:1). Bosch depicts her as the Virgin, with the Christ child in her lap. This is a commonplace translation of the cryptic sign: early Christian commentators understood the Woman of the Apocalypse to signify Mary and the Church, the former being "mother" of the latter. 's-Hertogenbosch honored both the Evangelist and the Virgin he mystically beheld. Her carved effigy made her numinously present to townsfolk and pilgrims. These local venerations converge on the event Bosch depicts: John's and 's-Hertogenbosch's epiphany.

Although beheld in the biblical past, the Woman of the Apocalypse points to the future. Revelation 12 weaves her into a plot encompassing the whole history of the world. In John's telling, she is pregnant and followed by "another wonder," an enormous dragon that seeks to devour the child as soon as it was born. But the child "was caught up unto God," the woman fled into the wilderness, "and there was war in heaven" (Rev. 12:3–7). In a single line that would underwrite the

Christian understanding of evil, John explains that this dragon is "that old serpent, called the Devil, and Satan, which deceiveth the whole world: he was cast out into the earth, and his angels were cast with him" (Rev. 12:9). In a beginning before the beginning, before God created heaven and earth, one angel rebelled. Defeated, he and his seditious followers, were cast down—in some cosmologies creating hell, in others infecting earth as primordial matter, as *hyle*, *silva*, *bosch*—thereafter to haunt creation, most egregiously in Eden. As the serpent, Satan seduces Eve who seduces Adam, bringing "Death into the World and all our woe," as John Milton put it in his epic poem about Satan's civil war. The serpent is "old," indicating that doomsday originates from an enmity pre-dating, and built into, the structure of the world. The serpent is also here and now, urgently so, because "he knoweth that he hath but a short time" (Rev. 12:12). This shrinkage of eons into days terrifies, because doomsday is about to happen. But it also consoles, because our sufferings are the next-to-last, and the worse things get, the sooner will our foes be punished.

The myth condensed in Revelation 12 underwrites the Christian world view, or *Weltanschauung*. Unique among artists, Bosch portrays "world view" literally, as a vast vista spreading forth before our eyes. In his surviving Last Judgments, and in *The Hay Wain* triptych, the Fall of the Rebel Angels backs the scenes of Eden (plates 9, 10, and 11). These scenes unfold in a spacious "worldscape" (as art historians term Bosch's expansive landscapes) that extends through across all three panels of these triptychs, placing catastrophe and hell on the same terrain. All other artists of the period represent doomsday as a dangerous moment, busy but sudden, in which God sends the saved up to heaven (at his right and our left) and thrusts the damned down into hell (at his left, our right). Instead, Bosch paints the historical paradise of Eden at our left, with the rebel angels crashing down. Judgment thus falls on a world-historical timeline from Satan's fall, via Eve's and Adam's, and via doomsday at the center, to hell, Satan's dominion, as the eternal end. In this visual telling, damnation so overwhelms the saved that one must almost use a magnifying glass to see those lucky few disappearing into a minuscule opening in the sky. This relentless downward story explains the Fall, and it elucidates the devils, Bosch's specialty. They are the seditious angels who, cursed and resentful, swarm God's oculus, tempt sinners and saints, and torture ceaselessly the damned. They use deception as a weapon, causing the phenomenal world, of which Bosch gives us a spectacular view, to be dangerous and illusory. Most of all they hurry, frenzied because they know better than we that time is short. That makes their job as tempters easier, because sin happens suddenly, in an *Augenblick*.

One of the devils that John on Patmos warns of has snuck into the picture. Larger than most of Bosch's *disparates*, this creature invites aesthetic appreciation of its polymorphous parts. Its insectoid stinger, amphibian legs, chitinous wings, pimply carapace, and humanoid face impossibly melded; the badge on its strangely organic cape visible enough to be observed but too small to be deciphered; the brazier atop its head burning with hellish fires; the pale bespectacled face glimpsing backwards from where its legs carry it: these make it a signature "Bosch," and not just in its playful inventiveness, but in its painterly panache as well. This devil belongs to a plot that the artist did not invent. Numerous Flemish manuscript illuminators and some earlier panel painters, too, portrayed John composing his Gospel or writing down his Apocalypse with a demon lurking beside him. Sometimes these adversaries steal the Evangelist's inkpot to thwart his scrivening or, diabolic scribes themselves, to write false accusations against the saint. The devil cunningly maligns—the Greek word *diabolos* comes from the verb "to slander."[210] Bosch outfits his demon with a pince-nez to flag his identify as hellish clerk, cleric, or scribe. He also has the creature look as if in flight just now, with the shoulder-pad hands signaling alarm and the webbed feet braced to run, leaving behind the three-pronged hook with which devils transport the damned, meat-like, to hell. Perhaps the stern eagle, John the Evangelist's symbol, hastened this departure—a farcical prelude to the war in heaven to come. Howsoever we read the devil's flight, beneath it, and with the meat hook pointing at the headletter "J," "Jheronimus Bosch" stands prominently displayed. Dating to the time of his admission as sworn brother to the confraternity, this is the artist's earliest extant signature.

Though made using black paint and a brush the letters look as if written with a quill in ink. Bosch's penmanship rivaled his painterly skills. His handling of the quill has no rival until Dürer, born a generation later. Indeed, Bosch's several pen-and-ink masterpieces are the earliest "autonomous" drawings of the Northern tradition; neither practice sheets nor preliminary sketches nor copies for workshop use, they each invite contemplation and collection as an aesthetic whole—even as they feature monstrous combinations of parts. The documents record that the artist "selver scrift" (himself wrote) the name "Jheronimus Bosch," as might a notary or scrivener.[211] In the *John of Patmos* panel, the fight over the inkpot, the pen-line form of the meat hook, and the signature's demonic haunting all tempt one—slanderously perhaps—to identify the artist with his bespectacled demon. No authenticated self-portrait of Bosch survives, though numerous faces in his paintings have been proposed as cameos. The portrait published in 1572, therefore long after his decease, shows a visage with a furrowed brow and "pallid," as the accompanying verse explains, due to his having "witnessed, face to face, the Lemures and the flying specters of Erebus (fig. 8)."[212]

Bosch's friends must have understood what he meant by signing his name where he did, in that dangerous spot above the altar where they performed their daily devotion. When they ritually mourned the artist's death, they did so with that panel visible in the chapel. They too hailed from 's-Hertogenbosch, that erstwhile realm of unruly Silva. The built fabric of St. John's Church questioned—with militant irony—people's nature, asking what kind of folk had access to the city and its precious sculptures of the Virgin. In Bosch's lifetime, during the completion of the side aisle, the exterior of the church came to be adorned with monstrous sandstone statuettes.[213] Demons straddled the top arches of the flying buttresses connecting the building's upper wall to the supporting piers. Intermingled with fools, drunkards, wild beasts, musicians, and artisans, they completed a haunting self-portrait of townsfolk and pilgrims visiting the church. Carved on site in the mason's lodge, their design would have been overseen by Alart du Hameel, perhaps with input from Bosch. Fantastical creatures also appeared inside St. John's, carved on the choir stalls and frescoed on the vaults. Monsters decorate many Gothic cathedrals. Symbols of evil, they served also to ward off demons by distracting, fooling, and terrifying them. But their dramatic flourishing would have had a specific meaning in the duke's forest. They warn that enemies, having penetrated the city walls, besiege the Virgin's sanctuary and weigh down its structural supports. In Bosch's grisaille, they even swarm God's all-seeing eye. Worse, the foes might be the townsfolk themselves, at war with themselves and with God. Friend and enemy, Hieronymus and Bosch, contend. Nothing has been decided, yet.

's-Hertogenbosch, 1504

In late summer of 1504, Philip the Fair, the duke of Burgundy and Emperor Maximilian's son and heir, arrived in Bosch's hometown armed for battle.[214] War for control of Guelders had raged throughout the reigns of Philip's predecessors, who sought to incorporate those neighboring lands into the expanding Burgundian state. In 1472, through bribery and force, Charles the Bold had compelled the reigning duke of Guelders to pledge fealty to Burgundy, but Charles's death in battle in 1477 made the region an independent duchy again, though nominally under Habsburg dominion. For four decades Charles II, duke of Guelders and count of Zutphen, battled Habsburg sovereignty, expanding his lands northward to Groningen and, allied with France, challenging Burgundy itself along its borders near 's-Hertogenbosch. For this reason Philip, brought back from Spain at the behest of his father, took up residence in that well-fortressed and well-provisioned city. From there his army, aided by Brabantine townsfolk, destroyed Gueldrian castles and villages to the north and east, while Charles II burned settlements along the Meuse, killing and imprisoning all who tried to flee—many drowned trying frantically to cross the river. When winter fell, Philip and his men were joined by Emperor Maximilian (Philip's father), Empress Bianca Maria Sforza, and other nobles, who "entertained themselves" with jousts, horseraces, handball, and dances "so that the streets resounded with trumpets."[215] The town government called its many citizens residing in Antwerp back to 's-Hertogenbosch to join in a special feast, ostensibly in honor of the Virgin's pregnancy but also to help amuse and placate visitors holed up for months in the city. Armed troops, including hardened mercenaries from elsewhere, were dangerous guests.

The dukes of Burgundy knew 's-Hertogenbosch well, having passed through its gates in festive *joyeuses entrées*—ritual entries by a ruler into a subject city. Charles the Bold in 1467, Maximilian and Mary of Burgundy in 1478, and Philip the Fair in 1496 all formerly "took possession of the land" by arriving at and being elaborately welcomed by the city.[216] Two milestones in Philip's youth were celebrated at 's-Hertogenbosch: in 1483 his admittance as a four-year-old to the Order of the Golden Fleece, and in 1496 his inauguration as duke of Brabant—the latter ceremony included the baptism of Jacob van Almaengian, elusive hero of Fraenger's fantasies. Nothing as momentous for Philip occurred during his 1504–5 stay, though thousands outside the city walls lost their lives and thousands more were rendered homeless. But it was in 's-Hertogenbosch that the duke received the world-changing news that his mother-in-law, Queen Isabella I, had died. Isabella ruled unified Spain jointly with King Ferdinand of Aragon. She had named Juana of Castile, her daughter and Philip's wife, heir to the throne. This made Philip (potentially) the first Habsburg king of Castile. After much conflict this came to pass in 1506, but Philip died soon afterwards. Only with the election of his son Charles V as Holy Roman emperor did Philip's line achieve worldwide rule.

Philip spent his last months in 's-Hertogenbosch raising money to travel with Juana to Spain. During those months he and Maximilian lived in the Dominican monastery while the empress (Lady White Maria, as the locals called her) stayed in a townhouse on the market square, right next door to Bosch's home. This remarkable proximity, plus the many other unrecorded links Philip had with the artist, helps explain Bosch's best-documented commission. Ducal accounts record that in September 1504 an advance was made "to Jeronimus van Aeken *dit* Bosch, painter living in Bois le Duc" for a "large painted tableau [...] on which should appear God's Judgment, which is to say, paradise and hell." This Bosch will do for Philip's "very noble pleasure."[217]

Published in 1858, this document proved that Bosch, during his lifetime, had been a favorite of potentates. They saw fit to record his name in full, a rare distinction for any non-noble, and certainly for painters.[218] Also unusually, Bosch received pre-payment for labor not yet commenced. Painters often had to beg for payment after delivering their work, especially from highborn patrons—Dürer complained of receiving nothing from Margaret of Austria for gifting her his entire corpus of prints. Finally, the phrase "for his very noble pleasure," while possibly a standard formula, chimes with Philip's expectations. The painting should entertain him like the other amusements he enjoyed in 's-Hertogenbosch in 1504. The contract states the ample size of the painting to be made: 9 feet high and 11 feet wide. These measurements agree with neither of the two extant Last Judgment triptychs by Bosch (one now in Vienna, the other Bruges) nor with Lucas Cranach's copy based on a lost third version nearly identical to the Vienna triptych. But just as Philip predicted what sort of picture might result, we too can imagine this creation.

Bosch's Last Judgments differ from all others in the tradition. Since at least the tenth century, on church tympanums, choir screens, altarpieces, and elsewhere, artists pictured doomsday as a dangerous moment, not quite instantaneous, but hectic and brief. The Creator will not suddenly blink the world out of existence, as Immanuel Kant (amused by apocalyptic imaginings) assumed an omnipotent deity should be able to do. Instead, enthroned as judge between the Virgin and John the Baptist as advocates, God decides judiciously, with due process followed and habeas corpus observed. The flesh of the dead must be resurrected either to be lifted to heaven or cast into hell. Giving up the corpses that had returned to dust, earth itself becomes a dusty waste before disappearing. When Netherlandish painters portrayed the event in triptych form, they balanced the drama unfolding on this disappearing waste between hell's soaring flames on the right panel, and heaven's lofty gate on the left panel. The saved escape the war zone not into a peaceable garden, but into a city with high defensive walls.

On Patmos, Saint John beheld this holy city with walls "144 cubits thick by man's measurement, which the angel was using" (Rev. 20:17). This Christian imagining reaffirmed visions that the Old Testament prophet Ezekiel had during his captivity in Babylon, after Jerusalem's walls had failed. Rebuking Israel as "a rebellious people" (Ezek. 12:2) who deserved their city's siege and destruction (587 BCE), Ezekiel also foretold a new Jerusalem with impenetrable walls. His extended verbal description of this future city had been preceded by a picture that God commanded Ezekiel to craft: "Take a clay tablet and draw the city of Jerusalem on it. Then lay siege to it: Erect siege works against it, build a ramp up to it, set up camps against it and put battering rams around it" (Ezek. 4:1–2). The prophet then had to lie for three hundred and ninety plus forty days immobile beside this drawing, eating bread baked over burning human excrement.

The earliest cities were built of clay. Each one of Babylon's 164 million baked mud bricks had "Nebuchadnezzar" stamped on them. Clay was also used for writing and drawing. Cuneiform tablets from ancient Nippur document siege conditions: parents selling their children for food, mothers eating daughters, and so on. One tablet contains a plan of Nippur, with walls and riverways scraped into the clay. Ezekiel survived one of Jerusalem's defeats. With Deuteronomy's ominous portrayal of siege states in the background of his vision, he takes on Jerusalem's future suffering as personal penance: during siege, cooking on human excrement became an exigency. Ezekiel also besieges the city in effigy. During the prophet's exile armies of Nebuchadnezzar breached Jerusalem's walls, destroyed the city, and enslaved its people. Ezekiel's wrathful prophecies thus came to pass. By a kind of sympathetic magic, the clay portrait of siege allowed the prophet both to punish and atone.

Bosch omits Heavenly Jerusalem. In its place he puts the landscape of paradise lost. More than a dangerous moment, his Last Judgments tell the world's history beginning to end, from the rebel angels in the sky through the baleful vector from Eve's formation from Adam's rib through the Fall and Expulsion (in a dark forest) directly to Judgment (plate 10). From Bosch's perspective all that happened in between, in the fissure separating the left panel from the central one, means nothing in the end. Bosch's reframing of time, bookending the last catastrophe with the cosmic and human first disasters, transforms space, as well. Without heaven's gates pressing forward at the left, landscape can plunge everywhere into depth. Bosch lifts us above ground—although cunningly not as elevated as heaven. Few in number and almost too small to see, the saved escape through a wormhole so high that any viewer who glimpses that painted detail will know themselves not to be among those lucky ones. Our paradise remains a vindictive one. "What a sight shall wake my wonder, what my laughter, my joy and exultation," wrote Tertullian around 197 CE when Christians were a persecuted minority in the Roman Empire, "as I see all those kings, those great kings [...] groaning in the depths of darkness [... and] those sages, too, the philosophers blushing before their disciples as they blaze together."[219] And suffer the sinful do in Bosch, the vast landscape setting allowing their torture wondrously to multiply. Following the old dictum that the punishment should fit the crime, the painter, assuming human history has yielded an infinitude of different crimes, can invent endlessly new varieties of torture, all administered by demons whom God, in his wisdom, allows to run the show. The punishments the damned endure begin already on earth, another of Bosch's artistic departures.

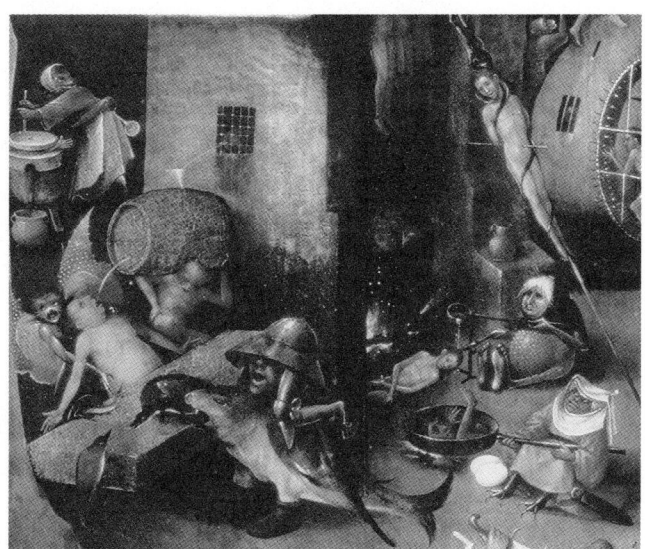

FIG. 14. Detail from
Hieronymus Bosch, *Last
Judgment*, open state, c. 1504.
Oil on panel. Gemäldegalerie
der Akademie der bildenden
Künste, Vienna

These tortures mobilize an intricate machinery assembled and powered up as
if suddenly. Wheels, levers, screws, and pulleys operate ceaselessly in sync, like a
perpetual judgment clock stuck on doomsday. Encyclopedic in their variety, each
of the torments has a subtly different tempo, expanding infinitely the painful
Augenblick. A she-devil in red robes and an escoffion waits for the chopped-up
sinner nicely to brown before adding the eggs to her omelet. Just to the left, the
body roasted whole on a spit will take longer, and it may be hours or days before
those unfortunates hanging above a simmering cauldron of heads will be warm-
smoked through (fig. 14). But this being hell, the cooking will go on forever, with
the victims perpetually at the apex of pain so unendurable death would be a mercy.
Bosch models his imaginings on justice exacted publicly on real-life perpetrators,
such as managed slow burning at the stake (for witches and heretics) and breaking
on the wheel (for highwaymen, street thieves, murderers, and arsonists), which
prolong painful death. Also eerily concrete is the setting Bosch conjures. Damnation unfolds in an urban landscape of ruined roads, bridges, hostels, and towns.
Across a vast terrain that, in hell, rises to conceal any endpoint on the horizon,
innumerable fortified cities burn brightly in the dark. Bosch sketches broken walls
and open gates negatively, swiftly applying red, yellow, and white flames on the
black underlying ground, thus conjuring the devastated City of Man in backlit
silhouette. The sieges have all ended and the foe has breached the walls and is
doing what victorious besiegers have always done: enemies "whose language you
will not understand" swoop down "from far away" and slaughter everything they
meet (Deut. 28:49).

In the hell panel of his *Last Judgment* preserved in Bruges, Bosch portrays siege from up close (plate 11). Devils equipped with flimsy ladders endeavor to scale the broken outer wall of the burning city. Some tumble to the ground as if repelled, but the joke is on the defenders, since their city is already conquered, its denizens violated (as always in Bosch) in physically invasive ways, with orifices—like city gates—violently entered. The invaders are monstrously open-ended, like the Tree-Man. In this triptych, as in the Vienna *Last Judgment*, the gates of hell at the lower right suggest that what happens across the infernal foreground, which extends from the central Judgment panel, occurs in some unwalled, undefended suburbs into which the displaced burghers have all been forced to flee—hopelessly, as citizens in Guelders learned in November 1504, when hundreds escaping Burgundian forces drowned in the Meuse.[220] The wholescale destruction of cities involved murderous clean-up actions against refugees. During the seven weeks it took in 1468 to burn Liège entirely to the ground, Charles the Bold braved bad weather and difficult terrain personally to slaughter a few surviving *liègeois* hiding in a forest to the west.[221] What looks fantastical to our eyes would have been familiar to Philip when he commissioned Bosch's tableau.

The dukes of Burgundy waged war incessantly during the century of their rule over the Netherlands. Seeking to establish a middle kingdom between France and the Holy Roman Empire, they fought against the French, who sought to hold or to regain territory; against neighboring lands such as Guelders and the Principality of Liège, which resisted Burgundian expansion; and against rebellious subjects, especially the prosperous towns in their realm. Through hard-won rights and privileges, the Flemish trade capitals of Ghent, Bruges, and Ypres had achieved the status of semi-autonomous city-states. Based on long-distance commerce and local industrial-style production, this densely urbanized region would become the chief source of Burgundian wealth and power, but not without constant struggle. Seven years after Philip the Good inherited the Duchy of Brabant in 1430, 's-Hertogenbosch refused to pay a tax contribution called the *bede* (benevolence), bringing the town into conflict with the duke. Impoverished and isolated, with the poor dying of famine, the town in 1438 capitulated to Philip's demands, remaining a relatively reliable subject of its Burgundian and later Spanish Habsburg overlords. In 1601 and 1603 's-Hertogenbosch withstood sieges by the Dutch, but in 1629, in the worst defeat of Habsburg power in northern Europe since the Spanish Armada, the city surrendered to Dutch and English armies after a violent six-month siege. Bosch's hometown remained a largely Catholic part of the Dutch Republic until French revolutionary forces captured the region in 1794.

The town of Ghent resisted the Burgundian state vigorously, with disastrous results.[222] Governed during crises by appointed "captains" loyal to the guilds, the city in 1452 refused to pay a new salt tax and engaged Philip the Good's armies in bloody skirmishes. Terrible losses provoked unrest in Ghent, violently deposing four successive captaincies. Finally, at the battle of Gavere on July 23, 1453, which saw tens of thousands killed and Ghent's bastions obliterated by artillery, the city capitulated. To dramatize the city's submission Burgundian negotiators demanded that its gates, towers, and walls be razed, a measure that, leaving Ghent undefended, would amount to urbicide. Philip the Good, burnishing his byname, softened the retribution. Seizing control over the city's governance, courts, and symbols, he demanded an elaborate ceremony of humiliation called the Honorable Amend. Ghent's leaders—at least those who had escaped execution—would march to some place far outside the city walls where, "nude, except for their undergarments, wearing cords around their necks," and followed by the whole citizenry, all "bareheaded and barefooted," they would "kneel and genuflect three or four times" before the duke.[223] Additionally, three crucial gates to the city were permanently sealed, turning the walls that protected them into an imprisoning enclosure.

For ten millennia cities were mostly walled enclosures. Jericho built its walls about ten thousand years ago, Catal Hüyük in Anatolia in about 6500 BCE. In Chinese, the pictogram for "city" (*chéng*) also means "walls." In Greek, the two are related, as well. *Polis* derives from the (hypothesized) Proto-Indo-European root *tpeH-*, meaning "citadel" or "enclosed space." Homer calls Athena the protectress of cities under siege.[224] Hector's name comes from the verb "to hold," as is appropriate to the prince who upholds Troy during its ten-year siege. While Priam, his father, stands on the ramparts pleading for him to come back inside the walls, Hector engages Achilles disastrously. Achilles chases Hector thrice around the city walls, kills him, and humiliates his corpse. The sack of Troy is near. The English word "town" evolved into words for fences and enclosures, such as the German *Zaun*. Civilization and siege thus go hand in hand. "What has a wall around it," wrote the town secretary of Eisenach in 1399, "that we call a city."[225] To demolish its walls was to turn a city back into a village. Dominating the conduct of war, siege shaped the European landscape: win the siege, win the war. Military campaigns progressed from siege to siege, with battles occurring intermittently, often when the besiegers came under attack.

The laws of war differed between battles and sieges. Understood as a trial arbitrated by God, a battle was supposed to keep non-combatants from violence and grant some mercy to the defeated. Changing technologies, from *en masse* longbows to gunpowder artillery, challenged chivalric codes of conduct.[226] The Burgundian court confined its revival of chivalry to ritual forms, such as jousts and hunting. Yet among Christians, battle remained a contest between enemies of roughly equal standing under God. In sieges God played no official role. Secular undertakings, they tested the sovereignty of rulers, hence the protocol of summons to surrender at the beginning and the harsh punishments at the end. Siege placed city governance in a double bind in which surrender meant treason against the citizenry and defense meant insurrection against the prince. An exception to the laws of war, siege turned enemies into criminals. After Philip the Good captured Luxembourg by force in 1463, he gave thanks at the Church of Notre Dame before commanding that the town be systematically sacked. Murder and plunder were not acts of war, but a sentence of justice against rebellion.[227]

In Bosch's culture, siege had an opposite: the *joyeuse entrée*. At key moments in their rule, when they acceded to power or married, or when their children came of age, the Burgundian dukes "took possession" of their principal cities by passing peacefully through their protective walls[228]. Between 1419 and 1477 the towns of Flanders and Brabant staged some two hundred such joyous entries, each a carefully orchestrated pageant in which the citizenry, assembled according to its own ranked order and affirming its local rights, privileges, and symbols performed their obedience to the duke. "If God himself had descended from Heaven," observed a councillor of Philip the Good in 1455 of the duke's entry into Arras, "I do not know if the citizens would have paid him this much honor."[229] Five years after their humiliating "honorable amends," the people of Ghent, made "melancholy" by his absence, begged Philip to enter their gates again, this time with jubilation. Among the many spectacles of adulation greeting the duke in 1458 was a *tableau vivant* of the Adoration of the Mystic Lamb, based on Jan van Eyck's altarpiece in St. Bavo's Cathedral. The city's most famous artistic wonder, the *Ghent Altarpiece* pictures Heavenly Jerusalem as imagined by John at Revelation 21, with "the people of the world" and the "kings of the earth" worshipping eternally the Lamb of God and with spires of a celestial city rising in the background. This vision Ghent staged as a living picture, casting itself as a blessed, peaceful city and Philip as a triumphant warrior God. Not all joyous entries passed as smoothly. When Ghent welcomed Charles the Bold in 1467, the duke found himself heckled and physically threatened by unruly guildsmen. Entering the Netherlandish cities that they ruled could be dangerous for the dukes. In 1437, Philip the Good and his troop of three thousand heavily armed Picard soldiers were almost defeated inside Bruges's city walls, narrowly escaping with their life.[230] Bruges was eventually subdued, but the perilous entry was forgotten neither by Philip nor by his successors.

In his *Hay Wain* triptych, Bosch gave the sin of avarice the shape of a joyous entry gone wrong (plate 9). The pope, an emperor, a king, a duke, and their motley entourage march behind a wheeled hay cart towed by demons and topped by a moralizing scene of lovemaking. The landscape background and figures in the foreground—beggars, vagrants, quacks, and mendicants—place the wagon out in the world, with the pile of hay or straw a misshapen emblem *of* the world, where pleasures are empty, like straw. The peddler on the triptych's closed state introduces this locality as a zone of wandering and exile beyond the safety of city walls (plate 8). But the hay wagon, resembling a wheeled allegorical parade float as commonly used in urban festivals, progresses towards a confused demonic entryway that gives way to hell. The gap between the central and right panels thus becomes a city gate, the entrance to which is dolorous in the extreme. The damned share the fate of a besieged citizenry whose walls have failed them and who now are gruesomely tortured for their disobedience. Bosch secularizes the scheme of his Last Judgment triptychs. He places the world in its everyday unfolding between the beginning in Eden and the end in hell. Doomsday has not yet come, but world history has been encapsulated in a *tableau vivant* of imminent damnation.

Damnation takes the form of urbicide. This was a punishment Bosch's noble patrons meted out with righteous ingenuity. The oldest form of total war, siege developed into a sophisticated art. Defensive poliorcetics focused mainly on fortifications. Gunpowder technology undermined the protective function of walls, challenging architects from Alberti and Filarete to professional military engineers like Vauban and Montalembert to imagine new solutions. Dürer dedicated his *Instructions on the Fortification of Cities, Castles, and Towns* (1527) to Ferdinand I, crowned king of Hungary after the death of his brother-in-law Ludwig II in battle against the Turks. By 1521 Belgrade lay under Turkish control, but in 1529 Suleiman the Magnificent would besiege Vienna unsuccessfully, though Ottoman expansion threatened Christian rulers for the next two centuries. "Now that in our time many strange things have come about," Dürer begins, improved fortifications should be built "so that not only is one Christian protected from another but also that those lands bordering on the Turks be saved from their violence and bombardment."[231] In a two-sheet woodcut folded into some copies, the artist—Hungarian on his father's side—imagines a German city under siege, its curtain walls, moats, and bastions inadequate to artillery of the day (fig. 15). In his *Four Dialogues on Painting*, Francesco de Hollanda has Michelangelo speak at length of the role of art in siege warfare: "What can be more serviceable in the business and enterprise of war than the art of painting, or what more useful to the stress of sieges and assaults." Citing his personal role in protecting Florence during its siege

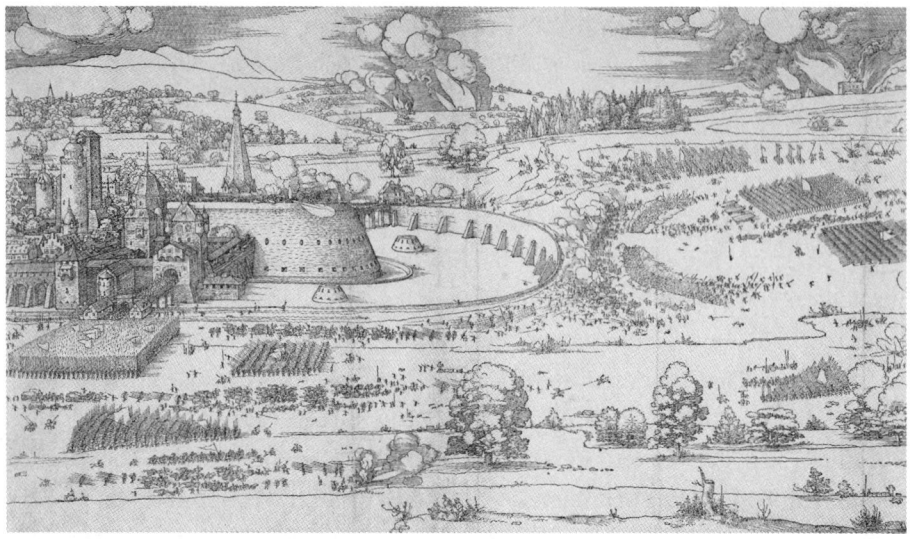

FIG. 15. Albrecht Dürer, *Siege of a Fortressed City*, c. 1527. Woodcut, 22.4 × 37.9 cm

by papal and Spanish forces, Michelangelo enumerates the usefulness of "great painting" to "the machinery and instruments of war," the shape and structure of fortifications, the design of weapons, armor, and banners, and to "making plans of distant places."[232] Tiny in the foreground of Dürer's print, a lamenting mother and cowering peasant bring vanquishment to mind. Already in the ancient world walls had been contravened by projectiles, scaling ladders, siege hooks, battering rams, siege towers, tunneling, and undermining. Wells, rivers, and arrowheads were contaminated, and sick livestock and diseased corpses were tossed or smuggled into the enclosure—a form of biowarfare. Time itself was a weapon, as hunger and thirst made the besieged surrender, or revolt against their leaders. As Machiavelli wrote, "[I]f the people hold you in hatred fortresses do not save you."[233]

Alart du Hameel, perhaps collaborating with Bosch, engraved a fantastical image of a war elephant besieged (fig. 16). Flying the crescent moon flag of Islam, the beast lumbers past walled castles and towns, assailed on all sides by engines of war. Prolonged siege exposes attackers to attack. A decade into their siege of Troy, the Greeks—in one day under the cover of night—constructed around themselves a huge defensive wall complete with towers, parapets, bastions, ditches, bolted gates, and sharp stakes; at Poseidon's demand, Zeus ultimately destroys the edifice for rivaling Troy's wall. Through contravallation and circumvallation besiegers thwarted the dangerous reversal of roles. In 1640, a Spanish army encircled a French army surrounding Italian troops besieging the French-occupied citadel of Turin: a triple siege. At Stalingrad in 1943, Soviet forces surrounded and defeated

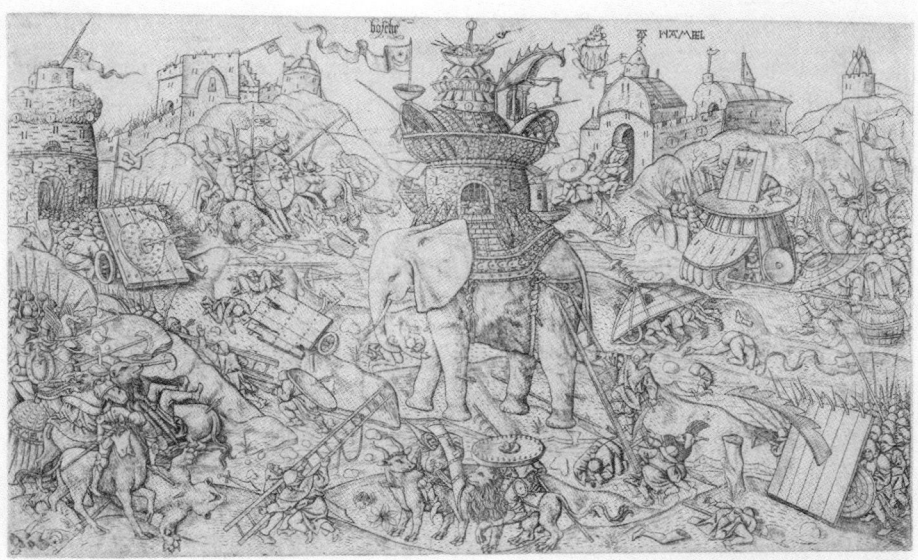

FIG. 16. Alart du Hameel, after Hieronymus Bosch, *War Elephant*, c. 1478–1506. Engraving, 20.3 × 33.6 cm

Hitler's 6th Army after some two million deaths—the siege had turned into a cauldron (*Kessel*) for the besieged Germans. Burgundian rule in the Netherlands ended in 1477 when Charles the Bold, besieging Nancy, died on the battlefield without a male heir. The decimation of Charles's forces, and hatred of Burgundian rule, compelled his daughter and heir, Mary, duchess of Burgundy, to wed Archduke Maximilian, passing the Low Countries into Imperial Habsburg hands.

In the weeks before his defeat, Charles pleaded with his allies for cash to pay his troops, and for gunpowder and artillery.[234] During Bosch's time firearms transformed siege warfare. Constantinople fell to the Ottomans in 1453 because its walls could not withstand bombardment by mobile cannons. One such weapon—the *bombarda horribilis* made for Mehmed II by an expert Hungarian foundryman— shot stone balls seven feet in circumference the distance of a mile.[235] Whole sections of the city's ancient fortifications collapsed in a day. By 1504 gunpowder artillery had become the weapon of choice. This did not fundamentally alter the experience of siege as the collective extreme. Time compresses as food runs short, wells go dry, and civic discord arises while the fortifications uncertainly stand. Space narrows drastically, too, intensifying its divisions. Walls that proudly embraced citizens suddenly press up against their deadly enemy. At its founding, 's-Hertogenbosch promised that "the gates and entry shall be open to him" who swears fidelity and pays the six-farthing citizenship fee.[236] Closed, such gates and exits imprisoned a restrictive regime, where small infractions were severely penalized and dissent and attempted flight were punishable by death. Siege brought war home. In 1472,

Beauvais withstood a four-week onslaught by Charles the Bold only because its women knew just how to respond, repairing breaches, dislodging siege ladders, and hurling stones and hot lime on attackers.[237] But when a siege dragged on—Ostend lasted four years against Spanish forces before surrendering, in ruin and with only two living denizens—the ties of community and kinship break. God's curses at Deuteronomy 28 portray this baleful state vividly: "The most gentle and sensitive woman [...] will begrudge the husband she loves and her own son and daughter the afterbirth of her womb and the children she bears. For she intends to eat them secretly during siege" (Deut. 28:57).

For the Deuteronomist siege was a concrete historical experience. Captured by the Babylonians, its denizens enslaved, Jerusalem was for them a memory and a pledge. God follows his curse with the promise of a new covenant (Deut. 29–30)—a passage probably written at the end of the Babylonian Captivity, when the Jews were able to return to Jerusalem and rebuild the Temple. But God's threat against those who disobey perpetually haunts this promise. Jerusalem would in fact be besieged, attacked, or captured at least fifteen times between the building of the Second Temple, circa 516 BCE, and its destruction in 70 CE.[238] In the Ki Tavo—the fiftieth weekly Torah Portion—the words about familial cannibalism, terrible to dwell upon, are read swiftly. A limit case of historical experience, mothers covetously eating their afterbirth collapses the human collective to a lone monster. Siege could therefore capture extremes endured in extreme solitude; hence the use of Old Testament laments in personal prayer. Christianity inherited from Judaism the image of Israel in siege. In the Passion-centered piety of the later Middle Ages, Christians applied it to Christ himself, but with a toxic twist: blamed for rejecting and murdering the Messiah they foretold, the Jewish people became besieging villains, legitimating future Christian violence against them.

Bosch used circular formats to portray Christ's encirclement. His *Seven Deadly Sins* wraps scenes of vicious humanity around its oculus containing Christ, and the verso of *Saint John on Patmos* rings episodes of the Passion around the pelican, symbol of Christ's redemptive bloodletting (plates 3 and 7). Two circular Boschian compositions (one in the Escorial, the other in Valencia) organize Christ's tormentors as a hostile wreath around Christ (fig. 17).[239] At the left, directing the procedure, a hook-nosed perpetrator bears a scepter topped by a golden figurine of Moses with the Tables of the Law. Probably the high priest Caiaphas, he gives the tormentors a Jewish identity. An echo of the central Man of Sorrows in *The Seven Deadly Sins* (note the identical placement of the stone bench and open tomb), this intimate siege is encircled by predatory demons who are themselves struck down by avenging angels. Concentrically arranged and, like the crown of thorns itself, viciously braided, Jewish and Satanic enmity radiates outward, asking whether we, the beholders, are friends or foes. A related panel by Bosch's hand poses this question more directly (fig. 18). Four torturers press up against Christ. One wraps an arm around his shoulder, another touches his overlapped hands. The wounds the tormentors mean to inflict, conveyed by the armored gloves that handling of the crown requires, mobilize our own feeling and imagination. Gazing at Christ, the foursome momentarily waver, the thorns not yet piercing their victim's flesh. The painting's radical close-up view thrusts us into this hesitant circle, as beholding Christ along with the villains we find ourselves already beheld by him. More personal than the all-seeing eye in Bosch's *Seven Deadly Sins*, that painted gaze makes our condition dangerous nonetheless, submitted as we are to Christ's judgment. Christ's white linen shirt places the event at a moment before the tormentors dress him (parodically) in royal purple robes (John 19:1–3). Over the centuries the painting's whites have become translucent, revealing a more elaborate cloak fastened with a pin that the artist drew but chose not to paint. Magnifying the blankness from which Christ's gaze stands forth, Bosch made the picture's emergency our own.

Nowhere is this collapse of historical time more disorienting than in the triptych Bosch painted for the Antwerp dignitaries Peeter Scheyfve and Agnes de Gramme (plate 13). With its prominent donor portraits, the work probably served both as an altarpiece for liturgical use and as a family memorial. Its outer wings visualize its sacramental use (plate 12). The semi-grisaille portrayal of the Mass of Saint Gregory affirms Christ's flesh and blood presence in the altar rite. According to legend, while Gregory (pope from 590 to 604) was saying Mass, a woman began to laugh, whispering to her companion that the consecrated bread could not be Christ since she herself had baked it. Gregory prayed for some sign to contradict the outrage and suddenly Christ—wounded and crowned with thorns—became visible above the altar. The story drew support from a venerable portrait of Christ in the basilica of Santa Croce in Gerusalemme in Rome, which was believed to have captured Gregory's vision, at the saint's own behest. From the Jubilee Year 1350 on, papal indulgences were granted for prayer to this picture. Israhel van Meckenem's engraving of the icon pledged ten thousand years of indulgence, upped to forty-five thousand years in the print's second state. Reducing by eons the punishment one might suffer for one's sins, such extravagant promises contributed to the flourishing of half-length effigies of the crucified Christ. Bosch's *Crowning with Thorns* and the Christ in *Seven Deadly Sins* reflect this trend, but his Mass of Saint Gregory transports us back to the miraculous event in Rome circa 600 CE, and through it to the moment in sacred history that the altar rite *re*-presents.

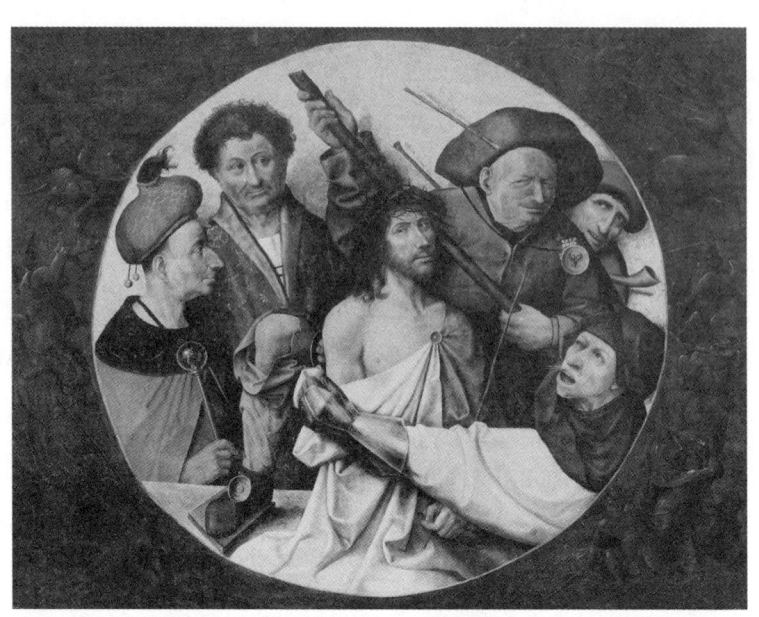

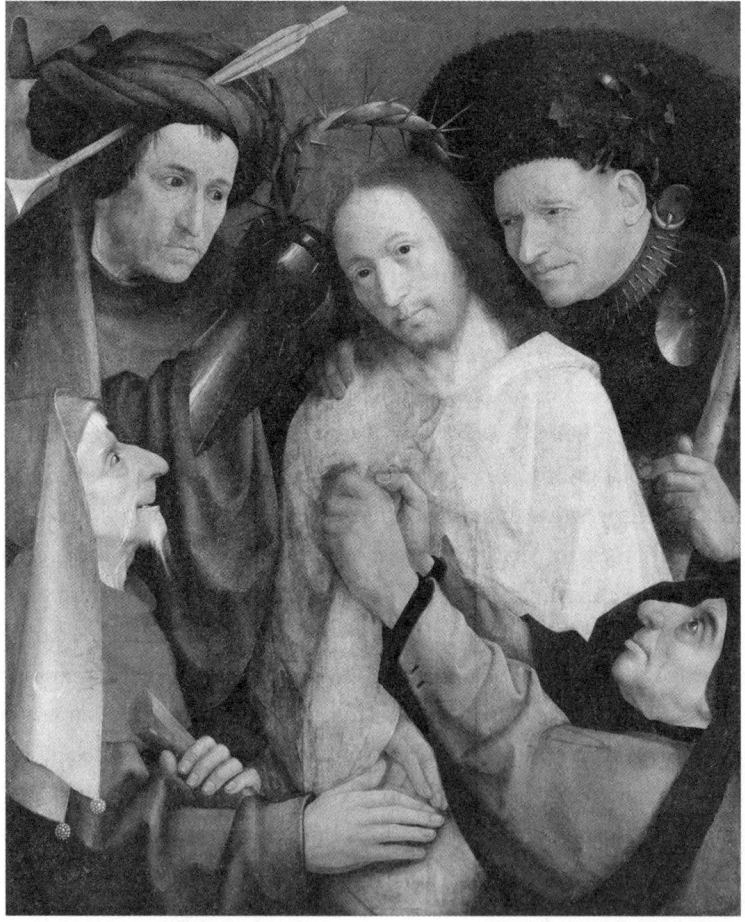

Christ rises from a stone tomb that resembles the supporting predella of a retable altarpiece—in German that part was termed the *Sarg* (sarcophagus). The marble slab behind looks to be carved with nine angels in relief. Passion scenes at the sides loosely maintain the fiction that Pope Gregory's Eucharistic miracle occurs before a retable altarpiece carved or painted with those episodes. But higher up the scenes unfold as if in a hellish vision, with Calvary's round summit echoing the painted panel's bell-shaped top. In the gloom of "the ninth hour," an angel, sized like ones carved in marble but airy and animated, hovers plaintively above the Penitent Thief, who sits beneath his cross. Christ is dying now, with his inner circle properly in attendance, but with the Bad Thief (below) still marching behind his cross. Calvary becomes a timeline, and at one of its moments, in a detail without precedent in Netherlandish art, Judas hangs himself on a tree. A winged devil bears the arch-traitor's soul away. Bosch sketches body and soul in transparent blacks and whites, and with paint still wet, he smears—perhaps with his fingers—a fiery explosion around the demon's head. The artist's direct engagement with his materials befits the pathos of this detail. Judas kills himself out of utter despair. More sinful than his greed and treachery, Judas's suicide sends him to the deepest depths of hell. "[B]y despairing of God's mercy in his sorrow that wrought death, he left to himself no place for a healing penitence," explained Saint Augustine.[240] Instead of exiting through the sinner's mouth, the soul of Judas exploded his body: hanging from a bough, writes the anonymous fourteenth-century poet of *Die Erlösung* (Salvation), "the traitor burst asunder."[241] Bosch intensifies the villainy around Christ. Besieged at death by perfidious friends and Jewish foes, insulted in sacrament by doubters, he appears now threatened by that dubious crowd pressing forward from behind the altar.

Depicting one continuous scene, these shutters open in a most peculiar way. Bosch painted Christ's two bodies—the historical one on the cross and the Eucharistic one in Gregory's vision—across raised frames and cut right through by the gap where the panels meet. When the shutters swing apart, both bodies split, like bread broken before Communion, or like those bodies' inner revelation. Lenten scenes of death give way to a colorful spectacle of Christ's Nativity. The Adoration of the Magi is the decisive scene of amity. Representatives of the multiple, far-flung "nations" (Hebrew *goyim*, Greek *ethnikoi*, Latin *gentiles*), inhabitants of the three known continents who—however—are not of God's chosen tribe, the Jews, they arrive before Christ, who was born Jewish, as outsiders, strangers, and

OPPOSITE: FIG. 17. Follower of Hieronymus Bosch, *The Crowning with Thorns*, c. 1540. Oil on panel, 157.5 × 195.8 cm. Monasterio de San Lorenzo de El Escorial/Patrimonio Nacional

LEFT: FIG. 18. Hieronymus Bosch, *The Crowning with Thorns*, c. 1500. Oil on panel, 73.8 × 59 cm. National Gallery of Art, London

potentially enemies. Paying homage to Christ in sight of their peers, they affirm publicly, with gifts and with worship, his status as king of kings. Bosch haunts this peaceful assembly with enemies. In the darkness between the Christ child and the Magi, an ass, an old emblem of the Jews who uniquely and stubbornly deny their own God, presses towards the godhead, its convex "Jewish" muzzle pressuring the flimsy post supporting the Virgin's canopy. Meanwhile, in the left panel, Joseph (a cuckold in Christian lore) sullenly dries Christ's diaper. In the central landscape background, warring armies contend, and at the right, wolves attack wanderers in a dangerous countryside.

Yet more discomforting is the abject troop crowding the manger's interior, their leader now setting foot on the sacred ground. Of all the enigmatic details in Bosch's oeuvre, this bizarre entourage has caused the most trouble. For Gombrich, the strange figure in the doorway proved that—contrary to Fraenger and others—visual images are not self-evident but need supporting texts and contexts for their correct interpretation. Gombrich argued this in the same year he published the early provenance of the *Garden of Delights*, toppling Fraenger's scholarly edifice. His 1967 lecture "The Evidence of Images" treats Bosch only in passing, via Gombrich's own wartime experience at a British listening post deciphering enemy communiqués, and after an analysis of visual perception and its pitfalls—what Gombrich terms "the variability of vision."[242] These high-stakes arguments give way to what purports to be a simple corrective. Bosch's mysterious group is King Herod and his scribes trying to spy out the Christ child. The proof is right there in the Bible, supplemented by medieval mystery plays, where Herod is a common villain.[243]

While never definitively refuted, Gombrich's identification has failed to convince. Rather than being a simple puzzle to be solved, the iconography is better left as a deliberately inscrutable malignancy, and inscrutable for iconographical reasons. According to an interpretation that Gombrich dismissed as baseless and anachronistic (its author, Lotte Brand Philip, had been a student of Panofsky), the mystery man at the doorway post is probably the Jewish Messiah arrived as Antichrist already at Christ's birth.[244] Recent work on Antichrist imagery in liturgical enactments of the Epiphany suggests that, though he would arrive in the future, Christians expected Antichrist to be temporally ubiquitous, circulating through world history.[245] The antitype of the Magi who identify Christ as king, Antichrist denies that identity as well as his own. The supreme illusionist, he deceives most effectively in his absence, when people, falsely believing he has arrived, proclaim the world's end is at hand and give up all respect for the law.

In the triptych, the armies mustered on the plain between Christ's Epiphany in Bethlehem and Jerusalem's distant walls have an apocalyptic charge. Saint John (at

Rev. 20:8) took a prophecy from Ezekiel—according to which Gog "of the land of Magog" will storm "the land of unwalled villages" (Ezek. 38:2, 18)—and imagined two evil nations, Gog and Magog, who will unite with Satan to battle God at the end of time. Legends also had it that Alexander the Great erected a great wall around his empire to repel Scythian horsemen. Over the centuries, attacks by nomadic peoples of the European steppe and the long walls erected to thwart mounted invaders made the Alexander legend one of the world's most often-told tales. The fourteenth-century *Travels of Sir John Mandeville* made Gog and Magog the Ten Lost Tribes of the Jews, whom Alexander confined to an inescapable region in the Caspian Hills; in the time of the Antichrist, they would escape to join the Jews of Europe and destroy Christendom.[246] Bosch's horsemen wear Turkish and Tartar headgear, making the catastrophe they foreshadow real and present. In the artist's time, Jerusalem stood under Mamluk control, falling then to the Ottomans in 1516. In the triptych's landscape a crescent moon atop an idol signals this hostile occupancy of the Holy Land. Bosch's *Ecce Homo* panel makes the point more vividly (fig. 19). While Jewish enemies demand Christ's crucifixion, in the background, in a scene echoing the foreground one, the Muslim foe musters under its red and gold banner.

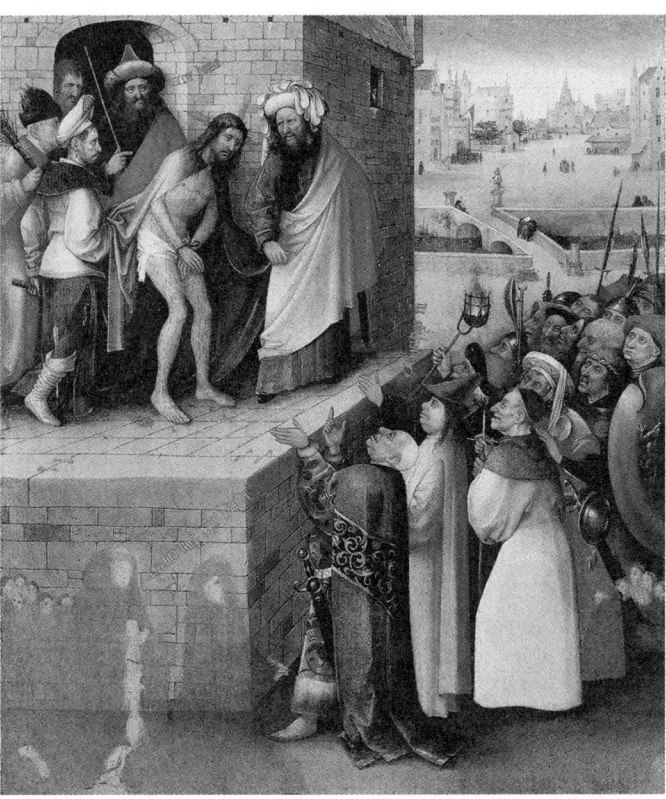

FIG. 19. Hieronymus Bosch, *Ecce Homo*, c. 1500. Oil on oak panel, 71.4 × 61 cm. Städel Museum, Frankfurt am Main

That flag flies again in the background of Bosch's *Temptation of Saint Anthony* triptych (plate 14). The founder of the monastic orders, Saint Anthony went into the Egyptian desert to pray alone, but his devotion was disturbed by a veritable army of demons. Earning the epithet of devil-maker, Bosch conjures a swarm of fantastical monsters tempting and tormenting the saint. They besiege and have begun to infiltrate the ruined tomb where he prays, while far off in the right panel's distant view, a Brabantine town, with windmills like the ones in 's-Hertogenbosch, has already fallen to hostile forces. Troops in Turkish turbans and equipped with siege ladders swarm the towers under the banner of the crescent moon. Supported by a globe carried on the back of a kneeling black man, the flag foretells Europe's enslavement if the infidel prevails. The demonic siege of the Christian self, pictured by Saint Anthony's temptation, thus expands to encompass the entire ecumene.

Bosch did not invent this siege mentality. He was just better at capturing what his public felt prevailed. Historians have debated the causes of this culture of fear that stretched back centuries before the Reformation, channeling terror into the hunt for enemies.[247] On a cosmic level, there was the old foe, Satan, whose rebellion God crushed, seeding the enmity that would bring Eve and Adam low. On a geopolitical level, the enemies could be distant ones, like the Turks or Hussites, or neighboring adversaries, like Guelders was to Brabant. Enemies lurked in the hearth and home. In war and hard times, floods of refugees wandered, peddled, and begged their way from town to town. In the Netherlands of Bosch's time, itinerants came to be vilified for belonging to a secret global order with arcane rules and symbols and an inverted honor code. Operating deceptively, they targeted the honest citizen. The widely circulated *Book of Vagabonds* claimed to capture this conspiracy in all its forms, including a cryptolect, or "cant," for which the book provided a glossary. Unintelligible to their victims, these words messaged fellow perpetrators. They were like arsonist's marks, telling which house or farm to torch and when and how.[248]

A painter of enemies, Bosch drew inspiration from such nefarious symbols. His villains often bear crafted marks of their demonic allegiance in the form of badges, shields, emblems, seals, and ensigns. Some of the imagery on the Magi's costumes and gifts is legible, most is not. The gold brought by the first Magus has been marvelously worked into a statuette of the Sacrifice of Isaac, a common Old Testament "type" foreshadowing Christ's sacrifice. But the beady-eyed frogs at the artifact's base, whether living creatures or enameled figurines, are not as easily digested. This chiaroscuro of the familiar and the strange befits the event, where at the Epiphany aliens become allies. The *Temptation of Saint Anthony* consists almost entirely of enemies and their insignia, artifacts, and rituals: behind

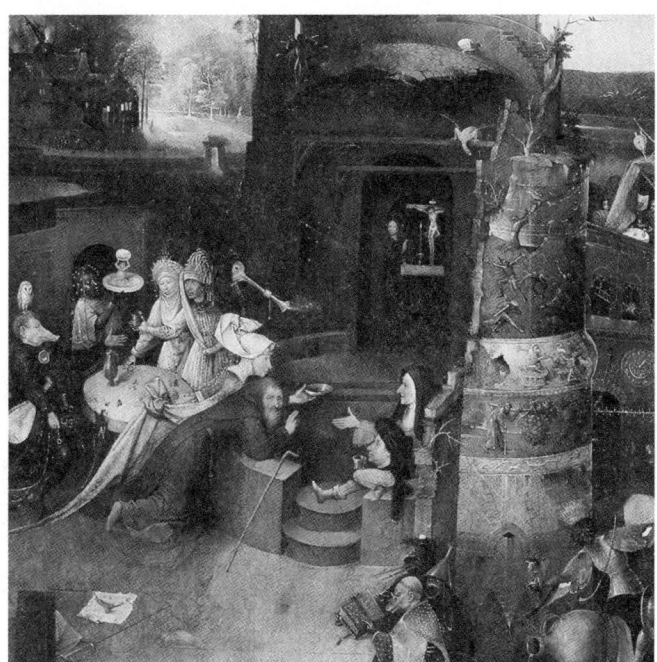

the saint, demons celebrate a Black Mass, with a frog elevating an egg-shaped
anti-Eucharist (fig. 20). Bosch sets two things apart from the diabolical tableau:
the scene around the saint's makeshift altar, where Christ appears as priest beside
the crucifix, and the hermit-saint himself, who looks out at us from the exact
center of the painting. A tiny point of paint, that outward gaze asks us to look
(like Anthony) inward, and away from the rest. Yet that hellish rest fascinates,
and gives pleasure, as Philip the Fair understood.

   The artist acknowledges this contradiction. Christ on the cross, a minimal
image of God, rises beside a polychrome imagery carved into, or frescoed on,
the toppling wall or column of the tomb. Some of this imagery is suitably inscrutable, since it means to conjure fallen and forgotten gods. Bosch paints, in
pinkish monochrome, a scene of abject veneration, with supplicants bringing
animal offerings to a demon-idol on a drum-shaped throne. But the scene above
it is legible: the primordial scene of Jewish image worship, the Adoration of the
Golden Calf, with the Israelites dancing the hectic *moreška* of Islamic infidels. The
tomb becomes a toppling monument to idols past and present. Bosch renders
these scenes in his signature sketchy style. Good for conjuring demons, it is at
odds with the meticulous finish of early Netherlandish art. The central panel of
the triptych that posterity calls the *Garden of Delights* bears a relation to this kind
of painting. Imagine if the murals on Anthony's place of prayer were restored to

their pristine condition and expanded to fill the entire visual field. We would be thrust so deeply inside the idol's illusion as to fancy we looked into another world. The painting's lure puts the Christian in a state of siege. A year after Bosch's death, such thinking would bring about a great upheaval. Instead of besieging, the visual image stood besieged.

Wittenberg, 1517

We in the field of Northern Renaissance art had hardly finished celebrating one big date when another was already upon us. In 2016, the quincentenary of Bosch's death occasioned books, shows, and research that brought the painter's life, work, and patronage into sharper focus than ever before. Then, in 2017, came the quincentenary of an historically more consequential event: Martin Luther's issuing and (ostensibly) posting on the door of Wittenberg's All Saints' Church of his "Ninety-Five Theses" against the power and efficacy of indulgences. The last Bosch centennial, in 1916, went unnoticed. The artist's death date itself came back to light again only in 1874, at a time when only a few specialists cared.[249] By contrast, each of the last five centenaries of the German Reformation's zero hour was in itself a defining event, a public remembrance when the Lutheran confession and eventually the entire German nation put its identity on display.[250] As one artist pictured the moment in 1917, a year before Germany's defeat in World War I, the Reformer looks sternly back at us while striking his epochal hammer blow (fig. 21). We, the image implies, are a world divided between friends and foes that Luther's decisive action clarifies. Four lines from Luther's hymn "A Mighty Fortress is Our God" offer militant solace, then and now, for troubled times.

One hundred years earlier, Protestant towns throughout Germany staged elaborate festivals and erected public monuments commemorating Luther, partly to affirm religion against enlightened detractors, partly to fuel nationalist passions in the aftermath of the Napoleonic Wars. In 1817, frustrated by their country's failure to unite, German university students held a "national festival" on the Wartburg, the hilltop fortress where Luther hid from Catholic and Imperial Habsburg foes and where he translated the New Testament into German. Gathered in dueling fraternities called *Burschenschaften*, they sang hymns, swore oaths, feasted, and burned books in imitation of Luther's burning of the papal bull that called for his excommunication—in 1933 book-burning students in Nazi Germany followed both historical precedents. The Wartburg Festival was intended to celebrate October 31, 1817, All Saints' Eve, the day associated with Luther's hammer blow.

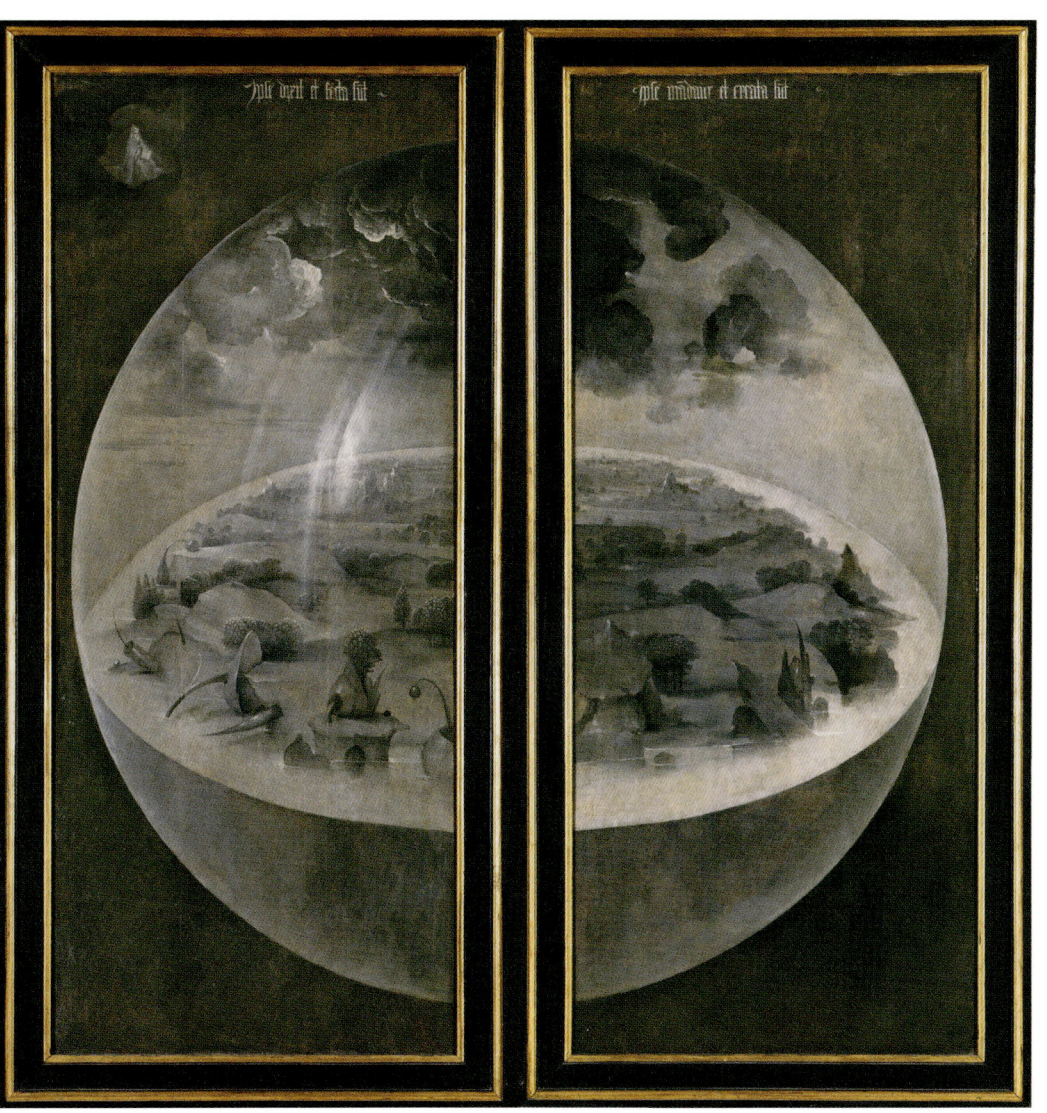

PLATE 1. Hieronymus Bosch, *The Garden of Earthly Delights*, closed state, c. 1500. Oil on panel, 220 × 390 cm. Museo Nacional del Prado, Madrid

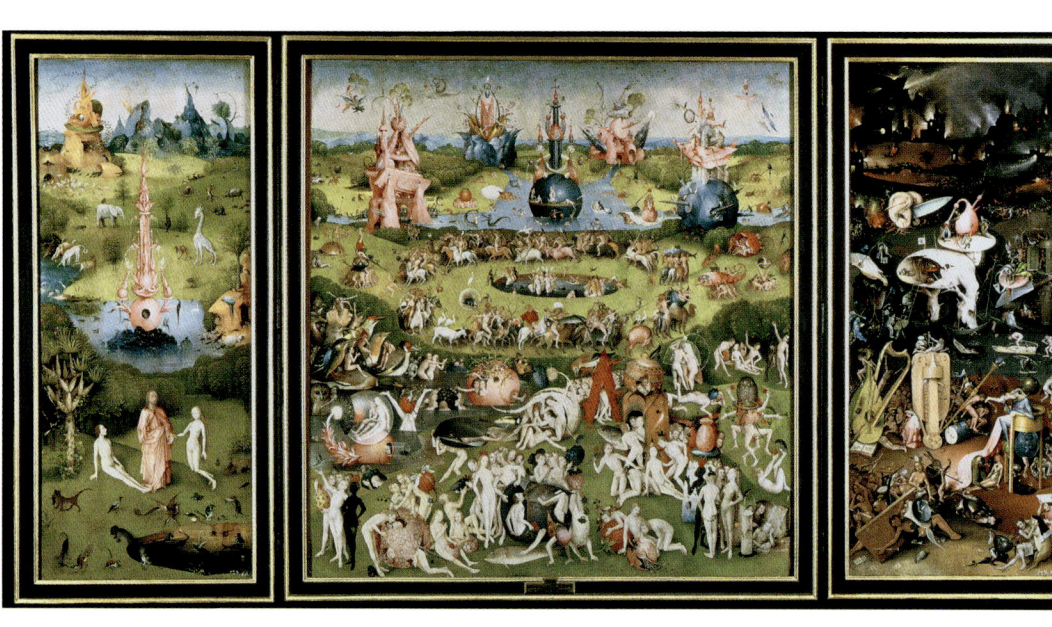

PLATE 2. Hieronymus Bosch, *The Garden of Earthly Delights*, open state, c. 1500. Oil on panel, 205.5 × 384.9 cm. Museo Nacional del Prado, Madrid

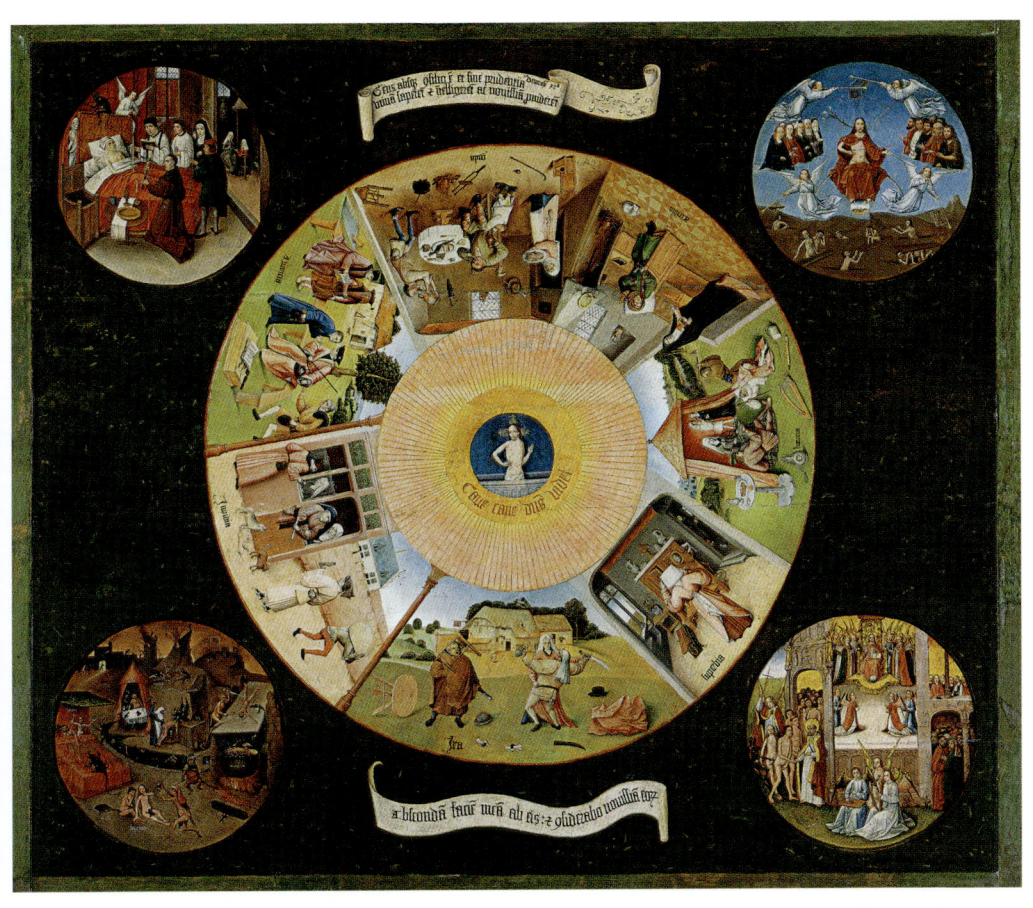

PLATE 3. Hieronymus Bosch and Workshop, *Seven Deadly Sins and the Four Last Things*, c. 1500. Oil on panel, 120 × 150 cm. Museo Nacional del Prado, Madrid

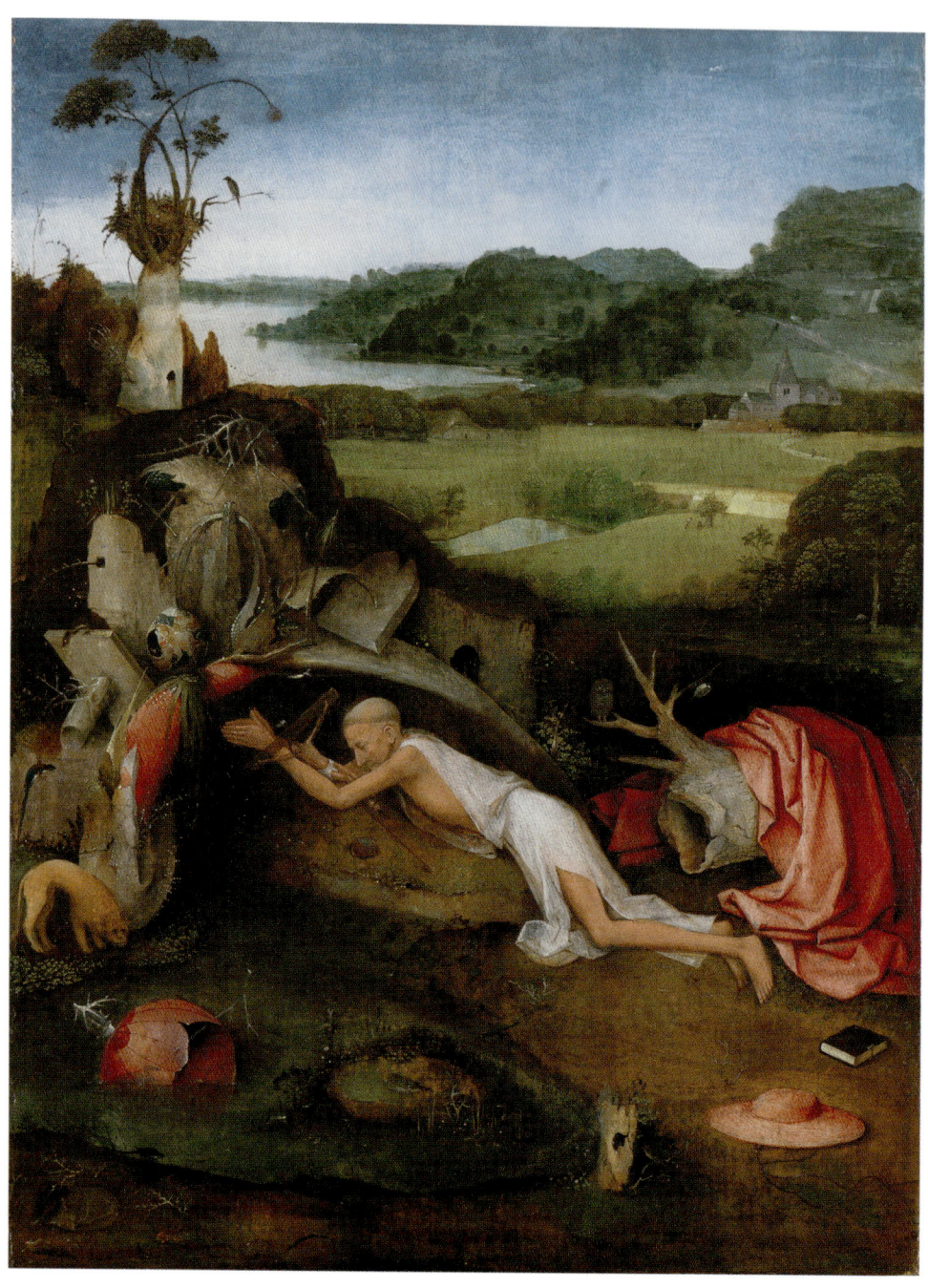

PLATE 4. Hieronymus Bosch, *Saint Jerome*, c. 1485–90. Oil on panel, 77 × 59 cm. Museum voor Schone Kunsten, Ghent

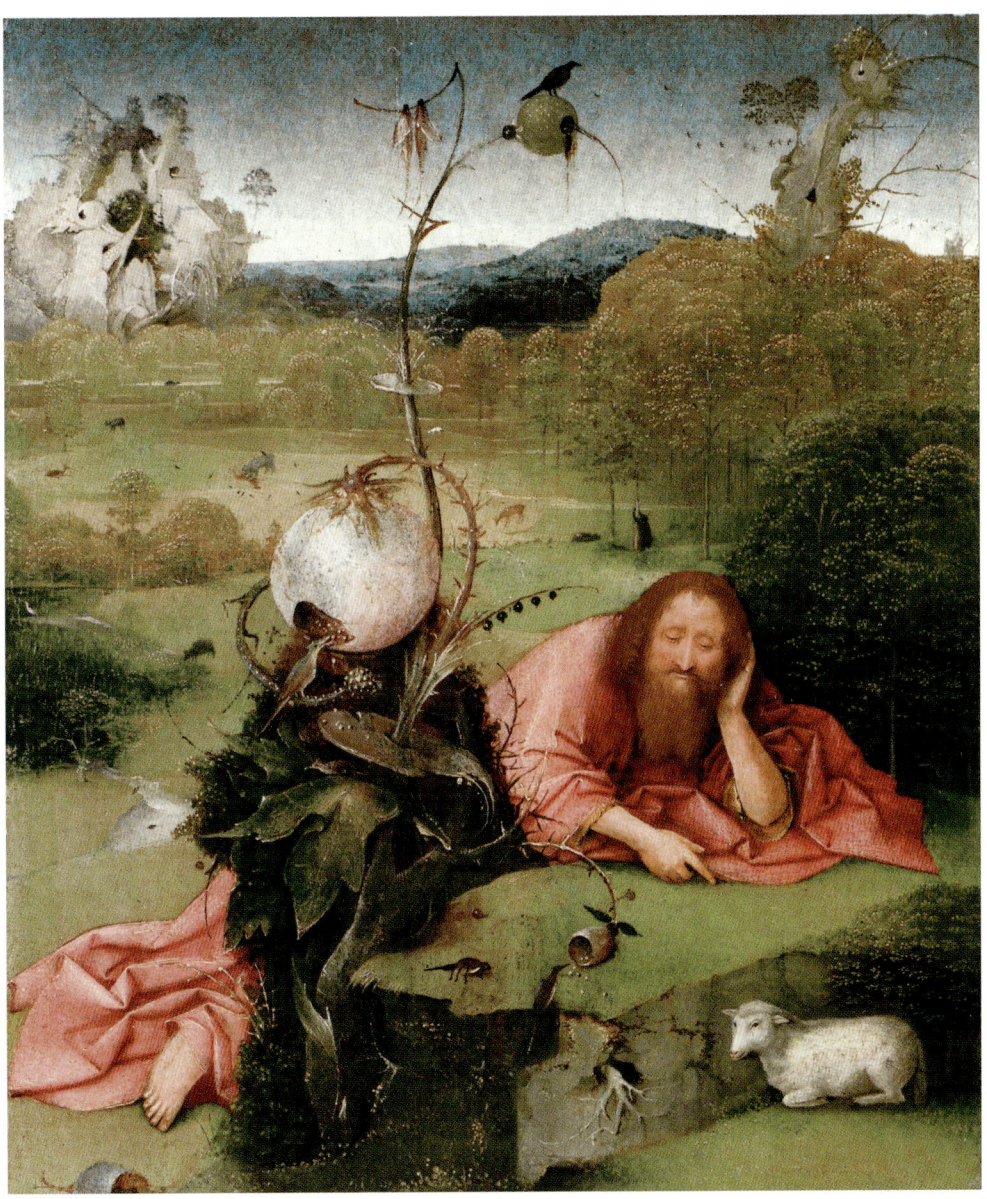

PLATE 5. Hieronymus Bosch, *Saint John the Baptist in the Wilderness*, c. 1490–95. Oil on oak panel, 48.5 × 40 cm. Museum of Lázaro Galdiano, Madrid

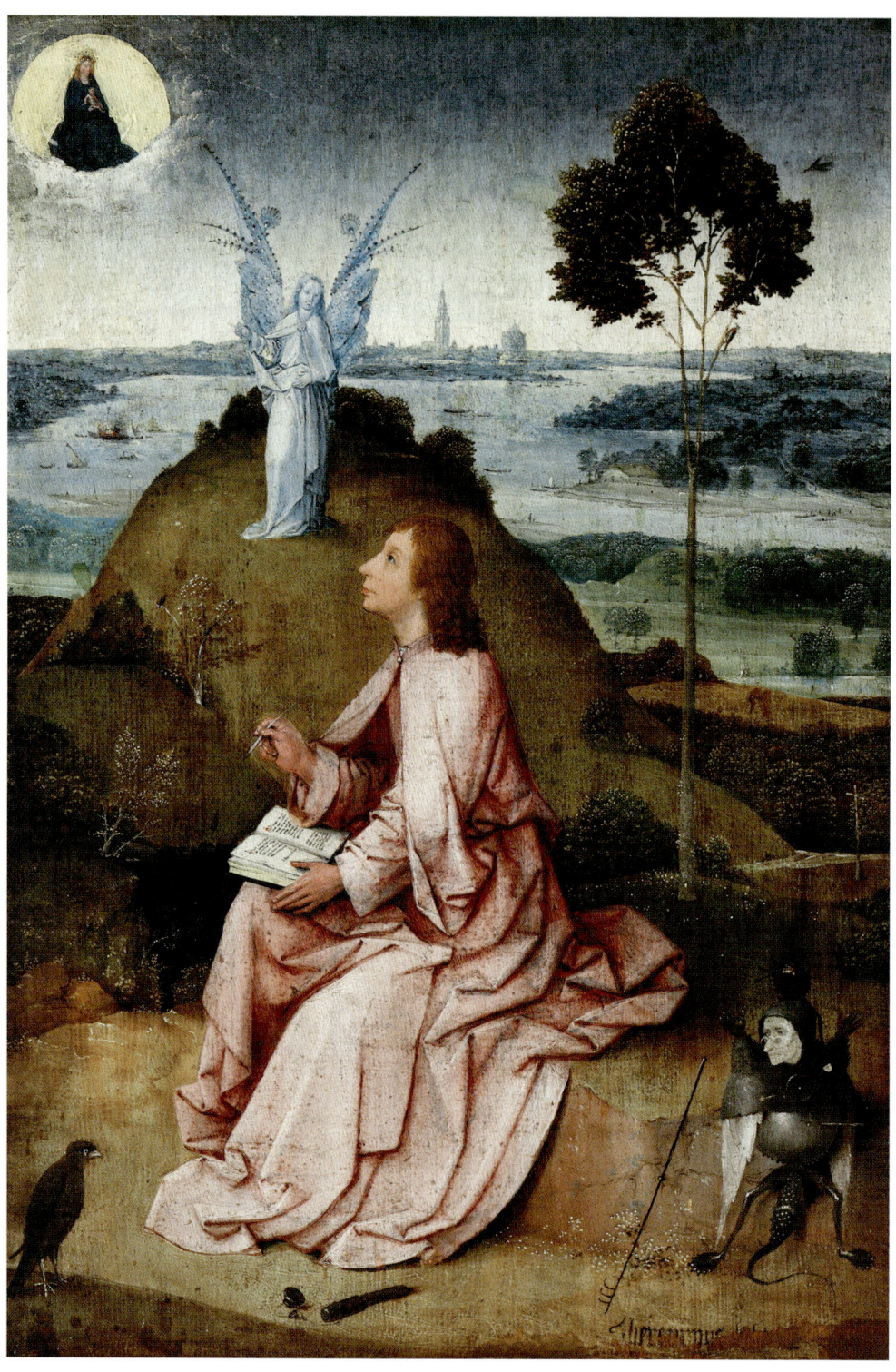

PLATE 6. Hieronymus Bosch, *Saint John the Evangelist on Patmos*, c. 1490–95. Oil on oak panel, 63 × 43.3 cm. Staatliche Museen zu Berlin, Gemäldegalerie, Berlin

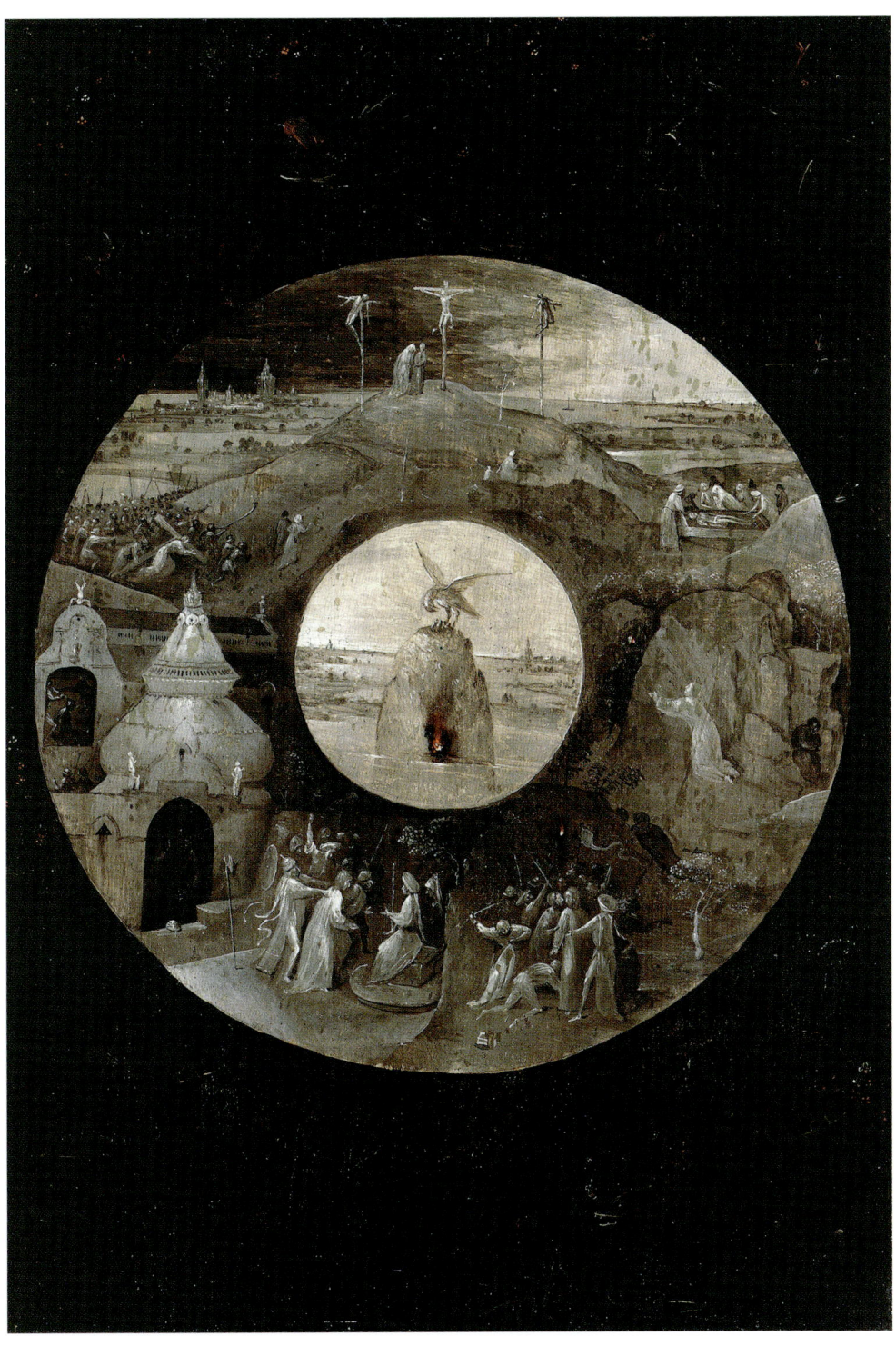

PLATE 7. Hieronymus Bosch, *Scenes of the Passion of the Christ*, reverse of *Saint John on Patmos*, c. 1490–95. Oil on oak panel, 63 × 43.3 cm. Staatliche Museen zu Berlin, Gemäldegalerie, Berlin

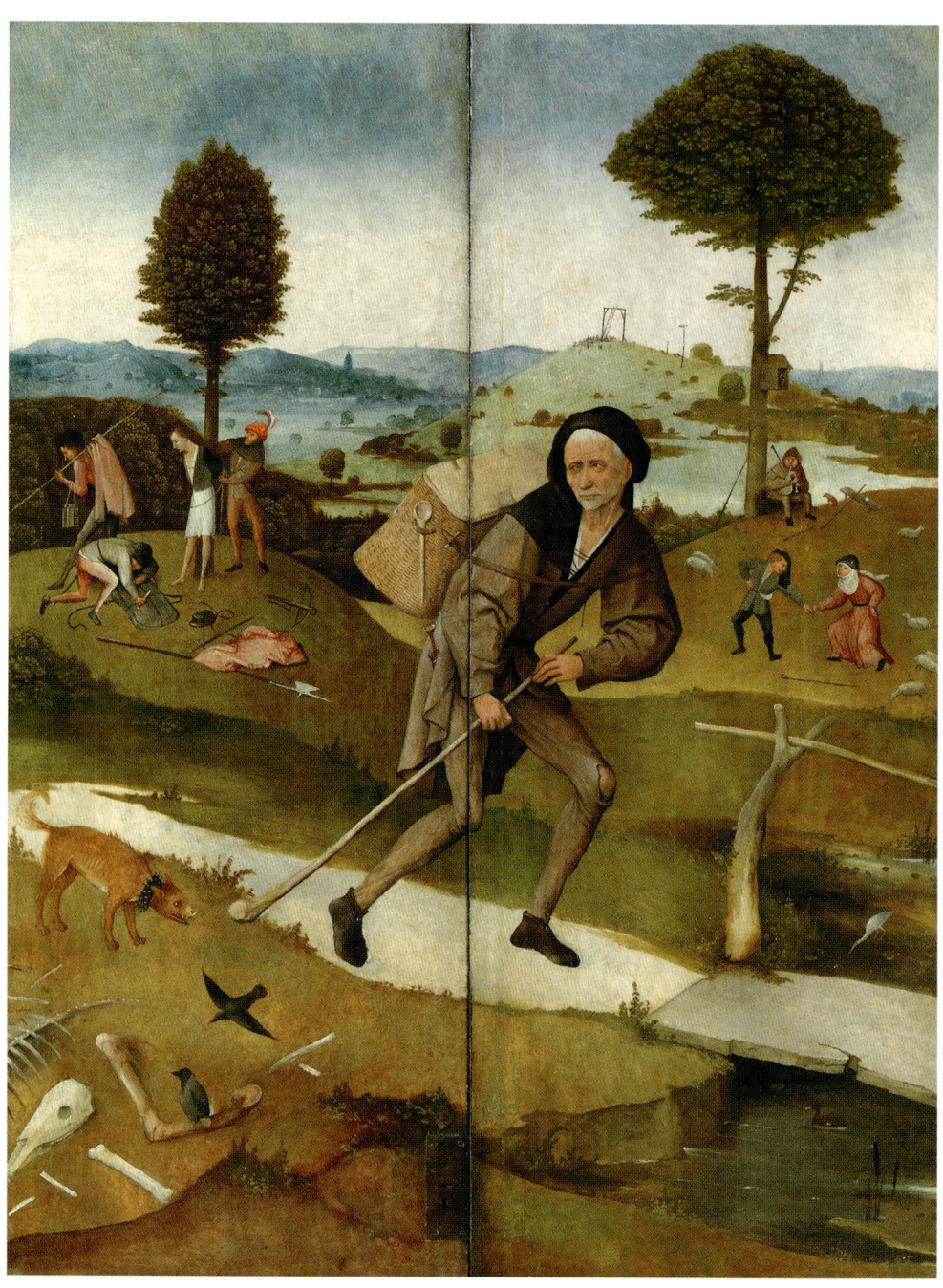

PLATE 8. Hieronymus Bosch and Workshop, *The Pedlar*, closed state of *The Hay Wain*, c. 1510. Oil on panel, 147.1 × 212 cm. Museo Nacional del Prado, Madrid

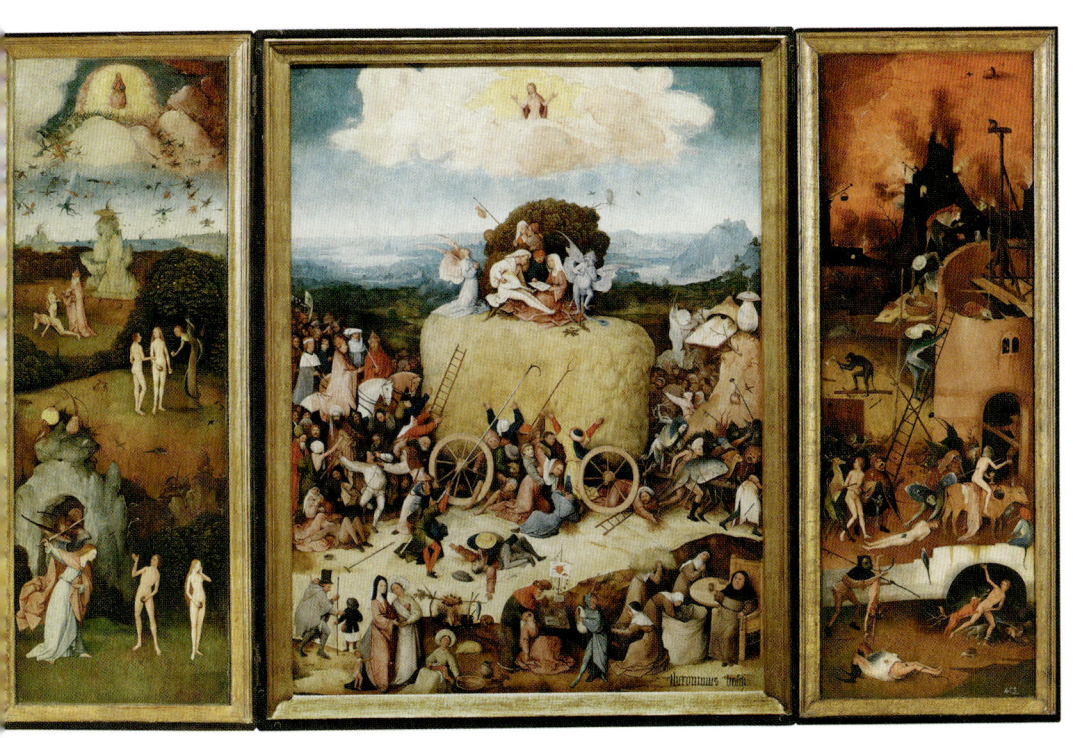

PLATE 9. Hieronymus Bosch and Workshop, *The Hay Wain*, open state, c. 1510. Oil on panel, 135 × 200 cm. Museo Nacional del Prado, Madrid

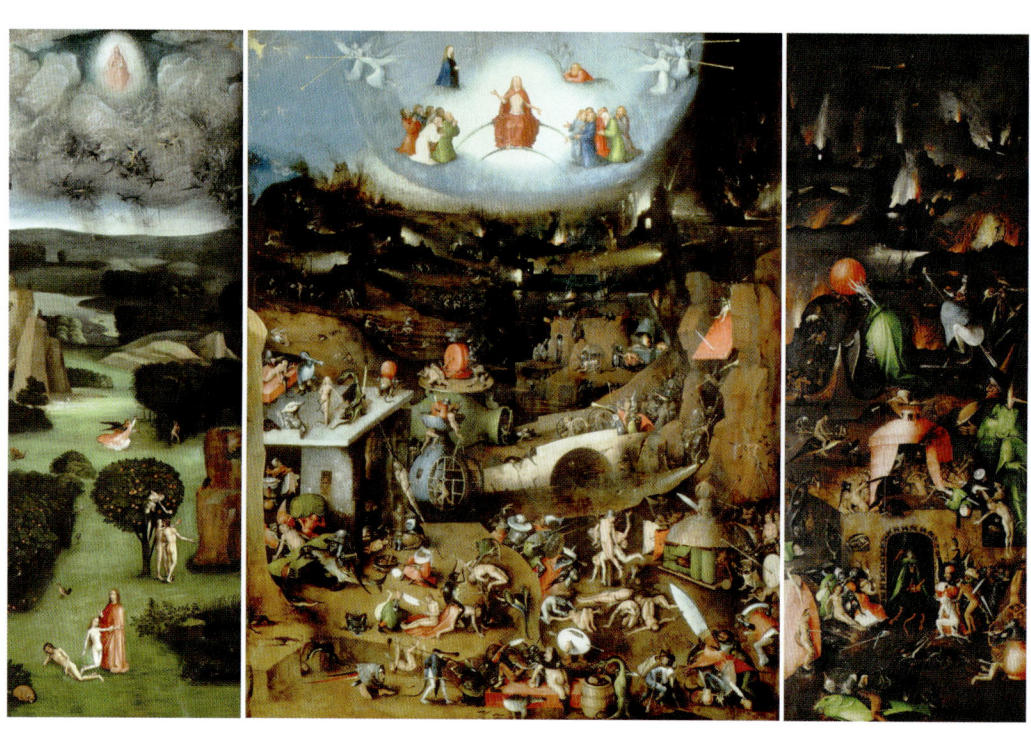

PLATE 10. Hieronymus Bosch, *Last Judgment*, open state, c. 1504. Oil on panel, 163.7 × 242 cm. Gemäldegalerie der Akademie der Bildenden Künste, Vienna

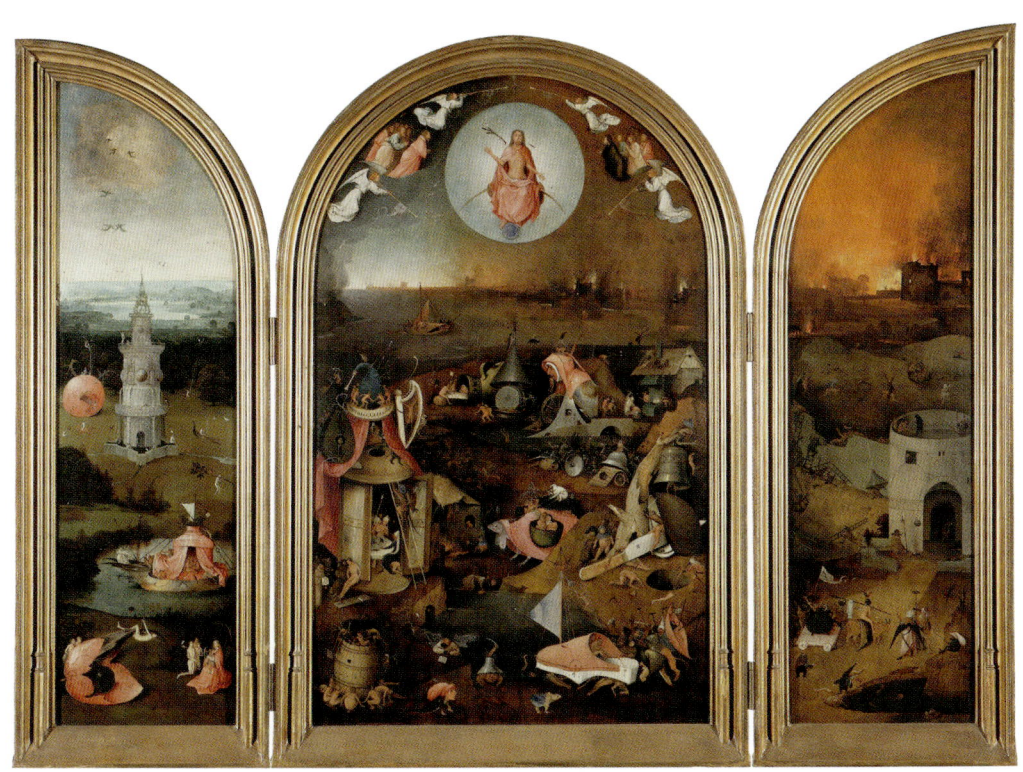

PLATE 11. Hieronymus Bosch, *Last Judgment*, open state, c. 1500. Oil on panel, 99 × 117.5 cm. Groeningemuseum, Bruges

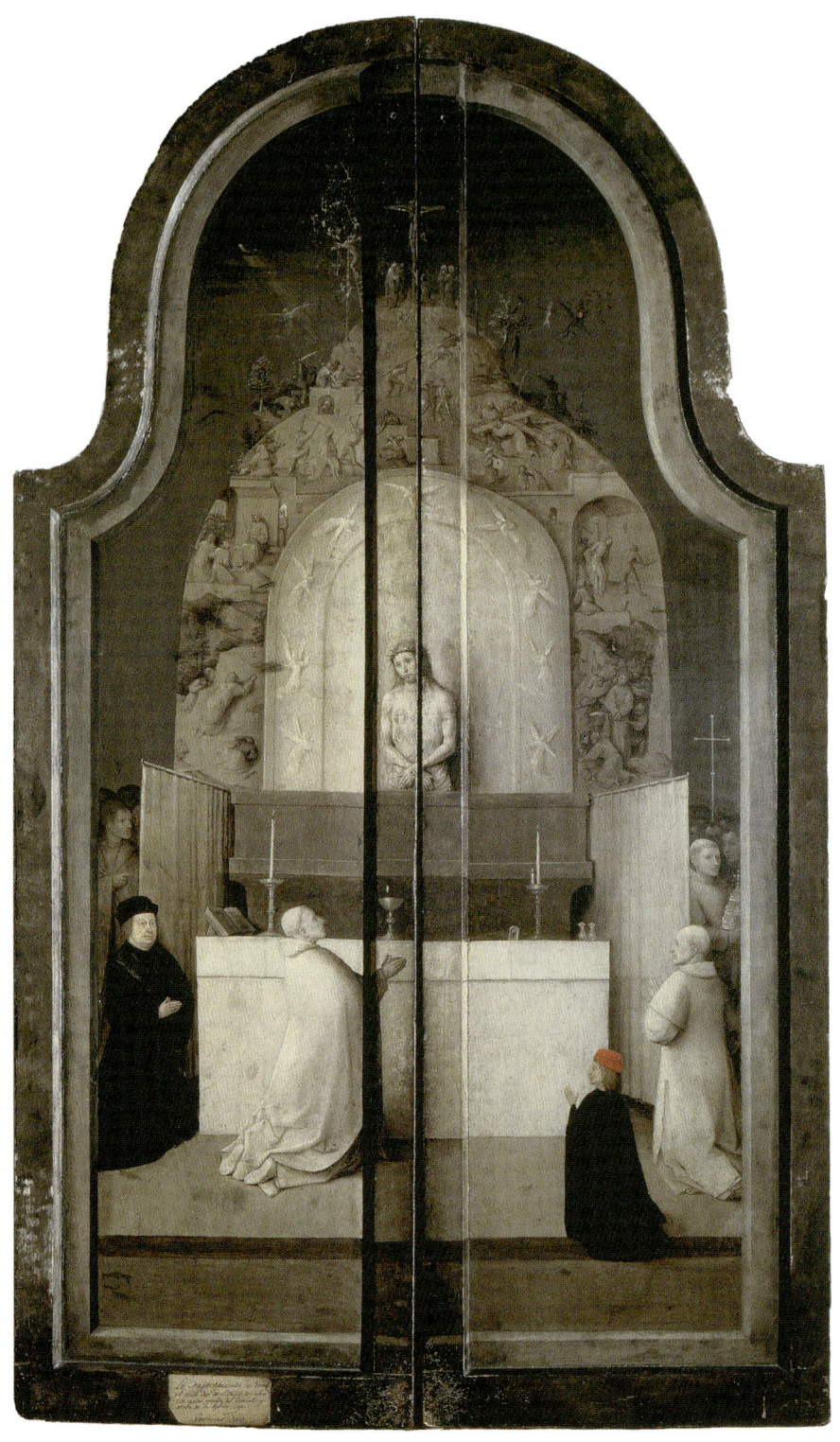

PLATE 12. Hieronymus Bosch, *Mass of Saint Gregory*, closed state of *Adoration of the Magi*, c. 1490–1500. Oil on panel, 138 × 72 cm. Museo Nacional del Prado, Madrid

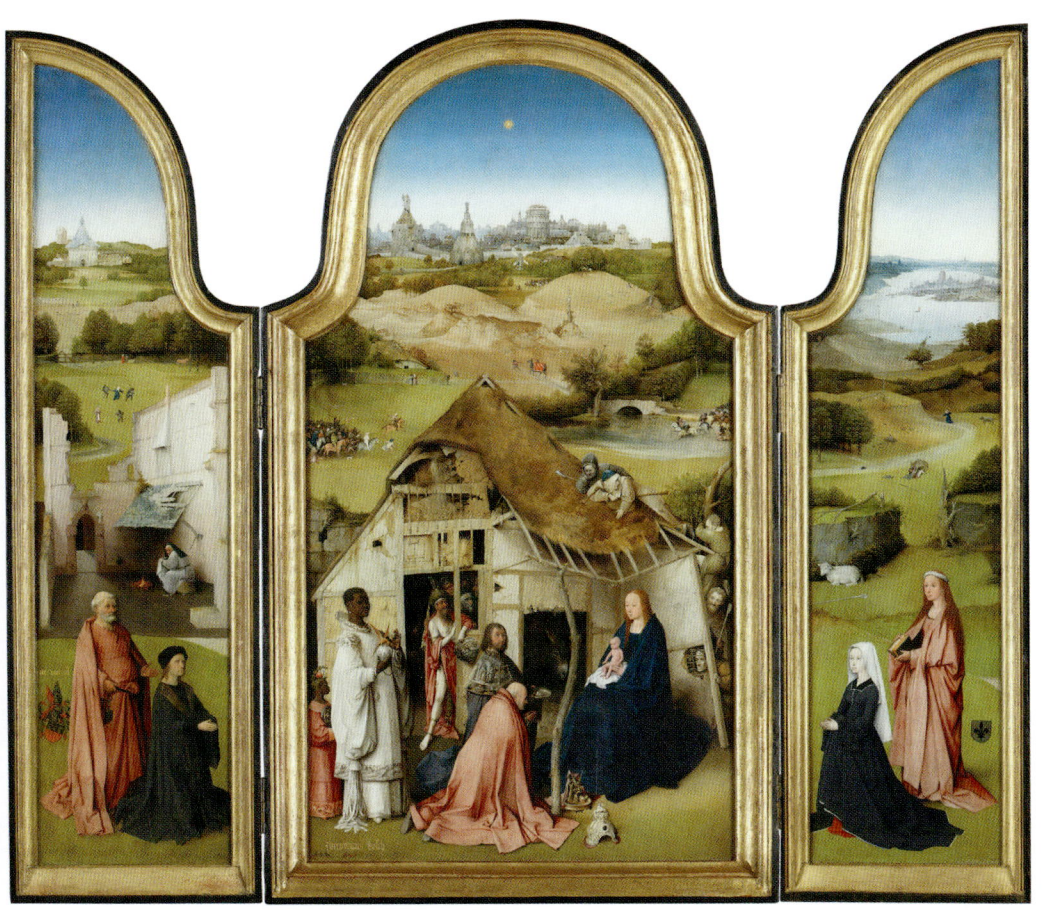

PLATE 13. Hieronymus Bosch, *Adoration of the Magi* (*Epiphany*), open state, c. 1490–1500. Oil on panel, 138 × 144 cm. Museo Nacional del Prado, Madrid

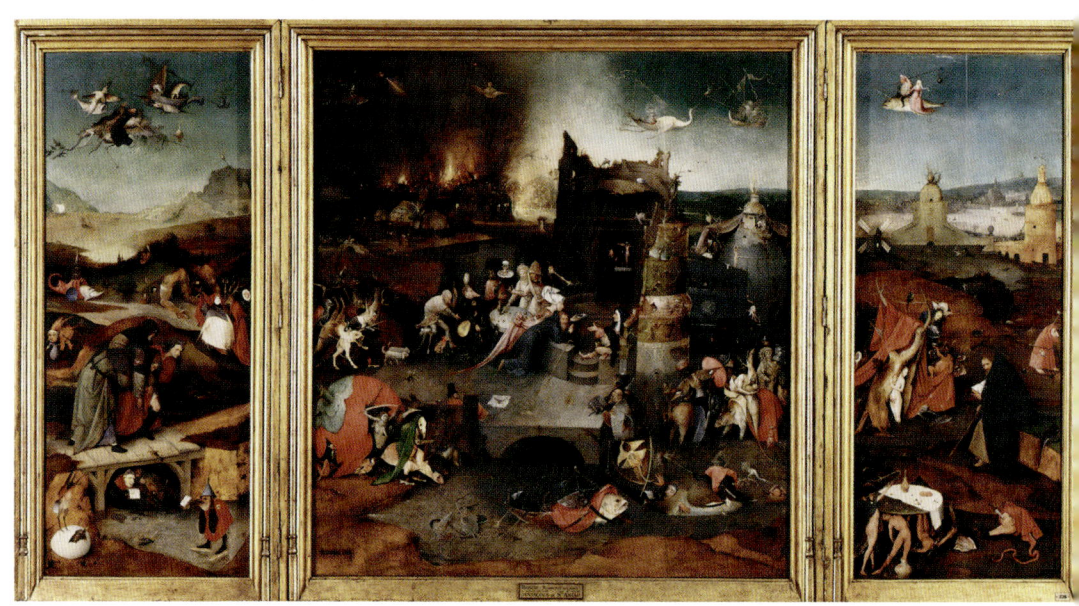

PLATE 14. Hieronymus Bosch, *Temptation of Saint Anthony*, open state, c. 1510. Oil on panel, 131 × 228 cm. Museu Nacional de Arte Antiga, Lisbon

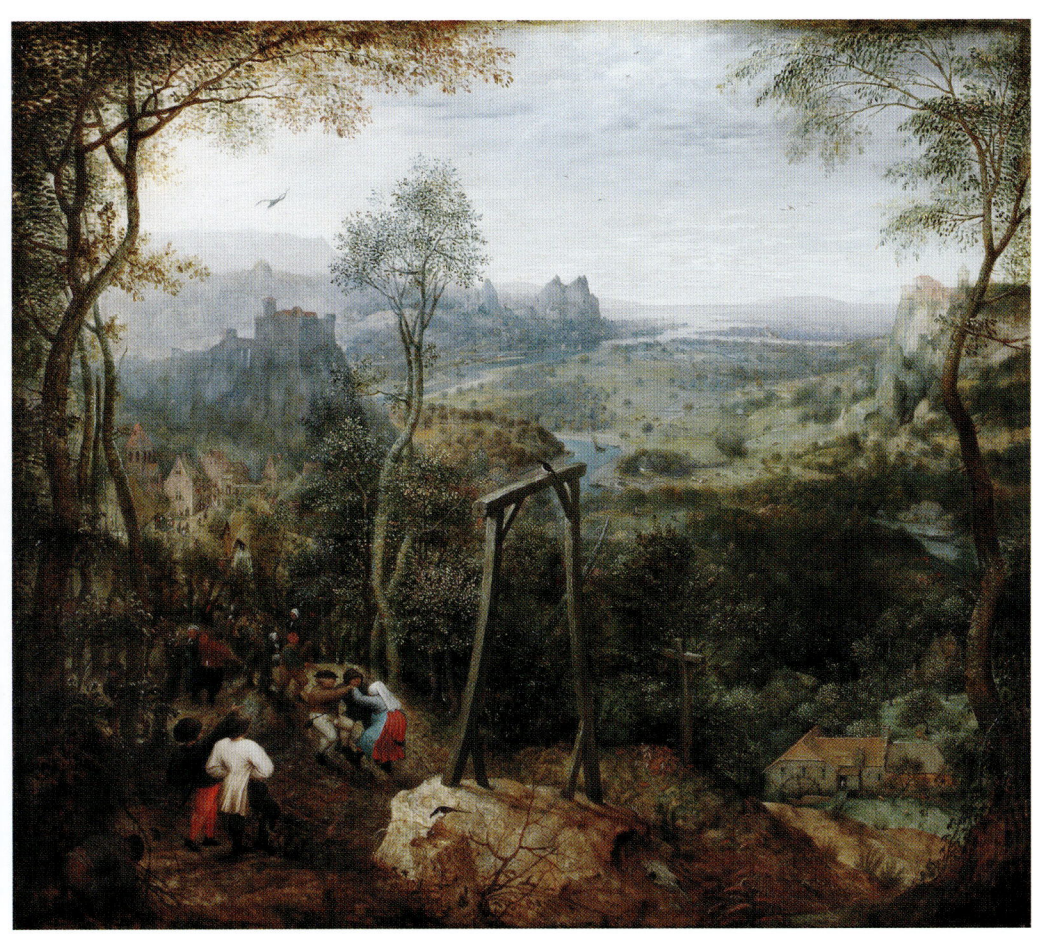

PLATE 15. Pieter Bruegel the Elder, *The Magpie on the Gallows*, 1568. Oil on panel, 45.9 × 50.8 cm. Hessisches Landesmuseum, Darmstadt

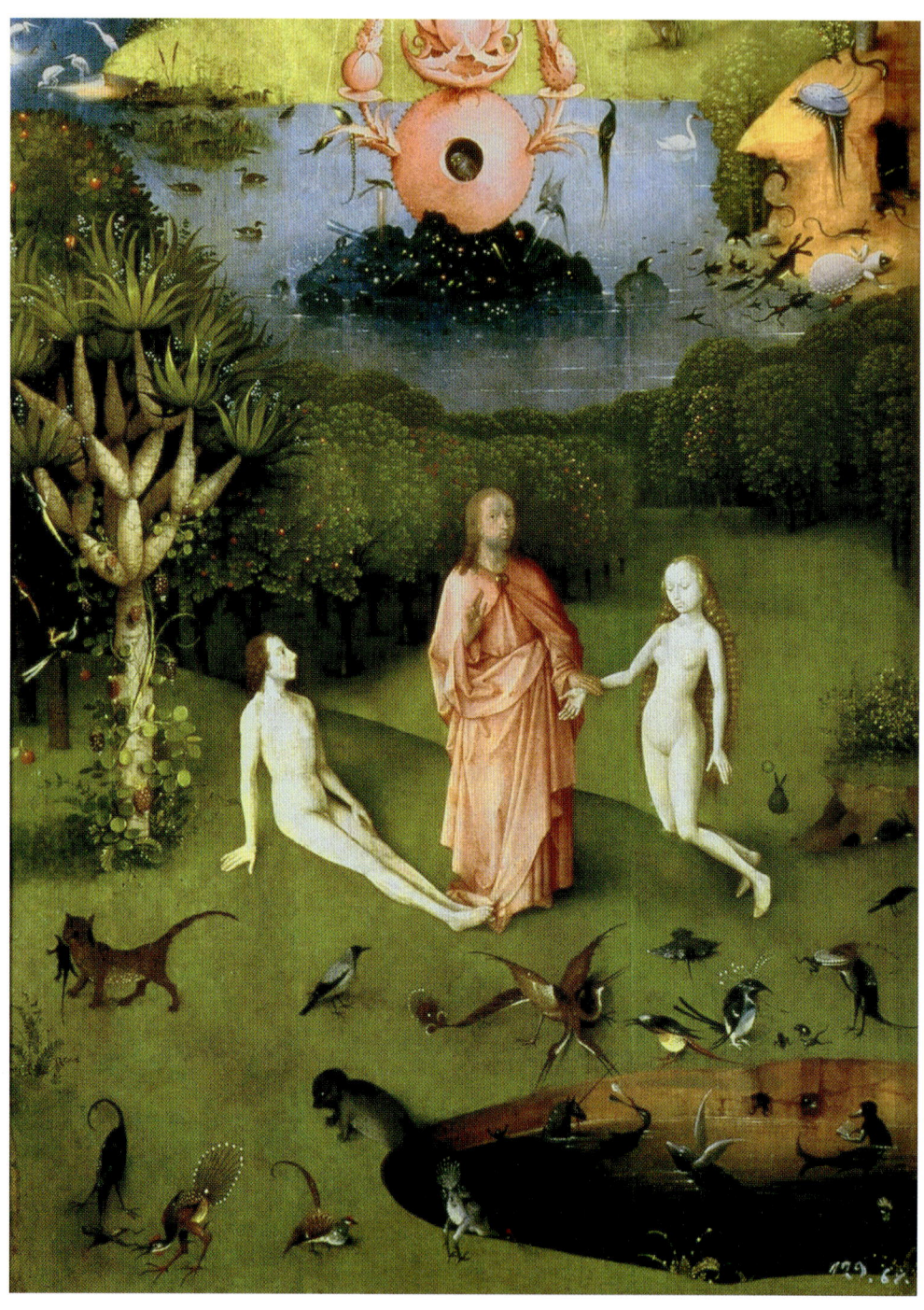

PLATE 16. Detail from Hieronymus Bosch, *The Garden of Earthly Delights*, open state, 1504. Oil on panel, 205.5 × 384.9 cm. Museo Nacional del Prado, Madrid

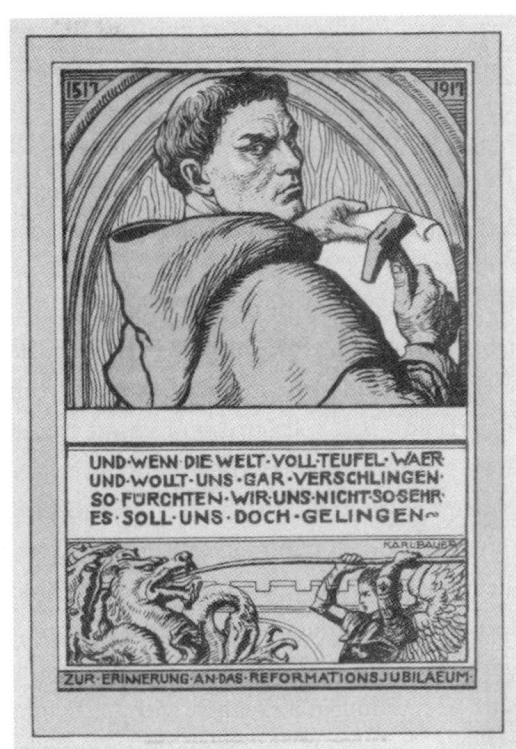

FIG. 21. Karl Bauer, *Luther Posts the 95 Theses*
(Invitation to a Reformation Jubilee), 1917.
Lithograph, 21 × 29 cm

Early biographies of the Reformer had recorded that date, but it took a century for people to make it, of all episodes in Luther's storied life, the focus of what became the very first large-scale modern centenary. A small administrative act—an obscure monk pasting obscure arguments (probably with sealing wax) to crowded noticeboards in Wittenberg—became an epochal turning point in history.

Luther centennials were an invention of 1617. In that year the Theological Faculty of Wittenberg University asked permission from the territorial church of Saxony to celebrate October 31 as the *primus Jubileus Lutheranus*. The idea was biblical. God had instructed Moses to keep each "seven sabbaths of years" (whether the forty-ninth or the fiftieth year remained open to debate) as a holy year of Jubilee, when debts would be forgiven and slaves and prisoners freed. On this model Pope Boniface VII made 1300 a jubilee year, granting plenary indulgence to pilgrims visiting Rome—this celebration was when veneration of the Christ portrait in Santa Croce took off, inspiring images of Pope Gregory's Mass (plate 12; fig. 24). Papal jubilees now came every fifty years. In 1470, Pope Paul II shortened the intervals to twenty-five so each generation could make the penitential pilgrimage to Rome and benefit from the indulgences received. The Ninety-Five Theses anathemized the efficacy of indulgence. Forgiveness for sins, Luther argued, came through faith alone, and not from any "treasure of merit" possessed by the Roman Church. Making this historical attack on the Church into a jubilee reactivated the cause of a divided Christendom.

1617 had started inauspiciously. On New Year's Day, Pope Paul V prayed for the eradication of heretics, effectively inviting Catholic princes to treat Protestants everywhere as absolute enemies to be attacked and exterminated. The extreme violence of the Thirty Years' War resulted in part from the weaponized theology of the conflict. Beginning in 1618 effectively as a civil war between German polities, it would leave central Europe ruined and decimated. Peace (in the form of confessional settlements) arrived when—so Schmitt argued—the jurists silenced the theologians' claims about just or unjust war, founding the *ius publicum Europaeum*. In 1617, both Lutherans and Catholics celebrated October 31, the former to vilify the papal Antichrist, the latter to repudiate the heretical jubilee.

A broadsheet commemorating the First Luther Jubilee visualizes the 1517 event for Protestant eyes (fig. 22).²⁵¹ As the text explains, the picture portrays a dream Elector Frederick the Wise of Saxony had during the night of October 30, 1517, the eve of the fateful date. The prince appears twice at the far right: asleep in bed and standing in his regalia, with Luther instructing and holy persons showing the way. The dream foresees the Reformer pen the words "On Indulgences" directly on a door, in the same letters as the printed text above. His colossal quill reaches to Rome, piercing the head of a lion labeled "Pope Leo X," and toppling the pope's tiara. A foreground scene recalls an earlier prophesy. Before his execution in 1415, Jan Hus was said to have proclaimed, "You may kill a weak goose [*husa*, "goose" in Czech], but more powerful birds, eagles and falcons, will come after me." Luther took Hus to be a spiritual precursor. He turned the Czech reformer's last words into a prophesy; at Luther's funeral in 1546 Hus's words became, "You may burn a goose, but in a hundred years will come a swan you will not be able to burn." In the print, Hus plucks from a burning goose the quill that will become Luther's pen. Foreseen by an evangelical martyr and dreamt by a sovereign prince, the Reformer's action was divinely inspired. In the sky above the turmoil in Rome, from a Trinity in the clouds, the Holy Spirit descends to illuminate the book that (small in the background) a young, tonsured Luther reads. This is evangelical doctrine at its core. Salvation comes not through merit earned or indulgences received, but through faith alone (*sola fides*), and faith comes alone through scripture, through God's word read or heard (*sola scriptura*). This the image legibly affirms, even for those who cannot read.

For art historians, the shift from celebrating Bosch to celebrating Luther was challenging. With Bosch's art, we wrestled with visual ambiguity and semantic

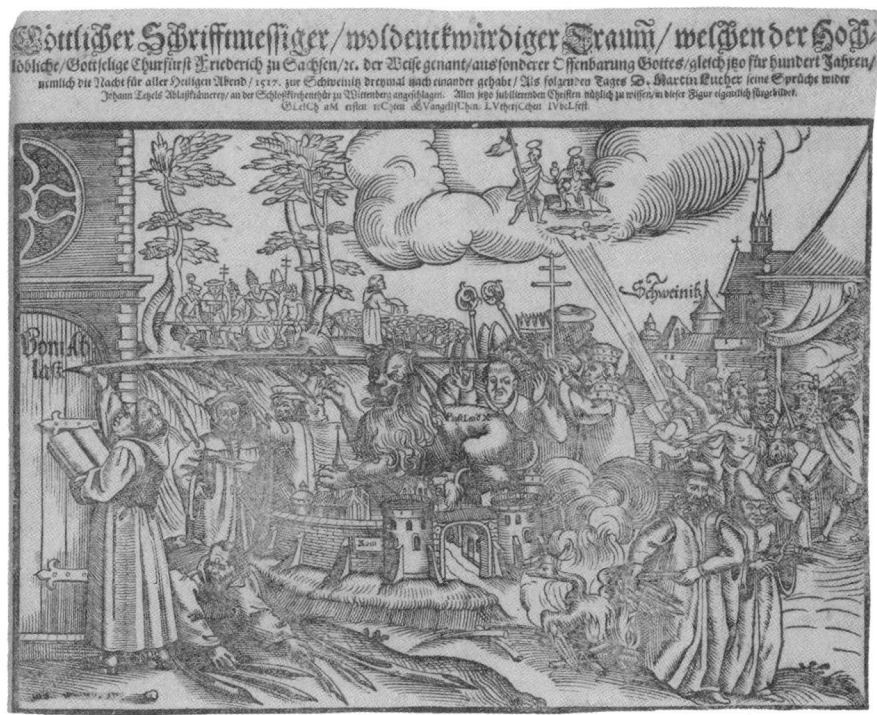

FIG. 22. Unknown artist, *Reformation Centenary Broadsheet*, 1617. Woodcut, 28.4 × 34.7 cm

overload. With Lutheran art, much of it polemical, we made do with pictures engineered for easy reading, or else we grappled with art history's absolute foe, the iconoclasts. The fact that Bosch died one year before 1517 colored perceptions of his art. Dürer lived until 1528, owned works by Luther, personally sympathized with the Reformer, and witnessed his native Nuremberg become Germany's first major Protestant city. Bosch, by contrast, rests sealed within an earlier epoch, hence his characterization as last medieval artist and perfect foil to the Renaissance that begins in the north with Dürer. This is not how Bosch was understood in his own century, as ambitious artists in the worldly city of Antwerp rushed to emulate his innovative manner. Imprecise in his chronology, but four centuries closer to Bosch than are we, Sigüenza portrayed the artist not as backward-looking, but as historically advanced. With the Escorial's collection of Italian masterpieces as his measure, the royal librarian placed Bosch after the Renaissance: "he knew that he had a great talent for painting and that in many subjects he did he had already been overtaken by Albrecht Dürer, Michelangelo, Raphael of Urbino, and others. Thus he embarked upon a new road, one on which he would leave the others behind while he was not behind anyone else and on which he would turn the eyes of all towards himself."[252] Novelty for novelty's sake, ostentatious self-display: these are values historians associate with European Mannerism, an artistic tendency begun around 1520 and still alive in Sigüenza's time. Our knowledge of Bosch's death date backdates him to the Gothic era, or places him in that historical twilight, the "eve" of the Reformation.

"Eve" conjures the darkness preceding day and an anticipated dawn. A creature of the waning Middle Ages, the thinking goes, Bosch could not fully comprehend the vector to which his art belonged. But his art does seem to belong to a future-directed vector, because it anticipates attitudes developed by Protestants. Bosch's scenes of sin, folly, and damnation show monks, priests, and the pope in compromising situations; and in his hands church ceremony takes a sinister or demonic turn (see fig. 20). Bosch introduced these satirical details to poke fun at his patrons, some of whom were erudite clerics able to get the joke. His moralizing struck home to the priestly and the lay order, and entertained them both. But in the wake of the Reformation, Bosch's anti-clericalism came to seem subversive, and it has led modern scholars to cast the artist as a reformer *avant la lettre*.[253]

A deeper premonition of evangelical piety in Bosch's art is his marked focus on the inner self. With few exceptions, this painter portrays not the militant martyrs but the hermit saints—spiritual loners like his name saint, Saint Jerome, or Saint Anthony, who turn inward to imitate Christ. Focused solely on their private devotions or staring calmly out at us from the vortex of their trials, Bosch's kneeling ascetics exemplify what the preachers of the day called "apathy": the elimination of any *pathos* for the world. Most painters inspire veneration for the miracles saints perform and the martyrdoms they suffer. Bosch refuses this activism, but he does make his saints look their viewer directly in the eye, effecting in him or her that inner turn to Christ celebrated as holy apathy. Neither martial nor merciful, his saints are powerless themselves, encouraging pious naysaying to any expectation of release except, in death, by faith in Christ. Christ himself withdraws from view, or is conspicuously obscured, and this too prefigures Luther, who held that Christ is the hidden god, the *deus absconditus* (plates 4 and 14; fig. 39).[254]

Concealment affects everything in Bosch's art, from his iconographic enigmas to his spontaneous and evasive mark-making. Bosch is most himself when he paints illusions. The demons he, "the devil-maker," makes are negative beings, manifestations of evil as the "privation of good."[255] Though they take sensible form, and can torment and tempt, their form is borrowed, privative, and hollow. Effective illusions, they mingle with mundane forms of trickery, such as witchcraft and conjury. Interchangeable with demons, idols are Bosch's other specialty (see fig. 20). To conjure strange gods Bosch paints in a strange way. To portray the idolatrous tomb where Anthony prays he becomes an idol-maker. Similar in morphology and facture to the demons that torment Saint Anthony, these abject artifacts make everything in the painting potentially idolatrous. Pitting this abject imagery against the true icon of Christ on the cross, the painting itself asks the question that will trouble painters mightily on the other side of 1517: Whose side are artists on? God's side, or the side of Satan, that other great illusionist?

But what most places Bosch on the brink of historical change are the emergency states into which he thrusts us. Siege is the occasion, theme, and aesthetic ground of Bosch's art. This gives it a special urgency in dangerous moments. Bosch portrays the human being as a creature pursued by clear and present dangers, rushing blindly towards a future catastrophe. The peddler on the shutters of the *Hay Wain* looks backwards towards thieves and a snarling dog, blind to the crack in the footbridge ahead and to the gallows above (plate 8). And these perils pale by comparison with what awaits him, as the panels swing open, cutting through him, to reveal humanity on the road to hell (plate 9). Bosch puts holy personages in states of siege, as well. Enemies haunt Christ at birth, mob him at death, and insult him during sacrament. The hermit saints pray while besieged outwardly and inwardly by demons. Doomsday takes the form of a siege not withstood. Before 1517, the sense of being under siege, physically or spiritually, made people feel that they lived on the eve of something huge and inevitable: not a new beginning, but the final end. At bottom, the artist's paintings are all Last Judgments. To historians, the siege mentality pervasive on the eve of the Reformation makes it look like 1517 had long been foreseen.

Luther's breakthrough took place while Bosch was alive. By Luther's own account, it occurred around 1515–16, while the Reformer, then a monk of the Augustinian order, was preparing his university lectures on Saint Paul's Letter to the Romans.[256] Luther found himself stalled at one sentence of the text: "For therein is the righteousness of God received from faith, to faith." What bothered him about these words also caused deep anxiety in the culture: God's righteousness as the demand that people obey him or else. In English, "righteousness" still has that sense of wrathful outrage. This understanding terrified because even if one wants to be good, even if one only does good, one cannot wean one's mind from vice. "In your sight," Augustine declared of the all-seeing God, "no man is free from sin, not even a child who has lived only one day on earth."[257] This meant that a full confession could never be made, and yet the Church required a Christian's confession to be complete. To take Communion without confessing everything was deemed a deadly sin. Father confessors went to great lengths to ferret out iniquities in their flock, turning confession and penance into an inquisitorial trial. With something always to hide, people felt perpetually licked by the flames of hell.

Bosch built his *Seven Deadly Sins* to induce such paranoia. Nothing escapes its eye, including our curiosity that, tilting our head, insults the upright righteous God.

Luther recollected the terror he felt as a young novice in the Augustinian monastery in Erfurt, where he glimpsed an effigy of the crucified Christ—such gruesome images surprised Antonio de Beatis when he entered German lands. The sight threw Luther into despair, since how could a wrathful God, brutalized and murdered by humans, ever have mercy on his soul? "I shrunk back and averted my eyes and would have rather glimpsed the devil himself!"[258] Once while saying Mass, he froze when the liturgy called for him to speak directly to God: his sinfulness made him want to run, but his novice master forced him to stay.[259] Such terror sparked Luther's exegetical breakthrough. What Saint Paul termed the "righteousness of God" was not divine juridical wrath, but the righteousness God gives us freely as a gift through Christ. Nothing we can accomplish affects this righteousness. Under the law, we will always be damned. All we can and should do is to hear Christ's promise announced in scripture and accept it inwardly through faith. This tiny, grammatical adjustment to the reading of Romans 1:17 changed everything. It underlay the Ninety-Five Theses, with their attack on indulgences and works-righteousness, and it explains the Church's aggressive response, for if salvation comes through faith alone, then the Church loses its entire economy.

Art had depended on that economy. Most of the surviving works from Bosch's period were originally gifted as pious donations to some church. They tell stories, convey messages, project status, arouse admiration, and give pleasure, but they functioned most basically to help speed to heaven those specified by their donation. With Luther's *sola fides* doctrine, all this was for nothing, or worse: filling the house of God with useless things, art came to be seen as a wasteful extravagance—wealth better distributed to the poor. A broadsheet from around 1524 pits representatives of the many crafts threatened by evangelical preaching against the common folk, with Luther as their advocate (fig. 23). Armed with the Bible and dressed as a doctor of theology, the Reformer refutes the artisan's complaint before God, suggesting that the judgment reached against the painters, sculptors, bellfounders, paternoster-makers, and their like will be dire. Through sly enchantments, art bamboozled people into believing it played a role in salvation. It was more than wasteful, since it concealed the essentials of faith, blocking the way to heaven. It deserved vengeance, and vengeance there was. Consider how one poor farmer explained his conversion in Niklaus Manuel's play *Die Totenfresser* (Eaters of the Dead) from 1523. He had once insulted the pope in public and had been placed under the ban. Fearing for his soul, he stole his wife's egg money, rushed to Bern, and spent everything on an indulgenced print. "I believed I had seen

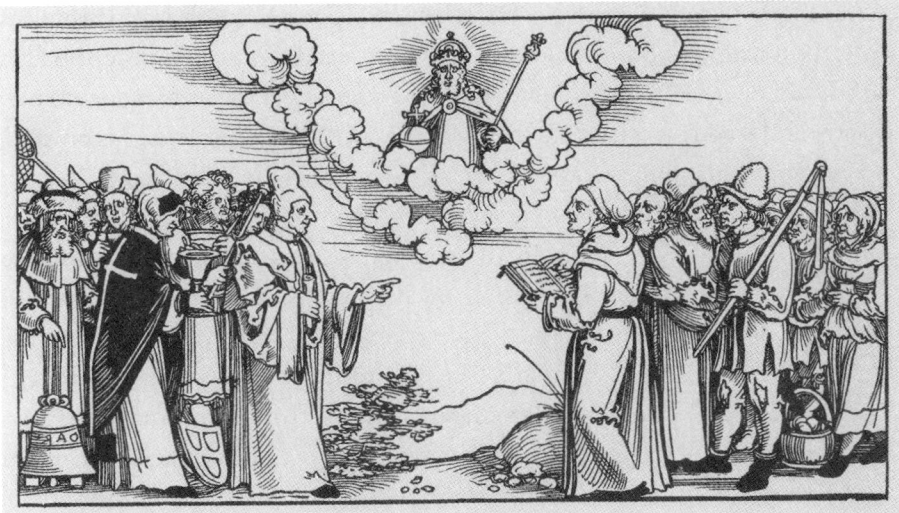

FIG. 23. Hans Sebald Beham (with text by Hans Sachs), *Luther and the Artisans*, c. 1524. Woodcut, 34.9 × 26.1 cm

God himself in it," the farmer recalls, repulsed by his former gullibility, because, "instructed by knowledgeable people to perceive the thing to be worthless," the scales suddenly fell from his eyes and he became enraged at his deception: "so I fetched the thing and wiped my ass on it."[260] Before 1517, art was expert at picturing its audience in a universal state of siege. After 1517, the tables turned and art itself came under attack.[261]

Iconoclasm is a polemic in the root sense of *polemos*, Greek for "war." Not only do iconoclasts break images they deem inimical; they also distinguish as enemies those who use such images. The Old Testament interdict against images transforms a pluriverse of multiple gods into a universe under one God. No longer rivals or subordinates, the other deities become falsehoods, which is to say, idols. Of all the commandments that Moses carried down from Mount Sinai, only the one forbidding image-making would have seemed strange to other cultures of the ancient Middle East. It alone singled out the law of the Israelites from the written or unwritten codes of other nations. What Jan Assmann termed the "Mosaic distinction" defined Israel internally, as well, because the chosen people—the Jews—were habitually straying from that one requirement peculiar to them.[262] The prophets, too, railed against their people's special propensity for worshipping false gods. Israel already strayed during the mere forty days when Moses, their leader, was away receiving the law: the impatient people fashioned the golden calf-shaped statue, worshipped it, and danced around it, "naked unto their shame among their enemies" (Ex. 32:25). Idolatry violated not just any law. It trespassed against monotheism's basic law, its *Grundgesetz*. On seeing the dance, Moses cast down the tablets engraved with *all* ten laws. Moses's next response was political in Schmitt's sense. It cut through all non-political ties. Blood, marriage, and friendship became but trivial associations compared to it. To the sons of Levi, who abandoned their idolatry and stood on the Lord's side, Moses said, "[S]lay every man his brother, and every man his companion, and every man his neighbor" (Ex. 32:27).

Iconoclasm occurs inside the enemy–friend distinction. Internally, the distinction looks to be the extreme one in which a group perceives its own very existence to be threatened by some other group. Such a conflict will therefore be hard to judge by a disinterested third party: for example, by historians observing the long and brutal war over images in Europe five centuries ago. Though quicker to do, the breaking of images is far more impenetrable than the making of images. With the making of images we have, first and foremost, the artifact itself, which bears eloquent witness to its manufacture. In the early sixteenth century, artists gave independent value to the mark itself. Already Bosch made drawings not merely as preparatory tools, but as valued collectables. Love of art had already become an affection for the making of art. This peculiarity caused art to become far and away the most documented of all forms of human fabrication. With the breaking of images, by contrast, we have next to nothing. The object of their wrath destroyed, iconoclasts leave—at most—suggestive gaps, targeted erasures, and conspicuous absences that *perhaps* can be read as evidence of some hostile intention, for destructive hammers are sometimes guided by more than blind fury.[263] People attack something or someone in or through the image. In surviving works bearing scars of an attack, it is sometimes unclear whether the assailants attacked hated figures portrayed by the image (devils, Jews, witches, etc.), whether they attacked the image itself as idol, or whether they attacked both: the enemy *in* the image and the image *as* enemy. On occasion, the alibi for image-breaking was disingenuously neutral: I bumped it, it was old and frail, it broke. But even then, there is an implicit target: the Church for cluttering God's house with junk.

A rich body of written diatribes against images survives. In Wittenberg in the winter of 1521, while Luther was in hiding in the Wartburg, the city's interim preacher, Andreas Bodenstein von Karlstadt, enumerated—first in sermons, then in a pamphlet—the reasons for image-breaking. And because of his arguments, the Wittenberg Council, on January 24, 1521, issued a new Church Ordinance requiring the removal of images from the city's churches—the first such ordinance ever in the Christian West. No figurative artifacts from the period before the Reformation survive inside Wittenberg's City Church, where Luther preached.

The assault on images followed from Luther's breakthrough. The Ninety-Five Theses called for a religion freed from intercessors. Around 1500, sacred effigies were among the most prominent of mediators. Their use and distribution under clerical control, they celebrated the salvific power of saints and ecclesiastics while also reinforcing the divide between the clergy, who could read, and the laity, who generally could not. In Pope Gregory's formulation images served as bibles for the illiterate. Others before Karlstadt had criticized the cult of images as corrupt and deceptive. Erasmus, in the *Praise of Folly* (1509), mocked as "superstition" popular devotion to miracle-working effigies. But it took Karlstadt to turn nuanced critique into iconoclastic fury. In the thunderous voice of an Old Testament prophet, he affirmed that the interdict "Thou shalt make no carved or graven image" belonged to God's first command, that it bound Christians as it had the Israelites, and that putting images on altars turned Christians into idolaters, adulterers, and whores. The Golden Calf linked image worship to carnal lust through the scandalous dance performed around it. Medieval illuminators paired idolatry with Eve and Adam's trespass. Both wove carnal desire together with the sense of sight. Images caused lustful looking as did the forbidden fruit—in Luther's translation, the Tree of Knowledge was *ein lustiger Baum* (Gen. 3:6). "God knows very well how dangerous and harmful images are," warns Karlstadt, "and how we can be violated by them in an instant."[264] The word for "instant" here is that standard German compound: *Augenblick*. Karlstadt separates the word into its two parts: images can violate us—or better, we can grasp them wrongly—in one *augen blick*. Writing when the word's meaning was more literal (*Augenblick* as "look of the eye") than figurative (*Augenblick* as "moment" or "instant"), Karlstadt proposes the image as a dangerous moment when seeing leads us fatally astray. The idea is familiar from the art of Bosch, but in Wittenberg after 1517 it had quite different results.

Whether church cleansing followed passionately from Karlstadt's arguments or obeyed dutifully the Council's decree, and when exactly the cleansing occurred and how long it took to complete, the records do not say, nor do we know what became of the debris. In the city of Bern, where iconoclasts rioted in 1528, fragments of ruined statuary have survived because the image-breakers buried the debris in a ditch beside the church. In Zwickau, the old images were removed from the church but preserved as objects of derision and—later—as historical curiosities. Kept in a room called the *Götzenkammer* (idol chamber), they survived to become, in 1857, the core of a newly created Museum of Church Antiquities.[265] But in Luther's preaching church in Wittenberg, the history of earlier art was eradicated and rewritten through new artifacts posing as apostolic. By the time of Luther's death in 1546, Wittenberg's City Church—like many medieval churches repurposed for Protestantism's preaching-based service—resembled a vast auditorium decorated with portraits of the congregation and its ministers.[266]

It is easy to understand how a person's devotion to sacred images could be converted into anger at having been deceived. Harder to imagine is the step to physically breaking church pictures, since so much beside their putative holiness would render violence against them taboo. Not just their beauty, antiquity, and cost, but their belonging to a familiar lifeworld would stay their destruction. A *Mass of Saint Gregory* painted in 1497 and signed by a certain Seewald testifies to this hesitancy (fig. 24). Probably in the early 1530s, someone attacked the panel, targeting the eyes of nearly all the represented persons save one. When it came to defacing Christ, the image-breaker faltered. Karlstadt confessed to the fear felt by a would-be iconoclast, how the hand refrains from breaking what the mind knows to be stock and stone: "Fear holds me and makes me in awe of the image of a devil, a shadow, the notice of a small falling leaf."[267] Karlstadt gets inside the mind of the spooked church-cleanser in order to comfort and encourage him. But the passage exposed Karlstadt to mockery. Luther returned from the Wartburg in March 1522 in order to halt iconoclasm in Wittenberg. He judged that image-breaking would jeopardize the civic order, alienate the common folk, and anger his princely protectors. Among his arguments against "fanatics" (*Schwärmer*) like Karlstadt was the claim, sarcastic but effective, that they so believed in the power of images that they had to smash them to break their spell. The image-breakers were secretly idolaters. Even before the Roman Church could formulate a response to this, the first outbreak of iconoclasm in the West, Protestants stood divided among themselves over image-breaking, with each side claiming the other to be its mortal foe.

Idolatry is an accusation, not a description. No one believes in the way the iconoclasts say the idolater does. Defenders of traditional religion responded to Karlstadt that his portrayal of images and their use was a caricature. Even simple folk distinguish the effigy from the saint it represents; they treat it as a mediator, and that separates them from that old foil, the idolatrous pagan. The iconoclast's concept of naïve belief is polemical. But iconoclasm suffers from polemical descriptions, too. A contemporary woodcut allows the images to have their say (fig. 25). While the iconoclasts break and burn them the "poor persecuted idols" do not quite deny their culpability:

> People flocked to us in great reverence
> From afar over land and over sea, at great expense,
> Made sacrifice, as if we were a god,
> To the real mockery of the True Lord.

TOP: FIG. 24. Master Seewald, *Mass of Saint Gregory*, 1497. Oil on pine, 101 × 76 cm. Stadtmuseum Münster

RIGHT: FIG. 25. Erhard Schön, *Complaint of the Poor Persecuted Idols and Temple Images*, c. 1530. Woodcut, 44.2 × 37.7 cm

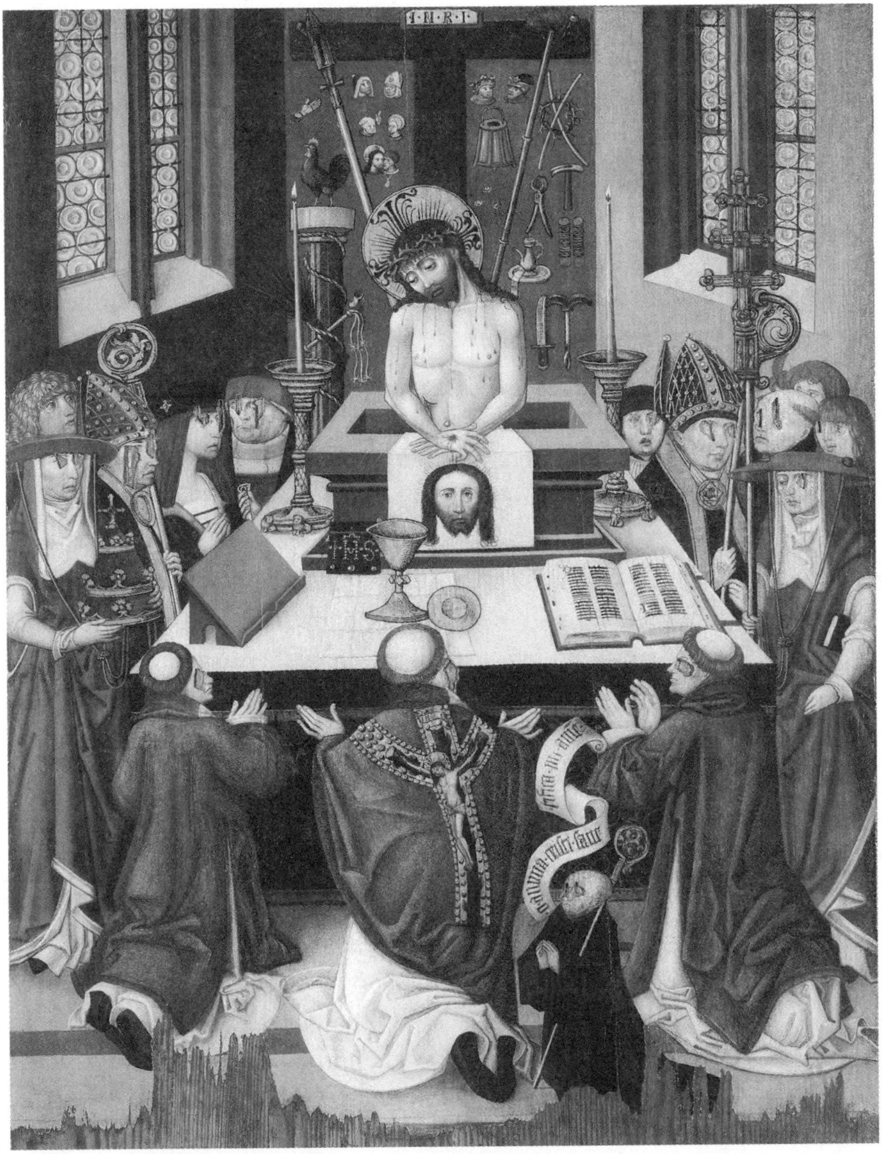

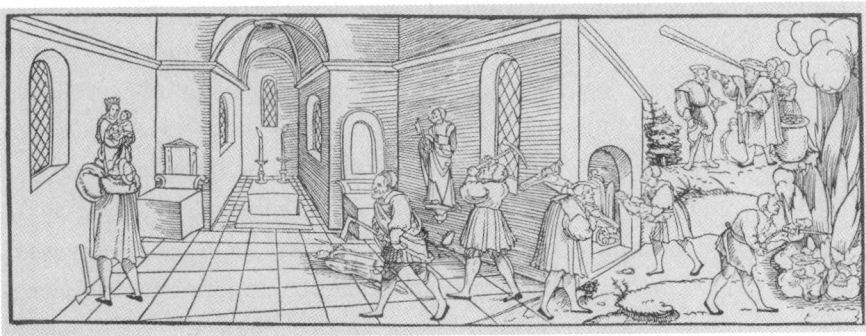

The images complain that they receive unequal justice, because they passively stood there, while their attackers did far worse, disturbing the peace, living in sin, and turning the church service into carnival. And those who break images were the very ones who had worshipped them. At the upper right, flanked by wine, women, and money, an iconoclast looks at the proceedings with a strange beam in his eye (an allusion to Matthew 7:3): "And why worry about a speck in your brother's eye when you have a log in your own."

Like Luther's diatribe against Karlstadt, the woodcut's argument against image-breaking is not an argument *for* images. If not directly under attack, art remained in a state of siege that lasted more than hundred years. So how did artists endure? Some increased their production of secular images, such as portraits, landscapes, and coats-of-arms, or they created exquisite objects for a small consumer base of art collectors. Others took to painting and carving words, like the elaborate text altarpieces created in Germany and Scandinavia. A few artists joined in the rites of destruction. Karel van Mander reports a painter covering with black paint a masterpiece by Hugo van der Goes.[268] In iconophobic territories where Catholics regained control, artists could engage in the task of restoration. Around 1600, the ruined remains of an *Adoration of the Magi* triptych painted in 1520 was remade into a single-panel monument to its own survival. In confessionally divided Augsburg, Christoph Amberger painted for the stripped high altar of the cathedral a new triptych after project drawings (by Hans Holbein the Elder) for the destroyed retable.[269] Meanwhile, artists on both sides of the religious wars reached back into their old repertoire of enemies and created images of a new foe: the *other* confession.

Before 1517 artists conjured monstrosities as signs of a world at the brink of the apocalypse. Now this imaginative expertise served polemical ends. The woodcuts of the *Papal Ass* and *Monk's Calf* show abnormal births (fig. 26). Portrayed with seeming verisimilitude by Lucas Cranach, these monsters were used by Luther and Philipp Melanchthon to evidence papal corruption. Pictured, explained, and printed, omens of cosmic catastrophe became weapons in a public battle over which religion is the true one. To deepen the rancor of their imagery, artists reached back to Bosch. Matthias Gerung's woodcut monstrosity slanders visually what Luther verbally criticized (fig. 27). A colossal demon rests its scaly ass on a papal letter of indulgence, identified as such by the seals attached to it. Its crutch, collection box, and cowl associate the monster with a mendicant monk, that hated agent of papal greed and corruption. The Ninety-Five Theses targeted especially the Dominican friar Johann Tetzel, who sold indulgences with the jingle, "As soon as the coin in the coffer rings, the soul from purgatory springs." Instead of releasing sinners from punishment, Gerung's monster draws them into

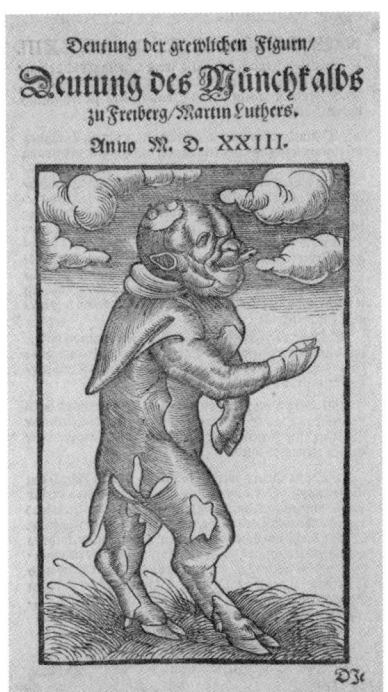

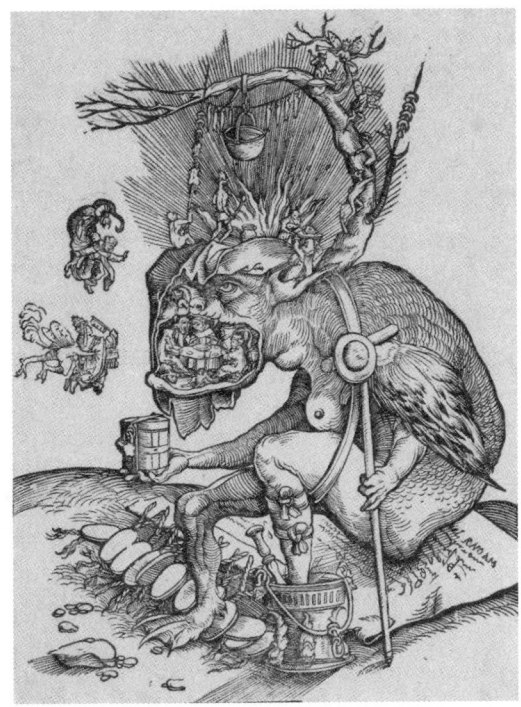

FIG. 26. Lucas Cranach the Elder, *Monk's Calf*, 1523. Woodcut, 25.6 × 14 cm (sheet)

FIG. 27. Matthias Gerung, *Satire of Indulgences*, c. 1530. Woodcut, 30.7 × 22.5 cm

a culinary inferno. The impish cooks and musicians are distinctly Boschian, as is the leafless tree that frames their activities. Indeed, Gerung's entire invention recalls Bosch's famous arboreal hybrid: the Tree-Man from the hell scene of the so-called *Garden of Delights* and the related drawing (plate 2; fig. 28). Both monsters suffer a wounded leg and contain in their orifices an abject scene of feasting. Both sport ungainly shoes: unsteady boats in Bosch; in Gerung a bucket for holy water. Bosch's "disparities" invited such variations of their parts. The Tree-Man would have come to Germany through copies, imitations, and reworkings, such as the pen-and-ink one Bosch himself made on a sheet preserved in the Albertina.

Gerung's remix unleashes on a specific enemy the diffuse animosities mobilized by Bosch. Some decades later, when Sigüenza defended Bosch from charges of heresy, a Protestant in flight from the Spanish-occupied Netherlands took the artist to be a prophet of the Reformation and applied his imagery to Europe's dire situation.[270] Paulus de Kempenaer was a polymath emblematist, heraldry designer, and writing master strongly committed to the Protestant cause. A supporter of William the Silent, briefly secretary to the Council of Brabant, and a close confident of the executed Count of Egmont's daughter Sabina, De Kempenaer fled from

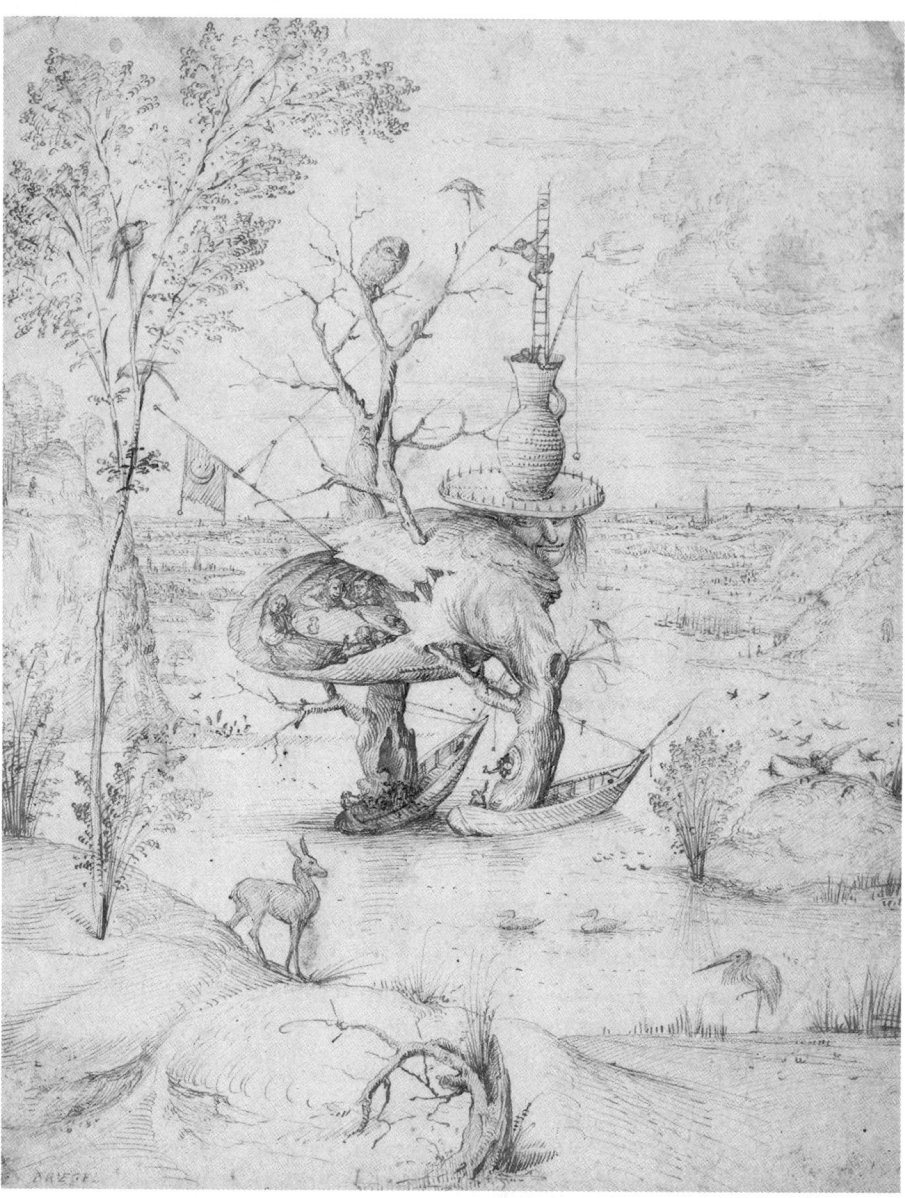

FIG. 28. Hieronymus Bosch, *The Tree-Man*, c. 1505. Pen and brown ink on paper, 27.7 × 21.1 cm. Albertina, Vienna

Antwerp to Leiden and Gothenburg before settling in 1593 in the Hague. There evidence of his activities becomes sparse, save for seven notebooks by his hand. Compiled from 1597 to 1618, these manuscripts crowded together adages, poems, calligraphy, Bible prophesies, biographical rambling, and allegorical drawings, much of this expressing the author's conviction that, thanks to the papal church and Habsburg Spain, world history was coming to a catastrophic end.

To visualize these dire times De Kempenaer turned to Bosch, about whom the diarist was astonishingly well informed. Four centuries before Steppe and Gombrich, he reported a "delightful large panel with wings" owned by William the Silent that had been seized by Alba and carried off to Spain for Philip II's enjoyment. De Kempenaer also reflected on the strangeness of this vicissitude. Catholic authorities recognized that the artist's pictures "uncovered the rogueries and the wickedness of the papists and the monks more than [did] ten Reformed preachers."[271] Collectors of Bosch had therefore to hide their possessions lest these be confiscated by the inquisitors and publicly burned as heretical and Lutheran. And yet Philip eagerly sought such pictures, De Kempenaer reports, acquiring at least six of the best for seventy thousand ducats. The "otherwise most Catholic King of Spain" treasured the "obscure, obscene, filthy, phantasmal, funny or disdainful spooks or drolleries," either ignoring or misunderstanding their message. As Sigüenza testified, people in Spain did fret about the paintings Philip hung in his palace at El Escorial. In De Kempenaer's eyes, Bosch vilified "the horrible idolatry," "ox-beliefs," and "childish and Apis-like vanities" of the papists—the reference here is to the bull-worship that provoked Moses's image-breaking fury.[272] Thus Bosch's images were iconoclastic to their core. The Catholics would have broken them were it not for Philip's aesthetic tastes.

Of the several small drawings De Kempenaer made in imitation of Bosch, one stands out as especially cunning (fig. 29). Executed in pen and brown ink, with pale brown and blue washes, the sketch conjures the famous Tree-Man—not the painted one in the *Garden of Delights*, but some variant that transplanted the Tree-Man from hell to an expansive harbor scene. The autograph sheet in the Albertina does this, and De Kempenaer follows its pattern in most details, including the crescent moon flag, emblem of lunacy and Islam. The circular format recalls an etching dating to around 1600 based on Bosch's design, though De Kempenaer follows the Albertina drawing's orientation and includes details present there and not in the print (fig. 30). Daan van Heesch proposed the existence of a lost version of the Tree-Man somewhere between the Albertina sheet and the etched roundel.[273] The etching's maker, probably an artist in the circle of David Vinckboons, with whom De Kempenaer collaborated, introduced two motifs. At the right, a crowd gawks at the monster as if it were natural curiosity, and at the base, three experts—a painter with his palette and brushes, a fabulist (perhaps) with an Aesopian fox, and an astronomer with a sextant—professionally portray, narrate, and interpret the bizarre arrival. The word "monster" comes from Latin *monstrare* (to show) and *monere* (to warn). By 1600, Bosch's monstrosity had become delightful to common folk and interesting to specialists.

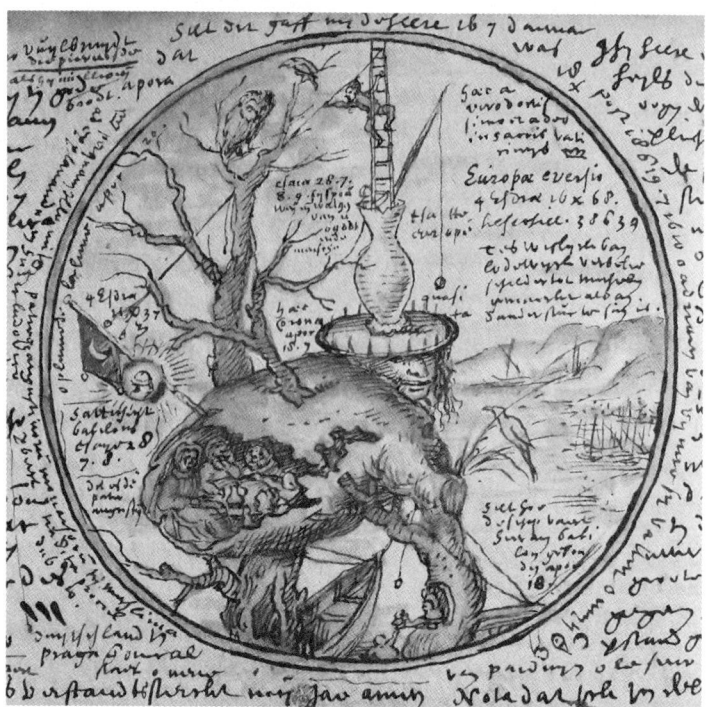

LEFT: FIG. 29.
Paulus de Kempen-
aer, *Tree-Man*, 1610
(*Perfer et obdura*,
p. 321). Manuscript,
19 × 25 cm. Private
Collection (Stichting
de Kempenaer)

BELOW: FIG. 30.
Anonymous Flemish
(circle of David
Vinckboons?) after
Hieronymus Bosch,
The Tree-Man, c. 1600.
Etching, 21 cm
(diameter)

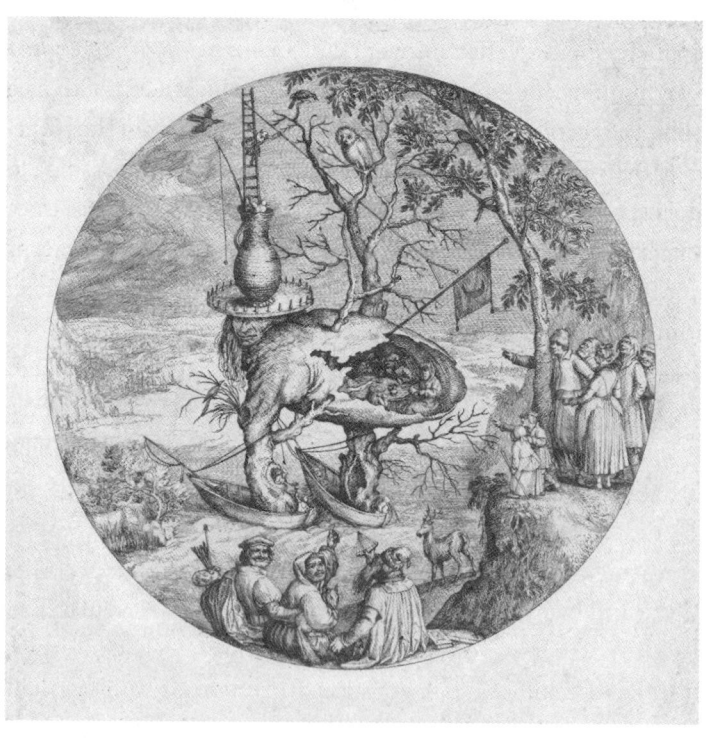

De Kempenaer was those three experts wrapped into one. An artist, calligrapher, and emblem-maker, he captured the Tree-Man capably, his pen able to follow the errant path of trunks and branches. A fabulist, he moralized the monster verbally, in texts squeezed into the drawing's blanks. Well versed in astral lore—he drew astronomers at least twice in his notebooks and obsessed about heavenly omens—he interpreted the Tree-Man astrologically, adding to Bosch's design one potent sign: below the crescent moon of Islam he sketched a solar eclipse in the form of a penis-capped man. At least thirty such phallic creatures appear in De Kempenaer's notebooks as emblems of clerical carnality. The texts added to the drawing explain this lewd addition. Bosch's Tree-Man stands for the Whore of Babylon, whom both the Catholic church and the Turkish foe idolatrously adore. The end of the world draws near. Gog and Magog, "Antichrists, namely the pope and the Turk," each with their ominous flags, have arrived to "overthrow Christendom." The revelers in the Tree-Man's anal cavity stand for "drunken Europe," divided internally by religious conflict and threatened at its borders by Islam.[274]

In the Escorial, Philip II saw the same depictions and interpreted them, similarly, as signs of Europe in siege. The Protestant emblematist and the Catholic monarch alike felt assaulted by an enemy "other" that Bosch, from the other side of a great historical divide, had prophetically portrayed. A dangerous *Augenblick* for dangerous times, Bosch's art gave form to every viewer's imagined enemy in every here and now. At once idolatrous and iconoclastic, his imagery spoke eloquently to both sides of the image wars, but in a language understood only by the combatants. Such imagery (writes Schmitt) "can neither be decided by a previously determined general norm nor by the judgement of a disinterested and therefore neutral third party."[275] Will this always be the case?

Madrid, 2023

Five centuries on and the naked revelers still pursue their pleasures on the grassy plane (plate 2). Hectic at the edges, their activities ring the center, as if what drives them binds them together by gravitational force. A perfect circle on green around a circular swimming pool painted a shadowy blue, the mounted parade resembles one feature of a painting today displayed nearby: the seven deadly sins in Bosch's panel of that title, with the sins paraded around the bluish center of God's all-seeing eye (plate 3). In the triptych, the circle lies flat on the earth, becoming oval in perspective. Time, and the garden's goings-on, seem to bend until, captured by the circle, they remain trapped in its rotation. From this eternal here and now—

in a painter's workshop in 's-Hertogenbosch, in a Brussels pleasure palace, near Philip II's place of prayer, in the Villanueva Building of the Prado, Room 56a—a host of tiny eyes look out at whoever stands before them. At the left, while Adam stares mesmerized at Eve, God sees me from the beginning, and in the middle and from out of hell a constellation of glances keeps the focus always on me. And me alone, because, especially with the central panel, it is so hard to say to you, who might stand beside me, where our eyes have wandered, mine pursuing monkeys in the shadow of a pierced spheric ruin, yours elsewhere, but each of us presently watched and watching.

There is another thing that keeps these revels contemporary. Nothing in this garden, neither the tents nor the towers nor the playthings, bears any trace of human manufacture. Whatever looks to be a tool, dwelling, or garment, everything that could count as culture, turns out to be a natural formation. Even the edibles are raw, not cooked: fruits, berries, and saps. This confounds historians. Bosch gives us nothing to date. He seems to have recognized that one bit of sewn apparel, a single artifact (some equipment, say, like the clubs Lucas Cranach gives his fauns and wild men, with one end sawed nearly off), would have looked to have been made in a period style that, imagined circa 1500, would therefore look of the artist's own period, and not our own. Bosch causes us to dig about like an archaeologist in empty sand, unable to fix the painting, the code, and the world these represent, in some context or history. Granted, deep time is present at the edges. The triptych's outer shutters portray the world in Day Three of its creation, when God separated land and sea and made self-seeding plants, living organisms that grow, reproduce, and adapt on their own, without divine intervention (plate 1). And these outer panels swing open to a beginning now occurring on a terrestrial paradise called Eden, and to a terrible end.

The Eden panel shows an event never before imagined by a work of art (plate 16). Not yet the marriage of Adam and Eve, when God joins the couple, Adam's hand with Eve's in mutual covenant; not yet even their meeting, when each rushes towards the other in reciprocated longing: this is the fleeting moment after Eve's creation from Adam's rib, when Adam opens his eyes from sleep and first beholds his mate. A nanosecond, this *Augenblick* is momentous, nonetheless. Divine creation now stands complete and natural procreation takes over everything: the seeding plants first, then the animals, and now the first humans, man and woman, must seed themselves "according to their kind" (Gen. 1:11). Now begins the course of a world left to its own devices, which the Bible tells as a story of interdict, trespass, and expulsion, then afterwards, of human history, Adam, Eve, and their offspring as they live, labor, and die from their catastrophic beginning to an end yet to come. Bosch urges us to think this way, to read the folding ensemble as a story unfolding step by step in time. Assuming that his triptych will, at the beginning of the tale it tells, be closed, he casts its outer panels as Act I: a cosmic prelude to Acts II–IV that follow when the shutters, still gloomy gray but already pregnant with water, earth, breathable atmosphere, and life, open to a blast of color. And in the right panel of that open state, in a different gloom than the grisaille one on the shutters, he displays the story's grim conclusion. The scenes taking place in hell make it hard not to read the triptych as showing, in reading direction left to right, a beginning, a middle, and an end. Of all the counts against Fraenger this was the most serious. A brilliant writer on art who, first among Bosch scholars, articulated the central panel's dangerous insinuation that the pleasures displayed are innocent ones, he must have sometimes wondered, while Allied bombs rained down on him, if the right wing panel did not prove him wrong. That hell must conclude the story compelled him to argue awkwardly that its punishment was for those who resisted the triptych's call for sexual freedom — and for Fraenger's scholarly foes.

Whatsoever they might represent, though, the "delights" result from Eden, and they result in hell. With terrestrial paradise to the left and an inferno to the right, the triptych resembles one of Bosch's Last Judgment triptychs. Half a century after its confiscation by the duke of Alba, Paulus de Kempenaer assumed the seized ensemble had Judgment at its center. Perhaps he heard a flawed description of the painting or mixed it up with a Boschian *Last Judgment* published by Hieronymus Cock.[276] The clever emblematist was thus spared art history's most intractable anomaly: Bosch's spectacle of pleasure unmitigated and unjudged between paradise and hell. As if in some cosmic suspension of the law, God does not sit in judgment even in Eden, because Adam and Eve's trespass has not yet occurred. What happens, then, in this beginning? Adam looks fixedly at Eve, who looks downward modestly, but shamelessly, as well she should. For as the Bible says, before the Fall they were both "naked, and they felt no shame" (Gen. 2:25). Mesmerized looking is the only human action in Bosch's scene, save perhaps for the blood involuntarily flushing Adam's cheeks. Up close that vermillion blush yields stereoscopic pleasures, not just of Adam's features rendered in the round. Closer still, microphotography reveals a craquelure of oil glazes — vermillion delicately brushed on lead white flesh — and leaner emulsions deeper down, and below those, visible even to the naked eye, underdrawings brushed in gray on a white chalk ground, all atop a panel made of Baltic oak — Bosch's preferred support. That is what close looking does for me. But what does it accomplish for Adam?

Bosch digs back to a beginning before the Fall, to an instant—unspoken in the Bible—after Adam wakes and before he exclaims, "This is now bone of my bones, and flesh of my flesh." And unlike in Bosch's other Edens, which include the remote backstory of Satan's fall, this backstory is immediately Adam's, occurring in the silent moment of his look. Bosch finds this story between the Bible story's compacted lines, and not surprisingly. Throughout history, humans have expressed their deepest ethical ideas through stories, and of all these the tale of Adam and Eve has endured the longest and impacted the most. For about three millennia Jews, Christians, and Muslims—peoples of the world's triad of monotheistic religions, all claiming descent from the Judaism of the ancient Israelites and worshipping Abraham's God—have reasoned ethically through the seedpod of this, even to its earliest audiences, unreasonable story, with its talking snake, magic trees, naked couple, and cruel conclusion.

Even the modern master of ethical reasoning granted this fable some rationality. Immanuel Kant professed to loathe the story, which he understood in its traditional Christian interpretation. This held that Adam and Eve passed their sin to the entire human species as an inborn defect. By this account, no one is ever innocent, not even at birth. Newly born infants are already sinful and—if they happen to die before being baptized—they go straight to hell. What had been voluntary and unnatural in Adam (created in God's image) became involuntary and natural ever after in the human species. Not only are our intentions and actions vicious; even our reasoning about how to act will have been corrupted by Eve and Adam's original sin. Concerning this doctrine, Kant wrote in 1793, "Of all the ways of representing evil in the human being, the most inappropriate is surely to imagine it as having come to us by way of our inheritance from our first parents."[277] This is because, from the point of view of reason, rather than faith or superstition, each evil action has to be considered "as if the human being had fallen into it directly from the state of innocence."[278] As if fallen directly from the state of innocence because, for Kant, every sin has to be understood as an original one: not an inheritance of the human animal but a fall enacted newly and freely in each individual. We are all Adams and Eves, each under the moral duty to obey the law, each capable of reasoning, and each free to choose whether or not to obey.

It was of paramount importance to Kant that moral behavior should not derive from fear of punishment. The natural world could be understood consequentially. Kant's *Critique of Pure Reason* demonstrates how human reasoning in terms of cause and effect accords with the laws of nature as described by Newton's physics. But the moral law was different, because it was built on human freedom, which was unconstrained and absolute. "Two things fill the mind with ever new and increasing admiration and awe," concludes Kant, "the starry heavens above and the moral law within."[279] And of the two mysteries, the latter—the moral law within—was the more intractable. Kant granted that the idea of a pure innocence from which we freshly fall is elusive. Reason can shift the blame for the most heinous crime to causes prior to the criminal act, such as coercion, passion, insanity, trauma, intellectual disability, and addiction. Evolutionary scientists have proposed that *Homo sapiens sapiens* has its closest living relatives in socially violent primates; genetically we are a murderous lot. To black box mitigating circumstances and imagine every moral action as a clean beginning, to glimpse behind every misdeed a root in evil of a radical kind: this remained inexplicable, even for Kant: "there is no conceivable ground for us, therefore, from which moral evil could first have come in us. — Scriptures express *this incomprehensibility* in a historical narrative."[280]

On the one hand, there is the patent incomprehensibility of evil. As Søren Kierkegaard put it in his sustained reflections on the biblical account, "no explanation that explains Adam but not hereditary sin, or explains hereditary sin but not Adam, is of any help."[281] On the other hand, there is scripture's *representation* of that incomprehensibility in story form. According to that story, radical evil arises at a moment in time, in the originating action of Eve and Adam's eating the forbidden fruit. As narration, scripture's representation itself happens in time: in words ordered into sentences that create a plot with a beginning, middle, and end. Kant will insist on representing the origin of evil not according to time, but according to reason.[282] Morality derives from certain maxims that humans freely make and follow somehow outside the temporal dimension of choice. Compacted like an algorithm, they seem to operate instantaneously, uncoupled from the time it takes to decide—or to read: "Act in accordance with the maxims of a member legislating universal laws for a merely possible kingdom of ends," goes one tricky formulation of Kant's supreme maxim.[283] Even for reason's great champion, people therefore need stories—Kierkegaard calls them "myths"—to reason ethically.

But what about images? Do they meet the ethical challenge of Adam and Eve? On the walls of several of the Christian catacombs in Rome, in a house church at Dura Europos, and in several late antique sarcophagus reliefs, there they already stand, a naked man, a naked woman, and between them a tree—enough to conjure the biblical episode (fig. 31). Artists mostly stuck to the facts. This made them "literalists" whether or not they had read Augustine's verdict: you have to accept on faith that the event really truly happened and leave its enigmas to God. "Hereditary sin is so deep and horrible a corruption of nature," states Luther in the *Smalcald Articles* (1537), "that no reason can understand it, but it must be learned and believed from revelation of Scriptures."[284] Yet in each of countless cases over

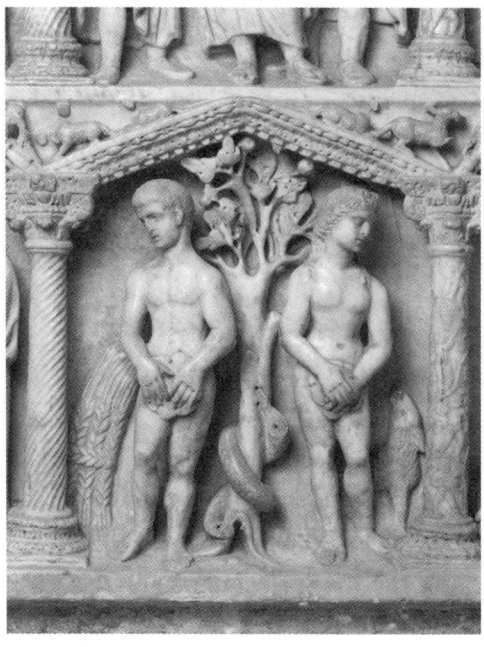

FIG. 31. Adam and Eve, Detail from the *Sarcophagus of Junius Bassus*, 359 CE. Marble, 122 × 245 × 122 cm (base). Museo del tesoro di San Pietro, St. Peter's Basilica, Vatican City

the centuries, image-makers had to make certain practical decisions, each of which involved some reasoning about the unreasonable.

One crucial and immediate choice concerned how to display Adam and Eve's nudity now, in the aftermath of humanity's fall from innocence. The Bible story has—built into it—a history and an ethics of vision. Again, at creation "they both were naked, the man and woman, and were not ashamed" (Gen. 2:25). Adam and Eve walked around the Garden nude, but they did not *see* their nudity in the way we inescapably do now. Then came the trespass. And that trespass—importantly and dramatically—was itself precipitated at least in part by something unruly about the sense of sight. The serpent promised that eating from the tree, the woman's eyes would "be opened," and the woman "saw that the tree was good for eating and that it was lust to the eye and the tree was lovely to look at"—*ein lustiger Baum* in Luther's German Bible (Gen. 3:5–6).[285] Some medieval commentators held that ocular desire triggered the Fall and the carnal desire that followed. Artists could thus link Adam and Eve's trespass to concupiscence and idolatry. Idols elicit sinful worship through their ocular appeal. An illumination from a so-called "moralizing bible" positions the Fall above an idolator and a fornicating couple—the lustful pair sport the same headband as the serpent in Eden (plate 17).[286]

The painted eyes form directional vectors. The frozen stares of Adam and the serpent at Eve, of Eve at the apple, of the idolator at his idol, of the lover at his love, and of that love back at him, or past him to the golden idol of remunerated sex: these gazes doom the actors in the present, giving the nudes no time to hide in shame. The French illuminator solves the problem of our lasciviousness by hiding his naked figure's genitals with a forward-striding leg. A seeming accident of their stance and our viewpoint, this arrangement moves the story itself a step forward. Eve sees the tree, feels lust in her eyes, and therefore eats, and Adam—suddenly, with no explanation—eats, too; and then what happens? "The eyes of them both were opened and they knew that they were naked, and they sewed fig leaves together and made themselves aprons" (Gen. 3:7). Portraying the symptomatic aftermath of transgression relieved most artists of the more difficult challenge of showing the moment, literally the *Augenblick*, of the Fall itself, when Eve and Adam were naked but not yet ashamed, while we ineluctably behold this innocent nakedness shamefully, with open, knowing, postlapsarian eyes. In the first of the Bible's two accounts of their creation, God "created the human in his image, in the image of God He created him" (Gen. 1:27). In the second account, Adam's formation becomes yet more artisanal: God "formed the man from the dust [or mud] of the ground" (Gen. 2:7). Image-makers themselves, artists could and sometimes did claim this special link to God. No wonder they were especially self-reflective about their agency when making likenesses of Adam and Eve.

A twelfth-century sculptural relief illustrates the depths of reasoning that medieval artists applied to their task (fig. 32). Discovered by chance in 1856 in the masonry of a demolished building, this object originally formed part of the upper support, or lintel, of the north portal of the cathedral at Autun, in eastern

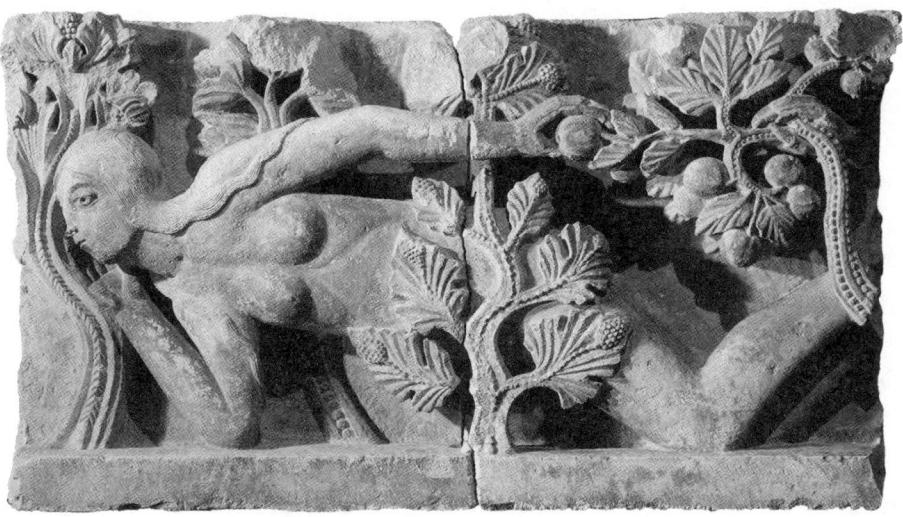

FIG. 32. Gislebertus, *Eve*, from the cathedral of St-Lazare in Autun, ca. 1130. Stone lintel relief, 72.4 × 129.5 cm. Musée Rolin, Autun

France. Most probably it was the creation of a sculptor who carved that cathedral's extant Last Judgment portal and signed it: "Gislebertus made this." The lintel fragment captures the moment of Eve's Fall. Left-handedly she plucks the forbidden fruit from a bough held by a clawed demon—the serpent in the role of the devil or Satan. Eve appears to recline or to creep on the ground. This posture would have been encouraged by the limitations of the sculptor's medium. Gislebertus's "given" was a narrow horizontal block of limestone intended to span a wide doorway—the fragment is 1.3 meters and the lintel spanned about five meters.[287] Carving Adam and Eve in upright positions in a block of this size and shape would have required them to stand no taller than the block's narrow height. The sculptor could have carved other scenes to fill the length of the lintel, or let Eden's vegetation flourish at the sides, but for practical, aesthetic, and narrative reasons, he lit upon the brilliant idea of carving Eve horizontally across the stubborn block and making her fallen, entangled in vegetation, and serpentine.

Gislebertus packed a lot into that posture. Eve leans her head towards her right hand, as if to support it as she reclines, which conjures the condition of sleep or dreaming. Natural to her reclining state, such a pose resonates with other moments in the story. In earlier manuscript painting, portrayals of Adam asleep during Eve's formation show him resting his head against his hand. In the relief, Eve's eyes, carved into the limestone (and originally filled in with shiny colored paste), are indisputably open. While connoting sleep or dreams, her gesture denotes sorrow, melancholy, and regret. Her entire posture also draws on images of the repentant Eve, who creeps for cover out of shame and to avoid God's notice. Gislebertus extends his carving's narrative reach. In Eve's elongated form, he makes the lintel she decorates span a story from her creation from Adam, through her temptation, Fall, shame, sorrow, and penance, and into the future. The fruit-bearing plant that covers her sex projects the story into the present day, since according to Christian doctrine, we who have all sprung from Eve's womb will be infected by her sin. Through a bit of pictorial irony, the sculptor causes us, Eve's offspring, to re-enact our connection to disastrous past. Eve's upper body manifests what, for the period, must have been a remarkably frank display of frontal nudity, particularly for an image above a cathedral door. To carve this female nude, the sculptor may have looked at antique survivals, which abounded in this formerly Roman part of Europe. By contrast to these, Eve twists awkwardly at the waist, her body's cylinder rotating ninety degrees, shifting the frontal view of her upper body to a profile view of her buttocks and legs.[288] Again, the thinking is that Eve becomes ashamed of her nether regions after the Fall. But built into this carving is an expectation of how it will be experienced, corporeally, by viewers here and now.

As for so many images of Adam and Eve, the "implied viewer" of this work is heterosexual and male. With this audience chiefly in mind, Gislebertus engineers Eve's body so that, through the erotic display of her breasts, she will cause in the beholder the very thing that, according to the Christian doctrine of Original Sin, was caused by the Fall: namely, carnal lust. The ethical salience of lust consisted in the fact that it is felt to arise involuntarily, literally as a movement of the body, indeed a body part, quite independently of a mind that might try to say "No!" Although death was the more terrifying punishment for the Fall, lust was experienced within life as a similar, spectacular rebellion of the flesh: flesh so alive that it becomes uncontrollably other. Experiencing this otherness as they gazed upon Eve's form, churchgoers would be encouraged to take the lead from Eve's lower form and turn away, from her and from the carnal world, in penance. Like his Last Judgment nearby, Gislebertus's carved lintel would have preached repentance before the house of God. Lust will remain, but reflective, guilty, and groveling. It is this perpetual circle of sin, shame, penance, and sin again that Eve's carved body mimes and aspires to effect.

While its ethics may be foreign to many of us today, the fragment constitutes a powerful instance of ethical reasoning, nonetheless. It gives a special place to unreason, showing the human being split between action and intent, instinct and knowledge, and compulsion and freedom. Whether or not such ethical reasoning engaged the image's audience, it had to engage its maker who, reasoning practically about the artisanal challenge at hand, had to reach decisions not only about materials, format, processes, and functions but also about the moment depicted. Image-makers may have been restricted (as Lessing would put it) to "forms and colors in space," but the act of making occurred as thoughts, actions, and choices unfolding in time.[289] The combined ethical and aesthetic challenge of Adam and Eve was met most enthusiastically by artists of the Renaissance. From Andrea Pisano, Jan van Eyck, and Masaccio through Dürer, Michelangelo, Raphael, and Titian to Rubens and Rembrandt, the most ambitious makers of the period proved their mettle by attempting to realize the unfallen beauty of the nude human body. This was one of the key challenges that brought artists to study and resuscitate the achievements of the classical past. For in ancient Greece and Rome—these artists knew—idealized nudes abounded, and human corporeality itself was both an aesthetic and an ethical ideal.

Ever since the itinerant artist Jacopo de' Barbari, visiting Germany, showed him "a man and woman that he made by measurements," Dürer became consumed by the desire to make nude human figures of perfect proportions.[290] The Nuremberg master had seen countless nudes of northern European manufacture,

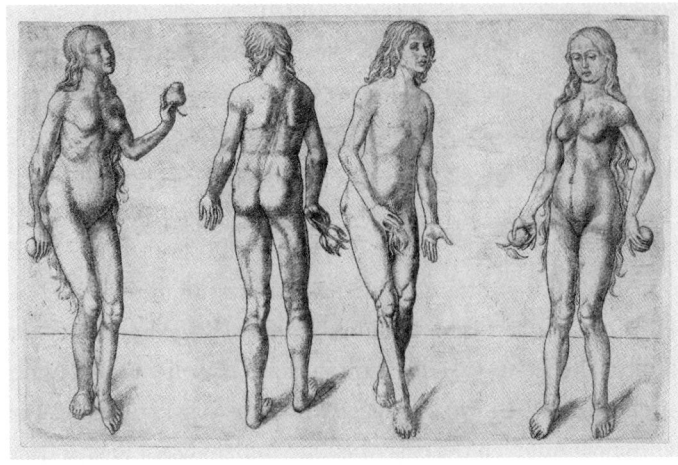

FIG. 33. Monogrammist PM, *Two Studies of Adam and Eve*, c. 1485. Engraving, 13.8 × 20.8 cm. British Museum, London

some disseminated in engraved or woodcut form. But evidently, by comparison with Jacopo's "man and woman" (the specific print or drawing he showed has not survived), the vernacular nudes of, say, the German anonymous Monogrammist PM seemed wanting, since nothing about them, not the limbs in themselves, not their relation to their bodies, not the link between one body to another, not even Adam, seen from the front, to Adam seen from the rear, conform to an underlying rule (fig. 33). Unfortunately for Dürer, the visiting Italian did not divulge the circle-squaring rule. Perhaps he wanted to keep it secret, or perhaps he did not understand the question. In any case, after years of labor, through nature studies, geometric construction, imitation of classical models, and some reading of Vitruvius, Dürer staged his beauty ideal in a scene of humanity's fall *from* perfection.

Never had the Renaissance received as public an expression as Dürer's engraving of 1504 (fig. 34). Adam and Eve regain their lost Edenic bodies through forms borrowed from another lost paradise, that of classical antiquity: Adam is based (broadly) on the Apollo Belvedere, Eve on the Medici Venus. Yet in his writings Dürer acknowledged that the task he set for himself ultimately eluded him: "I believe there is no one alive capable of perceiving the ultimate ideal of beauty embodied in the least of living creatures, let alone in a human being, which is the special creation of God with dominion over the rest of creation." This deficiency was both objective and subjective, and both theoretical and practical, and Dürer explains it with reference to our fallen vision: "Our knowledge is undercut by deceit, and darkness is deeply embedded within us, so that our fumblings lead us nowhere."[291] Not just for decorum's sake do the leaves of the fig tree and mountain ash just happen to cover Eve and Adam's groin. The moment of the Fall has already arrived. But there's an "almost," and even a "not-yet," prompted by the

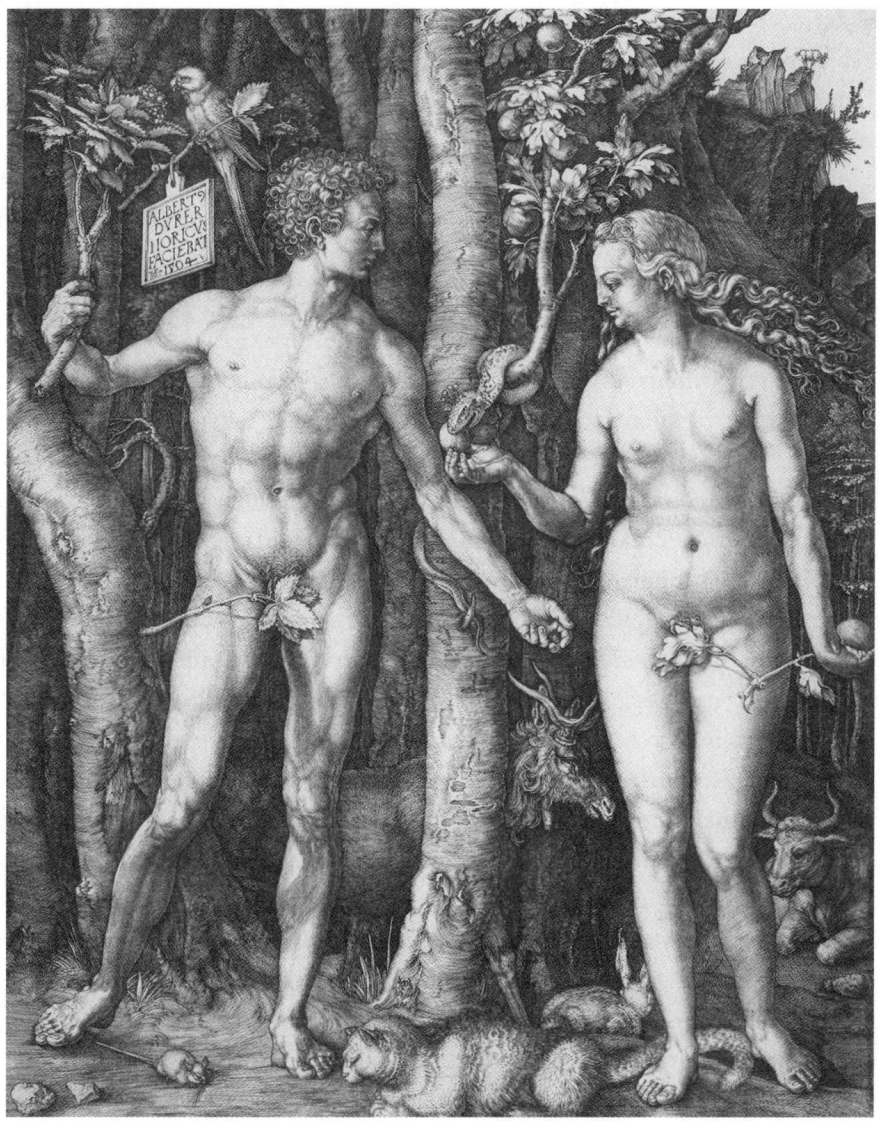

FIG. 34. Albrecht Dürer, *Adam and Eve*, 1504. Engraving, 25.1 × 19.2 cm

teetering goat, upper right, and by the still-vegetarian cat who only seems to be lazing peacefully before the innocently ambling mouse whose tail seems just now released from under Adam's forward-striding foot.

In fact, everything's slipping, just now, into the "always already" of the lapse, through Eve's grasping fingers, through Adam's willing reach, and—perhaps most decisively—through Adam's fixed gaze, which seems to blast Eve's tresses, as if with "a storm [...] blowing from Paradise."[292] Observe also how the dimorphic covering leaves mime the carnal inclination of the parts they cover. Dürer places the "now" of the moment of the Fall at the instant of Adam's look. He makes that *Augenblick* into just that—in German of the time the word had distinctly erotic connotations, conjuring (like cupid's arrow) sexual desire as both ocular and sudden. Adam's *Augenblick* is not quite lustful yet, but it is clearly energetic, or "libidinal" in the biological sense of expressing an urge or instinct: hence those windblown tresses. And by a simultaneity to which image-makers are especially attuned, the instance of Adam's intensive looking has to coincide with our pro-longed—because aesthetically engaged and wondrous—ocular appreciation of the engraving.

Every artist who has ever tried to picture it has been forced by the limits of their medium to reduce the Fall to a single moment. The Renaissance doctrine of poetry and painting as "sister arts" might have sent Dürer to Aristotle for lessons on the "unities" required of art—the *Poetics* had just become available to humanists in Germany. But the creator of the woodcut *Apocalypse* did not need books to teach him about dramatic narrative, or about how his medium confined storytelling to a single *Augenblick* and (because he was committed to linear perspective) to a single viewpoint on that *Augenblick*. He therefore had to make the most of the depicted moment, and that meant allowing it to conjure what came before and what will follow. As Lessing wrote, the *Augenblick* had to be *fruchtbar*, "pregnant."[293] Even though the biblical story gets told in multiple sequential scenes, the ethically chal-lenging one, where innocence flips ineluctably into guilt, requires freeze-framed movements that beg the question of when and why. The choices painters make can seem to be purely aesthetic ones, tricks of the trade: how to paint a hand that gives the fruit or takes it, who to show looking and who looked at, whether to pose the figures standing, reclined, or tumbling right now below the tree, and so forth. Yet these artisanal choices require and provoke reasoning of an ethical kind because, in imagining this story, every decision implies culpability.

Dürer labored long and hard on this dilemma. A study sheet with five sepa-rate drawings of Adam's right hand documents this struggle (fig. 35). The artist wants to get that hand and those fingers right, what they look like, down to their minute veins and wrinkles, reaching, about to take, or already taking the fruit. This exploration involves Dürer's own hand: he practices manually making Ad-am's hand in pen and ink so that, when he engraves it with a burin on a copper plate, he will know exactly how to do it, and will perform each of his manual op-erations well. But such practical concerns mobilize reasoning of another kind, since each of the five exercises suggests a subtly different movement and has a subtly different take on the "when" of the Fall. The tiny movements of the model's fingers—perhaps Dürer's observed in a mirror—look candid and random. Like

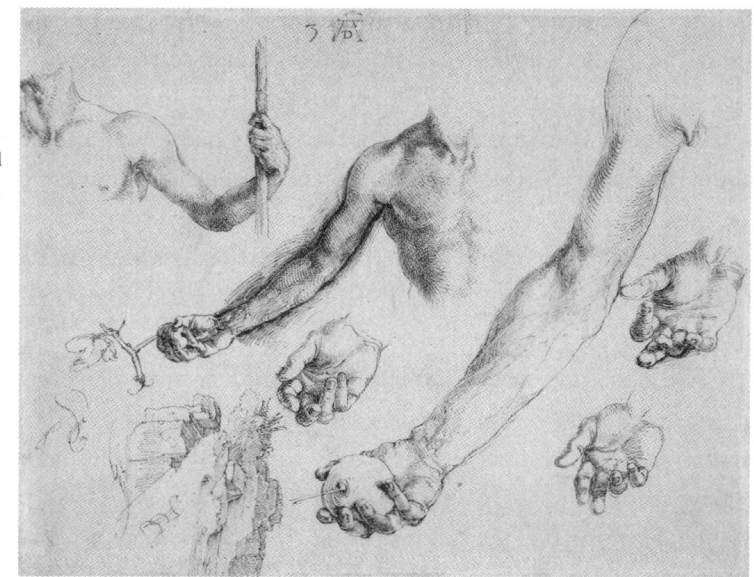

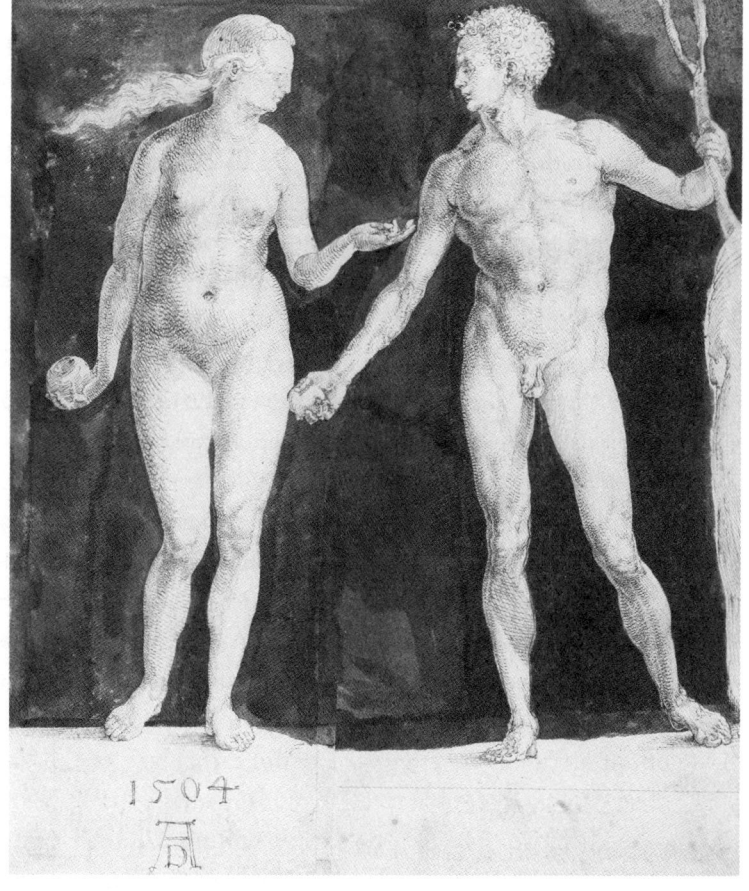

Eadweard Muybridge's stop-action photos of a pencil passed from hand to hand, these contingent views give optical expression to unconscious action, for surely Adam did not choose to fall, but fell unthinkingly. In the 1504 engraving, Dürer settled on the reaching rather than the taking hand, but not before micromanaging the gesture's placement in the scene. In a drawing preserved in the Morgan Library, he sketched Adam and Eve on separate sheets of paper—or on one sheet then cut in two. This allowed him to play with the distance separating them before pasting them together using a third bit of paper and merging the collage with white gouache and brown wash (fig. 36).

The engraving freeze-frames Adam and Eve in their places and poses, but Dürer does everything he can to picture them still mobile and free. Unable to show actions in sequence, image-makers need to collapse causes and effects. This might relieve them of engaging with the question of theodicy: *unde malum*—where does evil come from? But the limitations of their medium allowed image-makers to engage in this great question creatively, speculatively, and outrageously without answering it in heretical ways. With the advent of printing, artists could avail themselves of decisions previously taken. Dürer's engraving stopped the clock for artists who followed his example. Afterward, northern European paintings, drawings, and prints of Adam and Eve pictured moments unfolding after the one finalized in the 1504 print, as if Dürer had copyrighted the "not-yet" leaving others only the "already" to explore. Hans Baldung Grien worked in Dürer's workshop from 1503 until 1509 as assistant, collaborator, and (during Dürer's sojourn in Venice 1505–7) manager. Established as an independent master in Strasbourg, Baldung produced in 1511 a rival print of the Fall in the new medium of chiaroscuro woodcut (fig. 37). The gray or reddish-brown tone block of extant impressions thrust Adam and Eve into a visual and ethical shadowland at odds with paradisiacal Eden. But as the prominent text tablet announces, this is already the Fall of everyone, the *lapsus humani generis*.

Adam grabs the apple in the instant he also gropes Eve's breast. Collapsing together—now explicitly—the trespass against God and sexual desire, Baldung makes it impossible to see which came first.[294] Adam takes the apple because he lusts, and lusts because he takes the apple. Augustine held that before the Fall, Adam controlled his procreative power. To reason otherwise, to blame the lapse on the body or Eve or nature would grant evil independent powers and contract God's omnipotence. Only after the Fall did carnal lust, or the "law of the members," arise.[295] No longer able to control his genitals, Adam passed his sin to us through the behavior of our bodies. Men neither will their genitals into action nor voluntarily rein them in. This carnal penalty infects us from our biological

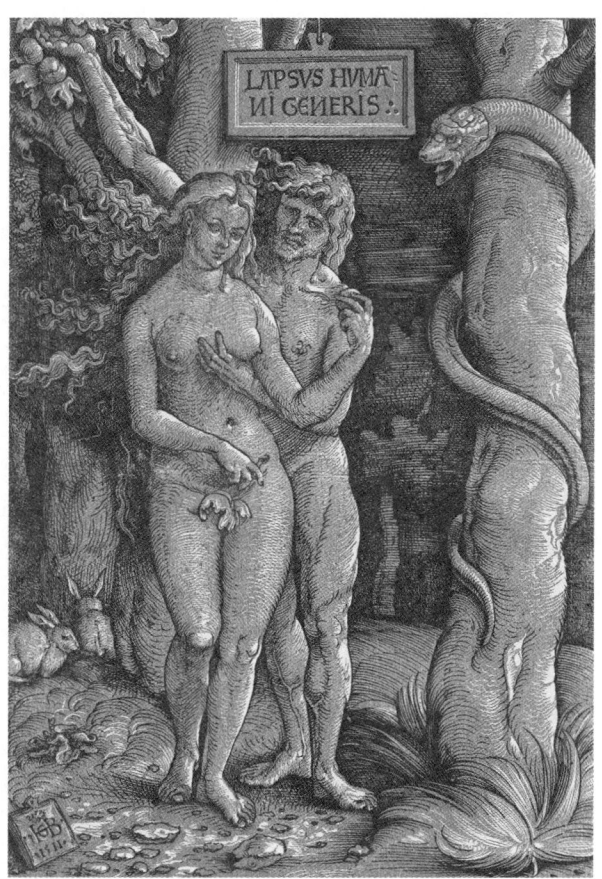

FIG. 37. Hans Baldung Grien, *The Fall of Mankind*, 1511. Chiaroscuro woodcut in two blocks, 38 × 25.8 cm

conception, because human beings are produced through the lust-driven coupling of their parents. Again, doctrinally, lust is the effect, not the cause, of the lapse, but due to the constraints and opportunities of their medium, image-makers tell a story of sin that has no history. Collapsing time into a pregnant moment and turning Eve's body and gaze to the picture's viewer, Baldung expects him (the implied audience of heterosexual men) to be aroused and to fall with Adam. The world's first catastrophe happens in the present tense.

Bosch similarly collapses evil's origins into the moment of his painting. But he rolls the story back to an instant well before the Fall, when the only action was looking. What happens in Adam's *Augenblick*? To glimpse the revolution now occurring, Bosch invites us to follow the directional vector of Adam's gaze out of the left panel and through the triptych's other scenes. This sightline first passes through Eve's downcast eyes to what looks to be Eve minutes later, now grabbed at the wrist by an Adam doppelganger, who looks blankly our way. In between, the couple in a veined translucent pod, and countless intimacies spread throughout the landscape, enact further steps before the visual vector reaches the counter-clockwise parade. Waylaying time's arrow and repeating the story like a broken record, the circle—wrongly termed by some observers a "rite" or "ritual," since the beasts create the circle, not the riders—captures our gaze just as Adam's eye was trapped by Eve at the start. Bending the line of Adam's sight, the men on male priapic mounts circling the pool of bathing women seem to act out the desire that came into the world with the first libidinous regard.

Bosch highlighted Eve's blond hair with lines of gold paint, so that the fascination the image portrays gets repeated in the fascination the image visually causes. Her tresses, and likewise those of the blond bathing women are the stuff of idols: "gods of gold you should not make for yourselves," is God's first commandment (Ex. 20:23). And as in the beginning, so at the end, the vector of Adam's sight terminates in a vortex. The Tree-Man—Bosch's signature motif—looks rearward over his ruined body and via the pleasures that ruined him, back to Adam whose facial features he shares. The triptych thus tells a story of desire. Beginning before the Fall, in the vitality of procreative nature, it traverses a humanity dehumanized by desire and burning itself out in hell. It is a story, a narrative, yet because Bosch expresses it in the form of an image, innocence and guilt, cause and effect, origin and end have to appear all at once. Pushing three timeframes together, his triptych captures what Kant called "radical evil" and admitted was elusive both to storytelling and to reason. "And what is the origin of our evil will?" asks Augustine, answering that "pride is the beginning of sin."[296] Eve loved herself, asserting

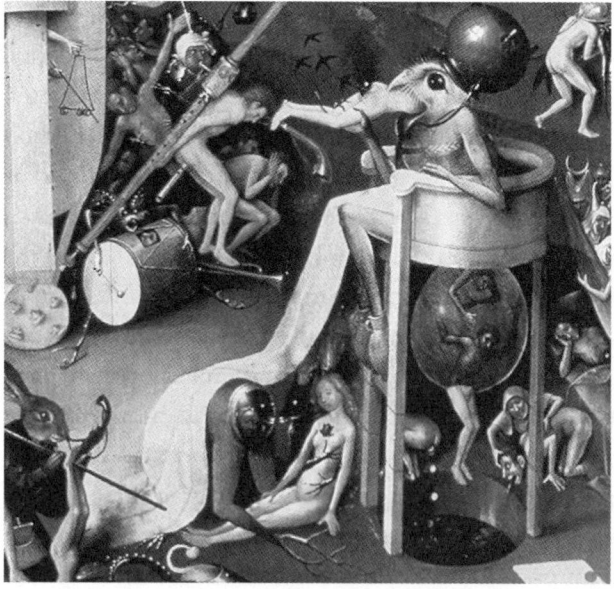

FIG. 38. Detail from Hieronymus Bosch, *The Garden of Delights*, open state, 1504. Oil on panel, 205.5 × 384.9 cm. Museo Nacional del Prado, Madrid

her rights and manipulating Adam's infatuation with her. And Adam, loving his appetite for Eve, preferring it to the whole of God's creation, turned self-ward, too. In the hell panel, Bosch visualizes this idea. He builds his personification of pride or *Superbia* out of parts of Adam and Eve in the garden (fig. 38). But in Eden, hell breaks out before either of our parents could even begin to be prideful. We do not decide but have been decided on, from the moment Adam set eyes on Eve.

The artist's reasoning might be hypothesized as follows. Tasked by his patron to create an allegory of lust, Bosch knew from the outset its beginning and end. Lust should start and finish where his triptychs typically begin and end, in Eden and hell, perhaps with a cosmic prelude attached: the Fall of the Rebel Angels, or an abbreviated Hexameron, like the one he painted for the high altar in 's-Hertogen-bosch. Only the middle called for a new invention, one rooted in lust's paradisiacal commencement (whenever that was) and exhibiting lust's vicissitudes, which human experience shows are many and diverse. Aware—as Christian artists long had been—that the Fall was a story of the eye, Bosch postulated (unconventionally but plausibly) a starting point before the doctrinal one: the instant Adam first glimpses Eve. What that "pregnant" moment contained, the central panel then displayed: libidinal pleasure for pleasure's sake, and with seeding not as God commanded it, "according to their various kinds" (Gen. 1:11). Men with men, women with women, peoples of different continents and tribes couple not in matrimony or in families, but collectively and promiscuously, some spilling their "seed on the ground" (Gen. 38:9), and with no children anywhere in sight.

In the Netherlands in Bosch's time, inquisitors, confessors, and magistrates obsessed about sodomy. Terming it variously a sin "against nature," an "unspeakable crime," a "red, screaming crime" that is mute, they included in this capital offence all sexual acts not performed for the purpose of producing offspring.[297] Refraining from speaking the unspeakable, Bosch hid these trespasses in the eye of the beholder; for who visiting the counts of Nassau in Brussels, or Philip II at El Escorial, would publicly say what privately captivated them? The artist cleverly disavowed his own imaginings. Nowhere does the triptych say that Adam's gaze caused the spectacle that follows. What happened in Eden becomes merely an occasion for an anomalous—an exceptional—painting of this kind, and one in which the visual itself is freely and expansively explored. Not law-obeying cause, but the contingency of occasion brings the center about. The "moral" remains perpetually in play, hence the conspicuous absence of final judgment above.

Bosch openly acknowledged that his paintings can be dangerous. His *Seven Deadly Sins* screams "Beware, beware God sees" (plate 3). But with a cruelty attuned to its princely setting, Bosch's unnamed and unnamable triptych reveals its danger only when it is too late. In hell, the body, the city, and Christian Europe are being plundered and sacked. But already at its first *Augenblick* the image will have conquered whoever lays eyes on it. Reflecting on how sin enters the world newly both in Adam and in any individual, Kierkegaard observed that the moment, the sudden, the *Augenblick—øieblikket* in the Danish—escapes the grasp of reason, even though reason fixates on transition, negation, mediation, and dialectic.[298] The sudden, the moment, the exception, the siege: therein lies the core of the ethical. To approach this state Kierkegaard reaches back to the most enigmatic of Plato's dialogues. In the *Parmenides*, Plato imagines the moment, Greek ἐξαίφνης, interposed between movement and rest, being and not-being, life and death, the many and the one. The fleeting "now" as if racing forward from past to future, the moment does not exist "in any time. [... I]n changing, it changes instantaneously, and when it changes it can be in no time, and at that instant it will be neither in motion nor at rest."[299] The moment is "wondrous," ἄτοπος, literally, that which has no place. "The Greek word is especially appropriate," notes Kierkegaard parenthetically.[300] It fits perfectly for Bosch. Centered on a non-biblical, ahistorical nowhere, his triptych is decidedly atopic no matter where it stands.

The picture looks at us, puts us at its center, and at first this order seems to belong to the world Bosch places on display. Fountain, pool, and parade align along the picture's central vertical axis and the four surrounding formations—despite their wildly capricious shapes—flank perfectly that center. The garden's symmetries resemble those of a pinnacled Gothic cathedral, crystalline structures occurring out there in the landscape. Symmetry receives support from outside, from the physical framework as a triptych with shutters that neatly close, and with a structure borrowed from churches, where altarpieces originally customarily appeared. Yet upon closer inspection, nothing is ordered within this painted world. The tips of those distant towers only *look* aligned. But they are in fact protean, consisting of fragile pinnacles, shimmering foliage, and birds in flight. If I were to stand on the grass among the revelers on the green, a single step to the left or right (necessary to walk through their multitude) would make the order the picture gives me collapse. The garden's symmetry is a purely contingent structure, an order dependent wholly on the viewing eye. At one with the tunnel vision of desire that trapped Adam, it has trapped Bosch's viewers for a half-millennium. The brilliant colors of the central panel belong to this optical allure. Those pastel blues and pinks appear nowhere else in the whole history of early Netherlandish painting, causing Bosch's triptych to stand out from all the other paintings in the Prado. Like flowers to insects or apples to Eve or golden effigies to the impious Israelites, Bosch causes us to see idolatrously.

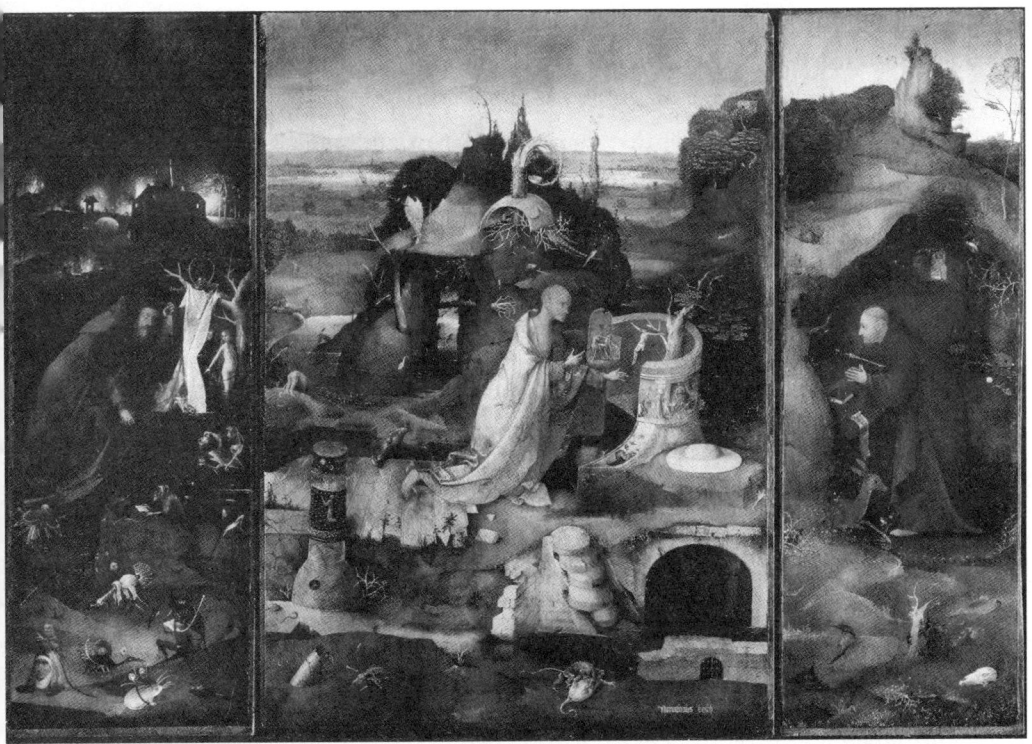

The artist was as good at painting idols as he was at painting devils—the two went hand in hand. His paintings of the abject paintings on the tomb where Saint Anthony prays look eerily self-illuminating, like Bosch's hellish tableau itself, which contains them. Crumbling at their edges these idols—in stripes of pink, green, and blue—look solid, but are thin veneer: an owl peers from behind them as if past a broken eggshell. In his *Hermit Saints Triptych*, Bosch imagines *Saint Jerome*, his namesake, in the ruins of a decorated sanctuary (fig. 39). As with the moldering images in the *Saint Anthony Triptych*, some of these decorations belong to Judeo-Christian iconography, but most do not. The unicorn figurine and the Judith and Holofernes relief make sense in light of Jerome's predicament, as he struggles to master his instincts. Less legible are the lewdly perched owl mobbed by songbirds and the stargazing mystic on a cylinder. Belonging to a derelict tomb or temple of an unknown religion, such fragments conform to the familiar Christian story that Christ, the true image of God, caused the pagan idols to fall. Other artists portray such doomed artifacts as mere bizarre formations vaguely evoking antique statuary. Bosch instead conjures idols as belonging to a sedimented history of false religions, or of syncretic mystery cults long forgotten, in which what resembles an Old Testament episode is but an accidental homology, the Judith and Holofernes story, but with altogether different names. Bosch's *Epiphany* triptych plays the same game with the gifts of the Magi. Such "found imagery" mingles with the devilish temptations that early Christian hermit saints steadfastly resist. Besieged, engulfed, and overshadowed by enemies, Christ's truth persists. But what if those luminous idols, tamed by appearing as details in scenes of devilish temptation, took over the whole painted panel? That is the conjecture this dangerous masterpiece answers: an enemy image beheld by enemy eyes.

Nuremberg, 1947

Museums never display Bosch's triptych in its intended resting state, with shutters closed and the newly created world, drab grays on gray, hovering "over the surface of the deep" (plate 1). A perfect sphere but stormy inside, the world looks volatile in this dormancy, its curvature pressing restlessly up against the slit between two panels that support it, urging them to open. With his creative fiat (from Psalm 33:9) written beside him, God casts the panels as a painted incipit. In Schedel's *World Chronicle*, God dominates the world's beginning (see fig. 13). In Bosch, creation dwarfs the Creator, causing the Psalmist's "it stood firm" to sound like a question. And when the shutters open, the bewilderment increases. Bosch built his triptych to be experienced as a spectacular event. The opening's blast of color, movement, and life should *happen*, and happen *suddenly*. In the Nassau palace this would have been performed at special occasions. The Prado hangs the triptych as it does the framed gallery pictures of later eras, always open, available, and underway, at any viewer's pleasure.

But even in its open appearance Bosch's tableau blasts open the temporality of the museum. You can spot it in the gallery from far away, thanks to the crowds it draws, as if the erotic energy of the revelers converts efficiently into a visual hunger that, now five centuries on, shows no signs of abating. These crowds behave differently than do visitors to a merely iconic masterpiece, where they check it off their to-do list, take selfies, and move right along, sometimes without even looking at the thing. Bosch's crowds stray from their plan, selfishly lingering, their nose right up against the picture, to the annoyance of others behind. This rudeness is collective. Everyone jockeys for the best position but the experience is solitary. Wherever the eyes wander they wander alone, since close pointing is forbidden in the museum, and by the time I explain where I am looking, you will have stalled elsewhere. We become incommunicative, speaking unhelpfully of things so fantastic that they "could not be properly described in any way to those who do not know them," or reporting about "figures who defecate cranes" when there are no such things.[301] Appearances are sudden and fugitive.

The anonymous etcher of Bosch's Tree-Man understood stupefied looking (fig. 30). At the edge of a precipice, a crowd behaves as people do when something this big and strange arrives on their doorstep: they gawk and point, like the children and the fool among them. They are Bosch's regulars, for whom mute eyewitness will have been sufficient. To these common folk the etcher contrasts the foreground trio, those experts in marvel who treat the phenomenon as a question. "It is owing to wonder that men both now begin, and at first began, to philosophize," wrote Aristotle. People wondered "originally at the obvious difficulties"—such as the Tree-Man. Then they advanced "little by little and stated difficulties about the phenomena of the moon and those of the sun and stars, and about the genesis of the universe."[302] The etching's astronomer sits at the end of a progression from the painter who merely pictures the perplexity, through the fabulist—Aristotle's "lover of myth"—to the stargazing prognosticator.

The Tree-Man is hyperbolically evident. The impression it makes on the eye is that of an object which actually exists and the mind grasps correctly. When Karlstadt castigates idols for causing the eye to grasp erroneously (*vergreuffen*), he blames them for the false sense impressions they produce.[303] Eyewitness certifies the Tree-Man as an impossibility made real: rootless trees balanced on boats allowing the precariously top-heavy entirety to walk on water. To the experts, the Tree-Man's evidence is insufficient. In their eyes it must be, or mean, something other than it is, a monstrance that warns of something else. To Matthias Gerung it signified the idolatrous Roman Church; to Philip II's librarian it warned that pleasures vanish the instant you enjoy them; to Paulus de Kempenaer it augured a Europe besieged and divided. The nineteenth-century rediscovery of Bosch brought a new type of expert to the question. Not content silently to gaze, the historian of art looked for bygone beliefs in the old pictures. Leaving no evidence about his intentions, Bosch presented to these professionals a challenge. No survey can be complete, stated Panofsky at the close of his survey, without a discussion of Bosch. Yet Bosch made concluding impossible: we "have bored a few holes" but "have not discovered the key."[304] Gombrich issued a similar warning: "visual evidence never comes neat, as it were, unmixed with imagination."[305] Impossible figures like the Penrose triangle require critical scrutiny, and so do works by Bosch. This Gombrich undertook. He argued that the triptych portrayed the world before the biblical Flood, and that "its Christian name is *Sicut erat in diebus Noe*," or "As it was in the Days of Noah." As evidence, Gombrich adduced a reference to a painting of that title recorded in a Brussels inventory.[306] The argument did not convince.

For Fraenger, Bosch's triptych was its own key. To solve the riddle, one just had to accept what it showed: Eve, Adam, and the revelers all innocent of sin. Aware that others of his trade needed supporting evidence, Fraenger trawled the Dutch archives for Adamites and Jews, but in his eyes they were right there before us, hundreds of them pursuing their erotic rites. That he understood the picture erroneously, and that others remain persuaded, derives from the painted spectacle itself. Bosch causes our eyes to grasp his artifact cultishly, in line with our idolatrous forefather Adam. To Schmitt in Nuremberg, Fraenger's answer was convincing and appalling. It is time to circle back to that episode and consider why the expert on enemies got Bosch's enemy painting wrong.

In prison on possible war crimes charges, Schmitt felt himself naked like Adam and Eve "upon their eviction from the Garden of Eden."[307] In other words, the jurist imagined himself a victim of one of Bosch's terrifying juridical regimes. The people questioning him—in Berlin in 1945 and in Nuremberg in 1947—formed an abject court. Neither a jury of peers nor even typical victors' justice, they were an enemy tribunal. The US Military Government employed as interrogators Schmitt's former vocational foes. Robert Kempner had been a prominent member of Schmitt's profession until 1933. His prewar activities included defending an Armenian assassin on the grounds that Armenians had suffered genocide, and seeking to charge Hitler with high treason, both commitments radically opposed to Schmitt's. Now as assistant US chief counsel, Kempner sought to determine whether Schmitt, his old adversary, could be prosecuted for "participating directly or indirectly in the planning of wars of aggression, war crimes, and crimes against humanity."[308]

That question had been long in coming. As early as 1916, in a book on the poetry of Theodor Däubler, Schmitt railed against the modern "age of security," with its dreams of a fully pacified world. An idling machine without purpose or end, liberal democracy outlawed conflicts, turned politics into "everlasting conversations," and reduced states of exception to a constitutional loophole.[309] Such an apparently peaceable world, Schmitt predicted, would eventually turn a hostile eye towards enmity itself. This "war against war" would "necessarily" be "unusually intense and inhuman" because

> by transcending the limits of the political framework, it simultaneously de-grades the enemy into moral and other categories and is forced to make of him a monster that must not only be defeated but also utterly destroyed.[310]

In Nuremberg Schmitt became that monster. Beyond his legal opinions supporting Hitler's seizure of power, beyond the imperative "to shed blood, and kill other human beings"[311] in order to protect German blood, beyond his *Großraum* theories justifying the murderous resettlement of the east, Schmitt's hatred for the Jews as threatening his "whole way of life" aligned him with Nazi extermination policies. Writing in 1935 to Ernst Jünger about "Jewish dominion" he cited Léon Bloy approvingly: "war makes no sense if it does not exterminate." It was while revisiting Bloy—and while gaining insights into the developing "situation" through the art of Bosch as explicated by Fraenger, "a specialist"—that Schmitt, in 1943 again to Jünger, wrote about "a Jewish art historian, Panofsky" arrested for his insolence.[312]

Contrary to what Schmitt predicted, Kempner's questions were gentle. And the answers Schmitt gave were evasive and self-serving. He did not promote Hitler's legal order but only "diagnosed" it; he was at worst "an intellectual adventurer;" and when finally asked if, in light of the murder of millions, he felt "ashamed," he admitted only this: "Today, yes. I don't find it proper in this humiliation that we suffered to root about in it." Under interrogation, it is he who is the victim at the hands of Jews. When kindly told by Kempner to "go home," he agreed "to root about" some more in his shame, his Schmittian decisionism fawningly abandoned for the "everlasting conversation" he loathed.[313] But not before turning the tables on his questioners and, in the texts he had written in prison and published in 1950, portraying them as the monsters of history.

Bosch's triptych triggered the most vivid of these enemy imaginings. The "Adamic happiness of the garden of earthly delights" was the Bosch of Fraenger's antinomian fantasies.[314] Originally unfolded to Schmitt alone in letters privately exchanged, those fantasies were jointly made. Free to travel to Spain, the jurist inspected for the art historian Bosch's works in the Prado; hunkered down in Päwesin, the art historian tantalizingly intimated to Schmitt that the artist's patron was a backsliding Jew. And what Schmitt, in Nuremberg, saw in Bosch was fully the jurist's own, his sinister vision of liberal democracy as an evil machine. Already as a young Catholic conservative, Schmitt portrayed earthly paradise as the ultimate abomination. Writing in 1922, he noted that the great counter-revolutionary philosophers of the state—especially the Spanish reactionary and champion of dictatorship, Juan Donoso Cortés—recognized the dangers posed by theories of the natural goodness of man. Without a recognition of humans as dangerous animals there would be anarchy: "all moral and political decisions are thus paralyzed in paradisiacal worldliness of immediate natural life and problem-free corporeality."[315] Three decades later, Schmitt reshuffled those very words to characterize Bosch's *Garden of Delights*: "This is nature and the natural law, the suspension of self-alienation and of self-externalization in a problem-free corporeality."[316]

The sentence is meant to sound like philosophical gibberish. Schmitt mocks the post-Hegelian writings of Max Stirner, whose egomaniacal effusions fascinated Schmitt in high school: "At this moment, Max is the only person who visits me in my cell."[317] Stirner, the "rabid egoist," made sense when Schmitt first read him in his youth, and he made sense at Nuremberg, as Schmitt contemplated his situation. "Problem-free corporeality" (*problemlose Leibhaftigkeit*) stands for a wholly materialistic, or monist, understanding of the universe: the not-I as pure body without soul. That "corporeality" should be "problem-free" accords with the machine-like progress of the modern age, where decisions—key to sovereignty—never have to be made, since everything runs according to rule, with no resistance or exceptions. The marked presence of *Leib* (body) in the German *Leibhaftigkeit* allows prurience to stick to the secular world view, clogging its gears. Compared to Fraenger's understanding, however, Schmitt's *Garden of Delights* is not a sexual utopia, but a political one. Bosch "cast in white nakedness upon a panel" a world of friends without enemies. In such a world, there would be no politics and no state, for "the concept of the state presupposes the concept of the political," and the political presupposes an enemy.[318] Catholic reactionaries like Donoso Cortés despised the anarchists for denying monogamy, not so much because it led to sinful behavior but because it destroyed sovereignty in the primal form of "the family resting on the authority of the father."[319] Political theorists from Plato and Aristotle to Locke and Rousseau took the family to be the original organizing principle—Hobbes's "dominion paternal." First cities, then empires, and finally nation states would extend that family principle without changing what made it necessary. Humans seek to exert a certain degree of dominance in life. They are by nature political animals.

Schmitt drew from Donoso Cortés the theological starting point for politics: the dogma of Original Sin. For the "Catholic Spaniard" Adam and Eve's trespass did not corrupt us merely or chiefly in "the ridiculous vitality" of our carnal longings.[320] The Fall made us wholly depraved and nowhere more obviously than in our lust for domination. "The denial of Original Sin destroys all social order," wrote Schmitt in 1933, for the crux of God's punishment is enmity: "I will put enmity [...] between thy seed and her seed" (Gen. 3:15).[321] From that moment on until the end of time, humans will have to decide between God and Satan, good and evil, and obedience and disobedience. And "the last moment of the last battle [had] arrived," for Cortés in the form of liberalism and atheistic socialism, for Schmitt in Nuremberg in the form of the final "war against war," of which he was the victim.[322] Bosch's *Garden* was the face of this enemy. The "ridiculous vitality" of carnal desire destroys the principles of matrimony, patriarchy, and dominion to which human life must be bound. Although he does not say it openly, Schmitt—who based his friendship concept on homogeneity of blood—must have looked with terror at the triptych's erotic mixing of gender, family, and race—Antonio de Beatis's astonishing "men and women, white and black." In 1948 Schmitt wrote of Bosch's revelers, "The state of the spirit is more gruesome than the state of nature in Hobbes."[323] In the jurist's mind, assimilated Jews are the preachers of this new state. Wearing constantly changing "masks of demonic enigmaticness," dissimulating their being a distinct race, they promise world peace, tempting Christians to deny inborn corruption and thus reject God.[324] In another text from 1948, Schmitt summons his nemesis, the Jewish-Austrian legal theorist Hans Kelsen, along with the other framers of Austria's and Germany's postwar constitution, and compares them to "the little helper demons in the hells of Hieronymus Bosch."[325] Behind their gentle sermons lay Satan, who whispered in Eden and whispers still, "There are no enemies!"

The odd thing about Schmitt's prison epiphany is that he of all people should have gotten Bosch right. His *Leviathan* book took Bosch to have been serious about evil: that artist's devils "are ontological reality," unlike Bruegel's. Schmitt may have borrowed this contrast from Jünger, for whom Bosch was a constant aesthetic touchstone. In December 1933, nine months into Hitler's dictatorship, Jünger wrote to Schmitt to compliment him on the third edition of *The Concept of the Political*, which the jurist had extensively revised to reflect the new situation in which his own friend–foe politics had become explicit. Jünger, in his autobiographical novel *Storm of Steel* (1920) and in influential texts on "total mobilization," had celebrated the "pure form" (*Gestalt*) of mechanized warfare as "a gripping spectacle to behold."[326] Seven times severely wounded, and one of only eleven shock troop commanders to be awarded the *Pour le Mérite*, he knew violence from up close, and on an epochal scale. Jünger unfolds his praise of Schmitt's text kaleidoscopically, in thoughts and images that flash up, vanish, and reappear.

Bosch, Jünger begins, has long been known to him through a copy hanging in Cologne (presumably the Boschian *Nativity* now dated to after 1570), which he often visits. In the artist's works animals appear in a wholly medieval fashion, divided into two halves, each half diverse in itself but ontologically distinct from the other, and transitioning—foreground to background—from good to evil. This dualism estranges them: "that these pictures are of an alien kind lies in the fact that this kind of distinction has become alien to us." Bruegel's paradises, by contrast, "portray plants and animals as *species* in relation to one and the same diversity."[327]

Jünger is probably thinking not of Pieter Bruegel the Elder, but of his son Jan "Velvet" Brueghel, whose meticulous renderings of nature graced the best early modern art and wonder cabinets of his day. The "process that we term modern" therefore consists in the "disintegration of evil," and this makes amoralists particularly modern. Schmitt's thought defies this process: "Your distinction between friend and enemy is, by the way, not of a modern nature." It lies both closer to Bosch while also projecting "beyond the modern" into the future. Jünger, for his part, takes Bosch's paintings and Schmitt's friend–foe distinction "not as a reality but as a measure" or "method" through which "one and the same diversity" can be reworked and attacked.[328]

Schmitt must have remembered Jünger's letter when, in writing about Hobbes, he contrasted Bosch's "medieval belief" in demons to Bruegel's aestheticization of evil and located the emergence of secular concepts of sovereignty and international law—the *ius publicum Europaeum*, of which he, Schmitt, was "the last knowing representative"—in the civil wars raging in the half-century between the two painters. In his unshaken faith in Genesis 3:15, Schmitt would also have appreciated being paired with Bosch, the painter as medieval, and the jurist as modern, portraitist of the enemy. Why instead of accepting Fraenger's analysis did he not challenge or correct it? Why, in other words, did Schmitt fail to see his *own* perspective in the spectacle of earthly paradise exterminated by secret sovereign decision?

Schmitt insisted that the enemy is a concrete adversary intending to negate his opponent's own way of life. Neither objective nor subjective, the enemy is born in his attack and in the decision about the attacker as the enemy. Both the enemy's power and what is "one's own"—friends and a way of life—originate as the answer to the one event: the enemy first, then "one's own." And just those two: no third party observing the conflict from outside can properly grasp the enemy. The enemy is self-evident, but only to the combatants: "Only the actual participants can correctly know, understand, and decide the concrete situation and settle the extreme case in conflict."[329] Yet in Nuremberg, called into question, terrified by shame, and haunted by Bosch, Schmitt's certitude falters. Pacing his theories as if they were walls of a cave, he asks and asks again the question, "Who is my enemy?" Two lines of poetry come to mind, a sentence from Theodor Däubler, whose poem *Das Nordlicht* Schmitt had analyzed back in 1916. It had been through Däubler that Schmitt and Fraenger became acquainted, and *Nordlicht*, "using the form of a triptych for a poem" of an immense size, may have focused them both on Bosch's triptych.[330] Echoing through Schmitt's postwar writings until they become a personal mantra, these gnomic lines allow the crown-jurist of the Third Reich to turn an eye on himself: "The enemy is our own question as form [*Gestalt*]."[331]

Our own question. This was the interrogators' question, and Bosch's also, cast in white nakedness upon a panel. We see ourselves only in that question. "Eureka, I have found him, namely my enemy. Woe unto him who has no enemy, for he will be his enemy at the end of time."[332] The enemy is therefore intimate, like a friend or brother: "The other is my brother," Schmitt concludes, thinking both of his situation in Nuremberg, imagined as a state of universal civil war, and of the first brothers, Cain and Abel. Cain kills suddenly, before Abel can know it, and without the face to face of duel or battle that would give time for recognition.[333] "Tell me your enemy and I will tell you who you are," wrote Schmitt in the notebook he kept upon his release from prison.[334] Those words could be written below Bosch's triptych. "Form," or *Gestalt* in Däubler's German, comes close to what Christian theology termed *figura*: something concrete and historical that, through a likeness, reveals something else that is also concrete and historical. The likeness can be vague, its vagueness multiplying its deictic power. If Adam is the *figura* of Christ, writes Tertullian, then Adam's sleep is Christ's death, his borrowed rib, Christ's wound, and Eve, the Church, "the mother of all living."[335] The similarities that connect the two may be indefinite but what they connect is real. Unlike the modern idea of an event, as something singular and self-sufficient, figural understanding of history was at once concealed and concrete: a cloaked reality pointing beyond itself to the final end. "The enemy is our own question as *Gestalt*," writes Schmitt, remembering silently Däubler's next line: "And he will hunt us, and we him, to the same end."

Kurinskij, 1942

In May 1944, Schmitt spent three days in Lisbon in the company of Mircea Eliade. The Romanian novelist, folklorist, and philosopher of religion had been an ardent supporter of the Christian fascist Iron Guard and António Salazar's authoritarian rule. He also served as Romania's cultural attaché in Portugal after his country entered World War II on Germany's side. He had met Schmitt in Berlin in 1942, "a small man with a face not very impressive but luminous, animated." They discussed Salazar, aquatic symbolism, and Schmitt's influence on Romanian political thought, and Eliade was impressed with the German's "metaphysical courage."[336] Two years later in Lisbon, when Schmitt gave lectures there on international law, the two often dined together and visited the museum in the Palace of Janelas Verdes, gazing "for more than an hour" at Bosch's *Temptation of Saint Anthony* (plate 14). The jurist apprised Eliade of the work of a "friend," Wilhelm Fraenger, who had written "a huge monograph of over a thousand pages—as yet unpublished." Bosch's art, Schmitt reported, contained biographical and historical facts, including the existence of secret societies that, protected by the emperor, seized corrupt magistrates and killed them "according to all the legal formalities." In the Lisbon triptych, Schmitt ventured, the envelope in the beak of a bird "probably contain[s] the death sentence." Schmitt "tells me," Eliade reports, that Bosch had become "the latest fashion" in Germany: "Everyone is interested in him, although very few speak or even fewer publish. The air raids and the insecurity help the Germans to understand Bosch and to rediscover themselves in him."[337]

What the Germans rediscovered—presumably—was a triple siege: by Allied forces, by the Gestapo, and (perhaps) by compunction. Among those Germans obsessed by Bosch was Ernst Jünger, whose engagement with the Netherlandish artist profoundly impacted his literary output. In their letters, Bosch circulates between Schmitt, Fraenger, and Jünger less as an artist they mutually appreciate or as a historical riddle they try to solve than as a prophet of current doom. When Jünger, in 1933, likened Schmitt to Bosch it was Schmitt's "projection beyond the modern" that linked the jurist to the premodern painter. And in Schmitt's letter of 1943 that pairs Bloy's *Salvation through the Jews* with Panofsky's insolence, Bosch signals an unspeakable foreboding that the Germans will lose the war and be delivered to their enemies.[338] Nothing prevented anyone from speaking or publishing about Bosch, but because the artist himself seemed inherently secretive, he became the shared cipher for remaining silent during states of siege. Whispered, the name "Bosch" could telegraph a furtive, belated disavowal of the Nazi regime—what came to be called "inner immigration," or it could encrypt an ineffable mixture of terror and guilt. Jünger crafted the most remarkable communication of this kind in the Christmas greeting he sent to Schmitt in 1942. Dated December 23, it was posted from "the East" (*Osten*).

Jünger did not divulge his exact position in the Caucasus. Army Group A, to which he was attached, stood catastrophically stalled in its southeastward push to the oil fields by the Caspian Sea and Jünger's movements (better kept secret) shifted daily. However, Schmitt did receive an unforgettable portrait of his friend's predicament. In this "kingdom of pain," Jünger writes, "mechanical processes, as crystallizations of pure violence, along with pain as their passive correlate, recall powerfully certain paintings by H. Bosch."[339] Dangling midair in a goods cable lift, high above a deep and jagged ravine, he observes swarms of captured war prisoners loading the dead and wounded onto barges while horses tumble into the river and jets of flames from the heavy artillery tear the air. From a small opening in a ruined bridge abutment, an officer barks orders down to the cannoneers, his shouts mingling with the strains of "Silent Night" blasted through the valley from loud-speakers. "Too bad," Jünger writes, "that Bosch could not paint what I saw," this "ice landscape" that the Netherlandish artist had seen already in his time, though the battle back then was one-sided—a "war against unbelievers"—whereas today "the war between atheists takes the crown." What Jünger projects into the valley below him, at a distance that enables him to mingle what he has personally witnessed with what he heard rumored, were German atrocities against so-called "partisans" (in the Caucasus these were often just children orphaned by the war), as well as the mass extermination of the Jews "certainly occurring on a huge scale."[340]

This Boschian inferno glimpsed in the Caucasus mountains became the dramatic climax of *Strahlungen* (Emanations), the edited version of Jünger's war journals.[341] German readers had to wait until 1949 for this book to appear, in part because the author refused to submit to the "denazification" process, which imposed on him a four-year publication ban. Unlike Schmitt, Martin Heidegger, and many other prominent German thinkers, Jünger never joined the National Socialist Party. He refused a seat offered to him in the Reichstag in 1933, and ignored Goebbels's frequent invitations to meet with Hitler, who venerated the author of *Storm of Steel*. Jünger's politics were nationalist, authoritarian, and ruthless, but he rejected Nazi race theory: for him blood was a metaphysical life-force, not a biological value.[342] Nonetheless, his literary treatment of the front-experience as a positive existential extreme, his radical rejection of Weimar liberalism, and his vision of "total mobilization" of society around a national idea helped shape Nazi ideology. After 1933 Jünger fraternized with anti-Semites like Schmitt, and in the Caucasus he served directly under mass murderers. Portrayed in his diaries as observers like himself, these were in fact high-ranking army officers who cooperated with the *Einsatzgruppen* (mobile killing units) and led the liquidation campaign against imagined partisans (mostly just local civilians), even if his diaries put the perpetrators at a polite remove.[343] Like *Ex Captivitate Salus*, but without Schmitt's cringeworthy self-pity, *Strahlungen* was a moral reckoning on the author's own terms.

Jünger had been called back to the army in 1939, and by summer 1940 he headed an infantry division in the Battle of France. A year later he took his unit to Paris to serve as a guard regiment while he, famous and well-connected, spent the next four years (minus the months in the Caucasus) living expansively in the French capital. Jünger kept his diaries with the intention of putting them into literary form. His journals chronicling the outbreak of the war, published in 1942 as *Gärten und Straßen* (Gardens and streets), established the style of, and an eager public for, *Strahlungen*: finely wrought descriptions of everyday life abruptly intercut with dream sequences, historical reflections, and botanical, antiquarian, and (intensively) entomological research reports. Jünger termed these intensely visual collages "picture puzzles" (*Vexierbilder*) and likened them to Bosch's imagery, where, in "a moment of shock," one thing shifts over unexpectedly into something completely other: in Jünger, an herbivore beetle camouflaged as a leaf, in Bosch, a harp used as a torture instrument.

> When we solve a picture puzzle, bewilderment, astonishment, fright, but also exhilaration can result [...]. Such exercises were intended to show that even the world in a greater sense is composed like a picture puzzle—that its secrets lie exposed on the surface and that only a minimal adjustment of the eye is required to view its wealth of treasures and wonders.[344]

Underlying these transformations, and pushing desire and history forward, was life as a demonic energy that animated creatures (beetles and their observers) as well as machines (harps, tanks, and artillery).

In 1930, Jünger published a book of catastrophe photographs under the title *Der gefährliche Augenblick* (The dangerous moment). Snapshot photography had made the fatal instant of the car crash, parachute fail, gas explosion, and combat kill newly available to the human eye, the ocular instant conveyed by the German word *Augenblick*. That word had appeared more than a hundred times in *The Adventurous Heart*, first published in 1929. Jünger's introductory essay to the photographs, titled "On Danger," links the camera's capacity to capture disaster with technology's disastrous power. "The mathematical demonism" of machines becomes "in a special way visible" through the camera lens.[345] It had also been prophetically evident in Bosch. Newly arrived in Paris, Jünger takes a young female office clerk to the cinema: "there I touched her breast. A hot iceberg." The lights stay on, a newsreel shows German offensives, and "the mere glimpse of the weapons of annihilation produced screams of fear." Motion pictures of the "automatic nature" of modern weaponry—tanks gliding on steel plates, ammunition belts "swallowed as they fire"—cause terror: "The rings, hinges, armor, observation slits, sections of the tank, the arsenal of life-forms that harden like crustaceans, toads, crocodiles, and insects—Hieronymus Bosch had already envisioned them."[346] Filmic before the invention of film, his hell scenes spectacles of overabundant energy, Bosch predicted the transmutation of life into machines and machines back to life.

Set in Paris, the birthplace of the *flâneur*, *Strahlungen* follows Jünger—an unattached man of quasi-aristocratic leisure—through ephemeral episodes which he rapidly sketches, like Baudelaire's painter of modern life. And as in Baudelaire, these encounters unfold at the rapid pace of a modern metropolis. Experience shocks the voyeur. The erotic encounter ("I touched her breast") happens suddenly and confusingly: "a hot iceberg." But so do all the dangerous moments wherein flânerie in the modern metropolis mostly consists. But in Jünger's case, after nearly four years on the front line in World War I, and now an officer in his country's second catastrophic war, shock takes more violent forms.

Anecdotes of military violence become "capriccios," in homage to Bosch and Goya.[347] From a commander returning from the East, Jünger gathered these gruesome vignettes: an army regiment wiped out by frost is dubbed "The Asthma Division"; a slain Soviet commissar frozen solid in a standing position is shown off by his killer "like a sculptor displaying his work"; a captured Russian colonel, besieged for weeks and surviving on human flesh, explains that "he himself had eaten only the livers."[348] Carl Schmitt visits Jünger and, during the night, "images in the style of Hieronymus Bosch" materialize. In the foreground, before a crowd of naked victims and executioners, a "woman of great beauty" is decapitated with one blow. "I saw the torso stand for a moment before it crumpled—yet even headless, it seemed desirable." Without warning, Jünger returns to earth: "The ducks in the garden. They mate in puddles on the lawn left by the rain."[349] Used to cruelty, and viewing violence with a cruel detachment, the eye becomes cruel itself.

Jünger writes differently about mass killing than he does about erotic and martial violence. Wide-angle views replace the close-up focus of the "picture puzzle" as he reports on "butchers in the large charnel houses [...] who have single-handedly slain enough people to populate a midsize city." He hears terrible rumors, presumably of Operation Reinhard, commencing in Occupied Poland at the time, and involving the gassing and mass burial of over two million people, followed by the exhumation and burning of the camps and the content of their graves: "Corpses are hidden from adversaries so that they cannot be exhumed and photographed." He turns these into fables, casting Nazi butchers as *lemures*, the malignant ghosts of Roman mythology and imagining their extermination sites as *lemures*-forests:

> Feast days of the *lemures*, including the murder of men, women, and children. The gruesome spoils are hurriedly buried. Now there come other *lemures* to claw them out of the ground. They film the dismembered and half-decayed path of land with macabre gusto. Then they show these films to others.[350]

Lemures are the hellish spirits that, in the sixteenth-century poem describing him, Bosch "witnessed, face to face," and in Goethe's *Faust* lemures serve as Mephistopheles's gravediggers. It may have been a desire to witness for himself "the forests of the *lemures* in the East" that sent Jünger to the Caucasus. To Schmitt he wrote simply that he was ordered there "for my information." To Hans Speidel, a friend then serving on the Eastern Front as chief of staff of the 5th Army Corps, he confided that, although his journey was not undertaken out of "conscientiousness," the desire "to make a full judgment about the war as well as the second half of the twentieth century" nonetheless played a role.[351]

Jünger arrived at Voroshilovsk, headquarters of Army Group A, on November 21, 1942. Further to the east, the Germany armies—anticipating easy victory—had encircled Stalingrad only to be themselves encircled by Soviet troops. Meanwhile, with winter closing in, Army Group A, comprised of the 11th and 17th Army and the 1st Panzer Army, stood mired in difficult mountain terrain. Prussian military doctrine called their predicament a "cauldron" or "soup kettle" (*Kessel*).[352] Rather than engaging the enemy along a hostile front line, as happened in trench warfare in World War I, troops might, using new mobile armed elements, break through the foes at a "pressure point" *(Schwerpunkt)* in a "wedge" (*Keil*) movement. Those breaking through would then eliminate enemy artillery and supplies, while the infantry turned sideways towards the enemy's vulnerable flanks, dispersing and trapping them in cauldrons. Hitler intended the invasion of the Soviet Union to be a "wedge and cauldron" war on a continental scale, with Moscow (the pressure point) taken swiftly by tanks and airpower and other troops fanning out to besiege, in "cauldrons," other Russian cities. But where it succeeded in Poland and France, against Stalin the blitzkrieg strategy failed. In the 872-day Siege of Leningrad, during which more than a million civilians died of starvation, and in the Siege of Stalingrad more swiftly, the German besiegers were attacked from the rear and surrounded. "I shared my room with an officer from World War I who had come from the Stalingrad cauldron," wrote Jünger from Kiev, on his way back to Paris.[353]

Almost immediately on his arrival at the Eastern Front, Jünger recognized the hopeless situation. "A cauldron like this," he wrote on day two of his stay at Voroshilovsk, "has to be supplied by air until a land bridge can be established." The predicament conjures sieges of the past:

> The threat resembles that of a besieged city from classical times when no one could expect mercy. [...] For weeks and months, death could be seen approaching from afar. Many scores are settled in this way, for the political structures that the states had assumed have been turned inside out.[354]

Political structures invert because those in the cauldron become divided among themselves in ways that reveal the primal animosities of brothers—Schmitt's Cain and Abel as the origin of politics. For Jünger as for Schmitt, this inversion sparks a bizarre fantasy: surrendered to their enemies, Germans who showed no mercy can expect none and will be exterminated by surviving Jews. "The cauldron is the purest expression of our situation," wrote Jünger in 1944, "that was obvious to me before this war began. It was prefigured by such as the fate of the Jews."[355] This diagnosis, articulated by many Germans after the war, involved imagining a double siege: German troops surrounded by Stalin's Red Army and trapped by their own commanders, and perhaps also by their conscience at having once supported Hitler's regime. "When someone is not allowed to go back and cannot go forward," explains a German prisoner to his American interrogator in Hans Werner Richter's 1949 novel *The Defeated*, "he gets stuck in the middle. Behind us stood the trees on which we would be hung, and in front was the artillery." The cauldron becomes an apologetic symbol of Germans under Hitler's rule: "The German people were in the same situation as we were on the front. One can survive an enemy barrage, but not a firing squad."[356]

In a siege, space compresses. "Ever further. The cauldron tighter. Men perish uncounted," writes Theodor Plievier in *Stalingrad* (1945): "In shrinking space they withdraw concentrically back to the middle," only to be delivered to the annihilation they collectively unleashed and the judgment each individually deserves.[357] At the extremes, time shrinks with space: "The dimensions vanish," observes Jünger.[358] And in the so-called "cauldron literature" of the late 1940s and 1950s, as German soldiers trickled home from Soviet prison camps, the besieged were imagined to have been jettisoned from the historical continuum: "These service-men were 'finished,' [...] were without a past and without a future."[359] Jünger experiences siege in flashbacks to some distant past—the Persian Wars, classical times, Jerusalem's destruction in 70 CE, Bosch's "war against unbelievers"—that suddenly become present. After Voroshilovsk, the situation worsens. In Maykop on the banks of the Belaya, Jünger learns there are "too many places that are off limits to me" and wonders "if it might be good to visit these places of terror as a witness in order to see and remember what sort of people the perpetrators and the victims are."[360] But then he hesitates: "There are also limits to what we are capable of seeing." Ascending the notched ravine of the Pshish to the "utterly devastated town of Kurinskij,"[361] he passes spectacles that "the eye notices": a dead horse, the flesh of its upper body stripped clean by starving soldiers, "its ribcage and frozen blue and red intestines [...] like a detail from an anatomical atlas"; woodpeckers pecking at brittle wood, as "their bright raspberry breasts shone here and there against the snowy tree trunks."[362]

The approach of Christmas increases Jünger's forebodings. Sinking deeper into the cauldron, which in the steep, narrow, flame-filled ravine looks indeed like a hellish kettle, he receives from Gretha, his wife, "a holiday cake with hazelnuts from the vicarage garden"—and from Schmitt, a letter announcing that nihilism "is the urge to be incinerated in a crematorium."[363] Jünger would later seek to answer this provocation through the image of soldiers in trench warfare. Knowing they have nothing to lose, they go "over the top." Junger had just posted his letter to Schmitt describing the vision from the goods cable lift. The event happened a day before, on December 22—that is when *Strahlungen* dates it. The published account intensifies the Boschian optic. Now the ruined abutment has "Romanesque windows" and the shouting officer "peers out through one of the fissures in the way people look out of those hollow eggs in Bosch paintings, and glimpse bizarre machines."[364] Jünger peers down at the Pshish valley and its hellish travelers— like ants, hundreds and thousands of bearers in long lines. From an even greater height, "swaying" next to the crumbling abutment "on a narrow board swinging over the river, both fists clenched around a cable," he gazes at the prospect below.

> I comprehend the landscape like a picture in one of those moments that goes deeper than any painting. The little ripples down below take on something stiff and eternally frozen in time, a bit like the pale edges of the scales on the body of a snake.[365]

This "picture deeper than any painting" channels Bosch in both structure and detail. Elevated high above ground, from the position *sub specie infernitatis* that the Netherlandish painter established as his triptychs' characteristic point of view, a groundless eye looks down into the depths, there to lose itself in the visual— seeing "figures who defecate cranes."[366] For Jünger, Bosch was not just a painter among painters, but the complete realization of the pictorial itself: a synopsis, or "seeing together," of the whole of life as an excessive energy that equally and interchangeably fuels humans, animals, plants, molecules, and machine.[367] The force that caused Lucifer to revel and fall to earth, there to corrupt Eve, Adam, and humankind, and that fuels the engines of hell for all eternity, is the same force that makes each and every element within the visual synopsis become, upon inspection, something different: the man that is a tree, a boat, a brothel, an anus, and a duck.

At Kurinskij the Boschian worldscape sparks an equal Bosch-like inward turn—an introspection like the world-renouncing one that the hermit saints perform themselves and demand from us. On December 31, New Year's Eve, Jünger confronts the "forest of the *lemures*" head on. Hearing of "monstrous atrocities," of trains "mentioned that carried Jews into poison gas tunnels," he suddenly remembers "good old Potard back in Paris," a Jewish apothecary, "who was so worried about his wife" and who, by now, had probably been killed in one such train. "I am overcome by a loathing for the uniforms, the epaulettes, the medals, the weapons, all the glamour I loved so much." Where before he saw men "as though through a telescope pointed at the moon," now the *lemures* have become concrete and real, as has the perpetrator. "That terrible old saying applies to him as well as to his victims: 'This is you.' "[368]

Jünger left the Caucasus a week later, returning first to his home in Kirchhorst, then back to Paris for his second two-year sojourn. On January 4, 1944, he reports, "Air-raid alarms [...] are almost a regular occurrence. I use the time to examine the *Altar of the Last Judgement* by Hieronymus Bosch in a book by Baldass. Dr. Göpel gave me this recent publication as a present."[369] An art historian and an important collector and supporter of Max Beckmann, Erhard Göpel traveled Europe gathering looted Jewish art for an unrealized Führermuseum in Hitler's hometown of Linz. Together with SS-Officer Bruno Lohse (Hermann Göring's chief art-looter) he helped steal large parts of the vast Alphonse Schloss collection from its Jewish owners. After the war, and the painter's death in 1950, Göpel would remake himself into the pious protector of Beckman's legacy, co-founding the Max Beckmann Society and compiling, with his wife Barbara Göpel, the definitive catalogue raisonné of Beckmann's paintings.

The Nazi art agent gifted to Jünger Ludwig von Baldass's 1943 monograph on Hieronymus Bosch. The book sparked revelations. "These paintings," writes Jünger, "are puzzle pictures of horror that continue to reveal new and frightening details." What distinguishes Bosch from all other painters is "his literal vision," which also has a "prophetic" character. "One can actually discern the shapes of fighter bombers and submarines on these panels." Bosch's monstrosities do not merely resemble or foreshadow weapons of mass destruction. By a quantum wormhole in time, they already *are* those weapons. But neither do Bosch's visions stand outside the flow of time. "How apposite is the image of the naked man: in order to propel weird machines he runs like a squirrel, on a spoke-studded wheel."[370] Time passes manically on, but the human remains trapped in the permanent emergency of its own volition.

On January 2, 1943, on embossed letterhead, the "Prussian State Council Professor Carl Schmitt" wrote to Gretha Jünger hoping to ease her fears during Ernst's mission to the Caucasus. He reports that her husband, in a recent letter just received, had portrayed the "muddy forests of the East very vividly as a H. Bosch landscape." That portrayal, Schmitt adds, was "a magnificent document of his physically and mentally secure eye."[371] The jurist's praise, that Jünger—a writer famous for his acute and dispassionate gaze—could behold unspeakable carnage that implicates him with a safe and certain eye, brings to mind the infamous words

Heinrich Himmler spoke in secret to senior SS officers in Poznań in October 1943: "Most of you know what it means when 100 bodies lie together, when 500 lie there or when 1000 lie there. To have seen this through, and—with the exceptions due to human weaknesses—to have remained decent [*anständig*], that has made us tough. It is a never written, never to be written page of glory."[372] Detachment, the ability to perpetrate the killing of millions of innocent men, women, and children while remaining a respectable father, husband, and German: that, for Himmler, was the highest virtue. In Schmitt's estimation, Jünger's Boschian epiphany in the Caucasus documented such detachment magnificently.

Berlin, 1947

By coincidence Bosch's art first fell into my hands thanks to Ludwig von Baldass's Bosch monograph—the book Jünger pored over in Paris in 1944. That big volume had a special meaning for me as a child because of its special provenance. My father had literally pulled it out from the rubble of a collapsed apartment building in postwar Berlin. Until recently gray dust was discoverable in its binding. Born Jewish in Vienna, he had fled his native city in 1938 after Hitler annexed Austria. He managed to escape via Italy to New York, where he worked as a graphic designer creating posters and book jackets. Drafted into the US Army, he served in Washington and in London in the propaganda branch of the Office of Strategic Services (OSS)—the predecessor of the CIA. After the Allied victory in Europe, he traveled in the entourage of General Lucius Clay designing posters and informational brochures for Germans under occupation while also documenting the devastated country with his pen and Leica camera. By August 1945 he had settled in Berlin. Wandering the divided city in an officer's uniform, he filled scores of tissue-paper sketchpads with intimate drawings of life among the ruins. He reported to us that whereas some of his fellow officers had the entire content of abandoned houses packed up and shipped back to the States, he took the Bosch monograph as his sole salvaged souvenir. His paintings, drawings, and photographs were mementos enough.

Late in 1945 the OSS sent him to sketch from life the chief defendants of the war crimes trials at their arraignment at Nuremberg. He came down with shingles and, furloughed on medical grounds, he made his way alone by train to Vienna. There he confirmed what he had long suspected: that his entire extended family had been forcibly transported from Vienna and murdered, most of them at a secret extermination site near Minsk—the specific location outside the village of

Maly Trostinets would come to light only decades later.[373] Profoundly shaken and unready to move back to New York, he joined the Office of Military Government, United States (OMGUS) in Berlin and began obsessively to paint. On March 30, 1947, fifty-five of his drawings and paintings went on display at the Haus am Waldsee. Built in 1922 for a wealthy Jewish clothier, this small mansion in the district of Berlin Zehlendorf had been turned into a gallery and performance space, with a program aiming to recuperate artists who had been ostracized or persecuted during the Nazi period. The first nine exhibitions held there were group shows of established German artists, but the tenth was the solo exhibition of my father, an unknown thirty-two-year-old Viennese American painter living in Berlin.

The curators of my father's exhibition in Berlin were mostly Americans serving in OMGUS's Monuments, Fine Arts, and Archives Section—the famous "Monuments Men" charged mainly with recovering artworks stolen by the Nazis from Jews, museums, universities, and religious institutions. In the first months after the war ended, the United States had been most concerned with denazification. Insofar as it reached out in an organized way to ordinary German people, OMGUS did so according to what it termed the "confrontation policy." The aim—thus ran a memo of the Office of War Information already in 1944—was "to make them [the German people] realize that they are guilty."[374] The most famous instances of this were the twenty-four or so "confrontation visits," in which American field commanders forced Germans living in the vicinity of concentration camps to tour the sites. But by June 1945, American and British intelligence communities grew concerned about the wisdom of this approach, particularly in light of a powerful propaganda campaign by the Soviet occupiers, who shifted the blame for Nazi atrocities from the German people to external forces: big business, monopoly capitalism, and Western imperialism, all—it was claimed—presently threatening Germany anew in the form of the American occupiers.[375] US policy therefore shifted to winning German hearts and minds in the hopes of containing Soviet expansion and establishing a strong constitutional democracy. This new strategy placed an emphasis on visual propaganda, mostly through the medium of film, but also through painting, photography, and the graphic arts.

My father's show at the Haus am Waldsee belonged to this endeavor. The first exhibition of American modern art in postwar German, it remained a singularity: the next exhibition in that venue showed American children's drawings, and OMGUS never again sponsored modern art in this way. To peer into the minds of Germans in a state of siege, the show's organizers created a special printed questionnaire, with eleven questions prefaced by a paragraph stating that responses were not mandatory and could be made anonymously and at home: "Don't be afraid! This questionnaire is not a questionnaire."[376] Germans were used to frightening questionnaires inquiring about affiliations with the Nazi Party: recall the questionnaire given to Schmitt during his first detainment, with its embarrassing question, "Who are you?" By answering such questionnaires, many Germans hoped for clearance certificates—*Persilscheine*, as they were nicknamed, after the Persil brand of laundry detergent. Only 14 percent of the fifteen hundred visitors to my father's exhibition completed the form. Some respondents said that they went to the show to see modern American art but left with an impression that the artist was not a typical American. To the penultimate question, "Do you believe the painter intended to cause an emotional shock in the viewer?" the answers were mixed. Some praised the artist's honesty, others objected to his bleak outlook. One complained that whoever the painter was, he portrayed the Germans as an outsider and had not experienced all that Germans had had to live through.[377] Many of the works on display clearly referenced the disasters of war, and one or two gestured towards the Holocaust. The show's centerpiece, an autumnal landscape titled *My Parents*, portrayed my father's murdered mother and father on separate paths in the Vienna Woods. In this the exhibition was unique. It was the only show sponsored by the US Military Government that concerned recent German history, and it would be decades before Holocaust-related art would be shown in Germany in such a prominent way.

The exhibition was a considerable success. German newspapers compared my father's satirical fantasy to Bosch and Bruegel. American magazines picked up on the exhibition and the artist's unusual story, paving the way for successful shows in New York in 1947 and 1948. *Life* magazine reported that the exhibition "created a sensation in Germany." The journal's chief critic lauded the paintings contained in it as "the best to date to have come out of the aftermath of the war." *Time* magazine praised the painter as "the find of the year" and predicted for him a brilliant career. A few reviewers were more critical, objecting to the painter's "hysterical I-told-you-so" attitude and advising him to get over his "savage bitterness."[378] Such bitterness, they conceded, may be understandable, given the painter's personal circumstances: his entire family had been murdered by the Nazis, so of course he feels bad, but it is 1947 and time to get over it! In the German press, these circumstances remained wholly unmentioned, and even the exhibition catalogue speaks of the paintings only in formal and art historical terms, as negotiating between the two tendencies in modern art: abstraction on the one hand, and storytelling on the other. One prominent German critic noted vaguely that the painter had lived in Vienna, but when that was he did not say.[379] These reviewers surely knew more than they chose to write, and some had interviewed

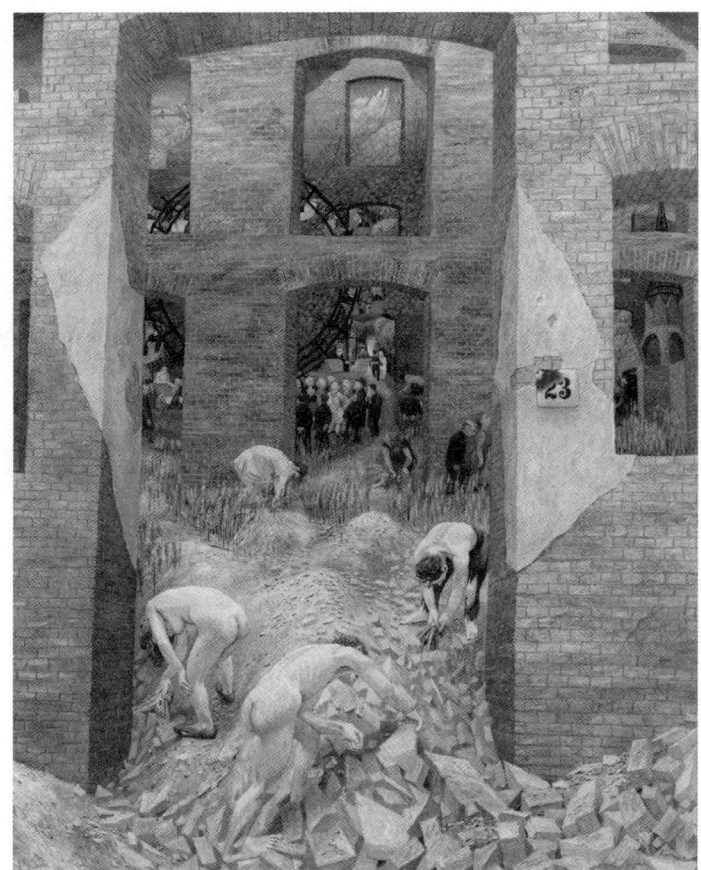

FIG. 40. Henry Koerner, *The Skin of Our Teeth*, 1946. Oil on masonite, 111.7 × 90.2 cm. Sheldon Museum of Art, University of Nebraska-Lincoln, Lincoln, Nebraska

the artist, whose native tongue was German, and who spoke English with a thick Viennese accent.

Returning to America in 1947, my father brought with him his prodigious artistic output and nothing else, save for army badges, his officer's uniform, an air pistol, and Baldass's *Hieronymus Bosch*. To that book was attached the tale of its discovery in the rubble. In picturing this event I was also guided by one of the pictures my father painted in Berlin. It featured a bombed-out apartment building with naked survivors pulling rags from heaps of bricks. In 1948 the Sheldon Memorial Art Museum in Nebraska acquired the painting, so I knew the work only from a reproduction (fig. 40). I also understood that my father based the foreground ruin on his own apartment building in Vienna, which he had documented in 1946 in a slightly blurred snapshot labeled (on the back) *My Home*. The Ferris wheel in the background was also Viennese. Evoking the Prater amusement park, which stood a few blocks away from his home, it juxtaposed bare survival to the tendency to forget. For me this painting depicted my father discovering Baldass's

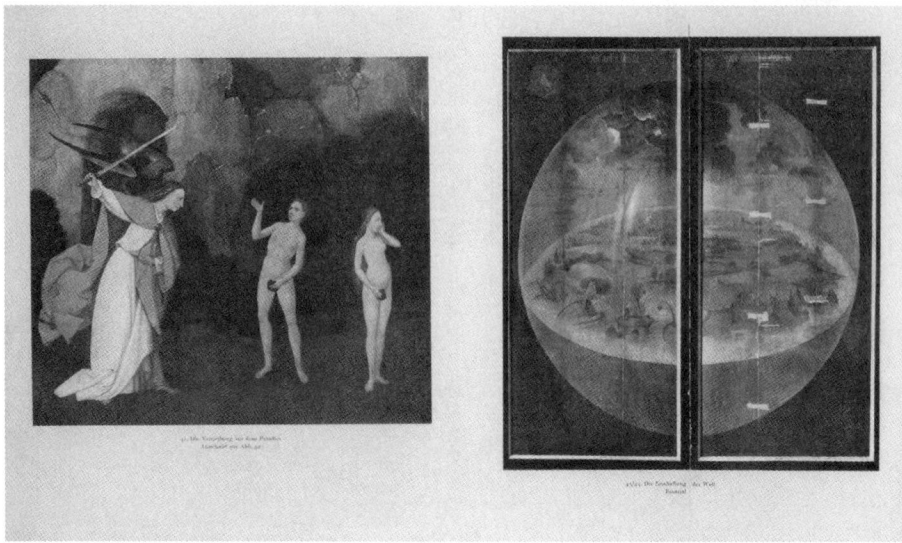

FIG. 41. Pages from Ludwig von Baldass, *Hieronymus Bosch* (Vienna: Schroll, 1943). 52 × 35 cm

monograph in the rubble. And to my eyes as a child, the illustrations contained in Baldass's book also looked eerily like my father's paintings. The old black and white illustrations of judgment and hell became my mental picture of Germany after the war. I was certain that there existed only one such book in the world and that it had been created for me.

The book's binding has disintegrated and the cheap wartime paper on which the text was printed has become so brittle that I have not dared to leaf through the pages in decades. Gently opening it today I observe that the plates—printed separately on glossy stock—are excellent and pristine, although the *Garden of Delights*, at the time it was photographed, was in its poor pre-restoration state. Paint surfaces appear severely abraded and deep vertical fissures have opened where the panels' wooden planks are joined. I also notice that Baldass, or his Viennese publisher Anton Schroll, printed, on the left page facing the gatefold plates of the triptych, a color detail from one of Bosch's Expulsion scenes. With one hand Eve covers her sex, with the other, she touches her cheek. By this arrangement, she seems embarrassed and shocked not by the world into which she and Adam will be exiled, but instead by Baldass's gatefold illustration, with the *Garden*'s outer shutters, leaves of paper, waiting to be opened (fig. 41). Bosch's puzzle pictures never solace. Instead, they besiege everywhere always.

Max Beckmann

Cambridge, Massachusetts 2014

On November 16, 2014, Harvard's art museums reopened their doors. Closed for six years during renovation, they presented to the public not only a new building, Renzo Piano's enlargement and stratified elevation of a Georgian Revival edifice built in 1925. The museums proposed for themselves a new identity, or rather *identities*, plural: because the one building now houses three museums, each of which previously had its own building, each with a different history, collection, and purpose. The oldest is the Fogg Museum. Founded in 1895, and housed after 1925 in the edifice that Renzo Piano was to transform, the Fogg served to train scholars, conservators, and museum professionals in the history of art. With an extensive study collection of casts and originals, labs for conservation and material analysis, a specialized library, and classrooms and auditoria equipped with state-of-the-art lantern projectors, it was the world's first integrated art history facility. The youngest of the three, the Arthur M. Sackler Museum, was founded in 1977. Housed in 1985 in its own building across the street from the Fogg, it took possession of the Asian, Islamic, and ancient Mediterranean collections of the Fogg. The third museum, the Busch-Reisinger, was founded in 1903 as the Germanic Museum. Ninety years later most of its holdings were moved from their imposing home in Adolphus Busch Hall to a new wing of the Fogg—the narrow, leaky, short-lived Werner Otto Hall. Its identity also morphed from "Germanic" art to the nebulous but more palatable one of "art from central and northern Europe, with an emphasis on German speaking countries."

Of the three museums now under one roof, it is the Busch-Reisinger that has the most contested identity—leaving aside the heated debate over the Sackler's name. Its holdings overlap with the Fogg's, which collects "Western art from the Middle Ages to the present day," including some German art. The confusion has not been helped by the fact that Piano's new building, being an expansion of the old Fogg Museum, is still called by almost everyone the Fogg. In the current installation, moreover, all Busch works that date from before 1900 and after 1945, along with many in between, have been integrated into the Fogg's non-national display—Beckmann's 1941–42 triptych *Actors*, currently in storage, concluded the original "Modern and Contemporary Art" hang. But for largely legal reasons, the Busch also maintains its own designated suite of galleries. So, to give this museum within the museums a distinctive face, the curators decided to hang, as the focal point of a long architectural vista visible free-of-charge from the public courtyard, a most eye-catching object (plate 18).

Their decision makes sense. Max Beckmann's *Self-Portrait in Tuxedo* is the Busch's most famous treasure, the artifact most often requested for loans. It is an "iconic" work—to use that overused expression. It is iconic of the Busch, having graced the cover of most general publications on the museum. It is iconic of its maker, portraying him, exemplifying his art, and giving his likeness an aura like that of sacred images. The painting is also iconic of an entire artistic style or movement, that of Expressionism. And it's iconic of the Weimar Republic and therefore of a decisive epoch in the history of Germany, and of the Europe centered on, and unsettled by, Germany.

In the 2014 installation, Beckmann presided over an art historical trajectory that ran from the Munich, Berlin, and the Vienna Secessionists through German Expressionism to the Bauhaus. In singling out this historical era and this trajectory, the curators reached a decision about their museum's identity. No longer housing the thousand-year span of German art, and jettisoning postwar and contemporary art, the Busch galleries time-capsule one brief epoch, what might be termed German "Modernism." This decision also makes sense. For the general public, this epoch represents an important climax in the history of art. German art is felt to have only two internationally recognized highpoints. One flowered during the early sixteenth century, in the art of Albrecht Dürer and his contemporaries—Lucas Cranach, Hans Holbein, Matthias Grünewald, Albrecht Altdorfer, etcetera. The other unfolded in the early twentieth century, in the art of Franz Marc, Emil Nolde, Käthe Kollwitz, Ernst Ludwig Kirchner, and (though he developed later and had a different approach) Max Beckmann. Due to this renown, German Expressionist works from the Busch, including Beckmann's large, three-canvas masterpiece *The Actors*, have also been inserted into rooms elsewhere in the museum dedicated to international Modernism. The distinctive "Modernism" displayed in the dedicated Busch galleries therefore required a local identity, and it is this that Beckmann's *Self-Portrait* was meant to evidence. And understandably so, for as one admirer put it in 1924, in the volume that included Wilhelm Fraenger's Beckmann text, "If I should now attempt to conceive of a specifically German art, its name would be Beckmann."[1]

Beckmann's *Self-Portrait* does exert a defining force over the surrounding artworks, as if they all stood under its dominion. This is partly because all seem, as we do when we glimpse it, subject to the sitter's penetrating gaze. From afar, the work looks less like an artist's self-portrait than like one of those large, official portraits you sometimes see at the entrance to single-collector museums, with the donor presiding in effigy over his or her holdings—Baron Hans Heinrich Thyssen-Bornemisza's portrait by Lucien Freud at the Thyssen museum in Madrid comes to mind. Beckmann looks less like a painter than like a noble patron. He might be mistaken for Adolphus Busch, the beer magnate after whom the Busch Museum was named. One critic, writing in 1927 when paint on the canvas was still wet, noted that Beckmann, while posed as a "deadly-earnest" critic of society, "presents himself in pristine evening wear like a young baron of industry."[2]

To do justice to the impact of this person, this persona, one ought to stand before the original picture, or better yet: to enter into a conversation in front of it. It has been mainly in my role as an ambassador for the Busch-Reisinger Museum, rather than as a scholar, that I have engaged with Beckmann's *Self-Portrait*. I have a much narrower purview on this artist than I do on Bosch, whom I have grappled with for decades, or on Kentridge, where my connections are deep and personal. I have become familiar with this one object and its remarkable career while remaining largely oblivious to the extensive literature on Beckmann and to the artist's arcane personal mythology. For if I am asked to excite visitors from the general public using one object always on display in Harvard's museums, I always choose this work over ones I know more about. In a gallery setting, I anyway much prefer to stand back and let an object speak through others in the room. Or as Sigmund Freud wrote of psychoanalytical practice in its mature phase, when he realized that no amount of memory-retrieval and interpretation could effect a cure, I try to stay "content to study the prevailing surface-level" of the group's response and use my "interpretative skills chiefly for the purpose of identifying the resistance manifest there," and making the group "conscious" of those resistances.[3] And this painting, for me more than any in the Harvard Art Museums, lends itself magnificently to this. Through repeated sessions with Beckmann's *Self-Portrait* I have learned to manage conversation, leaving openings for surprise, disagreement, emotion, and doubt. Historical questions inevitably arise—about tuxedos, cigarettes, the artist's biography, and the work's initial impact: what people thought of it back then, when the paint was still wet. Most of these queries can be answered with dispatch. Indeed, the conversation requires little outside information to keep it flowing, and where it flows remains comfortably within the bounds of what the work was meant to achieve—if such a thing can be measured by published critical responses of the time and by the written testimony of the artist himself.

From these sessions, I have gathered some common themes that typically arise. Such themes serve as talking points for further conversations undertaken in front of the painting. The first is usually Beckmann's pose. That he has had to pose for himself, standing still before a mirror while also painting his likeness, sparks comment on the puzzling quirks of self-portraiture—how, because Beckmann painted from a mirror, the cigarette in what seems the artist's left hand would have been held in his reflected right hand, and how, because he is both the painter and the sitter, Beckmann could not have used that hand simultaneously for smoking and painting. Recognized as artificial, the entire pose gets labeled variously as confident, dandyish, boastful, masculine, feminine, queer, and self-ironical, although with a certain agreement that Beckmann seems comfortable where he is. His relaxed *contrapposto* stance signals a casual coming to rest, and his hands—the one resting on his hip, the other held close—gather his body at its center of gravity. This man, the picture tells us, can stand here for a long time. The cigarette gives him something to do, although he has allowed the ash precariously to build up as he looks out at you.

This is probably the image's most remarkable feature: its confrontational relation to the viewer. Like Bosch's dangerous tableaux that warn, "Beware, God sees," Beckmann's *Self-Portrait* dramatizes its sovereign apriority, as it will be looking at you before you glimpse it, and after. The painter's gaze is too unblinking to be felt as friendly. Locking eyes with this larger-than-life-sized effigy, you will be the first to back down. Frontality comes naturally to self-portraits, because the maker will tend to look straight at the mirror. But as everyone who has tried to make a self-portrait will soon discover, it is especially difficult to paint a convincing frontal likeness. Physiognomic peculiarities are better rendered slightly from the side, in three-quarters view—profile views may be easier still, although these are hard work for a self-portraitist. In three-quarters, the bridge of the nose has one silhouetted outline, and the characterizing projections of cheek and chin are easier to capture. Beckmann insists on the frontal pose, and instead of clarifying his features in relief, he cuts them through by a wildly erratic, formally disintegrating shadow. In front of the actual canvas on the gallery wall, the shadow has an even more divisive effect. Its surface is matt, being built up of layers of lean paint, whereas the lighter passages are executed in oilier paint and therefore are shiny. The represented highlights on Beckmann's face thus become reflective highlights on a painted surface. But instead of contributing to the illusion of volume, the play of light and shadow fragments the likeness dramatically.

The shift from the painting as image or likeness to the painting as brute fact of oil paint on canvas is something Beckmann engineered his *Self-Portrait* to accomplish. The flickering contrast of light and dark on which the portrait's illusions rest stands off against the undifferentiated flatness of the black tuxedo. And that all-over black is in fact composed of a complex mix of lamp blacks (from soot collected from burning oil), bone blacks (from charred bones), and lead white. Beckmann conjures the tuxedo's flatness over against the bewildering abstraction of the picture's background, which suggests at once a curtained balcony and a painter's studio, and features complexly abraded, scraped, and layered areas that baffle the eye even on close inspection. With this collapse, where there is neither space nor light nor likeness but only that painted *thing* made of paint-covered fabric and hanging framed in the gallery, someone in every group will likely refer to the work's place in the history of art—how many painters in Beckmann's time and earlier had aspired to achieve a flatness that would undo centuries of illusion-making, thereby putting their art on a new path, the so-called "modern" one, where the medium itself *is* the reality. That path haunted Beckmann throughout his career, from his 1903 encounter with Paul Cézanne—in his words the last old master who became the first "new master"—through his enmity, raging in the 1930s, against the "clique" of collectors of Picasso.[4] He addressed this, the dominant artistic tendency, throughout his writings. Taking up the challenge of Modernist abstraction, he proposed that painting should not merely show painting itself, since that would make it mere decoration. Instead, painting is, in his words, "the single true reality that there is," because it alone traverses both the illusory and the real.[5] We will return to this inflated claim, but at this point I would note that through his divided likeness, and with the background play between light and dark, Beckmann asks us actively to realize his effigy, bringing his person into focus. Observe also how the artist cast his eyes almost completely in shadow, dramatizing his epiphany.

For this particular confrontation, Beckmann has donned what in German is called a *Smoking* and in Britain a dinner jacket. A hundred and fifty years ago a prototype of this outfit was worn at the Autumn Ball at Tuxedo Park, a country club south of New York, hence in America the term "tuxedo." Used for evenings in a club or private house rather than at formal dinners or public occasions, which required white tie and tails, the tuxedo bespoke casual elegance and membership in an exclusive social set. Encountering Beckmann today in this dress makes one feel excluded and underdressed, unless, of course, one was fortunate enough to be at the museum's festive reopening dressed, as many were, in a tuxedo. But even then, Beckmann will have been there before you and seems more at ease. And in how and where he stands, it's clear he can leave, perhaps through the door just to the left. Again, the sense that he belongs creates the impression that instead of you being the audience to him, he is giving you an audience with him.

What better image for the Busch to station front and center in its galleries than this picture that seems so eminently to belong! But the tuxedo also signals a certain kind of belonging. The Viennese critic and architect Adolf Loos captured this in his commentary on men's clothing. Loos wrote that an article of dress is modern if, "when wearing it on a particular occasion in the *best* society at the center of one's culture, one attracts as little attention to oneself as possible."[6] Loos published this statement in 1898, in Vienna's progressive *Neue Freie Presse*,

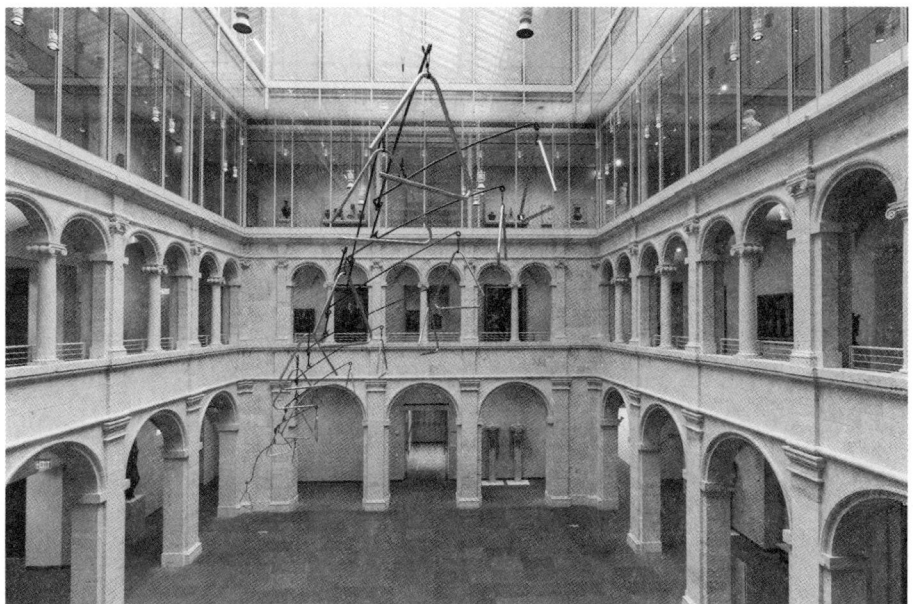

FIG. 42. Harvard Art Museums, *View of Interior Courtyard*. Installation shot from the Harvard Art Museums, Gallery 1000, *Calderwood Courtyard*, featuring Carlos Amorales, *Triangle Constellation* (2015)

and what he meant was that one should disappear into the woodwork, but only at the center of society—which for him meant high society in London. Loos noted that if you actually showed up in Vienna wearing casually fitting London attire you might be laughed at, but only because the Viennese were still backward in their dress. Viennese elegance would stand out in London, but to a well-traveled person it also stood out in Vienna, as it seemed ridiculously conspicuous. Loos was saying that to become *cosmopolitan* was to disappear into one's surroundings, and that to do so was the mark of being a *modern* person. Modern persons do not distinguish themselves as individuals through their clothing. Instead, they endeavor to vanish into the crowd—but then to distinguish themselves elsewhere: in government, commerce, or art.

Beckmann's *Self-Portrait* thus looked right at home in the new Harvard Art Museums. Icon of both an individual and a specific culture, it signaled in 2014 the Busch-Reisinger's distinct identity. But dressed in the uniform of the cosmopolitan, it projected German art into an international framework. That was the framework that Renzo Piano gave to the building's design (fig. 42). The original Fogg Museum had been cosmopolitan already, with its classicizing Georgian exterior and arcaded, two-story travertine courtyard replicating the façade of Antonio da Sangallo's beautiful canon house at San Biagio, in Montepulciano. Opening that courtyard to glazed study rooms above, and to conservation labs higher still, and with galleries reached from a public indoor thoroughfare, the new museum preached the values of transparency, openness, and borderless exchange. How then did Beckmann's canvas enter this cosmopolis?

Frankfurt, 1927

Beckmann probably began work on the self-portrait in August 1927. By November he was strategizing its unveiling, juggling offers from the Mannheim Kunsthalle and the Flechtheim Gallery in Berlin. In the end, he premiered the painting at the 1928 Berlin Secession, then showed it at the exhibition "Deutsche Kunst" in Düsseldorf, where it received the Gold Medal. By June 1928 it had been sold to the Nationalgalerie in Berlin through the intervention of Germany's greatest champion of modern art, the critic and novelist Julius Meier-Graefe.[7] By that time Beckmann referred to it as "das große Selbstporträt im Smoking."[8] The title indicates the importance of the costume for him. That this "large self-portrait" needed a distinguishing label, though, derived from the fact that Beckmann made so many of them—about a hundred self-portraits in various media, far more even than other prolific German and Austrian self-portraitists such as Lovis Corinth, Kokoschka, and Egon Schiele, indeed more than any significant artist since Rembrandt. Like Rembrandt, and—for the German tradition that would have been foremost in mind—like Albrecht Dürer, Beckmann cast his person in a variety of characters and roles: as medic, as manic, as dandiacal man about town; also, as sailor, *flâneur*, Jupiter, prisoner, conjurer, circus barker, tightrope walker, clown, and mysterious king. "What are you? What am I? Those are the questions that constantly persecute and torment me, and perhaps also play some part in my art," noted Beckmann in a lecture delivered (in German) in London in 1938: "For the self is the great veiled mystery of the world."[9]

Of these personae, the clown and king are perhaps the most telling. A master of masquerade, the clown projects the artist as a lowbrow entertainer, and also as a fool, outsider, victim. In a self-portrait of this variety, painted in 1921, Beckmann, carrying what looks to be a bloody slapstick, twists his stiff right arm (really his left arm as beheld in the mirror) around towards us, as if to display a malady or a wound, as Christ does his stigmata in the often gruesome iconography of German "Man of Sorrows" effigies (fig. 43). The gesture also repeats that of the torture victim in the large breakthrough canvas *The Night*, begun in 1918, right after the war, and completed in 1919 (fig. 44). There the arm's awkward pose suggests that it has been wrenched and broken, as is happening to his other arm—observe

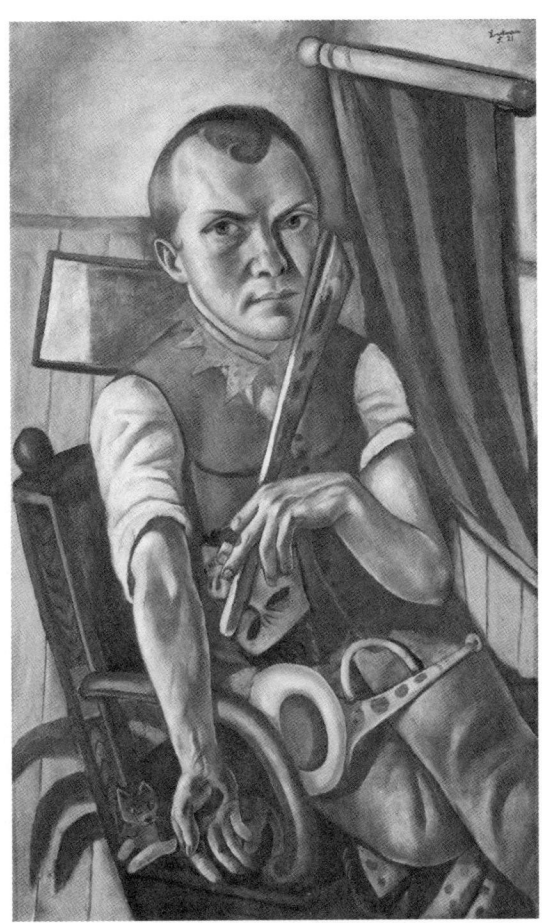

FIG. 43. Max Beckmann, *Self-Portrait as Clown*, 1921. Oil on canvas, 100 × 59 cm. Von der Heydt Museum, Wuppertal

how the woman between the bandaged torturer and his strangled victim wears a zigzagging clown's collar. It was a guiding principle of Expressionism that artists not only feel the intense sensations they depict; they should allow unbridled lust, violent loathing, orgiastic pleasure, and convulsive pain to direct and misdirect their pen, burin, or brush. In *Self-Portrait as a Clown* Beckmann's mask has come off (it grimaces from under his slapstick), revealing the backstage of artistic performance. In 1950, just months before his death, Beckmann wrote that the cardinal virtue for painters was "keen awareness and uncompromising self-criticism."[10] Amplifying the public scorn for modern artists as charlatans, his clown persona mixes self-criticism with self-pity, subversion with docility.

The mysterious king, ostensibly standing for authority, is the clown's dangerous alter ego—Beckmann's monumental *Departure* triptych focuses on him (plate 20). In the German Baroque theatrical tradition of the *Trauerspiel*, the prince, whether tyrannical like Marlowe's Tamburlaine or melancholy like Shakespeare's

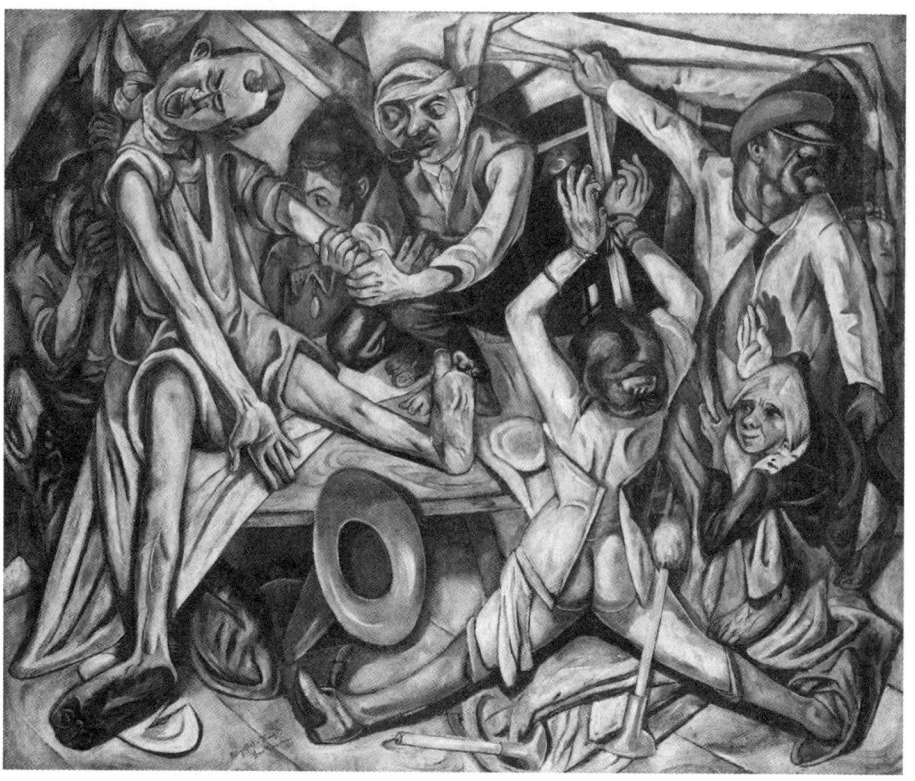

FIG. 44. Max Beckmann, *The Night*, 1918–19. Oil on canvas, 133 × 153 cm. Kunstsammlung Nordrhein-Westfalen, Düsseldorf

Hamlet, is buffeted by history. He is the sovereign, defined by Schmitt as "he who decides on the exception." In 1925, Walter Benjamin submitted (unsuccessfully) his study of this material to the Philosophical Faculty of the University of Frankfurt as his academic *Habilitation*. By Benjamin's account—written in response to Schmitt's—the prince of the *Trauerspiel* is fatally unable to decide, since already in the early modern period, during the permanent siege-state of confessional warfare in Germany, secular sovereignty lost its connection to salvation history. The jester becomes a king, and comedy (the *Lustspiel*) "migrates" into *Trauerspiel*: "The physical appearance of the actors themselves, particularly of the king, who shows himself in full regalia, could have a rigid, puppet-life effect: 'Princes, / to whom the purple is inborn, / are sick without their scepter.'"[11] Beckmann never read Benjamin, but he understood the theatrical origins of his puppet-king persona. In *Actors*, another monumental triptych gifted to Harvard in 1955, a garishly costumed king with features of the artist as a young man stabs himself on the boards of a crude stage, with the orchestra pit occupied by thugs. The collapse—in 1942, when Beckmann completed the work under dire conditions in Amsterdam—of any dream of artistic sovereignty takes the histrionic form of self-immolation and of histrionics per se. Decisive action becomes play-acting and history turns into farce, as happens in the *Trauerspiel*.

What, then, does the tuxedo project? Beckmann had already dressed up in one for a self-portrait from 1923 (plate 19). But how differently he wears it. With his bowler and scarf left on, he looks to be either coming or going, but not comfortably remaining. Tensely erect, with one arm pressed to his side and the burning cigar held like a weapon, he appears uneasy in his role, as if he were forced into it. In 1924 Beckmann is reported to have arrived in a tuxedo for a casual lunch at an elegant home. Some guests laughed at the misstep, while others were impressed by his audacity. Having "singled himself out by selecting a costume," he promptly sat down right beside the wealthy aristocrat Lilly von Mallinckrodt-Schnitzler, who would become one of his major patrons.[12] The 1923 canvas's cramped vertical format enhances the feeling of unease, as if posing were something Beckmann did half-willingly. Beckmann's stiff uprightness clashes with the kaleidoscopic backdrop. The curves of the curtain and moldings, together with the meanders and candy-striped fringe, subject the sitters to mechanical forces and counterforces, suggesting that equilibrium, both corporeal and formal, can only be achieved with effort. Beckmann's bright scarf wraps around his neck like a tentacle reaching from the backdrop to strangle him. It articulates a condition painted often by this artist and often diagnosed: the modern urban individual having to hold himself up against an increasing onslaught of sensations. The sociologist of the metropolis Georg Simmel, analyzing the gravity of Auguste Rodin's sculpture, wrote of the "latent heroism of every natural movement": the feat of the modern hero is merely to stand or successfully shift one's weight against a background of violent contesting forces.[13]

From its fragmentary features we can identify the self-portrait's setting as a theater. Pressed up against what looks to be the edge of a stage, Beckmann assumes a liminal identity between audience and performer. In other self-portraits, he inhabits this borderland in the guise of a circus barker. Even as artists project self-sovereignty, they have to drum up a public to pay for their art. In a 1927 essay titled "The Social Stance of the Artist by the Black Tightrope Walker," Beckmann declared—mockingly—that "the talent for advertisement is the prerequisite for the pursuit of the artistic calling [...]. Woe betide that miserable creatively inclined creature not able to subdue his obdurate spinal column in the course of daily bowing and scraping."[14] In the 1923 canvas, the dark tuxedo projects the persona of an impresario possessed—ironically—with too rigid a backbone to bow and scrape.

How then are we to parse the balance that Beckmann's later 1927 likeness displays? During the intervening five years the artist's fortunes had improved. In 1925, he accepted a professorship at the Städelschule in Frankfurt, and in that same year he married his second wife, Mathilde von Kaulbach, a singer and the patrician daughter of the distinguished Munich painter Friedrich August von Kaulbach. Nicknamed Quappi by her friends, she introduced Beckmann to an elite circle of patrons and cultural leaders. Germany's economic condition had also improved. The rampant inflation of the early 1920s gave way to fiscal stability (though only briefly: on May 13, 1927, "Black Friday," the Berlin stock market dropped by almost 40 percent, a harbinger of the global financial disaster that would strike two years later). But there is more behind Beckmann's comfort in his tuxedo than personal success and a strong economy. In 1918, after Germany's crushing defeat in World War I, Beckmann made headlines with shocking portrayals of human depravity. Executed over almost a full year, from 1918 to 1919, *The Night* transports the violence of war into a domestic interior. For the strangled man, the sexually violated woman, and the abducted child Beckmann used himself, his then-wife (Minna Beckmann-Tube), and their son Peter as models. At the time of its unveiling, the canvas would have had an explosive topical significance. On January 15, 1919, right-wing militia kidnapped, tortured, and murdered Rosa Luxemburg and Karl Liebknecht, dumping her body into Berlin's Landwehr Canal and his anonymously in a morgue.

This execution of two prominent revolutionary socialists had been tacitly sanctioned by the country's weak new Social Democratic government. That government, the first popularly elected one in all of Germany's history, had been formed in the city of Weimar, hence why the turbulent fourteen-year-long experiment in parliamentary democracy, between Germany's capitulation and Hitler's takeover in 1933, is commonly referred to as the Weimar Republic. We have already explored that polity's fatal flaws. Challenged economically by poverty, rampant inflation, unemployment, and the war debts levied by the Treaty of Versailles, destabilized politically by expansive emergency powers written into its constitution and by conspiracy theories—including the most poisonous one of an international conspiracy of Jews vengefully engineering the country's demise—the country stumbled from crisis to crisis in a perpetual state of exception. The defeated German army brought war back home, literally. With the republic's military restricted by treaty to one hundred thousand men, millions of demobilized veterans returned—defeated, traumatized, and often in possession of their guns and ammunition—to unemployment and poverty. Forming paramilitary groups, each protecting its political party, they substituted, officially or unofficially, for the police. The right-wing Freikorps quelled socialist and Communist uprisings, thus upholding the liberal regime that they loathed. Beckmann's *The Night* took aim both at the brutal assassins and at the politically paralyzed liberal bourgeoisie, who leave the dirty work to others. "Do you believe, you who ask, that you may already forget, that the war is over and done with? That it is history?" asked Benno Reifenberg in 1921 about *The Night*: "War *is*." It is true, the young critic adds, Beckmann's vision had the "blessing" of old German masters Matthias Grünewald and Gabriel Mälesskircher, who "saw" Christ's feet "swollen into lumps." But bridges back are of no help: "It is not about the past. It is about the here and now."[15]

Before World War I Beckmann had been a painter of outsize ambitions, though firmly on the measure of past artistic achievements. Working on large-format canvases in the grand tradition of Eugène Delacroix and Théodore Géricault, he specialized in disasters: the earthquake of Messina, the sinking of the Titanic, the Last Judgment, the biblical Flood, a sea of well-painted nudes in mortal combat titled simply *The Battle*. Real catastophe changed everything. After his first impressions of war as an observer on the eastern front, he volunteered for paramedical service, serving in the violent battles around Tannenberg, where almost a hundred thousand soldiers lost their lives, mostly Russian, but including his brother-in-law. In Belgium in 1915 he worked in a typhus unit and operating theater, suffered a nervous breakdown, and, after treatment in Frankfurt, returned to civilian life in 1917. His wartime letters to his wife, published in 1916, evince fascination with the horrors observed: "I saw fantastical things. In the half-lit shelter half-clothed men streaming with blood, being bandaged in white. Huge and painful in expression. New conception of the flagellation of Christ."[16] Artmaking became his purpose, and a defense: "I have been drawing, that safeguards one against death and danger."[17] Graphic media, especially resistant ones—sketching with a hard sharp reed pen or scratching with a metal or diamond needle on a metal printing plate—suited this endeavor. A drypoint from 1915 predicts these developments. The grenade of the print's title explodes not just the bodies, the coherence of which Beckmann had formerly preserved even in torture, mortal combat, and damnation; the sudden carnage of modern weaponry—what Ernst Jünger aestheticized as a "storm of steel"—ruins pictorial form, as flesh, blood, and shrapnel seem to splatter wildly across the picture plane.

For Benno Reifenberg "war *is*" because, once suffered, the wounds it inflicts, too terrible to be remembered, instead are repeated. In 1920, Freud wrote that the recurrent nightmares dreamt by shell-shocked war veterans fulfilled no wish. They thus contradicted the mind's normal regulatory principle, that of avoiding pain

and procuring pleasure. Freud argued that the sudden impact of extreme experience overwhelms the mind's representational abilities: "the effect of mechanized
violence" is caused by the "lack of any preparedness for anxiety." Traumatized
individuals deliberately re-experience the original distressing situation, repeating the past but without the means to recall its prototype. The living organism's
most elemental line of defense, repetition masters "the stimulus retrospectively,
by developing the anxiety whose omission was the cause of the traumatic neurosis."[18] If hysterical symptoms functioned like the protective bastions and glacis
built around a city, keeping dangerous memories out of mind—Nuremberg's
medieval bastions gave Freud this model—then repetition was what remains when
the siege walls fail.

Beckmann publicly promoted the understanding of his art as a nervous symptom of war trauma. *Hell*, a portfolio of eleven lithographs published in 1919 by
Israel Ber Neumann in Berlin, explores the inescapable after-images of combat.
Comparable in size to paintings, these sheets include a version of Beckmann's
much-heralded canvas *The Night*. During the war and for several years after, prints,
being cheaper and easier to transport, found more buyers than paintings. *Hell*
capitalized on Beckmann's notoriety in a way that suited the market. Printed
portfolios also furthered the artist's purpose by telling a backstory *about* his own

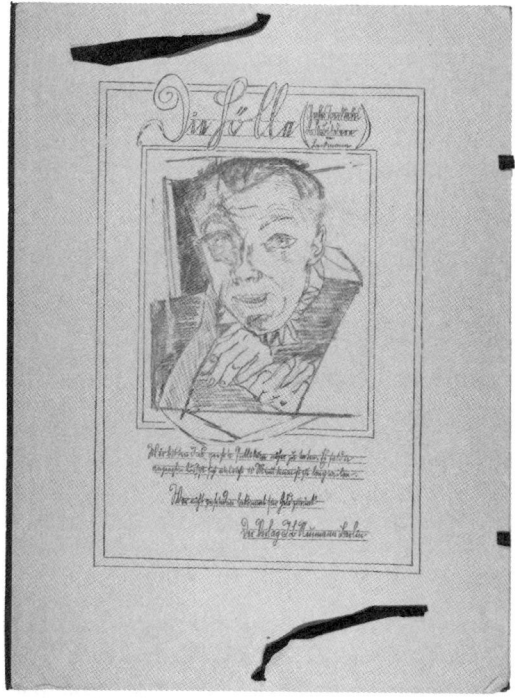

FIG. 45. Max Beckmann, *Self-Portrait*,
cover from *Hell* portfolio, published 1919.
Lithograph, 63.4 × 41.7 cm. Museum of
Modern Art, New York

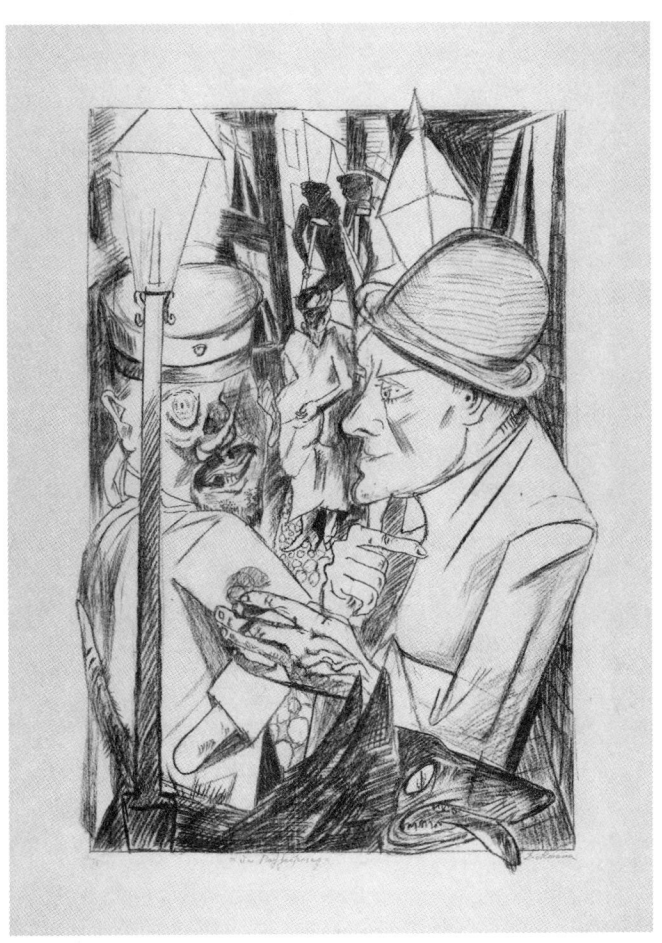

FIG. 46. Max Beckmann, *The Way Home*, plate 2 from *Hell* portfolio, published 1919. Lithograph, 87.3 × 61.2 cm. Museum of Modern Art, New York

imagery. If the *Seven Deadly Sins* best introduces viewers to the Bosch's outlook, *Hell* is the most efficient primer for Beckmann's art. Although a self-portrait appears only in three of its lithographs, the portfolio implies a passage, in first person, through postwar Germany, pictured as an infernal city. In the author's portrait featured on the title page, the artist dressed in circus garb, and looking straight out at us, invites "honored ladies and gentlemen of the public" to "step right up" and behold "the pleasant prospect of ten minutes or so in which you will not be bored. Full satisfaction guaranteed, or else your money back" (fig. 45). But when the curtain rises on the first lithograph, the dramatic performance is squeezed into its fictive enclosure, and the mood darkens as Beckmann begins his underworld journey as errant pilgrim and Virgilian guide (fig. 46).

The journey is a dangerous homecoming, like the mythical ones of Odysseus or Agamemnon. But it captures the fate of countless ordinary German soldiers returning defeated and damaged from the front. In *The Way Home*, we meet

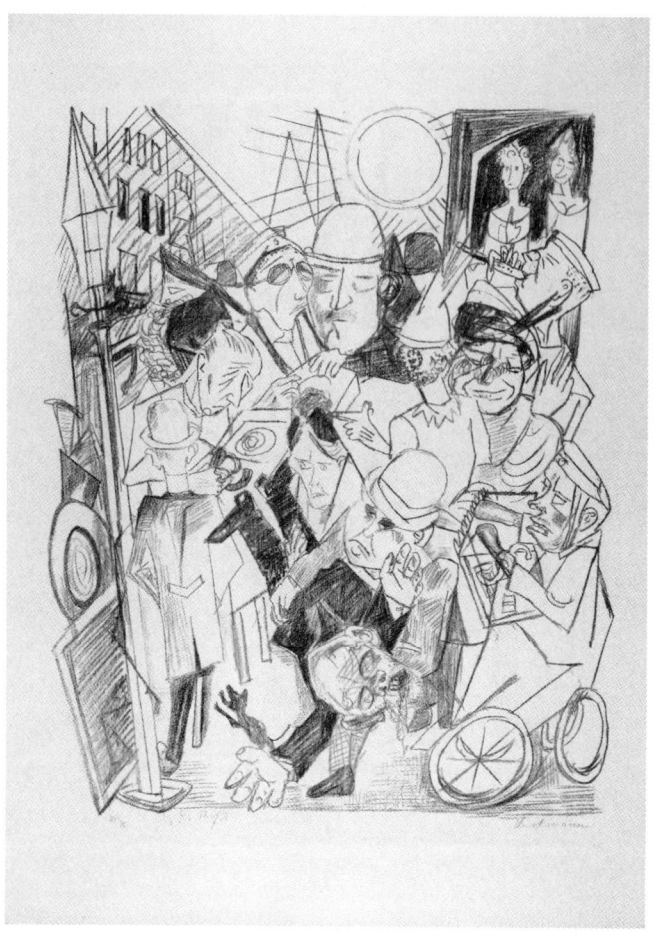

FIG. 47. Max Beckmann, *The Street*, plate 3 from *Hell* portfolio, published 1919. Lithograph, 87.3 × 61.2 cm (sheet). Museum of Modern Art, New York

Beckmann lost in the streets of a modern metropolis at night, seeking direction from a horribly scarred war invalid—the opening of the *Divine Comedy* finds Dante similarly "astray in a dark wood where the straight road had been lost." Whether, in *The Way Home*, he has mistaken the uniformed beggar for a policeman, or whether, hardened to the sight of battle-scarred beggars, he simply asks for directions in exchange for a tip, Beckmann leaves open-ended. The encounter is anyway accidental and fleeting, like urban experience itself. With the lamplit flash of the invalid's ruined visage—one eye directed blind yet omniscient out at us—the vicissitudes of shock begin. This dangerous *Augenblick* also recollects—by involuntarily repeating—the mechanized violence that caused the invalid's disfiguring wounds, his *traumata*. "I stared, with a queasy feeling of unreality, at a blood-spattered form with a strangely contorted leg hanging loosely down, wailing 'Help! Help!' As if sudden death still had him by the throat," writes Jünger at the opening of *Storm of Steel* of his first real experience of war.[19]

For Baudelaire's painter of modern life, the sudden intensifies the experience of the new and the now which defines modernity. The postwar *flâneur* encounters increased bombardments. Suddenness punctuates all of Beckmann's lithographs centrally, in the violent event presently occurring, and at the periphery, in innumerable disturbing details abruptly glimpsed. *The Street*, the portfolio's second print not counting the title page, features an explosive confusion of bodies through which an old man's corpse (bleeding from the mouth) is lugged unceremoniously away (fig. 47). Beckmann pictures the metropolis as that onslaught of conflicting forces and sensations which makes uprightness—as Rodin put it—heroic. Among scenes of accidental catastrophe appear intentional atrocities: *The Night* in its lithograph remake and the newly conceived *The Martyrdom*, portraying Rosa Luxemburg's murder under the cover of darkness (figs. 48 and 49). How the wanderer comes on these hidden passions the portfolio need not explain. Like Dante, Bosch, and Grünewald, Beckmann visits circles of a visionary inferno. An impoverished family sits at a table with nothing to eat, stereotypical ideologues argue interminably in a crowded cafe, the rich entertain themselves in clubs deep into the night, patriots sing drunkenly at their *Stammtisch*, and, in *The Last Ones*, members of a Freikorps unleash crazed violence against their enemies (figs. 50 and 51). The latter scene predicts the February 1934 siege of socialist insurgents in Vienna's Karl-Marx-Hof. Bombarded with light artillery by army and right-wing paramilitary "home guard," the socialists surrendered, after which the First Austrian Republic's constitution was effectively suspended. When, in the final sheet, Beckmann finally reaches his destination, the violence outside—on the battlefield and in the streets—has penetrated the domestic interior (fig. 52). A boy, presumably the wanderer's neglected son, plays soldier with live grenades. Siege has brought war home.

In a seminal text published in 1924, Wilhelm Fraenger, writing on *The Dream*, argued that Beckmann's baffling formal departures had their origin in the traumas experienced personally and collectively during battle (fig. 53). In *The Way Home*, the abrupt revelation of the invalid's "shot-through face" causes Beckmann "suddenly to shy away." Panic spread to the surroundings:

> Under the pressure of such a shocking experience under the streetlamp, the ordinarily solid image of three-dimensional space evaporates. The street sneaks away somewhere into the unknown. It no longer contains and houses the human being but slips away in fatal flight between skewed houses and streetlamps that are now nothing but a swaying stage setting.[20]

Our footing lost, we tap about for something solid: here, the outline of a streetwalker; there, an invalid, shadowed and on crutches, approaching from behind;

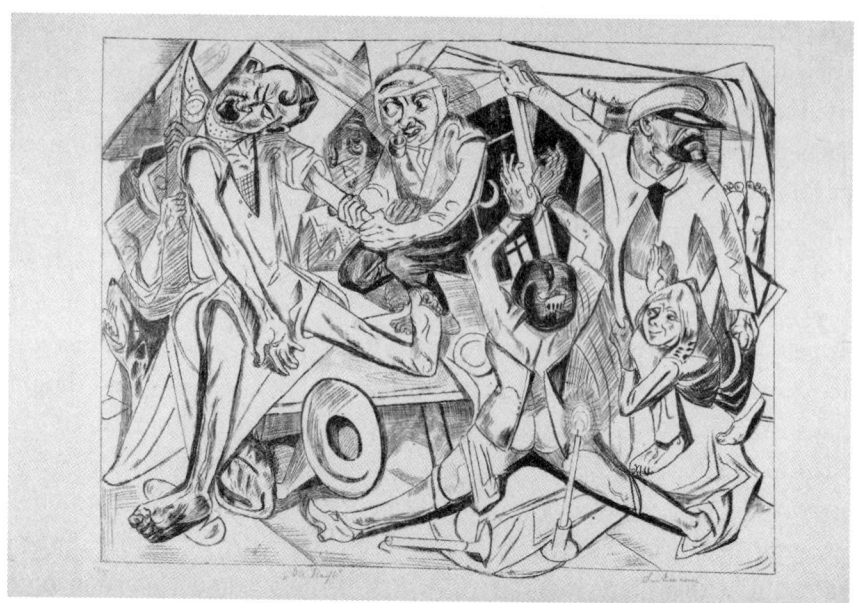

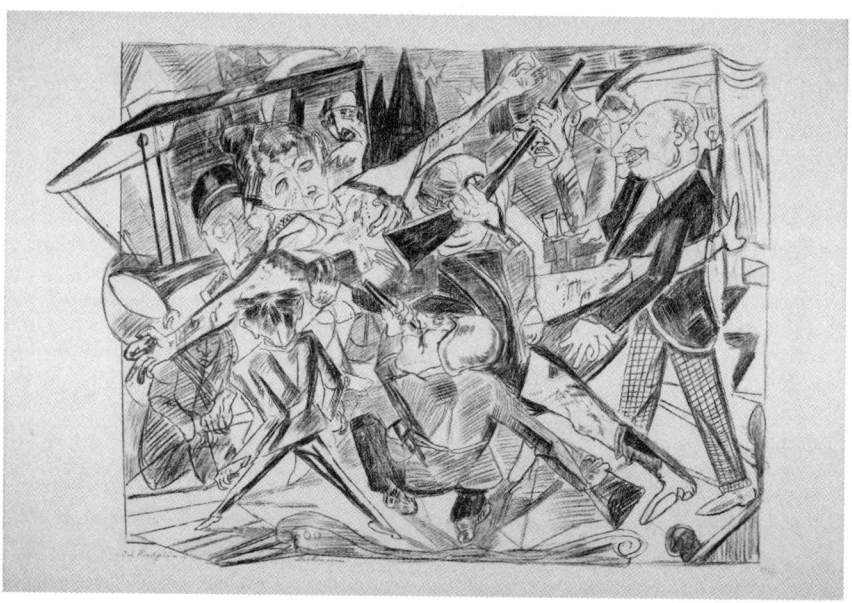

TOP: FIG. 48. Max Beckmann, *The Night*, plate 7 from *Hell* portfolio, published 1919. Lithograph, 61.4 × 87.2 cm. Museum of Modern Art, New York

ABOVE: FIG. 49. Max Beckmann, *The Martyrdom*, plate 4 from *Hell* portfolio, published 1919. Lithograph, 61.7 × 87.2 cm. Museum of Modern Art, New York

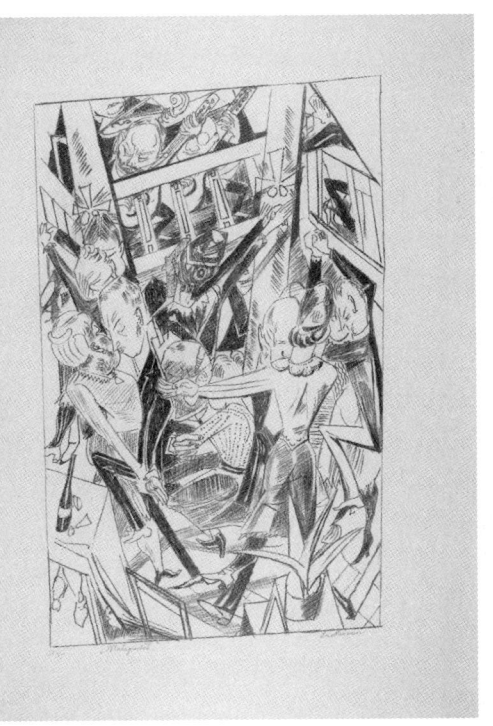

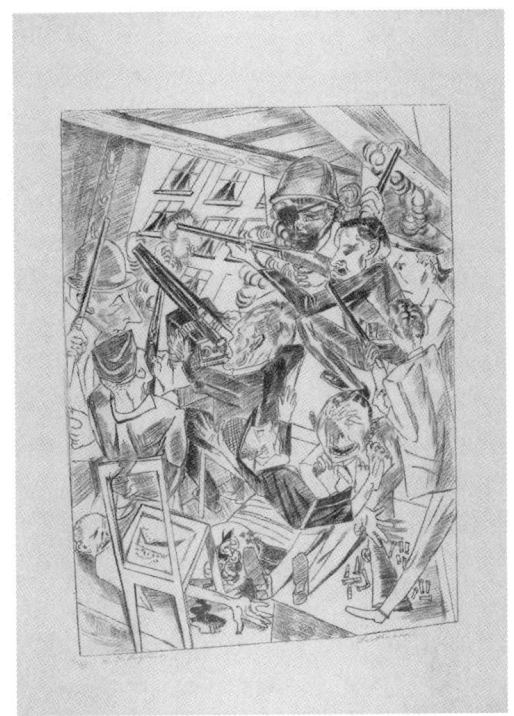

ABOVE: FIG. 50. Max Beckmann, *Malepartus*,
plate 8 from *Hell* portfolio, published 1919. Lithograph, 87.5 × 61.3 cm. Museum of Modern Art,
New York

ABOVE RIGHT: FIG. 51. Max Beckmann, *The
Last Ones*, plate 10 from *Hell* portfolio, published
1919. Lithograph, 86.8 × 61.2 cm. Museum of
Modern Art, New York

RIGHT: FIG. 52. Max Beckmann, *The Fami-
ly*, plate 11 from *Hell* portfolio, published 1919.
Lithograph, 86.5 x 61 cm. Museum of Modern Art,
New York

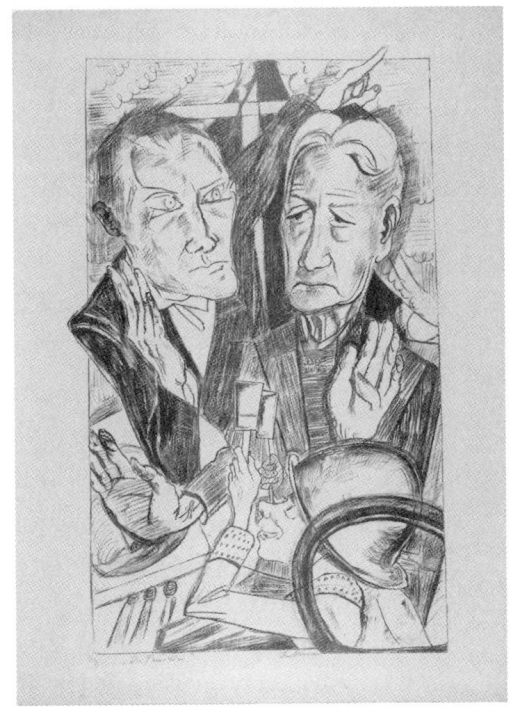

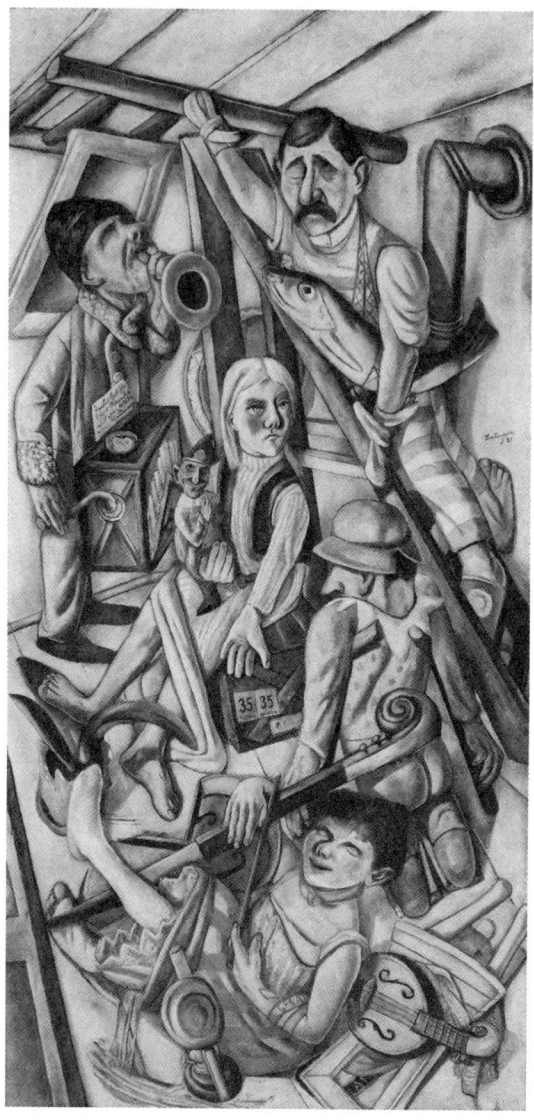

FIG. 53. Max Beckmann, *The Dream*, 1921. Oil on canvas, 182 × 91 cm. St. Louis Art Museum, St. Louis, Missouri

and along the whole lower framing edge, black triangles depicting a blind man's dog. The creature's tongue exceeds the picture's frame because that is how the world in a state of emergency appears, exploding grenade-like towards the eye.

Two decades before Bosch's *Garden of Delights* would seduce and deceive him, Fraenger delivered this trenchant early analysis of art in a state of siege. Part of the Beckmann "almanac" that included texts by Curt Glaser and Julius Meier-Graefe, Fraenger's 1924 essay on *The Dream* still stands as a benchmark analysis of Beckmann's art, comparable in its perceptiveness to Kahnweiler's Picasso. Beckmann's epochal descent into ugliness is, in Fraenger's reading, an artistic "necessity" in the deep sense of that word: necessity as *Notwendigkeit*, a turn (*Wende*) towards dire need (*Not*). Unlike Cubism's playful abstraction of forms, and different from the subjective vagaries of Expressionism, Beckmann's departure responds to a collective emergency state, giving exception an aesthetic form.[21] In the ensuing years, Beckmann's art grew calmer and—in the term of his day—more "objective." And then it morphed from the "return to order" called for by German champions of "New Objectivity" (*Neue Sachlichkeit*) to imagining that art had the power to create a new world order.

This, roughly, was the intention of the *Self-Portrait in Tuxedo*. And unusually in the case of *this* image, we possess a detailed and public manifesto articulating its objectives. Written in tandem with the painting, and published before work on the painting was complete, this text—titled "The Artist and the State"—is less an explanation of the image than the image is an explanation of the text. For Beckmann's statement needs all the explaining it can get. In the face of its obscurity, its publisher, Prince Karl Anton von Rohan, issued this disclaimer: "We are proud to publish the great artist's moving confession, although we do not want to associate ourselves with certain extreme metaphysical conclusions."[22] Beckmann's essay appeared in the July 1927 issue of Rohan's journal *Europäische Revue*, in a series of commissioned articles titled "The European." An Austrian champion of Pan-European unity, Rohan invited luminaries to contribute ideas towards a new world order centered on the Occident, or *Abendland*. It was to the question of being "European" that Beckmann addressed himself. Here are the opening lines:

> The artist, in the new sense of the times, is the conscious shaper of the transcendent idea. He is at once shaper and vessel. His work within the state is of fundamental significance because it is from him alone that the law of a new culture can emanate. Without a new common transcendental idea any new concept of the state remains incomplete. The concept of the state must form itself out of this idea, and the artist in the new sense is the true creator of a world that did not exist before him. Self-reliance is the new idea that the artist, and with him humanity, must form. Autonomy in relation to eternity. The solution of the mystical riddle of balance, *the final deification of the human*: this is the goal.[23]

Art historians have difficulty using these words to clarify Beckmann's image because little about them is self-evident, including the keyword: "balance."

Some of the ideas that seemed obscure or extreme are easier to explain. Beckmann addressed the series's title, "The European." That title begs the question of the state, since it contrasts to another label, "The German" or, for Rohan, "The

Austrian." According to Beckmann, the state, whether national, continental, or intercontinental, presupposed a transcendent idea. This sounds metaphysical but is an historical fact. Until about the sixteenth century, if and when there was such a concept as that of a sovereign state, it was founded on an otherworldly idea, that of God as omnipotent lawgiver. In the modern era, especially after the American and French Revolutions, but already in the wake of confessional conflict and civil war, the state came to be understood as founded on mutual consent, and law itself became the transcendental idea. We assume we live under the protection and the threat of laws passed by our elected representatives and in accordance with the constitution. Otherwise, there would be anarchy, a war of everyone against everyone. Such faith in the rule of law was sorely tested in Beckmann's world by the political conditions of the Weimar Republic. Communists and fascists, both heavily armed, fought each other in the streets (witness Beckmann's *The Last Ones*), with the ruling centrist parties having the narrowest of mandates.

As a German rather than as a European, the artist belonged to a manifestly weak state, one that would in six years become the paradigm of a "failed state." Germany's weakness lay in the breakdown of the legal order through which conflict is normally mediated. The Weimar Republic failed to contain division through constitutional means—that is, through political debate in parliament and through elections overseen by a politically neutral police force. In allowing the Freikorps to fight the Communists, it ignored its fatal enemy, the militarized, anti-constitutional National Socialists. The president of the Republic therefore proclaimed frequent "states of emergency." As we have seen, states of emergency suspend the rule of law, which is the modern state's transcendental idea. This crisis was Carl Schmitt's juridical domain. The Republic's first president, the Social Democrat Friedrich Ebert, declared no less than 136 states of emergency during his seven years of governance. The law allowed him to do this. Article 48 of the Weimar Constitution sanctioned the president to take emergency measures if "public security and order are seriously endangered." He could do this without parliamentary consent, and could even dissolve parliament, as often he did. Though inscribed in the rule of law, the exception in Weimar Germany became the rule. The office that enforced the law became the office that makes the law, creating a dictatorship. It was this state that Schmitt diagnosed, and that Hitler used for terrible ends.

This was the backdrop to Schmitt's famous thesis, stated in 1922, that the state is founded on the exception: "Sovereign is he who decides on the exception."[24] Like Beckmann, Schmitt diagnosed the crisis of the state as the loss—precisely—of a transcendental idea. Schmitt proposed that the vanished idea had been a mere secularization of a theological idea: that of God as ultimate decider who can transgress even the laws of nature. Beckmann's essay responds to the same conditions as those that motivated Schmitt's *Political Theology*, and it traverses the same ground, but in Beckmann the decider is not a prince, president, or dictator, but the artist. The artist shapes the boundaries of a new culture and dispenses its laws. Where those boundaries are, whether they are the disputed ones of post-Versailles Germany or the nebulous ones of Europe, Beckmann does not say. But it is the artist alone who gives them shape, because he fashions worlds that do not exist before him. For he alone creates *ex nihil*, as God was once thought to do. Had not Dürer in his 1500 *Self-Portrait* transferred to himself the idea of divine sovereignty? Artistic genius, what that German painter called "inspiration from above," rendered him godlike while also endowing him with sovereign powers on a par with those of princes.[25] Although he associated his artistic agency with unruly nature, or Silva, Bosch, like Dürer, boasted of his genius that made him capable of producing new creations rather than imitating created nature or previous art.

For Schmitt, such inflated thinking derived from the loss of a transcendent idea. It involved the modern secularization, or making "this-worldly," of an ancient theological idea: that of God as the ultimate decider who transgresses even the laws of nature. Like Schmitt, Beckmann understood this condition to be distinctly modern and secular. "The old gods lie in smithereens at our feet," he writes, and in place of the ruined idols he proposes the deification of man: "For we are God—by Jove, perhaps an altogether inadequate and pathetic God, but God all the same." Through the power of creating something out of nothing, the artist shows this to be true: "What we have here is a picture of ourselves. Art is the mirror of God embodied by man."[26] Where Dürer cast himself in the likeness of Christ, Beckmann in *Self-Portrait in Tuxedo* makes God in the image of the painter. The belief that, in the value vacuum of modernity, the objectified will of one exceptional subjectivity should lead the collective was widespread at the time. In the revolutionary winter of 1918–19 the leading sociologist of the day, Max Weber, asked not just of the would-be professional politicians he was addressing but of all Europeans at this troubled moment in time, "What kind of person does one have to be, to be allowed to lay one's hand on the spokes of the wheel of history?"[27] Many hoped that artists would take the lead. Max Kommerell's catchphrase "the poet as *Führer*" embraced the notion that artists could—willfully, violently, and irrationally—lead the state and that the state should be irrational and willfully like a work of art.[28] Rooted in a politics of sovereign decision, such ideas appealed directly to the failed artist and architect Adolf Hitler.

But why the tuxedo? Beckmann explains: "The new priest of this new cultural center must be dressed in dark suits or on state occasions appear in tuxedo, unless we succeed in developing a more precise and elegant piece of manly attire."²⁹ The painting's imagined event is thus an occasion of state. It is also the foundational occasion when, through the artist-priest, the state receives its transcendental idea. The painting achieves this transcendent idea by solving the riddle of balance. The word balance—in German *Gleichgewicht*—appears no less than ten times in Beckmann's short text. Sometimes an underlying law, sometimes a synthesis or "sum," sometimes a fugitive aim, balance gives artists and statement the same purpose: "Like the artist, the statesman seeks the realization of the transcendent idea in the concrete expressive product of the effective balance, that is, in the organization of the state."³⁰ Under the tangle of abstractions lies a period cliché. Writing in 1926, Carl Schmitt reports mockingly on the prevalence of an expansive meaning of balance: "Of the images which typically recur in the history of political thought and state theory, and whose systematic investigation has not yet begun—for example, the state as a machine, the state as an organism, the king as the keystone of an arch, as a flag, as the soul of a ship—the imagery of balance is most important for the modern age. Since the sixteenth century the image of balance can be found in every aspect of intellectual life [...]: a balance of trade in international economics, the European balance of power in foreign politics, the cosmic equilibrium of attraction and repulsion, the balance of the passions [...], even a balanced diet."³¹ In modern theories of state "balance" names, variously, the division of powers (executive, legislative, and judicial), the relation between opposing political parties (Republican versus Democrat, Labour versus Tory), the partitions of chambers of parliament, and the economic and military power relations among sovereign states. Schmitt pours scorn on what Beckmann calls "the new cult of balance," because for Schmitt, balance is just an image, and a deceitful one at that. It conceals the true character of the legal order, which is founded not on the equilibrium of conflicting interests but on an original decision reached—unilaterally—on the exception. The decision reached is on the enemy, and the enemy seeks not balance with, but annihilation of, its opponent's entire way of life.

Schmitt was also a contributor to Rohan's *Europäische Revue*, and although Beckmann reaches different conclusions, his essay engages with some of the questions that concern Schmitt. The artist is the decider. Through his "great and decisive works" we will find "the strength in ourselves to become God—that is, to be free, to decide for ourselves whether to live and die."³² The dream of the artist as *Führer* who decides for the whole culture in the form of the aesthetic creation was a widespread one among contributors to Rohan's journal. Beckmann may have cast himself more specifically in the hypothetical role as a leader. His *Self-Portrait in Tuxedo* echoes Lovis Corinth's 1924 *Portrait of Friedrich Ebert* (fig.

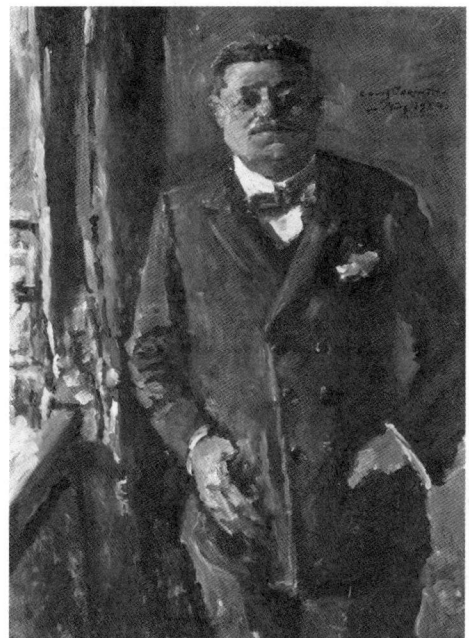

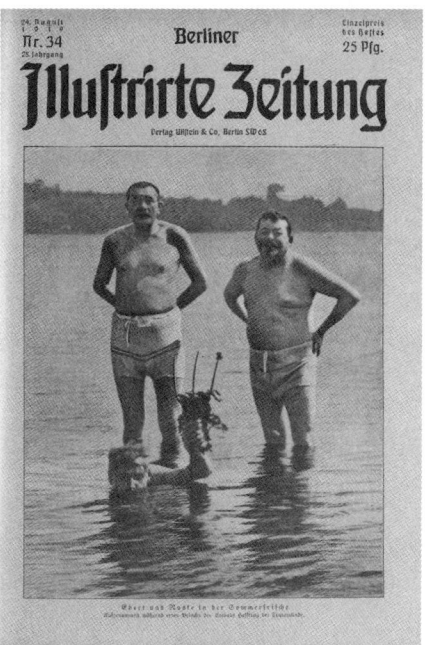

LEFT: FIG. 54. Lovis Corinth, *Portrait of the Reich President, Friedrich Ebert*, 1924. Oil on canvas, 140 × 110 cm. Kunstmuseum, Basel

RIGHT: FIG. 55. Title page of *Berliner Illustrirte Zeitung*, August 24, 1919. 29.21 × 40.4 cm

54). On August 24, 1919, a Berlin newspaper displayed on its cover a scandalous photograph of Ebert as a portly old man in swimming trunks (fig. 55). Published on the day Germany's first democratically elected president swore his oath of office on the country's constitution, newly ratified in Weimar, the picture—surreptitiously obtained—was meant to be malicious. Cartoonists and artists on both sides of Germany's political divide (including Hannah Höch in her 1919 collage *Dada-Rundschau*) turned the photo into a symbol of the country's leadership vacuum. Beckmann, by contrast, gives his own likeness a balanced and physically imposing stature.[33] He also carries that strength over into the painting's form, thus rectifying the sensation-based disequilibrium of Corinth's late Impressionist style.

For Beckmann, the proof of the artist's sovereignty lies in the evidence of the image itself. (That may be why Fraenger understood Beckmann perfectly but was wrong about Bosch.) Getting to work on the canvas while his confession went into print, Beckmann shaped his painted likeness to be the concrete instance of balance achieved. How are we to evaluate the evidence? Are we each individually to appraise, discover, and be somehow shaped, individually and collectively, by the painting's balance? And wherein does balance reside? In the pose of the subject, who is also the image's maker? In the work's concrete forms, since—as Beckmann asserts—painting is "the only true reality?" Does balance lie in both of these and more, as a balance between figuration and abstraction, creation and reception? Sitting for his own portrait, Beckmann performs equilibrium physically through his *contrapposto* pose; painting, he organizes the picture's formal balance on this pose, as that wavering meeting place between dark and light, intensified as contrasting values of black and white. Beckmann admitted that "black and white are the two elements that concern me." In a lecture delivered in the rooms of London's New Burlington Galleries in 1938, one year into his exile from Nazi Germany, the painter gave his bipolar palette an ethical charge: "All things come to me in black and white, like virtue and crime [...]. It is my misfortune, that I can see neither all in black nor all in white. One vision alone would be much simpler and cleaner, but then it would not exist. It is the dream of many to see only the white and truly beautiful, or the black, ugly and destructive. But I cannot help realizing both, for only in the two, only in black and in white, can I see God as a unity creating again and again the great and eternally changing terrestrial drama."[34] The *Self-Portrait* balances and unifies these opposites on his living person: the lights, layered over black ground, bring forth his flesh, with blood pulsing in the veins underneath. But the balance the painting imputes to Beckmann's person remains unstable—more subtly than in the 1923 *Self-Portrait*, but nonetheless unstable. Its fulcrum is the wavering chiaroscuro that divides the face in two. Beckmann's took his persona as "black tightrope walker" from Nietzsche. Re-entering the human world, Nietzsche's Zarathustra comes upon a tightrope walker and exclaims, "Man is a rope stretched between the beast and overman—a rope over the abyss."[35] In the margin of page 72 of his marked-up paperback copy of *Thus Spoke Zarathustra*, Beckmann scribbled, "Why the stupid word 'overman'?—individuality is the right word."[36] Beckmann wants the concrete individual, himself especially, to hold the precarious balance.

But to take a step backwards: is it through an individual interpretation such as mine that balance is measured? Beckmann claims that, through balance, the artwork can shape the state. Might this balance thus be better measured by a collective response, in a conversation occurring where the picture physically hangs, or less democratically, among what the artist calls "responsible" people, meaning special persons responsible for the state? "The decision about the achievement," writes Beckmann, "is an aesthetic question to be measured by the highest degree of the collective vitality of the engendered balance."[37] The decision is therefore collective. Its measure is the state—aesthetic and political—that the artwork concretely engenders.

The *Self-Portrait in Tuxedo* created a stir at its unveiling. "The effect is brutal," wrote an anonymous reviewer in the *Kölnische Zeitung* early in 1928, "but the work is certainly in the spirit of the newest art."[38] To some the effect was politically worrisome: "A Caesarean mask, frowning forehead, tyrant's stare, every inch the great man," wrote Fritz Stahl. "Such faces must disappear again from the world if humanity is to be restored." But to Heinrich Simon, the publisher of the *Frankfurter Zeitung*, the work promised needed leadership: "This lonely maverick may become the only personality in European painting who will form a style for the future."[39] "He's afraid of nothing," wrote Bruno Erich Werner, adding: "but—and that significantly distinguishes him from a number of more limited contemporaries—he refrains from taking any one position."[40] Meanwhile the Nationalgalerie secured its purchase, and it was hung in the galleries of the Kronprinzenpalais. On February 15, 1933, the gallery's director, Ludwig Justi, dedicated a whole room to Beckmann, with the *Self-Portait in Tuxedo* as its anchor. The state had decided favorably on the artist in the state. Balance had been achieved.

Munich, 1937

The decision lasted a few scant weeks. On February 27, 1933, an unemployed bricklayer with Communist affiliations, perhaps aided unknowingly by the Nazis in a false flag operation, set fire to the German parliament building, and on the 28th, as if to restore order but clearly to assume total power, Hitler suspended the Weimar Constitution, allowing him to issue a host of draconian decrees. This suspension was never repealed: legally, the Third Reich was a twelve-year emergency state. By March 1933, Ludwig Justi had been fired from his directorship of the Nationalgalerie, Beckmann and all artists of his ilk lost their jobs, the Kronprinzenpalais was cleared of anything smacking of modernism, and the *Self-Portrait in Tuxedo* was put away. Four years later, in Munich on July 19, 1937, a bizarre exhibition would open that called on the German people to reach a new decision—advertised as the *Volk*'s own decision—on the art that had previously represented them. Ten of Beckmann's oil paintings and a number of his works on paper were placed on display for public mockery and potential destruction.

The Nazis invented a term for all these administrative measures. The term was *Gleichschaltung*, and like so many Nazi euphemisms, it is difficult to render adequately in English. Sometimes translated as "coordination," sometimes as "synchronization," but having a distinctly mechanical ring, like the "shift" or *Schaltung* of a locking clutch or the moving parts of a machine gun, *Gleichschaltung* was the process by which Nazi Germany established its total control of all aspects of society. The first *Gleichschaltung* laws dissolved the diets of the German federal states, removed non-Germans from civil service posts, abolished trade unions and other free associations, and declared the Nazi Party to be the country's only legal party. The climax of this process occurred in 1935 in Nuremberg, when the symbols of Party and State were fused, and Jews were forbidden to marry or have sexual relations with non-Germans and were stripped of their citizenship.

Gleichschaltung was a weapon against the ground norm of the modern state: equality under the law. It was also a weapon against the modern state's solution to political conflict, namely balance (*Gleichgewicht*). Within weeks of Hitler's take-over, as we have seen, Carl Schmitt had joined the Nazi Party. Aspiring to become crown jurist of the Third Reich, he tried to clarify the new order by—among other things—contrasting the liberal ideal of *Gleichheit* to the new equality which Nazi law should bring about. Schmitt first termed this new kind of equality *Gleichartigkeit* (being of the same kind), then switched to the even more severe *Artgleichheit* (equality of kind). "*Artgleichheit* of the German people, unified in itself," wrote Schmitt in 1933, "is the most indispensable premise and foundation for the concept of political leadership of the German *Volk.*"[41] The term was chiefly a biological one for the identity of a species: the common scientific definition has it that a species is a group of organisms that can reproduce with one another in nature and produce fertile offspring. Charles Darwin's *On the Origin of Species by Means of Natural Selection* (1859), became, in Heinrich Georg Bronn's first German translation, *Über die Entstehung der Arten im Thier- und Pflanzen-Reich durch natürliche Züchtung* (1860). The idea had a foothold in scripture, where, at the beginning of the world, God commands plant life to reproduce "according to their various kinds" (Gen. 1:11)—a rule that the promiscuous but childless denizens of Bosch's *Garden* seem to disobey.

Schmitt aimed his polemic at the Jews as a different race, one unequal and inimical to Germans and separate from them, like a species. Jewish difference was not self-evident, however. German children were trained to interpret the evidence using images. *The Poison Mushroom*, published by Stürmer Verlag in 1938, announces that "just as it is often hard to tell a poison mushroom from an edible one, so is it often very difficult to recognize the Jew as swindler and criminal." An illustration by the cartoonist Philipp Rupprecht, under his pseudonym Fips, shows seventh graders learning this lesson: Young Karl explains that the Jewish nose "is hooked and looks like the number six" (fig. 56). Some non-Jews are hook-nosed, too, Karl explains, but not at the bottom, and this sparks lively conversation about confusing deviations, like blond Jews, and about differences in voice (Jews speak through their nose) and odor (they have a sweet, repellent smell).

Racial difference had also to be disclosed to adults in all spheres of life. Schmitt focused his efforts on law, organizing in 1936 a conference on Jews in jurisprudence.

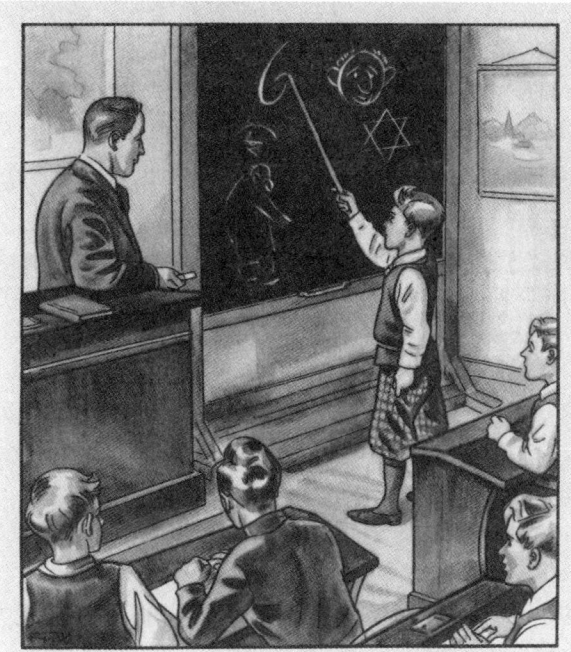

FIG. 56. Philipp Rupprecht, illustration from Ernst Hiemer, *The Poison Mushroom* (*Der Giftpilz*) (Nuremberg: Stürmer Verlag, 1938), 27 × 20 cm

„Die Judennase ist an ihrer Spitze gebogen. Sie sieht aus wie ein Sechser..."

He admitted that books by Jewish jurists dominated German law and did not obviously betray their Judaism, nor did Jewish authors' taken names, which were German and Christian. Schmitt therefore ordered that these books be destroyed or re-catalogued as 'Judaica' and their authors designated as "Jew." Schmitt's rival and early patron Hans Kelsen thus became "the Jew Kelsen."[42] And his most prescient interpreter, presumably, became the Jew Leo Strauss. For Schmitt, the hiddenness of Jewish difference was what made it so dangerous. Tradesmen and parasites, Jews were virtuoso mimics and tacticians. This explained why, though Jews have no talent as painters, "a Jewish art dealer can nevertheless discover a genuine Rembrandt faster than a German art historian can." The same is the case in legal studies: "Jews quickly recognize German substance."[43] The Jewish art experts and legal scholars represent the most dangerous of parasites because they feed off something Germans have, and Jews do not: namely, authenticity. "It is often said that such and such a person is 'honest subjectively,' and this might be the case. But I have to add that I cannot see into the soul of these Jews and that we have no entrance into the inner being of Jews. We only recognize a false relation to our kind. He who grasps this truth knows what race is."[44]

Gleichschaltung proved harder to pursue in the realm of art. The Nazi leadership stood divided over which among the many current artistic tendencies should be the official one. Joseph Goebbels, chief propagandist of the Nazi Party, collected Emil Nolde, an avowed racist, virulent anti-Semite, and early member of the Nazi Party. But Goebbels also collected Ernst Barlach, a passionate socialist. Goebbels's rival, Alfred Rosenberg, championed a German-looking "folkish" kind of art over anything modern or international, but he admired Expressionists for their strength and their roots in old German art—Rosenberg compared stormtroopers to Dürer's *Knight, Death, and the Devil* engraving. Art was central to Nazism, not just as a political tool but as a biopolitical end. In 1937 Hitler staged in Munich, in a purpose-built "Temple" of art, *The First Great German Art Exhibition*.[45] During his impoverished years in Vienna (1909–13), he sold postcard-sized paintings by his own hand, and he twice applied to Vienna's Academy of Fine Arts and twice failed, to his bitter disappointment, as his autobiography *Mein Kampf* records. To the British ambassador in 1939, in the midst of the Polish crisis, he is said to have confided that he was a painter not a politician, and that his only ambition was to retire to the Berchtesgaden hills and paint.[46] For him art was not merely a tool of propaganda but an ultimate aim. He proclaimed that the German, or "Aryan," race was superior because it alone created authentic culture. The state was a work of art, a "dictatorship of genius." Through his personal genius, he would create a Thousand Year Reich, with its enemies annihilated or enslaved, and its lands encompassing most of the Eurasian continent. "A statesman is an artist," wrote Goebbels in a novel composed in the 1920s and published in 1934: "For him the people is merely what stone is for a sculptor. The Führer with the masses poses no more of a problem than does a painter with color."[47] Works displayed in the First Great German Art Exhibition were classicism on steroids. And they were overtly racist: they imagined a new human species with perfect, muscular warrior bodies bred to kill or be killed at the will of the artist-dictator.

These are terrible fantasies of art and modernity. But what was it that turned the Nazi leadership against modern art? Both Rosenberg and Goebbels rejected artists like Beckmann because of their perceived corruption by Jewish art dealers, critics, and tastemakers. This hostility found its most powerful public expression in 1937, in the exhibition *Degenerate "Art"* (fig. 57).[48] Billed as a defamatory show or *Schandausstellung*, its purpose was to vilify: note the scare quotes around "art" (*Kunst*) in the show's official title.[49] In his speech at the opening ceremonies, the nominal curator, Adolf Ziegler, described his purpose as "placing before the eyes of the German people" works of recent (so-called) "art" which, formerly dominating Germany's museums, had embraced everything sick and corrupt. With this exhibition—650 works out of many thousands deaccessioned—such artmaking was declared, by the Führer himself, "finally over and done with."[50]

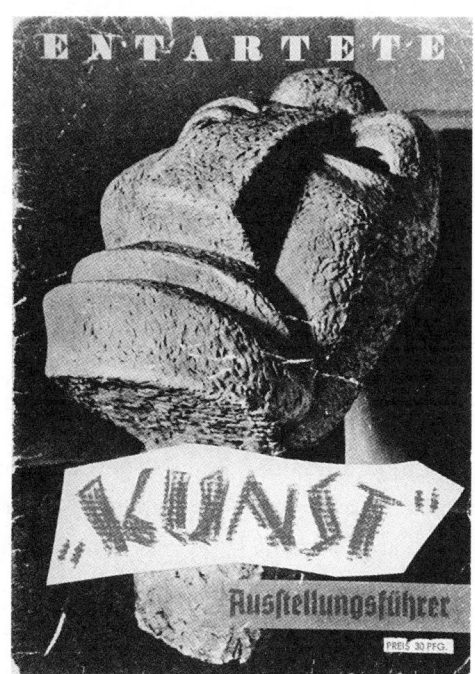

FIG. 57. Cover of *Degenerate "Art"—Exhibition Guide* (Berlin: Verlag für Kultur- und Wirtschaftswerbung, 1937), showing Otto Freundlich, *Der neue Mensch*, 1912, plaster cast, 21 × 15 cm

However, before its destruction it was to be publicly exposed for its trickery and murderously mocked.

The success of this display astonished even its organizers. More than two million people saw the show—five times the number visiting the *First Great German Art Exhibition* that opened in the House of German Art (Haus der deutschen Kunst: "built by German people for German art"), right next door.[51] Indeed, *Degenerate "Art"* in all its venues drew more than any other exhibition of modern art in history. We are used to images *of* the enemy. Bosch's demons, heretics, and sinners are, to his audience, implacable foes, and in the way Bosch imagines those enemies, through their hideous faces, diseased bodies, crude gestures, and outlandish garb he also slanders them. We are also familiar with images being treated *as the enemy*. For Wittenberg's iconoclast, graven images were themselves the foes to be destroyed, sometimes with their ruins preserved as a *damnatio memoriae*, as in the "idol chamber" in Lutheran Zwickau, which preserved the town's broken effigies as evidence of popish folly and deceit. Modernist works deaccessioned by the Nazis but neither destroyed nor resold languished in rooms nicknamed "poison chambers" (*Giftschränke*). But there is that other, more fugitive category: that *of enemy images themselves*: which is to say, the enemy's *own* images, the ones he or she uses against *us*. These are less familiar, although in certain details within Bosch's paintings (the gifts of the Magi, the garb of Antichrist, the ruined décor of

Saint Anthony's place of prayer), and—arguably—in the *Garden of Delights*, as the whole of the triptych's central panel, we have seen such objects before. Inimical to us, they will be dangerously elusive, like arsonists' signs or camouflaged weapons, or like the wooden horse the Greeks placed before the gates of Troy. This is what *Degenerate "Art"* proposed to display. Exhibiting objects that had been acquired by the state as amicable, it exposed these as having been, all along, enemy images intending to negate Germany's very way of life. To art historians today, conversely, that exhibition is itself the enemy, a teaching moment *par excellence* when everything went wrong.

Ziegler ended his speech with an imperative: "German *Volk*, come and judge for yourselves."[52] The exhibition of course steered the public towards a negative decision. It did this openly. Where curators (from Latin *curare*, "to take care of") typically preserve lovingly what they collect and display, here they endeavored to deface and destroy. Paintings were torn from their frames and hung tightly and haphazardly, with their purchase price displayed for ridicule and derisive slogans smeared on the walls (fig. 58). Labels slandered their objects, rather than identifying or explaining them. Again, the intent was conspicuously political, in Schmitt's sense: to distinguish friends from enemies. The overtly propagandistic character of the show was billed as a necessary antidote to the secretly propagandistic tenor of modernist art, where "art for art's sake" was a concealed weapon in the war of worldviews, Jewish against German. The section devoted to Dada is particularly instructive here. Hung in parody of the First International Dada Fair, the installation played a cruel trick on its target (fig. 59). Dada assumed the bourgeois public would be antagonistic to it. It parried this aggression with blatant provocation. It was a "fighting" movement, like all avant-gardes. Ziegler notes this in his remarks, "The degenerate artists said, 'Away with the whole bourgeois culture! Topple the old idols in the name of a proletarian culture to be!'" To which Ziegler responds, "My dear German comrades, what those pen-pusher types wanted now will become reality. We are going to toss out *their* old idols on a scale never seen before."[53]

It is hard to capture the menace, where deathly threats are laced with cruel humor. Originally, the motto "Take Dada Seriously! It's Worth It!" was meant half-ironically, in the spirit of absurdist play. The Nazis turned those words back on their enemies. Now we *have* taken you seriously, the exhibition says, and you're in a prison where the motto is ironic: "Arbeit macht frei." Christopher Isherwood, at the close of *Goodbye to Berlin*, writes of a young Communist and his boy-scout palavers: "I'm thinking of poor Rudi, in his absurd Russian blouse. Rudi's make-believe, story-book game has become earnest; the Nazis will play it with him. The Nazis won't laugh at him; they'll take him on trust for what he pretended to be.

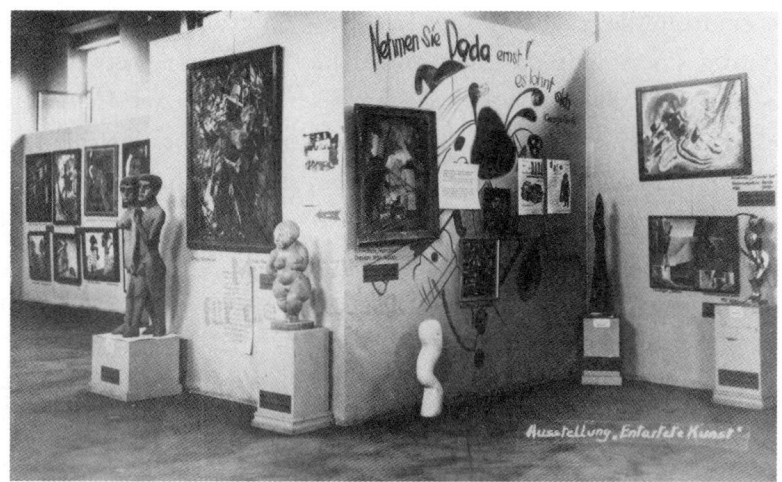

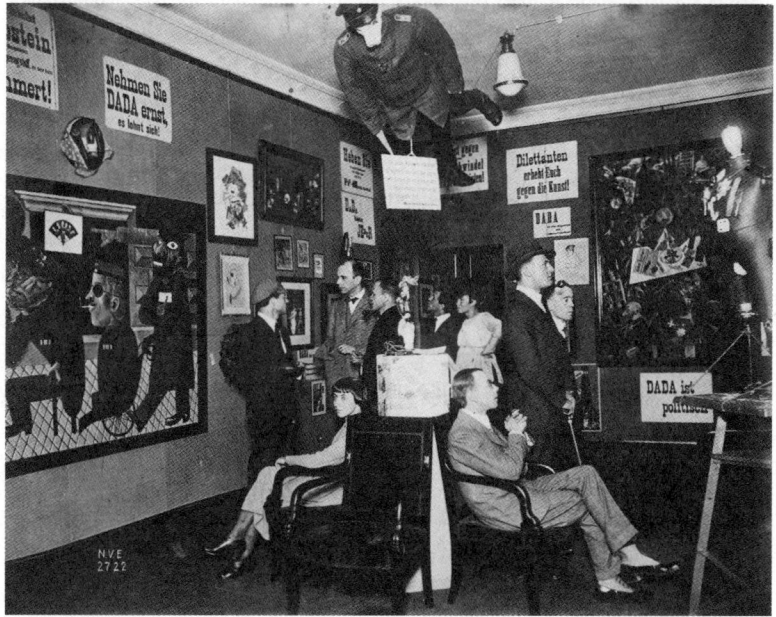

TOP: FIG. 58. Photograph of *Degenerate "Art"* exhibition, Archäologisches Institut, Munich, 1937

ABOVE: FIG. 59. Photograph of First International Dada Fair, Gallery Dr. Otto Burchart Berlin, June, 1920

Perhaps at this very moment Rudi is being tortured to death."[54] There are reports that visitors to *Degenerate "Art"* were expected to talk loudly in the galleries and groan and laugh in disgust, or to ask for their money back from the former museum directors who had purchased the "stupid" works.[55] The exhibition's noisiness set it apart from the hush of museums. Photographs of the public milling through the installation make it impossible to tell who went to hate, and who to silently say farewell. Hostile hilarity was the official response, yet the show drew unruly inspiration from the art it attacked. Take the exhibition catalogue's infamous cover (see fig. 57). Its indecorously upturned head intervening between *Entartete* (degenerate) and *"Kunst"* ("art"), Otto Freundlich's 1912 *The New Man* is intended as a shocking example of non-art. But Freundlich built shock into his sculpture and the cover designer redirected the blow. Crayoned forcefully on rough-woven stock, " *"Kunst""* looks the work of an erstwhile Expressionist: an Emil Nolde, say, but with sharper political instincts.

The exhibition's organizers dressed as a "fighting administration," and rumor had it that the uniformed gallery attendants monitored the reaction of visitors. But *Degenerate "Art"* also assumed that the broader German public harbored a simmering hostility towards modern art. "What is caused in all of us," states Ziegler with a not unreasonable certitude, "is shock and revulsion."[56] Take the pages from the original exhibition catalogue, with their terse comment, "All commentary is superfluous!" (fig. 60).[57] For art historians this is a troubling claim. It shows that commentary is sometimes an ethical necessity. It is necessary for when my students glimpse in a film of the 1937 exhibition a painting now prominently displayed in the galleries of the Busch. It is urgently necessary when that work is *Mulattin* (literally "Mulattress") by Nolde, an artist who held views similar to those of the organizers of *Degenerate "Art"* (fig. 61). In 1913, when Nolde painted the picture, Germany passed legislation making "German blood" the sole criterion for citizenship, excluding colonial and mixed-race subjects. Combining erotic fascination with repugnance—Nolde makes the sitter's heavy makeup clash mockingly with the skin of her neck and shoulders—*Mulattin* vacillates between the pictures *Degenerate "Art"* vilifies and the exhibition's own shock value aesthetics (fig. 62).

What made the images for which "all commentary is superfluous" so self-evident to people of Ziegler's ilk? To the show's target audience, the "works" (again the scare quotes) were patently nauseating both for the seeming physical deformities of the depicted human figures and for the deformity of their modernist depiction. A page from Paul Schultze-Naumburg's notorious 1928 picture book *Art and Race* tries to make the case entirely by visual means, juxtaposing details "from pictures of the 'Modernist' School' " with photographs of physical *and* mental disabilities (fig. 63). Inextricably bound together, such "deformities" also suggested a deformity in the artists themselves, who were not only sick like their models, but insolent, too, for pompously parading their depravity. "Either what appears on the market and elsewhere as art is really the expression of the whole *Volk*, in which case our culture is ripe for collapse [...] or the *Volk*-body is in mind and body differently directed and healthier, and it is only the art of today that concerns itself with such symptoms of decay and degeneration."[58] In 1939, Carl Schmitt celebrated the

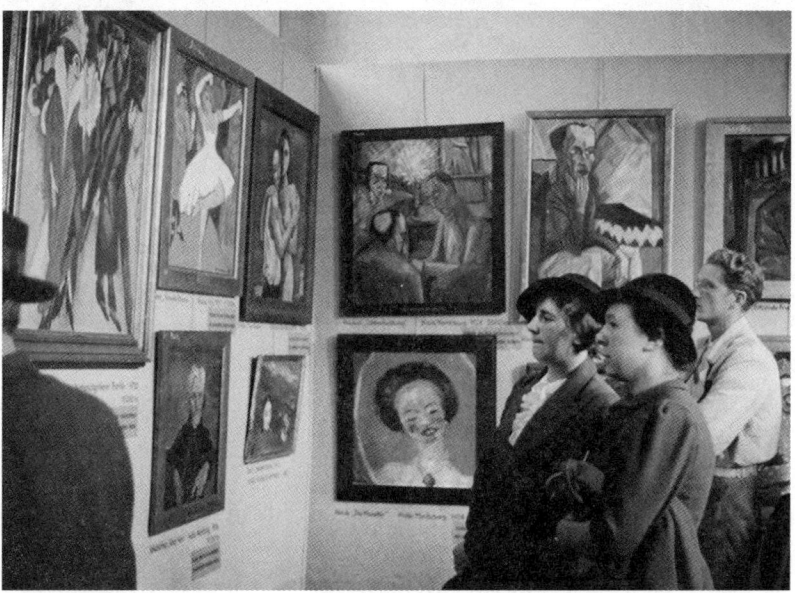

TOP: FIG. 60. Pages from *Degenerate "Art"—Exhibition Guide* (Berlin: Verlag für Kultur- und Wirtschaftswerbung, 1937), 21 × 15 cm

ABOVE: FIG. 61. Visitors at *Degenerate "Art"* exhibition, Munich, 1937; Nolde's *Mulattin* on side wall. Film still

violent assertion of a new *nomos* of the earth in the form of a "strong and untouchable middle of Europe."[59] Balance would be accomplished not, as Beckmann had it, in the free play between contradictory aesthetic forms—Schmitt had satirized that in his 1919 *Political Romanticism*. Instead, balance must be achieved by one blood bloodily seizing enough soil to stand on. A balanced and pacified world might

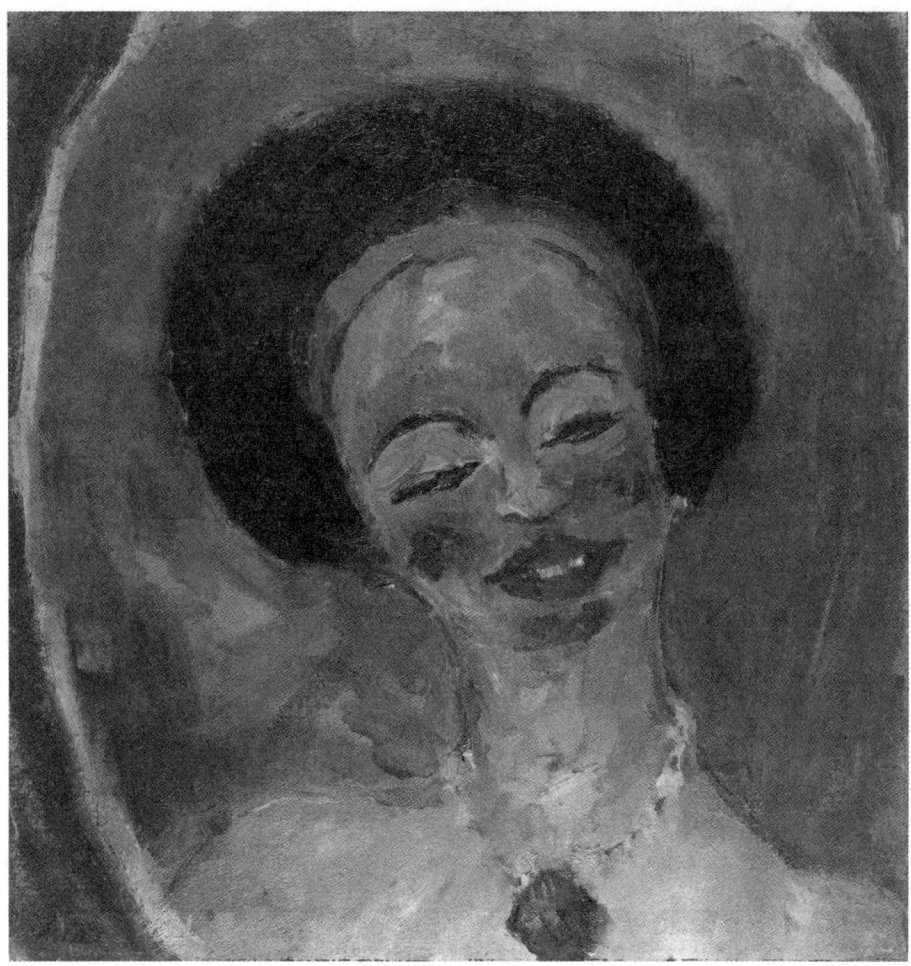

FIG. 62. Emil Nolde, *Mulattin* (*Woman of Mixed Race*, formerly *The Mulatto* and *Mulatto*), 1913. Oil on canvas, 77.5 × 73 cm. Harvard Art Museums, Cambridge, Massachusetts

contain some "interesting antitheses and contrasts, competitions and intrigues of every kind, but there would not be a meaningful antithesis whereby men could be required to sacrifice life, authorized to shed blood, and kill other human beings."[60]

Nazi race theory held that the physical defects of non-Aryan bodies as well as the aesthetic malformations of modernist art derived from a mental and spiritual deformity of artists who saw and represented the world in a degenerate way. And the way modernist artists saw and created was Jewish. Whether or not an artist was of Jewish descent, as "the Jew [Otto] Freundlich" was, Judaism had corrupted them. Only one section of the exhibition featured Jewish artists. These were displayed, the catalogue explains jeeringly, as a "special honor" in spaced type and between quotation marks (*"S o n d e r e h r u n g"*).[61] But Jewishness was omnipres-

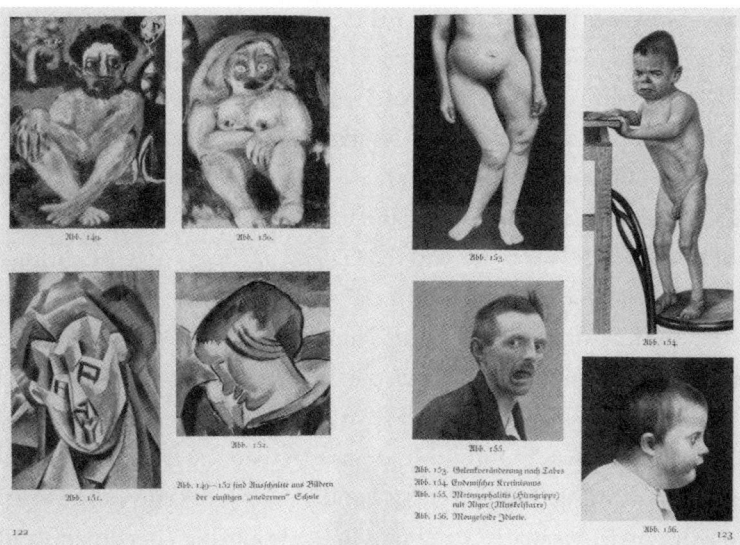

FIG. 63. Pages from Paul Schultze-Naumburg, *Kunst und Rasse* (Munich, 1938), 32 × 23 cm

ent in the form of the Jewish dealers and curators who peddled modernist art, and of the Jewish critics who foisted it on the public through their bamboozling interpretations. "Artworks that cannot be understood on their own," reads Hitler's statement printed across from the photo-collage of Expressionist sculpture, "but require for their right-to-life pompous user manuals in order to finally find that intimidated soul who can tolerate such stupid and brazen rubbish, will from as of now no longer find their way to the German *Volk*" (see fig. 60).[62] Ziegler's imperative "Judge for yourself!" was meant as retribution against the tyranny of Jewish deciders.

In the months following the exhibition, such judgment took many forms, from outright destruction (Freundlich's *New Man* disappeared) to putting the works on the auction block. Aware of the international market for modernist art, the Nazis profited from the sale of works deaccessioned from public collections. Moneys earned funded the German war effort. The *Self-Portrait* that Van Gogh dedicated to his friend Paul Gauguin, along with a number of other key works that found their way into Harvard's collections, was acquired by way of one of the public auctions held in the wake of *Degenerate "Art."* German museums sold off a total of 590 deaccessioned works by Beckmann. Beckmann himself left Germany on July 19, 1937, one day after hearing Hitler's radio broadcast against degenerate art.

When he had lost his teaching position in Frankfurt four years earlier, Beckmann relocated to Berlin, calling the move "a change of scenery." His forms changed, too. Started in Frankfurt in 1932 and finished in Berlin in 1933, on New

Year's Eve, *Departure* was the first of his nine monumental triptychs (plate 20). Evoking the sacred artifacts of the Christian Middle Ages, this antiquated format bolstered extravagant new claims. Freed from its service to religion but mindful of its spiritual calling, art—the tripartite structure suggested—could be redemptive on its own.[63] "Departure, yes departure, from the illusions of life towards the essential realities beyond," wrote Beckmann to his dealer Curt Valentin, by then in exile in New York. "It is to be said that *Departure* bears no tendentious meaning—it could well be applied to all times."[64] In this understanding, the triptych sustains the myth of artistic sovereignty launched in *Self-Portrait in Tuxedo*. Recall Beckmann's 1927 statement, "The artist, in the new sense of the times, is the conscious shaper of the transcendent idea."[65] And as late as 1941 he still could boast, "Creation is redemption."[66] But it is hard not to read the triptych tendentiously, so to speak, as reflecting the emergency condition in Germany at the time. When he began work on it, his works still hung in the honorific "Beckmann gallery" of Berlin's Nationalgalerie, but when *Departure* stood complete, tens of thousands of Jews and dissidents had fled Nazi Germany.

Beckmann refused to sell the triptych's middle canvas separately. "The center is the end of the tragedy," he explained to a client, "but its meaning can only be understood when all three panels are viewed together."[67] Viewed together, the triptych takes us from one hell, via the peaceful central scene, back to hell. Among the artist's most violent creations, the left panel thrusts us into the dangerous present moment. The first five letters of the word *Zeitung* (newspaper) peak from under a reflective globe on which rests, face down, a woman with hands sadistically bound. Time requires no crystal ball to foretell its outcome. The right panel (more obscure) features a man and woman roped together accompanied by a uniformed lift attendant—Beckmann's ironic "modern harbinger of fate."[68] The unfortunate couple has been understood as representing the war between the sexes, but the artist glossed the unfortunates as "you yourself dragging with you, as part of yourself, the corpse of your memories, your evil doings and failures, the murder that everyone at some stage in their lives commits."[69] Torture, rape, and murder committed on the left panel, and culpability figured on the right, thus converge on titular "Departure." Set apart from the claustrophobic flanking canvases, the boat at sea evokes—variously—Noah's ark, the sacrament of Baptism, the promise of redemption, and, through the warrior and king, some dream of sovereignty. But while prompting thoughts about their relation, there is no clear passage among the canvases. Prefigured by Bosch's enigmatic garden between paradise and hell, this will be the modern triptych's purpose: to bring disjunct times, places, and meanings together urgently—the format's numinous origins support this demand—but also inconclusively. Breaking the boundary between work and world, the triptych hails the beholding "you" as the site of synthesis and decision.

In 1937 Beckmann and Quappi packed their suitcases and fled to Amsterdam. The contents of Beckmann's atelier traveled separately to avoid confiscation. After taking refuge in Quappi's sister's home, the couple found a small apartment below an unused tobacco storehouse, which served as Beckmann's studio until 1945. Their exile would be permanent. Beckmann had hoped to emigrate to the States, where he had many émigré friends and clients, but Germany's invasion of Holland in 1940 kept him in Amsterdam. Like many Germans, his emigration had to be of an inner kind, where fear of the Nazi police state trumped guilt about German atrocities. To make ends meet Beckmann sold work from his studio. Erhard Göpel, the Nazi art agent who in 1944 gifted Jünger the inspiring Bosch monograph, smuggled rolls of Beckmann's canvas for sale back in Germany. He would claim to have protected the artist from persecution in exile.[70] But Beckmann painted chiefly—and prolifically—for himself, though hoping for a fitter audience in the future.

Among the first works begun in exile, *Death* features the artist in his old wartime role as medic (lower left), with Quappi fiddling with her shoes beside him (plate 21). Their patient, a blond, green-skinned woman lays already shrouded in her coffin, while something of her seems to slip away at the right. A woman and large fish in a tight embrace sweep magically towards an upside-down world of Boschian hybrids and musical performers. Although the artist's signature fixed its orientation, the canvas coheres as well hung the other way round. In that topsy-turvy upper zone, on yellow wooden floorboards suggesting a theater stage, a monstrous angel with its pink penis exposed blasts a trumpet towards a male choir singing from the shadows offstage. The formal principle of Beckmann's *Hell* portfolio, whereby artistic and historical emergency explodes the structure of space, causing the eye to grasp the picture part by shocking part, achieves a new intensity. "The viewer has to shift and change to complete the work," writes a contemporary artist who, for forty years, has kept a postcard of Beckmann's *Death* "close at hand" in his studio.[71] For this fervent admirer, Beckmann's canvas evokes "the world as a contested arena, where neither grace nor damnation are inevitable." The painting fills him "with awe and hope at the way painting or drawing could so evoke the ambiguities, uncertain and arcane ways in which we shape our sense of ourselves and our construction of the world."[72]

William Kentridge wrote these lines in 2003 for a Beckmann exhibition that traveled from Paris to London to New York. But *Death* gave direction to this artist long before, when he found his artistic calling during one of apartheid South

Africa's many official emergency states. The picture's spatial fragmentation—a condition amplified in Beckmann's triptychs—urged viewers to complete it, implicating them in its symbolic dilemmas, as Kentridge wished South Africans would be in their political ones. *Death*'s dense temporal palimpsest gave direction, too. Its layering of Greek myth, Hieronymus Bosch, Berlin cabaret, World War I field hospitals, Impressionist domesticity, and proleptic auguries of Francis Bacon and George Baselitz ("when I first saw Baselitz's work," Kentridge writes, "it was the other way around—the Baselitz reminded me of the Beckmann") allowed it to be both archetypal and topical, both a remembrance and a forgetting.[73] Beckmann's shrouded corpse, a form sinking into the painter's elemental mix of black and white, uncannily predicts the South African artist's key motif: the body in the veld.[74] In short, *Death* gave Kentridge his picture of what he in 1986 termed "art in a state of siege," the term this book struggles to explore.

While Beckmann was at work on this canvas, his *Self-Portrait in Tuxedo* went from the depot of the Nationalgalerie (where it had languished since 1933) to Karl Buchholz, a non-Jewish dealer specializing in selling works deaccessioned by the Nazis. Shipped in 1940 via Switzerland to New York, it was acquired by the Busch-Reisinger Museum from Buchholz's assistant Curt Valentin for the ridiculously low and unpublished purchase price of $600.

Cambridge, Massachusetts, 2022

This explains how the painting came to hang in the Harvard Art Museums, but it does not explain why it hangs there. Originally, the Germanic Museum, the Busch-Reisinger's precursor, collected only plaster casts and photographs of German monuments, historical artifacts, and masterpieces along with relevant books and journals. Founded in 1903 with the support of Emperor Wilhelm II, it was intended not as an art museum, but as a showcase, study collection, and archive that would foster a sense of German identity among German Americans. To some observers, Germans tended to shed their ethnic identity in the New World more rapidly than other immigrant groups. The museum's opening was ill timed. World War I began barely over a decade later, making celebrations of Germanness in the USA at first controversial and then—after America declared war on Germany in 1917—unthinkable. The museum's purpose remained in flux between the wars, but by the time World War II broke out another identity had been created for it. Instead of collecting reproductions, the museum began acquiring original works of art.

Beckmann's *Self-Portrait in Tuxedo* was one of the first modern works of art purchased by the Busch. And what a strange beginning it was. This painting de-accessioned from Germany's national gallery was accessioned by Harvard po-lemically, as representative of a Germany different from Hitler's, a progressive, peaceful, cosmopolitan Germany, where men wear American-style tuxedos in a setting that could be anywhere so long as it is sophisticated. This was a nation now exiled from its own lands, either physically, as refugees, or spiritually, through "inner immigration." Today, the canvas's vexed provenance has made it a fitting emblem of a museum that has been repeatedly called upon to redefine its identity. For me, teaching from the objects collected by the museum (including medieval and Renaissance ones now integrated into internationalizing hangs), this gives the Busch a distinct advantage over the Fogg.[75] The Fogg has always projected its identity as a cosmopolitan one, as the neutral given of art for art's sake, when in fact it has its own obvious biases. The Fogg does not collect, and until recent-ly refused to exhibit, African, Oceanic, Pre-Columbian, and Native American Art, these being the domain of Harvard's Peabody Museum of Archaeology and Ethnography housed—problematically—in the same building as the Harvard Natural History Museum. The Fogg defines its purview as "Western" art, but with contemporary art its collection suddenly becomes global. The Busch, by contrast, has been a troubled concept from the start, in its claim to represent for German Americans their origins on Germanic soil. And two wars, and Germany's Cold War division, further complicated these claims. But none of this would be of interest here if something of this conflict were not made evident by Beckmann's painting. One can learn about balance and crisis just by looking at how Beckmann depicts his thumb, or how the whole frontal representation of the body is negotiated, or crossed out, by the radical splitting of the body into two parts, black and white, a splitting that goes right through the sitter's face. Again, it is counterintuitive to place at the center of your own face this fragmenting device of chiaroscuro that neither unites the composition nor sets the body forth but instead fragments, flattens, and unbalances.

But what better emblem of the attempt to belong and at the same time to be always moving elsewhere, to be at home and at the same time be in exile? That one painting can do this, and do so in a university setting, with classes grouped thoughtfully around it and countless discussions provoked by it, is extraordinary. More remarkable still is that, throughout the classes and discussions, the painted cigarette still seems to burn, making us feel that the picture is happening right now, and that its modernity, flashing forth in 1927 and almost liquidated in 1937, is with us still. This goes some way towards demonstrating the power of images in difficult times: one dab of lead white paint provoking questions that stay urgent for a century.

During the pandemic, when the Harvard Art Museums closed for nearly two years, the collection waited while out in the world monuments toppled and racism, anti-Semitism, and White supremacism were on the rise. In October 2022 I went to the Busch to film Beckmann's *Self-Portrait* in its mothballed hang. Teaching it on an online course, I wanted to provide students with some sense of how the work looked in situ, and how it responds to one's movement in the gallery and to changing ambient light. Strict protocol dictated that I enter the galleries sanitized, masked, and alone, with the one on-duty guard a good city block away. With the whole museum to myself, I filmed multiple routes to the picture, from the entranceway, through the Renaissance-style courtyard, past Ernst Barlach's monumental 1930 ceramic *The Beggar* (the Busch's first modern art acquisition), and into the Busch, taking in, as I wandered, Erich Heckel's marvelous triptych *To the Convalescent Woman*, or else finding Beckmann's canvas among neighboring pictures that, through its size and placement, it seems to dominate: George Grosz's satirical *Nutcracker* that turns German militarism into surreal kitsch; Ernst Ludwig Kirchner's *Self-Portrait with Cat*, with it cadaverous skin tones and unsettling checked cloth support; and, facing off stylistically and ideologically against Beckmann's effigy, Nolde's offensively titled *The Mulatto*. In a gallery talk, these adjacencies come to the speaker's rescue. Asked about Expressionism, one can point to Kirchner's green skin, bloodred coat, and pink surrounds. Queried about toxic Weimar politics, Nolde's canvas stands ready at hand.

Beckmann's *Self-Portrait* also raised very basic questions that close looking alone could address. The picture's background tended to confuse and deceive. Viewers read into its simple forms all sorts of fantasies that careful inspection can confirm or dispel. Close-up viewing never fully resolves such questions, revealing instead that visual confusion was an intended effect. Although it resembles a simple blank canvas, the rectangle behind the sitter, rendered in white over a black ground, is visually complex and representationally fugitive, while the dark zone along the left framing edge, which in photographs swallows up Beckmann's sleeve, is overpainted, black on black, and is texturally and tonally distinct from the tuxedo's black. Some of this I recorded as best I could, hoping to counter the frustrating distance experienced in distant learning.

Meanwhile, around the time of my visit, the career of Beckmann's canvas took a new turn. The curators decided that, when their museum reopened in September 2021, the work would be removed from the public sightline to the furthest corner of the Busch galleries. In its place would hang that other picture acquired from

German collections via Nazi deaccessioning: Nolde's *Mulattin* (see fig. 62). This change belonged to a larger museological initiative. ReFrame, as the initiative was called, aimed to "reimagine the function, role, and future of the university art museum." It sought to shine light "on difficult histories," investigate "untold stories," and experiment with "different approaches to storytelling."[76] To this end, Kehinde Wiley's 2020 *Portrait of Asia-Imani, Gabriella-Esnae, and Kaya Palmer*, on long-term loan to the Fogg, occupied one new sightline, while the entrance to David Hammons's video installation *Phat Free* occupied another. From the courtyard, where it could be seen free of charge, *The Mulatto* looked to have been hung in order to complement Wiley's and Hammon's work. Only inside the gallery, and only as ticketholders, could the public read that the hang "situated Emil Nolde's painting [...] and its unnamed subject in the context of the Black German experience and the 'Degenerate Art' campaign." Of the sightlines created in the pandemic's wake, alone the Busch galleries' vista was vexing in this way. Nolde railed against racial mixing. And although he made sure this would be forgotten after the war, when he would be celebrated as a victim of the Nazi regime, after 1933 upon finding he had been categorized as "Degenerate" he did everything he could to persuade the Nazis they had got him completely wrong, producing (among other things) a plan for "de-Jewifying" Germany and circulating it among members of the government with the hopes that Hitler might read it.[77] The Busch's curatorial decision had a good effect. It invited difficult conversations and new reckonings with the present and past, as has been the norm for this anomalous collection. For one thing, during this hang, the picture's museum title changed from *The Mulatto* to *Woman of Mixed Race*.

Beckmann's *Self-Portrait* looked at home in its reduced position in the back corner of the Busch. Students found it slightly harder to see and to discuss its painterly subtleties (the lighting makes the play of glossy and matte paints almost invisible), but they adapted, and so did the painting.[78] The artist had, after all, engineered it for change. In his Frankfurt studio, it would have looked as if it were itself set *in* an artist's studio, with frames and canvases stacked up on the wall behind the sitter, and the tuxedo but one of the artist's many histrionic props. Then, at its unveiling at the Berlin Secession, it might have seemed audacious: its maker overdressed for the occasion, yet, a Gold Medal won, also equal to his ambitions. Ascended to Germany's Nationalgalerie, the portrait's chameleon backdrop would again mutate, becoming elegant, festive, and official. The picture's question—the artist and the state—receives its answer in this ultimate tableau: Beckmann as the artist of the state. Even deaccession and debasement could be absorbed into the painting's iconography. A poignant photo survives of the *Self-Portrait* standing

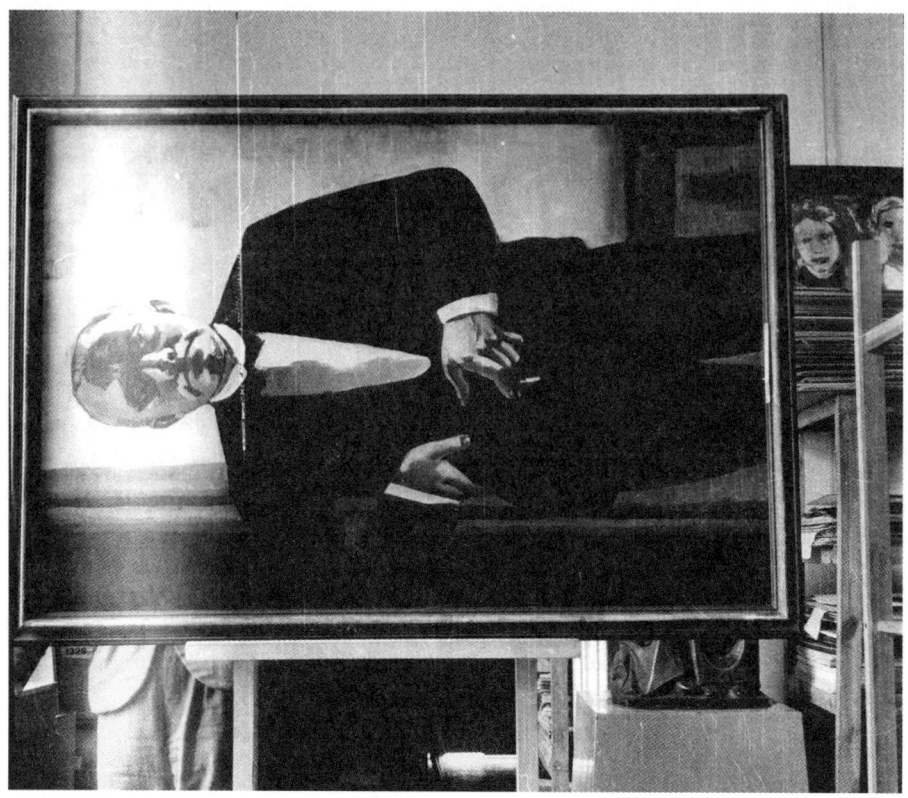

FIG. 64. Photograph of Max Beckmann's *Self-Portrait in Tuxedo* in Schloss Schönhausen, 1938. Zentralarchiv, Berlin (SMB-ZA, V/Slg. "E. K." u. KP, Roters Liste 51)

haphazardly on its side in 1938 in a depot in Schloss Schönhausen (fig. 64). Now the white blank of the painting's background echoes the "degenerate" artworks stacked on the shelves behind, anonymizing the *Self-Portrait* as a document in an historical archive. That, too, is art in a state of siege. Camouflaged among the ruins of an idol chamber, Beckmann's cigarette burns dangerously still.

William Kentridge

Johannesburg, 1993

At the time, the drawing would have looked complete (fig. 65). A dead body filled the sheet from end to end, and patchy ground covered the rest. The cause of death held center stage. A gaping exit wound below the chest indicated a bullet, presumably taken in the back. A disheveled shirt, torn open to the shoulder, registered the tumult of the moment when the victim fell to the ground, perhaps while running, perhaps away from the shooter, the impact causing the tear. Sheets of newspaper under and around the body extended the evidence to moments before and after sudden fatal one, when others, chased or chasing, whipped up the printed sheets. One sheet rested over the victim's feet, arriving there after the shot and the victim's fall, after his body lay inert.

Compared to the suddenness it conjured, the drawing looked slowly made. The body's torqued pose, the newspapers in proper perspective, the gray ground a lively chiaroscuro, the bright parts left in reserve, as unmarked paper, evinced effort, knowhow, and forethought. The sketch could have been exhibited as it was: an artwork of dramatic urgency made in charcoal on heavy cotton stock an impressive five feet wide. Even its messiness would have looked deliberate: artistic finish restrained by an ethical demand for fact.

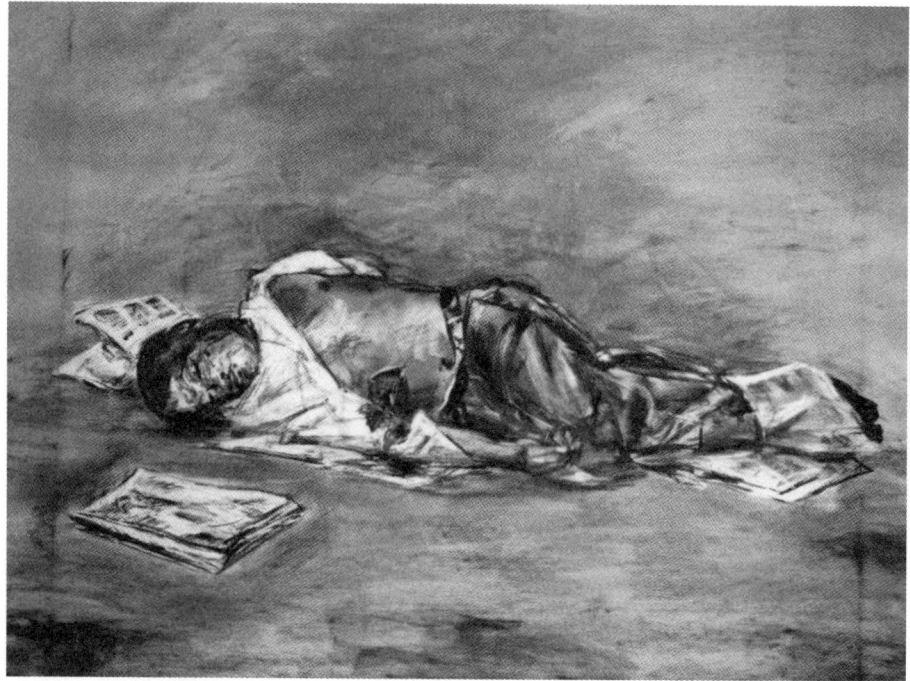

FIG. 65. Still from William Kentridge, *Felix in Exile*, 1994. 35mm film transferred to video

This drawing's eloquence would have already seemed more forensic than aesthetic. Silent witness to a crime, the sketched corpse looked as if testifying before a public forum—a law court, medical board, or government commission. Yet something about the drawing, its stiff outlines, calligraphic reserve, and labored illegibility in the area of the face, also suggested that the fact conveyed had already circulated in the public sphere, and that the body was neither drawn from life nor dreamt up by the artist, but had been copied, sometimes point by point, from another image, presumably from a photographic one as might appear in black-and-white halftone in a newspaper. The drawing's creator, William Kentridge, reports that a filmmaker friend had mentioned certain photos he had seen of bodies in the veld. Whether this friend used those exact words—"bodies in the veld"—the artist can no longer remember. But picturing to himself those photographs, he imagined individual bodies lying in the type of open rural landscape that in South Africa is called the veld. When he finally got hold of the actual snapshots of Black South Africans killed in the political violence raging in the country at the time, the bodies turned out to lie in interior spaces: rooms, doorways, and corridors.[1] The artist therefore sketched carefully a single body from one of the photographs, and for reasons not evident yet, but important to the drawing's future, he surrounded it with indications of the misheard or misimagined veld.

And that was when the real work began. Late in 1993, as spring in the southern hemisphere turned to summer, Kentridge approached this drawing pinned up on a wall in his studio and with his sharp charcoal made what might have seemed a trivial addition (fig. 66). In the area of the wound, where blood spilled over the shirt, he extended by a few millimeters one dark rivulet staining the victim's sleeve. Further up, closer to the wound, he also wiped over a highlighted droplet so that it lost its shine, and where the blood-soaked sleeve met the newspaper, doubling as shadow to define the underlying contour of the arm, he added reinforcements. In ordinary drawing practice, such strategic marks and smudges might amount to finishing touches—cautious efforts to clarify the image without overworking it. Detected by a connoisseur of master drawings, they might be understood as telling "pentimenti," from the Italian *pentire*, "to regret." But Kentridge's was no ordinary drawing practice, and the changes made from here on in served a purpose altogether different from remorse. For in his studio, behind him as he as he drew, stood a film camera, with the oblong sheet perfectly framed in the viewfinder.

Once previously, before he made these changes, Kentridge had clicked the camera's shutter three times. Three frames of film, amounting to a quarter-second

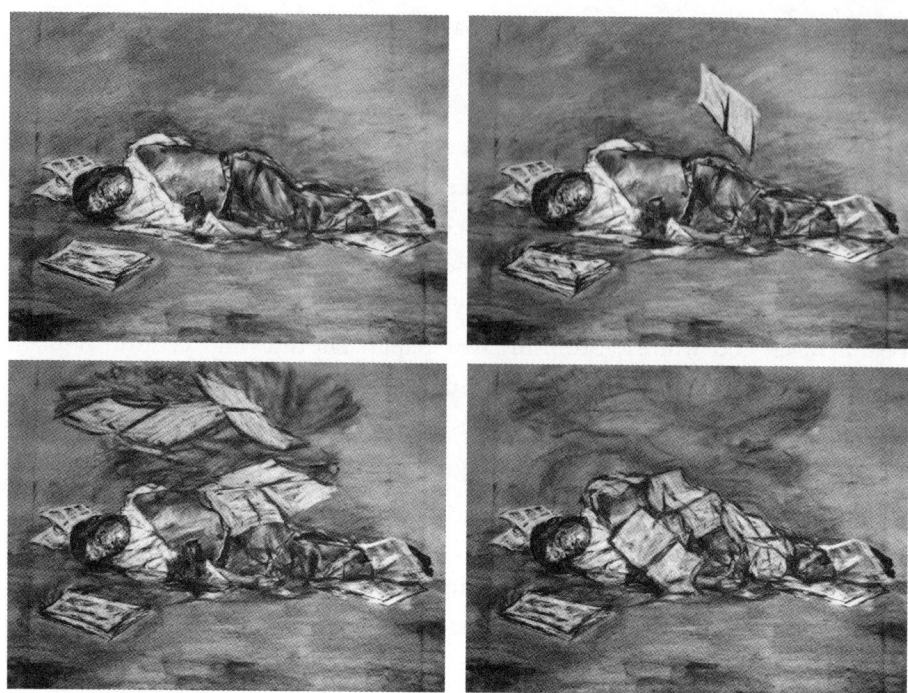

FIG. 66. Stills from William Kentridge, *Felix in Exile*, 1994. 35mm film transferred to video

of screen time, are all that remain of the finished-looking drawing described above. The new state, the one with the minor changes that buried the earlier state into the past, would share this fate—three clicks, three frames, a split second of film time—since it would be altered too, as would the scores of successive states, allowing, among other things, the wound to seem, in the film, still to bleed and the left tip of the foreground newspaper gently to rise and then to fall, as if lifted by a breeze. Extinguished in the original charcoal, the suddenness of a real time event returns in the twelve frames-per-second flash of 35mm film projection. In the studio, however, work was anything but swift. A minute of film could take months to create, far longer than it took to complete the drawing for the opening shot. Making came almost to a standstill, while also propelling the maker into motion between the drawing and the camera. Kentridge has made the claim that the directions his animations take are never planned. Following no outline or storyboard, they unfold fortuitously and playfully in the curious gap between creating a mark and beholding it from the camera's point of view, and in the walking that joins the two. "Left foot, right foot, go back to the beginning," explained the artist in a lecture while miming on stage how he paced, "Something about the action that can provoke thinking—a change from the physical to the mental, a truce between the artist as maker and the artist as observer."[2]

The newspaper's momentary flutter may have begun as an afterthought, an economical way of animating the rest of the drawing while making the wound appear to bleed. But just two seconds of screen time and many charcoal interventions later, Kentridge drew the top sheet peeling off from the pile to soar up above the body and come to rest over the victim's hip. Marginal at first, the newspapers stole the scene, their expressive shape-shifting a virtuoso demonstration of what successive phases of a charcoal drawing, filmed, could achieve. Now a whole sheaf of pages leapt up and divided into three, each gliding in the air like a bird or angel, then shrouding the body where they land. Out of the drawing's periphery, from impulses arriving from the charcoal medium, came a story: the body disappearing into the veld.

The body bore witness to a traumatic event. Its vanishing into the veld projected that testimony into a future when memories fade, or are censored or repressed, and when human history passes into the landscape, becoming natural history. Kentridge conjured this flashing forth and disappearance in the sitting room of his parental home. That domestic space served as his studio at the time, with the charcoal drawing and the camera forming an enclave within an enclave within an enclave. Like most homes in the Upper Houghton area of Johannesburg, the Kentridge residence itself stands inside a gated compound, with high walls and fences around the perimeter. Behind the main house, terraced gardens rise steeply up a hillside, with vistas northward, over the Highveld, towards Pretoria. The only member of his family remaining in South Africa, Kentridge returned to his childhood home in stages. In 1993–94, he only used its sitting room as his studio, residing in the Bertrams district, a few miles to the south. A few years later, he moved with his wife and children into the Houghton residence, and in 2000, he erected on the grounds, and set apart from the house, a purpose-built studio in the form of a tall, square citadel.

The summer of 1993–94 was a dangerous time in South Africa. After the formal end of apartheid on February 2, 1990 and Nelson Mandela's release from prison nine days later, the country had moved haltingly towards democratic rule, with factions of the White minority violently resisting change, and formerly silenced or outlawed opposition groups wrestling for power. In April 1993 the murder of Chris Hani (leader of the Communist Party) by right-wing extremists brought the crisis to a head. Fighting between White supremacists, Zulu nationalists, and the African National Congress pushed the country to the brink of civil war, with thousands murdered in street violence, massacres, and reprisal killings. The situation improved after Mandela's victory on April 28, 1994, as the first democratically elected president of South Africa. But when Kentridge drew the body disappearing in the veld, the outcome was uncertain.

The image of the body in the veld projected the dangerous moment occurring outside, in the Black townships, into the protective enclosure of a family home, and into the studio space within that enclosure where, between the drawing and the camera, Kentridge worked alone. Keeping the freedom of the graphic line rigorously in check, Kentridge drew the one corpse with forensic care, but also moved it to the veld—less to distance the image than to take stock of distancing mechanisms themselves. Newspapers screamed of atrocities from all corners of the country; now they flutter about in an unnoticed, unnewsworthy afterwards, gently blanketing but ultimately concealing the evidence. Historical amnesia, South Africa's refusal to come to terms with its violent, unjust, racist past, is thus called to account—in *Ubu and the Truth Commission* (1997), Kentridge, with playwright Jane Taylor, would address how to retrieve the testimony of victims.

In admonishing against forgetfulness through the medium of charcoal drawings, however, something peculiar occurred. It happened already in those first tiny alterations, although almost imperceptibly: erased or drawn over, the marks of the original drawing remained detectable as traces. But it was when the first newspaper rose above the body into the neutral ground of the veld, twisting about as if with aesthetic abandon, that these traces became dramatically indelible images of the past.

For their illusion of movement motion pictures depend on the persistence of vision. The human eye can only process ten or so separate images per second. If within about a fifteenth of a second one image is replaced by another, the first will persist, creating the semblance of continuity. Rather than making hundreds of slightly different drawings and projecting their image in rapid succession (how animation is ordinary done), Kentridge altered the same drawing hundreds of times, engendering motion and plot. Because the charcoal marks cannot be completely erased, all previous images persist not just in the eye, but materially on the sheet of paper. Animated, the drawing tells the story of the body disappearing in the veld. But it also tells a story of its own making. In its palimpsest of marks and erasures it testifies to the ineluctable persistence of the past. In a moment of danger an image of the past flashed forth. It was this artist's calling not only to seize hold of the image, but also to retain it in the conviction that, written by the victors, history conceals the victims. "*Even the dead* will not be safe from the enemy if he wins."[3]

Grahamstown, 1986

"Art in a state of siege" is an artist's motto born *in extremis*. At midnight on June 12, 1986, South Africa's White minority government imposed a nationwide state of emergency granting authorities extraordinary powers, including immunity from prosecution and the right to impose curfews, seize property, ban journalists, search without warrant, arrest without charges, and use of any kind of force to disperse crowds. The emergency was only announced twelve hours later. By then thousands of anti-apartheid activists had been detained and Black townships locked down. Giving police the advantage of surprise, the delayed public notice also accorded with the state of emergency's liminal legal status. Government actions acquired the force of law by suspending the law, creating an orderly disorder—something different than anarchy and chaos. "Because the exception is different from anarchy and chaos, order in the juristic sense still prevails, even if it is not of the ordinary kind."[4] That is how Schmitt put it in the 1920s, a time Kentridge acknowledged was similar to his own: "The artists working in Weimar were working in a state of siege."[5]

"I am of the opinion," declared President P. W. Botha to Parliament on the afternoon of June 12, "that the ordinary laws of the land at present on the statute books are inadequate to enable the government to insure the security of the public and to maintain public order." Having taken the decision on his own, without consulting Parliament or his cabinet, Botha spoke ominously of "plans which have been made by radical and revolutionary elements for the coming days, which pose real danger for all population groups in the country." Though he would not say what plans these were, the state of emergency anticipated unrest foreseen for June 16, the tenth anniversary of the Soweto Uprising when police violence left hundreds dead and many more wounded. And by the government's account, domestic protest, in 1986 as in 1976, worked hand in glove with foreign foes. A constant and "total onslaught" of Soviet-backed neighbor states required "total control" externally through direct and covert military action, and internally through martial law. Botha acknowledged that the state of emergency would further isolate South Africa internationally: "stricter security action will elicit strong criticism and even punishment measures from the outside world." Besieged by enemies within and beyond its borders and, through economic and cultural sanctions, by a liberal world order, South Africans had "to go it alone" in order to preserve (in Botha's words) "their heritage of 300 years."[6]

This was the state of siege referenced by the motto. Needless to say, it was understood differently by those who imposed and supported it than by those who contested or were targeted by it, and differently again by White South Africans—reactionary or progressive—than by the country's Black majority who, ever since the 1913 Native Lands Act, had been placed under executive rule rather than under Parliament and thus stood already under siege. Lifting constitutional and judicial restraints, the state of emergency made the ruling National Party the all-powerful decider over everyone, eliminating differences because nothing escaped its reach. Not just dissent, protest, and resistance, but everyday life in its private forms was abandoned to this non-judicial law. Art came under siege, as well. In normal conditions presumed to be autonomous from politics and law, art found itself forced either to justify or to challenge, in dwindling outlets, the legitimacy of the regime, while the regime, forbidding criticism, widened the parameter of what it deemed political to include, among other things, arts festivals. It must have been some of this that went through his mind when, on June 15, 1986, with South Africa entering its darkest hour, William Kentridge typed, underlined and in capitals, ART IN A STATE OF SIEGE.

The words headed the script of a public talk delivered some days later at the Winter School, the lecture venue of the National Festival of the Arts in Grahamstown (renamed Makhanda in 2018) in South Africa's Eastern Cape province.[7] Today their author is one of the world's most celebrated artists, a prolific creator of prints, drawings, animated films, tapestries, sculptures, multimedia installations, colossal murals, public monuments, and historical pageants, and an acclaimed designer and theatrical director of major opera productions. Over two random days in mid-December 2014, he could be observed collaging wall-size paper trees in his home studio, monitoring the casting of small bronzes at a collaborating foundry, checking progress on a public sculpture of welded steel plates that form a walking globe when looked at from a certain spot, tinkering with his multimedia backdrop for live performances of Schubert's *Die Winterreise* song cycle, overseeing the computer programming of mechanized drum sets for an upcoming exhibition, inspecting at his bustling downtown studio a series of cut-out profiles to be carried in a new multimedia "dance of death" installation *More Sweetly Play the Dance*, visiting a print workshop where his ink drawings were being transferred onto linoleum matrices, taking a stroll through a retrospective of his tapestries based on his designs about to opening at Wits Art Museum, stopping in a satellite gallery exhibit of new landscapes sketched in charcoal on pages from a salvaged cash book once used by a local mining company, and giving a guided tour of his installation *The Refusal of Time* on view at the Johannesburg Art Museum—while also genially preparing delicious meals for his family, office and assistants, and visitors, including myself, my wife, and six astonished students from Harvard.

But in June 1986, when he coined the motto, there was scant evidence of what art in a state of siege might be.

Born in 1955, William Kentridge had reached the age of thirty-one with only a modest creative output to his name. His decision to become an artist had been late and wavering. In South Africa, his surname is still powerfully associated with a distinguished line of lawyers, all cosmopolitan, progressive, and politically engaged.[8] William's paternal grandfather Morris Kentridge, born Kantrovich in Lithuania, studied law in Scotland and served for over forty years as a Laborite member of South Africa's Parliament—one of the few Jews to hold such a position.[9] William's maternal grandmother, also with Jewish roots in Lithuania, was the first female advocate in South Africa and the second in the British Empire. Her daughter—Felicia Geffen, William's mother—was an esteemed civil rights lawyer, a fierce anti-apartheid activist, and the co-founder of the Legal Resource Centre, which litigated many of the country's landmark rights cases. William's father, Sir Sydney Kentridge (knighted in 1999), looms large in South African legal history, among other things for his defense of Nelson Mandela in the Treason Trial (1956–61) and his role in the inquest into the death of Stephen Biko (1977). Law was, in William's words, the "family business," and becoming an artist was "a completely unnatural thing to do."[10] When, around 1984, he finally settled on that calling, he did so with a unique sense of what law, by contrast with art, could achieve, but also with a certain rivalry, a wish to engage in a different and, at this dire moment, a perhaps more effective sphere.

The lawyers in William's family had operated in a field of conflict between law and politics, which is to say, between the statutes passed by Parliament and respecting rights enshrined in the country's constitution, and the execution of such statutes by the majority-party government. The government meanwhile clung to power by harassing or outlawing opposition parties and, via apartheid law which it pushed through starting in 1948, by preserving Whites-only voting. The creation of a patchwork of powerless, pseudo-autonomous homelands effectively rid South Africa of its Black citizens. The state of emergency further reduced this narrow field, since law fell wholly to the executive. Through his family William could grasp the nature of this legal vacuum. Whatever art might accomplish under siege would somehow have to stand apart from politics and law.

Kentridge's circuitous formation as an artist would have sharpened this understanding. At university he majored in African Studies and Politics.[11] In the mid-1970s, this meant heavy doses of Marx, and an approach to history less as a collection of facts than as a dynamic process, a ceaseless struggle between oppressors—whose victories and achievements tend to be the facts written down—and the largely unrecorded but far more numerous oppressed. This meant engaging critically with South Africa's past and perceiving the challenge that colonialism posed to history itself as a victor's story told largely about Europe by Europeans. If Hegel could declare, high-handedly, that "after the pyramids, World Spirit leaves Africa, never to return," Kentridge (in his words) would try "to see if a riposte could be given."[12]

Artmaking remained extracurricular. In studio classes at the new Johannesburg Art Foundation, Kentridge struggled with oil painting (central to the European tradition) but excelled in printmaking. This affinity was fortuitous, for although he engaged explicitly with European artist-printmakers—his works reference Dürer and Rembrandt, and especially the great satirists Hogarth, Goya, and Beckmann—printing linked him to Black South African artists working in the cheap but expressive medium of linocut. Compared to painting, prints were also more bookish, because of their shared materials, use of a press, intimacy, and storytelling capabilities. The readerly nature of prints, as well as their being issued in multiples and in serial form, also made them useful as visual communicators. Some of Kentridge's best early works are posters made for anonymous public display.

More crucial to his later development, though, was the way prints exposed the element of process. Compared to the immediacy of drawing and painting, printmaking segmented production into discrete stages, each involving different technologies, tempos, attitudes, and actors. The marks created on a pre-prepared matrix, meticulously inked and decisively wiped, leave behind a reversed and unpredictable impression on paper through pressure applied by a press operated by a collaborating master printer, or by the artist, but only if he or she has special training in that craft. Kentridge experimented widely with the whole range of print techniques—engraving, drypoint, etching, linocut, lithograph, silkscreen, aquatint, and sugar lift. And already in his earliest prints process was no mere means towards an end, but acquired a symbolic value in its own right. Though technically refined (from 1979 to 1980 he taught etching at the Art Foundation), his prints look deliberately like protracted struggles with their materials. Initial, seemingly rejected marks remain not fully burnished out of the matrix, and later lines, more nervous than sure, and sometimes differently inked, foretell future revisions, more difficult erasures, and denser palimpsests. All this visible facture makes the viewer's experience a process and a struggle, too. Counteracting blind empathy, where the beholder is sucked unthinkingly into the image's illusion, the artwork acquires what Kentridge, schooled in Marxist aesthetic theory, would have understood as a *critical* function: the familiar, which in normal conditions

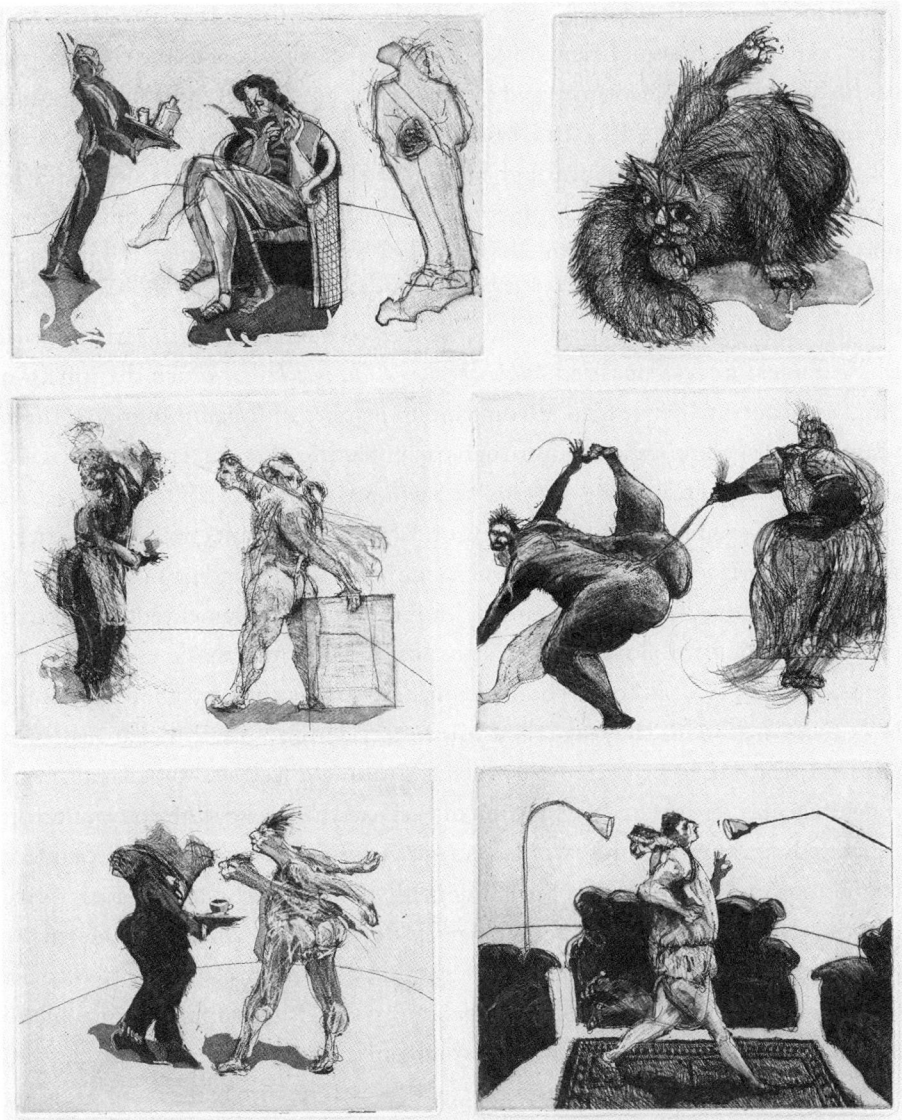

FIG. 67. William Kentridge, *Domestic Scenes (They also wait who only)*, 1980. Etching with soft ground and aquatint, 49 × 37.5 cm

seems true, right, and natural, suddenly reveals its contingent, historical, humanly constructed character and thus its capacity for change.

This was certainly a factor in the series *Domestic Scenes*, etched and printed in 1980 and shown in a solo exhibition at The Market Gallery in Johannesburg in 1981. In forty capriccios printed individually and in groups, Kentridge satirized the relation between privileged White employers and Black "domestics" (fig. 67). The closed, familial, and apolitical space of house and home—the *domus* contained in the word "domestic"—turns out to be a battlefield of racial warfare. The series previewed many of Kentridge's signature motifs: dance-like contortions of the human body, Goya-inspired experimentation with etching and aquatint in the service of Goya-like satire, cameo self-portraits with a confessional edge, filmic movement expressed through half-erased corrections, and erasure itself as a figure of repressed history. Predictive too was the etchings' dialogue with live performance. In 1975 Kentridge and some fellow students founded the Junction Avenue Theatre Company, South Africa's first non-racial theatrical group. While making *Domestic Scenes* he wrote and co-directed a farce about the struggles of Black domestic servants titled *Dikhitsheneng (The Kitchens)*, which the Junction Avenue Company performed at community centers in Johannesburg. In these years he engaged more in theater than in artmaking. The latter brought scant income: the only gallery sale of *Domestic Scenes* was to his mother.

Junction Avenue productions drew on Kentridge's talents not just as writer, director, and actor but also as poster artist and set designer and painter. Dramatic dialogue combined with dance, music, and mime, all supplemented by placards painted with political slogans, cryptic mottos, and plot information supplementing the action. Actors broke character mid-action or changed their makeshift costumes on stage as they switched roles—anything to prevent that fusion of elements into an illusionistic whole which had characterized traditional realist European theater. This jarring separation of parts had been a key doctrine of Bertolt Brecht's dramaturgy. "Music, words, and setting must become more independent of one another," wrote Brecht. Such independence served the elusive goal of epic theater, the "estrangement-effect" (*Verfremdungseffekt*).[13] Working in Germany when states of emergency were the governmental norm, Brecht proposed an art form that might overturn tyranny by defamiliarizing the ordinary: "turning the object of which one is made aware, to which one's attention is to be drawn, from something ordinary, familiar, immediately accessible, into something peculiar, striking, and unexpected."[14] In other words, fight the political state of emergency with subversive aesthetic emergencies.

The Junction Avenue Theatre followed Brecht in method and politics. Productions transposed events of South African history into dramatic conflicts between individuals and the races, classes, and ethnicities they represented. By exposing contradictions—between, say, the apolitical lazy tranquility of home life for Whites and the oppression of Black migrant domestic labor—they might transform the audience. Human life was a condition that could be changed, not a fate to be endured. Realist theater's fusion of elements, it was believed, pacified spectators, merging them with the spectacle. Separating the elements kept the

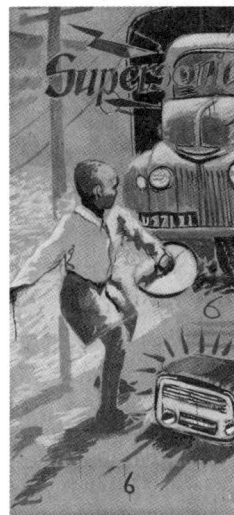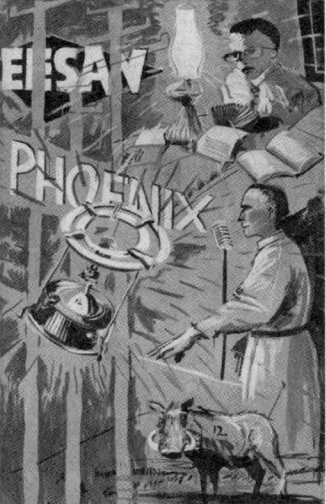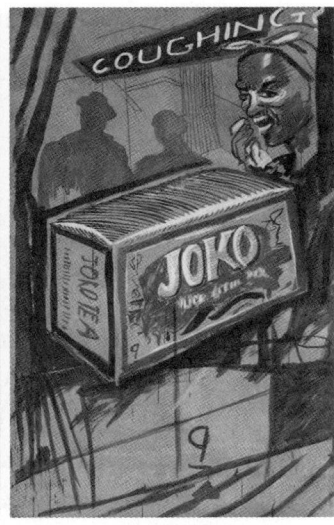

FIG. 68. William Kentridge, backdrop drawings for Junction Avenue Theatre Company's production of *Sophia-town*, 1986–88. Gouache on butcher paper

audience distanced, mobile, and alert. Separation also mirrored radical politics, exposing the structural differences of gender, class, and race. Kentridge made the backdrops for these productions. Painted mostly in black and white on big sheets of brown butcher paper tacked to the stage walls, these were roughhewn and collaged like the performance they backed, with mottos, slogans, and brand names clashing with images that were themselves fragmented. Surviving pieces of these wall-size backdrops have been framed and exhibited in roughly their original arrangement (fig. 68). Brecht would have approved. He championed storytelling that could playfully be extended, rearranged, or excerpted: narrative that "one can as it were take a scissors and cut it into individual pieces, which remain fully capable of life."[15]

When exhibited alongside his later art, these backdrops illuminate Kentridge's connection with theater. It is not just that, in his recent opera productions and multimedia performances, drawing remains a setting for music and words, or that exhibitions of his work often have the character of Brechtian tableaux, with the artists' banners outshouting the curator's wall labels and kinetic noisemaking sculptures standing in for stage props and orchestra. Kentridge's images pose as if they were merely the setting for something activated elsewhere, in that space in which the audience "meets the image halfway." However, this artist also gives "setting" a terrifying density, since it encompasses his studio, the domestic world within and around it, the surrounding city of Johannesburg, the Highveld land-scape beyond, and the human violence, that "never-ending chronicle of disasters or almost disasters," etched into the landscape like skid marks on a road (plates 27 and 32; fig. 98).[16] What has been pushed to the background steps forward to testify.

Changes in his family life moved image-making to the foreground of Kentridge's activities. In 1981, tired of facing "the terrible South African judges," his parents emigrated to London. That same year Kentridge moved to Europe and in London he married Anne Stanwix, an Australian-born medical doctor and his partner since university. When they resolved to return to Johannesburg in 1982, William became the only Kentridge to remain permanently in South Africa. No longer under his father's shadow, he worked restlessly at first, in theater, film, and television, but the birth of a daughter in 1984 brought focus: "That's the point where I began to write 'artist' on application forms, rather than 'technician.' Sink or swim I was reduced to being an artist."[17] He swam, thanks mostly to an ambitious group of drawings made in 1984–85 in charcoal on big heavyweight sheets of paper. Some of them grouped together as triptychs, like the painted ones by Bosch and Beckmann, these drawings amplified the storylines of his prints, with their kaleidoscopes of private and public life and their mix of humor, sentiment, and cruelty. Their sheer scale signaled importance and encouraged drawing with the whole body, something familiar to Kentridge from acting in the theater. Their rough texture, or tooth, grabbed the charcoal easily, as compared to the effortful marks prints required. And their thickness allowed the charcoal to be blended, rubbed, erased, reapplied, and erased again without damaging the sheet, although no matter how assiduously it was done, erasing left traces of the obliterated marks. This ability to transform but not to forget suited Kentridge and spoke to the historical moment. His etchings had achieved a palimpsestic look through multiply reburnishing and reworking their plates, and his films would take the fluid but indelible charcoal mark into uncharted territory. In the 1980s in South Africa, erasure also had a special meaning, due to the country's strict censorship laws. Reporting on censorship was itself censored, causing the editors of the liberal *Weekly News* defiantly to print redacted news items as black and white squares. Meanwhile, in the wider spheres of collective memory, in the history taught in school and commemorated in monuments, public holidays, and anniversaries, whole chapters of the country's past were forcefully repressed.

It was largely based on these new drawings, first exhibited in 1985 at Cassirer Fine Art Johannesburg, that Kentridge received from the Standard Bank its Young Artist Award. This distinction required the honoree to deliver a talk at the arts festival in Grahamstown followed, a year later, by a traveling solo exhibition. When Kentridge took to the podium in 1986 to speak of "the work I do," he was looking forward beyond his artistic output thus far to an oeuvre yet to be created.[18] Judging by the surviving typescript, he choreographed his talk carefully, with images and phrases projected behind him by a slide projector organizing, amplifying, and playing off against his script. Some of the slides were made by hand, by scratching what would be projected directly into the emulsion. More a multimedia performance than a conventional lecture, the collage of pictures, text, and theater inaugurated Kentridge's public presentation style. He perfected the style in his Norton Lectures, delivered at Harvard University in 2012, sixty-five years after Panofsky's talks on early Netherlandish art.

Handwritten notes, reminders, boldfaced emphases, and unspoken (because supplied by slides) mottos—some erased and corrected, some added on Post-its— fill the margins of the Grahamstown lecture's dot-matrix printout, suggesting that Kentridge worked on the script up to the last moment. These efforts paid off, as the text now stands as the artist's first and most important manifesto. It is as foundational to Kentridge's undertaking as the 1927 essay "The Artist in the State" was to Max Beckmann's. Excerpted in monographs and exhibition catalogues, the text has shaped the public understanding of Kentridge's practice particularly as it relates to apartheid—the context in which his work, when it began to appear in international venues, tended to be set. The lecture also laid down a program for what he would go on to make as he worked out, in productive dialogue with events unfolding in South Africa, what this strange thing, "art in a state of siege," might be.

In the lecture, that phrase names the last stage of a three-stage history of art. Although they belong to a chronological sequence, Kentridge considers the three stages as the different directions any artist might take. "The pictures I love," he explains, "are not for me."

> The great impressionist and post impressionist works, like the Big Seurat in the National Gallery in London and those Tiepolo skies are the paintings that give me the greatest pleasure. Immediate pleasure in the sense of well-being in the world. They are visions of a state of grace, of an achieved paradise. This state of grace is inadmissible to me.

This expulsion from paradise results partly from an artist's temperament. In Kentridge's experience, "lyricism" descends "into kitsch or sentiment." But the expulsion also follows from the ethical predicament of art making under apartheid:

> Lyricism seems to need a certain self-confidence and clear conscience that I lack [...]. Here, more than most other places one's nose is rubbed in compromise every day, and our compromises are more grotesque than most.

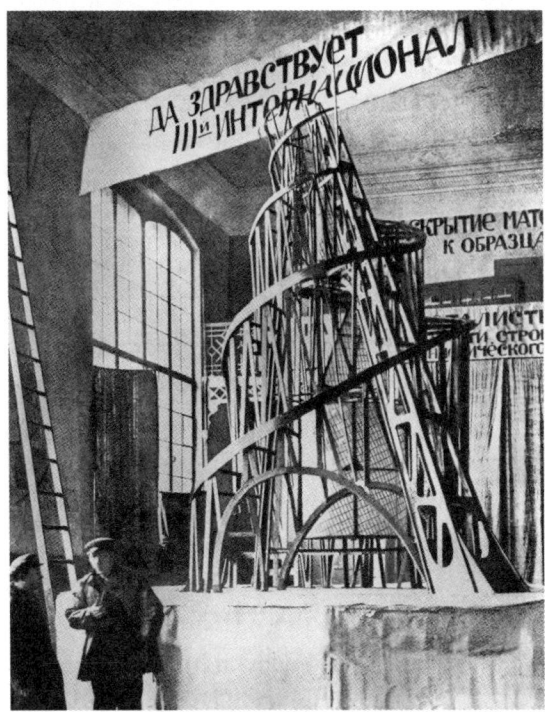

Beautiful paintings by Seurat and Tiepolo—epitomes of the European aesthetic tradition of disinterested pleasure and art for art's sake—did not achieve grace because they were created in a more just society. They conjured "a benevolent world" despite the "human misery" that already abounded. However: "It is one thing to be grateful for those lies and quite another to perpetuate them."[19]

Also denied to Kentridge is a different art, the revolutionary one rising from the ruins of those last beautiful illusions (fig. 69). This utopia is exemplified by Vladimir Tatlin's *Monument to the Third International*—not the concrete colossus Tatlin hoped would be built, which would have been "monstrous," but the wood and wire model of it as captured in an old photograph, "with Tatlin and his assistants clambering around [it], huge enough in itself, a hope and certainty I can only envy." Kentridge explains:

> Such hope, particularly here and now, seems impossible. The failure of those hopes and ideals, their betrayals are too powerful and too numerous. I cannot paint pictures of a future like that and believe in the pictures.

No longer able or willing to recuperate what he calls "art in a state of hope," Kentridge finds solace in the picture painted by Max Beckmann in 1938, when the artist had fled to exile in Amsterdam (plate 21). Painted in a dangerous moment,

Beckmann's *Death* flashes forth in Kentridge's present moment as "a beacon for endangered souls."

It accepts the existence of a compromised society and yet does not rule out all meaning or value nor pretend these compromises should be ignored. It marks the spot where optimism is kept in check and nihilism is kept at bay.[20]

In the typescript, Kentridge underlined, highlighted, and rewrote the words "optimism in check nihilism at bay," as if to make it his mantra.

When Kentridge declared art to be in a state of siege and reached back to Germany in the 1930s for a comparable example, his country stood in one of many emergency states. The 1986 decree renewed and expanded to the whole country a decree of July 20, 1985, which declared an emergency in thirty-six magisterial districts. That emergency state, in turn, reiterated one imposed in March 1960 after the massacre of unarmed protesters in Sharpeville, and that imposition was sanctioned, in turn, by Public Safety Act No. 3 passed in 1953 and empowering the government to deem a state of emergency to exist at any time, and "in any area within the Union."[21] Over and above these acts and decrees stood the pathological legality of apartheid itself, in which the ruling White minority National Party annulled decisions made by the courts and retroactively passed laws supporting its racialist rulings and policies. The 1986 State of Emergency, imposed three days before Kentridge typed out the text of his lecture, would be renewed annually until 1989, when radical change finally came to South Africa. During these four tumultuous years, thousands died at the hands of security forces and state-sponsored assassins, and in violence among opposition groups.

Kentridge's audience in Grahamstown would have grasped what art in the states of grace and hope meant for South African artists. Apolitical art in the modernist forms of Post-Impressionism, Abstract Expressionism, and Color Field Painting continued to be taught and practiced, despite political circumstances that appalled most of its champions. Kentridge termed this disconnect "the disease of urbanity" and defined it as "the refusal be moved by the abominations we are surrounded by and involved with." In his view, art cannot overcome the disconnect altogether, because human passions and memories are short-lived. Artists can, however, capture the different "impressions and impulses"—rage, guilt, apathy, denial, cynicism—before they solidify into "some moral bedrock (opportunism is the word that comes to mind)." Revolutionary art, with its utopian hopes, also existed in South Africa, variously as "resistance" and "struggle" art, although the government suppressed it, forcing it underground or into exile. Kentridge's early posters fell somewhat into this category—what Albie Sachs, its first politically progressive critic, called "fists and spears and guns art."[22] But it had proved politically ineffective and ethically and aesthetically limiting, as it did not address the "ambiguities and contradictions" (Sachs) of life as lived in a state of siege.

For Kentridge the choice was less between politics and art than between law and art as alternative vehicles for dissent, the former based on argument, the latter on ambiguity. All choices were anyway limited. In Beckmann's *Death*, in the canvas's dizzying, uncertain, and contradictory vantage point, Kentridge glimpsed "a narrow gap" that he could work in and through,

> aware of and drawing sustenance from the anomaly of my position. At the edge of huge social upheavals but removed from them. Not able to be part of these upheavals nor to work as if they did not exist. This position—neither active participant nor disinterested observer—is the starting point and the area of my work. It is not necessarily the subject of it. The work itself is so many excursions around the edge of this position.

The gap, spot, edge, area, and "fox hole" offering protection from enemy fire: these are Kentridge's figures for the state of siege, a state the artist asserts is "the condition of many people if not all of us."[23] After all, siege had become, just days before under a slightly different name, the country's *official* state. Kentridge took the word "siege" (instead of "emergency") from Costa-Gavras's 1972 film *État de Siège*, which dramatized the struggle between Uruguay's repressive right-wing government and leftist guerrillas. Closer to home, André Brink, already in 1983 under the title *Writing in a State of Siege*, had called on South African writers to take moral responsibility for their society—Brink's 1988 novel *States of Emergency*, set in 1985, would weave public and domestic emergencies together into a fiction about fiction writing.[24] Siege was the condition the government claimed the country was in, in order to call a state of emergency: a nation surrounded by hostile Soviet-backed neighbor states, threatened from within by insurgents, and hypocritically shunned by the international community. Siege was also the condition felt by the opposition, besieged as it was publicly and privately now by the police and security forces. Importantly, siege was a state South Africans, and artists especially, experienced working in a country culturally boycotted by most nations of the world. But siege was finally the juridical fact of a legally sanctioned and legally binding suspension of law.

Siege is in fact the oldest of the several terms used in legal doctrine for what the South African government called an "emergency." It is a surprisingly recent term, the artifact not of absolutist regimes but of revolutionary and democratic ones. There must exist a secular concept of the "rule of law" to require a loophole wherein, temporarily, under conditions of armed conflict, natural disaster, unrest, and pandemic, the laws that constrain government power can lawfully be suspended. In English, these states are mostly termed "emergencies" (from Latin *emergere*, "to rise out or up"), with accidental catastrophe as their model, although the peculiar law they trigger is often called "martial," thus evoking the human activity of war. As we have seen in Schmitt's response to Bosch and in the emergency states of the Weimar Republic, under which Beckmann worked, German legal doctrine uses the terms "necessity" (*Not*) and "exception" (*Ausnahme*). The latter, "exception," has the advantage of capturing, without analogy to a different kind of law (e.g., "martial"), the status of a lawful suspension of the law itself.

Antedating these, the term "state of siege," when used outside its common meaning as that dire form of warfare dating back to the earliest cities, originated as a technical term during the French Revolution.[25] It was coined to describe a condition distinct both from peace, where military and civil authority each act in their own sphere, and from war, where civil authority acts in concert with the military. In the *état de siège*, "all functions entrusted to the civil authority for maintaining order and internal policing pass to the military commander, who exercises them under his exclusive responsibility." Devised in 1791 for situations at seaports and around military strongholds, where the word "siege" clearly applies, this third state was soon declared for entire cities and municipalities inside France. On December 24, 1811, Napoleon gave himself the power to declare a state of siege whether or not a city was actually besieged by enemy forces. Aimed at suppressing civil unrest, Napoleon's *état de siège* received a telling qualification. It was "fictitious" (*fictif*) and "political" (*politique*). It has little to do with the situation of a fort or town surrounded by enemy troops, since the foe lies diffused within the polity. Such a siege is therefore *fictitious*, and it is also *political*, because to decide there exists an internal adversary who should be treated *as if* it were an enemy outsider—that is politics at its extreme.

South Africa's siege states were patently political, the desperate measure by the National Party to keep its decades-long hold on the government. Siege was also transparently fictitious, and not just in old juridical sense. After the National Party's 1948 victory in the general election, politics—the activities of political parties, elections, and parliamentary dispute and legislation—operated within the limits set by apartheid law, which (in 1950) ruled that "white" South Africans (people of "European" descent) should be juridically, territorially, and conjugally set *apart* from "non-whites."[26] Prohibiting Black South Africans from living in cities and certain areas, imposing pass laws that effectively defined Blacks as foreigners in all but their pseudo-national "homelands," and constructing a fictional system of "separate but equal," the ruling majority, in fact a small minority within South Africa, constructed a topography that, in times of unrest, placed the White minority in a state of siege. To be White but opposed to apartheid was to be, as Seamus Heaney wrote for a different context, "besieged within the siege, whispering morse." Heaney built his metaphor for Catholic rebellion in 1970s Northern Ireland on that oldest story in all of European fiction, the ten-year Siege of Troy: "Where half of us, as in a wooden horse / Were cabin'd and confined like wily Greeks."[27]

A key aspect of siege is that it is meant to be temporary. Special articles and provisions in a legal code can provide some emergency powers under certain circumstances, but these powers are limited in time and in scope. They do not extend to changing the law permanently. Once in force, however, emergency powers can be renewed, sometimes interminably. This had been the case in Nazi Germany, as we have seen, and it must have seemed the case in South Africa in 1986—the state of emergency's annual renewal ceased only on June 7, 1990. Dates matter to the history of emergencies, as they locate in time what should be temporary. South Africa's history unfolds through watershed dates: 1948, 1950, 1953, 1960, 1985, 1986, 1989, 1990, 1994. Inside a state of siege, however, time seems to stand still. Fictive and political ones terminate arbitrarily, since the decision to end them stands outside the legal norm. Ancient Rome had an institution analogous to the state of siege, the name of which expresses vividly this legal and temporal suspension: when, due to war or civil unrest, an emergency (*tumultus*) was declared, this could lead to the proclamation of a specific legal order, termed an *iustitium*. Charisius, a fourth-century Latin grammarian, explained the word etymologically: "Iustitium: when the law stands still, just as [the sun does in] the solstice."[28] Interrupting the flow of time, each standstill makes earlier ones seem contemporaneous. Apartheid South Africa in its final days, Weimar Germany as it veers towards dictatorship, the presidency of Donald Trump: "an old story [...] all cousins."[29]

From another perspective, states of siege are not time-limited, but interminable, because for some people living within a legal order, and arguably for all legal orders in their violent or arbitrary beginnings, siege conditions are the norm. This was what Walter Benjamin, writing in 1940, in flight from the Gestapo, articulated in his *Theses on the Philosophy of History*: "The tradition of the oppressed teaches us that the 'state of exception' in which we live is the rule. We must arrive at a concept of history that is adequate to this."[30] The experience of the oppressed speaks against the assumption that emergency powers are easily surrendered and that siege states will be temporally limited. According to Benjamin, knowing this is the case is necessary not just for understanding this or that dangerous event or period in history, but for understanding history in general. One should not be surprised that something like fascism can arise "even" today. Refusing the enlightened expectation of progress, the surprise is that anyone should be surprised. But what about the history of art? What kind of history might be written about it?

Paris, 1981

No matter how strong the walls and ample the supplies, the besieged cannot foresee the outcome of their plight or its duration. "I have to be precise but I don't know when the invasion began," explains the chronicler in Zbigniew Herbert's 1982 poem "Report from a Besieged City":

> two hundred years ago in autumn perhaps yesterday at
> dawn
> here everybody is losing the sense of time[31]

Battles are swiftly won or lost. News of their conclusion arrives only after the event. Sieges can last for months, even years. During the temporal and legal standstill, the besieged must endure, negotiate, and delay. Delay tests the besiegers and the besieged. Enemy forces surrounding a city can be attacked from behind. In time, they can suffer famine, plague, and internal strife, like the besieged. In the period between the Reformation and Napoleon, when rulers preferred siege warfare to battle and news could travel in printed form, a lively literature arose that reported on sieges in real time, while they were underway, publicizing each turn of events to a polarized international audience. From March through May of 1631, Imperial forces of the Catholic League besieged Protestant Magdeburg. Hearing accounts of Catholic defeats elsewhere, Magdeburg's citizenry held out, hoping for a relief attack from Lutheran Swedish troops. No help arrived, and Imperial forces breached the walls, torched and plundered the city, and murdered almost all its twenty-five thousand inhabitants. Widely broadcast, this destruction—nicknamed Magdeburgization—etched itself into the European imagination. For both sides of the confessional divide, but initially for vengeful Protestants, to exterminate defeated foes was to give them "Magdeburg mercy." Written in 1939 after Hitler invaded Poland, Brecht's *Mother Courage* includes a visit to Magdeburg just after its sacking. During the early modern Wars of Religion of the sixteenth and seventeenth centuries, siege was all-pervasive, as it was in Europe in 1939 and in apartheid Johannesburg, where the Market Theatre performed Brecht's play. People were "losing the sense of time" again.

Once concluded, the story of a siege tends to be written by the winners. If its walls withstand the enemy, a city can boast of its endurance. If its fortifications fail, a city can lose not just freedom, treasure, and lives. It loses its past, too, since history belongs among the conqueror's spoils. Testimony of the utterly defeated is rare. The little that has survived speaks of unspeakable hardship, of "going into misery" (*ins Elend gehen*) and wandering robbed of *Heimat* "and everything else," as one Catholic victim of Swedish urbicide put it.[32] A stock phrase, *ins Elend gehen* implies exile from home and from history. Benjamin's point in calling states of exception the rule was to avoid an unreflective "empathy with the victor" that, beneficial to rulers, characterizes supposedly objective history. The past "as it really was" is only what victors want to be written and remembered. The besieged see history differently, but rarely get to tell their tale. As an African proverb has it, the lion's story will never be known as long as the hunter is the one to tell it.

Histories of art are triumphal, too. Most artists work for the rich and powerful, aggrandizing them and theirs; whether by plunder or purchase, artworks remain with the victors. Histories of the art deemed to matter historically—art that shapes the future by breaking with the past—tend to be more subtly triumphal. In them, artists win more than their patrons. They overcome philistines, teachers, rivals, tradition, prejudice, museums, capitalism, and the art world. They struggle with materials, techniques, conventions, poverty, misunderstanding, neglect, and self-doubt, and they triumph. But what about art in a state of siege? Unable to conquer, such art can at most endure. Keeping optimism in check and nihilism at bay, it broadcasts its efforts minute by minute, losing the sense of time and borrowing liberally from art of the past, which in dangerous moments seems like yesterday. But while it cannot be victorious, it is also not a victim. Art in a state of siege requires a history of the *not yet*: not yet triumph, not yet lament.

The story of Kentridge's artistic development might be written in two parts, with 1986 and South Africa's state of emergency as its turning point. In the first part, the artist's diverse activities stay in their separate spheres. Forms, themes, and motifs from his theatrical work enter into his prints without those prints becoming theater, and without theater becoming an extension of the prints. In the second part, his activities become even more diverse, but now they orbit around a single center. Drawing becomes a form of film and film becomes a form for drawing; posters become artworks with posters as one of their themes; theatrics are internalized into the work of art. Collaboration with other makers still flourishes, but the results are, from the public point of view, works by "William Kentridge." The transition to being an Artist with a capital "A" is not simple. When he steps into his works, Kentridge does so in character. These excursions link back to his pre-1986 work in dramatic ensembles, when he changed roles and costumes on stage, and before sets that just happened to be by his hand. But now pretending to be someone else makes everything that much more recognizably Kentridge's own. This change is partly the artist's doing, his unwavering commitment to art as a calling. Partly it results from an audience perspective that draws diverse objects, films, texts, and performances into the artist's "oeuvre."

From 1986 on, Kentridge has handled his oeuvre with great care. Working mostly in charcoal or India ink on paper, even dressing in black and white, he gives everything he makes a tonal and material consistency. Color rarely enters into his work, and almost never mixed and layered in the way painters handle color. Crimson red and lapis blue flash up in this largely monochrome oeuvre as distinctive leitmotifs: crimson for forensic interventions, the red of rubrics and redactions; lapis, rarer than the crimson but more generous when applied, aqueous, consoling, and lifegiving (plates 27, 29, and 32). In recent works, rich samplings of individual colors in geometric shapes appear printed on encyclopedia pages, a color vocabulary for others besides Kentridge to use.

Like colors, dramatic characters appear sparingly, with enough backstory to make them last through his oeuvre, shaping it into an epic cycle or *comédie humaine*. His experiment, begun in 1986, of filming drawings as they come into being benefits this endeavor. It gives images, usually freeze-framed at the moment they are deemed complete, time to tell a story. At first mere records of the drawing's line-by-line production, these plots could be embellished into dramatic conflicts, and these could develop serially, from one film to the next, to form a cycle. Although Kentridge accepts the most diverse commissions with almost playful abandon, even this variety contributes to the oeuvre. His production of Dmitri Shostakovich's *The Nose* reworked imagery, techniques, and styles from his earlier work, imagining the opera from a new perspective. But from Shostakovich Kentridge himself received new myths and motifs, each complete with layered backstories. Henceforth any disembodied proboscis in a work by Kentridge, whether drawn, etched, cut with scissors, hand-torn from construction paper, modeled in clay, cast in bronze, or woven in tapestry, carries rich constellations of meaning: utopian hopes and Stalinist terror, corrupt politics and the aesthetics of the grotesque, Shostakovich and Nikolai Gogol, and much, much more.

In 2007, Kentridge designed a production of *The Magic Flute* to discover, in that paean to Enlightenment over darkness and night, a new critical perspective on Africa's violent colonialist past, as well as on the artist's medium of black and white that will inform future projects. In 2018, to commemorate the centenary of World War I, he collaborated on the performance piece *The Head and the Load*, remembering the forgotten million Africans killed in that war. A year later, he directed Alban Berg's *Wozzeck*, with its worm's eye view of army life, absorbing into his oeuvre Austro-Hungarian and, through Georg Büchner's 1836 play (*Woyzeck*), Prussian military history. Although in hindsight inevitable, these increases could not be predicted in advance. They arose through a managed form of accident, what Kentridge terms "fortuna": "something other than cold statistical chance, and something, too, outside the range of rational choice."[33]

One summer, while Kentridge was behind in his work, an army of ants invaded his studio. Fascinated by how their thick black trails looked like living drawings, he decided to take time off to film the ants, using sugar-water to lure them from the garden to paper placed on the studio floor. Filming them from above, he tried to write with the ants, painting letters with sugar-water and expecting the creatures to march in orderly lines. Instead, they clustered around bits of the letters, consuming all the sugar before moving on. Undeterred, the artist realized that by turning the positive film into a negative, which makes the black on white of ants on paper appear as points of light swarming a black field, he could turn the insects' troublesome clumping into something visually striking and usable. And because the work that had been delayed through this detour dealt with Georges Méliès and his 1902 film *A Trip to the Moon*, Kentridge utilized the strange footage to suggest both vintage cinema and constellations wandering the night sky (fig. 70).

Kentridge made this backstory public when he exhibited *7 Fragments for Georges Méliès*.[34] The ants entered his oeuvre on film and as a parable illuminating the work. Kentridge frames the ant siege as a delay that ends up clinching the work delayed. But the episode also highlights the importance of preparedness and knowhow. The artist had to have an overhead camera at hand and be good at operating it. And drawing with sugar-water came easy to this draftsman expert in working with variable fluids in brush on paper. It made special sense to a creator of sugar-lift prints. Each of the artist's moves derived from free association: ants on the breadboard looked like marks on paper, zooming in on the ants looked like satellite surveillance, ants clustered in one spot looked like an aerial shot of cars at a mall. But it is one thing freely to associate and another thing to make something remarkable out of an association: for example, reversing the film to represent stars. The anecdote reveals the artist's ant-like industry even as it projects agency to the ants. Teaching them to write fails. Using them to represent stars is the next best thing. Kentridge calls this victory snatched from defeat "the less good idea." You start with a good idea "but when you take it off the proverbial drawing board, cracks and fissures emerge in its surface, and they cannot be ignored."[35] Decisions remain indecisive. In stark contrast to the ideal of artistic sovereignty launched in

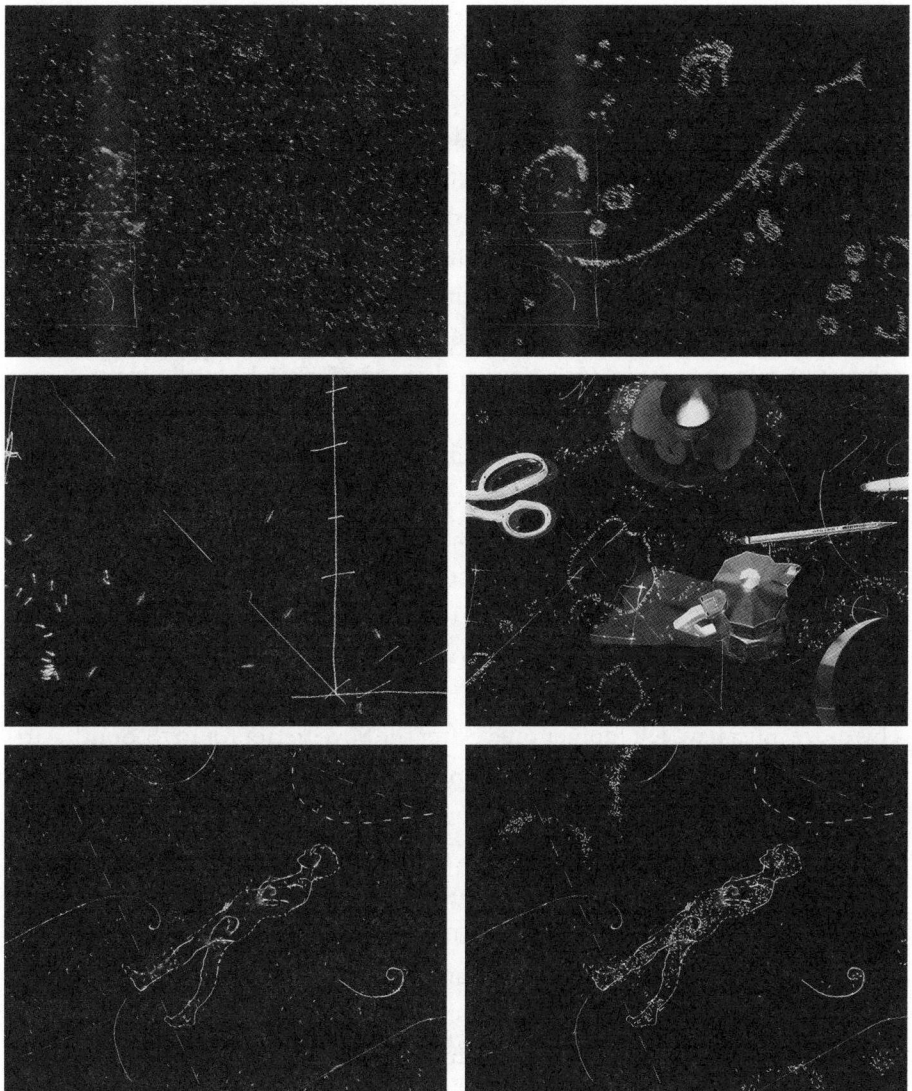

FIG. 70. Stills from William Kentridge, *Day for Night*, 2003. 16mm film transferred to video

Bosch's time and resuscitated in Beckmann's tuxedoed decider, artmaking consists in playfully circumventing defeat.

The short film *Day for Night* chronicles silently, in 16mm black and white, the invasion of Kentridge's studio by ants. Starting with the ants themselves, in reversed film up close, then zooming out, it captures both the chaotic swarming of the invaders and a human presence observing, recording, and experimenting. Thirty-five seconds in we see the sugar-solution's effects. Ants cluster amorphously where the nourishment has pooled, overrunning boundaries outlined in pen.

Suddenly, the ants comply, gathering within, and making visible and alive, sugary flourishes freely rendered by the artist's broad brush, though still crawling heedlessly over penned axes and measure markings that evoke control. The film ends ambiguously. A human figure appears in outline striding forward and upward among loops and broken lines. Ants swarm over it, although some halt fleetingly when a line falls in their path, evidencing that not just the sugar trails but pen marks, too, are known to the ants in some antish way.

The ants create the finishing touch when almost every one of them sprints into the outlined human interior, animating and decomposing it from within. The film ends with a colophon representing two authors: the artist who outlined the human figure and the ants who completed it. The partnership between Kentridge and his non-human collaborators achieves equilibrium. Following a less good idea, the experiment succeeds and the delayed Méliès homage gets finished. The ant-filled outline forms a self-portrait of Kentridge striding the closed universe of his studio. Although decidedly not following the straight path of progress, everything the artist makes circles back to his oeuvre. How was this convergence achieved when earlier, before 1986, his work seemed to drift apart?

In 1981 Kentridge left Johannesburg for Paris with no fixed plans of returning. This move must have felt momentous. After the Soweto riots of 1976, South Africa became increasingly a pariah state cut off from the global community. Sanctions imposed by other nations made it difficult for South African artists to exhibit their work abroad. Isolation, censorship, violence, and political repression caused artists, writers, and intellectuals to emigrate, including, in 1981, Kentridge's parents, who settled in London. Paris was an obvious choice for William. When he spoke of "art in a state of grace," he pictured French Impressionism, Seurat, "and the park-like edge of the Seine."

Kentridge arrived in Paris at the start of a decade-long boom in the market for European and American contemporary art. Supported by a surging global economy, a new generation of artists was turning away from the anti-commercial practices of performance and Conceptual Art and back to figurative canvas painting. When Kentridge came to Europe, Anselm Kiefer was completing his important canvas *Innenraum*. Exhibited at the Centre Pompidou in Paris in 1982, this huge, rigorously perspectival rendition of a soaring skylighted interior derived from a postwar photograph of Albert Speer's Reich Chancellery in Berlin. In an ambiguous gesture foreshadowing some of Kentridge's engagements with colonial violence, Kiefer's recovery of traditional forms of representation, narrative, and history served a new aim. History painting had become the overcoming of a toxic past: *Vergangenheitsbewältigung* in German. Painting of Kiefer's generation might have interested an émigré artist from South Africa, a nation state founded on and sustained by violent colonialist power. But Kentridge did not go to Europe to learn to paint. Instead, he went to study mime, having secured admission to the École internationale de théâtre Jacques Lecoq.

Of all his unlikely career moves, learning mime in the city of painters is the least likely. The idea followed from the onset of an artistic paralysis that would last until 1985. As Kentridge remembers it, by 1981 he found himself trapped in a specific form of spatial representation: a stage-like three-walled "pit" with a single vanishing point. Used in the prison-like settings of his prints, the formula had the effect of bringing brought his own art to a standstill: "I had a block; I felt that I no longer knew what I was drawing or even how to draw."[36] Working at the periphery of the art world, he also had few models that could solve his predicament. He knew the Abstract Expressionists—their champion, Clement Greenberg, had been a guest at his parent's home. But their work provided little guidance in the intensely political context of South Africa. Even less relevant to Kentridge were the departures of installation, performance, and body art. "I was aware of Joseph Beuys," he recalls:

> Beuys and his honey pump, which was supposed to be political art. But politics is not spreading honey around the main building at the Documenta art exhibition. It's putting electrodes on people's testicles, locking them up, putting them in fear of their lives.[37]

Displayed at *documenta* VI in Kassel in 1977, Beuys's *Honeypump in the Workplace* sent two tons of liquid honey through plastic tubes using a pump greased by masses of margarine. The idea of a rejuvenated and non-hierarchical social body modeled on bees did not convince. Creating art in the extreme state required a different apprenticeship from what avant-garde artists in Europe or America could offer. Mime was, at this point, the "less good idea," Kentridge's way of moving forward by stepping backwards and around.

In hindsight the move made sense. Mime is a visual medium. It tells a story silently, through bodily movement alone. From the Greek *pantómimus* ("imitator of everything"), its roots lie in ancient theater. In 467 BCE, during the tragedy *Seven Against Thebes*, Aeschylus employed a dancer named Telestes to mime the entire story of the Egyptian's city's mythical sevenfold siege. But mime has a history independent from that of the theater. Working its magic offstage, on the street, it became a form of popular entertainment especially in nineteenth-century Paris. By way of vaudeville and *théâtre de variétés*, it had a brief flourishing in silent film. By 1981, though, mime was a marginal genre confined mostly to the pedestrian zones of big cities. Yet precisely its obsolescence made it a plausible alternative to current aesthetic opinion.

In Jacques Lecoq's practice, moreover, mime was not the mere niche art of silent acting and illusionistic performance—Marcel Marceau walking against the wind or pulling an invisible rope. It encompassed an entire philosophy of art that began with the body in motion. Developed through physical exercises and group improvisations, this discipline stood in contrast to schools of acting that delved inward, accessing an actor's personal memories and emotions to give depth to a dramatic role. An emphasis on inner life suited conventional theater, where language, gesture, and plot express conflicts in the subjective sphere—Hamlet's indecision, Hedda Gabler's suppressed emotions, Willy Loman's broken dreams. Lecoq's approach stood diametrically opposed to the "method acting" pioneered by Konstantin Stanislavski and made famous in the 1950s by American film stars schooled in Lee Strasberg's Actors Studio. Method acting demanded truth in performance, and truth meant accessing "artistic emotions [...] shy as wild animals [that] hide in the depths of our souls."[38] By contrast, Lecoq prioritized "the external world over inner experience." Training started with performing efficiently and compellingly simple actions. In a gymnasium converted into a performance hall, Kentridge practiced relaxed and hurried walking, rising smoothly from a seated position, and breathing and speaking in increasing levels of tension.

Kentridge has claimed he was a mediocre mime: "Every week, we had to do a series of improvisations, and every week mine would look exactly the same."[39] Within a year he was back in Johannesburg, still undecided about the future, but his training in Paris stayed with him. Wordless storytelling, in the forms of silent film, slapstick, procession, triumph, *danse macabre*, pageant, and puppet show, forms the core of Kentridge's art (figs. 71 and 97). And even after he resolved to pursue the visual arts full-time, he remained an actor, casting himself as a character in his works, sometimes as several conflicting characters. Already the "Art in a State of Siege" talk of 1986 doubled as a performance piece, with its hand-drawn slides and choreographed presentation. Within his films and animations, he can often be seen practicing the simple movements of a Lecoq disciple: pacing, walking at different speeds and states of tension, shadowing the agile moves of a professional dancer, stepping again and again over an overstuffed chair in looped sequence.

Whether directly on film or transferred from film to animated drawings or flipbook pages, he performs these actions as "himself," dressed always in his trademark black trousers, white cotton shirt, and pince-nez (fig. 72). He in fact wears these clothes always when working—and he is almost always working. Neat, re-

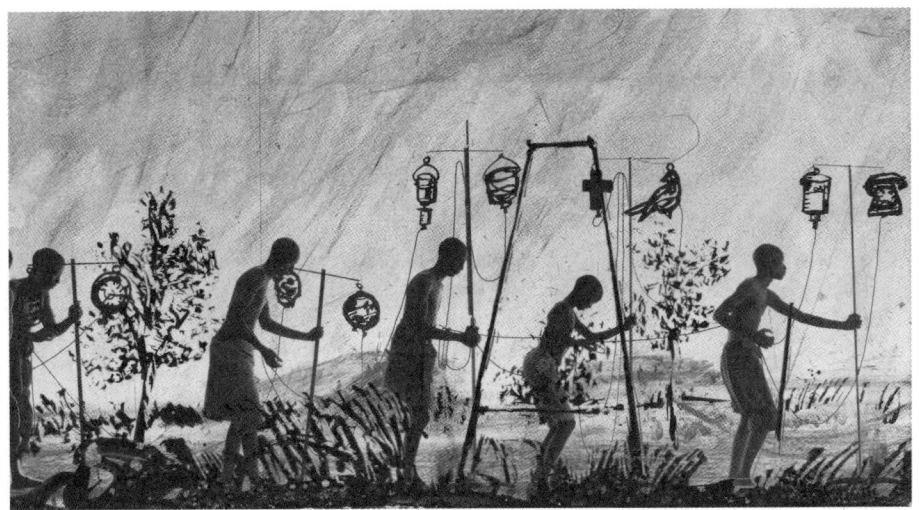

laxed, and practical, and in sync with his monochrome palate, the outfit began as a practical expediency. Black trousers do not show ink stains, white shirts easily bleach clean, and (with the exception of the pince-nez) the components are common and timeless. If a work in progress suddenly suggests he step into it, he always looks the same. The costume thus insures what film editors call "continuity," the consistency of details from shot to shot. When called upon to speak about his art in studio visits, interviews, and public talks, the outfit allows him to multiply, first as the artist talking about his work in real time, then in the work displayed or screened behind him, sometimes joined by proliferating, superimposed doppel-gängers, who sometimes comically contest what the other Kentridges say. These self-portraits are impersonal. They stage Kentridge as a dramatic persona along with other characters developed in his oeuvre. This persona is external. It is body like any other body, expressive through its motions and conveniently the artist's own.

In lectures, these personae often make a simple point. Everything this artist does starts "with the desire to draw," and drawing begins with the body, and not just the hand and eye, but the whole body, controlled but playful and spontaneous, as Lecoq had taught. Mime thus prepared Kentridge for his unexpectedly decisive performance, which through its success turned him from theater back to art. In 1984, he began to draw again, this time in charcoal on big sheets of paper, some more than a meter high. Working in this medium on this scale could not be accomplished by drawing with one's knuckles, wrist, or even arm. It required gesture committed from head to toe—Lecoq's simple exercise of standing up in

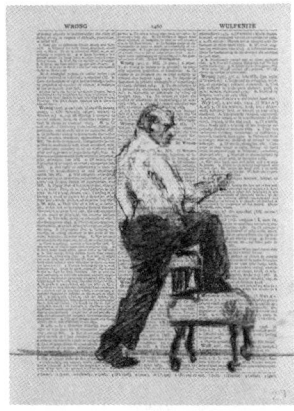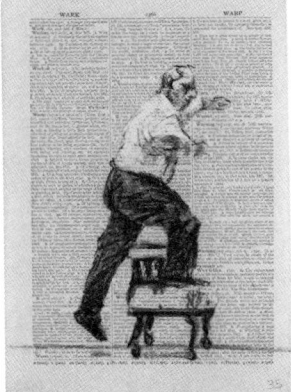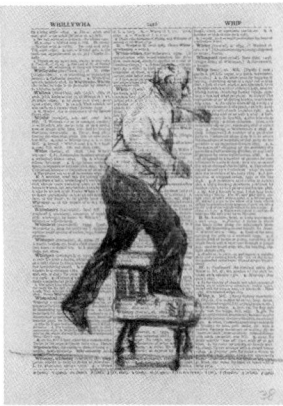

FIG. 72. William Kentridge, three sheets from *Second Hand Reading*, 2013. Charcoal, ink, and watercolor on *Cassell's Cyclopedia of Mechanics* (1914) and *Shorter Oxford English Dictionary* (1936), each 27.2 × 28.5 cm

one smooth go. Drawing in this way also required something to be committed to. This he found not in political engagement, or in a story or motif he himself had devised, but in someone else's image, a picture that took him back to Paris fifty years past.

Paris, 1932

Kentridge had not drawn with charcoal before, not even in art school, where he experimented widely with pen and ink, pencil, graphite, and shoe polish. He thought of charcoal as a painter's medium, the first step towards creating an image in oil on canvas. Even though at the moment, in 1984, when he chanced to reach for charcoal simply to draw, he also hoped—now that he was finally writing "artist" on application forms—to reach eventually from working on paper, the medium he had some success with through his prints, up to painting on canvas, the *ne plus ultra* of the Western tradition and still the most prestigious art form. But when charcoal came to hand, Kentridge's ambition was to escape from the artistic paralysis that had seized him four years back and sent him to Paris to study mime.

The idea was just to draw, pure and simple, without having to decide on a motif, tell a story, or serve a political purpose. The exercise resembled the warm-ups actors do, loosening up their body, face, mouth, and voice before going on stage. To embark on drawing without thinking about what or how to draw, Kentridge took some images—random photographs, prints, and reproductions—that he thought he would enjoy drawing and simply tried to sketch these on large, thick sheets of paper. Why he reached for charcoal he can no longer remember, but the scale of those sheets, and the hope the drawings might—after years of blockage—be fluid and free, recommended charcoal.

The breakthrough, as Kentridge now remembers it, came while making one drawing in particular (plate 22). Signed and dated 1985, the sheet is executed all in charcoal except for foreground details, principally the *Carica papaya*. Rendered in vivid orange and yellow pastel, that fruit, called pawpaw in South Africa, gave the work its humorous title *Tropical Love Storm*. Kentridge depicts a couple embracing in the mirrored corner of a café. Though pressed cheek to cheek, their faces take them elsewhere: hers sharply lit, suggesting flickering pleasures which her cigarette-holding hand suggests are kept under control; his hidden behind hers, but revealed in a reflection that, at first sight, looks like the face of another man peering intrusively at the kissing couple from the next booth. To the right, a reflection of this ambiguous reflection captures the man's highlighted face yet again but adds more faces, now in fact of other men. However, instead of simply conjuring a crowded café, these strangers, through the logic of the mirror, press in on the lovers, even as the lovers, at this moment of intimacy, diverge into separate worlds: in the reflection, the man's shadowed eyes seem to look elsewhere, perhaps at us, while the woman looks, as it were, lost in herself.

The drawing is full of surprises. At the lower right, a pair of clasped hands introduces a body uncomfortably close to the couple, and to us, who find it hard to read them. A potted plant puts an ironic twist on the "tropical" of the title. A champagne flute teeters on the table's edge and the image's ragged border, activating the wide margin that makes the drawing resemble a print, where the borders around the impression are reserved for artist's signature, date, and edition number. Most striking is the shadowed visage that peers from behind the plant in our direction. With nothing on our side of the mirror corresponding to it, this interloper looks to be the lone creation of artistic license in an image broadly true to life. Even those clasped hands seem plausibly to have strayed there by accident, as if captured in a snapshot. And the skewed geometry of the mirrored corner along with the many distortions of bodies, objects, and reflections all bespeak a depiction drawn by hand but faithful to some model. Like the "body in the veld" (see fig. 65), there is something distinctly photographic about the drawing, particularly the mirroring, analogous to camera's operation, of things and their images.

Kentridge did in fact work from a photograph. It was shot in Paris, as its title indicates: *Couple d'amoureux dans un petit café, quartier Italie* (fig. 73). Already here the mirrored corner plays tricks, although different from the ones Kentridge's charcoal draws. The woman looks her lover directly in the eye, though his gaze,

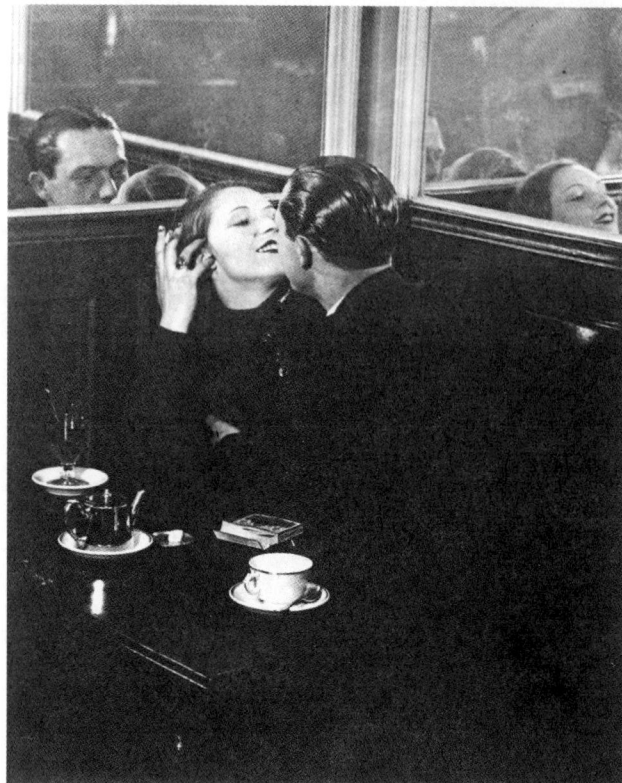

FIG. 73. Brassaï, *Couple d'amoreux dans un petit café, quartier Italie*, c. 1932. Silver gelatin print, 24.9 × 19.8 cm

detached in the reflection behind her, undoes the togetherness of their embrace. Stranger still is the reflection to the right, where Kentridge added the cyclopean intruder. The woman's mirrored face appears uncannily like its prototype: uncannily, because reflecting the opposite half of the face visible to us, and subject to intervening obstacles, displacements, and distortions, such a perfect doubling would be unlikely. Its softer focus, an artifact of the camera's focus and the mirror's sheen, makes the reflection suggest an idyllic moment, or actors kissing on the silver screen. Like frames of a film, the four reflections capture different views of the rapturous instant. And although all are of that one moment freeze-framed on the photographic plate, we, whenever we behold them, look at each of those captured reflections sequentially, sending the one we just beheld into the past but recapturing the present in the one we currently observe.

It matters that the frozen moment is an amorous one. Their desires for coffee, cigarettes, and drink well supplied, the man and woman are in the throes of a bigger desire, the erotic one that pulls them together and spins them around in a revolving door of reflections. The camera participates in this embrace. Pressing intrusively in on the couple, it captures their chemistry with its chemistry, the café's chiaroscuro received on its light-sensitive plate. Developed (in this case, years after the photograph was taken), the high-gloss gelatin silver print draws us into this circle, both because of the desire it documents and because of its autonomous aesthetic allure. "Of all printing papers I love the glossy," this photographer once remarked, "it's the only type which tells you straight away that you have to do with a photograph and nothing else."[40]

Gyula Halász, alias Brassaï, was born in 1899 in the Transylvanian town of Brassó, at the eastern edge of the Habsburg Empire. Trained at the academies of Budapest and Berlin, he arrived in Paris in 1924 in hopes of becoming a painter. Photography happened by accident. Working for German and Hungarian newspapers, he wrote stories about Paris and illustrated them with photographs he found or commissioned. To avoid paying others, he started taking the photos himself. In the 1920s, photography was more a technical craft than an artistic vocation, although avant-garde artists in Paris before Brassaï—especially Man Ray and Francis Picabia—had begun to explore the camera's new image-making potential. In 1930, Brassaï acquired a Voigtländer Bergheil with the Heliar f/4.5 lens. This state-of-the-art folding camera worked well in low light and could take close-up and distant shots without having to change lenses. This he brought with him on nightly wanderings that took him into the streets, cafés, brothels, and ballrooms of Paris—places more alluring to him than a painter's studio. Soon he was selling his photographs to *Vu*, the first large format weekly to feature photographs in essay form, and in 1932, under the assumed name of Brassaï (i.e., "from Brassó"), he published a collection of his photos titled *Paris de nuit*. The American novelist Henry Miller, who wandered the city with Brassaï, dubbed him "the eye of Paris." The epithet stuck.[41]

With double-page photos of cobblestones as its first and last pages and cobblestones on its cover, *Paris de nuit* wanders the city as if compulsively, encountering its nocturnal denizens working, playing, lovemaking, and sleeping, some bedded down on the street. Captions written by Brassaï made the photos into *Denkbilder*. Homeless beggars asleep on straw under an elegant, curved portico become "modern descendants of medieval vagabonds." A prostitute on her stroll becomes "Venus of the Street." Thought provoking, the photographs look thoughtfully made. Brassaï's Voigtländer used 6.5 × 9 cm glass photographic plates, limiting the shots he could take per night to a portable twenty-four. Fastidious about what and how to shoot, he eschewed the accidents that were a hallmark of 1930s photographic realism. The fleeting instant in *Couple d'amoureux* must have taken time to set up. Most photographers shoot hundreds of pictures before selecting one for printing. Brassaï limited himself to one or two. That way, he once explained to the novelist Lawrence Durrell, "I feel that I have really made it myself, that picture, not won it in a lottery."[42]

Brassaï visited Durrell in Paris in the late 1960s to photograph him for an American periodical. While exploring the writer's room in search of the right angle and light, Brassaï explained that where others try to catch their subject off guard, he insists that his sitter be "as fully conscious as possible—as fully aware that he is taking part in an artistic event, an *act*." His portraits should evoke those made by village photographers of long ago, when the whole community would come to the shoot and "'having a picture took'" was "an act of innocent majesty." In those days, slow shutter speeds meant posing for several seconds: "You had to hold your breath, sit still, and stare 'at the dicky bird.'" *Couple d'amoureux* endeavored to look somehow antiquated, as if it had been taken in a bygone era when cameras were "large as an oak tree."[43] This gives the moment captured in the photograph a peculiar duration.

Brassaï was an avid reader of Marcel Proust—he claimed to have learned French by working his way through the 3,200 pages of *In Search of Lost Time*. The photographer encountered in Proust's novel an interplay between a fugitive present—captured in accidental events, fleeting perceptions, and changing fashions synonymous with modern city life—and a sedimented past that flashed up involuntarily, eclipsing the here and now. Proust turns out to have been a brilliant commentator on photography, as Brassaï himself detailed in *Proust in the Power of Photography* (1997). Brassaï explored the novelist's account of photographic time, how the instant eternalized by the camera was inaccessible at the moment it was taken, being hermetically deposited on the light-sensitive plate or film. Only later, in an interior space set apart from the events that drew the camera to them, did the instant get developed into the photographic print. "Pleasure [...] is like photography," Proust wrote:

> What we take, in the presence of the beloved object, is merely a negative film; we develop it later, when we are at home, and have once again at our disposal that inner darkroom, the entrance to which is barred to us so long as we are with other people.[44]

The amorous instant pales by comparison to the image arising in the darkroom. But what if a negative never gets developed? By Brassaï's account, this is equivalent to Proust's central question: What is a memory we no longer can recall?[45] *Couple d'amoureux* was shot circa 1932 in the café on the ground floor of the cheap hotel where Brassaï lived. Prints taken from the glass plate came later, some far in the future—most extant prints of *Couple d'amoureux* date from late 1960 or after. Yet through its multiple reflections and deliberately retrospective feel, this image already has a time lag built right into it.

It must have been those different mirrored versions of the one "real" instant that caused the photographer to aim his lens at an otherwise ordinary kissing pair. Reflections make the familiar strange—or "marvelous": *le merveilleux*, as the Surrealists in Paris at the time called it. In the conclusion to his 1926 prose poem *Le paysan de Paris*, Louis Aragon contrasted "reality," defined as "the apparent absence of contradiction," to "the marvelous" as "the eruption of contradiction within the real." Love, meanwhile, was "a state of confusion between the real and the marvelous," in which contradictions "seem *really* essential to being."[46] Like Brassaï, Aragon found the marvelous abounding in the streets and arcades of Paris late at night, when love flourished in its licit and illicit forms, and the transitions from darkness to light are at their most extreme, and sudden. Suddenness itself— the fleeting, dangerous "now"—disrupts the flow of time in which it erupts. Like Proust's "involuntary memory," when, accidentally, through the taste of a tea-soaked madeleine his entire past returns to him with "a shudder [...] through [his] whole body," so too the utopia of Brassaï's amorous instant flares up marvelously and unpredictably at moments long after the original one.[47]

Kentridge worked from the famous photograph. Remembering, repeating, distorting, forgetting, and remembering again, he worked playfully *through* it, with the serious purpose of escaping paralysis by letting the charcoal itself lead the way. With attention evenly suspended on his source, the artist allowed himself, in the safe space of his studio, freely to draw plants, imagine papayas, and shuffle reflections. Kentridge understood the analogy between such goal-oriented free play and Freud's so-called "talking cure." The fundamental rule of psychoanalysis requires the patient to say whatever comes into their head, no matter how irrelevant, unpleasant, or ridiculous it may seem. Speech itself—in echoes, puns, and lapses—produces associations, too, as if independent of the patient.

Kentridge's "drawing cure" was shaped, similarly, by accident and the materials used. Dusty charcoal cannot imitate the sharp chiaroscuro of Brassaï's high-gloss print, so Kentridge makes do with shadows and highlights his medium can handle. The now-illuminated foreground allows him to outline the objects on the table, rather than having to leave them in reserve, as islands of unmarked paper in a sea of sooty black. And because, cast in a different light, everything effectively has to change, objects can be easily added, moved, or omitted. Now another cigarette has previously been smoked, its burnt butt resting on the saucer's edge; now the spoon that was in the glass—presumably for absinthe's sugar cube—has been set to the side to become a small reflective still-life convincingly drawn. And now the woman's eyes, open in the Brassaï, appear closed, thanks to charcoal's low resolution. Characteristics of the charcoal mark must have encouraged Kentridge to render the man's suit—in the photograph a subtly undulating surface that reveals the underlying body—as a pattern of broad strokes that can read as pinstripes but that, carried over to the woman's blouse, make both bodies seem to shimmer and move in the corner shadows.

These marks look impetuously drawn. But long before making them, Kentridge would have already pictured to himself, like an actor imagining an action before miming it, *how* to draw with charcoal in this particular way. And this he would have learned, decisively for the entire exercise of letting drawing show the way, from certain drawings contemporary with the Brassaï. Kentridge draws the old photograph in an old style. His choice and handling of the charcoal medium; his studied distortion of objects, bodies, and space; even his abandonment of conscious design for involuntary gesture: all this and more channels the art of the German and Austrian Expressionists. Their strategy had been to replace mimetic accuracy (obsolete after photography) and virtuoso draftsmanship (token of academic training and taste) with impulsive, unconscious gestures, the artist's hand guided less by what the eye sees than by what the whole body feels and does. Drawing is nervous response to what is drawn.

Expressionists drew with charcoal because of its responsive force, and they drew subjects that elicited forceful responses. Sketches of erotic, violent, or morbid subjects cast the respondent—the artist as well as the viewer—into managed states of emergency, the artist registering nervousness while controlling the messy medium, the viewer agitated by the imagery and style but calmed by artfulness. Strong affect was explored through "primitive" artifacts. These did not have to be discovered in exotic locations, like Gauguin's Tahiti or for Picasso the ethnographic collection of the Palais du Trocadéro. They could be found at home. Take, as one of countless possible examples, Erich Heckel's 1913 *To the Convalescent Woman* (plate 23). Fate has it that this triptych of canvases hangs near Beckmann's *Self-Portrait in Tuxedo*, having arrived at Harvard's Busch-Reisinger Museum in 1950 via a similar itinerary to the one Beckmann's canvas traveled: deaccessioning from a public museum in Germany, mocking display in the 1937 *Degenerate "Art"* exhibition, sale to Curt Valentin, transport to Buchholz gallery in New York, and purchase by Charles Kuhn for Harvard.

Heckel poses his bedridden fiancée (the avant-garde dancer Sidi Riha) against an African textile gifted to the artist by his brother. What appears to be a wooden statue in the style of so-called tribal art stands at the far left, as a sort of magical sickbed attendant. Heckel probably carved the piece himself. In the painting, he has the sculpture's rough-hewn contours carry over to his bride, eclectically mingling fantasies of Africa, fetish objects, Gothic religiosity, and old German woodcuts. The plants dominating the flanking canvases introduce nature into the cultural collage, but with the pots maintaining domestic decorum. Even with its exotic artifacts and sacral triptych format, the painting stays true to ordinary life. Heckel's studio and home were decorated in a fashionable bohemian style. The primitive artifact, collected or created, discloses something uncanny (*unheimlich*) in the home (*Heim*). Heckel's beloved has been called back from death. The German title, *Zur Genesung der kranken Frau* ("To the Recovery of the Sick Woman"), styles the painting as votive offering for her recovery.

Kentridge's cyclopean intruder has a similar uncanny feel. Where Heckel looks back from present circumstances to some paradisiacal past, Kentridge reaches back to the art that cultivated that rearward look and he exoticizes it, making a love scene in Europe of the 1930s "tropical." The evocation of painting from that period in history becomes specific in the one detail. The intruder's mask-like frontality and heavy-lidded eye references German Expressionist and post-Expressionist style. More narrowly, it evokes the faces Beckmann painted in his 1938 masterpiece *Death*, especially the Boschian three-eyed gastropod on the ceiling-cum-floorboards (plate 21). From about the age of fifteen Kentridge kept a postcard of that painting always "close at hand," and he came to understand that upside-down face as "a kind of self-portrait" of Beckmann. In his Grahamstown lecture, Kentridge called *Death* "a beacon for endangered souls," and made it the archetype of "art in a state of siege." The topsy-turvy elements made everything in the painting seem provisional, even the canvas's upright orientation—the artist's signature, lower right, "marks the decision as to which way it should be seen." But Beckmann's decision cannot be a sovereign one, for the work still "evokes the world as a constructed arena, where neither grace nor damnation are inevitable."[48]

The tropics of Kentridge's love storm are not paradisiacal but sad, *tristes*, though not from the familiar disillusioned European perspective. The artist would go on to develop an ambiguous iconography of Africa, from Lilliputian rhinos dancing on a White mine owner's desk to the text-cluttered acacias, bushwillows, and mongongo trees of his monumental tree collages, to the trauma-scarred countryside around Johannesburg—what the artist in 1988 will call "landscape in a state of siege" (plate 27; figs. 75 and 95). But in drawing after Brassaï, Kentridge takes an ironic distance from European models chiefly through that orange-fleshed topical fruit spilling seed between the lovers. Refusing the charcoal monochrome, the papaya also indicates that, contrary to what Kentridge claims, the decision to draw rather than to paint was not because of art school defeat or inborn want of color sense. Instead, it derived from an ambivalence towards painting, as the victor's medium. The pastel intrusion exudes pleasure in the making—Kentridge's "desire to draw" fulfilled.

Making *Tropical Love Storm* transformed Kentridge: "I realized, I can do this."[49] "This" did not mean "I can draw." That he could draw he knew since he was a child, when his mother lovingly preserved his works. And it meant more than the one drawing's achievement. If drawing Brassaï's photograph proved that, as an artist, he would not "sink" but "swim," this was because whatever he did in this case he could successfully do again and again, launching the remarkable oeuvre that flourishes to this day. But what exactly was it about *Tropical Love Storm* that gave him confidence? Kentridge's lecture "Art in a State of Siege" had a subtitle: "Caution: For External Use Only." The words seem humorously to warn that the lecture's medicine has at most a limited, topical application. But Kentridge also states from the outset that whatever he says about his work "comes after the event" and cannot grasp "the mental processes behind it." The "this" that making *Tropical Love Storm* proved he could do cannot be spoken. Yet it is possible roughly to grasp the drawing's premonition. At some level, "this" meant working from found images, rather than from life, or by using his imagination, or drawing automatically, through chance or unconscious movements of the hand. In this case, the found image happened to be a famous artful photograph, but others could also be discovered, among old prints, book illustrations, advertisements, anonymous snapshots, forensic photos, film stills, and so forth, just as long as they are images *of* something, thus affording Kentridge's art its representational core. It matters even more that the Brassaï is "historical," in the sense that the world it captures, and the medium it employs, belong to the past, the specific one of Paris 1932 time-capsuled in a silver gelatin print. Thanks to its mirrored café setting, the photograph also combines the public sphere with private intimacy in a manner amenable to Kentridge, who portrays siege states largely from the perspective of everyday life, and especially through erotic entanglements.

Then there is Brassaï, out of view but implied as a curious, mobile, and aestheticizing observer of the everyday. In Paris in 1932, such an observer had a name. He was the stroller, in French the *flâneur*—the veritable avatar of the modern life, according to Charles Baudelaire, and later to Aragon and Benjamin. Kentridge reaches back to the constellation of subject, medium, and viewpoint epitomizing the "modern" in its—paradoxically—past formation, the "historical" modern of Modernism as a movement born in Paris, flowering in early Soviet Russia and Weimar Germany, and shaken to its foundations just after Brassaï shot the photo, with Hitler's permanent emergency and the politically motivated Great

Famine in the Soviet Union. But where the would-be painter from Brassó strolls through Paris in search of the marvelous, Kentridge, returned to South Africa, explores the archives of European Modernism in search of cracks, fissures, and breaking points.

In 1985 Kentridge showed *Tropical Love Storm*, together with other drawings made before and after its breakthrough, in a one-person exhibition at Cassirer Fine Art in Johannesburg. It was this show that led to the Young Artist Award and the work that followed. The gallery's founder, Reinhold Cassirer, hailed from an illustrious Jewish-German family. Its members included the publisher Bruno Cassirer, his brother Paul, also a publisher and an important art dealer, and the philosopher Ernst Cassirer, whose work on symbolic forms (undertaken at the Warburg Institute) influenced his fellow-Warburgian, Panofsky. Paul and Bruno Cassirer, Reinhold's uncles, played a key role in introducing modern art to Germany, serving as founding secretaries, in 1898, to the Berlin Secession. A major early supporter of Max Beckmann, Paul exhibited the painter's work in 1907, and later published many of Beckmann's prints. Born in Berlin in 1908, Reinhold Cassirer was completing a political science doctorate at Heidelberg when Hitler seized power. He fled to South Africa in 1935 after his stepfather, forbidden from practicing medicine in Germany and about to be arrested, committed suicide. Family ties and shared progressive politics brought Kentridge to Cassirer Fine Arts. William's parents were close friends of Reinhold and his wife, the Nobel Prize-winning novelist Nadine Gordimer. But its multiple links to the triumphs and tragedies of European culture made Reinhold Cassirer's gallery a fitting venue for launching Kentridge's career.

Dreams of Europe, completed in 1985, must have had a powerful resonance in that space (fig. 74). Even from a distance, and without its evocative title, the triptych of charcoal drawings evokes the legacy of German art between the two world wars. It was then that Beckmann explored dream states and that he started creating triptychs. Like Heckel and others, Beckmann had resuscitated that format, which had been canonical for painted and sculpted altarpieces in northern Europe (plates 13, 14, and 20; fig. 39). Usually hinged, so that the outer panels could close over the larger, more elaborate inner panel (called the "corpus" or "shrine"), triptychs served to embellish with pictures and stories the rites performed at the altar. Evocative of the Holy Trinity, their tripartite structure supported the surrounding symmetries of built architecture and liturgical performance, centering church, village, countryside, and world on the images and the histories that matter. In the sixteenth century, Protestant iconoclasts attacked altarpieces for the idolatry they encouraged, while to Catholics the triptych form started to look old-fashioned.

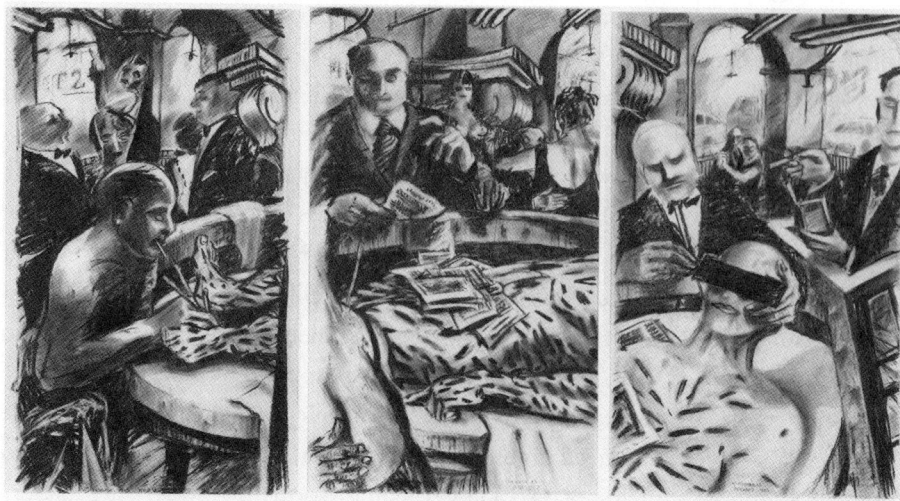

FIG. 74. William Kentridge, *Koevoet* (*Dreams of Europe*), 1984–85. Charcoal, each panel 100 × 73 cm

These once remarkably ubiquitous ensembles thus passed into obscurity. In the nineteenth century, when "old German art" became the focus of aesthetic adulation, the paintings and sculpture contained in triptychs were torn from their scaffolds and reframed as individual works of art. The early twentieth-century revival of the triptych was nostalgic and critical. A local variant of "primitivism" in modern art, it sought to break with recent tradition by reaching back to a buried past, a time when painters and sculptors—skilled craftsmen still integrated into the social order—made numinous objects festively displayed to an undivided community of believers.

Before the Reformation, the triptych had been a powerful symbolic form or "pathos formula," in Warburg's sense of the word.[50] Encompassing in its framework the myths that mattered for this life and the next, it was the way people made visual sense of their world. Bosch made triptych altarpieces and collectable artworks in triptych form, and he assumed that the latter—most confusingly in the so-called *Garden of Delights*—would be understood in ways cultivated by the former. Modern painters revived this format in the mournful awareness that it could no longer be symbolic in its original way, not least because, instead of being rooted to altar, church, and concrete locality, modern triptychs wandered from place to place, country to country, at the whims of taste and the art market. The divisions between Heckel's canvases break the sickbed scene into three paintings, each aesthetically balanced yet also fragmentary in feel. The sunflowers that turn their blossoms to the sitter, the sitter's sidelong glance, the vigilant statue at far left evince an impulse towards, rather than the achievement of, unity.

It was precisely this ambiguously "panoramic, patchwork" character of the format that attracted Kentridge. Reflecting—years later—on *Dreams of Europe*, he reports seeing triptychs by Beckmann and Francis Bacon and being fascinated by their dislocations of time and space. "Time has passed between each image, objects have been rearranged [...]. The view point is slightly changed and the perspective altered." The effect reminded him of photography before shots get developed. "The impulse derives from successive images of the same place on a roll of film," implying that *Dreams of Europe* predicts his transfer of charcoal drawing to film. Later he learned that "triptychs were originally used as altarpieces," yet *Dreams of Europe* already has a decidedly archaic look.[51]

Beckmann had no place in the advanced art world of the early 1980s—not one of the major modernist art historians ever reflected publicly on his art. Yet there he was, brought urgently back to life in a gallery in Johannesburg, at the start of South Africa's four-year long state of emergency. Beyond its format, Kentridge's triptych dreams "Beckmann" through costume, architecture, ambience, and style. The drawings' background projects the gruesome goings-on into interwar Berlin or Paris. Tuxedoed gentlemen carouse with women in flapper attire in a spacious nightclub or dance bar. Beckmann had included one such scene in his *Hell* portfolio (fig. 50). Ornamental volutes, envoys of Europe's "classical" tradition, push rudely forward; and the thick black strokes with which the capitals are drawn, and, more crucially, Kentridge's cartoonish handling of the café revelers, come from Beckmann. Caricature flourished in German art in the turbulent years following World War I, functioning publicly both to shame power and to communicate more directly than "fine art" could to an imagined audience of the powerless. Already in Kentridge's early works exaggerated bodies, gestures, and physiognomies worked, similarly, as a visual *J'accuse*. *Dreams of Europe* sharpens its outrage through the violence unfolding in the foreground, in a strange, elliptical space evocative of a table, a drinks counter, and a theatrical stage.

Kentridge's triptych has ties to Beckmann's *Hell* portfolio. Framed as a nocturnal stroll through a city, those large-scale lithographs visit bars, cafés, political clubs, and torture chambers—they are a German cousin to Brassaï's *Paris de nuit* (see figs. 46–52). As we have seen, the plate titled *The Martyrdom* portrays, in thinly veiled terms, the murder of Rosa Luxemburg by right-wing militia. Sanctioned by the Social Democratic government, her murder exposed the Weimar Republic to be a non-democratic polity permanently in siege. Beckmann's martyr vaguely resembles Luxemburg, and the two visually prominent rifles allude to the established facts of her execution: she was knocked down by a rifle butt and shot in the head, and her body was dumped into a canal and only retrieved six months later. But the artist deliberately generalizes the event, giving it a quasi-religious status of a martyrdom.

Kentridge adopted a similar strategy. Apartheid violence produced highly publicized corpses, including photographed ones of murdered activists. Several photos of the body of Stephen Biko circulated widely. Biko died in police custody in 1977, and a year later Sydney Kentridge, the artist's father, represented Biko's family at the famous inquest into the activist's murder. The post-mortem photographs formed part of that judicial dossier. It is tempting to imagine that the crude sutures stitching the autopsied corpse closed are recalled—involuntarily perhaps—by the wound-like marks in the drawing. *Dreams of Europe* struggled with "the evidence of images." For Sydney Kentridge, photographs served legal arguments mounted within the juridical limbo of apartheid rule. For William, they functioned within the alternative form of resistance that he termed "art in a state of siege."

Brassaï's photograph cleared the ground for drawing in this way. The plants, the intruder, and the papaya are free improvisations on the photo as well as the vagaries of charcoal itself—its point and edges always changing, its line hyperreactive to the paper's grip and shifting pressure from the hand. The ground that drawing Brassaï's photograph cleared was a playground, and like a playground it had protective limits. The found photograph restricted freedom, forcing drawing always to circle back to it. Such a deliberately curtailed space for play, as well as this asynchronous working from the past, comes close to what Sigmund Freud, defining the physical arena of the talking cure, termed a *Tummelplatz*.[52] In his thickly draped, carpeted, and ornamented consulting room in Vienna, Freud created a safe space for the dangerous acts of remembering by patients "who suffered mainly from reminiscence," with the goal of finally experiencing the present presently: that enclave "creates an intermediate realm between sickness and a healthy life by means of which the transition from one to the other is accomplished."[53] The "this" Kentridge realized he could do was not simply working from Brassaï and Beckmann. Remembering, repeating, and working through past imagery served the dangerous moment, the siege state unfolding then and there in "Johannesburg, 2nd Greatest City after Paris."

Johannesburg, 1989

"JOHANNESBURG" appears in the opening shot of the first so-called "Drawings for Projection," Kentridge's interconnected series of the now thirteen animated films that have defined his oeuvre (fig. 75).[54] He wrote with charcoal on paper those twelve uppercase Times New Roman letters, but from the moment the writing—filmed—flashes on screen, it becomes a flickering rectangle of light, with the city's name hovering in the lower third, where captions, credits, and chyrons typically appear. For eight seconds the handwriting shivers nervously alone, its tiny movements the result of the film's slow projection speed and glacial production method. Those eight seconds took ninety-six manual clicks of the shutter of Kentridge's Bolex camera perched on a tripod in his studio in Johannesburg, and miles of his pacing back and forth between the drawing and the camera. Before it was transferred to digital format, the film was screened to the whir and clack of 16mm projection. Current digital and 35mm transferals include, for seven seconds at the beginning, a black screen with ambient projector sounds edited in. Having already converted the static charcoal drawing into the timebound medium of film, Kentridge wants his viewers to be conscious of machinery and time. The Bolex is antiquated; the office equipment, architectural settings, and industrial landscapes featured in his films are, too. They date from his grandparents' era. And his animation technique is deliberately archaic, "stone age filmmaking," in his words.

When "JOHANNESBURG" flashes up on screen, it does so to the sound of a needle drop, followed by the crackle of the lead-in groove of a 78 rpm shellac. The stylus catches the groove of Duke Ellington's 1929 "Harlem Flat Blues," and on the syncopated beat of the Jungle Band's guitar and trio of clarinets, drawing commences. Big strokes of charcoal swipe the page, then straight lines, decisive marks and smudges, split-second additions, and shading bring into view an atmospheric landscape setting. The setting is *somewhere in Johannesburg*, and that *somewhere*, at the instant of the completion of its drawing, has wholly concealed the charcoaled "JOHANNESBURG." It is a strange place, concrete and dreamlike. A billboard or drive-in movie screen—at first oblique to the picture plane—swivels forward to suggest, in the gathering dusk, that a feature film set in Johannesburg will begin, projected on the rectangle. Across from it, a two-tiered stadium stand rises from furrowed, pitted, and weedy ground, with floodlights for a nighttime event. The setting is thus a stage, the empty seats and screen ironical ciphers for Johannesburg's expectations in 1989, when the film was made. An attentive viewer might notice blurred blotches and flickering along the opening scene's edges. They are shadows of a person—evidently shadows of Kentridge's head, shoulder, and active right hand cast on the drawing and caught on film. The accidents are deliberate. Nowhere else in his "Drawings for Projection" does Kentridge allow such intrusions. In sync with the playful animation, which records the drawing's entire genesis from a blank sheet, the shadows project onto the stage-like setting a split-second cameo of the artist.

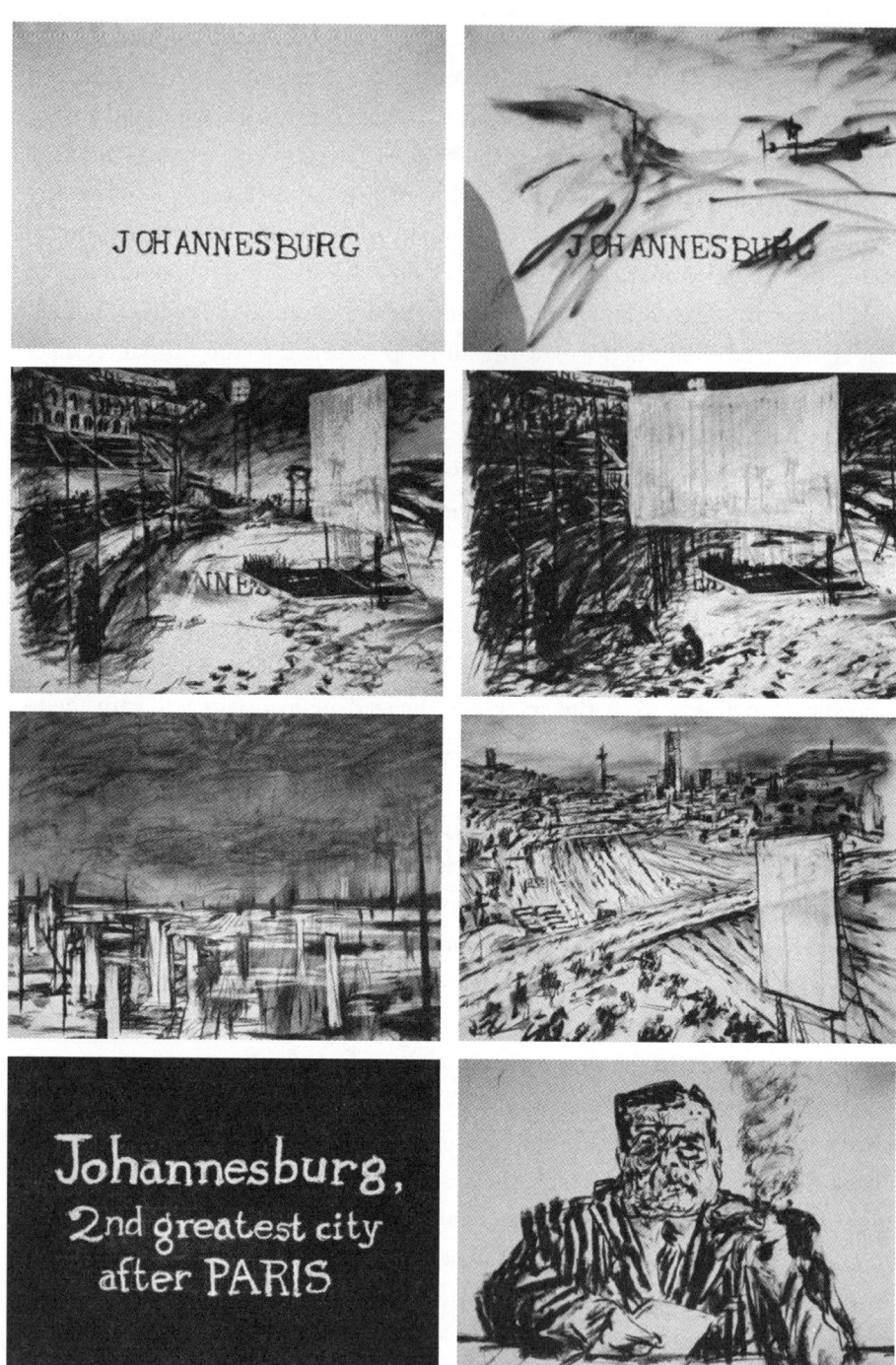

FIG. 75. Stills from William Kentridge, *Johannesburg, 2nd Greatest City after Paris*, 1989. 16mm film transferred to video

Two more landscapes quickly follow. A flat expanse punctuated by vertical rods has us looking out from the city into the surrounding veld. A swelling noise, high-pitched like birds or crickets but increasingly mechanical, drowns out Duke Ellington, but the clarinets return when the scene switches to Johannesburg's urban core, with its proud modern landmarks: the Carlton Center, in 1986 Africa's tallest building, and Hillbrow Tower, the continent's tallest structure. The opening vistas are "establishing shots" that set the upcoming action in a place. Here each setting is also a drawing that will be, or already has been, used for animations shown later in the film. Time and space merge in these sheets. In the "veld" setting, traces of a naked body in half length complicate the sky. The establishing shot does not simply show where future action will take place. It is the repurposed material remnant of the future. Kentridge dubbed such sedimented vistas "landscape in a state of siege,"

> images that seem solid and dark can be removed with a swipe of a cloth. Traces are left. Even after scrubbing the paper there is evidence of some disturbance. But this is easily overgrown and incorporated into the drawing. A few of the drawings are of specific places but most are constructed from elements of the countryside around Johannesburg.

The mutable but never fully expungeable charcoal mark is the aesthetic correlative of the setting, an essentially urban terrain "articulated, or given meaning, by incidents across it: pieces of civil engineering, the lines of pipes, culverts, fences." The result is neither picturesque, like Claude Lorrain's Roman ruins, nor sublime, like the Highveld of Jan Volschenk's and Jacobus Hendrik Pierneef's art. South Africa's colonial legacy makes them disturbing and dangerous: "A never-ending chronicle of disasters or almost disasters in the sets of skid marks that punctuate the road."[55]

These are the siegescapes that open *Johannesburg, 2nd Greatest City after Paris*. That title appears one minute into the film, handwritten in white on black, like a silent era title card or a clapper chalkboard. It marks the appearance of the chief protagonist of all Kentridge's films: Soho Eckstein, seen at his desk smoking a cigar. By the artist's account, the phrase came in a dream. A man in a pinstriped suit outside EMI headquarters works ten hours to document "Johannesburg, the second greatest city after Paris." The phrase resembles the hundreds of aphorisms, mottos, and trade idioms that populate Kentridge's drawings and prints, such as "shrapnel in the woods," "silent in the region," and "thick time." Gathered while reading or from conversations, the words teeter on the edge of nonsense, rescued only by the reader's sense-making impulse. The film title's boast sounds antiquated, for Johannesburg and for Paris. Had not Adolf Loos, writing in the backwaters of Austria-Hungary, already proclaimed New York and London to be the dawning century's capitals? Through its flickering picture, Roaring Twenties jazz, and boosterish title, Kentridge's opening sequence reaches back to an obsolete past.

Time itself must have seemed presently out of joint. Nineteen eighty-nine was a watershed year when change became inevitable in South Africa, though in which direction no one could safely predict. Violent domestic protest, weakening commitment by the White minority, tightening international sanctions, and the end of the Cold War (the government projected itself to the West as a bulwark against Soviet expansion in Africa) made the end of apartheid increasingly inevitable. In February, P. W. Botha, state president since 1984 and a fierce opponent of Black majority rule, resigned after suffering a stroke. Meanwhile, nearly a thousand "State of Emergency" detainees—individuals interned from one state of emergency to the next with no hope of a trial—went on publicized hunger strikes, forcing the minister of law and order to release many hundreds, while others escaped from hospitals and took refuge in foreign embassies, subjecting the country to further international scorn. Attention turned to the wretched "Section 29" detainees, individuals arrested without warrant and incarcerated indefinitely on the authority of the 1982 Internal Security Act. By August 1989, F. W. de Klerk was sworn in as the new president. Within a year he would declare the formal end of apartheid, un-ban the main opposition parties, and release Nelson Mandela from prison. On June 6, 1990, he lifted the state of emergency that had been invoked in 1986 and annually renewed. But in 1989 the siege state remained in force, with protests banned, demonstrations suppressed, and protestors detained. It was over many months of this uncertain year that Kentridge, holed up in his studio, created *Johannesburg, 2nd Greatest City after Paris*.

The film centers on a love triangle between the property tycoon Soho Eckstein, Mrs. Eckstein, and Felix Teitelbaum, the latter an idle, anxious, and infatuated "captive of the city." The film surrounds this domestic drama of White South Africans (akin to his 1980 print series titled *Domestic Scenes*) with siegescapes: a homeless Black man in a barbed-wire pit dodging missiles; displaced Black workers processing from and to the horizon; enemies locked in combat on the veld. The genesis of this plot reaches back to the 1986 Grahamstown lecture. Kentridge's immediate purpose in that talk had been to clarify what he hoped to make, most urgently for the solo exhibition that, by the terms of the Young Artist Award, would be mounted in 1987. To meet the challenge of creating "art in a state of siege," Kentridge returned to a work that political circumstances had provoked and aborted.

Johannesburg was founded in 1886 following the discovery of gold on Lang-laagte farm, on the Witwatersrand. The city celebrated its centenary in the *annus horribilis* of 1986. To sabotage the jubilee, a group of artists resolved to make agitprop works and sneak them into public places. Kentridge drew his contribution on acetate sheets to be printed in silkscreen and put up at night, as a parody of a boastful poster. But the protest sputtered, leaving the acetate drawings to languish in the artist's studio. Following the Grahamstown lecture, a collaboration with a skilled silkscreen printer brought these unused sheets back to mind. Kentridge's lecture supplied the work's new pseudo-typewritten mottos as well as its eventual title: "Art in a State of Siege"—these came from the slides that had accompanied the talk (plate 24).

The silkscreen does not hide its agitprop origins. Emblazoned across the lower third, "100 Years of Easy Living" satirizes a centennial motto, and the city's abbreviated name and heraldic symbol (three stamps from a stamp battery mill for crushing gold ore) appear at the upper right, with stamps upside down and with ink bleeding downward into the fountain, pond, or vlei at the base, as if the print's impression had been wet when hung. The image's two-tone ground supports this sense of haste. The edges appear frayed or poorly printed, and from a distance the mottled colors look like cheap brown paper unevenly pasted to a wall. Kentridge devised this ground to enliven the image and to simulate the butcher paper he used for posters and theater sets, although its pattern resembles camouflage. Dense associations, meticulous design, and professional printing on heavy Velin d'Arches paper exceed the original requirements of public protest. But collective political action—art in a state of hope—remains, like a layer of silkscreen ink.

Of all the print's layers, the densest is the personification of "Easy Living." We have seen the type before: the fat-cats in *Dreams of Europe* and their predecessors in Weimar art (see fig. 74). Three guard their profits in George Grosz's 1922 *Die Besitzkröten* (The property toads)—the *Degenerate 'Art'* catalogue used Grosz's drawing to exemplify the pernicious "political tendency" of modern art (fig. 76). Kentridge has his property toad melt into the waters below him, as if into one of the mining-related sinkholes in the Johannesburg veld that suddenly swallow up whole families living above them. Based in human and ecological exploitation, easy living stands on catastrophic ground. Kentridge adds a personal layer to this conceit. A cherished photograph shows Morris Kentridge, his grandfather, dressed in a suit and seated between his sons on Muizenberg beach. This family portrait inspired one of the artist's first successful works, the linocut *Muizenberg 1933* (fig. 77). By Kentridge's account, the pinstripe patterns in the print derived from the medium:

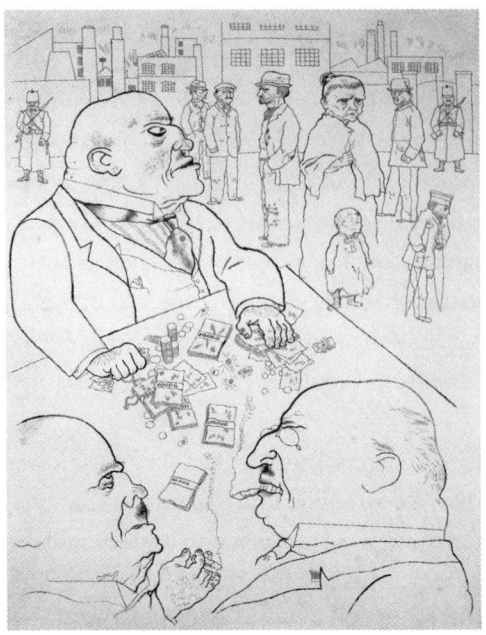

FIG. 76. George Grosz, *Property Toads* (*Die Besitzkröte*), 1920. Pen and ink, 52.7 × 41.1 cm. Scottish National Gallery of Modern Art, Edinburgh

> If you cut thin lines, eventually you produce a pinstripe—a dark background with a thin white line [...]. I didn't want a suit or a grey one where you have to suggest a lightening of the tone of the black of the print, so a pinstripe was the answer because the thing I was doing—cutting lines in the lino—had the same quality as the object I was drawing: the suit.[56]

Kentridge has many stories of imagery born from processes outside of the artist's intentions. To make the unintentional work, the artist must give it "an impulse, an object, a material, the benefit of doubt."[57] Attached to family history, the pinstripes draw a line through the artist's oeuvre. In 1980 Kentridge had directed and acted in a satirical play called *Secrecy*, performing in a pinstriped suit the role of a White tycoon with a Black employee as his guard dog. In 1989 this figure, now named Soho Eckstein, became the chief protagonist of the "Drawings for Projection," transforming from tyrant and cuckold to martyr and artist's alter ego. The silkscreen *Art in a State of Siege* was Soho's debut.

Francis Bacon called the distortions he applied to his painted faces "injuries" and confessed he found them difficult to do when his subject was with him in the studio: "I would rather practice the injury in private."[58] Kentridge did not need the print's bloodred blotches to practice the injury. The black lines that portray the face already deface it. Bloated features explode from the nose, the warts on his forehead project upward like debris. The cigar-puffing mouth also spits, shouts,

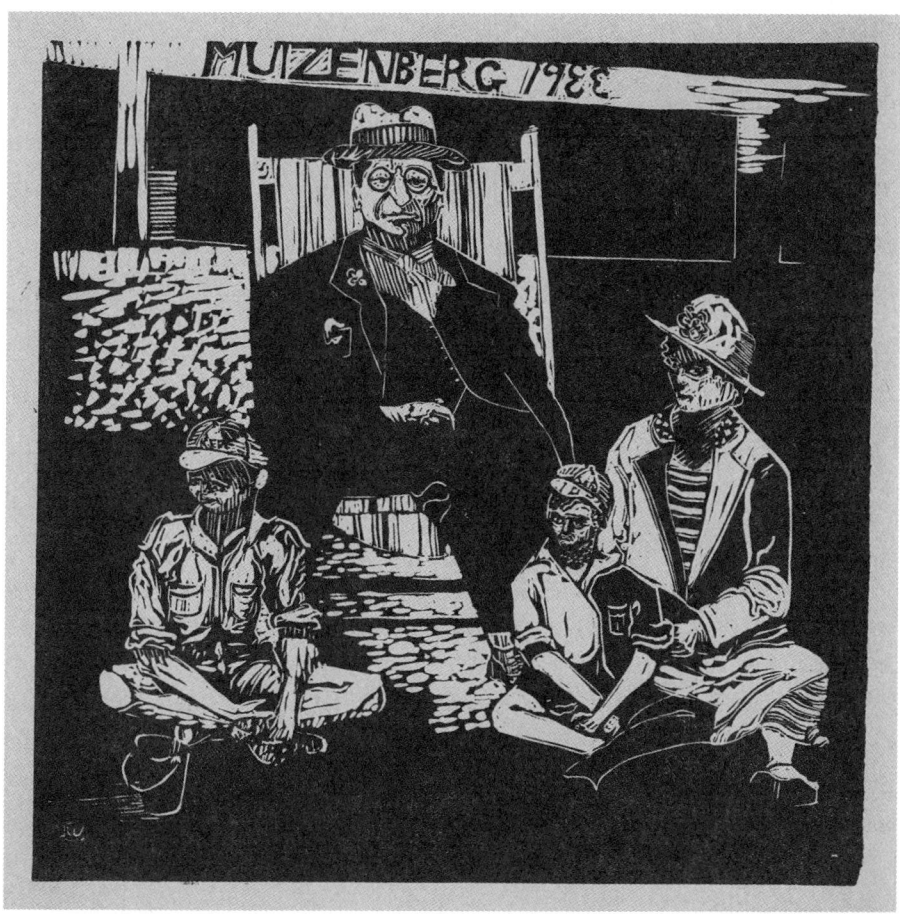

FIG. 77. William Kentridge, *Muizenberg 1933*, 1975. Linoleum cut, 47 × 60 cm

sneers, slobbers, and devours, while the intestinal jowls and the veiny cigar turn it grotesquely inside out. Multiplication and displacement—inheritances from Cubism—serve to vilify and mock: the repeated monocle cords enter the jumbled visage like leaky feeding tubes. To practice an injury is to injure coldly. Well-practiced in printmaking, Kentridge insures that the monocle's round glinting rim stands clear of the tangle around it, and he gives menace to the eyes by printing them on white paper meticulously left in reserve.

Caricature levels its accusation craftily and with foresight. Invested with personal meaning and politically charged, pinstripes acquire a new dimension. Kentridge forms the pattern's black ground out of human bodies squeezed together in rows, with the small, wavering space between them reading as white stripes on a creased dark suit. The artist derived his motif from a famous poster published in 1788 by British abolitionists and widely reproduced in recent times. Printed in the port city of Plymouth, it depicts the Brookes slave ship, a British vessel used in accordance with the Regulated Slave Trade Act of 1788. By means of its precisely engraved and mechanically multiplied images, the poster visualized for a wide public what British law sanctioned for the transport of Africans to America: six feet by one foot four inches (1.8 × 0.4 meters) of space for each man and five feet by one foot two inches (1.5 × 0.35 meters) for each woman. An icon of colonialist violence, the engraving also exemplified the evidentiary power of images, their ability both to present evidence to the court of public opinion and to make their case self-evident. Born into a family of lawyers, Kentridge brings the two-century-old testimonial to bear on the present. Johannesburg's hundred years of easy living are not a mere legacy of colonial violence. As Kentridge's film *Mine* (1991) extensively explores, Black goldminers continue to suffer enslaved conditions both underground and above, in stone barracks almost as cramped as the Brookes ship's lower deck (see fig. 101).

The bodies turn the suited business tycoon into a composite colossus. Kentridge has made printed paper collages on recycled pages of Thomas Hobbes's *Leviathan* (fig. 78). Medieval political theology conceived of the sovereign as a hybrid of two bodies, one human and one divine. Hobbes may have known that the biblical Leviathan—his name for the state or commonwealth—means "composite," from the Hebrew *liv'iah* (putting together). According to Hobbes, humans in the state of nature live perpetually at war, "and such a warre, as is of every man, against every man." To escape "continual fear, and danger of violent death" and a life that is "solitary, poor, nasty, brutish, and short," a disunited multitude unite themselves under a sovereign, making them one person, "*Feigned* or *Artificiall*," who represents them all. They make artificial chains, called laws, and fasten one end to the sovereign's lips and the other to his subject's ears. This animation or "automaton" prevails unless civil strife again plunges all into war against all, as happened in Hobbes's England.[59] The engraved frontispiece to *Leviathan* (1651) pictures the sovereign as a giant looming over a landscape and composed of the multitude he impersonates, all facing him. Made up of enslaved Africans, Kentridge's colossus impersonates the fraudulent body politic of White-minority rule. In *Johannesburg, 2nd Greatest City* this pseudo-sovereign (a private nobody who only represents himself) will be domestically betrayed and drawn into combat. But before this caricature could be transformed into a dramatic character, Kentridge had to expand the setting and bring his drawings mechanically to life.

The phrase "ART IN A STATE OF SIEGE" does not appear in the silkscreen of that title. It stands instead in typewriter font at the lower left of another print.

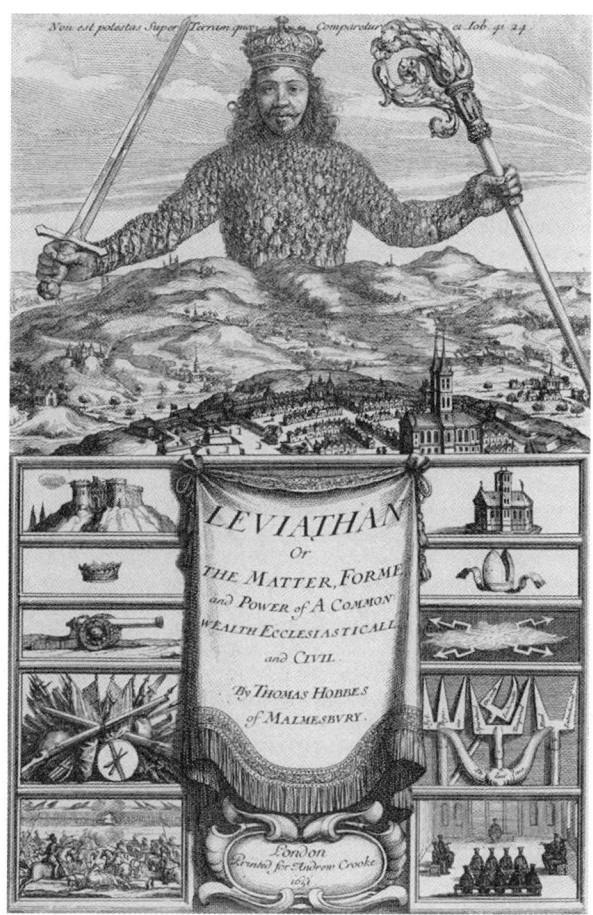

FIG. 78. Abraham Bosse, title page of Thomas Hobbes, *Leviathan* (London, 1651). Engraving, 24 × 15.5 cm

This sheet belongs to a massive triptych that incorporates the earlier "Easy Living" sheet and completes its program (plate 25). Representing Kentridge's three states of art, the silkscreens are sometimes hung in the sequence of phases outlined in the Grahamstown lecture: left to right, art in the states of "Grace," "Hope," and "Siege." Hanging *Art in a State of Grace* at the left also makes sense because it alone features the three typewritten titular phrases, thus introducing the group. However, Kentridge typically exhibits the triptych with "Siege" at the left, "Grace" at the right, and "Hope" in the middle, more in line with the chronology of the prints' creation. He began "Siege" in the emergency and centennial year 1986 and made the other two later, in 1988. This arrangement works well visually. The "Easy Living" tycoon and the bespectacled woman with a catfish hat gaze inward to the mysteriously receding central tableau: "Hope" as a turned-away woman with a fan for a head and bleachers for a dress—Tatlin's utopian *Monument* scrambled up and trivialized (see fig. 69). In fact, the triptych can be hung in any order, because in 1988 art of any kind, whether non-political or political, stood under siege, making aestheticist grace inadmissible and revolutionary hope absurd.

Kentridge defined his own position as one where "optimism is kept in check" and "nihilism is kept at bay." *Johannesburg, 2nd Greatest City* opens with the abandoned bleachers from the "Hope" silkscreen, but adds the billboard-like projection screen, proposing that hope and (in the film's own beauty) grace might survive. Recall that it was Beckmann's painting *Death* that, for Kentridge in 1986, marked "the spot" between optimism and nihilism. The silkscreens mark that spot themselves, but in a Beckmann-like style. They also realize, Beckmann-like, the public written manifesto that precedes them, in the way the German painter's *Self-Portrait in Tuxedo* fulfilled the program announced in "The Artist in the State" (plate 18). Kentridge's printed triptych has been a model for me, as well. Just as each of his three states contains the other two, "art in a state of siege" is best not pinpointed to a single work, artist, or era. In the extreme state, chronology becomes reversed, collaged, and voided. There is Beckmann in Kentridge, Bosch in Beckmann, and Kentridge in Bosch. Aesthetic grace and redemptive hope glimmer in all three, and just as the silkscreens can be hung in any order, I could just have well begun with Kentridge and ended with Bosch, with the contemporary artist looking forward and Bosch beheld in retrospect.

Kentridge has described his triptychs as filmic, because each panel reads like a different shot of a single scene. The silkscreens relate to film in more specific ways. In scale and format they resemble movie posters for promotional public display, and their ragged margins suggest long billboard use. Their settings, motifs, texts, and trio of characters also preview elements of the film series that Kentridge himself was about to begin. The artist later made large, printed posters for exhibitions of his "Drawings for Projection," adjusting the horizontal film images to the upright poster format. The triptych is oblong when hung and reads like three festive banners, each a collage of stills. The silkscreens thus festively announce the coming attraction: a major motion picture about art in a state of siege.

This is all hindsight. The triptych only seems filmic. The collaged imagery and frame-like jumps from print to print that resemble film montage; the cigar smoker's many mouths, the rotary fan, the fish popping up here and there; the two women becoming one woman turned towards us and away; the characters enacting a domestic scene: these add movement and narrative to images by nature motionless and mute. An impulse to go beyond the stubborn restriction of medium is there, though. Endowed with artificial life, the animated drawing would tell a novelistic story that unfolds serially over many years, with characters growing old

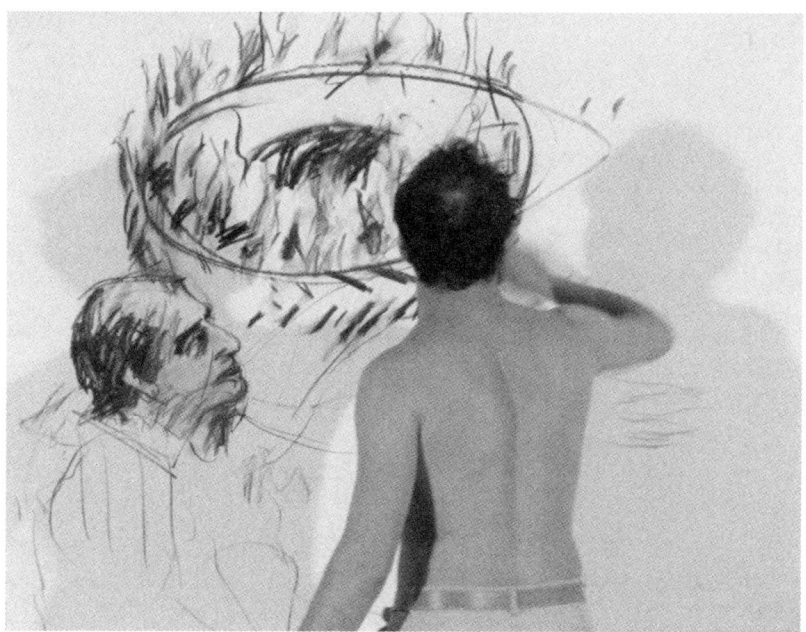

FIG. 79. Still from William Kentridge, *Vetkoek–Fête Galante*, 1985. 16mm film transferred to video

with their maker. Kentridge has offered different accounts of his breakthrough. By one of these, his "Drawings for Projection" arose out of his filmmaking activities in the early 1980s—from an urge to make movies cheaply and independently. By another, they offered the artist an escape from the relentless pace of artmaking: "I could see my life ahead of me, so I decided I had to do something for my own pleasure."[60] More compellingly, they originated from complex struggles with drawing.

He had been filmed painting a theater set. Interested in how the camera captured the image-making process, he kept the camera on loan to track, frame by frame, the development of a charcoal drawing. Kentridge wanted to see where things go right or wrong, when a good drawing became overworked, and when drawing flowed or got stuck. Printmaking archives these changes naturally, through proof impressions checking the current state of the matrix. In response to the 1985 State of Emergency, Kentridge had made the three-minute animated short *Vetkoek/Fête Gallant* featuring, in speeded-up film, people clownishly marking, erasing, and writing on a charcoal drawing (fig. 79). The erasing parodied the censorship imposed by the emergency—the film was screened at an exhibition contesting the suppression of the free press; its title linked White South Africa, symbolized by popular *vetkoek* (Afrikaans for "fat-cake") pastry, to the *ancien régime* in France at the eve of the revolution. In 1989, therefore, Kentridge must have had some idea of a public outcome for his solitary experiment with a borrowed Bolex.

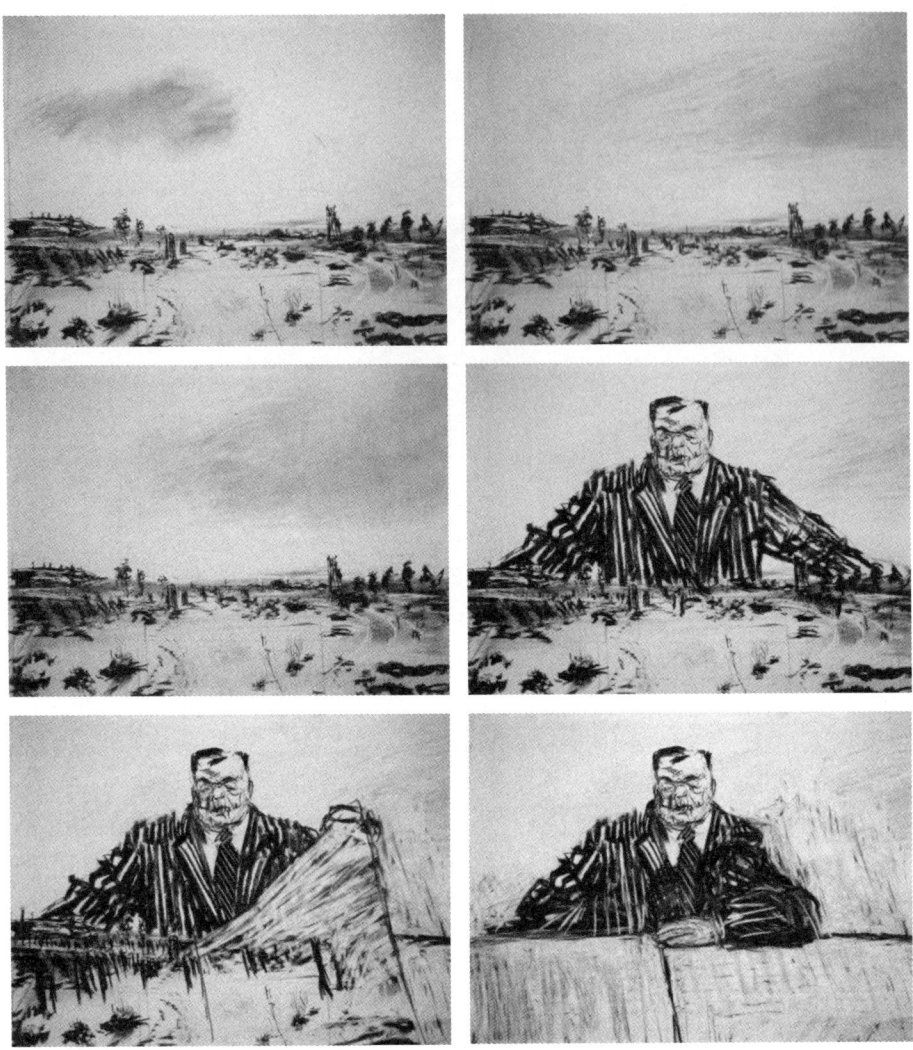

FIG. 80. Stills from William Kentridge, *Johannesburg, 2nd Greatest City after Paris*, 1989. 16mm film transferred to video

He began with a siegescape. The first drawing filmed while being made flashes up in edited form halfway through *Johannesburg, 2nd Greatest City*. The sheet already has clumps of grass in the foreground, a ridge in the distance, faint placeholders for undulations in between, and two poles establishing spatial recession (fig. 80). Over ten seconds a dense panorama materializes, each new detail capturing chiefly human interventions in the landscape, as if without the paths, pits, culverts, pipes, powerlines, and slag-heaps both the vista and the drawing would be blank. The buildup of setting shifts almost imperceptibly into the animated event. Stray dots in the distance multiply, cluster, and move, and the instant they move, we recognize the dots as people wandering the waste. Converging, they form a procession that snakes its way towards the foreground, revealing who they are: South Africa's oppressed Black majority unhoused by forced removal and the state-sponsored destruction of shanty towns and squatters' camps. Kentridge has noted that crowds, and especially ones gathered in lines, seem to draw themselves. A minimum of marks conjures a multitude, and a fuzzy serpentine makes a plausible parade. What would take a cast of thousands in a live action film is done with a few strokes of charcoal.

When Kentridge first showed his animations, he treated them as sideshows to exhibitions of the drawings in their final state. He still premiers new "Drawings for Projection" together with drawings that made them. It is the art historian's dream: a chronicle of an artwork's formation that also tells backstories of its motifs and metaphors. In fact, Kentridge's films rarely show the whole process of a drawing's production. Instead, they combine edited clips from many filmed drawings, turning the available footage into a cinematic montage with pans, crosscuts, and shifting focal lengths, and accompanied by a rich and evocative soundtrack. This transformation happened rather by accident. A filmmaker friend, Angus Gibson, saw the early footage and started working with it on his Steenbeck 16mm flatbed editing table. That was how drawings in motion became motion pictures complete with plot, characters, melody, spectacle, and (through intertitles) thoughts.

Johannesburg, 2nd Greatest City weaves together two stories, one private, one public. The private story follows the adulterous affair of Felix and Mrs. Eckstein from its yearnings and consummation through its discovery by Soho to a final showdown. The public story concerns Soho's commercial dealings and their impact on the people. It unfolds in the space between Soho at his desk, where he "takes on the world," and the veld, where the homeless oppressed ceaselessly march. Thanks to his charcoal medium Kentridge can shift swiftly and seamlessly between the domestic and the political plots. Twice he erases and redraws the lower third of one sheet, turning the veld into Soho's desk and back again in just fourteen seconds of screen time. Compared to the film's dazzling visual spectacle, the plots themselves are commonplace. Love triangles are archetypal domestic dramas because they throw the house—the *domus*—into conflict.

The public story about Soho, his property, and the oppressed is the standard Marxist one of history as class struggle. Those who, like Soho, control capital struggle continuously against those who provide the labor—in the racial capitalism of South Africa, the Black majority. Soho's specific interactions with the people are textbook features of class conflict. A 1911 poster, *Pyramid of Capitalist System*, shows the wealthy bourgeoisie eating "for you" while farmers and

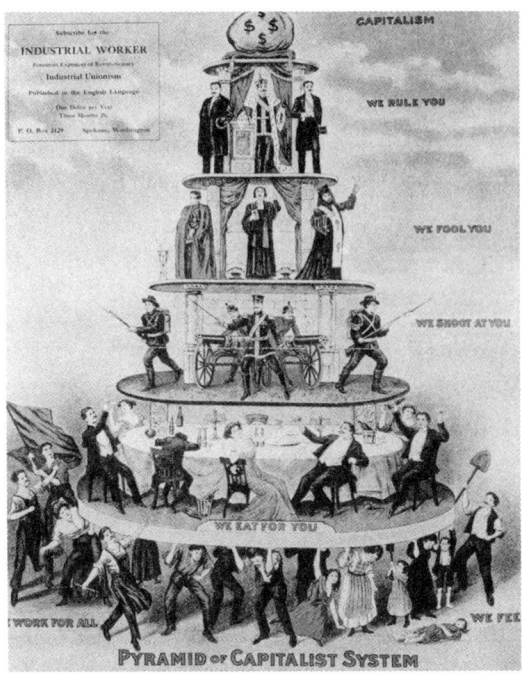

FIG. 81. Nedelkovich, Brashich, and Kuharich (attributed to), *Pyramid of the Capitalist System*, 1911. The International Publishing Co., Cleveland, Ohio

laborers who toil "for all" are crushed underneath (fig. 81). When Soho "feeds the poor"—the intertitle is poster-like—he gorges himself instead, pelting with food the supplicants arriving for his benefaction. Capitalism's "we fool you" and "we shoot at you" are thus combined, while "we rule you" takes the Hobbesian form of Soho, the Leviathan of racial capitalism, looming over his desk as veld, or world.

The stock nature of both these plots is deliberate. Kentridge wants his stories to pass into the setting. The love triangle begins in interior settings but moves out into the landscape, where the film begins and ends. Felix first appears, naked and with his back to us, on his apartment balcony beholding (while his bathtub fills) the pulsing city that holds him "captive" (plate 26). Immersed in the tub, his "ANXIETY flood[ing] half the house," he dreams of Mrs. Eckstein, his erotic and dangerous imagining flashing up as moving pictures in the book he peruses. Mrs. Eckstein herself then appears "waiting" alone in a glazed pool or bathhouse interior (fig. 82). Felix arrives outside the glass wall, which he magically penetrates when the lovers lock eyes. Soho meanwhile inhabits workspace, an interior blank save for the cluttered desk that morphs into blueprints, landscapes, and a feasting table. From his desk Soho buys "half of Johannesburg," but "Rumors of a different Life" reach him by telephone at the moment of his cuckolding. Felix entered and exited Mrs. Eckstein as a tiny fish, and later that fish, flapping about on Mrs. Eckstein's

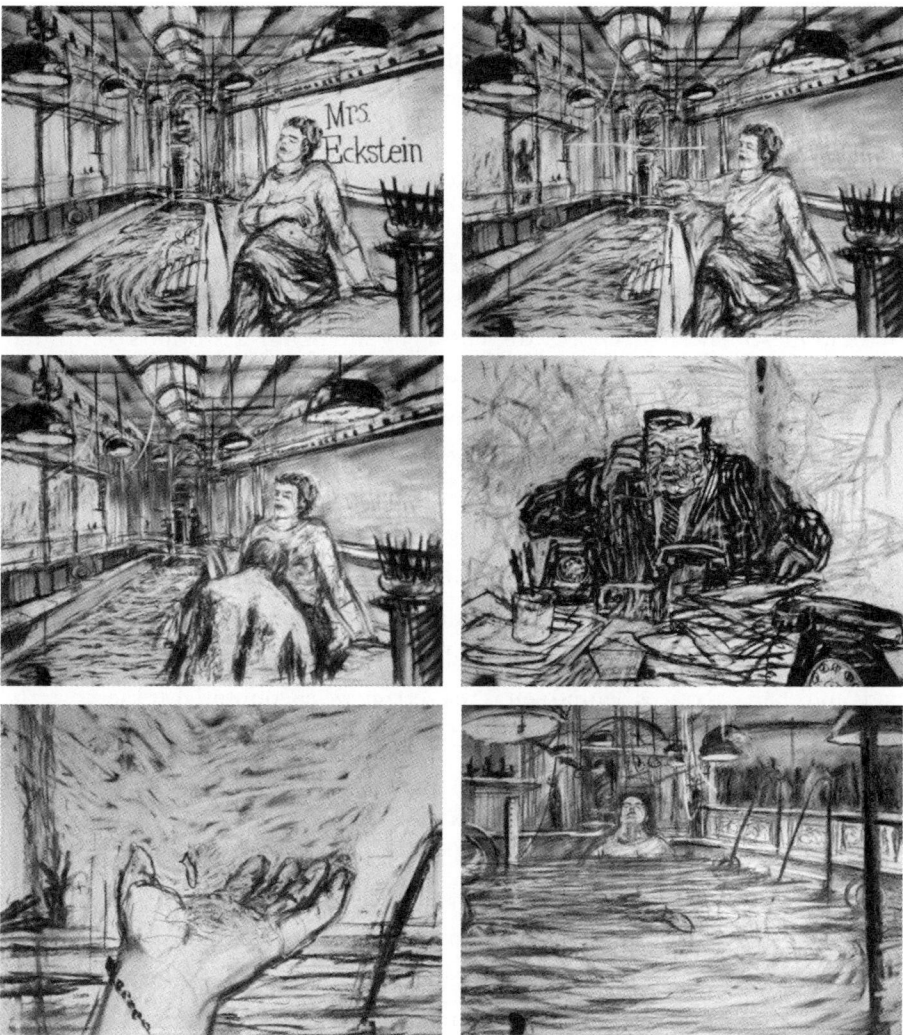

FIG. 82. Stills from William Kentridge, *Johannesburg, 2nd Greatest City after Paris*, 1989. 16mm film transferred to video

palm and then on Soho's, evidences the affair. Felix's aqueous nature allows him to breach the boundaries of body and home. Half the city may be Soho's, but Felix has penetrated Mrs. Eckstein, her name marking her as Soho territory.

Adultery breaches boundaries—hence its ancient associations with siege. The siege of Troy began with Paris abducting Helen from Menelaus's home, causing generations of devastating conflict within and between families and tribes. Hopeless in war, Paris—like Felix—prefers the bed to the battlefield, and private dalliances to historical action. When Aphrodite whisks him from death in combat to Helen's chamber, he becomes invisible: "None of the Trojans or their famed allies could then discover [him] to Menelaus."[61] Tristan, Paris's medieval counterpart, is slippery, too. His affair with Queen Iseult betrays her husband, King Mark, who is also Tristan's uncle and liege lord. "Leave this castle," the king commands, "and having left it, remain apart, and do not think to return to it, and do not repass its moat and boundaries."[62] But Tristan (from French *triste*, "sad," thus opposite to Latin *felix*, "happy") finds ways back in, using waters that leak from the castle to carry secret messages to Iseult. It is a version of chivalric courtship, as a knight besieging his lady, but with ruinous consequences. Kentridge gives Felix's breach of the domestic enclave its public dimension by entangling it in Soho's confrontation with the masses. The landscape view with Soho looming Leviathan-like over it suddenly shifts to Felix's adulterous entrance into Mrs. Eckstein. The tyrant becomes a fool, the besieger becomes besieged.

When they first appear, the oppressed wander as refugees (*ins Elend*) in their own land.[63] But "Eckstein Territory" has been transgressed, and now they crowd in on Soho, their leader opening his arms in a desperate gesture of petition (fig. 83). From his table, where he gorges himself, Soho bombards the supplicants with bits of his feast until, defaced and dejected, they fade away, leaving vertical rods and charcoal traces behind—it is the setting we encountered at the start: the veld landscape with traces of a body in the sky. Now Felix, large, naked, and seen from behind, steps forward to face Soho in combat. Their fight takes them into the open, into the ankle-deep waters of a vlei. The image evokes Francisco Goya's enigmatic *Fight with Cudgels*, a picture painted in oil on the plaster walls of Quinta del Sordo (House of the deaf man), where the artist lived from 1819 to 1824. Those were the years of Spain's Trienio Liberal, when, after the Peninsular Wars' half a million casualties, a military uprising brought a liberal government briefly to power, only to be defeated by a coalition of European monarchs lead by France. Goya's combatants, called "strangers" and "cowherds" in the Spanish inventories, might represent opposing sides in civil war, although their crude execution on the wall of a private interior links them and Goya's other "hermetically private" Black Paintings to the graffiti that madmen drew in bedlam.[64] A paradigm of the artist in a state of siege, Goya had already made a huge impact on Kentridge early on (see fig. 67). His visions of Soho looming over the landscape recollect Goya's *The Colossus* (1808–1812), and his processions echo the many that Goya painted, including two in the Quinta del Sordo itself. Soho and Felix's fight with cudgels connects domestic conflict in the home to unrest on the streets. And as in Goya, the duality of their battle also blinds the combatants to the condition that dooms them both. The oppressed Black majority, in an endless procession towards the horizon, brings the film to its close.

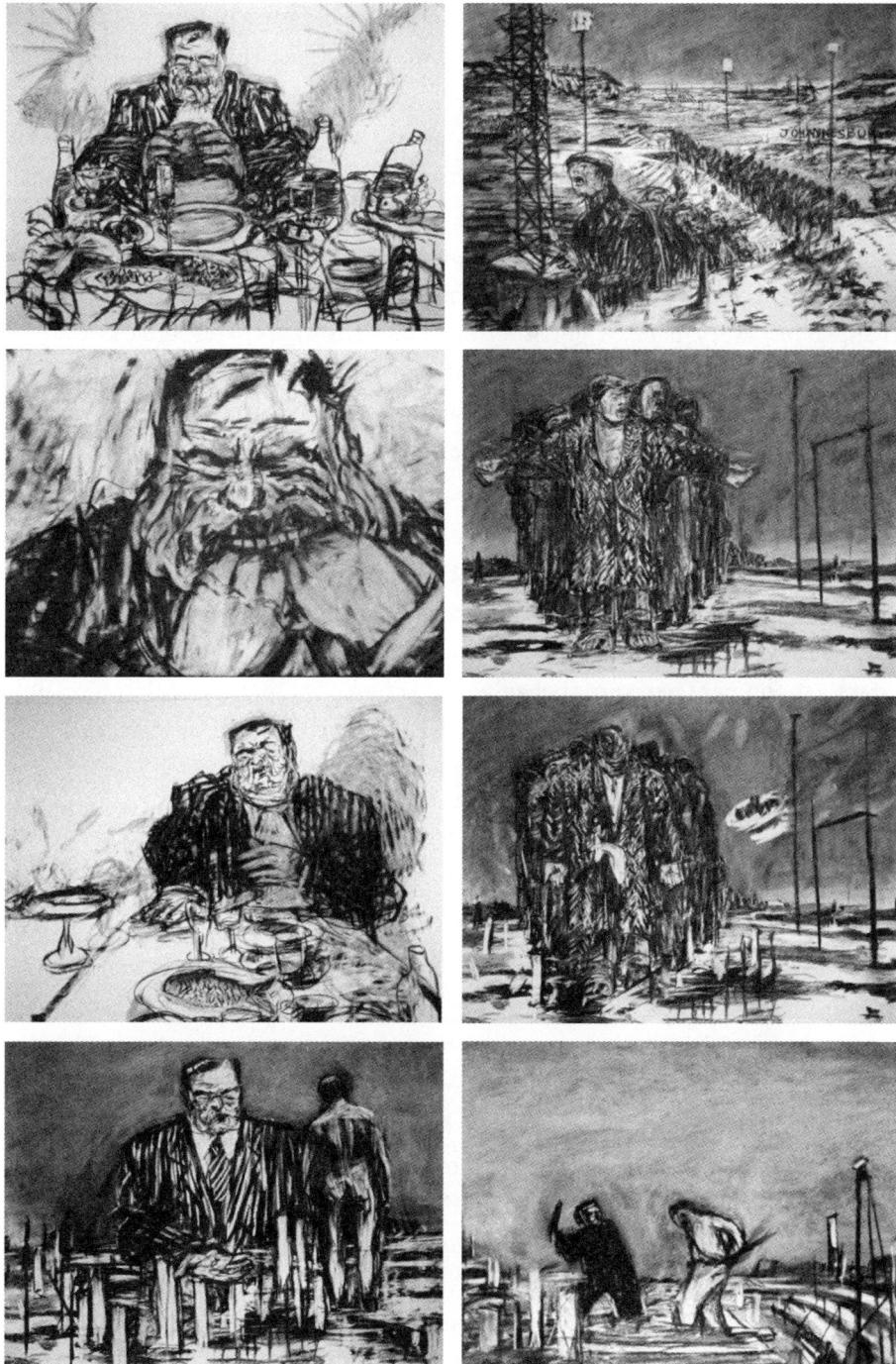

FIG. 83. Stills from William Kentridge, *Johannesburg, 2nd Greatest City after Paris*, 1989. 16mm film transferred to video

For Hobbes, the human condition in a state of nature consists of ceaseless one-on-one skirmishes, because "if any two men desire the same thing, which nonetheless they cannot both enjoy, they become enemies." Only by covenanting with would-be enemies to form a state do individuals escape interminable one-on-one conflict (see fig. 78). Covenanting also replaces such quarrels with perpetual war between states, sovereigns "in continuall jealousies [...] having their weapons pointing, and their eyes fixed on one another."[65] But civil war overturns the covenant, returning humans to their solitary, poor, and nasty state "of every man, against every man." Siege conditions, and Kentridge's perspective as a White South African, recommended his critical focus on the domestic, on ordinary persons, everyday actions, and mundane objects. But in 1989, that enclosure, long besieged, was breached, bringing conflict into the open.

The siege spills over into the landscape. *Johannesburg, 2nd Greatest City* opens and closes on that outdoor setting, as did the experiment with which "drawings for projection" began (see figs. 75, 80, 83). In the end, while Felix and Soho fight, ruins of colonial history clutter the waste. Refiguring the imagery of slave ship and miners' barracks, a bookshelf overstocked with severed heads appears and disappears, a monument to trauma behaving like trauma, in repressed and irrepressible returns. And in the final landscape, the besieged continue to process, this time marching into the distance and leaving an empty setting behind. The drawing reverts almost to what it was when drawing began, a sheet of paper, almost blank.

New York, 2009

Ideally you would happen on them by chance: you, exploring a private study not your own, or visiting a library or archive for another purpose; they, a sheaf of eighteen empty pages pressed into their slipcase so tightly that accessing them feels risky, and returning them unscathed harder still (figs. 84–91).[66] You contemplate their white perfection, admire their untrimmed deckle edges accomplished by artisanal hands, and (imagining you've come upon unused paper) resist the craving to put their pristine surfaces to use. "The blank sheet of paper awaits its mark," wrote Kentridge of this inclination. "There is an urge, an impulse to make the mark."[67] But a label urges caution. Printed in black on delicate paper punctuating the slipcase's linen covering, the words "SHEETS OF EVIDENCE" demand that the pages be inspected as a detective would a fingerprint. And it may be that lynx-eyed looking would have already espied in the complete simplicity of one page a figure. As if scratched into the paper's surface, this flashes forth

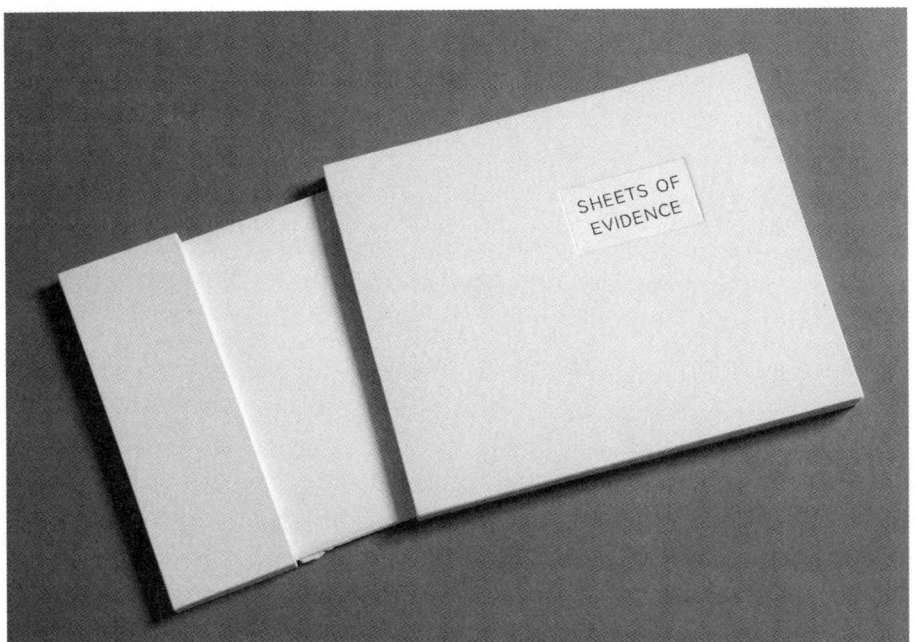

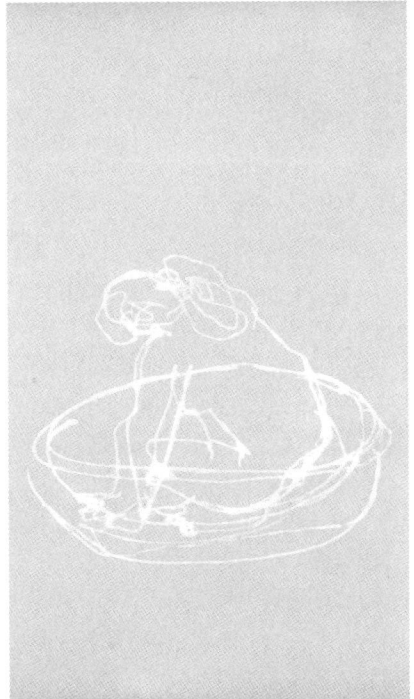

FIGS. 84–86. William Kentridge, *Sheets of Evidence* (New York: Dieu Donné, 2009). Artist's book of eighteen watermarked drawing collages, 31.75 × 28 × 3.2 cm closed

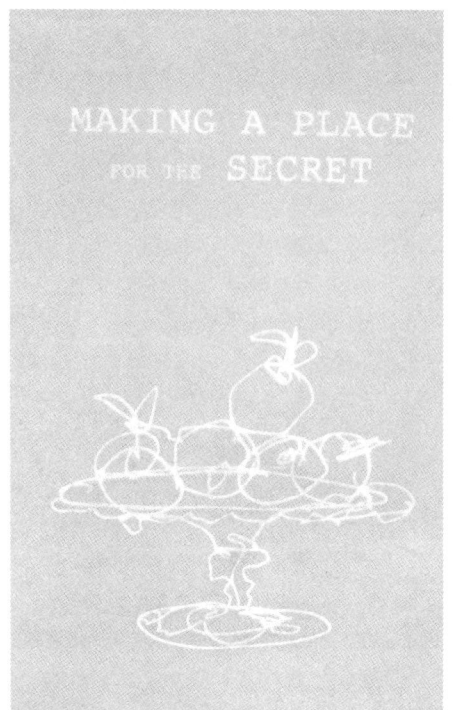
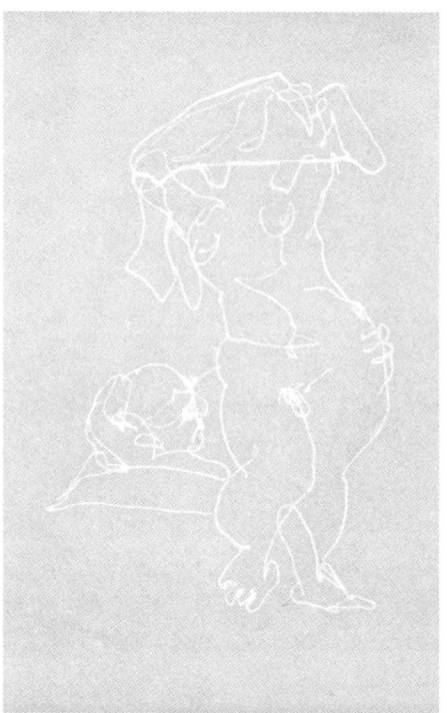
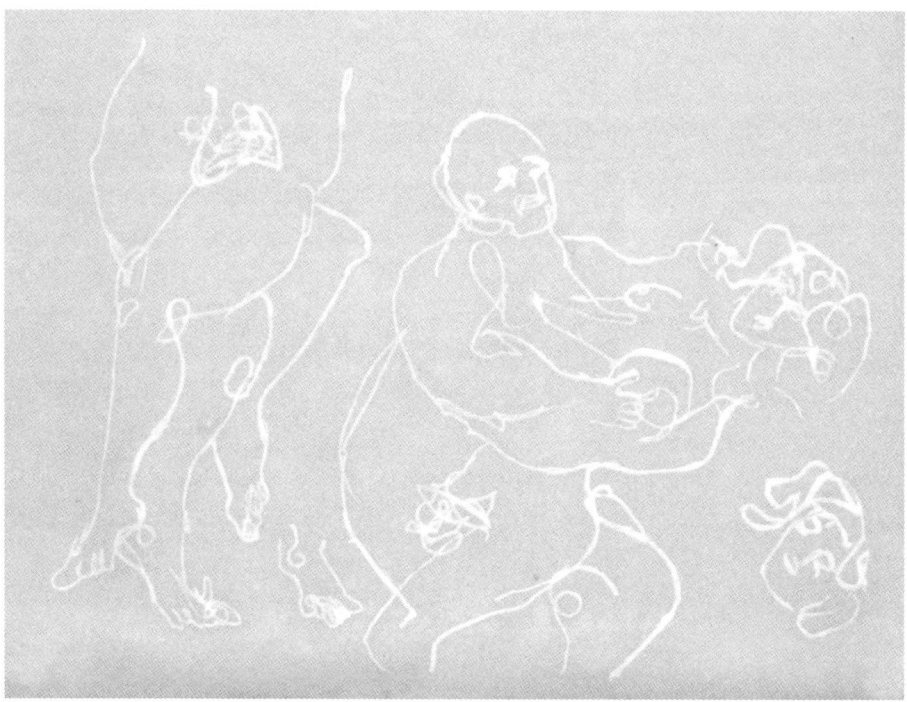

FIGS. 87–89. From William Kentridge, *Sheets of Evidence* (New York: Dieu Donné, 2009). Artist's book of eighteen watermarked drawing collages, 31.75 × 28 × 3.2 cm closed

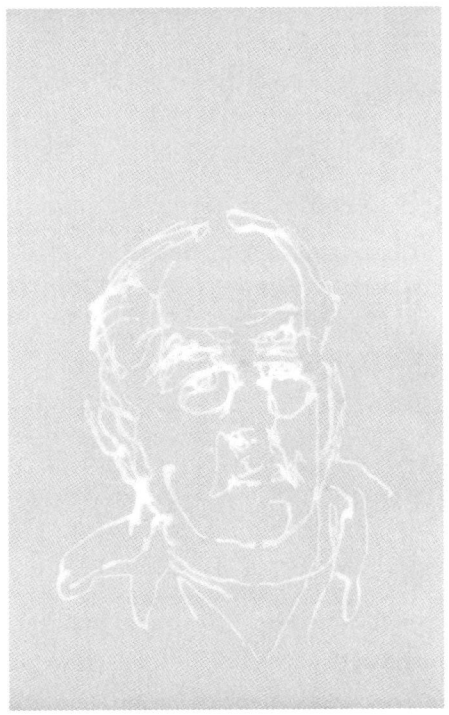
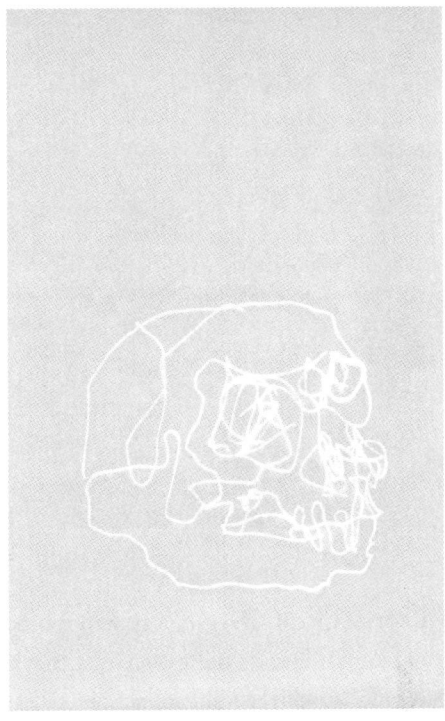

FIGS. 90–91. From William Kentridge, *Sheets of Evidence* (New York: Dieu Donné, 2009). Artist's book of eighteen watermarked drawing collages, 31.75 × 28 × 3.2 cm closed

fleetingly, while the page is turned. Only when the sheet is held up to light does the evidence become evident.

Watermarks, as these crafted variations are termed, escape simple definition. Slight differences in the density of the pulp of which the sheet consists, they lie not on or under the paper. Features *of* the paper, they cannot be printed—in paper currency this helps foil counterfeiting—and should be noticeable only when looked for. Artists may attend to them, but only to make sure that, on the paper a watermark guarantees, their pen or brush will leave its mark smoothly and dependably, heedless of the watermark.

The term is a misnomer. Better termed papermark, a watermark has little to do with water. It arises when something solid—typically a bit of bent wire attached to the papermaker's woven screen—disrupts the even flow of pulp when wet. Marks made directly by water, when a droplet falls on a sheet after it is formed, are called "papermaker's tears," indicating their status as blemish. In *Sheets of Evidence*, the watermarks appear watery nevertheless, seeming to have been fluidly sketched in a liquid medium like ink. Whole figures have been conjured from extended squiggles that swell, taper, and pool. Some sheets include water as a

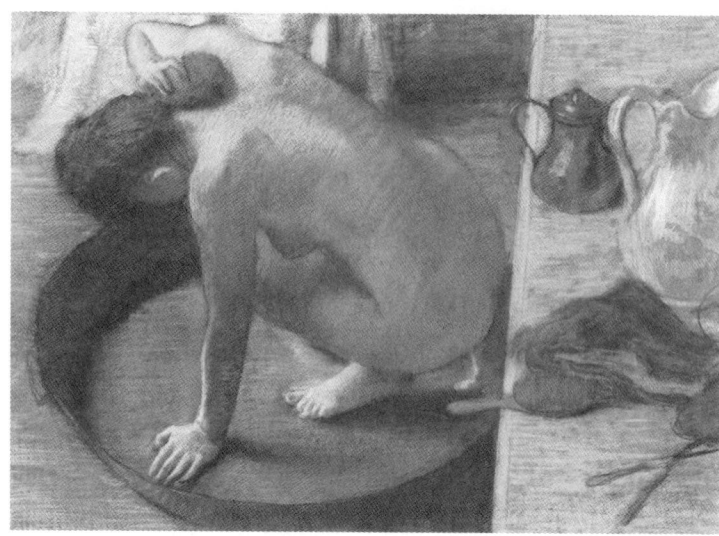

FIG. 92.
Edgar Degas, *The Tub*, 1886. Pastel, 60 × 83 cm. Musée d'Orsay, Paris

pictorial motif. In one, a naked woman crouches in a shallow tub; in another, the woman stands bent over in a tub holding a bath sheet (fig. 85). Her towel is twofold, since the "sheet" where she appears was itself made of cut, macerated, filigraned, and fermented rags.

The two images of women bathing recall pastels and monotypes by Edgar Degas (fig. 92). They also give the portfolio a voyeuristic charge. Degas intended his bathers to seem surreptitiously beheld. "Hitherto the nude has always been represented in poses which presuppose an audience," he explained to the Irish writer George Moore. "But these women of mine are honest, simple folk, unconcerned by any other interests than those involved in their physical condition [...]. It is as if you were looking through a key-hole."[68] Degas did not actually observe his subjects secretly. He stood in their space, sometimes capturing their candid movements, sometimes posing them in postures he wanted to draw, including ones with classical prototypes. The nude in his 1886 pastel *The Tub*—a model for one of the *Sheets of Evidence*—channels ancient statues of the crouching Aphrodite. Aphrodite is an aqueous goddess born from floating foam. By Hesiod's account, Cronos castrated his father, the primordial sky god Uranus, and tossed his genitals into the sea. Congealed into foam—*aphrós* in Greek—the fecund blood and semen birthed the love goddess fully formed, beautiful, and infinitely desirable. Viewers of Degas's art were unlikely to have taken the bathing women to be "simple, honest creatures," since such intimate visual encounters with unknown women could be had in brothels and bathhouses. *Sheets of Evidence* connect the dots. Three pages show a couple copulating, in one case with a third lover potentially involved (fig.

89). A sheet watermarked with texts sustains this line of thinking. "Three-in-a-bed / gambler / wins bet, / loses lover" derives from a 2006 tabloid headline about a sexual threesome gone wrong—though a non-sequitur follows: "When you drink tea / you are bringing a thief into the / body."

Sheets of Evidence is not about facts, but about fact finding. The innuendos in its pages spark investigative thinking. Formed of short cotton linter pulp pressed to 2,300 pounds per square inch, the sheets display bodies, lips, and tongues pressing tightly together, mimicking what brought the pages about. These erotic watermarks activate a second meaning of work's title. Sexual liaisons happen between the sheets. Made—potentially—of recycled bedsheets, paper remembers its private past. The watermarks' loopy lines resemble stains left by lovemaking, like the evidence on Monica Lewinsky's blue Gap dress. Papermakers themselves use a vocabulary rich in connotations. Bad sheets of paper are "kissed off" from the mold. Paper distorted during the drying process is "cockled." Fresh sheets flipped from the mold to the felt are "couched," from French *coucher*, "to put to bed." The texts in *Sheets of Evidence* come from technical manuals, news reports, and advertisement copy. Taken out of context and collaged, they waver between specialized, common, and slang usage. The word "lies" appears three times on one sheet: "What Lies / in Store / What Lies / in Wait / What Lies / Asleep" (fig. 86). Each means something slightly different, but all converge around the idea of potentiality. Capitalized and (through the line break) isolated for scrutiny, "Lies" also summons its homonym: "untrue statements." Hidden, the watermarks deceive; in store, they await discovery.

"MAKING A PLACE FOR THE SECRET" heads a drawing of fruit (fig. 87). The innocent still-life—art in a state of grace—may be a hiding place for ordinary secrets, the intimate, bodily matters of food, sex, illness, and death. In the left canvas of his triptych *Departure*, Beckmann paints a still-life behind the kneeling woman (plate 20). She is a nightmare version of Degas nudes, but whether the oversized fruits are as cruelly ironic, whether they are a last vestige of "art" in a state of siege remains deliberately unclear. The *Sheets of Evidence* was called by its maker a "pillow book," meaning a private miscellany, one accidentally discovered under a pillow and therefore private and obscure. In her famous work of that title, Sei Shōnagon claimed that she intended it for her eyes only, but accidentally left it on a cushion put out for a visitor, who carried it away despite her pleas. Like its tenth-century precursor, *Sheets of Evidence* points beyond its variety to a singular person. Although he figures in the lovemaking scenes, the portfolio's author makes his unmistakable appearance as a sort of colophon on the penultimate sheet, after "What Lies / Asleep" and before a final, finalizing drawing of a skull (figs. 90 and 91). To anyone familiar with the artist's oeuvre, filled as it is with self-portraits of all kinds and in nearly every medium, the balding man with pince-nez and an open collar will be recognizable at once.

William Kentridge made this ego document in 2009 in partnership with Dieu Donné, a nonprofit artmaking papermill in New York City. Kentridge had already held an artist-in-residency there seven years earlier. Initiated by Susan Gosin into the papermaker's craft, he had experimented with producing watermarks that appear to be drawn in pulp. Titled *Thinking in Water* (2003), the suite of three sheets used wire watermarks bent in the shapes of drawn lines. Dieu Donné stood on 36th Street in Manhattan, near Hudson Yards. A windowed gallery and shop for displaying finished works fronted the two-story balconied studio space. "Think carwash" is how Gosin describes the physical plant required for the operation she co-founded in 1976. Papermaking begins dry, with the rags and linter. Then it goes very wet, where pulp is mixed, beaten, and manipulated, new sheets are hydraulically pressed, and vats and screens are emptied and cleaned. At the end is the Dry Room, where sheets are dried and curated. Water will henceforth be—after fire—paper's chief enemy.

Paper can be made anywhere. The simple technique allowed wide variations in the materials and processes used. Invented in China before the second century BCE, papermaking arrived in Europe after a journey lasting more than a thousand years. Europeans forgot paper's Chinese and Muslim-Arab origins. They fancied they had invented it themselves. Despite this geographic diffusion, good papermaking retains a distinctly local character. It requires plenty of clean water to liquify the pulp and, in pre-industrial manufacture, to power the hammers that beat the rags to pulp. Wire watermarks first appear in Italian paper in the late thirteenth century. They coincided with European advances in wire-making and the development of wire mesh paper molds. Made using brass wire attached to the mold, these marks advertised the local mill and the purity of its water to consumers far away. Working with Dieu Donné, Kentridge grasped immediately the distinctiveness of watermarks. Unconcerned that the resultant work would be invisible under ordinary circumstances, but enjoying the humor and the personal resonance of the undertaking, he used his time at Dieu Donné to probe the subconscious of paper, that medium most integral to his art.

Soon after its emergence in Europe, paper became a ubiquitous material for painters, sculptors, and architects, first for designs, studies, copies, contracts, and training, then, in tandem with the proliferation of woodcuts and engravings, as a support for the "master drawing" as an autonomous creation and valued collectables. This expansive use followed from paper's low cost and homogeneousness:

paper's ubiquity derived from its being everywhere roughly the same. Although produced in a variety of sizes, colors, and quality, European paper was, by comparison with the creative heterogeneity of, say, Chinese-made paper, produced predominantly in clean white sheets. The material's early modern champions celebrated this homogeneity. In *The New Organon* (1620), Francis Bacon, observing paper's capacity to "masterfully rule [nature] and transform her completely," marveled above all at its continuous surface. This material consistency—how it "has fibres, but not distinct threads"—made it akin to, and thus an extension of, the human mind, which Bacon imagined, accordingly, as "a fair sheet of paper with no writing on it."[69] Expanding this metaphor, John Locke, in his *An Essay Concerning Human Understanding* (1689), famously described the mind as a *tabula rasa*: "white paper devoid of all characters, without *Ideas*."

Almost as much a feature of European paper as blankness, watermarks smuggle memory and geography into the pristine sheet. Importantly, the indelible nature of anything deposited on or in paper recommended the material for its initial use. Not only was paper cheaper to produce than parchment (made of prepared animal skins); marks on parchment could be completely scrubbed and scoured away, whereas paper cannot tolerate total erasure, tearing before the mark disappears. This fragile permanence made paper ideal for recording legal and economic transactions during Europe's revival of Roman law. Kentridge's "Drawings for Projection" engages with this property of paper. In these films, charcoal makes its marks as if effortlessly. Birds in flight, ocean waves, gathering clouds, undulations of the veld seem magically to draw themselves, and this expansive imagery can just as easily be brushed away and drawing can begin anew. But traces remain. The several drawings used in making one film contain in their fibers the film in its entirety. For Kentridge, paper's inability to forget has an ethical charge. While the artist explains his abstention from painting on grounds of want of color sense, oil paint has inherent powers of concealment that the graphic arts can resist. Painters, wrote Giorgio Vasari in 1550, can patch up their errors with the very brush that made them, "which brush, in their hands, has this advantage over the sculptor's chisels, that it not only heals, as did the iron of the spear of Achilles, but leaves its wounds without a scar."[70] Five centuries on, painting remains the art of arts thanks to the "finish" it achieves. Works in this medium look as their maker intends them, whereas works on paper appear impermanent, provisional, and in process.

Even when done in pencil, charcoal, or chalk, drawing on paper leaves behind a scar. Two short films of 2003 (the year of *Thinking in Water*) show paper returning to an unmarked Eden. Filmed from above Kentridge's drawing table, with the

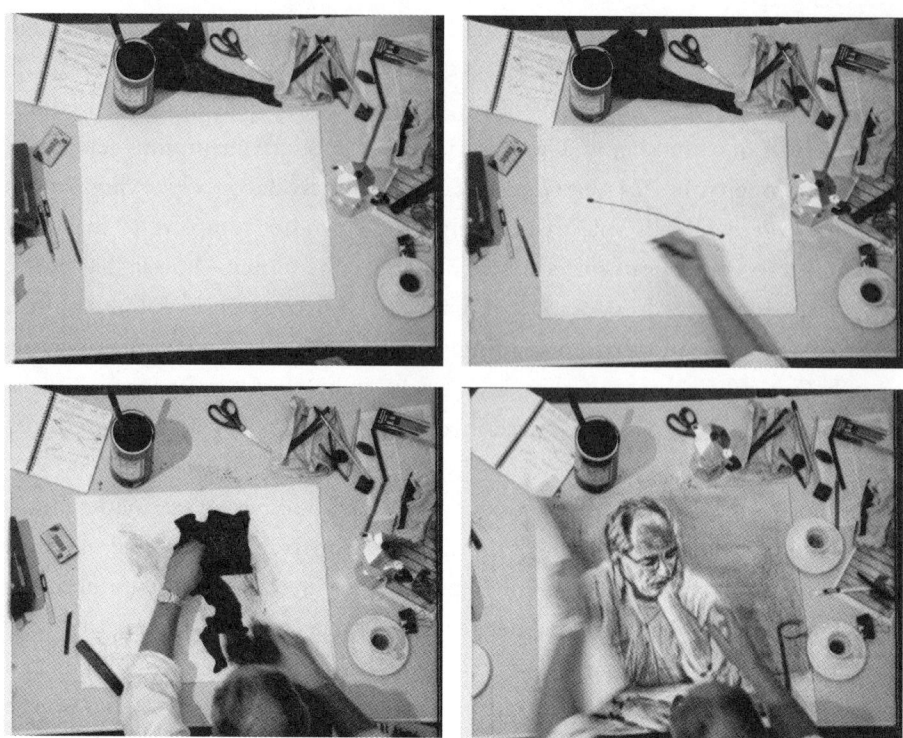

FIG. 93. Stills from William Kentridge, *7 Fragments for Georges Méliès, Tabula Rasa I*, 2003. Video

artist's hands captured at work, *Tabula Rasa I* and *II* begin and end with shots of a pristine deckle-edged sheet (fig. 93). The two films belong to the suit *7 Fragments for Georges Méliès*. In *Tabula Rasa I*, a medley of Kentridge's graphic practice flashes up in between the empty sheets: live action film of charcoal drawing intercut with drawing in animation; torn construction-paper puppets manipulated on the page; a stop-motion dance of a coffee pot, spilled coffee, a cup, and a saucer. Images flourish far beyond what the draftsman makes, creating the illusion they are products of the paper's volition—the blank sheet as "a Robert Ryman of possibilities" (Kentridge) where the imagination, seeing things in the paper, outshines whatever an artist imperfectly makes.[71] In the penultimate shot, Kentridge lays down a finished charcoal portrait of himself in melancholy inactivity at the table we observe from above—an authorial colophon that turns to nothing.

Tabula Rasa II ('good housekeeping') has a simpler plot. Over the opening blank page are spread, first, a sheet splashed and wiped to its edges in ink from a coffee pot, then another brushed all over with charcoal dust (fig. 94). Rolling the film of their messy production backwards, each of these monochromes is unmade to produce a tabula rasa. Good housekeeping ends with the blank sheet that "awaits

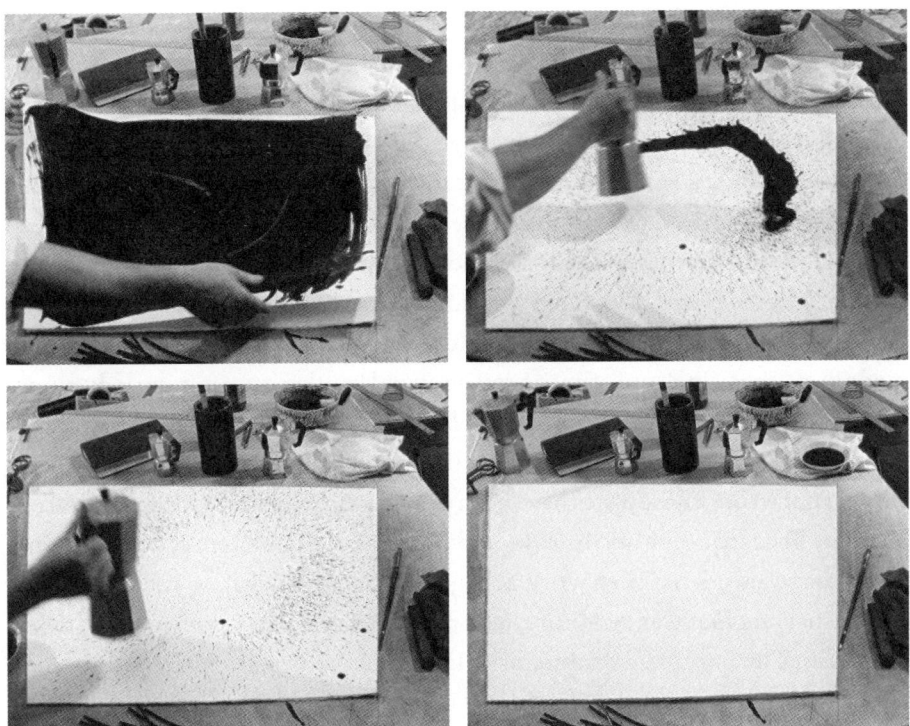

FIG. 94. Stills from William Kentridge, *7 Fragments for Georges Méliès, Tabula Rasa II*, 2003. Video

its mark."[72] It was the "impulse to make the mark" that, in Johannesburg in 1985, launched the artist's successful career (plate 22; fig. 73). Miming with charcoal Brassaï's photograph, Kentridge allowed his big sheet of paper to bring *Tropical Love Storm* about, enabling him to affirm, "I can do this." Earlier, wavering between theater and the visual arts, he had used paper as an intermedium: quality stock for his etched "domestic" dramas, and the cheap butcher paper for his posters and backdrops. He silkscreened *Art in a State of Siege* on paper printed with a mottled ground resembling imperfectly mounted butcher paper (plate 25).

From his early works on brown paper Kentridge knew how to use an off-white ground as a volume-creating middle tone between the black marks that outline forms and whites that highlight them (see fig. 68). Later he achieved this effect by drawing or printing on paper disbound from old books. Their text-covered surfaces served as a gray middle tone while dispelling the illusion of artmaking on a clean slate. Figure and ground stand in a shifting relation. In Kentridge's 2012 flipbook film triptych *No, It Is*, pages from Robert Burton's *Anatomy of Melancholy* (1621) play off against exuberant imagery and a pensive soundtrack. The disassembled pages set the organized knowledge they originally contained off against the words and images they now, recycled, randomly support (see fig. 72). A paradigmatic Enlightenment project, Denis Diderot's original *Encyclopédie* (1751–72) assumes the mind at birth as a tabula rasa to be filled—quasi-mechanically—through the ordered acquisition of rational knowledge. Kentridge's playful re-use of encyclopedia and technical manual pages contests this legacy, a European one that he, from his South African perspective, associates with colonialism. Europeans seized territory as if it were a tabula rasa without peoples or histories, or if inhabited, then only by "natives" who, not possessing history, are doomed to go extinct.

The most densely layered of Kentridge's contestations are the drawings he made in charcoal, ink, and crimson red on an old handwritten mining ledger purchased at a Johannesburg bookshop (plate 27). Their support is quality paper sourced from in an Italian mill. Darkened only slightly since their nineteenth-century manufacture, these pages have been printed with a delicate scaffolding of red and blue lines that serve as the rows and columns of double-entry bookkeeping. On this latticework has been written, beginning in 1906 in various hands, records of wage payments and expenditure, with red-penciled corrections and blue-ticked approvals. The East Rand Proprietary Mines Cash Book is an eloquent document of Johannesburg's economic foundation. From the year 1906 through to 2008 the city's mines made South Africa the world's leading gold producer. On the recommendation of anthropologist Rosalind Morris, Kentridge had the volume photographed, archived, and analyzed.[73] Morris studied the cash book vertically, from the layered historical evidence it gives of mining and miners, while Kentridge, beginning in 2012, utilized the disbound sheets horizontally, for landscape views. Based on photos the artist took of the barren veld around Johannesburg, these un-picturesque vistas get structure through the slag-heaps, water towers, fenceposts, utility poles, trees, and old machinery that, rising at different points on the receding ground plane, plot spatial movement into depth. Yet these verticals are falling into ruin. Even the slag-heaps come and go according to the price of gold. If the price is high the slag gets reprocessed to recover trace metals, and the terrain becomes flatland again, though more intensely scarred. Verticals collapse into ruts, sinkholes, and pole-shaped gullies etched into the earth's surface.

In one of Kentridge's drawings, red cones and circles refer to a massacre that had just occurred (plate 27). On August 16, 2012, the leadership of the National Union of Miners, backed by the police, opened fire on wildcat strikers in Marikana. Forty-four were killed—the greatest use of force since the 1960 massacre at Sharpeville. Created on August 19, 2012 Kentridge's drawing reaches from the investigation underway, through the killings and previous massacres, to 1905, when the cash book was inscribed with notes about native, European, and "coolie"

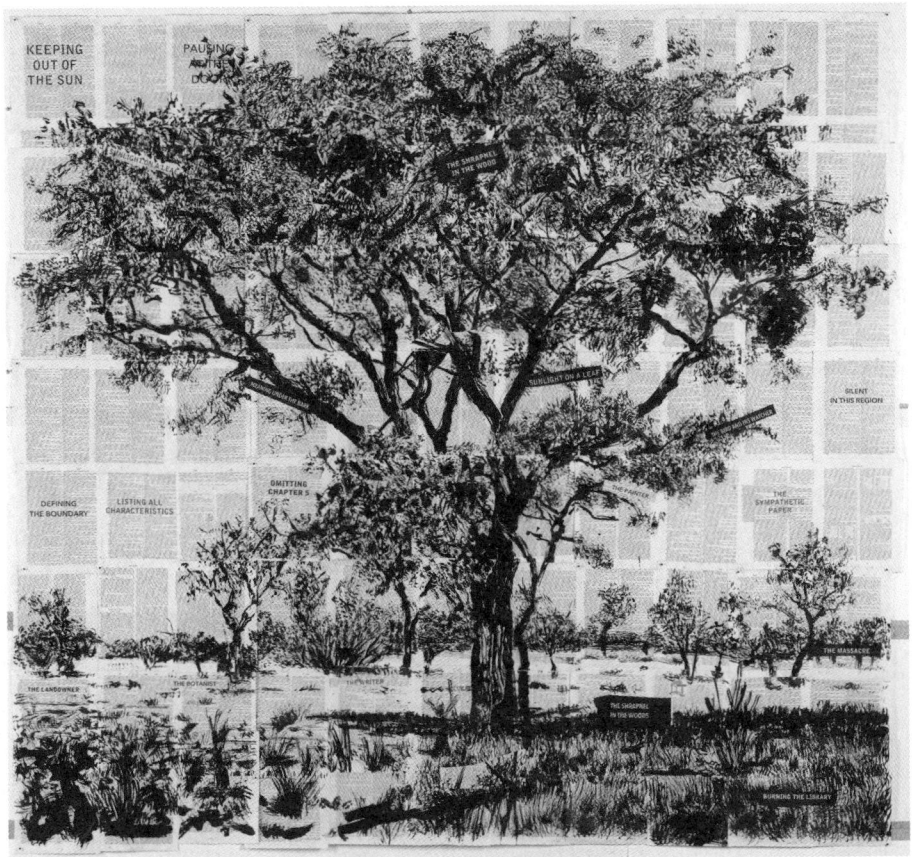

FIG. 95. William Kentridge, *The Shrapnel in the Wood*, 2013. India ink on pages from Crabb's *Universal Technical Dictionary* (1826), 210 × 220 cm. Private Collection

wages. History dissolves into natural history, but traces remain. Kentridge's crimson Prismacolor pencil dramatizes the recovery of such traces. Drawn over the landscape view, these decisive circles, lines, and inscriptions submit the charcoal sketch as evidence of a crime. Red like the cash book's scaffolding and corrections circa 1906, the marks connect the violence etched into the landscape to the violence secreted on the underlying paper. *Terra nullius*, "land belonging to no one," is the colonizer's myth. Even the scraggly trees that dot the veld contain remnants of human history. Some of Kentridge's large paper-collages of South African trees feature a phrase that hints at this hidden apriority of violence (fig. 95). Printed in black and white on re-used dictionary pages and mounted on or around the ink-on-paper tree, the words "SHRAPNEL IN THE WOODS" look like a warning label pertinent to that bit of the scene. As the artist tells it, the phrase derives from carpenters' lingo in Germany, where timber from regions where war once raged still contains shrapnel that can suddenly break a sawmill's blades. The tree, nature's thing-in-itself, harbors evidence of human cruelty. Materials remember. Woodworkers know this about woods—and Bosch knew it about forests. Kentridge knows it about paper.

Creating *Sheets of Evidence* took ingenuity. Instead of bending wire into the shapes of hand-drawn lines, Dieu Donné's papermakers photographed Kentridge's sketches and text collages and had them laser cut, line by line and letter by letter, in vinyl. Backed by a powerful adhesive and bonded firmly to the mold, these delicate watermarks registered their precise shapes in the paper, provided the sheet was expertly formed and couched. Dipped into the pulp, the watermark mold had to be given a gentle shake, allowing the fibers to line up evenly in all directions. Gosin divided this work with Paul Wong, he, in a "Zen frame of mind," forming the sheets, she meticulously curating each page—Gosin deemed less than a quarter of the sheets formed good enough to use. Expensive and time-consuming to make but difficult to see, the completed *Sheets of Evidence* were displayed on backlit shelves, each sheet with a timed LED panel that brightened and dimmed, revealing and concealing the watermarks dramatically. Solutions were proposed for packaging the portfolio so that their watermarks might be visible without special lighting: for example, by interleafing the sheets with delicate cream-colored abaca paper. But Kentridge was adamant. His work should be invisible, like the emperor's new clothes.

The inconspicuous nature of *Sheets of Evidence* stood in striking contrast to work the artist was doing elsewhere in New York in 2009. Kentridge came to the city in that year to direct Shostakovich's *The Nose* for the Metropolitan Opera. This production was large even by the Met's standards. Thirty artists in some eighty solo roles ran about a moveable, three-story stage. Continuous animated projections formed a backdrop as absorbing as the opera, while conductor Valery Gergiev summoned the intended cacophonies of Shostakovich's revolutionary score. Kentridge's *The Nose* was transformative for the artist and for the Met. While opera companies tend to enlist ambitious artists and dramaturges to give bite to the repertoire, this can be to the dismay of many opera lovers, who applaud the performers but boo the director. Incomprehensible already at its 1930 premier and with no tried-and-true staging to contest, *The Nose* demands directorial ingenuity. This Kentridge richly supplied, to the delight of critics and the public, and of the Met, whose gamble this time paid off. And if some experienced sensory overload, this encouraged returning a second time. For Kentridge, *The Nose* also brought his art before a new audience, and even those familiar with his work experienced it on a different scale.

Rare is the artist who can master both the miniature and the colossus. John Constable took years to translate his small, swift oil sketches to the "six-footers" exhibited publicly. Even Rubens, whose gigantic canvases could dominate the largest built interiors of his day, collaborated with "fine" painters like Jan Bruegel when the commission demanded. Miniatures lose their magic if simply expanded. Meticulous brushwork extended over large surfaces looks inert, and filling the void with detail destroys a painting's coherence. For an artist working chiefly on paper, the challenge is increased, and not only by the limit of standard sheets. Whether of ink, pencil, charcoal, or chalk, the graphic mark remains its own stubborn shape and width. It is not merely their fragility that makes works on paper less prestigious and costly than paintings on canvas. Known for their stamp-size prints, Nuremberg's Little Masters (*Kleinmeister*) are historically minor no matter how masterful and intriguing their products. In the Western tradition, artistic importance requires grand-scale products.

Kentridge is no *Kleinmeister*. Created in 2016, his *Triumphs and Laments* stretched for half a kilometer along the Tiber River, and *The Head and the Load*, a multi-media performance honoring the million plus Black Africans who died in WWI, required a stage the size of a football field. And in the beginning of his career, he committed his artistry to paper only after having drawn huge works on that support—those early theater backdrops made of sheets mounted together into paper murals. His mature drawings reached monumental proportions. The seminal *Arc/Procession* (1990) spans eight meters, and at two meters high, *Casspirs Full of Love* (1989/2000) is one of the largest etchings ever produced by a major artist. Theatrical work continued to force Kentridge to think big. His six collaborations with Handspring Puppet Company (1992–2002) and a *Magic Flute* premiered in Brussels in 2005 featured animation that can be projected large. Directing operas like Berg's *Lulu* (200 minutes) demanded long-form storytelling, as well. None of "Drawings for Projection" runs longer than ten minutes, but the footage can be recut, reversed, montaged, and paused, extending their projection time considerably. The twenty-four stop-action films for his *Winterreise* production run to eighty-five minutes. Experience taught Kentridge how, by making one element in the picture seem to move just slightly, still shots can be animated, saving on production time. Before directing *The Nose*, he had also mixed the labor-intensive animation of "Drawings for Projection" with faster, more flexible techniques, including live action, reworked archival footage, animated collage, and shadow shows. This last, crucial to his work since at least 1999, thematized the variability of scale, since the visual magic of shadows consists partly in how they stretch and shrink depending on their projection. Cleverly projected, the silhouette of a nose can fill a three-story stage.

The Nose was an overwhelming aesthetic totality that asked, among other things, how one person, clearly a virtuoso draftsman, could also be a skilled animator, filmmaker, set painter, collage artist, costume designer, prop master, and choreographer, and an expert in sound and image pairings. (Kentridge co-designed the sets with Sabine Theunissen and the costumes with Greta Goiris, but the concepts and aesthetic were his—though the insistence on collaboration was, too, born from the collectivism of his early theatrical work.) For the artist's long-time devotees, this *Gesamtkunstwerk* was also a *Gesamtwerk*: Kentridge's oeuvre (Latin *opera*) manifested in one place and time and bringing other works into its orbit. Shostakovich; Nikolai Gogol, whose short story the composer put to music; the lost noses in Laurence Sterne and Miguel de Cervantes: all seemed made for adaptation by Kentridge, founded, as his creative output had been, on channeling the satirical energies of European art. Fortunately (in this artist's sense), admirers old and new could visit, at that very moment in New York, an exhibition that anatomized the components of Kentridge's wizardry. *William Kentridge: Five Themes* opened at the Museum of Modern Art on February 28, 2010, a week before *The Nose* premiered. It surveyed chief themes, motifs, and mediums of the artist's output roughly from *Johannesburg, 2nd Greatest City after Paris* of 1989 to the 2009 workshopping of *The Nose*.[74]

Those previous twenty years had established Kentridge as a global artist, with exhibitions in the world's great cities, each show a site-specific installation expanding the artist's compass. Being South African had delayed his career through a besieged public sphere at home and cultural boycott by the international community. After 1990, group shows of post-apartheid South African art and film festival screenings of his animations brought Kentridge acclaim, but it was not until 1998, when he was in his mid-forties, that major museums mounted solo exhibitions of his work. But though a late arrival, his starting point had been global. The eureka moment of *Tropical Love Storm* came through citation: Brassaï with the papaya, Beckmann of a Litvak South African's dreams. When, in the 2000s, European cultural institutions had dreams for him, he was prepared. His *Magic Flute* told a calamitous history of colonialism to Mozart's sublime music; his Shostakovich tested hope in a post-9/11 global state of siege. Each new challenge expanded Kentridge's reach, but each was met back at home in Johannesburg, in drawings made on paper. An emphasis on process over finished product enabled *William Kentridge: Five Themes* to end where it began, in the artist's studio conjured in looped projections of *7 Fragments for Georges Méliès*.

I first encountered Kentridge's work in the Vienna venue of this exhibition. *Tabula Rasa I* stopped me dead in my tracks as I hastened through the Albertina's enfilade rooms, pulled by my two young kids eager to get to the gift shop. As the son of an obsessively productive artist, I had grown up in a household where drawing was so often to be observed that not having to watch my father at work was the challenge. But Kentridge's film self-portrait moved me deeply, and not just because of its visual tricks. Poetical, humorous, and unpretentious, the installation greeted me like a long-lost friend, and for the first time since my father died I felt sad not to be able to introduce him to this rarest thing: a younger artist who would have amazed him. The experience was intense and brief—my son succeeded in pulling me physically through the rest of the show. But I never forgot the artist with his humble materials: paper, charcoal, and ink to draw with, and stovetop espresso-pot to stay sharp.

The Nose was a paper pageant. Kentridge workshopped it with paper cutouts for actors and backed its performance with projected drawings and newsprint collages. The opera's protagonist (a nose detached from its owner's face to pursue an independent career) was performed by an actor concealed under a giant papier-mâché nose, with the wearer's legs running grotesquely under the nostrils. The costume's surface displayed the "mâché" newsprint from which it was made, and above its left nostril a red cross, legible perhaps as blood spilled during its escape from the face, paid homage to the paper constructions of Shostakovich's avant-garde contemporaries. In his children's book *About Two Squares*, El Lissitzky, revising Kazimir Malevich's painted monochromes, made a letterpress red square the avatar of the new Soviet order. In Kentridge's visual language, crimson on black and white connote juridical scrutiny. Turning images into evidence, they evoke law, the state, and—in Russia under Stalin and South Africa under apartheid—terror. It mattered to Kentridge's decision to direct *The Nose* that the central character was an antihero, since in ordinary circumstances noses are small and vaguely comical and base. In Shostakovich's libretto, the Nose become human sized, and rises to an official rank higher than that of its petty-bureaucrat owner. But beaten and shrunk for trying to escape St. Petersburg, it is reattached in the end, and normal conditions are restored. In Kentridge, rogue noses lingered on, featuring in drawings, prints, tapestries, statuettes, and—at the Toledo Underground Station in Naples—in a six-meter-high public equestrian statue made of rust-finish steel. Escaped from Shostakovich's opera and mounted on a rearing steed, *Il Cavaliere di Toledo* (2012) mocks its own monumentality. Kentridge's colossal frieze on the banks of the Tiber did this, too. Formed by jet-cleaning away centuries of patina, its imagery has by now disappeared beneath new layers of grime.

In New York in 2009, the artist's work was therefore not as divided as it might seem. To the colossus under production uptown, at the Met, the watermarks made at Dieu Donné give a critical reply. *Sheets of Evidence* takes its imagery from a pivotal moment in Kentridge's films. In *Johannesburg, 2nd Greatest City after Paris*, a sequence headed "But still his dreams were filled with Mrs. Eckstein" finds a naked Felix Teitelbaum reading in a bath (or his "anxiety"-flooded house). His dreams unfold as a succession of images on pages of a floating oblong book (plate 26). Mostly erotic, these aqueous figures closely resemble the watermarked *Sheets*. Like *Sheets*, Felix's dreams include anxious intrusions. A bust portrait of Soho—a miniature of the colossal Eckstein who, in the scene before, "takes on the World"—flashes up but is quickly charcoaled out, and the sequence ends with a split-second close-up of Soho's eye glancing ominously at Felix. The sequence is a *mise en abyme*: animation within animation, a dream within a dream. Kentridge has insisted that his "Drawings for Projection" unfold associatively, without outlines or storyboards, out of the free play of charcoal on the page. But like dreams, these drawings make sense. Felix's reveries go to the heart of the matter, to the love triangle that throws the domestic sphere into a state of siege.

In the film, these images of flagrant adultery precede the "Rumors of a different Life" that reach the cuckolded Soho, contesting his sovereignty (see fig. 82). *Sheets of Evidence* makes more diffuse allegations, perhaps against some unnamed perpetrator, perhaps against the artist present in his likeness, or perhaps against us. Discovered through overzealous scrutiny, the portfolio's imagery incriminates its hapless beholder, who comes on secrets unauthorized, not as judge or magistrate, but as voyeur or snoop. In conjuring this scenario, Kentridge re-stages encounters he had in childhood, in a home filled with top-secret documents pertaining to his parents' dangerous legal work, not meant for innocent eyes. Written boldly on the slipcover in black and white, the words "Sheets of Evidence" place everything in the miscellany before the law.

"Someone must have slandered Josef K., for one morning, without having done anything wrong, he was arrested." In Kafka, this occurs at home, in the bedroom, with the accused "halfway up in bed."[75] Based—presumably—on an anonymous, unstated allegation, the arrest seems completely arbitrary and juridically exceptional, with no charge issued and no prosecutor or venue named. The allegations suggested by Kentridge's sheets are obscure or hidden. Their title word—*evidence*—has two different meanings, as we have seen. In common parlance, it denotes an appearance that makes something else evident that is not apparent: tracks read by hunters in pursuit of quarry, symptoms that, to the medically trained, reveal the underlying malady. But evidence can also denote the quality or condition of being conspicuous, vivid, and self-evident. This, the older meaning, reaches back to a Greek word, *energeia*, translated into Latin as *evidentia*:

energeia denoting manifest presence in sense perception. The idea—held by Aristotle and the Stoics—is of a mind bombarded by uncertain sensory impressions. Evidence names the impression made upon the mind of something physically present to the beholder's eyes, something that the mind can grasp immediately, without engaging reason or understanding.

These divergent meanings of "evidence" form a twisted thread connecting our triptych of artists in the state of siege. The "evidence of images" was the question begged by Bosch. Pivoting from visual ambiguities to art historical ones, Gombrich summoned up Bosch to demonstrate how iconographies are not self-evident, but require texts and contexts for their decipherment. But mere caution proved inadequate for Bosch, who built his demons, illusions, and dreams to appear inscrutable, because he intended them to be inimical to us. When Antichrist finally arrives, as he does in Bosch's *Adoration of the Magi* altarpiece, he will be the opposite of self-evident, thus keeping Christians vigilant for encrypted signs (plate 13). No amount of evidence will definitively resolve the arch-deceiver's identity, at least until the final struggle, when the guessing ends. Yet Bosch would not fascinate were his works inconspicuous. His art mightily grabs and holds our attention. Through symmetry, coloring, and nudity, the *Garden of Delights* does the opposite of hide: it brazenly evidences, for which reason Fraenger took it to be its own key (plate 2). The putative altarpiece for an Adamic sect, the triptych straightforwardly showed initiates what to do: get naked and copulate. Fraenger's error was in tune with the painting. He beheld it as it asks to be beheld: idolatrously.

Evidencing was the goal of Beckmann's *Self-Portrait in Tuxedo* (plate 18). Not only did the canvas depict "the artist in the state," that extravagant vision of the painter as decider. The painting made artistic sovereignty self-evident. With movement and repose, black and white, matte and shiny contending, it evidenced restless balance—personal, political, and metaphysical—here and now achieved. But not for long, for after Hitler came to power, the painting would be made to manifest not sovereignty but degeneracy, sending the work and its maker into exile. After 1937, Beckmann would become the artist in the state of siege—and for Kentridge "a beacon for endangered souls" (plates 20 and 21). Kentridge's images stand out conspicuously, black on white, and never as conspicuously as (up until then) in New York City in the months after *Sheets of Evidence* stood complete. But the artist's blacks are ephemeral. Made of charcoal, they can easily be erased: "you can just wipe away a whole drawing with a flap of a cloth."[76] And his whites are a shadowy palimpsest, not a tabula rasa. Concealing its imagery in the stuff of paper, *Sheets of Evidence* makes explicit what was the case even for Kentridge's biggest creations. Nothing is self-evident. Placing image and viewer in a dangerous predicament, these sheets beg the question: what does the "evidence of images" look like in a state of siege, when the law is at once in force and suspended?

Cambridge, Massachusetts, 2012

"As an artist working in the field of illusion, I have of course a motive for trying to move the field of images, and hence, illusion, up the ladder."[77] Kentridge spoke these words from the stage of the three-tiered Sanders Theater, Harvard's grandest auditorium, to a capacity crowd. We are back where we began, at the Charles Eliot Norton Lectures, the festive academic event at which Panofsky surveyed the development of early Netherlandish painting until Bosch stymied him. Here in Cambridge, in the years between 1926 and 2012, distinguished scholars, writers, artists, architects, and composers explored, in six to eight lectures over as many weeks, some aspect of "poetry in the widest sense." Their task was difficult, as audiences expected to be instructed and entertained over an entire academic term. Fame could make a speaker's first lecture sell out. What happened afterwards could not be controlled. Audiences sometimes dwindled pitifully to the size of a modest seminar.

By "poetry in the widest sense" the drafters of the Norton Professorship meant *poiesis*, the bringing forth of something new. Creative artists were expected to reveal the how and why of their creativity. But creation is not easily explained, because—by some definitions—it does not submit to reason and cannot easily be put into words, especially by artists. The poetics of tragedy were explained by Aristotle in ways that the playwrights themselves, composing their tragedies a century earlier, may not have recognized. The publisher of Beckmann's "The Artist in the State" fretted about the painter's verbal obscurity. As a public lecture Beckmann's argument would have been even harder to digest. And although I would give almost anything to hear Bosch explain his works, my hunch is that his own explanations would not completely satisfy. When poets and novelists have given Norton Lectures, they tended to expound the poems and novels of other writers rather than explaining their own writings. For that reason, over half of the Norton Professorships have gone not to makers, but to historians of making, like Panofsky.

When Kentridge took the stage, he looked more the artist than the scholar. Wearing black trousers and a white button-down shirt left comfortably open at the neck, he appeared ready for work; and to those who knew his work, that costume made him resemble one of the many sketched, printed, and filmed self-portraits, especially when, after the long applause and standing comfortably at the podium, he finally clipped on his pince-nez. Worn in the neo-Gothic, wood-paneled splendor of Sanders Theater, the accessory conjured academics of old, as did the bound book from which Kentridge read as if from handwritten notes, rather than from a paltry printout. That book, a large black softcover Moleskine, allowed Kentridge freely to walk about the stage like an actor out of costume, running through his lines from "sides" held casually in hand. The role rehearsed was donnish, as befitted the Norton Professorship—the first incumbent of which, Gilbert Murray, since 1908 regius professor of Greek at Oxford, had lectured on "The Classical Tradition" dressed in full academic regalia.

In his opening words, Kentridge acknowledged the challenge of his incumbency. "About ten months ago," he began, "I telephoned my father to say that I had been invited to deliver this series of lectures. 'Well,' he replied, 'do you have anything to say?' " Mindful of Sydney Kentridge's paternal admonition, he therefore wrote down, before even starting to think about the lectures, the words—which he read from his notebook, with its page projected huge behind him, "Remember, you are an artist not a scholar, but avoid a six-hour parade of ignorance."[78] What followed were six hour-long talks that combined, in a synthesis hitherto not achieved by any Norton lecturer, historical analysis with creative artistry. This artistry derived, in part, from the fact that the challenge posed by the lectures was the same as the one posed for Kentridge's art:

> The thirty years in the studio are an attempt not just to answer the question, "Have you anything to say?" but rather to try to disempower the question. As I indicated at the start of the lecture, the presence of a father who was a lawyer was not incidental to this narrative. It became imperative to make something, a self, impervious to cross-examination. To assert the primacy and the necessity for stupidity, for the necessary stupidity that is essential in the studio.

"Stupidity" is Kentridge's disarming term for aesthetic play, understood—as it has been since at least the eighteenth century—as the freedom through which art can resist legal, political, and institutional forms of power. And the lectures were decidedly playful from the start, with Kentridge humorously imitating the movements of a seasoned speaker: the raised and the circling finger, the collar tug, open-handed tapping of the podium, "The apparent losing of the place in the notes. The real losing of the place in the notes." This catalogue of gestures, Kentridge observed, was "derived from a lecture I observed by Mr. Jacques Rancière."[79] The reference was weirdly apt. Although Kentridge claims not to understand him, Rancière explores how, over the centuries and especially under siege conditions, art offers a form of dissent (*dissensus*) different from that of politics and law because rooted in the bodily senses.[80]

Kentridge mimicked only the gestures, comically stripped of the arguments they support. His expert miming derived from that year in Paris studying under Lecoq. More fully than in his opera productions, Kentridge's Norton Lectures exhibited his creative oeuvre in *Gesamtkunstwerk* form. If the performances seemed effortless, urging an amazed Harvard professoriate to upgrade their clunky PowerPoints, it was because they had taken "thirty years in the studio" to accomplish. Decades of work as an actor, director, writer, and theater designer enabled Kentridge proficiently, and with the right team of collaborators, to orchestrate the six lectures as seamless multimedia performances, with a concluding fanfare blasted by a live brass band. The dazzling visuals behind him wove excerpts from his earlier films with new footage, both live and animated, shot and edited just for the lectures. They were his artistic specialty, what his spacious, light-filled studio, with cameras overhead and on dollies and a film editing room, had been built to create: drawings *for projection*.

Kentridge's seeming effortlessness was artful, and hard work. Before the first lecture, organizers of the Nortons complained of the artist's perfectionism, imagining talks of an ordinary academic kind. Little did they know just how perfect the lectures would be, and how approachable, speaking to a general public in a way Rancière, for example, could never do. Each of the six lectures' several arguments unfolded logically, illuminated by engaging examples and stories, bolstered by resumés of previous arguments made, and thus rendered "impervious to criticism." Kentridge called the talks "Drawing Lessons" not just because of the importance of drawing to his practice, but also because through drawing he met the audience halfway—for who has not taken a drawing lesson, and who does not sometimes draw, whether poorly or well? This manageable focus had historical depth, for it revisited what European art theory since the Renaissance maintained. Drawing—*disegno* in the Italian formulations—was synonymous with "poetry in the widest sense." Though displayed by bravura performances of an actual drawing, *disegno* was first and foremost creative design, a quasi-divine mental activity that raised painting and sculpture from manual crafts to an intellectual art and allowed them to compete with poetry. Kentridge's lectures entered the black box of artistic creativity with a drawing master as friendly guide, speaking not just live on stage, but sometimes doubled, tripled, or multiplied into a team of contrarian alter egos on screen behind him, comically voicing their prerecorded descent from his studio in Johannesburg.

Kentridge's likeness appears frequently in his work, not front and center, as self-portraits usually do, asserting their maker's authority, but fleetingly, in miniature, and not as ruler, but as clown. Somersaulting across pages of a flipbooks, he personifies the free play of drawing into which the artist, like everything else, gets helplessly swept (see fig. 72). *Sheets of Evidence* embedded his erotic acrobatics in the fabric of its pages, and allowed him, near the end, to take an author's bow. But like Shakespeare's Yorick, the artist-jester becomes a macabre skull (see figs. 90 and 91). In his one-minute film "Invisible Mending," Kentridge appears to draw a life-size portrait of himself, but only by reversing the footage of him erasing, defacing, and tearing up his effigy. In his "Drawings for Projection," Kentridge stands hidden behind the camera, but his person is distributed through the films' characters. At first, he gave his features to Felix Teitelbaum, the naked dreamer and lover. But as he aged, he wrote Felix out of his films and made Soho Eckstein, originally dressed in his grandfather's pinstripes, resemble himself. Opposites who love the same woman, Felix and Soho might be sides of one person: the White South African as contradiction. Their resemblance to the artist weaves personal confession with family romance, but it is also a practical expediency: creating his films alone in his studio over many months, Kentridge used his own person as a convenient available model.

His explicit self-portraits are playfully oblique. In one, the weavers at Marguerite Stephens's studio knotted into dense tapestry a loosely composed paper collage. *Self-Portrait as a Coffee Pot* acknowledges the dispersion of the artist's person into impersonal objects, inscriptions, and scraps (plate 28). The stovetop espresso-maker looks vaguely human (with a head, a skirt, and an arm on one hip), and through its placement high on the sheet and its association with caffeine, it conjures the sitter's stimulated brain. Between the hands and feet, a phallic megaphone introduces a crude mouthpiece for the texts mounted around it. Working equipment in the artist's Johannesburg studio, megaphones and Bialetti Moka Expresses recur throughout the artist's work, the latter starring in Kentridge's *A Universal Archive* (2012), a lithograph series created in conjunction with the Norton Lectures. There, and in his 2013 *Rebus* sculptures—cast bronzes that change from one object to another when viewed from different angles—the image of a coffee pot resolves and dissolves, demonstrating Gombrich's "variability of vision": the principle that objects appear to the eye mixed with false imaginings.

Paraphrased by Kentridge as "the object & its unreliable witnesses," this principle finds a telling expression in the tapestry. We think of self-portraits as celebrations of the artist in and beyond their creation. The tuxedoed Beckmann plays the role of exceptional individual who, via the achievement of the painting, is the sovereign "decider" in Germany's state of siege. This gesture proved to be spectacularly hubristic, in Beckmann's case, but the idea has deep historical roots—

think of the "christomorphic" portrait that Dürer painted of himself in 1500, the propitious year of the new half-millennium. Inspired by the anthropocentric thinking of the early humanists, Renaissance painters transferred to themselves a principle of sovereignty that, modeled on divine omnipotence, had been newly asserted by secular princes. Compared to princes, artists had an added claim to godlikeness, since through their *poiesis* they created something novel—what Dürer called the "new creature"—and distinguished from the mere imitation of nature. Self-portraits like Dürer's and Beckmann's testify to this human capacity by being in the "image and likeness" of their creators. Kentridge's self-portraits deflate that claim. And they, too, have predecessors.

Bosch left us no signed self-portraits, but he did create oblique ones. "Self," as the vector of a person's moral outlook towards or away from God, takes a generalized visual form either in world-renouncing hermit saints or in world-seeking wanderers. Through his namesake, Saint Jerome, Bosch associated himself with the pious ascetic, while diabolic imagery makes a grimmer confession. A cryptic pen and ink sketch of trees, birds, eyes, and ears probably evokes the Dutch proverb, "The field has eyes, the trees have ears; I will see, be silent, and listen" (fig. 96).[81] The drawing probably also stands for the artist who drew it playfully on a sheet of paper circulating in his workshop—the sheet's verso is a *Tummelplatz* of drawing, having been used for practice sketches by unskilled hands. Recall that Bosch took his moniker from 's-Hertogenbosch partly to associate himself with the forest (*bos*) in the toponym.[82] Figured by the dangerous and endangered tree, as well as by the owl (Middle Dutch *bosvogel*, "forest-bird," with a hint of evil, Middle Dutch *bós*), the self of Bosch's self-portrait is at once besieging and besieged. The artist is also "I" of the underlying proverb, a social being who, surrounded by eyes and ears, keeps his council. This secretive individual, then, created enemy pictures that behold, tempt, and potentially damn whoever looks at them. Above his drawing Bosch wrote (in Latin) a learned inscription: "miserable is the mind that [...] never invents anything new." The artist uses an unusual word for mind: *ingenium*. Precociously for northern Europe, Bosch links artistry to developing ideas of inborn genius. In its strangeness, the drawing evidences what genius brought about. But which side the creator is on, whether allied with God or with the entropic forces of nature, remains Bosch's secret.

And while the Netherlandish painter expanded it to encompass entire works by him, an ambivalence about image-making haunted other self-portraitists. Early modern artists represented themselves variously as conquered (Caravaggio as Goliath), disfigured (Hans Baldung Grien as witchcraft's victim), fragmented (Michelangelo as the flayed Saint Bartholomew), or bewitched (Salvator Rosa and

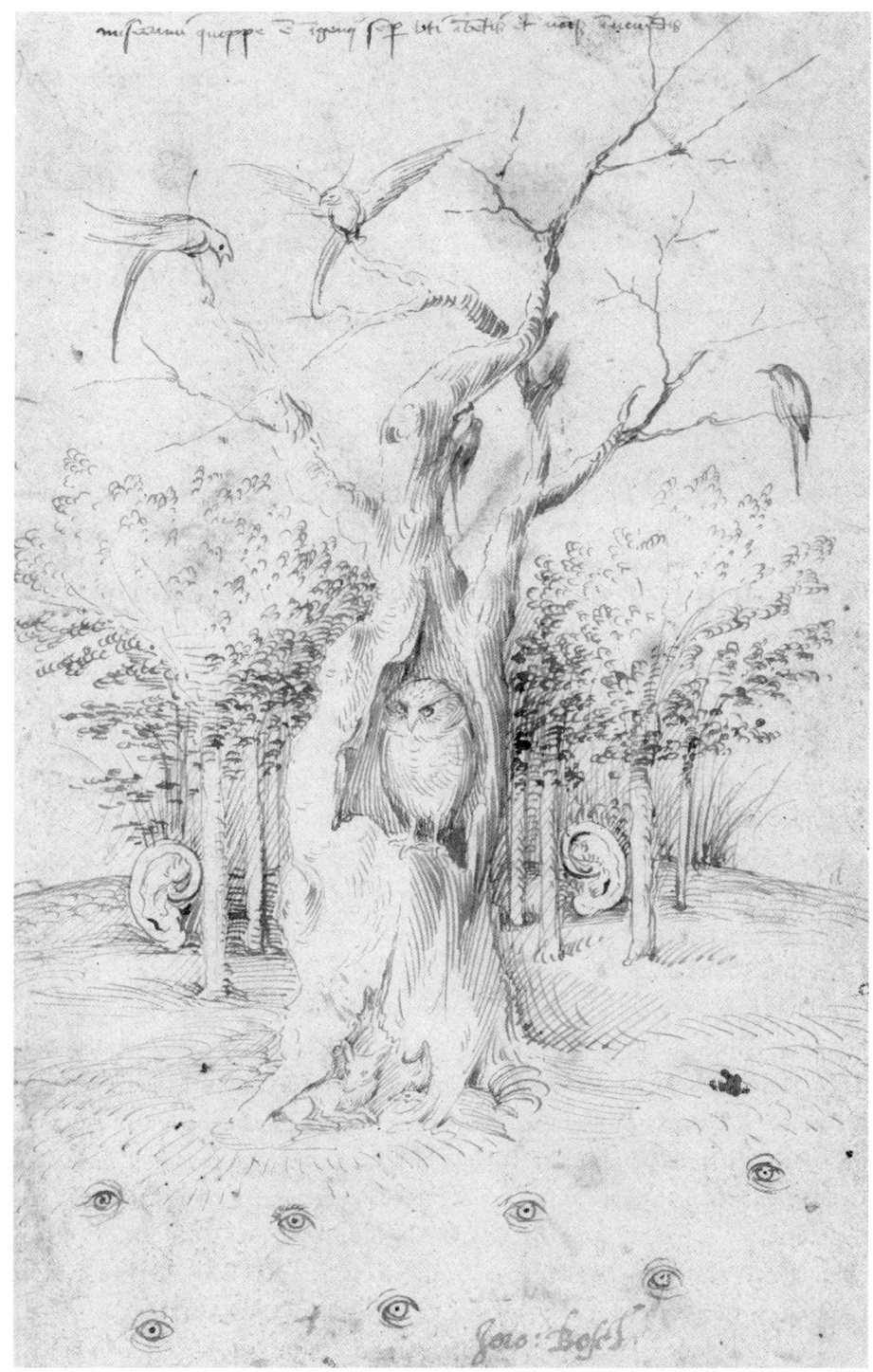

FIG. 96. Hieronymus Bosch, *The Field Has Eyes, the Trees Have Ears*, c. 1510. Pen and brown ink, 20.2 × 12.7 cm. Kupferstichkabinett, Berlin

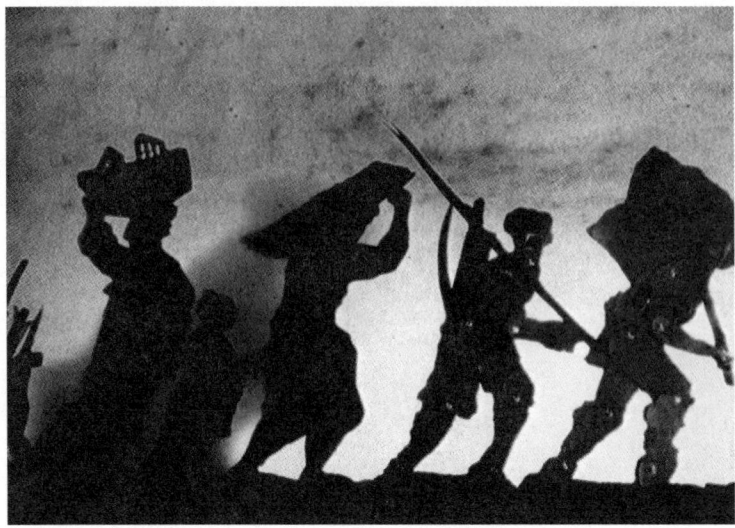

FIG. 97. William Kentridge, film still *from Shadow Procession*, 1999. 35mm transferred to digital

Pieter van Laer). In the early twentieth century, with artists such as Kokoschka, Schiele, and Beckmann, disfigured self-portraits became the avant-garde norm. Although Bosch's rebus resembles *Self-Portrait as a Coffee Pot* only accidentally, and I hesitate to bring the Netherlander back for one final bow, the drawing asks questions relevant to Kentridge's practice. Megaphone, feet, hands, and coffee pot are not objects cut and dried; rather, as the text in the picture puts it, they stand as "unreliable witnesses" of the object—things observed and drawn by a particular artist in a particular medium. The maker becomes a mere viewer of, say, coffee pots, or (a step removed) of the image of a coffee pot collaged or woven, while we beholders solving a similar puzzle become makers. It is this interplay that Kentridge's "Drawing Lessons" explore.

Those lessons began with images at their minimum: the shadow of the likeness of a thing. Such shadows had been the subject of Kentridge's *Shadow Procession*, a film he projected as overture to his Norton Lectures. Commissioned to create a work for the 1999 Istanbul Biennial, the artist filmed a shadow-casting parade and projected it deep under the Turkish city, in the vast and shadowy Yerebatan Cistern, ancient Constantinople's major reservoir and, under the Ottomans, water source for the Topkapı Palace (fig. 97). Unlike the processions in his "Drawings for Projection," which move to and from the horizon, this march, created by shadow puppets, moves only laterally, "neither advancing nor retreating, but passing," and with no representable starting point or end. It was the work's medium that gave the parade its particular form. "You have a light source, you have an object blocking the light," therefore the movement can only be lateral.[83] It was only when experimenting with these conditions in his studio, and predicting the impression shadows will make in their underground venue, that Kentridge made the association between his project and Plato's allegory of the cave.

In the seventh book of the *Republic*, writing in dialogue form in the voice of Socrates, Plato asks us "to make an image of our nature in its education." Imagine "human beings as though they were in an underground cave-like dwelling with its entrance, a long one, open to the light across the whole width of the cave."[84] Chained in the cave since childhood, these humans do nothing but behold a shadow play projected on the wall that they forcibly face. Cast by puppets, such shadows are the prisoners' sole reality, preventing them from knowing anything about puppets, the things the puppets represent, the light behind that makes shadows appear, and the outside world that shadow play dimly resembles. From this prison one inmate should then be imagined to be forcibly freed. Dragged first to the fire inside the cave, his eyes would so hurt him that, for a while, he would be unable to see the shadow-casting puppets. Hauled up from the cave to the light of the sun, his pain would be even greater, and his reluctance to see things as they really are—the objects in themselves, which the puppets merely resembled—would be stronger. Grown accustomed to the glare, though, and able finally to look at the sun from which everything visible proceeds, this prisoner would "already be in a position to conclude," on the self-evidence of the illuminated world, what is an image and what is reality, and that reality is the truer of the two.[85]

But then the recollection of his former home, and inherent pity for the prisoners left behind, might compel the prisoner to return to the cave, to convince its inmates of the unreality of their condition. In Plato, this homecomer is the philosopher who seeks to educate others on what he has learned. Kentridge read aloud large chunks of Plato's dialogue. He announced that it would be "the starting point" for all six lectures and advised his audience to go home and read the whole text "in its extended form." It was an audacious move, to reach back to philosophy's myth and to cross-examine it as might "a father who was a lawyer."[86]

Plato's shadow procession consists of "human beings carrying all sorts of artifacts, which project above the wall, and statues of men and other animals wrought from stone, wood, and every kind of material."[87] The gear and statues cast shadows but not their bearers. They march hidden below the wall and remain undiscussed by Plato. Kentridge steps backstage. Himself a dramaturge, he considers the shadows, the portable artifacts, and their porters. The latter are at once players and prisoners: "a catalogue of people on the move, specific people seen in newspapers and on the streets of Johannesburg."[88] In *Shadow Procession*, twelve men march in penal lockstep, each with his hand on the shoulder of the man in front. Cipher of South Africa's

Black majority in a permanent state of siege, they also stand for refugees displaced worldwide by poverty, war, and persecution. In Kentridge's recent work, these processions achieve huge proportions, from the eight-screen video installation *More Sweetly Play the Dance* (see fig. 71), through *Triumphs and Laments* (2016), to the live pageant *The Head and the Load* (2018), this last performable only in venues such as turbine halls and armories. By showing the porters as well as the gear they bear, Kentridge opens for exploration the puppetry that Plato, proceeding "up the ladder" from shadows to puppets to objects to the sun, leaves unspoken.

Kentridge had two concerns in visiting Plato's cave. The first was political. It accords with the purpose of the dialogue, which in Greek is titled *Politeia*, usually translated "republic," but better understood as "regime"—the latter preserves the sense of something menacing that encompasses all aspects of life. The story of the one prisoner's progress from illusion to reality belongs to a lesson in politics. Plato wants to prove that the just city (*polis*) should be ruled by philosopher kings who are enlightened by knowledge of the transcendent "ideas" about beauty, the good, and justice. Kentridge responds with lessons drawn from historical experience: "We have reached the point where all destinations, all bright lights, arouse mistrust. The light at the end of the tunnel turns too quickly into the interrogator's spotlight." Like his suspicion against "art in a state of hope," this wariness derives from what he takes to be the primary political manifestation of philosophical enlightenment: "the calamitous history of colonialism," and especially that violent history in Africa, imagined by the "enlighteners" as a dark continent, but engendering the oppressive regime of apartheid. Kentridge's ideas about Plato's allegory only occurred to him after he tried to cast and film real shadows. In creating *Shadow Procession*, he discovered that movement towards the light source is technically unfeasible, since the shadow grows and obliterates everything. The medium allows only interminable passage. But retrospectively, after he had beheld the shadows, they yielded this political idea: "The procession could not end with the *fête galante* on the island of Cythera of Watteau, nor could it arrive at a civic state, nor a collective farm."[89]

Kentridge's second concern in considering Plato's cave was aesthetic. In the allegory, shadows represent the lowest order in the hierarchical ladder of being. On top are the "ideas," the eternal, perfect, and transcendent forms of all things and concepts. Virtues such as justice, as well as physical things like chairs or shovels, receive their reality from these "ideas." The objects paraded in the puppet show, depicting a chair, a shovel, a Bialetti 3-Cup Moka, and so on in silhouette: they stand one step lower still. Mere likenesses of things, they are third-order imitations: likenesses of real things that are images of the ideas. In Book Ten of

The Republic, Plato censures representational art for creating dangerous illusions. But the shadows cast by the puppets languish at the very bottom, especially as they appear to the cave's prisoners, who cannot see what caused them and who never behold the things (equipment, men, animals) that the puppets represent. Physically ungraspable, shadows evidence nothing but themselves: there can be no proper comprehension of the sense impressions they make. In Stoic terms, there is no grasping or comprehension (*katalepsis*) of the elements of sense experience (*phantasiai*); in Boschian terms there is "nothing but devils, buttocks and cod-pieces."[90] The modern philosopher of symbolic forms Ernst Cassirer used these non-referential shadows to picture what symbols proper are not. For Cassirer, who influenced Panofsky's method of translating images into meanings (the method that failed when it came to Bosch), shadows are of no epistemic value whatsoever: "Without the symbol the life of man would be like the prisoners in the cave of Plato's famous simile. Man's life would be confined within the limits of his biological needs and his practical interests; it could find no access to the 'ideal world' which is opened to him from different sides by religion, art, philosophy, science."[91] But what if one suspends judgment about the existence of an external world and reduces the situation of the cave to its essentials?

In a world that knows nothing about the puppets, porters, fire, and caves, shadows would function as symbols in some way. And in Plato's allegory they do. In a key passage concerning the enlightened prisoner's altruistic return to the cave, Socrates reports that the prisoners "form judgements" about the shadows.[92] Competing among themselves about who best recognizes, remembers, and predicts them, they behave like priestly diviners. In Greek mythology, caves were the birthplaces of gods. The earth goddess Gaia, fearful of her husband Uranus's wrath, gave birth to her children hidden in a cave, as did Rhea, Gaia's daughter. Fearful of her infanticidal husband Cronos, Rhea bore Zeus in a cave under Mount Ida. The goddess of childbirth, Eileithyia, daughter of Zeus, was cave-born like her father, and the Nymphs whisked Dionysus, born prematurely, to be incubated in a firelit cave.[93] Fabricating a myth about philosophy, Socrates might have tunneled back into an even deeper past, when the earliest humans sought refuge in caves and painted shadowy likenesses "of men and other animals" on the walls as magical entertainment. Kentridge reminded his audience that under Johannesburg a seam of gold pressed up two billion years ago almost to the earth's surface was discovered 130 years ago, establishing his city's wealth, and, further, that "in dolomite caves twenty kilometers north of my studio two skeletons were found" of human cousins two million years ago, "somewhere between small-brained Australopithecus and the large-brained Homo sapiens, who died while caving."[94] As an artist, Kentridge has good reasons to rethink the shadow play, "to move the field of images, and hence, illusion, up the ladder," and "to show the place illusion has in the making of knowledge itself." He aims to show that perceiving shadows, like beholding crafted images, is never passive. Symbol-making is resemblance-finding. Finding an image in the shadow begins in the cave.

In *Shadow Procession*, the shadows were cast by jointed bits of torn black construction paper moved past the camera. These puppets had only the barest resemblance to figures in a procession, and even less to "specific people in Johannesburg." Yet we mentally grasp the blurry shadows nonetheless, and perhaps more pleasurably and richly than had they been meticulously cut. Our mind compensates for their imprecision, actively completing them more perfectly than any scissors might. Kentridge calls this "meeting the world halfway" and explains: we see "[s]omething we don't know that we know. Something we can recognize without knowing."⁹⁵ Great painters understood this principle. Titian and Rembrandt, especially in the paintings they made in old age, give us much work to do, as by stepping back from their surfaces, we find their subjects within the obscure buildup of paint. As Gombrich explains, what we enjoy "is not so much seeing these works at a distance as the very act of stepping back, as it were, and watching our imagination come into play, transforming the medley of color into a finished image."⁹⁶

Kentridge wants makers and viewers to share in this transformation. The creation of "Drawings for Projection" proceeds, frame by frame, with the artist contemplating from behind the camera the charcoal sketch in whatever is its current state, then transforming it minutely into a slightly different sketch to be beheld and altered in its turn. Like Plato's cave, the artist's studio is the framework for this activity, an image-filled interior set off from the world. A space for productive play, the studio also resembles the setting of psychoanalysis, a "playground" (*Tummelplatz*) with only one rule: patients must say whatever comes to mind. The working-through of memories, dreams, and symptoms unfolds "in almost total freedom."⁹⁷ A playground, a dreamscape, a puppet-theater, a cave: the studio is "a safe space for stupidity."⁹⁸ In this artist's practice it is a place literally adjacent to the memory-filled family home—as Freud's statue-filled treatment room was in his home at Berggasse 19. There are created images "impervious to cross examination." There defeat is as productive as victory.

The artist has illuminated the creative role of misunderstanding through a recollection from early childhood. From 1956 until 1961, 156 persons, including Nelson Mandela, stood accused in South Africa of treason. Sydney Kentridge served as a chief lawyer for the defense. Between the ages of three and six years,

William therefore frequently heard of his father departing from home to the "treason trial." Not understanding the reference, the boy grasped the phrase as "trees and tiles." He did this partly by accident, because the words sound alike, but he was also prompted by what he saw when he heard the words: at the bottom of the garden, near the property's gate, a cluster of fir trees; and up on the veranda, where people gathered in the sun, a table with a mosaic top.[99]

"It is perhaps altogether questionable whether we have any conscious memories *from* childhood," warned Freud; "perhaps we have only memories *of* childhood."[100] Kentridge's story celebrates the child's ability to make sense of the world. Although treason and trials are unknown to him, he grasps something in the image of what he does know. Enlisting rhyme and simile, his misunderstanding is poetical. It belongs to language in a state of innocence, as when Adam "gave names" to the beasts and the birds. But it matters to the memory that the words innocently misheard refer to crime and punishment. Kentridge remembers being oblivious to treason and trials, yet in his home, through words and actions of his parents, he must have been aware of something dangerous. "Trees and tiles" is not just any poetical creation, but one that transforms original painful information about the violent world into a scenario of shady groves and shiny mosaics.

Kentridge's is hardly the first attempt to move illusion "up the ladder." Plato provided a template in his imagined competition among the prisoners over who interprets the shadows best. Rethinking this detail of Plato's allegory, Aristotle imagined people living underground "in comfortable well-lit dwellings, ornamented with statues and pictures and furnished with all the luxuries enjoyed by persons thought to be supremely happy." Ignorant of the world above, these inhabitants heard stories about divine powers. Plato's cave thus contains not only art, but myth and religion, as well. Were suddenly "the jaws of the earth to open," Aristotle proposes, these people would realize in the beauty of the above-ground world "that the gods exist and that these mighty marvels are their handiwork."[101] The cave becomes a cultural edifice that knows of, and in being "handiwork" already imitates, divinely created nature. Release from the cave becomes unnecessary. One need only see the world artfully to grasp its truth. The Christian Middle Ages imagined Plato's cave mostly in negative terms, as a figure for the world as a sinful, illusory prison that can be escaped only at death. On the example of the hermit saints, the Christian should renounce life already in life, by retreating into caves, tombs, grottos, and deserts to pray. The subterranean shadow play now becomes devilish deception—those flickering resemblances that Bosch excelled at depicting, to the point of seeming diabolical himself. But while coded as false, this free play of the imagination would become a sign of creative genius.

Modern theories of *poiesis* emerged from a new, positive understanding of play. Kant wrote that "poetry plays with illusion, which it produces at will." But Kant distinguished poetry from political oratory, which employs illusions to persuade: "Without using illusion to deceive us [...] poetry tells us itself that its pursuit is mere play."[102] Extending this idea, Friedrich Schiller observed how the free appearance of art, exemplified by Greek statues in their semblance of movement and life, elicits in the spectator a vital free play of response: "man only plays when he is in the fullest sense of the word a human being, and *he is only fully a human being when he plays*." Asking how illusion can exist in the moral world, in the realm, as it were, of treason trials, Schiller admitted a crucial limitation. It can exist in the moral world "to the extent that it is aesthetic semblance; that is to say, semblance which neither seeks to represent reality nor needs to be represented by it."[103] Aesthetic play must be purposeless and pure. Nietzsche took the further step. The worlds experienced in dreams are illusions, but they leave the dreamer with a real and powerful perception of them. Their appearance is of a particular kind: "the appearance of *mere* appearance."[104] Humans have a "primordial desire for mere appearance," and they satisfy it with works of art. Before a *Gesamtkunstwerk* the spectator should see and hear nothing but illusion—like the prisoners in the cave. "My philosophy," wrote Nietzsche in an early draft note for *The Birth of Tragedy*, is "*upside-down Platonism*: the farther removed from true being, the purer, more beautiful, and better it is. Living in illusion is the goal."[105] The doctrine of art for art's sake (Kentridge's repudiated "art in a state of grace") begins here, yet for Nietzsche illusion is never pure. In Greek tragedy, spectators, though they take pleasure in knowing them to derive from illusions, experience danger and terror. Original pain (*Urschmerz*) unites with the original delight of illusion itself.[106]

In 2014, Kentridge began a series of monumental trees consisting of tiled, inked, and torn dictionary pages. Working from squared photographs, he loosely drew on the unbound pages parts of the expansive whole: twists and turns of trunk and branches, grass and bushes fringing the foreground, expanses of field, and a dense chaos of leaves. Assembling the sheets took greater precision, as he patched the tree together, tiling, ripping, and layering ink-marked pages on the principle (articulated in the Norton Lectures) that to depict things as complex as a tree, an artist does better summarily to evoke than meticulously to copy it. Added to the painted pages were phrases, many previously featured in his work. The sheets circulate back to what they were made of—pulped wood—but produce a bookish tree with words as leaves (see fig. 95). These trees have ancient roots. The Cumean Sibyl wrote her prophecies on leaves, piling them at the entrance to her cave. Gusts of wind scattered the leaves, making the fate they foretell unreadable.

Dante remembered this image at the close of his *Divine Comedy*, in which "what is scattered through the universe in leaves is, with love, held together one volume." And James Joyce ends *Finnegans Wake* with a tree (that stands for the novel itself) bidding its last leaf farewell: "My leaves have drifted from me. All. But one clings still. I'll bear it on me. To remind me of. Lff!"[107]

Kentridge has linked the tree series to his "trees and tiles" recollection, though just as Plato's allegory occurred to him only after completing *Shadow Procession*, the memory returned belatedly, once collaging the trees had begun. Activating the beholder's share, the collages require viewers to see the trees for the tiles, and to put the trees on trial. Communicating definitions, the underlying dictionary pages conjure facts, suggesting that the tree they form is a tree of knowledge, and not just factual knowledge. Because it is a tree, the knowledge it imparts is the moral one of good and evil. Neither the tree nor the veld where it rises is innocent. The veld is Kentridge's ruinous setting, a siege-scape scarred by colonial conquest, violence, and exploitation. And printed scraps of paper in and around the foliage signal the *Urschmerz*: "SHRAPNEL IN THE WOODS."

The Norton Lectures say nothing about the conclusion of Plato's allegory, when the enlightened prisoner, out of pity, resolves to climb back down into the cave and teach the truth to his erstwhile companions. The homecomer, Socrates explains, would be blinded by the darkness. Out of practice in the agon in which the perpetual prisoners compete, he would seem foolish in his expositions. For in the cave there are "honors, praises, and prizes for the man who is sharpest at making out the things that go by, and most remembers which of them are accustomed to pass before, which after, and which at the same time as others, and who is thereby most able to divine what is going to come." Inside the cave, the cleverest among the prisoners—though they do not even know they dwell in a cave—tell stories and make prognostications, just as the returning prisoner will do. Desiring praise, they will now fervently compete against him, setting their stories off against his. And because their eyes see better in the dark, and because the shadows behave as the clever inmates predict, the enlightened homecomer will lose the competition. "And if they were somehow able to get their hands on and kill the man who attempts to release and lead up," asks Socrates, "wouldn't they kill him?"[108]

What is this dangerous agon in shadow world all about? Divining what is to come, the competitors resemble astrologers and charlatans who pretend to read the future in the stars. Virtuosos at pure argument, they behave like Sophists, whom Socrates resembled but repudiated. Experts of a formal order, they come closest of all to lawyers, as Socrates himself suggests. He imagines the enlightened prisoner "compelled in courts [...] to contest about the shadows of the just or the representation of which they are the shadows." In such a court of law, argued before "men who have never seen justice itself," the truth will not prevail.[109] The conclusion that, if the other prisoners could get their hands on him, the revenant would be murdered, is never contested, raising the question unanswered by Plato and perhaps unanswerable: how is justice to be achieved in a real-world regime?

Socrates's hanging question is a supreme example of dramatic irony. With it the philosopher predicts his own death. Tried in Athens for impiety and for corrupting the *polis*'s youth, Socrates defended himself unsuccessfully and was forced to drink hemlock. Socrates's question proves that there was nothing accidental about the outcome of his treason trial. In the regime in which the philosopher finds himself, justice cannot be reached through dialogue and debate, Socrates's form of argument. In the agon among prisoners, in their state of siege, the evidence of shadows wins over the self-evidence of truth. This was something that Kentridge, in an early childhood encounter with a certain image, personally observed. "As I indicated at the start of this lecture," notes Kentridge, "the presence of a father who was a lawyer was not incidental to this narrative."

Johannesburg, 1961

Flashbacks to early childhood come easily to Kentridge because he lives and works in his parental home. Fir trees still shadow the driveway where his father left for work. The mosaiced garden table still glitters in the sun. Home still presses up against the terraced hillside planted by his father, with its vistas of Houghton's purple-blooming jacaranda forest. In his mother's eyes, William was already an artist at three, bringing her beautiful drawings as gifts. "Every child draws. I just kept on drawing," remembers Kentridge, "I found I could get approval just by making things."[110] Where the ground slopes steeply to the compound's gated exit, there now rises a modern edifice, square and tall, a citadel for making. Reached from the house by a short footpath, Kentridge's purpose-built studio lies closer to home and hearth than other any artist's atelier I know. Even Bosch, raised in a medieval urban milieu of home-based crafts, moved (when his advantageous marriage allowed it) from his father's workshop and home to his own residence on the statelier side of the market square. No wonder trees, tiles, trials, and treason haunt Kentridge's art, created in that familial enclave. No wonder that, wherever it travels, whether to a cistern under Istanbul, a medieval hospital in Bruges, a contemporary art museum in Beijing, or the Tiber river embankment in Rome, the things Kentridge makes remain domestic.

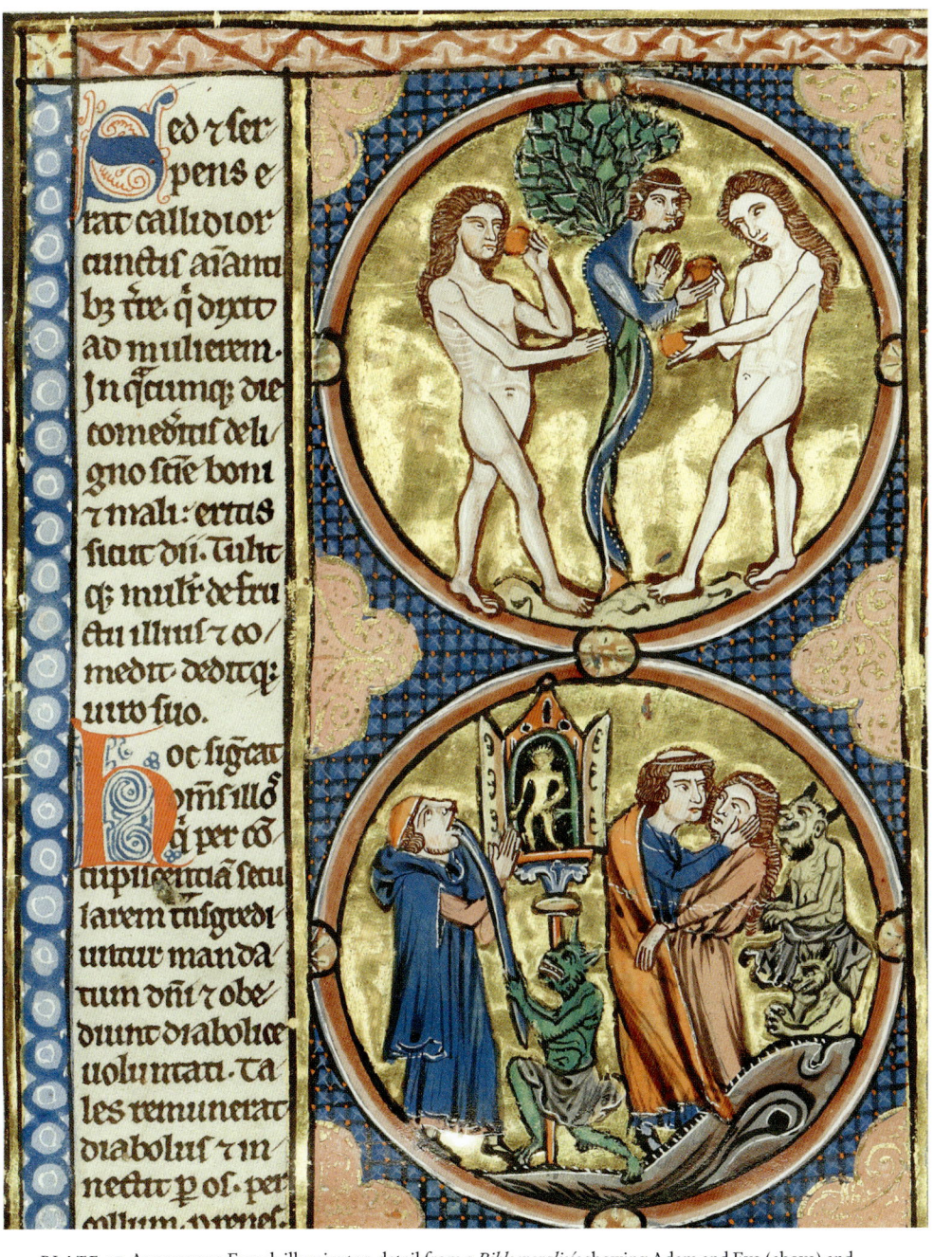

Sed & ser
pens e
rat callidior
aunctis aïanti
b3 tre. q̃ dixto
ad mulierem.
In quacumq; die
comeditis de li
gno scïe boni
& mali: eritis
siait dii. Tulit
q; mulr de fru
ctu illius & co/
medit deditq;
uiro suo.

Hoc sigẽat
hõis illos
q̃ per con
cupiscenciã secu
larem tñsgredi
untur manda
tum dñi & obe
diunt diabolice
uoluntati. Ta
les remunerat
diabolus & in
nectit p os. per
collum. uipnes

PLATE 17. Anonymous French illuminator, detail from a *Bible moralisée* showing Adam and Eve (above) and idol worship (below), 1230–40. Oxford, Bodleian Library, MS Bod. 270b, fol. 7v

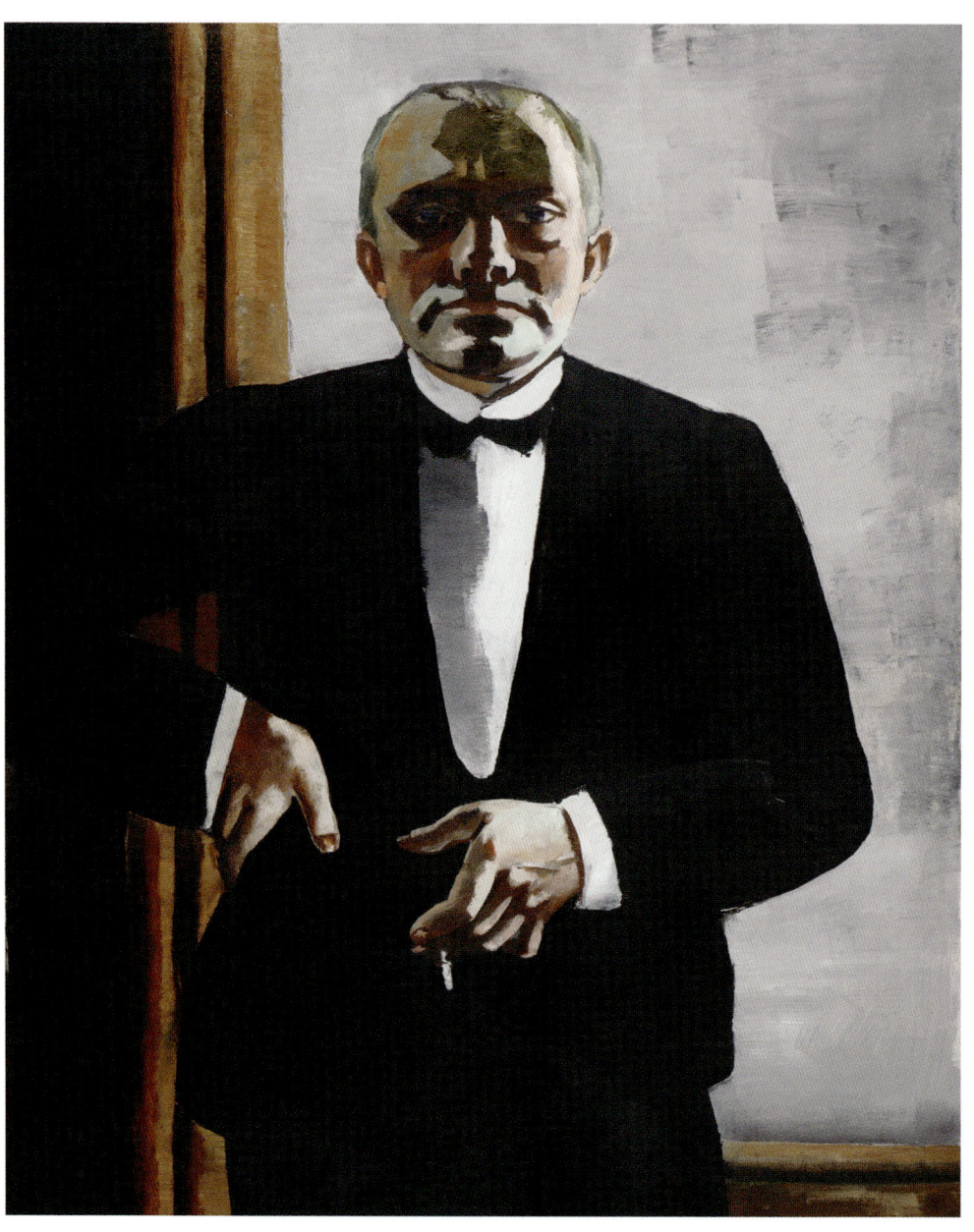

PLATE 18. Max Beckmann, *Self-Portrait in Tuxedo*, 1927. Oil on canvas, 139.5 × 95.5 cm. Harvard Art Museums, Cambridge, Massachusetts

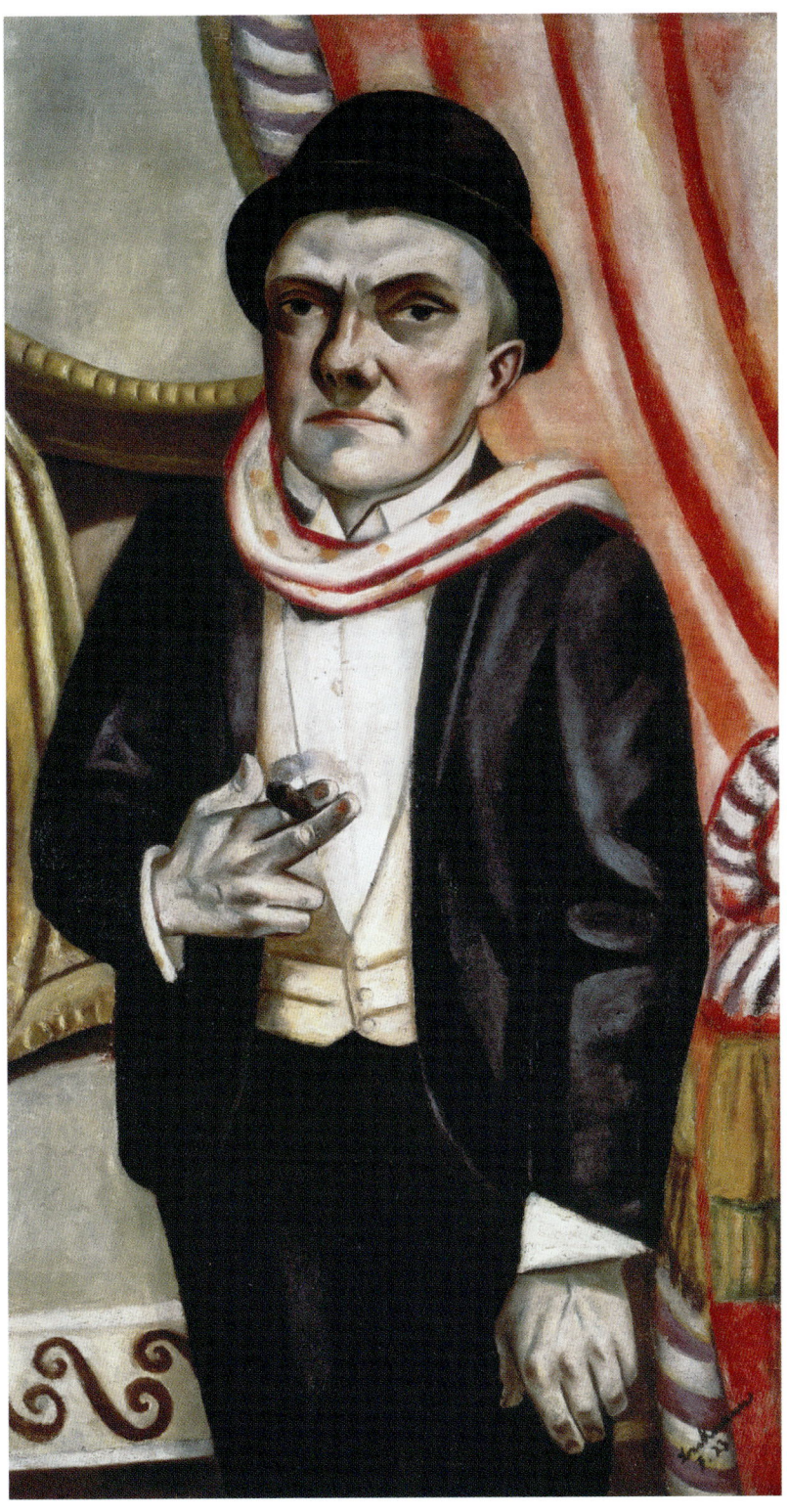

PLATE 19. Max Beckmann, *Self-Portrait with a Red Curtain*, 1923. Oil on canvas, 110 × 59 cm. Neue Galerie, New York

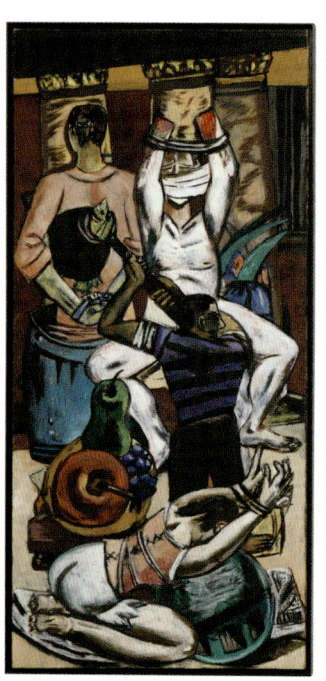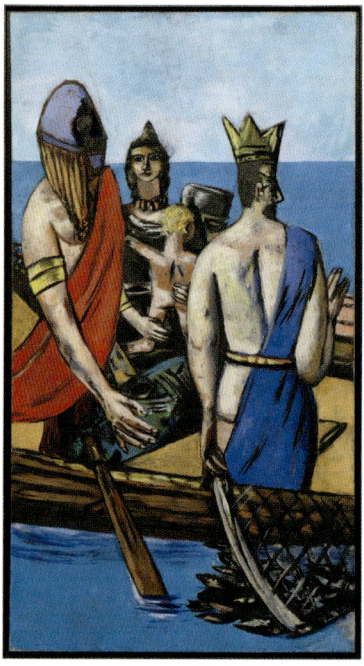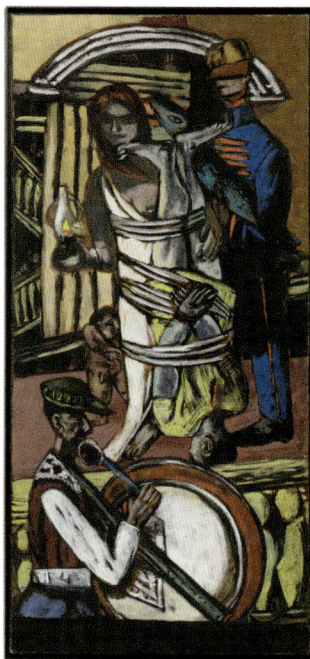

PLATE 20. Max Beckmann, *Departure*, Frankfurt 1932 and Berlin 1933–35. Oil on canvas, three panels, side panels 215.3 × 99.7 cm, center panel 215.3 × 115.2 cm. Museum of Modern Art, New York

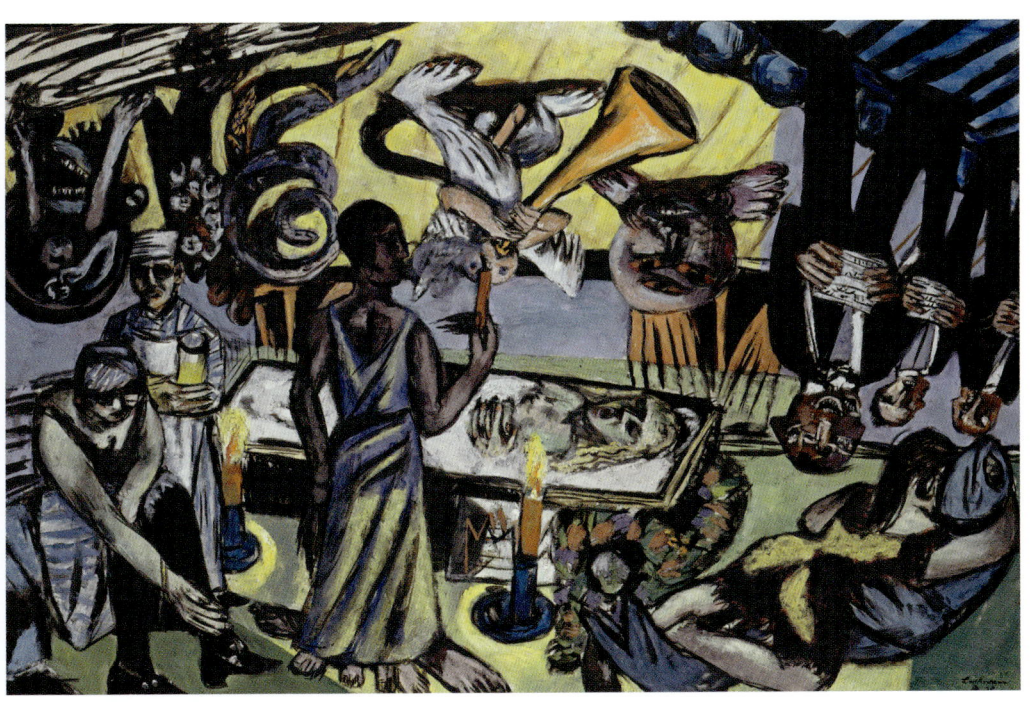

PLATE 21. Max Beckmann, *Death* (*Tod*), 1938. Oil on canvas, 121 × 176.5 cm. Neue Nationalgalerie, Berlin

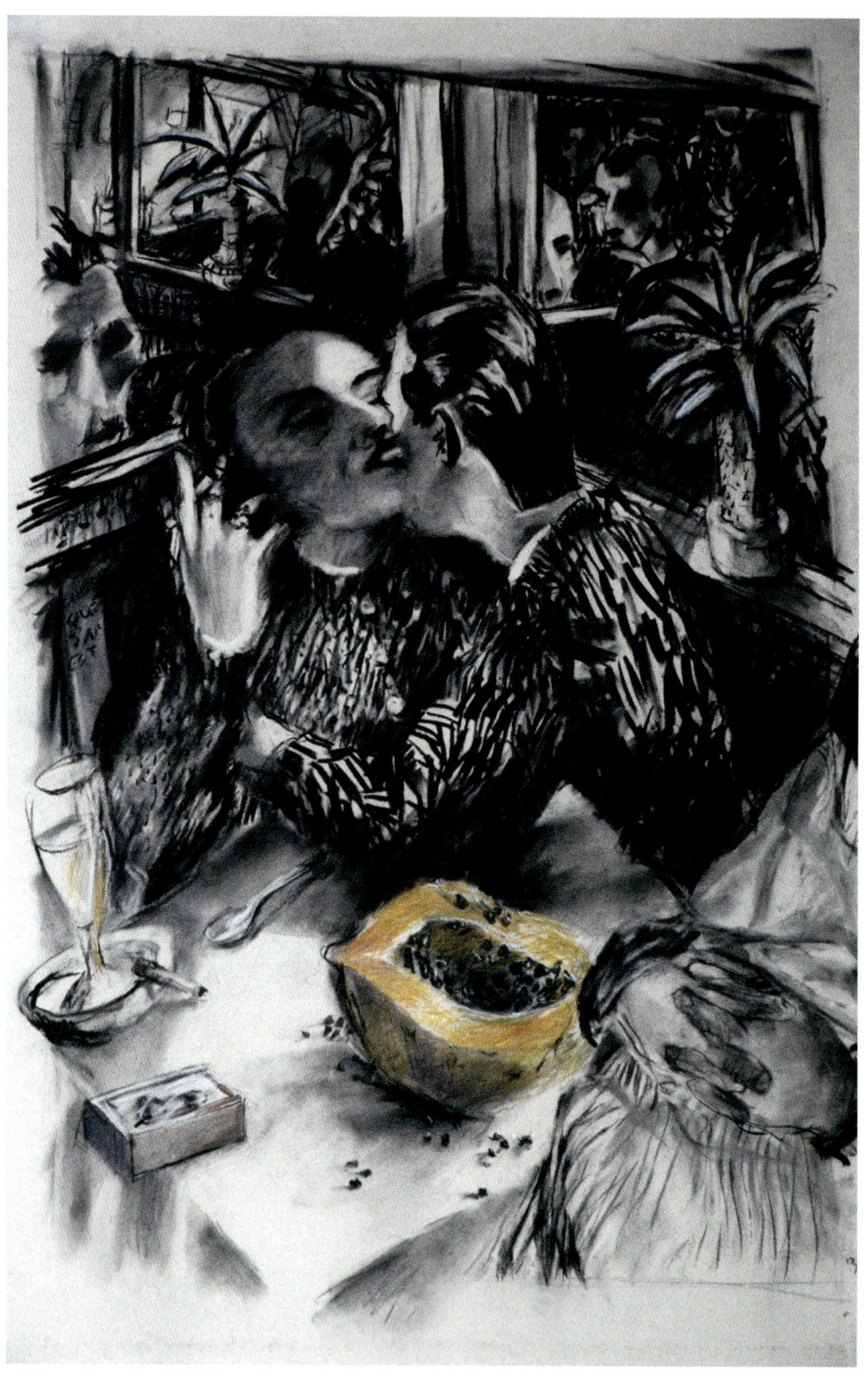

PLATE 22. William Kentridge, *Tropical Love Storm*, 1985. Charcoal and pastel on paper, 98.5 × 69 cm

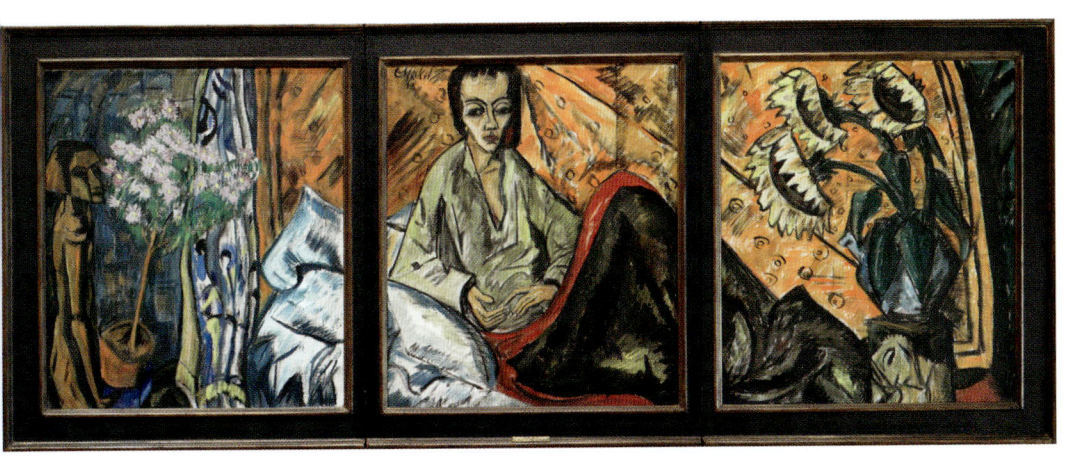

PLATE 23. Erich Heckel, *To the Convalescent Woman* (*Zur Genesung der kranken Frau*), 1912–13. Oil on canvas, triptych, 98.7 × 244.8 × 4.4 cm (framed). Harvard Art Museums, Cambridge, Massachusetts

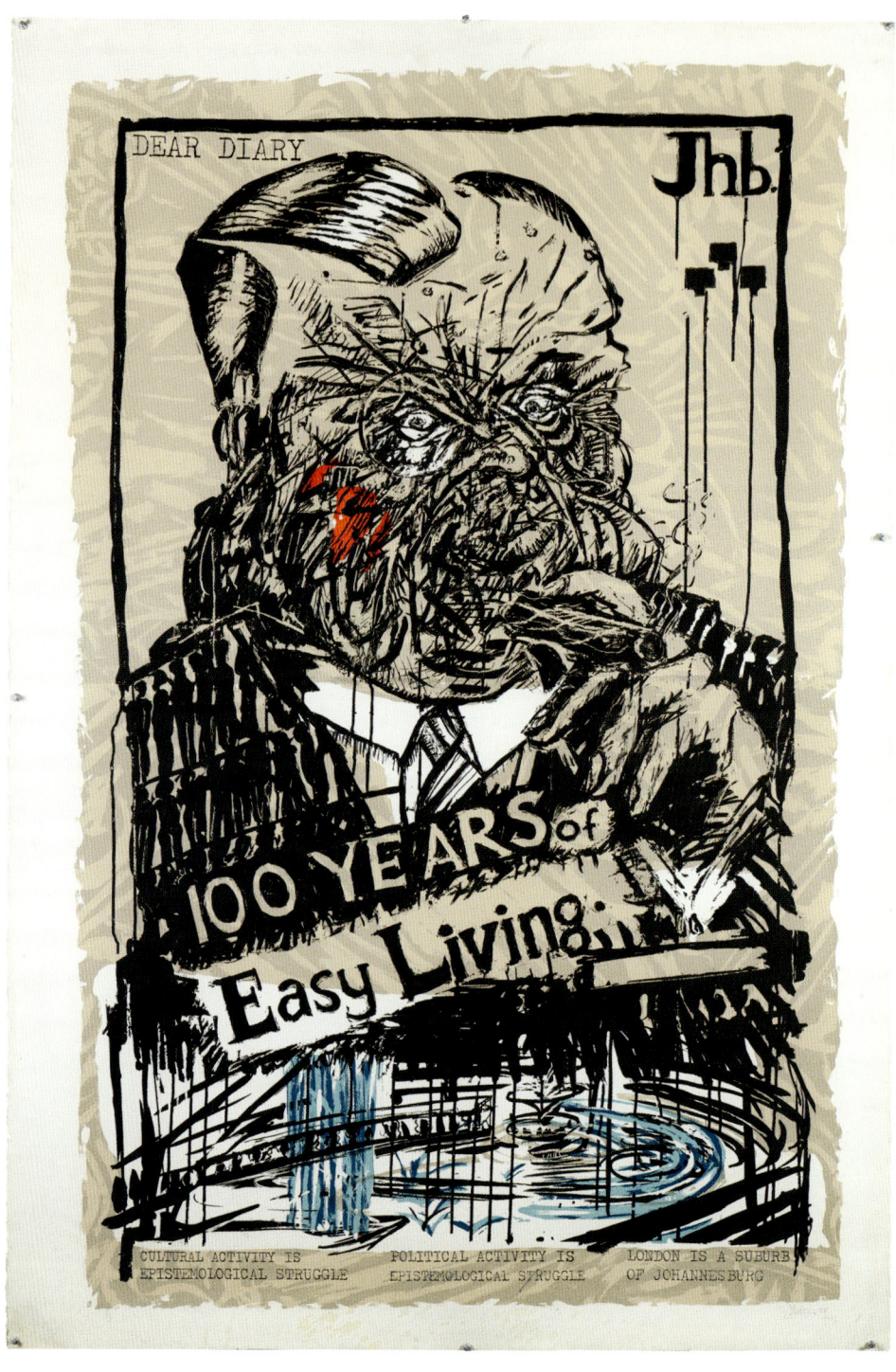

PLATE 24. William Kentridge, *Art in a State of Siege*, 1986–88. Silkscreen on velin d'arches creme and brown paper, 160 × 100 cm

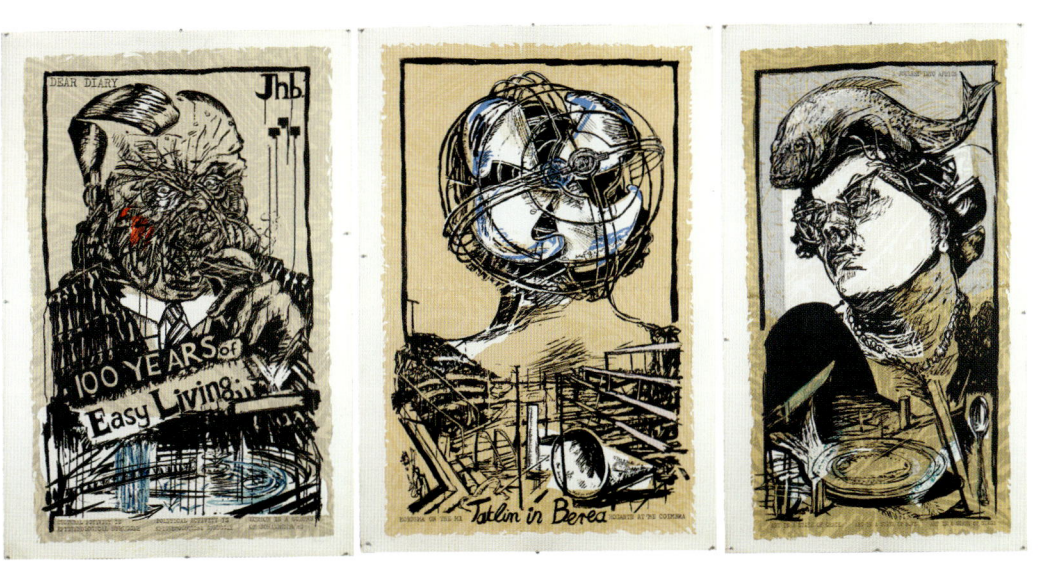

PLATE 25. William Kentridge, *Art in a State of Siege, Art in a State of Hope, Art in a State of Grace*, 1986–88. Silk-screen on velin d'arches creme and brown paper, each 160 × 100 cm

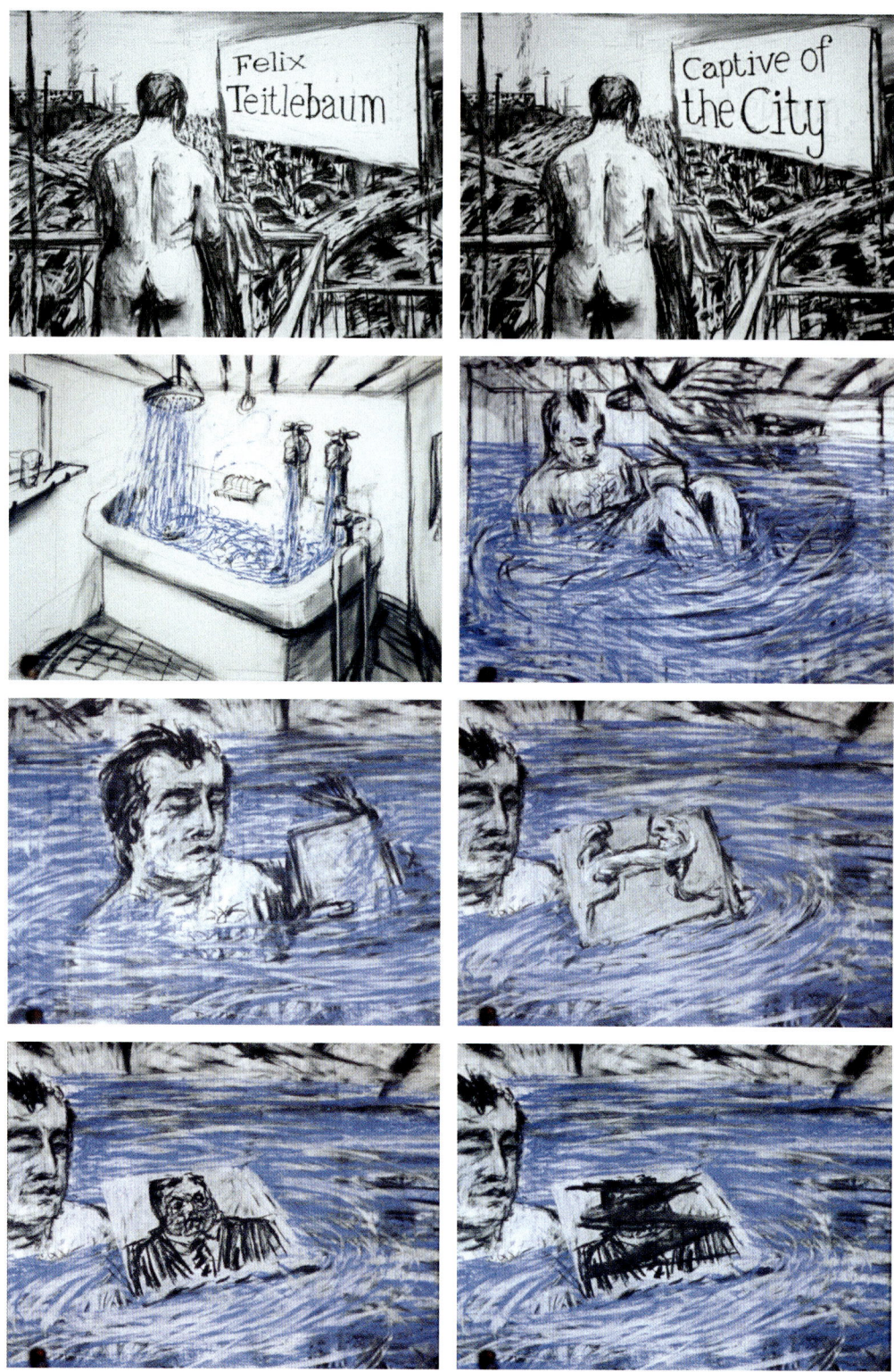

PLATE 26. Stills from William Kentridge, *Johannesburg, 2nd Greatest City after Paris*, 1989. 16mm film transferred to video

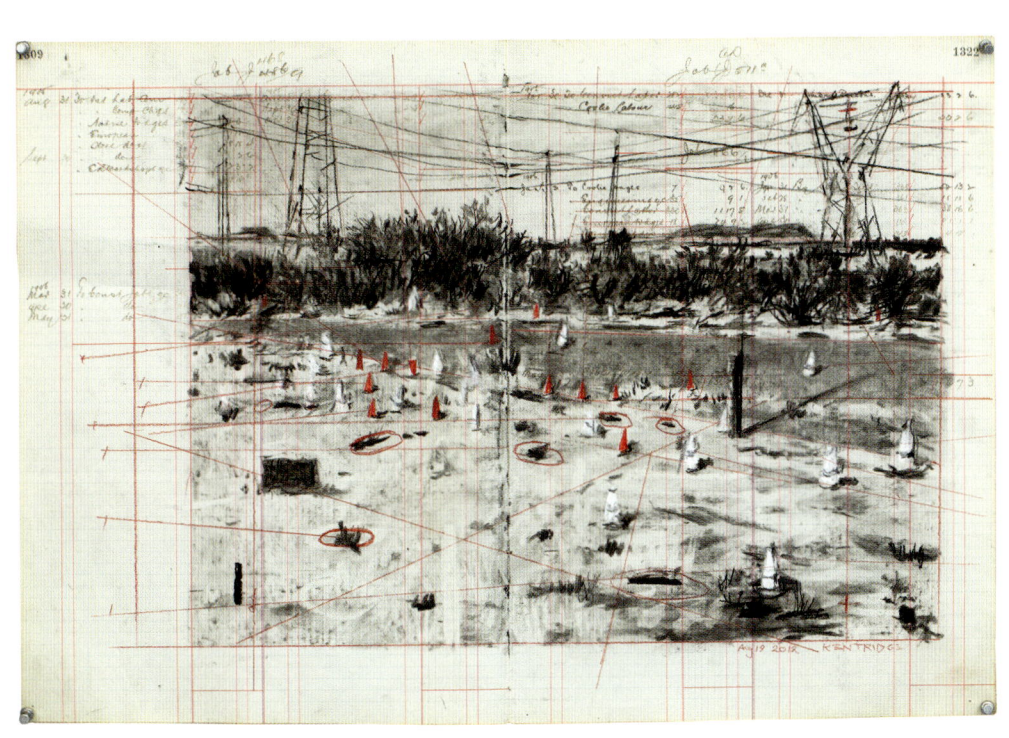

PLATE 27. William Kentridge, *Untitled* (53), 2012. Charcoal, pastel, and colored pencil on ledger pages from *East Rand Proprietary Mines Cash Book*, 47 × 66 cm

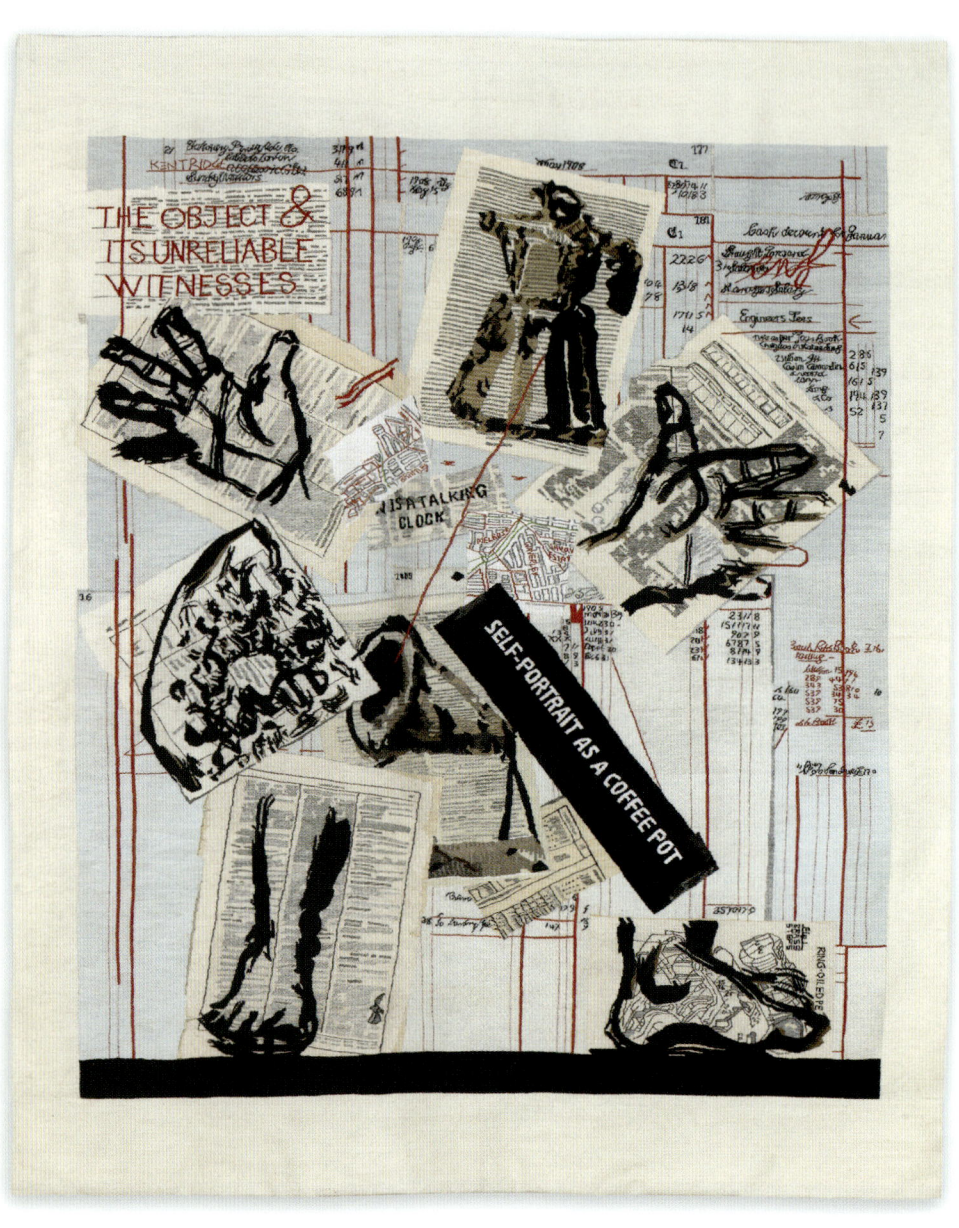

PLATE 28. Stephens Tapestry Studio after William Kentridge, *Self-Portrait as Coffee Pot*, 2012. Tapestry weave with embroidery (warp: polyester; weft and embroidery: mohair, acrylic, and polyester), 282.9 × 229.9 cm. Graphische Sammlung Albertina, Vienna

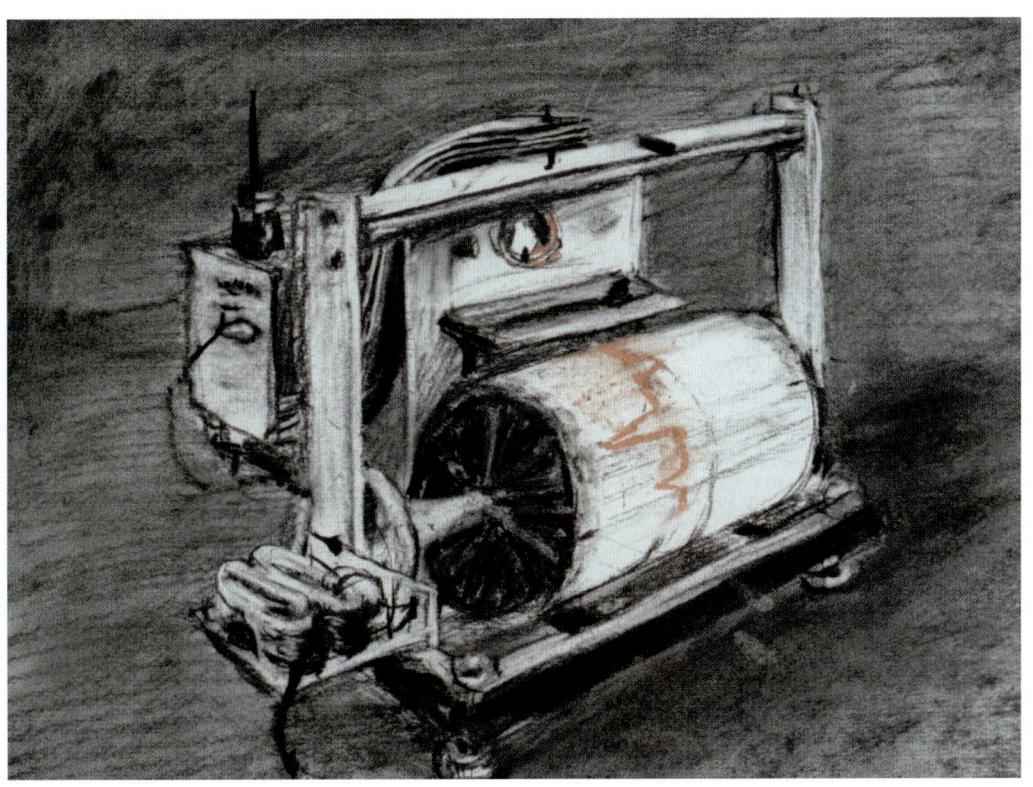

PLATE 29. Still from William Kentridge, *Felix in Exile*, 1994. 35mm film transferred to video

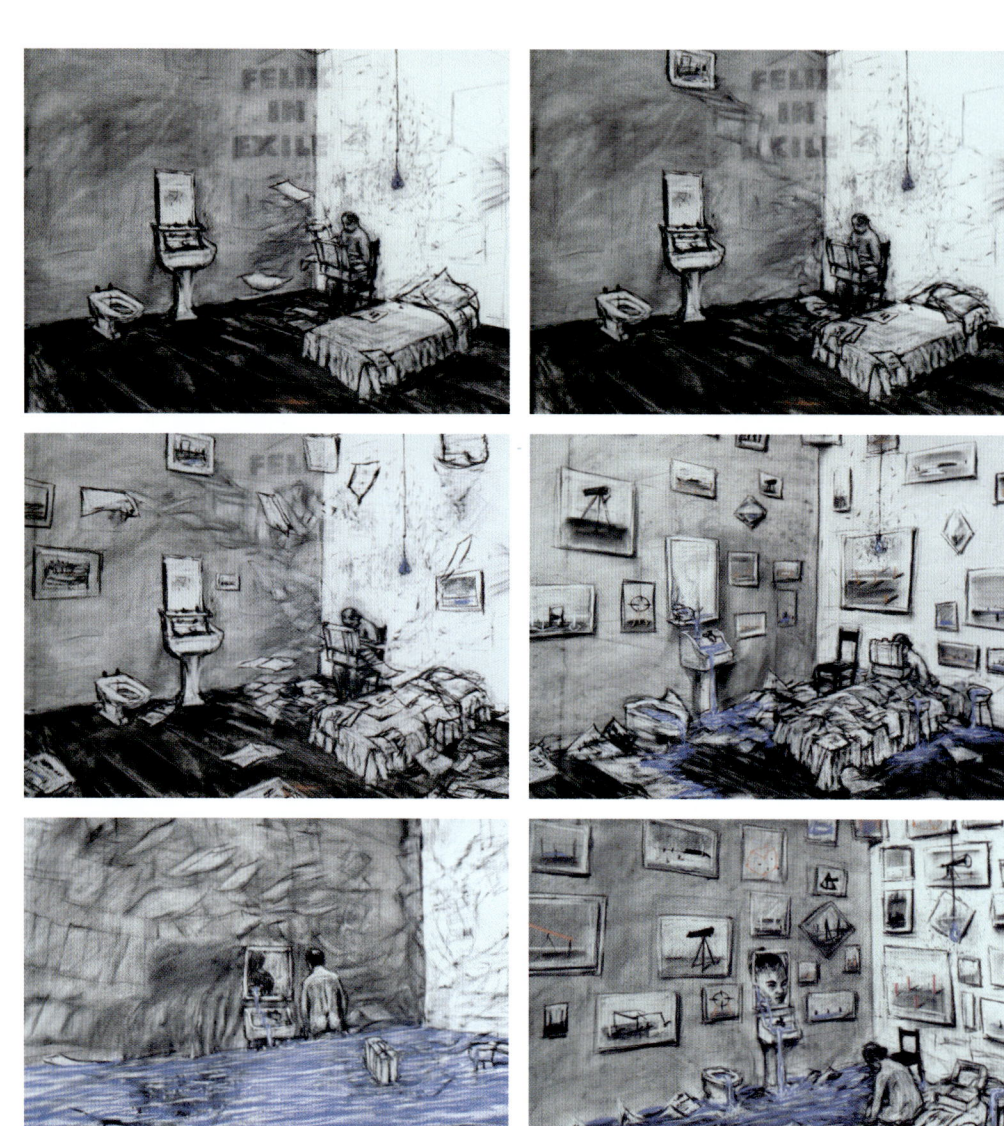

PLATE 30. Stills from William Kentridge, *Felix in Exile*, 1994. 35mm film transferred to video

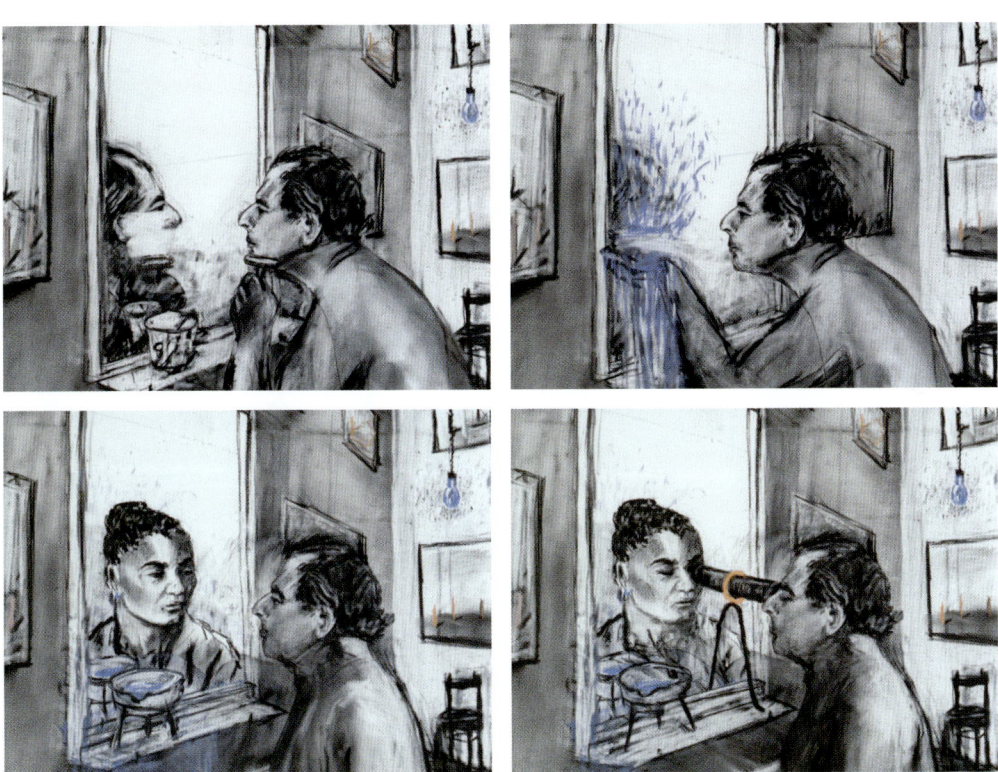

PLATE 31. Stills from William Kentridge, *Felix in Exile*, 1994, 35mm film transferred to video

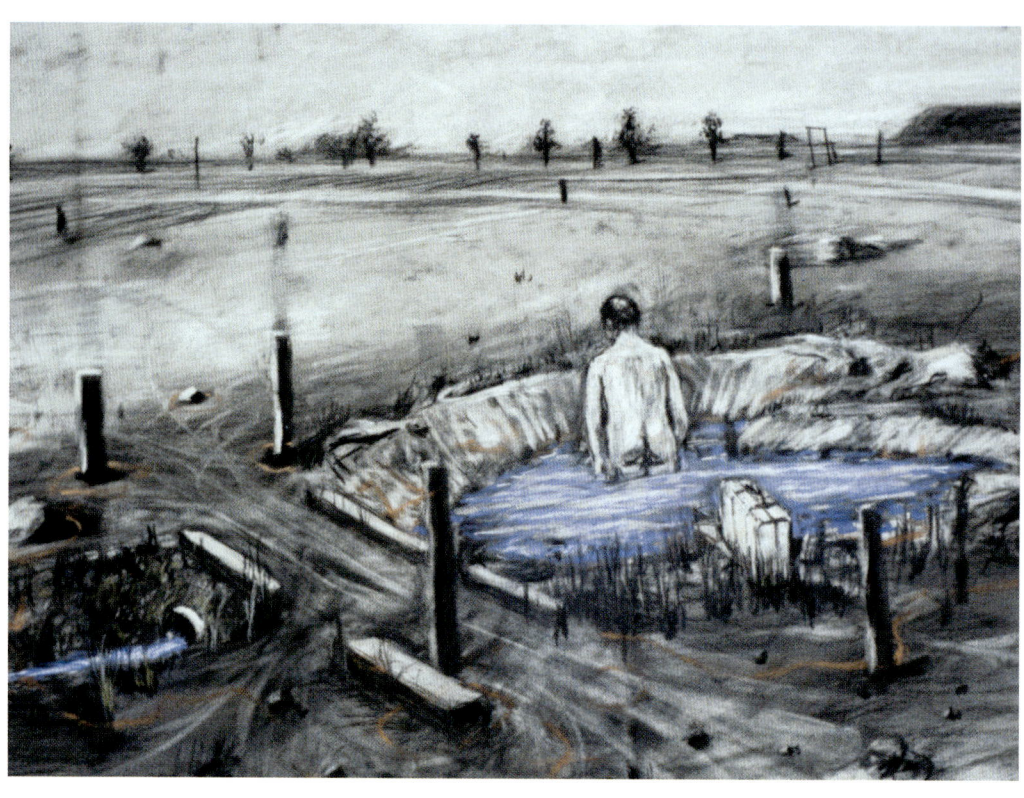

PLATE 32. Still from William Kentridge, *Felix in Exile*, 1994. 35mm film transferred to video

"London," the silkscreen *Art in a State of Siege* declared, "is a suburb of Johannesburg" (plate 24). As a boy, Kentridge imagined Johannesburg as suburbs of his desk at school. Further afield were Transvaal, South Africa, the Earth, the Milky Way, a "spiraling outward, a huge tornado upward from the exercise book, out to the edge of the universe [...]. Pinpointing who I was. I was in that city. At that desk. At that time." Another of his imaginations was generational, from himself back to sixteen great-great-grandparents in Lithuania and forward to "XX NUMBER" great-great-grandchildren spread everywhere, with himself "as a pinhole like the eye of a needle."[111] Everything starts with him and with the tip of his instrument making a point that becomes a line that forms an image, there and only there. And when he takes the drawing out of the studio, with the help of set designer Sabine Theunissen, he turns every gallery into the semblance of his studio, with atelier props, handmade signage, and gray workaday walls casting the audience in the role of assistants. *The Nose*, under Kentridge's direction, "spiral[ed] outward" from the artist's studio to the St. Peterburg of Gogol and Shostakovich to the Met in New York, where the final opera production had a workshop look, as if we were back in the studio. Kentridge's *Winterreise* places the singer and pianist before films projected on a wall hung (as the artist's studio is) with leaf-like sketches. At the performance's Vienna premier, Schubert's rustling lime tree mingled with the trees in Kentridge's leafy compound in Houghton, Johannesburg.

Made in the studio, Kentridge's drawings and films are obviously or subtly set in the studio. The marchers in the video installation *More Sweetly Play the Dance* wander through a vast Highveld terrain, but Kentridge makes that landscape look as if drawn in the narrow confines of his atelier (fig. 71). Measurement marks in red and black—residues of the filming process—clutter the drawn panorama, announcing it as set design. *Johannesburg, 2nd Greatest City after Paris* began with a landscape and empty bleachers facing a blank screen; but this sketched stage setting was ultimately a phantom of the studio, Kentridge's cave, his *Tummelplatz*, where everything imagined as outside is the likeness of a likeness of a shadow.

In Plato's allegory, the prisoners have been in the cave "from childhood." Not born there, they arrived from outside, but so early that they have forgotten everything that came before, including their passage through the "entrance, a long one, open to the light." The liberated prisoner, by contrast, "recalls his first home." Pitying his old companions, he climbs back home to illuminate them—an impossible task, since the prisoners have different recollections and award prizes to the one who "most remembers" which shadows "are accustomed to pass before, which after, and which at the same time as others."[112] Though ignorant of origins and blind to the truth, such cave-bound champions excel at re-cognition, at seeing things again and in sequence. In revisiting Plato's cave, Kentridge wants us to forget the liberator and work with the situation of the prisoners, which—the artist implies—resembles the life of the oppressed, for whom the state of siege is the norm. That means working with images, as Kentridge does enclosed in his studio.

Such work consists of "meeting the world halfway." Like the champions of the shadow game, we see something "we can recognize without knowing." Work proceeds associatively, one image leading to another, or appearing "at the same time as others," or reversing course. The memory of "trees and tiles" came to mind only after Kentridge made trees with paper tiles, Brassaï's Paris mattered only after Kentridge left his own Paris behind, and Plato's allegory became relevant only after *Shadow Procession* stood complete. Deferred, involuntary, and phantasmagorical, the flashbacks are disproportionally intense, like screen memories. "I have the impression that there's something not quite right about this scene," writes Freud of a vivid memory of "the glorious woods of my childhood [... :] the yellow of the flowers is far too prominent in the overall picture." Out of all that happened over many decades in Kentridge's garden, the mosaic's tessellations shine brightly forth as in an exaggerated "hallucination" or "parodistic exhibition."[113]

Kentridge punctuated his Norton Lectures with recollections from childhood. "Let us go back to the cave and its prisoners deceived by the shadows," he announced in an early segment headed "Our Eight-Year-Old Shadows."

> And I think of an eight-year-old on the beach, and the long shadows cast by the sun close to the horizon. The shadows are a version of you. Lift your arm and the shadow lifts its arm [...]. The shadow of the head now up at the dunes at the top of the beach moves twenty meters as I duck down, quick as that.

The breathless "and" introduces "an eight-year-old," at first any eight-year-old, then "a version of you," but finally William himself casting first-person shadows on the dunes: "It is an extension and more than an extension of me." Three lectures later he spirals out to the next generation:

> In the studio I film my eight-year-old son. He takes a jar of paint and a handful of pencils, some books and paper. He throws the jar of paint across the studio walls, scatters the pencils, tears the papers, and scatters the shards. We run the film in reverse. There is utopian perfection. The papers reconstruct themselves perfectly every time.

Both anecdotes celebrate child's *poiesis*, his "power to remake the world." On the beach, William delights in shadow-making that, in turn, reveals "a speed and dexterity I did not know I had." In the studio a lifetime later, his son "catches all the paint—not a drop is spilled. The wall is pristine." There's a joy in making: "Can I do it again?" the son asks. But reality is messy: "Yes. But first we have to clean the studio," Kentridge says to us, the audience, as if we were children.[114] The materials, not the maker, lead the way, and the delight resides in the beholder's share, in the shadows out there on the dunes that move more skillfully than the child who casts them. That the virtuosos are children fits the lectures as drawing *lessons*, and it accords with the old idea that art is a form of play, that the artist is a perpetual child, and that artworks are toys for adults.

But in the earliest memory that Kentridge recounts, child's play takes a different turn. The event occurred at home in 1961. When Kentridge recounted the story half a century later, he did so under the rubric—unspoken, but included in the lecture's published form—"KNOWLEDGE AS SHAME."

When he is six, he goes into his father's study and sees a thin yellow box, which looks like a box of chocolates. The lid is carefully opened. Inside is not the thin wax paper covering the first layer of chocolates, but a sheaf of glossy 10 × 12-inch black and white photographs. A man lies face downward, a dot and a dark stain in the center of his checkered jacket. The next photograph? The man rolled over. An incomprehensible confusion of shirt, jacket, viscera; the whole chest disintegrated by the exit wound of the bullet.[115]

The event is sudden, like a wound. Only seconds separate seeing the yellow box and opening it from realizing what the photographs show. Peaceable "meeting the world halfway" is overturned: chocolates to photographs, stain to wound, confusion to a disintegrated chest. It matters that the images are snapshots taken in the heat of the action. The link of photography to violence allows Kentridge to reach back another fifty years to the suddenness of mechanized warfare suddenly captured. Beckmann's art in a state of siege depended on surprise. Through shocking portrayals of veterans disfigured in battle, the artist assailed the public conscience while also reopening—therapeutically—the psychic wounds his generation tried unsuccessfully to forget (see fig. 46). Beckmann experienced warfare at first hand, as a medical orderly on the Eastern Front, and sketched what he saw. But the Great War's "world-festival of death," in Thomas Mann's phrase,[116] found its most adequate expression in photographs and film. Jünger relished Bosch's painted demons because, in their machine-like energy and form, they predicted the posthuman reality of mechanized killing. A machine that aims and shoots, the camera captured the dangerous moment best.

"Images thus arise from a mathematical demonism by way of which the new relation of people to danger becomes, in a very special way, visible," notes Jünger in

Der gefährliche Augenblick.[117] The six-year-old William examines the photographs one by one: "people lying spread across the veld. A man sitting dazed, his head in his hands. A policeman standing on top of the armored vehicle. Another chest—is it a man? Is it a woman?—blown apart." The beholder's share repeats itself in a terrible succession. "The six-year-old closes the box. Puts it back on the shelf. Puts a book on top of it to hide what he has done." Trespassing in the father's office, lured by the promise of chocolates, seeing what should not be seen, the child tries guiltily to hide his tracks. "It is more than 'this should not happen.' THIS SHOULD NOT BE SEEN." The shame enlarges: "He should not have seen it. Not as strong as that his seeing it has made it happen, but a complicity between the event and the sight of it."[118]

"Trauma" comes from the Greek word for wound. In its original use as a medical term, it denotes both an injury where, due to external violence, the skin is broken, and the effects of such an injury on the whole organism. At the turn of the last century, psychologists likened wounds on the body to injuries of the mind. "Certain reminiscences of the shock fall into the subliminal consciousness," wrote William James in 1894 in a review of Pierre Janet's work. "If left there they act as permanent 'psychic traumata,' thorns in the spirit, so to speak."[119] Caused by suddenness, psychic trauma is permanent. Happening within such a short span of time, trauma cannot be processed, staying in the mind "like a foreign body [*Fremdkörper*] which long after its entry must continue to be regarded as an agent that is still at work."[120] "This," that "should not be seen," cannot be unseen. It keeps returning, as the bodies "spread across the veld" do, involuntarily to Kentridge as a child, and more safely in the studio, his *Tummelplatz* for remembering, repeating, and working-through.

Based on clinical evidence of "shell shock," Freud developed his account of living organisms so incessantly assaulted by the external world that "[*p*]*rotection against* stimuli is almost more important than [...] *reception of* stimuli."[121] For Warburg, scholarship about the Great War brought about his own psychic collapse; for Beckmann, trauma invaded ordinary experience through sudden glimpses of disfigured invalids; for Freud, war neurosis, as a test case for trauma generally, revealed modern life to be a perpetual state of siege, with the mind bombarded by shocking sense perceptions and unprocessed memories. Happening suddenly, trauma can only be mastered retrospectively, "by developing the anxiety whose omission was the cause of the traumatic neurosis." And such anxiety is developed by compulsively repeating the trauma in dreams, symptoms, and fantasies. What one could not have seen coming is now always about to come. Early on, around the time when he first concluded that his patients "suffer principally from reminiscences,"[122] Freud observed that the mind turned traumatic memories into "scenes," with the subject as a dramatic protagonist and the event vividly unfolding in a sort of "private theater." Freud went on to propose the content of one such scenario: the "primal scene" of sexual intercourse between the parents observed by the child. This proposal generated much debate as to whether it had been experienced or merely fantasized. But Freud's more productive insight was of the scene-like form of childhood memories.

Kentridge's story of the photographs has the hallmark of a primal scene. Told in third person present-tense, it has the six-year-old observing his own actions passively, as if from outside: "The lid is carefully opened." And what he observed has a dreamlike intensity: the thin yellow box, the thin wax paper, the "10 × 12-inch" glossy prints. Like the "trees and tiles," the memory begs the question whether it is *from* or *of* childhood. In Freud, primal scenes are comprehended long afterwards, with details retrospectively fantasized. Like collective myths, these scenes represent, and by representing process, some experience that is to the child an unfathomable enigma. Instead of establishing facts or proposing theories, they tell a story—about seduction, castration, procreation, and so forth. The tale of the six-year-old's discovery of the chocolate box of photographs is the primal scene of evil—"the shock of adult violence." It functions for Kentridge as his personal theodicy in scenic form. The ethical begins here, and here it will remain, in drawn, filmed, and reimagined bodies in the veld.

The photographs were of the Sharpeville massacre. They had been taken by the British-born photojournalist Ian Berry, who happened to be in Sharpeville covering pass-law protests for *Drum* magazine. On March 21, 1960, the protests turned violent when the police, assembled at their station off Seeiso Street, fired with submachine guns at the crowd, killing sixty-nine protesters, including women and children, and injuring another hundred and eighty. The slaughter caused an uproar among Black South Africans. Strikes, riots, demonstrations, and marches led the government on March 30 to declare, for first time in the country's history, a state of emergency. Police detained over eighteen thousand people without warrant or stated cause. The country's governor-general outlawed the two main Black opposition parties, forcing them into a thirty-year exile. The massacre and the draconian measures taken in its aftermath outraged the world community. On April 1, The United Nations Security Council unanimously passed a resolution deploring South Africa's actions and calling on the government "to abandon its policies of *apartheid* and racial discrimination." International condemnation and pressure from White South Africans forced the government, in 1961, to form a Committee of Inquiry to investigate the killings. Sydney Kentridge agreed to serve as chief counsel for the Sharpeville community. This gave him special access to the relevant evidence, including the prints of Ian Berry's publicly inaccessible photographs that William, thinking they would be chocolates, came upon.

The inquest hinged on whether, as the police claimed, an angry crowd confronted inexperienced officers who spontaneously opened fire in self-defense, or whether, as Kentridge's team argued, the officers used excessive force deliberately, and on command, in order to disperse a largely peaceful gathering of Black protesters marching against pass laws. "The photographs," as William Kentridge in 2012 explained, "were part of the evidence presented at court (the court exonerated the policemen)."[123] His father used them to prove the direction of the gunshots. The disposition of the bodies and shape of entrance and exit wounds allowed forensic specialists to deduce that the victims had been shot in the back while fleeing from the police. Based on that evidence, a fair judge could be convinced of the culpability of the officers. And incriminating the police would bring the government to justice. Because law enforcement is a direct extension of the executive branch of the state, free and fair scrutiny of the police affirms the independence of judges and, thus, the rule of law. From his years on the defense team in the Treason Trial, Sydney Kentridge knew that, in the courtroom, the law itself could successfully be put on trial. In 1961, nearly six years after their arrest, the last thirty defendants not yet acquitted of treason were found not guilty. The laws were rotten but the legal system itself was not, or at least not yet.

Apartheid's pathology as a legal order consisted most basically in its exclusion of the majority that stood under it. Disenfranchised in 1948, Black South Africans, representing about 70 percent of the country's population, had no say in Parliament—the body that made the laws. Displaced to urban townships like Sharpeville, which were run by powerless local councils, or to the ten nominally independent "homelands" (in reality, corrupt dependencies of South Africa), and with political parties and extraparliamentary politics effectively banned, Blacks could be tried by a state legally external to them, both in standard criminal procedures and in the more fraught case of treason. After the failure of the Treason Trial to convict, Parliament in 1967 passed the Terrorism Act expanding the definition of treason to include any act that could be proven to endanger law and order. The Act shifted the burden of proof from the prosecution to the defense and abolished due process, permitting arrest without warrant, allowing hearsay evidence, suspending habeas corpus, and dispensing with the right to bail, legal representation, and a speedy trial.

Apartheid was an administrative labyrinth larger than most countries' tax code, regulatory apparatus, criminal law, and welfare system combined.[124]

Constructed by the law, it could be challenged legally. With political opposition restricted, media censored, and public protests forbidden, law became the chief weapon against it. Anti-apartheid legal activists like William's father and mother litigated cases contesting pass laws, torture, mandatory military conscription, the suppression of labor unions, and forced resettlement of Blacks. In an article published in 1980, Sydney Kentridge contended that "the traditional forms of legal process have not been abandoned." At the start of this text, written for an international readership, he observed that the courts of South Africa dealt with laws and institutions bearing a "close resemblance to those with which American courts had to deal in the fairly recent past."[125] The irony was that US courts worked to *remedy* discrimination on racial grounds, whereas the South African Parliament sought to *ratify* segregation. A year before *Brown v. Board of Education*, the 1953 Reservation of Separate Amenities Act did not merely legalize separate but equal public premises and vehicles. It forbade integration, stipulating that setting apart *un*equal premises and vehicles for other races could not be legally contested.

By Sydney Kentridge's account, the rule of law in South Africa stood in jeopardy. Legislative supremacy subordinated all aspects of the state to Parliament, enabling the introduction of countless procedural novelties, unchecked by any juridical body and unfettered by a bill of rights. Claiming to be besieged externally by hostile neighboring states and internally by sedition, the government, through the Terrorism Act, could label almost anything as treasonous and bypass due process. According to English law—South Africa's inheritance—conviction for treason required a higher burden of proof than for other crimes, because charges of treason were more apt to be politically motivated and more likely to enlist "fictitious conspiracies" for their proof.[126] Treason therefore required at least two independent witnesses to testify to the treasonous act. Finally, most judges—by South African law the sole triers of fact—were reluctant to stand up in defense of the law, and the ones who did risked prosecution for obstructing justice. This put lawyers in a predicament. Their calling obliged them to defend clients who wanted to be defended, but their efforts presented a false image at home and abroad of judicial integrity.

Internationally, the country projected itself as a *Rechtsstaat*, in contradistinction (for example) to the racialized justice of the Nazi state, which had compelled defense lawyers to place their loyalty to the state over any obligation to clients, and which deemed the *Rechtsstaat* to be a Jewish-Liberal invention. "Even South African's severest critics readily conceded that the standard of the administration of justice in South Africa is of the highest order," boasted a Nationalist MP in 1985.[127] Since they interpreted the laws rather than making them, lawyers could preserve the illusion of that high standard, defending the rotten state against critics. Sydney Kentridge ended his article by asking, "What has the exercise in court been worth?" Venturing an answer, he noted that when change comes to South Africa, "those newly in power will remember the legal process either as a protection against power or as power's "convenient instrument." Given the direction his country had taken, however, the latter would be the stronger memory. But foreshadowing his son's artistic credo—"optimism in check nihilism at bay"—Sydney Kentridge concluded, "It is not necessary to hope in order to work, and it is not necessary to succeed in order to persevere."[128] A final footnote attributes those words to William the Silent, Prince of Orange, owner of Bosch's triptych and the duke of Alba's foe, who fled his country during its state of siege.

The inquest on the Sharpeville massacre absolved the officers of wrongdoing: the decisively parenthetical "(the court exonerated the police)" is all that William Kentridge said about what happened publicly with regard to the photographs he found. "I would have been six years old," he adds, as if personally to verify the story's impersonal beginning, "When he was six."[129] Despite his father's arguments, the survivors' testimony, and the evidence of images, the truth did not come to light. South African law made the judge, and not experts or a jury, the sole trier of facts. He alone decided whether the shots in the back really occurred. Sydney Kentridge refused an appointment to the bench. He preferred to argue the truth rather than to decide it, given that such decisions would have to be made according to laws abhorrent to him. "There is no need to search for the truth behind these laws," he announced in an article of 1982 published in *The South African Law Journal* under the provocative title "Telling the Truth about Law." The truth behind these laws, he continues, "is apparent on the face of them. They are openly discriminatory and oppressive."[130] In the courtroom, as in Plato's cave, victory goes to whoever "is sharpest at making out the things that go by." Contesting "in courts and elsewhere [...] about the shadows of the just or the representations of which they are the shadows," the homecomer would have to "dispute about the way these things are understood by men who have never seen justice itself." And if the others get their hands on him, the truth-teller will "no doubt" be killed.

Sydney Kentridge obtained the photographs as *forensic* (from the Latin adjective *forensis*, "of a forum") evidence, to serve as proof in the forum of public inquiry. Grown up, his son would display forensic evidence, too, but differently, through crimson pencil marks. The color of annotations and of blood, this form of drawing turns landscapes into scenes of a crime. Under apartheid, Black South Africans were tried in a forum to which they did not belong. After Sharpeville, when the government declared a state of emergency and replaced law by force, the whole country stood exceptionally under the normal condition of the Black majority. Walter Benjamin's observation—that "the tradition of the oppressed" teaches how emergency states are not "the exception but the rule"—became self-evident. Two years after stating that there was "no need to search for the truth behind these laws," Sydney Kentridge left South Africa for good.[131] But what of his son who stayed behind, building his studio at home, at the primal scene of the photographs' discovery? And how strange that, in retelling the allegory of the cave, moving shadows "up the ladder," he left out the implied prophecy of Socrates's judicial murder.

The six-year-old closes the box, puts it back on the shelf, wishes what was seen could be unseen. "I did not ever tell my father that we both had looked at those photographs," he publicly announced in Cambridge in 2012.[132] Both looked: the father, for evidence in court; the son, for candy that turned out to be images that, explosive to behold, could not be forgotten. To call the child's look merely traumatic would flatten its long, productive duration. Typeset in red in the lecture's published version, the words "THIS SHOULD NOT BE SEEN" are the artist's foundational dissent, his refusal of the parenthetical "the court exonerated the policemen" as the final word. Distinct from expressing a divergent legal opinion, aesthetic dissent differs from how his father beheld the photos. The artist in a state of siege will allow the bodies in the veld to bear witness differently than in law and politics, and in a different forum.

Johannesburg, 1994

When the bodies appear in works by his hand, Kentridge builds them into a scenario that renders nearly unrecognizable the primal scene of his beholding them in photographs kept in his father's office (see figs. 65 and 66). Elaborately developed through plot, character, theme, and melody, the new scene extracts, combines, and shuffles details of the six-year-old's discovery, like letters in an anagram. The artist himself recognized where these bodies came from only belatedly: "only after the drawing was finished did I remember the Sharpeville photographs." Over six months, from September 1993 to February 1994, he had sketched the bodies from police photos of violence occurring presently; much later, reflecting on the drawings, he discovered their hidden prototype: "I remembered what I had been drawing, long after the drawing was finished."[133] Kentridge does not say, "what I *unconsciously* had been drawing." His activity had been fully conscious. He drew in the deliberately associative process of finding what the drawing wants to be, of discovering *Tropical Love Storm* in Brassaï's amorous couple. In the studio, it

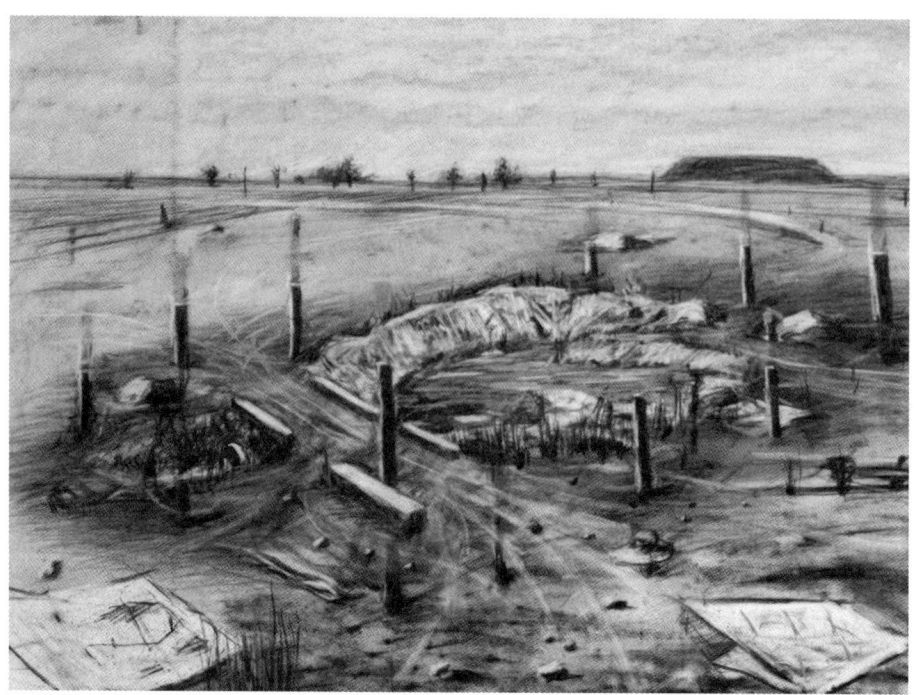

FIG. 98. Still from William Kentridge, *Felix in Exile*, 1994. 35mm film transferred to video

is drawing itself that lies on the couch, with the artist seated on a chair behind, encouraging, managing, and recording what happens in the *Tummelplatz*. Freud calls what happens there the transference: the process by which past prototypes reappear "as a chunk of real life."[134]

In memory, the bodies lay "spread across the veld." And when the bodies first reappear in Kentridge's art, the veld is just a smudged ground around the body, graying the whole sheet to its edges. That ground, the body's physical setting together with its paper support, might go unnoticed—absorbed, as viewers of the animated film will be, in rapidly unfolding action within which the drawing appears initially as a cut-away shot—were Kentridge not to have made drawings on paper into key actors in the plot. The film immerses us in a story that unfolds in a fitful montage of scenes. Fluent in the language of film, viewers will distinguish two main ones: a "here" in the form of an enclosed interior and a "there" figured as an out-of-doors landscape view (fig. 98). In the interior scene, the protagonist, a naked man resembling Kentridge sits passively in a room without doors or windows; he is the Felix of the film's title, *Felix in Exile*. Initially empty save for bare necessities (a bed, chair, toilet, and sink), Felix's cell-like interior will get flooded with images arriving from elsewhere (fig. 99).

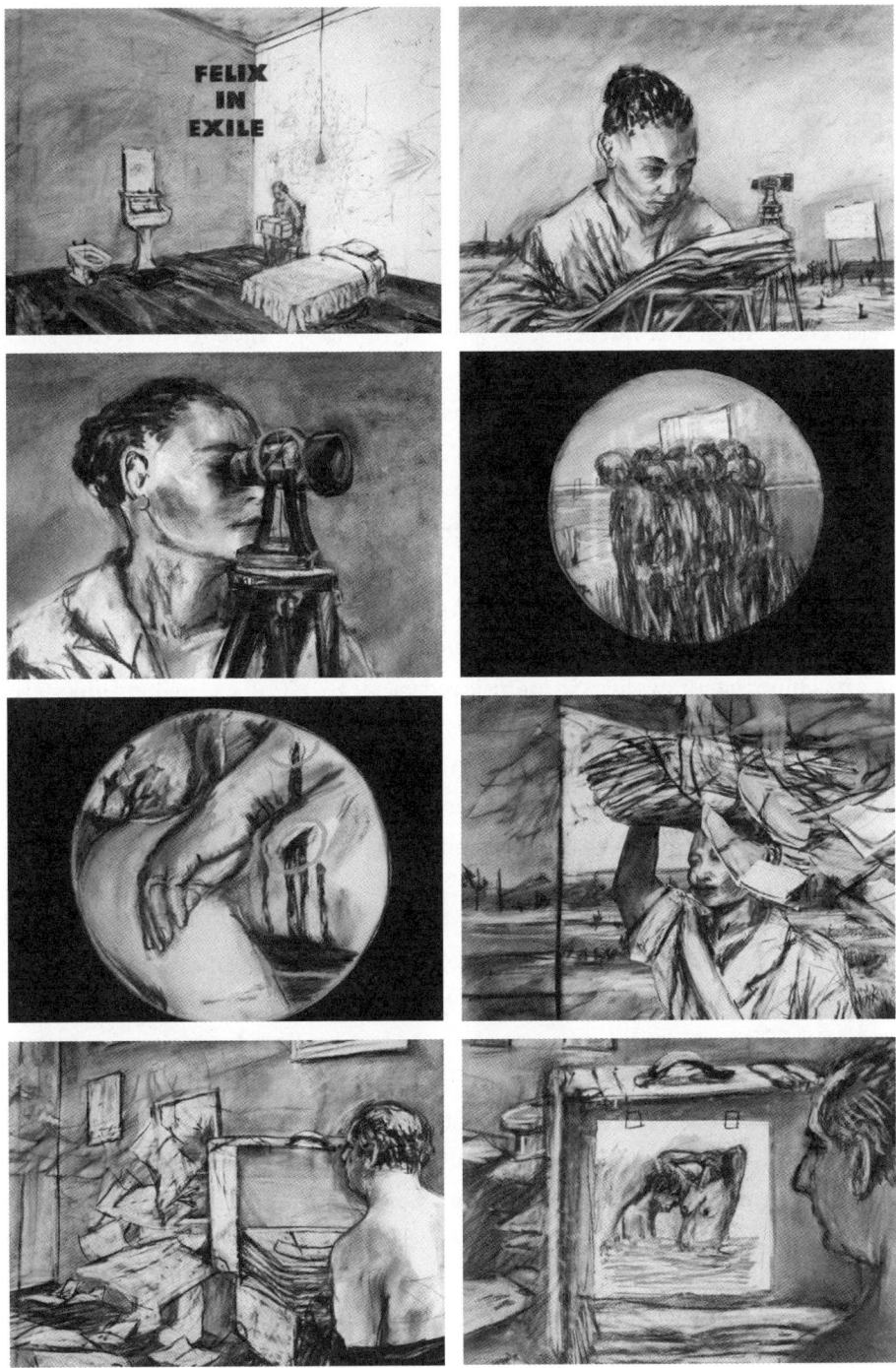

FIG. 99. Stills from William Kentridge, *Felix in Exile*, 1994. 35mm film transferred to video

In the outdoor scenes, actions of a momentous and violent kind occur against a landscape background, in the veld as out in the "world." There Black South Africans gather, march, and perish, shot by unidentified snipers. There Kentridge also conjures a new character, the film's second protagonist: a Black woman, nameless in the film but called Nandi by the artist, who draws, surveys, and variously records the veld, the bodies, and the stars above. The film links her amorously to Felix, who longs for her from his prison-like interior. His yearning takes the form of leafing through sketches Nandi has made. These include the drawings of bodies in the veld. These "sheets of evidence" pass between the interior and exterior settings in a way that is both plausible and dreamlike. Scene changes are plausible, because the paper sheets remind us that the film consists of nothing but drawings, which is to say, illusions that can take us anywhere. The changes are also dreamlike, because the film unfolds not as events do in the world, but as thoughts do in the mind.

The film abounds in puzzling imagery. White dots on a black, round ground become stars observed through a telescope. Connected by chalky white lines, these stars form constellations that turn into objects: a human head, a faucet that runs blue water, a suitcase filled with drawings (fig. 100). A rotating cylinder appears as a machine that draws lines in forensic red (plate 29). Its mark-making links it to the charcoal sketches, newspaper pages, surveyors' maps, and the hand-drawn film itself. The cylinder resembles a seismograph registering underground vibrations and a cardiograph measuring movements of the heart. By way of similarities and contiguities, cylinder, suitcase, faucet, and head gesture towards some idea lying restless and urgent under the surface.

Dreams turn thoughts into dramatic scenes. Freud marveled at the filmic character of dreams: how, apart from whatever they might mean, they present the sleeper with something that could be "perceived through the senses like a waking experience."[135] Like plays and films, dreams require scenic consistency, which they supply by reworking—or "revising"—incoherent thoughts, wishes, and stimuli into something like lived experience. Kentridge only once made a film of a dream he had dreamt. As the deadline for a group exhibition in Italy drew near, he dreamt he was at that exhibition and saw it was hung with other artists' works, each eliciting in him the same response: "Damn, if only I thought of that myself, I could have done that for this exhibition that I have to do now."[136] Created for the show that had worried him, *Sleeping on Glass* (1999) realized the works he had beheld in his anxiety dream.

Made to be displayed on a mirror above an actual antique wooden dresser, that film was an anomaly. Kentridge's "Drawings for Projection"—*Felix in Exile* included—arose out of his wakeful associative method. Working without a sto-

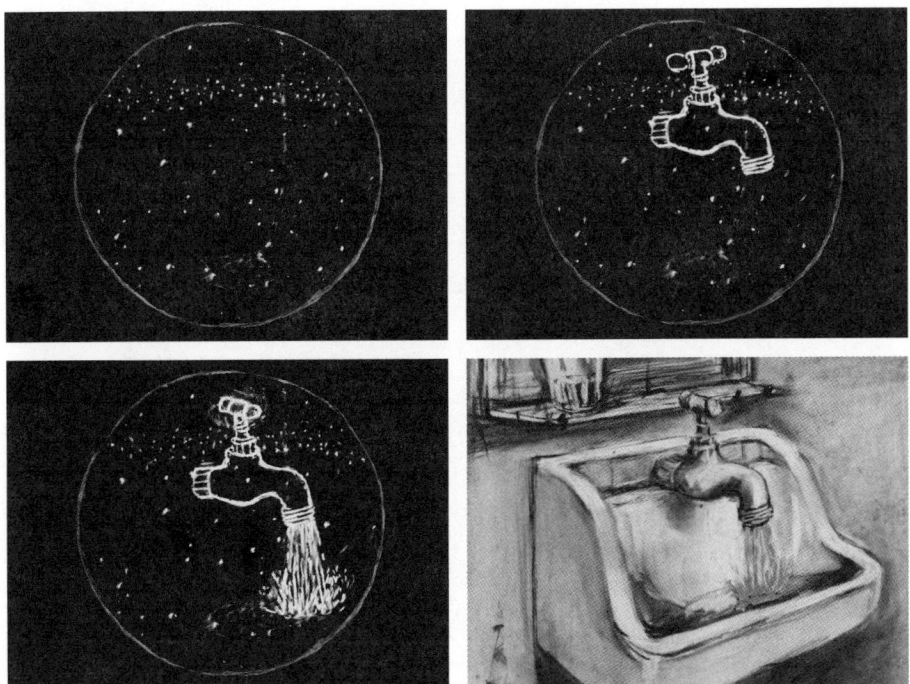

FIG. 100. Stills from William Kentridge, *Felix in Exile*, 1994. 35mm film transferred to video

ryboard, he allows the plot to arise from the drawing that hangs before him, following the impulse to add or subtract from it. In 1991, planning to make a new film about Soho Eckstein's daughter, dubbed Liberty, he spent weeks drawing the opening scene: Soho in bed with his breakfast tray, lowering the plunger of a cafetière. "Thinking like a novelist," Kentridge pondered Liberty's character, all the while unthinkingly drawing the plunger's descent, millimeter by millimeter, through the cafetière, the tray, and the bedsheets, then—this was free association's breakthrough—to plunge underground, via showering and sleeping miners, into the gold-containing bedrock under Johannesburg (fig. 101).[137] A tour-de-force of animation and a *mise en abyme* of the artist's method, the sequence confirmed to Kentridge his method of working. The plunger had found the film's subject. Liberty and her story abandoned, *Mine* unfolds between Soho's comfortable bed and underground tunnels and caves where the miners work and sleep.

Kentridge's films do not unfold exactly as the drawings' making did. Stories and settings take shape on the editing table, and with sounds and music as powerful unifiers. From 1989 to 1998, Angus Gibson edited the rushes shot in the artist's studio, submitting them to the sort of "revision" that dreams require for their reality effects. The mind, Freud wrote, demands unity, and if it cannot establish

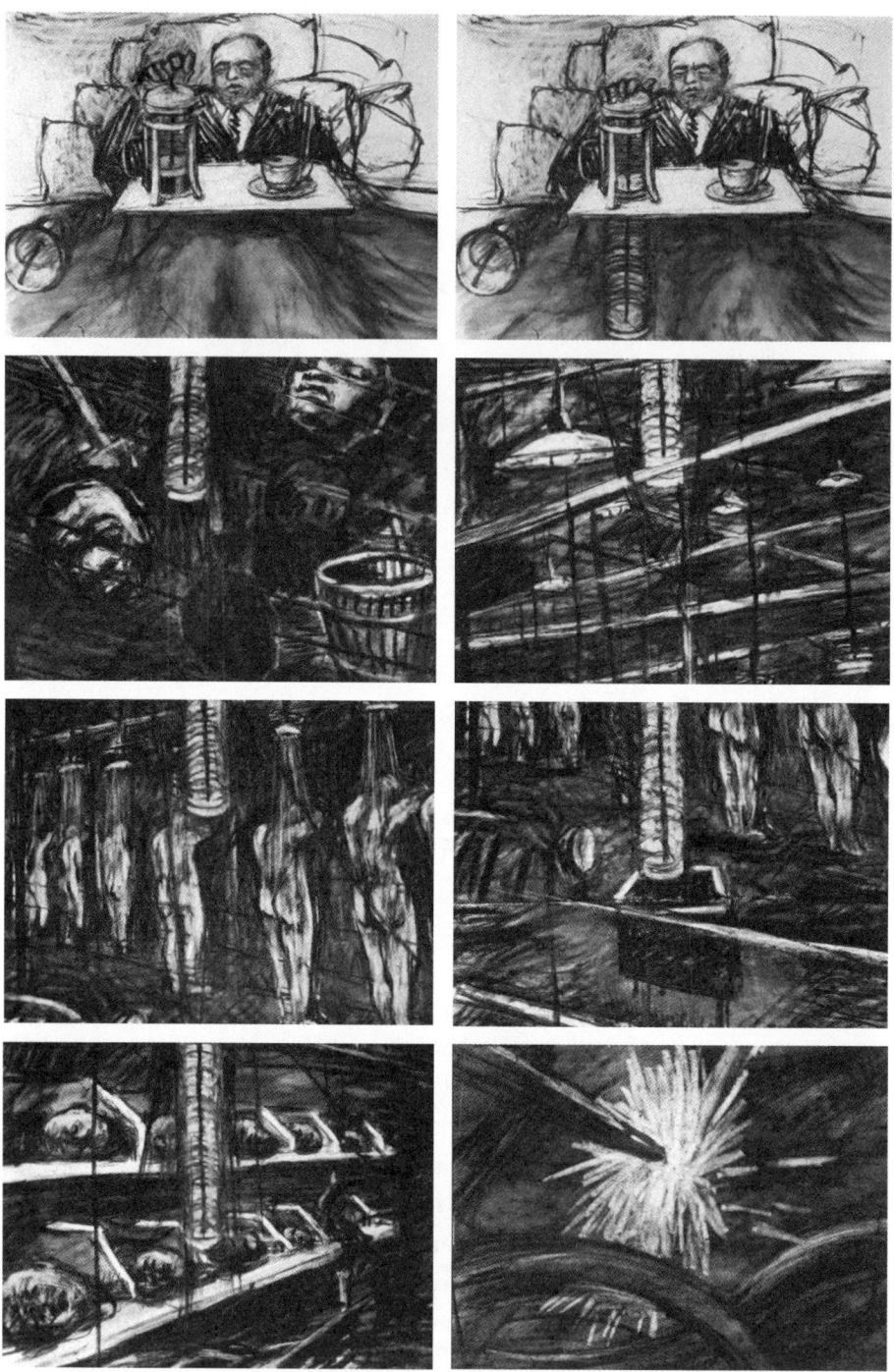

FIG. 101. Stills from William Kentridge, *Mine*, 1991. 16mm film transferred to video

true connection between thoughts or perceptions, "it does not hesitate to fabricate a false one."[138] In *Felix in Exile*, this cutting and pasting accomplished the dreamlike transitions between the landscape and interior, as well as the pivotal scene change from a body in the veld to a drawing of the body in the veld.

We are back where we began, at our first look at *that* drawing, finished and complete: an *Augenblick* before the animation began, permanently turning the drawing, mark by mark, into a different drawing (see fig. 65). And with this artist's practice, we have never really left that beginning, never escaped from his home studio, where Grahamstown, Paris, Cambridge Massachusetts, and London are all suburbs. Made in that studio, *Felix in Exile* takes place *in* the studio. Kentridge tells the story differently. In a text written for the film's first showing, Felix "is alone in a room (I assume in Paris, from the title of my first film)." *Johannesburg, 2nd Greatest City after Paris* had Europe in mind as a place to which Felix, consumed by his affair with Mrs. Eckstein, and last seen battling Soho, would escape (plate 26). Kentridge moved to Paris in 1981, and although he, alone of his family, returned to South Africa, the French capital remained an imaginary refuge. After the First World War and during the ensuing turmoil in eastern Europe, Paris did become home to artists from Russia, Ukraine, Belarus, Poland, Transylvania, and Lithuania. Dominated by foreign-born painters, the so-called School of Paris established the city as, artistically, the Greatest City. But exile was a more general condition for European Modernists in the interwar years. In 1937, when his works went on display in Nazi Germany as "degenerate," Beckmann fled to Amsterdam and painted *Death*, Kentridge's "beacon for endangered souls."

Whatever his inventor's assumption might have been, Felix could be in exile anywhere. With one electric bulb to light it and bare walls smudged as if with years of graffiti, the protagonist's dwelling place looks less like a hotel room than a prison cell. When they first appear in the film, those walls feature faint squares and rectangles (plate 30). These are ghosts of artworks to come. Several scenes later in the film, Nandi's drawings will flit through the air and stick to those walls like flypaper. Within the actual making of the film, though, the picture-filled walls came first. Kentridge created the empty room of the film's opening shot by erasing large swaths of the one drawing's earlier state, and as usual charcoal residues remained. From the start it is evident that Felix's place of exile is glimpsed in retrospect, literally marked by events to come. Fortuitously, those smudges also resemble picture-frame marks left over from a past occupancy—that is why if you take down a painting you often have to repaint the wall. Naked but always with his suitcase by his side, Felix hovers between arrival and departure. The film ends with him standing in a sinkhole in the veld, as if he has finally departed from the room, with the drawings in the suitcase nearby (plate 32). But this may be flash-back, just as the film's beginning was (see fig. 99). This makes Felix a prisoner of eternal return. But the palimpsest has more layers than this. Foretold initially by the charcoal traces on the walls, the gathering of Nandi's drawings conjures famil-iar scenarios. Each sketch is a blurred replica of one of Kentridge's "drawing for projection." The display is of semblances thrice removed, a drawing of a drawing of a photo of bodies in the veld, like the shadows in Plato's cave.

Another famous image, one culled from the story of European art, casts a shadow on this interior. The structure of Felix's gallery brazenly paraphrases the one surviving photograph of Kazimir Malevich's paintings as they hung in St. Petersburg in 1915 (fig. 102). Titled "The Last Futurist Exhibition 0.10," this legendary show announced an end of art history and a beginning. It is a "last" exhibition because Malevich will replace its so-called Cubo-Futurism (fusing French Cubism and Italian Futurism) with Suprematism. But the cryptic "0.10" announces that a new count has already begun. In Malevich's understanding, his abstract paintings turned the bend from past to future. Not only did they empty out (in his words) "any attribute of real life," causing the art of painting to become a wholly autonomous "end in itself."[139] By repeating, in white, red, or (especial-ly) black, the square format of the canvas, painting negates its material support. Like the show's contradictory title, however, Malevich's iconoclasm can be read in reverse, as a rival and reformation of *the icon*. The artist hung *Black Square*—the show's pivotal work—across the upper corner of the room, in the spot where, in Russian Orthodox homes, sacred effigies are traditionally hung—their east-fac-ing corner placement intensifies the visual concentration holy icons demand. Mounted in the second year of the Great War, during domestic turmoil in Russia that would lead to revolution in 1917, the exhibition envisions redemption beyond the current emergency.

Kentridge's art abounds in monochrome rectangles, triangles, and circles, and his limited palette of black and white accented in pure reds and blues pays homage to the Russian experiment in art. In 1986, he called that experiment "art in a state of hope." But he also announced that, in his "here and now," and know-ing what happened in post-revolutionary Russia in the name of the future, such hope seemed impossible: "I cannot paint pictures of a future like that and believe in the pictures." In a catalogue essay for the major Kentridge exhibition in Old St. John's Hospital in Bruges (2017), Benjamin Buchloh argued that the Malev-ich reference in *Felix in Exile* expresses a sense of "disenchanted belatedness, or marginal exclusion from the grand narratives of avant-garde history." Kentridge relishes superseded things, media, and styles. Among familiar objects to draw, he

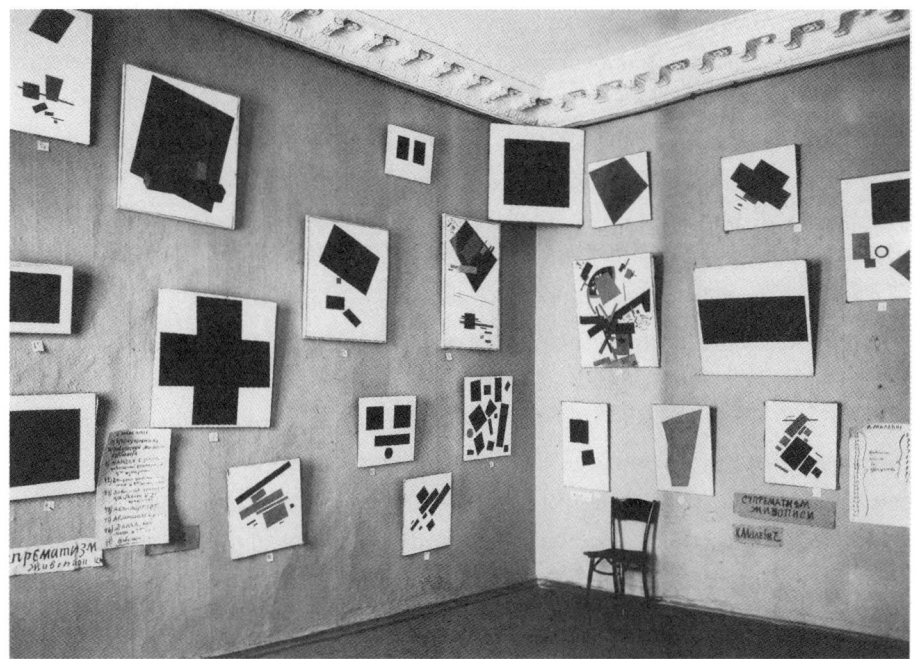

FIG. 102. Kazimir Malevich, *The Last Futurist Exhibition of Painting, Petrograd*, Winter 1915–16. Photograph, 67.7 × 49.2 cm. Russian State Archive of Literature and Art, Moscow

prefers outdated machinery: Bakelite telephones, hand-cranked record players, and office equipment of his grandfather's generation. His animation techniques reach back to the prehistory of cinema—to the phenakistiscope, zoetrope, flip-book, and stereoscope; he calls his animation technique "stone-age filmmaking"; and when he found his calling through the medium of charcoal, it was by way of a revival of interwar European art, and particularly of Beckmann. While admired by collectors and the public, Beckmann exerted little influence on other artists of the 1980s. Obsolescence functioned for Kentridge as an aesthetic and political counterstrategy responding to the conditions of South Africa, for which the adventures of the then-current avant-garde were hopelessly irrelevant. It was not just that the times were different under apartheid. Controlled, distorted, and resisted under colonial rule, time per se passed asynchronously as the siege state within which artists in South Africa lived and worked. From Kentridge's place of exile, avant-gardist redemption looked obsolete. In the transformed image of the Last Futurist show, the mysterious chair gets sat on, the lightbulb swarms with flies, and a bed appears for the weary. Attaching a dingy washbasin to the interior wall of Felix's cell, Kentridge "deletes all hope for the wall to retain any of its original pathos of austere abstraction."[140]

Yet like Malevich in his *Black Square*, Kentridge breaks and makes. In 1913 the Russian artist painted a version of *Black Square* on a backcloth he produced for *Victory Over the Sun*, a Futurist opera with atonal music and a libretto written in a nonsense language called Zaum. A stage designer himself, Kentridge would have appreciated the theatrical origins of European abstraction—how, in the 1915 installation, display walls replaced what had been a painted textile curtain. Behind that curtain, the actors could don their bizarre costumes, designed by Malevich, or retire to rest. Kentridge would also have recognized that, with its dynamic geometry and prop-like chair, the photograph of the "0.10" exhibition documents Futurist theater design. *Felix in Exile* builds on these and other resemblances, perhaps on photographs of the 1920 Dada Fair as well as ones of its Nazi parody (see figs. 58 and 59). Kentridge returns abstract painting to its origins as a stage setting. And while the bed, lightbulb, and sink domesticate the space, the pictures that come to hang there—drawings of Nandi's drawings of the veld—transform this interior into the image of the setting where the film itself was actually made. For in its hybrid of workspace, gallery, theater set, and home away from home, Felix's high-ceilinged prison cube stands for Kentridge's studio.

Felix in Exile began as work typically does in the studio, by playing with images and words: "Let me stress here that it is the process of working that gets my mind in gear." Having decided to make a film that could fit into an ongoing series of films, he started shuffling the letters in the name "FELIX," yielding the imperfect anagram "EXILE." Visual play commenced with two images, one fictional, the other real. The fictional image was of Soho shaving and losing his face in the mirror; the suggestive anagram put Felix in Soho's place. The real image consisted of those forensic pictures of bodies in the landscape that we have explored. Nandi was originally one of the murder victims. In the filmmaking process, her corpse preceded the development of her character, and in the film's storyline, we see her posthumously as flashback (fig. 103). The view of the veld into which her body vanishes opens and closes the film (plate 32; fig. 98). Drawing animated her. Kentridge's "dumb physical activity of stalking the drawing, or walking backwards and forwards between the camera drawing: raising, shifting, adapting the images," brought her to life.[141] With *Felix in Exile*, though, the play of words and images was checked by a requirement. Drawing and filming functioned "as a diary. That is to say a record of images and thoughts occupying me at the time of making it."[142] The bodies, Nandi, and all the rest belong to a record of the artist's internal life. This requirement helps explain the film's two scenes: one outside in the world, the other inside, with the sole inhabitant engaged with his mirror reflection.

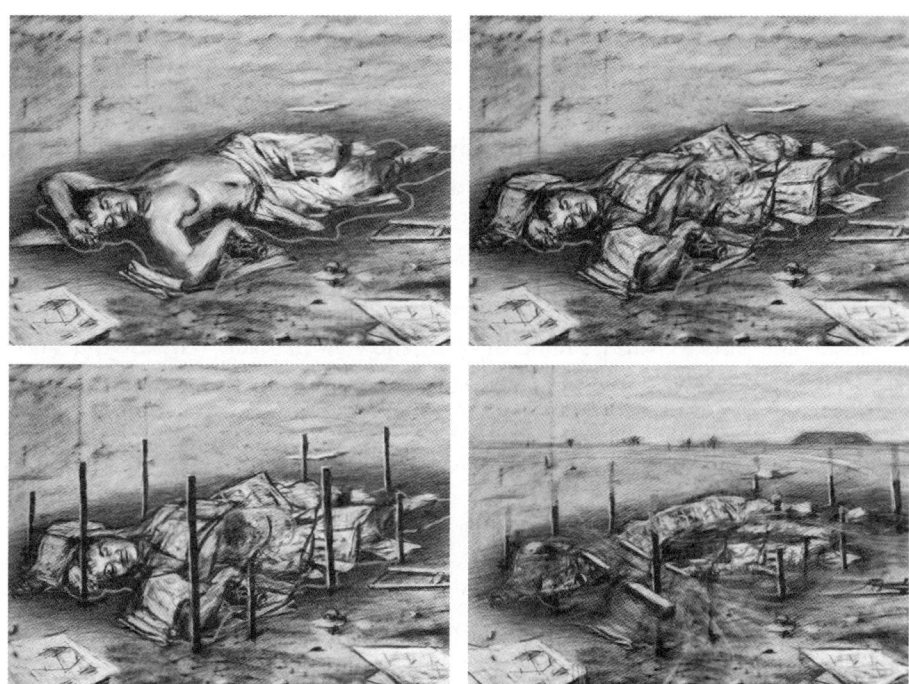

FIG. 103. Stills from William Kentridge, *Felix in Exile*, 1994. 35mm film transferred to video

While making the film, Kentridge would have received images from, and had thoughts about, events outside his studio. In April 1994 the formerly outlawed African National Congress (ANC) defeated the National Party, in power since 1948, in the country's first multiracial election. In May, Nelson Mandela took the oath of president of the National Unity Government, with F. W. de Klerk, his rival, as deputy president. But while *Felix in Exile* was being made, in the seven months preceding the peaceful transfer of power, the country came to the brink of civil war. The murder, on Easter Sunday 1993, of the charismatic Communist Party leader Chris Hani shook the period of relative tranquility following Mandela's release from prison in 1990. Key to a negotiated settlement between the ANC and the National Party, Hani had support among the militant youth in the townships. His assassination stoked fears that the ANC could not control its followers and that White South Africans, foreseeing chaos, would refuse compromise. A fair and efficient police investigation found Hani's White nationalist murderer to have been a recent immigrant from eastern Europe with possible ties to overseas neo-Nazi organizations. These facts blunted somewhat the divisive effect of the assassination. But continuing killing and torture by security forces, and massacres of ANC supporters in Boipatong and Bisho, dimmed prospects for non-violent change. Attacks against White civilians by the "military" wing of the Pan-Africanist Congress fostered an impression among affluent South Africans of being a people under siege. Leaving the country remained an option. The White population declined precipitously after 1994, but exile meant something different now from what it did under apartheid, while earlier forms of political activism became irrelevant or obsolete. This new state of siege presented a new artistic challenge.

The film begins out of doors. A sinkhole in the veld, filled with water rendered in pastel blue, cuts to Nandi's hand drawing the view in black, red, and blue, not as a landscape artist would, but as a surveyor might (see fig. 99). Nandi aims her vintage instruments (a theodolite, a sextant, and an extending telescope) at poles that rise like remnants of a border fence. What had been the labor of colonial appropriation, treating the land as *terra nullius* to be seized, divided, and owned, becomes in Nandi's hands an investigation of the crimes committed by the colonizers. The poles and sinkhole mark, and Nandi maps, bodies disappearing in the veld. In the past, in an era evoked by Nandi's vintage instruments, land surveying erased prior histories. But even in 1994 violence continued to rage in "new South Africa," the evidence of it again vanishing into landscape. This disappearance Nandi's drawings resist. They pass like wind-tossed leaves between the world and the studio to collect in a sheaf in Felix's suitcase. Whereas in earlier films Felix, as surrogate for the artist, would have made the drawings, here that activity passes to Nandi. Stepping into "tricky terrain" Kentridge observed, "There is a similarity between a painting or drawing—which is oblivious to its position in history—and the terrain itself, which also hides its history. I am really interested in the terrain's hiding of its own history, and the correspondence this has not only with painting, but with the way memory works."[143] Oblivious landscapes are the ones by South African painters a hundred years past, such as Pierneef and Volschenk: "A kloof and escarpment, a tree is celebrated. A particular fact is isolated and all ideas of process or history is abandoned. These paintings, of landscape in a state of grace, are documents of disremembering."[144]

There is no forest without shrapnel in the woods, no field path without bodies underfoot. "Landscape in a state of siege"—Kentridge's 1988 term for drawings he had undertaken—is a confusing motto. Is siege not something coming from outside, the enemy surrounding an enclave to force a surrender? Even the "political" or "fictional" sieges that a president or parliament might declare preserve this basic topography by treating perceived internal dissent like an external foe. Kentridge sometimes portrays the oppressed as a procession out on the veld turning towards the city, home, office, or studio, but such a confrontation would not yet be landscape in a state of siege. The phrase pictures an inverted topography in which an interior besieges the space around it. Its temporal analogue would be when, instead of being a brief interim, a siege would be the permanent condition—"not the exception but the norm," as Benjamin described siege states from the viewpoint of the oppressed.

Landscapes in a state of siege bear witness to the innumerable sieges that have occurred and will occur in them, shaping and scaping land into an historical palimpsest. And because at some time in its past every terrain has been the setting of human killing, landscapes in a state of siege are everywhere. Kentridge arrived at the phrase by reflecting on a faraway setting: forests in Poland, "deep gray-green pine trees and rolling hills in the soft European light," where a million people were gassed, buried, and burned. "The traces in the landscape are thin," new growth lower than the forest around, striations where buildings stood, "a null expanse that once was one of the Auschwitz crematoria." The veld around Johannesburg manifests its scars more openly. The only features an artist can fix upon to organize the ground plane into a receding vista are the residue of human incidents: overgrown traces of an abandoned foundation, "pieces of civil engineering, the lines of poles, culverts and fences."[145] Examined closely, the tabula rasa proves to be poorly erased and provisionally rescripted.

When he began to draw landscape in a state of siege, he did so in a deliberately arbitrary way, by driving some precise but random distance, "say 6.3 or 19.8 km," and sketching what happened to be there, avoiding any aesthetic preference for one view over another while also proving siege's ubiquity.[146] All the same in their setting, format, medium, and repertoire of features, the drawings executed on mining cash book pages nonetheless each offer a singular view: not posts, culverts, and pylons in general, but this stunted post, yawning culvert, pylon twisted in just this way. Their specificity makes the remnants into poignant ruins, as if, because it holds little interest yet has been drawn with such care, the view must be of huge interest to someone. The Romantics charged commonplace particulars with overwhelming personal emotion. Wordsworth finds his happiness collapse because of

> a Tree, among many, one,
> A single Field, which I have looked upon,
> Both of them speak of something that is gone.[147]

A unique tree remembered uniquely in poetry can affect others. William Blake confessed to being profoundly moved by Wordsworth's tree and field. Kentridge's trees and fields have a different charge, closer to Brecht's ethical despair. In response to Nazi book-burning, Brecht wrote of "dark times"

When talk about trees is nearly a crime
For it implies staying silent about injustice.[148]

Kentridge captures the "Tree, among many, one" for the evidence it gives of other people's losses. That makes his drawings emotional and ethical, and tender and terrifying (see fig. 95).

"The land is an unreliable witness," writes Kentridge, "It is not that it effaces all history, but events must be excavated, sought after in traces, in half-hidden clues."[149] His cash book drawings dig through the present killings documented on them, also through the remembered Sharpeville photographs and the East Rand Mines' cruelly factual inscriptions, to strata lying deeper underfoot: to gold that, discovered 130 years ago, brought Johannesburg about, and to the meteor strike, two billion years ago, that tilted up the earth's gold-filled crust. It matters to the drawings and to the films made of the drawings that Kentridge worked in charcoal. Easily made and easily wiped away, charcoal marks are impossible completely to erase. Like tiny splinters, the black particles—residue of twigs of wood that has been heated under oxygen-starved conditions—lodge too far into the paper's pulp to be removed. At first Kentridge considered this a liability:

> I got every kind of eraser, even an electric one. I tried to use shiny paper, different materials. It took me about a year and a half to understand that the erasures were part of the films. More than that—they were part of their meaning and part of their interest. They had to do with the sense of things.[150]

What does he mean by the "sense of things"? "Sense" encompasses practical, moral, and aesthetic senses as well as a bedrock in visual sensation. It connotes something important but ineffable: a structure of feeling that the artist wants to convey. The phrase fits the fugitive presence of the charcoal mark and of images themselves. Images may be divergent in the sense we make of them—witness the responses that Bosch's paintings have elicited—but they are nonetheless persistent and conspicuous. Instead of truth, they give us the *sense* thereof.

That charcoal cannot be completely eradicated also affirms a fragile hope. Kentridge often evokes reflections of the nineteenth-century German jurist and popular astronomer Felix Eberty. Eberty postulated that the light illuminating from every event on earth moved out from our planet at 186,000 miles per second. The *Augenblick*, as it were, travels with the light. Therefore, if someone were to stand at the right point in space, they could observe again every event that ever happened. "The air is thick with images," writes Kentridge, "time made dense with each event and its image, as if one could take a sheet of paper and swing it through the air, catching the images as they crashed into it."[151] Kentridge's 2012 installation *The Refusal of Time* updates this thought experiment through the science of black holes. Although they suck up everything that approaches their event horizon, including light, black holes are believed by most physicists to preserve all the information they swallow. The hope that evidence will remain, that it lies perpetually in wait, extends to the image-maker: "With each breath, we pump out images and transmit ourselves and traces of ourselves, sending our images [... :] here I am, here I am, here I am."[152]

Nandi drew the landscapes that Felix peruses. Felix has done something similar before. In *Johannesburg, 2nd Greatest City after Paris* he leafs through a sheaf of images mostly of Mrs. Eckstein, for whom he yearns. The watermarks in the pages of *Sheets of Evidence* recollect this episode by placing fugitive erotic imagery in the beholder's hands. Some of Nandi's drawings are erotic, as well. They feature her naked, bathing, and embraced by Felix, who arrives through his aqueous avatar, the fish (see fig. 99). Quick flashbacks of lovemaking establish a domestic perspective that the film will also transcend. Felix's exile is inward. A predicament and a privilege of White South Africans, it is reminiscent of what some Germans who stayed behind in Nazi Germany later called "internal immigration" and compared problematically to the difficulties actual émigrés endured. In the film's most famous portrait of inner exile—also Kentridge's first idea for the film—Felix looks at himself in the mirror while shaving and sees his face disappear with the razor's edge. "I will not survive my life" was Kentridge's diary association with this imagining.[153] In a meticulously engineered transition, Felix leans towards the mirror as if to find his reflection, his proximity now suggesting that his breath fogged up the glass. Splashing water on the surface, it clears not to his reflection but to redemptive waters, and through these to Nandi looking back at him (plate 31). Comforted, Felix's eyelids close, but a telescope extending through the mirror allows Nandi and him to see eye to eye. Having structured the film between divergent scenes, one inside Felix's prison, the other out of doors, one based on the original fantasy of the protagonist shaving, the other based on police photos of murdered bodies in the veld, Kentridge imagines ocular contact. Their *Augenblick* travels with light.

In *A Midsummer Night's Dream*, Tom Snout—one of the amateurs performing the play within the play—pretends to be a garden wall that separates Pyramus from Thisbe. Forming a slit with his hand he mimes the chink through which the lovers whisper (with tragic results). Although walls appear to imprison Felix, the wall in front of him is open to the audience. Angled to form a corner, the walls behind him operate like a theatrical set to divide and connect successive scenes. The language of theater took the word "scene" from the Greek *skēnē* (from *skia*, "shadow"), meaning the place of dramatic action. More specifically, it means the stage along with the front side of any background structure through which the actors enter and exit. In Plato's cave allegory, which like *Felix in Exile* hinges on a scene change between inside and outside, that theatrical background would be the wall or screen where the shadows are projected. When in *Romeo and Juliet* Shakespeare writes, "fair Verona, where we lay the scene," he meant that the stage in London where the company performed should be imagined as Verona. Classical drama as described by Aristotle observes a unity of place, but even dramas that moved across space and time preserve the impression of continuity on the understanding that a "scene" is simply "what is *seen* at a given moment."[154] Medieval morality plays focused the audience's attention on one figure who moved from episode to episode as stages in a continuous progress and illustrating one instructive truth. Flitting easily from drawing to drawing, but inhabiting continuously their own time and place, Kentridge's cameo self-portraits recollect the allegorical Everyman, Pilgrim, or Death of earlier drama. His film characters—Soho, Felix, Mrs. Eckstein, and Nandi—have to navigate, with at least a dream-like plausibility, space divided into scenes.

Historically, scenic space has been intimately bound up with siege. In countless cases in European theater the decisive events of war occur out of sight, on a battleground far away or in combat around the besieged castle where the scene is laid, to be described by an actor standing besieged, perhaps atop the defensive wall itself—Christopher Marlowe's *Tamburlaine*, Shakespeare's *Hamlet*, *Henry V*, and *Henry VI*, and later Restoration siege plays by John Dryden and William Davenant offer vivid examples. The stage constitutes a place besieged. Its back wall, in English dramatic practice termed the tiring-house wall, divides inside from outside, fiction from life, such that any backdrop might be imagined as a defensive wall.

Besieged in the stage set of a room, prison, cave, gallery, or studio, Felix assumes the familiar role of melancholic protagonist who, imprisoned literally or psychologically, perceives life as shadow or dream. "What is life?" asks Calderón's Segismundo, sent back to his eternal prison cell after an artfully staged and dream-like release: "A frenzy. What is life? A vain hope, a shadow, a fiction. The greatest good is fleeting, for all life is a dream and even dreams are but dreams."[155] Benjamin preferred the term "mourning play" (*Trauerspiel*) for post-classical tragedy, because in such plays the hero does not decide, as Greek heroes do—tragically to their ruin, though confirming by their difficult choice the structure of the cosmos. The mourning play, by contrast, divides action between impulsive violence and indecision. Its heroes are tyrants or martyrs. Kentridge's Soho is both.[156]

Benjamin rethought Schmitt's definition of the sovereign as "he who decides on the exception."[157] He proposed instead that rulers, through their decision, resolve the state of exception: they seek to end the state of siege that is the mourning play's essential setting. But the heroes of the obscure German dramas he studied, plays written and performed during a disastrous century of confessional conflict and civil war, cannot decide, or do so impotently, like King Herod, in frenzied rage, destroying themselves and their court. Although they focus on history—the worldly domain of significant events—human action is either random or wanting, and ultimately fails. As Benjamin put it, "History wanders into the setting"—that is, in German, into the *Schauplatz*, literally "show place." Along with Freud's *Tummelplatz*, "show place" serves as another analogue to Kentridge's studio.[158] What Benjamin means is that human action passes into the scenery behind the actor, in the form of ruinous nature, of natural history.

In Kentridge, history wanders into the veld. His films are mourning plays, and these, according to Benjamin, "are not so much plays that make one mournful as plays through which mourning finds satisfaction: plays for the mournful."[159] *Felix in Exile* ends where it begins: in a landscape in the state of siege (plate 32). The initial view of the watery sinkhole turns out to be Nandi's grave. Her body, like the murdered ones she drew in black and red, has disappeared into the veld. In the film's final shot, which uses the same charcoal drawing as the initial scene, Felix stands in the sinkhole of mourning. With his back towards us, he agitates the waters with his hands as if to see through its surface, as he did with the mirror, when he saw his image disappear. This may be yet another of Felix imaginings, a drawing or shadow observed by him inside his cave. Yet he stands decidedly out of doors, not quite under the sun, because the charcoaled sky forbids such illumination.

Socrates gives no answer to the question raised by his allegory. How can someone who has seen the real world convince those who haven't that they behold mere illusions? How can the homecomer explain the situation to those who do not even know what a cave is? One answer is, you invoke an image, a fiction, of a cave with shadow-casting puppets, and you ask your listener mentally to behold it: "See human beings as though they were in an underground cave-like dwelling," instructs Socrates, to which Glaucon, having dutifully pictured it, exclaims, "It's a strange image." Making an image evades arguments that cannot be won in politics or in court and that, in the extreme case, doom the truth-teller. Socrates does not say that his imagining, with its scene changes, below ground and above, solves the dilemma. The image is simply self-evident: "I see," says Glaucon from beginning to end. The image will contain the fact about truth-telling (" 'Would they kill him?' 'No doubt about it,' he said"), yet can remain "impervious to cross-examination."

This is perhaps the best strategy for art in a state of siege. Kentridge is the home-comer who has seen the body in the veld and returned to give evidence in artful forms. *O felix culpa.*

Acknowledgments

This book took shape through several campaigns waged over fifteen years. Its triptych structure preserves the three-lecture format of the E. H. Gombrich Lectures on the Classical Tradition, which I was honored to deliver at the Warburg Institute in 2016. In turning these talks into a book, the structure's aptness came slowly to light, partly through comment by an anonymous reader, who spotted the resemblance. Many of the key works I explore were triptychs: panels, canvases, and prints displayed in threes, with connections and ruptures among the parts. It had been art history's most disruptive triptych—the winged ensemble by Hieronymus Bosch titled, provisionally, *The Garden of Delights*—that originally sparked my pursuit. Long engaged with Bosch's imagery but not wishing to get trapped in the maze of interpretations this famous triptych had generated, I ventured to explore, originally in the Louise Smith Bross Lectures delivered in Chicago in 2007, not the painted ensemble itself but the responses it had elicited from viewers in the past. My engagement with the writings of Carl Schmitt, reaching back to 1983, when my friend Frank Schirrmacher introduced me to them, led me to the jurist's interpretation of Bosch. Making sense of this reception, penned in a prison in Nuremberg in 1947 and yielding Schmitt's motto "the enemy is our own question as *Gestalt*," became the initial impulse of this book.

Current events magnified this impulse. The global "War on Terror" after the September 11 attacks, the administration of US domestic emergencies by a new Department of Homeland Security, the legal status of the Guantanamo Bay detention camp, and the posthumous return of Carl Schmitt to intellectual preeminence: these and more persuaded my colleague Noah Feldman and I to launch a new course—shared between Harvard Law School and the Graduate School of Arts and Sciences—on "the enemy." The course's second iteration coincided with Donald Trump's election to the US presidency. On the eve of the inauguration, students explored scenarios in which, through gray areas in the Constitution and during the next transfer of power, the United States might be ruled by emergency decree. Schmitt's Weimar-era writings on the crisis of constitutional democracy and on "states of exception" suddenly became plausible descriptions of America today. I am grateful to Noah for blazing a trail between law and the human. My collaborations with Bruno Latour related to the politics of climate change engaged critically with Schmitt's idea of a "nomos" of the earth and helped me understand emergency states also from a wider perspective. This the COVID-19 pandemic further encouraged.

While the feeling of being besieged became increasingly familiar, the phrase "state of siege" entered my vocabulary only lately, through the work of William Kentridge. For this illumination, for my reaching forward from Bosch to contemporary art, and for so much in my life I am grateful for, I am indebted to Margaret Koster Koerner, my dear wife. Inspired by Kentridge's 2012 Norton Lectures at Harvard, Meg—like me a specialist in Renaissance art—resolved creatively to work with the South African maker's relation to the art historical past. In 2017–18, at the Sint-Janshospitaal in Bruges (one of Europe's oldest extant hospital buildings), she curated a landmark exhibition centered on Kentridge's macabre masterpiece, the video installation *More Sweetly Play the Dance.* With key Early Netherlandish paintings displayed in the same sepulchral space, Meg drew a line from Bosch's time, when Bruges began its decline from global trade capital to melancholy Bruges-la-Morte, through Belgium's violent colonization of Africa and the experimental works of Marcel Broodthaers, to Kentridge. Written while the exhibition *William Kentridge: Smoke, Ashes, Fable* was being prepared, my Gombrich Lectures, and thus this book, followed with deepest gratitude Meg's brilliant design.

Curating the Bruges show took Meg often to Johannesburg. In 2014, we brought our co-taught Harvard graduate seminar on Kentridge to South Africa to observe the artist and his collaborators in action. For William Kentridge's friendship and generosity I will always be profoundly grateful. A pale shadow of his eloquent self-analysis, this book would not have been written without his inspiration and could not have been written without his sustained support. Deep thanks go to Anne Stanwix, who graciously hosted us on many occasions, and even with a troop of students in tow. I am also hugely indebted to Anne McIlleron for her help over these many years, and to her colleagues at William Kentridge Studio—Natalie Dembo, Damon Garston, and Joshua Trappler—who helped gather so many of the images and film stills reproduced in these pages.

Along with "art in a state of siege" another of Kentridge's mottos applies to the present book. "Finding the Less Good Idea" signals how, when pursuing the "best idea," cracks start to form, forcing the maker to decide whether to bandage those cracks with claims of certitude or instead to improvise with fragments and discover what might be made of them. Kentridge advises the latter, and founded Johannesburg's "Centre for the Less Good Idea" on this advice. For years my putative best idea had been a book on Bosch and Schmitt, but it remained "limping"—that was Bruno Latour's curt judgment of a draft. Progress was also interrupted by my work on a movie about Viennese homemaking. At the center of *The Burning Child* stood a portrait painted by my father—an artist by trade—in

1944 in Washington, DC. The painting depicted his mother and father safe in their upholstered apartment in Vienna's Leopoldstadt district. When he painted it, my father did not know of his parents' fate, but by 1941 letters from them had stopped arriving. Painted from memory, their portrait hints subtly at their state of siege. A window in the room gives a glimpse of top-story apartments across the street. From windows directly facing us, two denizens, tiny in their portrayal but disturbing in their effect, stare blankly back at us. Before he fled Vienna in 1938 my father heard from the shelter of that parental apartment the roar of his gentile neighbors' jubilation when Hitler marched into Vienna in triumph, and during the Nazi Party rally on April 9 in the Nordwestbahnhof, a block from his home. Interior design had been Vienna's signal contribution to modern architecture, yet home, however densely curtained and decorated, could not keep out the enemy. If anything, beauty pacified the homemaker and sparked envy in others. Expelled from their beloved apartment—their next-door neighbor, an early member of Austria's Hitler Movement, "Aryanized" the whole building—my grandparents were deported in 1942 to a camp outside Minsk, where they were killed on arrival.

I wrote my Gombrich Lectures in the midst of filming. Inspired by Meg to trace a vital arc from Bosch to Kentridge, but unsure what to speak about in the second lecture in between, I reached for a good idea: a streamlined survey of sieges in art from Nikolaus Meldemann's 1530 woodcut view of Vienna surrounded by Ottoman troops through Jacques Callot and Francisco Goya to Costa-Gavras's 1972 film *State of Siege*, which inspired Kentridge's phrase. Unfortunately, such a talk was not in my power, so I reached instead for a less good idea: the career of Beckmann's *Self-Portrait in Tuxedo* from its making to its current display. I had given casual gallery talks about Beckmann's canvas, which for some years hung one floor below my office at Harvard. I had used it as an ambassador to our museum and a prompt for conversation, but never studied it in depth. On an invitation from Yukio Lippit to speak at the Radcliffe Institute about universities as collectors, and stimulated by Jennifer Roberts's call for "slow looking," I improvised a lecture on Beckmann's *Self-Portrait*. With the editorial support of Jonathan Shaw and help from Lynette Roth, I published a transcription of that talk in *Harvard Magazine*. My less good idea of expanding this text into a Gombrich Lecture seems to have been a fortunate one, for the deeper I dug into Beckmann's art the more uncanny links to Bosch, Schmitt, and Kentridge I discovered.

Kentridge calls this method of anxious, hope-filled discovery "fortuna." I have been extremely fortunate to have benefited from many responsive communities to test my ideas. At the Warburg Institute, special thanks go to David Freedberg, my incisive discussant for the Gombrich Lectures. At U.C. Berkeley's Townsend

Center for the Humanities, thanks go to Whitney Davis, Timothy Hampton, Margaretta Lovell, James Porter, Jane Taylor, and Winnie Wong. At the University of Chicago, to Christine Mehring and Richard Neer. At Rice University, to Graham Bader, Leo Costello, and Joseph Manca. At the University of British Columbia, to Julia Orell. At the University of Antwerp and at Bad Homburg, to Vivian Liska. At the Center for Ballet and the Arts at NYU, to Jennifer Homans. In Vienna, to the late Wolfgang Achbauer, to Sylvia Liska and Catharina Kahane, and to my *Burning Child* collaborator, Christian Bruun. And on the storm-tossed summit of the Weissmies (4017m), to Valentin Groebner. To friends and colleagues in the Cambridge, MA area, several of whom engaged in teaching contexts with my work on Beckmann, I owe my heartfelt gratitude, in particular Quincy Amoah, Benjamin Buchloh, Homi Bhabha, Bo-Mi Choi, Bill Connor, Thomas Cummins, Hilary Field, Peter Galison, Eleanor Goerss, Jeffrey Hamburger, Caroline Jones, Daniel Jütte, Jinah Kim, Ewa Lajer-Burcharth, Matthew Liebmann, Sarah Mallory, Cristina Morilla, Lydia Mullin, Tamara Morsel-Eisenberg, Gregory Nagy, Veronika Poier, Sarah Rosenthal, David Roxburgh, Sebastian Smee, Paris Spies-Gans, David Stern, Ramie Targoff, and Sloane Volpe. Co-teaching two seminars on monuments with Sarah Eizabeth Lewis clarified this book's framing narrative. Conversations with Shawon Kinew about Aby Warburg and the autobiographical side of art history inspired my re-examination of Warburg's Kreuzlingen lecture. Co-teaching with Felipe Pereda a seminar on the imagery of witchcraft illuminated the "militant irony" (Northrop Frye) of the artists treated in this book and confirmed that the visualized symbols of the enemy were built to be inscrutable. And in joyous co-taught courses on Adam and Eve, Early Modern Curiosity, Ego Documents, and Art & Literature in a State of Siege, Stephen Greenblatt has been for years a defining interlocutor for my work. I owe an outsize debt of gratitude to these wonderful colleagues.

Further afield, thanks go to Daan van Heesch, for new research on Bosch, to Caroline Fowler and Hanneke Grootenboer for inspiring suggestions, to Alexander Nemerov for encouragement and critique, to Vivienne Koorland for insight into apartheid South Africa, to Susan Gosin, for firsthand insight into Kentridge at work, and to Stephanie Koerner, for inspiration and much more. I am grateful to my editor at Princeton University Press, Michelle Komie, who waited patiently for this, our second happy collaboration, and to Francis Eaves, Dave Luljak, Annie Miller, Terri O'Prey, and Jodi Price for shepherding the manuscript into print. It would be impossible to name all the students whose insights have influenced my work. Emphatic thanks go to Trent Barnes for exploring before me Kentridge's *Sheets of Evidence*, to Harmon Siegel for illuminating Kentridge as a mime, to Rosie

Collier for exploring subterranean Bosch, to Clio Takas for brilliantly glossing the English Renaissance stage as a siege space, and to Kirsten Burke, for innumerable insights, archival and bibliographical wizardry, and infectious love of art history. Without Kirsten's support as teaching fellow, virtual classroom aficionado, research assistant, and text editor, this book may never have come to print.

The year I finished this book I lost three luminous friends. Peter Weibel served, in my imagination, as my long lost Austrian brother. His insights into Vienna's siege mentality changed how I understood my childhood in that city. Francesco Pellizzi had been an alert and supportive reader of my work since my days in graduate school. My thoughts about the *Augenblick* of Bosch's triptych were written with him in mind. Bruno Latour had been, for thirty years, the implied reader of everything I wrote. The passing of my courageous and compassionate friend has made this book a lonelier communication than I could have imagined. Painfully aware of the calamitous nature of the present moment, Bruno directed this thought towards the next generation. In Bruno's spirit, and in deep gratitude for their patience with me, a scribbling father, I dedicate this book with love to my four children.

Notes

Kreuzlingen, 1923

1 Annotated typescript, Warburg Archive, Warburg Institute, London (Box 93, Folder 4).

2 Ernst H. Gombrich, *Aby Warburg: An Intellectual Biography* (London, 1970), pp. 23–24.

3 A. M. Meyer, "Aby Warburg in His Early Correspondence," *The American Scholar* 57, no. 3 (1988), p. 447.

4 Ibid., pp. 451–52.

5 Carl Georg Heise, *Persönliche Erinnerungen an Aby Warburg* (New York, 1947), pp. 20 and 42–50; Gombrich, *Aby Warburg*, p. 51.

6 Ron Chernow, *The Warburgs* (New York, 1994), pp. 224–30.

7 Ludwig Binswanger and Aby Warburg, *Die unendliche Heilung: Aby Warburgs Krankengeschichte*, ed. by Chantal Marazia and Davide Stimilli (Zurich, 2007), p. 252.

8 Ibid., p. 40.

9 Gerhard Fichtner, ed., *Sigmund Freud–Ludwig Binswanger: Briefwechsel 1908–1938*, (Frankfurt am Main, 1992), pp. 175–76.

10 Ben Shepherd, *A War of Nerves: Soldiers and Psychiatrists in the Twentieth Century* (Cambridge, MA, 2000), p. 21.

11 Franz Kafka, *The Office Writings*, ed. by Stanley Corngold, Jack Greenberg, and Benno Wagner, trans. by Eric Patton with Ruth Hein (Princeton, NJ, 2015), p. 339.

12 Sigmund Freud, *Beyond the Pleasure Principle*, trans. by James Strachey (New York, 1961), p. 35.

13 Ibid., p. 37.

14 Ibid., p. 30.

15 Sigmund Freud, "The Architecture of Hysteria," in Freud, *The Origins of Psychoanalysis: Letters to Fliess, Drafts and Notes, 1887–1902*, ed. by Marie Bonaparte, Anna Freud, and Ernst Kris, trans. by Eric Mosbacher and James Strachey (New York, 1954), p. 203.

16 Joseph Roth, *The Radetzky March*, trans. by Joachim Neugroschel (New York, 1996), p. 187.

17 Gombrich, *Aby Warburg*, p. 228; Claudia Naber, "'Heuernte bei Gewitter': Aby Warburg 1924–1929," in Robert Galitz and Brita Reimers, eds, *Aby M. Warburg: "Ekstatische Nymphe ... trauernder Flußgott"—Portrait eines Gelehrten* (Hamburg, 1995), pp. 104–29.

18 Binswanger and Warburg, *Unendliche Heilung*, p. 122.

19 Chernow, *Warburgs*, p. 206.

20 Ulrich Raulff, "Zur Korrespondenz Ludwig Binswanger–Aby Warburg," in Horst Bredekamp, Michael Diers, and Charlotte Schoell-Glass, eds, *Aby Warburg: Akten des internationalen Symposions, Hamburg 1990* (Weinheim, 1991), pp. 68–69.

21 Ludwig Binswanger, *Henrik Ibsen und das Problem der Selbstrealisation in der Kunst* (Heidelberg, 1949); Paul de Man, *Blindness and Insight* (New York, 1971), p. 39; Joseph Leo Koerner, *Die Suche nach dem Labyrinth* (Frankfurt am Main, 1983), pp. 19–23.

22 Galitz and Reimers, *Aby M. Warburg*, p. 8.

23 Gertrud Bing, "Aby M. Warburg: Vortrag anläßlich der feierlichen Aufstellung von Aby Warburgs Büste in der Hamburger Kunsthalle am 31. Oktober 1958," in Aby Warburg, *Ausgewählte Schriften und Würdigungen*, ed. by Dieter Wuttke, 2nd edn (Baden-Baden, 1980), p. 455.

24 Claudia Naber, "Pompeji in Neumexiko: Aby Warburgs amerikanische Reise," *Freibeuter* 38 (1988): 88–97.

25 Aby Warburg, *Images from the Region of the Pueblo Indians of North America*, trans. by Michael Steinberg (Ithaca, NY, 1995), p. 38.

26 Ibid., p. 1.

27 Ibid., p. 54.

28 Aby Warburg, *Bilder aus dem Gebiet der Pueblo-Indianer in Nord-Amerika: Vorträge und Fotografien*, ed. by Uwe Fleckner (Berlin, 2018), p. 33.

29 Warburg, *Images*, p. 30.

30 Uwe Fleckner, "'Almost No Picture is Free of Errors ...:' Distance and Its Loss in Aby Warburg's Photographic Practice," in Christine Chávez and Uwe Fleckner, eds, *Lightning Symbolism and the Snake Dance: Aby Warburg and Pueblo Art* (Berlin, 2022), p. 145.

31 Gerald Vizenor, *Manifest Manners: Narratives on Postindian Survivance* (Lincoln, NE, 1994).

32 Aby Warburg, *Schlangenritual: Ein Reisebericht*, ed. by Ulrich Raulff (Berlin, 1988), p. 60.

33 Cited in Gombrich, *Aby Warburg*, pp. 226–27.

34 Hans Prinzhorn, *Bildnerei der Geisteskranken* (Berlin, 1922); Karl Königseder, "Aby Warburg im 'Bellevue'," in Galitz and Reimers, *Aby M. Warburg*, p. 88.

35 Cited in Naber, "Pompeji," p. 88.

36 Gombrich, *Aby Warburg*, pp. 106–27.

37 Aby Warburg, *The Renewal of Pagan Antiquity*, trans. by David Britt (Los Angeles, 1999), pp. 90–108.

38 Warburg, "Fragment on the Nympha" (1900), cited in Gombrich, *Aby Warburg*, p. 108.

39 Gombrich, *Aby Warburg*, pp. 88.

40 Ibid., p. 71; Aby Warburg, *Frammenti sull'espressione: Grundlegende Bruchstücke zu einer pragmantische Ausdruckskunde*, ed. by Susanne Müller (Pisa, 2011), p. 26.

41 Bing, "Warburg," p. 464.

42 Naber, "Pompeji," p. 91.

43 Gombrich, *Aby Warburg*, p. 88.

44 Ibid., p. 20; Berndt Roeck, *Der junge Aby Warburg* (Munich, 1997), pp. 16–17.

45 Bing, "Warburg," p. 463.

46 Heise, *Persönliche Errinnerungen*, p. 43.

47 Werner Rappl, Gudrun Swoboda, Wolfram Pichler, and Marianne Koos, eds, *Mnemosyne-Bilderatlas: Begleitmaterial zur Ausstellung "Aby M. Warburg. Mnemosyne"* (Hamburg, 1994).

48 Peter H. Wilson, "Under Siege? Defining Siege Warfare in World History," in Anke Fischer-Kattner and Jamel Ostwald, eds, *The World of the Siege: Representations of Early Modern Positional Warfare* (Leiden, 2019), pp. 298–303.

49 Jean de Léry, *Histoire mémorable de la ville de Sancerre* ([Geneva], 1574), p. 135, 137–38. I am grateful to Stephen Greenblatt for bringing these recipes to my attention.

50 Ibid., p. 138.

51 Ibid., pp. 147–48.

52 Bertolt Brecht, *Mother Courage and Her Children*, trans. by Eric Bentley (New York, 1955), p. 34.

53 Giorgio Agamben, *State of Exception*, trans. by Kevin Attell (Chicago, 2005), p. 11.

54 Mikhail Bakhtin, *The Dialogic Imagination*, trans. by Caryl Emerson and Michael Holquist (Austin, TX, 1981), p. 84.

55 William Kentridge, "Beckmann's *Death*," in Sean Rainbird, ed., *Max Beckmann* (New York, 2003), p. 183.

56 See Michael Rothberg, *The Implicated Subject: Beyond Victims and Perpetrators* (Stanford, CA, 2019), pp. 87–118.

57 Gotthold Ephraim Lessing, *Laocoön: An Essay on the Limits of Painting and Poetry*, trans. by Edward Allen McCormick (Baltimore, 1962), p. 78.

58 See pp. 224–28 below.

59 Northrop Frye, *Anatomy of Criticism* (Princeton, NJ, 1957), p. 223; I am grateful to Felipe Pereda for reminding me of Frye's trenchant concept.

60 Walter Benjamin, "Theses on the Philosophy of History," in Benjamin, *Illuminations*, ed. by Hannah Arendt, trans. by Harry Zohn (London, 1970), p. 257 (original emphasis).

Hieronymus Bosch

1 Erwin Panofsky, *Korrespondenz 1910 bis 1968*, ed. by Dieter Wuttke (Wiesbaden, 2001–3), vol. 2, pp. 790–91.

2 Ibid., pp. 796–97.

3 Josef Derbolav, "Poiesis," in Joachim Ritter and Karlfried Gründer, eds, *Historisches Wörterbuch der Philosophie* (Basel, 1971–2007), vol. 7 (1989), p. 1023.

4 Erwin Panofsky, "Iconography and Iconology," in Panofsky, *Meaning in the Visual Arts* (New York, 1955), p. 32.

5 Ernst Cassirer, *The Philosophy of Symbolic Forms*, trans. by Ralph Manheim, 3 vols. (New Haven, CT, 1955); the original 1923–1929 German edition was published by Bruno Cassirer, Ernst Cassirer's cousin, who also published Max Beckmann.

6 Ernst Cassirer, *Die Idee der republikanischen Verfassung: Rede zur Verfassungsfeier am 11. August 1928* (Berlin, 1929).

7 Karen Michels, *Transplantierte Kunstwissenschaft: Deutschsprachige Kunstgeschichte im amerikanischen Exil* (Berlin, 1999), pp. 10–27.

8 "Panofsky Lectures," *The Harvard Crimson*, Febuary 14, 1934.

9 Erwin Panofsky, *Early Netherlandish Painting* (Cambridge, MA, 1958), p. 141.

10 Ibid., p. 141.

11 Ibid., p. 144.

12 Thomas Aquinas, *Summa Theologiae* 1, q. 1, a. 9. c; Panofsky, *Early Netherlandish Painting*, p. 142.

13 Panofsky, *Early Netherlandish Painting*, p. 141. For books written in the heyday of this critique, see Christopher Wood's review of Craig Harbison, *Jan van Eyck*; Joel M. Upton, *Petrus Christus*; and Jan Baptist Bedaux, *The Reality of Symbols*, in *Art Bulletin* 75, no. 1 (1993): 174–80.

14 Hugh of St. Victor, *De tribus diebus* 4.3; *Dies Irae* 5; see Hans Blumenberg, *Die Lesbarkeit der Welt* (Frankfurt am Main, 1981), pp. 51–53.

15 Erwin Panofsky, "Zum Problem der Beschreibung und Inhaltsbedeutung von Werken der bildenden Kunst" (1932), reprinted in Panofsky, *Aufsätze zu Grundfragen der Kunstwissenschaft*, ed. by Hariolf Oberer and Egon Verheyen (Berlin, 1992), pp. 85–89; Panofsky, *Studies in Iconology* (Oxford, 1939), pp. 3–32; and Panofsky, "Iconography and Iconology," pp. 26–54.

16 Panofsky, "Iconography and Iconology," p. 26.

17 Martin Heidegger, *Kant und das Problem der Metaphysik* (Bonn, 1929), p. 192; Panofsky, "Zum Problem der Beschreibung," p. 92.

18 Panofsky, "Iconography and Iconology," p. 26

19 Ibid.

20 Ibid.

21 Ibid., p. 27.

22 Aristotle, *Nicomachean Ethics* 8.1.4, Bekker 1155a25 (trans. by David Ross and Lesley Brown [Oxford, 2009]).

23 Leon Battista Alberti, *On Painting*, trans. by Cecil Grayson (London, 1972), p. 60.

24 The diptych is divided between the Royal Collection, Hampton Court and the collection of the earl of Radnor, Longford Castle.

25 *Frankfurter Zeitung*, November 19, 1935; Gopal Balakrishnan, *The Enemy: An Intellectual Portrait of Carl Schmitt* (London, 2000), p. 188.

26 Ernst Fabian, "Der erste Versuch, in Zwickau ein Museum zu errichten," *Mitteilungen des Altertumsverein für Zwickau und Umgebung* 11 (1914): 1–13. See pp. 119–22 below.

27 Erwin Panofsky, "Jan van Eyck's Arnolfini Portrait," *Burlington Magazine* 64, issue 372 (March 1934), pp. 117–19, 122–27.

28 Margaret L. Koster, "The Arnolfini Double Portrait: A Simple Solution," *Apollo* 258, no. 499 (2003): 3–14.

29 Panofsky, *Early Netherlandish Painting*, p. 357.

30 Ludovico Guicciardini, *Descrittione di tutti i Paesi Bassi, altrimenti detti Germania Inferiore* (Antwerp, 1567), p. 98. Facts about Bosch have been greatly clarified and simplified by the Bosch Research and Conservation Project (BRCP). See Matthijs Ilsink et al., *Hieronymus Bosch, Painter and Draughtsman: Catalogue Raisonné* (Brussels, 2016), and Luuk Hoogstede et al., *Hieronymus Bosch, Painter and Draughtsman: Technical Studies* (Brussels, 2016), referred to henceforth as BRCP1 and BRCP2 respectively. For literature from before 1983, see Walter S. Gibson, *Hieronymus Bosch: An Annotated Bibliography* (Boston, MA, 1983).

31 Panofsky, *Early Netherlandish Painting*, p. 357.

32 Johannes Adelphus, *Das Buch des Lebens*, Part 2 of Hieronymus Brunschwig, *Medicinarius: Das Buch der Gesundheit* (Strasbourg, 1505), p. CXXXIVv; Panofsky, *Early Netherlandish Painting*, p. 358, where the page reference is in error.

33 Wilhelm Fraenger, *Hieronymus Bosch*, trans. by Helen Sebba (New York, 1983).

34 For example, already Panofsky, *Early Netherlandish Painting*, p. 511 n. 7.

35 The Wilhelm Fraenger-Institut Berlin. See Petra Weckel, *Wilhelm Fraenger (1890–1964): Ein subversiver Kulturwissenschaftler zwischen den Systemen* (Potsdam, 2000).

36 Max Beckmann, *Briefe*, ed. by Klaus Gallwitz, Uwe M. Schneede, and Stephan von Wiese, 3 vols (Munich, 1993–95), vol. 1: *1899–1925* (1993), p. 225.

37 Wilhelm Fraenger, "Max Beckmann: Der Traum; Ein Beitrag zur Physiognomik des Grotesken" (1924), in Fraenger, *Von Bosch bis Beckmann: Ausgewählte Schriften* (Cologne, 1985), p. 310.

38 Carl Zuckmayer, *Als wär's ein Stück von mir: Horen der Freundschaft* (Frankfurt am Main, 1966), p. 253.

39 Oskar Kokoschka, *My Life*, trans. by David Britt (New York, 1974), p. 21.

40 Zuckmayer, *Als wär's ein Stück*, p. 254.

41 Peter Laregh, *Heinrich George: Komödiant seiner Zeit* (Munich, 1992), p. 45.

42 Wilhelm Fraenger, *Jörg Ratgeb, ein Maler und Märtyrer aus dem Bauernkrieg*, ed. by Gustel Fraenger and Ingeborg Vaier-Fraenger (Dresden, 1972).

43 Fraenger, *Bosch bis Beckmann*, pp. 34–50.

44 Wilhelm Fraenger, *Der Bauern-Bruegel und das deutsche Sprichwort* (Zurich, 1922).

45 Weckel, *Wilhelm Fraenger*, pp. 53–65; Gombrich, *Aby Warburg*, pp. 30–37.

46 Walter Gibson, review of Wilhelm Fraenger, *Hieronymus Bosch*, in *Speculum* 72, no. 4 (1997), p 1171.

47 Elmar Jansen, "Vorbemerkung," in Wilhelm Fraenger, "Korrespondenz mit Hans Arp, Carl Schmitt, und Franz Roh," *Sinn und Form* 3 (2005), p. 306.

48 Ibid.

49 Max J. Friedländer, *Early Netherlandish Painting*, 5, *Geertgen tot Sint Jans and Jerome Bosch*, trans. by Heinz Norden (New York, 1969), p. 88, cat. no. 10.

50 Fraenger, *Hieronymus Bosch*, p. 10; Eduard Beuss, "Symbol," in *Die Religion in Geschichte und Gegenwart*, 3rd edn, Kurt Galling (Tübingen, 1962), vol. 6, col. 540.

51 Irenaeus, *Exposure and Refutation of Knowledge [Gnosis] Falsely So-Called.*

52 See pp. 52–60 above.

53 Fraenger, *Hieronymus Bosch*, pp. 20–24, citing Paul Frédéricq, *Corpus documentorum inquisitionis haereticae pravitatis neerlandicae* (Ghent, 1889), vol. 1.

54 Raoul Vaneigem, *The Movement of the Free Spirit*, trans. by Randall Cherry and Ian Patterson (New York, 1998), p. 189; Frédéricq, *Corpus*, p. 271.

55 Vaneigem, *Movement*, p. 189; Frédéricq, *Corpus*, p. 271.

56 Hugh Trevor-Roper, *The European Witch-Craze of the Sixteenth and Seventeenth Centuries and Other Essays* (New York, 1969), p. 116.

57 Gibson, review of Fraenger, *Hieronymus Bosch*, p. 1172.

58 Fraenger, *Hieronymus Bosch*, pp. 15, 14.

59 Sigmund Freud, "Negation" (1925), trans. by Joan Riviere, in Freud, *General Psychological Theory: Papers on Metapschology*, ed. by Philip Rieff (New York, 1963), p. 213; and Freud, *Dora: An Analysis of a Case of Hysteria*, ed. by Philip Rieff, trans. by James Strachey (New York, 1969), p. 75.

60 Adolf von Harnack, *Marcion: Das Evangelium vom fremden Gott* (Leipzig, 1921).

61 Benjamin Lazier, *God Interrupted: Heresy and the European Imagination between the World Wars* (Princeton, NJ, 2008); on Harnack's impact, see pp. 29–33.

62 Wilhelm Fraenger, *Hieronymus Bosch: Das tausendjährige Reich; Grundzüge einer Auslegung* (Coburg, 1947).

63 Weckel, *Wilhelm Fraenger*, p. 138

64 Ibid., pp. 154–55.

65 Ibid., p. 65.

66 Carl Schmitt, *The Concept of the Political*, trans. by

George Schwab, expanded edn (Chicago, 2007), p. 26.

67 Ibid.

68 Ibid., p. 30.

69 Ibid., p. 19.

70 Carl Schmitt, *Political Theology: Four Chapters on the Concept of Sovereignty*, trans. by George Schwab (Chicago, 1985), pp. 31–32.

71 Ibid., p. 5.

72 Schmitt, *Concept of the Political*, p. 7.

73 Schmitt, *Political Theology*, p. 5.

74 Reinhard Mehring, *Carl Schmitt: Aufstieg und Fall* (Munich, 2009), pp. 200–304.

75 Carlo Galli, *Janus's Gaze: Essays on Carl Schmitt*, ed. by Adam Sitze, trans. by Amanda Minervini (Durham, NC, 2015), pp. 12–26.

76 Carl Schmitt, *Dictatorship: From the Origin of the Modern Concept of Sovereignty to the Proletarian Class Struggle*, trans. by Michael Hoelzl and Graham Ward (Cambridge, 2014).

77 Carl Schmitt, "Der Führer schützt das Recht," *Deutsche Juristen-Zeitung*, 39, 1 August 1934, cols 945–48.

78 Carl Schmitt, *Antworten in Nürnberg*, ed. by Helmut Quaritsch (Berlin, 2000), p. 53.

79 Raphael Gross, *Carl Schmitt and the Jews*, trans. by Joel Golb (Madison, WI, 2007), pp. 31, 73.

80 Ibid., p. 26.

81 Schmitt, *Concept of the Political*, p. 27.

82 Gross, *Carl Schmitt and the Jews*, pp. 36, 178.

83 Letter from Günther Krauss to Carl Schmitt, May 18, 1932, cited in Mehring, *Carl Schmitt*, p. 362.

84 Heinrich Meier, *The Lesson of Carl Schmitt: Four Chapters on the Distinction between Political Theology and Political Philosophy*, trans. by Marcus Brainard (Chicago, 1998), p. 153.

85 Mehring, *Carl Schmitt*, pp. 330–33.

86 Carl Schmitt, *The Leviathan in the State Theory of Thomas Hobbes: Meaning and Failure of a Political Symbol*, trans. by George Schwab and Erna Hilfstein (Westport, CT, 1996).

87 Thomas Hobbes, *Leviathan*, ed. by Richard Tuck, rev. edn (Cambridge, 1996), p. 89.

88 Schmitt, *Leviathan*, p. 43.

89 Ibid., p. 9.

90 Gross, *Carl Schmitt and the Jews*, pp. 155–65.

91 Schmitt, *Leviathan*, p. 60.

92 Jansen, "Vorbemerkung," p. 306.

93 Schmitt, *Antworten*, p. 11.

94 Carl Schmitt, *Writings on War*, ed. and trans. by Timothy Nunan (Cambridge, 2011), pp. 125–97.

95 Schmitt, *Antworten*, pp. 11–27.

96 Ibid., p. 55.

97 Ibid., pp. 27 and 66.

98 Carl Schmitt, *Ex Capitivitate Salus*, ed. by Andreas Kalyvas and Federico Finchelstein, trans. by Matthew Hannah (Cambridge, 2017), p. 60.

99 Ibid., pp. 63–72.

100 Ibid., p. 63.

101 Ibid., p. 65.

102 Letter of Schmitt to Fraenger, January 5, 1947, in Fraenger, "Korrespondenz," p. 321.

103 Letter of Schmitt to Fraenger, February 7, 1947, in Fraenger, "Korrespondenz," p. 322.

104 Wilhelm Fraenger, "Hieronymus Bosch: Johannes auf Patmos; Eine Umwendtafel für den Meditationsgebrauch," *Zeitschrift für Religions- und Geistesgeschichte* 2 (1949–50): 327–45; in Fraenger, *Hieronymus Bosch*, pp. 247–55.

105 Aelbertus Cuperinus, *Merckelicke geschiedenis der stat vanden Bosch in tyden van hartoge Philips van Brabant*, in Cornelius Rudolphus Hermans, *Verzameling van Kronyken, Charters en Oorkonden betrekkelijk de Stad en Meijerij van 's Hertogenbosch* ('s-Hertogenbosch, 1848), p. 69; Fraenger, *Hieronymus Bosch*, p. 429 n. 95.

106 J. Becker, " 's-Hertogenbosch de oudste Joodse gemeente in de Noordelijke Nederlanden," *Studia Rosenthaliana* 18 (1984), p. 77.

107 Fraenger, *Hieronymus Bosch*, p. 255.

108 Fraenger, "Korrespondenz," pp. 311, 318.

109 Schmitt, *Antworten*, p. 60.

110 Fraenger, "Korrespondenz," p. 311.

111 Letter of Fraenger to Schmitt, May 26, 1943, cited in Weckel, *Wilhelm Fraenger*, p. 137.

112 Helmuth Kiesel, ed., *Ernst Jünger–Carl Schmitt: Briefe 1930–1983* (Stuttgart, 1999), p. 164.

113 Léon Bloy, *Le Salut par les Juifs*, rev. ed. (Paris, 1906), pp. 27, 29–30, 35.

114 Kiesel, *Ernst Jünger–Carl Schmitt*, p. 164.

115 Ibid., p. 167.

116 Fraenger, *Hieronymus Bosch*, p. 143.

117 Schmitt, *Leviathan*, p. 24.

118 Antonio De Beatis, *The Travel Journal of Antonio de Beatis: Germany, Switzerland, the Low Countries, France and Italy, 1517–1518*, ed. by J. R. Hale, trans. by J. R. Hale and J.M.A. Lindon (London, 1979), pp. 1–7.

119 Ibid., pp. 57, 9.

120 Ibid., pp. 82–83.

121 Ibid., pp. 132, 95.

122 Ibid., p. 94.

123 Ernst H. Gombrich, "The Earliest Description of Bosch's *Garden of Delight*," *Journal of the Warburg and Courtauld Institutes* 30, no. 1 (1967): 403–6; Jan Karel Steppe, "Bijdrage tot de historische en de ikonografische studie van zijn werk," in Steppe, *Jheronimus Bosch. Bijdragen bij gelegenheid van de herdenkingstentoonstelling te 's-Hertogenbosch* ('s-Hertogenbosch, 1967), pp. 7–12, 28–30; and Jan Karel Steppe, "Problemen betreffende het werk van Hieronymus Bosch," *Verhandelingen von de Koninklijke Vlaamse Academie voor Wetenschappen, Letteren*

en Schone Kunsten von België 24 (1962): 166–67.

124 Ernst H. Gombrich, *The Heritage of Apelles* (Oxford, 1976), p. 90.

125 De Beatis, *Travel Journal*, p. 95.

126 Jeffrey Ashcroft, *Albrecht Dürer: Documentary Biography*, 2 vols (New Haven, CT, 2017), vol. 1, p. 560.

127 Ibid.

128 Maryan W. Ainsworth, Stijn Alsteens, and Nadine M. Orenstein, *Man, Myth, and Sensual Pleasures: Jan Gossart's Renaissance* (New York and New Haven, CT, 2020), pp. 222–23.

129 Hans Cools, *Mannen met macht: Edellieden en de Moderne Staat in de Bourgondisch-Habsburgse Landen (1475–1530)* (Zutphen, 2001), pp. 268–72.

130 Ashcroft, *Albrecht Dürer*, vol. 1, p. 155.

131 Ernst Münch, *Geschichte des Hauses Nassau-Oranien*, 3 vols (Aachen, 1933), vol. 3, pp. 71–72; Pater Gerlach, "Hendrik III van Nassau, heer van Breda, veldheer, diplomaat en mecenas," *Brabantia* 20 (1971): 48–52, 87–94.

132 Richard Vaughan, *Charles the Bold* (London, 1973), pp. 84–122.

133 Pierre François Xavier de Ram, *Documents relatifs aux troubles du pays de Liège, sous les princes-évêques Louis de Bourbon et Jean de Horne, 1455–1505* (Brussels, 1944), p. 239.

134 De Beatis, *Travel Journal*, p. 94.

135 See p. 92 above.

136 Merriam Sherwood, "Magic and Mechanics in Medieval Fiction," *Studies in Philology* 44 (1947): 567–92.

137 Cools, *Mannen met macht*, p. 270; Münch, *Geschichte*, vol. 3, pp. 160–61.

138 Jos Koldeweij, Paul Vandenbroeck, and Bernard Vermet, *Hieronymus Bosch: The Complete Paintings and Drawings* (Rotterdam, 2001), p. 110.

139 Otto Kurz, "Four Tapestries after Hieronymus Bosch," *Journal of the Warburg and Courtauld Institutes* 30, no. 1 (1976): 150–62.

140 Ibid., p. 151.

141 Richard Clough to Sir Thomas Gresham, August 21, 1566; published in J.-M.-B.-C. Kervyn de Lettenhove, ed., *Relations politiques des Pays-Bas et de l'Angleterre sous le règne de Philippe II*, 11 vols (Brussels, 1882–1900), vol. 4 (1884), p. 338, cited in Andrew Spicer, *Calvinist Churches in Early Modern Europe* (Manchester, 2007), p. 109.

142 Jonathan Israel, *The Dutch Republic* (Oxford, 1995), pp. 155–68.

143 Felipe de Guevara, "Commentaries on Painting," in James Snyder, ed., *Bosch in Perspective* (Englewood Cliffs, NJ, 1973), p. 29.

144 Guicciardini, *Descrittione*, p. 19; Giorgio Vasari, *Le opere*, ed. by Gaetano Milanese, 9 vols in 10 (Florence, 1878–85), vol. 5 (1880), p. 439.

145 Dominicus Lampsonius, *Pictorum aliquot celebrium Germaniae Inferior effigies* (Antwerp, 1572), plate 7, p. Av; in Lampsonius, *The Life of Lambert Lombard (1565) and Effigies of Several Famous Painters from the Low Countries*, ed. and trans. by Edward H. Wouk (Los Angeles, 2021), p. 114.

146 Paul Vandenbroeck, "High Stakes in Brussels, 1567: The *Garden of Delights* as the Crux of the Conflict between William the Silent and the Duke of Alva," in Jos Koldeweij, Bernhard Vermet, and Barbera van Kooij, eds, *Hieronymus Bosch: New Insights into His Life and Works* (Rotterdam, 2001), p. 88.

147 Ibid.

148 Daan van Heesch, "Paulus de Kempenaer and the Political Exploitation of Hieronymus Bosch in the Dutch Revolt," *Simiolus* 41 (2019), pp. 6–7.

149 Vandenbroeck, "High Stakes," p. 89.

150 Schmitt, *Ex Captivitate Salus*, pp. 53, 56.

151 Schmitt, *Political Theology*, p. 36.

152 Schmitt, *Ex Captivitate Salus*, p. 60.

153 Schmitt, *Leviathan*, p. 24.

154 Carl Schmitt, "The Age of Neutralizations and Depoliticizations" (1929), in Schmitt, *Concept of the Political*, p. 95.

155 Karel van Mander, *Lives of the Illustrious Netherlandish and German Painters*, ed. by Hessel Miedema (Doornspijk, 1994), pp. 193–94.

156 Jan Grauls, *Volkstaal en volksleven in het werk van Pieter Bruegel* (Antwerp, 1957), p. 116.

157 Mander, *Lives*, p. 190.

158 Lionel Penrose and Roger Penrose, "Impossible Objects: A Special Type of Visual Illusion," *British Journal of Psychology* 49, no. 1 (1958): 31–33.

159 On picture puzzles, see pp. 291–94, below.

160 Julián Zarco Cuevas, "Inventario de las alhajas, relicarios, estatuas, pinturas, tapices y otros objetos de valor y curiosidad donados por el rey don Felipe II al Monasterio de El Escorial," *Boletín de la Real Academia de la Historia* 96 (1930), p. 657.

161 Matthias Wivel et al., *Titian: Love, Desire, Death* (New Haven, CT, 2021), p. 195.

162 Lodovico Dolce, in Giovanni Gaetano Bottari, ed., *Raccolta di lettere sulla pittura, scultura ed architettura, scritte da' più celebri personaggi [...]*, 8 vols (Rome, 1754–1825), vol. 3 (1759), pp. 259–60.

163 José de Sigüenza, "History of the Order of St. Jerome" (1605), in Snyder, *Bosch in Perspective*, p. 34.

164 Ibid., p. 37.

165 José de Sigüenza, *Historia de la Orden de San Jerónimo*, ed. by Juan Catalina García, 2 vols (Madrid, 1909), vol. 2, p. 637. The Bosch Research and Conservation Project deemed the panel "Workshop or follower of Hieronymus Bosch" and conjectures that its poplar support suggests a function as decorative tabletop (BRCP1,

p. 473; BRCP2, p. 34).

166 Sigüenza, "History", p. 37.

167 Fraenger, *Hieronymus Bosch*, p. 43.

168 Weckel, *Wilhelm Fraenger*, p. 137; Fraenger, *Hieronymus Bosch*, p. 298.

169 Geoffrey Parker, *The Grand Strategy of Philip II* (New Haven, CT, 1998), p. 17; Ernst H. Kantorowicz, *The King's Two Bodies: A Study in Medieval Political Theology* (Princeton, NJ, 1957). Kantorowicz's is a prehistory to Carl Schmitt's account of state formation.

170 George Kubler, *Building the Escorial* (Princeton, NJ, 1982), pp. 12–19.

171 Parker, *Grand Strategy*, p. 17; also, Geoffrey Parker, *The World is Not Enough* (Waco, TX, 2001).

172 Paul Vandenbroeck, "The Spanish *inventarios reales* and Hieronymus Bosch," in Koldeweij, Vermet, and van Kooij, *Hieronymus Bosch: New Insights*, p. 53.

173 As transcribed in Zarco Cuevas, "Inventario," p. 657.

174 Vandenbroeck, "Spanish *inventarios*," p. 53.

175 De Beatis, *Travel Journal*, p. 94

176 José Manuel Cruz Valdovinos, "La clientela de El Bosco," in *El Bosco y la tradición pictórica de lo fantástico* (Barcelona, 2006), p. 188 n. 38.

177 Sigüenza, *Historia*, vol. 2, p. 637.

178 *Madroño* is taken to mean "strawberry" in Walter S. Gibson, "The Strawberries of Hieronymus Bosch," *Cleveland Studies in the History of Art* 8 (2003): 24–33.

179 Sigüenza, "History", p. 38.

180 Ibid., p. 34.

181 Ignacio García Aguilar, "De saberes silenciados en la celda de fray José de Sigüenza," in Dámaris Montes, Víctor Lillo, and María José Vega, eds, *Sabres inestables: Estudios sobre expurgación y censura en la España de los siglos XVI y XVII* (Madrid, 2018), pp. 201–22.

182 Van Heesch, "Paulus de Kempenaer," pp. 6–7.

183 Sigüenza, "History", p. 35.

184 Francesco Pacheco, *Arte de la pintura, su antiguedad e grandezas* (Seville, 1649), p. 432.

185 Francisco de Quevedo, "Alguacil del Parnaso [...]" (1620), quoted in Helmut Heidenreich, "Hieronymus Bosch in Some Literary Contexts," *Journal of the Warburg and Courtauld Institutes* 33, no. 1 (1970), p. 182.

186 Francisco de Quevedo, *Dreams and Discourses*, trans. by Robert K. Britton (Oxford, 1989), p. 77.

187 Marcus van Vaernewijck, *Van die beroerlicke tijden in die Nederlanden en voornamelick in Ghendt 1566–1568*, ed. by Ferdinand Vanderhaeghen, 10 vols (Ghent, 1872–1881), vol. 1, p. 156.

188 Carl Justi, "The Works of Hieronymus Bosch in Spain" (1889), in Snyder, *Bosch in Perspective*, p. 52.

189 Godfried Christiaan Maria van Dijck, *Op zoek naar Jheronimus van Aken alias Bosch: De feiten, familie, vrienden en opdrachtgevers, ca. 1400–ca. 1635* (Zaltbommel, 2001), p. 186; account book of Illustrious Brotherhood of Our Dear Lady of 's-Hertogenbosch (1516–17, fol. 166v), published in J.C.A. Hezenmans, "Hieronymus van Aken," *Onze Wachter* 2 (1874): 1–35.

190 BRCP1, pp. 13–20.

191 Thomas à Kempis, *The Imitation of Christ*, trans. by Leo Sherley-Price (Harmondsworth, 1952), p. 174.

192 Jacobus de Voragine, *The Golden Legend*, trans. by William Granger Ryan, 2 vols (Princeton, NJ, 1993), vol. 2, p. 211; BRCP1, p. 118.

193 Voragine, *Golden Legend*, vol. 2, p. 213.

194 Van Dijck, *Op zoek naar Jheronimus van Aken*, pp. 182, 186, 107.

195 See pp. 65–68 above.

196 Koldeweij, Vandenbroeck, and Vermet, *Hieronymus Bosch*, pp. 25–27.

197 BRCP1, pp. 464–67; BRCP2, pp. 420–29.

198 For example, Dirk Bax, *Hieronymus Bosch, His Picture-Writing Deciphered*, trans. by Maria A. Bax-Botha (Rotterdam, 1979); Eric de Bruyn, *De vergeten beeldentaal von Jheronimus Bosch* ('s-Hertogenbosch, 2001).

199 Joseph Leo Koerner, "Impossible Objects: Bosch's Realism," *RES: Anthropology and Aesthetics* 46 (2004), p. 87; Matthijs Ilsink, *Bosch en Bruegel als Bosch* (Nijmegen, 2009), p. 47–50.

200 Bernardus Silvestris, *Cosmographia*, Megacosmos 1, lines 1–2, 18–19, in Silvestris, *Poetic Works*, ed. and trans. by Winthrop Wetherbee (Cambridge, MA, 2015), p. 9.

201 Voragine, *Golden Legend*, vol. 2, p. 211.

202 Van Dijck, *Op zoek naar Jheronimus van Aken*, p. 186.

203 BRCP1, p. 21.

204 Van Dijck, *Op zoek naar Jheronimus van Aken*, p. 175.

205 Koldeweij, Vandenbroeck, and Vermet, *Hieronymus Bosch*, pp. 69–79; BRCP1, p. 23.

206 Lucas van Dijck, "Jheronimus Bosch Inspired by People in His Environment: Research from the Archival Sources," in J.W.M. Timmermans, ed., *Jheronimus Bosch: His Sources* ('s-Hertogenbosch, 2010), pp. 119–22.

207 BRCP1, pp. 161–75.

208 André Lehr, "Het oordeelspel in de Sint Jan," in A. M. Koldeweij, ed., *In Buscoducis: Bijdragen* (Maarssen, 1990), pp. 403–10.

209 BRCP1, p. 165.

210 Jan Gerrit van Gelder, "Der Teufel stiehlt das Tintenfaß," in Artur Rosenauer and Gerold Weber, eds, *Kunsthistorische Forschungen: Otto Pächt zu seinem 70. Geburtstag*, (Vienna, 1972), pp. 174–82.

211 Van Dijck, *Op zoek naar Jheronimus van Aken*, p. 182.

212 Lampsonius, *Pictorum aliquot*, plate 7, p. Av; in Lampsonius, *Life of Lambert Lombard*, p. 114.

213 A. M. Koldeweij, Ernst van Mackelenbergh, and W. Adriaanse, *De Bouwloods van de St.-Janskathedraal te 's-Hertogenbosch* ('s-Hertogenbosch, 1989).

214 Johan Hendrik van Heurn, *Historie der Stad en Meyerye van 's-Hertogenbosch*, 3 vols (Utrecht, 1776–77), vol. 1, pp. 406–14.

215 Ibid., p. 408.

216 Ronald Glaudemans, Jos Koldeweij, Jan van Oudheusden, Ester Vink, and Aart Vos, *The World of Bosch* ('s-Hertogenbosch, 2001), pp. 54–56.

217 Van Dijck, *Op zoek naar Jheronimus van Aken*, p. 91.

218 Alexandre Pinchart, "Notes sur Jérôme van Aeken, dit Bosch, et sur Alard de Hameel, graveur et architecte à Bois-le-Duc," *Bulletins de l'Académie royale des sciences, des lettres et des beaux-arts de Belgique*, 2nd series, 27 (1858), p. 498.

219 Tertullian, *De spectaculis* 110, in *Tertullian, "Apology," "De spectaculis"; Minucius Felix, "Octavius,"* trans. by T. R. Glover and Gerald H. Rendall (Cambridge, MA, 1958), p. 297.

220 Van Heurn, *Historie der Stad*, vol. 1, pp. 407–8.

221 Vaughan, *Charles the Bold*, p. 37.

222 Richard Vaughan, *Philip the Good* (London, 1970), pp. 303–33.

223 Peter Arnade, *Realms of Ritual: Burgundian Ceremony and Civil Life in Late Medieval Ghent* (Ithaca, NY, 1996), p. 118.

224 *Iliad* 6.305.

225 James D. Tracy, "Introduction," in Tracy, ed., *City Walls: The Urban Enceinte in Global Perspective* (Cambridge, 2000), p. 1.

226 Geoffrey Parker, *The Military Revolution: Military Innovation and the Rise of the West, 1500–1800* (Cambridge, 1988), pp. 6–44; Peter Purton, *A History of the Late Medieval Siege, 1200–1500* (Woodbridge, 2010), pp. 274–80.

227 Marc Boone, "Destruction des villes et menaces de destruction, éléments du discours princier aux Pays-Bas bourguignons," in Martin Körner, ed., *Stadtzerstörung und Wiederaufbau: Zerstörung durch die Stadtherrschaft, innere Unruhen und Kriege*, 3 vols (Bern, 2000), vol. 2, pp. 97–117.

228 Arnade, *Realms of Ritual*, pp. 95–158.

229 Georges Chastellain, *Oeuvres* (Brussels, 1864), vol. 3, p. 35 n. 1, citing Jacques du Clercq.

230 Vaughan, *Philip the Good*, pp. 88–89.

231 Ashcroft, *Albrecht Dürer*, vol. 2, p. 837.

232 Francisco de Hollanda, *Four Dialogues on Painting*, trans. by Aubrey F. G. Bell (Oxford, 1928), pp. 50–54.

233 Niccolò Machiavelli, *The Prince*, trans. by Harvey C. Mansfield, Jr (Chicago, 1985), p. 87.

234 Vaughan, *Charles the Bold*, pp. 422–30.

235 Marios Philippides and Walter K. Hanak, *The Siege and the Fall of Constantinople in 1453* (Burlington, VT, 2011), pp. 397–425.

236 Glaudemans et al., *Bosch's World*, p. 28.

237 Purton, *History of the Late Medieval Siege*, pp. 312–13.

238 Eric H. Cline, *Jerusalem Besieged: From Ancient Canaan to Modern Israel* (Ann Arbor, MI, 2004), pp. 8–10.

239 BRCP1, pp. 348–59; BRCP2, pp. 378–94.

240 Augustine, *The City of God* 1.17, trans. by Marcus Dods (New York, 1950), p. 26; Friedrich Ohly, *The Damned and the Elect: Guilt in Western Culture*, trans. by Linda Archibald (Cambridge, 1992), p. 35.

241 Ohly, *Damned and the Elect*, p. 41.

242 Ernst H. Gombrich, "The Evidence of Images," in Charles S. Singleton, ed., *Interpretation: Theory and Practice*, (Baltimore, 1969), p. 40.

243 Ibid., pp. 75–89.

244 Lotte Brand Philip, "The Prado *Epiphany* by Jerome Bosch," *Art Bulletin* 35, no. 4 (1953): 267–93.

245 Debra Higgs Strickland, *The Epiphany of Hieronymus Bosch: Imagining Antichrist and Others from the Middle Ages to the Reformation* (London, 2016), pp. 71–111.

246 C.W.R.D. Moseley, trans., *The Travels of Sir John Mandeville* (London, 2005), pp. 165–66.

247 I relied on Will-Erich Peuckert, *Die grosse Wende: Das apokalyptische Saeculum und Luther*, 2 vols (Darmstadt, 1966); Jean Delumeau, *La peur en Occident (XIVe–XVIIIe siècles): Un cite assiégée* (Paris, 1978) and Delumeau, *Sin and Fear: The Emergence of a Western Guilt Culture, 13th–18th Centuries*, trans. by Eric Nicholson (New York, 1990); Carlo Ginzburg, *Night Battles* (Chicago, 1991), pp. 33–88; and Robert Ian Moore, *The Formation of a Persecuting Society: Authority and Deviance in Western Europe, 950–1250*, 2nd edn (Oxford, 2007).

248 Valentine Groebner, *Defaced: The Visual Culture of Violence in the Late Middle Ages*, trans. by Pamela Selwyn (New York, 2004), pp. 37–66.

249 Hezenmans, "Hieronymus van Aken."

250 Peter Marshall, *1517: Martin Luther and the Invention of the Reformation* (Oxford, 2017).

251 Neil MacGregor, *A History of the World in 100 Objects* (London, 2010), pp. 552–58.

252 Sigüenza, "History," p. 36.

253 For example, Rudolf Chadraba, *Dürers Apokalypse: Eine ikonographische Deutung* (Prague, 1964); contested by Gombrich, "Evidence of Images," pp. 91–104.

254 Joseph Leo Koerner, *The Reformation of the Image* (Chicago, 2004), pp. 201–11.

255 Aquinas, *Summa Theologiae* 1, q. 49, a. 3, reply to q. 3.

256 Gerhard Ebeling, *Luther* (Tübingen, 1981), pp. 33–35.

257 Augustine, *Confessions* 1.7, trans. by Richard Sydney Pine-Coffin (Harmondsworth, 1961), p. 27.

258 Martin Brecht, *Martin Luther*, trans. by James L. Schaaf, 3 vols (Minneapolis, 1985), vol. 1: *His Road to Reformation, 1483–1521*, p. 77.

259 Ibid., p. 72.

260 Niklaus Manuel, *Die Totenfresser*, ed. by Ferdinand Vetter (Leipzig, 1923), p. 53; Steven Ozment, *The Reformation in the Cities: The Appeal of Protestantism to Sixteenth-Century Germany and Switzerland* (New Haven, CT, 1975), p. 45.

261 Sergiusz Michalski, *The Reformation and the Visual Arts: The Protestant Image Question in Western and Eastern Europe* (London, 1993); Koerner, *Reformation of the Image*, pp. 27–169.

262 Jan Assmann, "Was ist so schlimm an den Bildern?," in Hans Joas, ed., *Die zehn Gebote: Ein widersprüchliches Erbe?* (Cologne, 2006), pp. 17–32.

263 Martin Warnke, "Durchbrochene Geschichte? Die Bilderstürmer der Wiedertäufer in Münster," in Warnke, ed., *Bildersturm: Die Zerstörung des Kunstwerks* (Frankfurt am Main, 1977), p. 93; Michalski, *Reformation*, pp. 75–98; Koerner, *Reformation of the Image*, pp. 83–93.

264 Andreas Karlstadt, "On the Removal of Images" (1522), in Bryan D. Mangrum and Giuseppe Scavizzi, ed. and trans., *A Reformation Debate: Karlstadt, Emser, and Eck on Sacred Images; Three Treatises in Translation* (Toronto, 1991), p. 35; Andreas Karlstadt, *Von Abtuhung der Bylder / und das keyn Bedtler vnther den Christen seyn soll* (Wittenberg, 1522), C4r.

265 Fabian, "Der erste Versuch," pp. 1–13.

266 Koerner, *Reformation of the Image*, pp. 402–44.

267 Karlstadt, "On the Removal of Images," p. 36.

268 Van Mander, *Lives of the Illustrious Painters*, p. 74.

269 Chambéry, Musée Savoisien, Inv. M914. Bord.244; Louis Réau, *Histoire du vandalisme: Les monuments détruits de l'art français*, 2 vols (Paris, 1959), vol. 1, p. 96; *Welt im Umbruch. Augsburg zwischen Renaissance und Barock*, exh. cat. Stadt Augsburg, 3 vols (Augsburg, 1980), vol. 2, pp. 109–10.

270 Van Heesch, "Paulus de Kempenaer," pp. 36–38.

271 Ibid., p. 10; see pp. 77–78 above.

272 Van Heesch, "Paulus de Kempenaer," pp. 9–10, n. 26.

273 Ibid., p. 33.

274 Ibid., pp. 34–35.

275 Schmitt, *Concept of the Political*, p. 27.

276 Van Heesch, "Paulus de Kempenaer," p. 12.

277 Immanuel Kant, *Religion within the Bounds of Mere Reason*, trans. by Allen Wood and George di Giovanni (Cambridge, 1998), p. 62.

278 Ibid.

279 Immanuel Kant, *Critique of Practical Reason*, trans. by Mary Gregor (Cambridge, 1997), p. 129.

280 Kant, *Religion*, pp. 64–65 (original emphasis).

281 Søren Kierkegaard, *The Concept of Anxiety*, ed. and trans. by Reidar Thomte (Princeton, NJ, 1980) p. 28.

282 Kant, *Religion*, p. 43.

283 Kant, *Grounding for the Metaphysics of Morals*, trans. by J. W. Ellington, 3rd edn (Indianapolis, 1993), p. 438.

284 Martin Luther, *Smalcald Articles* (*Schmalkaldische Artikel*, 1537), Part 3, Art. 1.3, in Friedrich Bente and William Herman Theodore Dau, trans., *Triglot Concordia: The Symbolical Books of the Ev. Lutheran Church* (St. Louis, 1921), p. 477.

285 Robert Alter, whose translation I use here, renders the Hebrew *ta'awah* as "lust" through its pairing with *nehmad* (that which is desired); Robert Alter, trans., *The Hebrew Bible: A Translation with Commentary*, 3 vols (New York, 2018), vol. 1, pp. 24–25.

286 Michael Camille, *The Gothic Idol: Ideology and Image-Making in Medieval Art* (Cambridge, 1989), pp. 60, 88–89.

287 Denis Grivot and George Zarnecki, *Gislebertus: Sculptor of Autun* (New York, 1961), p. 149; Otto Karl Werckmeister, "The Lintel Fragment Representing Eve from Saint-Lazare, Autun," *Journal of the Warburg and Courtauld Institutes* 35, no. 1 (1972): 1–30.

288 Werckmeister, "Lintel Fragment," p. 18.

289 Gotthold Ephraim Lessing, *Laocoön: An Essay on the Limits of Painting and Poetry*, trans. by Edward Allen McCormick (Baltimore, 1984), p. 78.

290 Ashcroft, *Albrecht Dürer*, vol. 2, pp. 710–13.

291 Ibid., pp. 875–76.

292 Walter Benjamin, "Theses on the Philosophy of History," in Benjamin, *Illuminations*, ed. by Hannah Arendt, trans. by Harry Zohn (London, 1970), p. 259.

293 Lessing, *Laocoön*, p. 99; Gotthold Ephraim Lessing, *Werke*, ed. by Herbert G. Göpfert, 8 vols (Munich, 1970–79), vol. 6 (1974): *Kunsttheoretische und kunsthistorische Schriften*, p. 25.

294 Ewald M. Vetter, "Necessarium Adae Peccatum," *Ruperto-Carola* 18, no. 39 (1966), pp. 153–54; Joseph Leo Koerner, *The Moment of Self-Portraiture in German Renaissance Art* (Chicago, 1993), p. 298.

295 Augustine, *Against Julian*, trans. by Matthew A. Schumacher (New York, 1957), p. 125, citing Romans 7:19 and 25.

296 Augustine, *City of God* 14.13, trans. by Dods, p. 460; Charles Dempsey, "Sicut in utrem aquas maris: Jerome Bosch's Prolegomenon to the *Garden of Delights*," *Modern Language Notes* 119 (2004): 247–70.

297 Jean Wirth, *Hieronymus Bosch: Der Garten der Lüste* (Frankfurt, 2000), p. 97; Joseph Leo Koerner, *Bosch and Bruegel: From Enemy Painting to Everyday Life* (Princeton, NJ, 2016), pp. 208–18.

298 Karl Heinz Bohrer, "Der gefährliche Augenblick: Zur Systematik des Plötzlichen," *Merkur* 32, issue 358 (March 1978), pp. 242–62.

299 Plato, *Parmenides* 156e; *Plato in Twelve Volumes; with an English Translation* (Cambridge, MA, 1914–30), vol. 9 (1928), trans. by Harold N. Fowler.

300 Kierkegaard, *Concept of Anxiety*, p. 83.

301 De Beatis, *Travel Journal*, p. 94.

302 Aristotle, *Metaphysics* 982b10–18, trans. by W. D. Ross, in Aristotle, *The Complete Works of Aristotle: Revised Oxford Translation*, 2 vols, ed. by Jonathan Barnes (Princeton, NJ, 1984), vol. 2, p. 1554; see Anton-Hermann Chroust, "Philosophy Starts in Wonder," *Divus Thomas* 75, no. 1 (1972), p. 56; and Lorraine Daston and Katharine Park, *Wonders and the Order of Nature 1150–1750* (New York, 1998), pp. 109–133.

303 Karlstadt, "On the Removal of Images," p. 35; see pp. 118–19 above.

304 Panofsky, *Early Netherlandish Painting*, p. 357; see pp. 32–33 above.

305 Gombrich, "Evidence of Images," p. 56; see p. 00 above.

306 Gombrich, *Heritage of Apelles*, pp. 90, 86–87.

307 Schmitt, *Ex Captivitate Salus*, p. 63.

308 Schmitt, *Antworten*, p. 52.

309 Schmitt, *Political Theology*, p. 53.

310 Schmitt, *Concept of the Political*, p. 36.

311 Ibid., p. 5

312 Kiesel, *Ernst Jünger–Carl Schmitt*, pp. 49, 164.

313 Schmitt, *Antworten*, pp. 53, 60, 66.

314 Schmitt, *Ex Captivitate Salus*, p. 65; see pp. 34–42 above.

315 Schmitt, *Political Theology*, p. 65; translation emended.

316 Schmitt, *Ex Captivitate Salus*, p. 65; translation emended.

317 Ibid.

318 Schmitt, *Concept of the Political*, p. 19.

319 Schmitt, *Political Theology*, p. 65.

320 Ibid., p. 58.

321 Schmitt, *Concept of the Political*, p. 68; Meier, *Lesson of Carl Schmitt*, p. 13.

322 Schmitt, *Political Theology*, p. 66.

323 Carl Schmitt, *Glossarium: Aufzeichnungen der Jahre 1947–1951*, ed. by Eberhard Freiherr von Medem (Berlin, 1991), p. 148.

324 Meier, *Lesson of Carl Schmitt*, p. 155.

325 Schmitt, *Glossarium*, p. 162.

326 Ernst Jünger, "Total Mobilization" (1930), in Richard Wolin, ed., *The Heidegger Controversy* (Cambridge, MA, 1992), pp. 122–23.

327 Kiesel, *Ernst Jünger–Carl Schmitt*, p. 18.

328 Ibid., pp. 18–19.

329 Schmitt, *Concept of the Political*, p. 27.

330 Carl Schmitt, *Theodor Däublers 'Nordlicht'* (Berlin, 1991), p. 24.

331 Schmitt, *Ex Captivitate Salus*, p. 71; translation emended following Meier, *Lesson of Carl Schmitt*, pp. 49, 53–54.

332 Schmitt, *Glossarium*, p. 146.

333 Schmitt, *Ex Captivitate Salus*, p. 71.

334 Schmitt, *Glossarium*, p. 243.

335 Erich Auerbach, "Figura" (1938), trans. by Ralph Manheim, in Auerbach, *Scenes from the Drama of European Literature* (New York, 1959), pp. 29–30.

336 Mircea Eliade, *The Portugal Journal*, trans. by Mac Linscott Ricketts (Albany, NY, 2020), p. 32.

337 Ibid., p. 108.

338 Kiesel, *Ernst Jünger–Carl Schmitt*, pp. 18, 164.

339 Ibid., p. 152

340 Ibid.

341 Ernst Jünger, *Strahlungen* (Tübingen, 1949); in English, with Jünger's "Second Paris Journal" and "Kirchhorst Diaries" (*Strahlungen II* [Stuttgart, 1979]), as Jünger, *A German Officer in Occupied Paris: The War Journals, 1941–1945*, trans. by Thomas S. Hansen and Abby J. Hansen (New York, 2019).

342 Ernst Jünger, *Der Kampf als inneres Erlebnis* (Berlin, 1922), p. 32; Nikolaus Wachsmann, "Marching under the Swastika? Ernst Jünger and National Socialism, 1918–1933," *Journal of Contemporary History* 33, no. 4 (1998), p. 576.

343 Hannes Heer, "Das Schweigen des Hauptmanns Jünger: Ernst Jüngers Reise an die Kaukasusfront 1942/43," in Moritz Bassler and Ewout van der Knaap, eds, *Die (k)alte Sachlichkeit: Herkunft und Wirkungen eines Konzepts* (2004), pp. 97–119.

344 Ernst Jünger, *The Adventurous Heart: Figures and Capriccios*, trans. by Thomas Friese (Candor, NY, 2012), p. 73; and Ernst Jünger, *Der Waldgang* (Stuttgart, 1980), pp. 31, 51.

345 Ernst Jünger, "Einleitung," in Ferdinand Bucholtz, ed., *Der gefährliche Augenblick: Eine Sammlung von Bildern und Berichten* (Berlin, 1931), p. 16.

346 Jünger, *German Officer*, p. 8.

347 Ibid., p. 56.

348 Ibid., p. 55.

349 Ibid., p. 37.

350 Ibid., pp. 173, 62 and 59; also pp. 65, 72, 229, 338, 346, and 381.

351 Kiesel, *Ernst Jünger–Carl Schmitt*, p. 148; Heimo Schwilk, ed., *Ernst Jünger: Leben und Werk in Bildern und Texten* (Stuttgart, 1988), p. 190.

352 Norman Ächtler, "Der reinste Ausdruck unserer Lage: Der Kessel als literarischer Chronotopos und existenzphilosophische Metapher bei Theodor Plievier und Ernst Jünger," in Matthias Schöning and Ingo Stöckmann, eds, *Ernst Jünger und die Bundesrepublik* (Berlin,

2012), pp. 269–94.

353 Jünger, *German Officer*, p. 160.

354 Ibid., p. 125.

355 Ibid., p. 314.

356 Hans Werner Richter, *Die Geschlagenen* (Munich, 1985), p. 123; Ächtler, "Der reinste Ausdruck," p. 271.

357 Theodor Plievier, *Stalingrad* (Cologne 2001), p. 104; Ächtler, "Der reinste Ausdruck," p. 274.

358 Ernst Jünger, *An der Zeitmauer* (Stuttgart, 1959) p. 191.

359 Plievier, *Stalingrad*, pp. 17, 404; Ächtler, "Der reinste Ausdruck," p. 273.

360 Jünger, *German Officer*, p. 135.

361 Ibid., p. 137.

362 Ibid., p. 136.

363 Ibid., p. 147.

364 Ibid., p. 146.

365 Ibid.

366 De Beatis, *Travel Journal*, p. 94.

367 François Poncet, "Ernst Jünger et Jérôme Bosch," *Revue de littérature comparée* 71, no. 4 (1997), p. 430.

368 Jünger, *German Officer*, p. 152

369 Ibid., p. 287; Ludwig von Baldass, *Hieronymus Bosch* (Vienna, 1943).

370 Jünger, *German Officer*, p. 287.

371 Ingeborg Villinger and Alexander Jaser, eds, *Briefwechsel Gretha Jünger und Carl Schmitt, 1934–1953* (Berlin, 2007), p. 72.

372 Bradley F. Smith and Agnes F. Peterson, eds, *Heinrich Himmler. Geheimreden 1933 bis 1945 und andere Ansprachen* (Frankfurt am Main, 1974), p. 170; Dirk Rupnow, *Vernichten und Erinnern: Spuren nationalsozialistischer Gedächtnispolitik* (Göttingen, 2005), pp. 61–63.

373 Joseph Leo Koerner, "Maly Trostinets," *Granta* 149 (November 2019), pp. 14–33.

374 Sybil Milton, "Confronting Atrocities," in Stephen Goodell and Susan D. Bachrach, eds, *Liberation 1945* (Washington, DC, 1995), p 61.

375 Cora Sol Goldstein, *Capturing the German Eye: American Visual Propaganda in Occupied Germany* (Chicago, 2009), pp. 20–39.

376 Insert in *Henry Koerner: Gemälde und Graphik, 1945–1947* (Berlin, 1947).

377 Goldstein, *Capturing the German Eye*, p. 94.

378 *Life*, May 10, 1948; *New York Times*, April 4, 1947; *Art Digest*, June 1, 1947; *Art Digest*, February 1, 1948.

379 Goldstein, *Capturing the German Eye*, p. 94.

Max Beckmann

1 Wilhelm Hausenstein, in Curt Glaser et al., *Max Beckmann* (Munich, 1924), p. 69.

2 Adolf Behne, "Schlichter und Beckmann," *Die Welt am Abend*, April 1938; cited in Lynette Roth, "New Identities: Type and Portraiture," in Stephanie Barron and Sabine Eckmann, eds, *New Objectivity: Modern German Art in the Weimar Republic, 1919–33* (New York, 2015), p. 265.

3 Sigmund Freud, "Remembering, Repeating, and Working Through" (1914), trans. by John Reddick, in Adam Phillips, ed., *The Penguin Freud Reader* (London, 2006), p. 392.

4 Max Beckmann, "Letters to a Woman Painter" (1948), in Max Beckmann, *Self-Portrait in Words: Collected Writings and Statements, 1903–1950*, ed. by Barbara Copeland Buenger (Chicago, 1997), p. 316; Hans Belting, *Max Beckmann: Tradition as a Problem in Modern Art*, trans. by Peter Wortsman (New York, 1989), p. 23.

5 March 1939 letter to I. B. Neumann, cited in Belting, *Max Beckmann*, p. 19.

6 Adolf Loos, "Men's Fashion" (1898), in Loos, *Ornament and Crime: Selected Essays*, trans. by Michael Mitchell (Riverside, CA, 1997), p. 90.

7 Lynette Roth, *Max Beckmann at the Saint Louis Art Museum* (St. Louis and Munich, 2015), p. 102.

8 Max Beckmann to Israel Ber Neumann, May 24, 1928, in Max Beckmann, *Briefe*, ed. by Klaus Gallwitz,

Uwe M. Schneede, and Stephan von Wiese, 3 vols (Munich, 1993–1995), vol. 2: *1925–1937* (1994), p. 113.

9 "On My Painting" (1938), in Beckmann, *Self-Portrait*, p. 306.

10 Max Beckmann, "Speech for Friends and Faculty during Commencement Week Activities, Washington University, St. Louis" (1950), in Beckmann, *Self-Portrait*, p. 320.

11 Walter Benjamin, *Origin of the German Trauerspiel*, trans. by Howard Eiland (Cambridge, MA, 2019), pp. 122–23; Benjamin Buchloh, "Figures of Authority, Ciphers of Regression: Notes on the Return of Representation in European Painting," *October* 16 (Spring 1981), p. 53 n. 18.

12 Käthe Rapoport von Porada, "Max Beckmann: Der Titan," MS, Städel Museum, Frankfurt am Main, p. 96; Roth, *Max Beckmann*, pp. 104–5.

13 Georg Simmel, "Rodin (mit einer Vorbemerkung über *Meurnier*)," in Simmel, *Gesamtausgabe*, 24 vols (Frankfurt am Main, 1989–2015), vol. 14 (1996): *Hauptprobleme der Philosophie; Philosophische Kultur*, ed. by Rüdiger Kramme and Ottheim Rammstedt, p. 339; Malika Maskarinec, *The Forces of Form in German Modernism* (Evanston, IL, 2018), p. 3.

14 Beckmann, *Self-Portrait*, p. 282.

15 Benno Reifenberg, "Max Beckmann," in *Ganymed: Jahrbuch für die Kunst* 3 (1921). p. 44.

16 Max Beckmann to Minna Beckmann-Taube, May 4, 1915, in Beckmann, *Briefe*, vol. 1: *1899–1925* (1993), p. 128.

17 Beckmann to Minna Beckmann-Tauber, October 3, 1914, in ibid., p. 97.

18 Sigmund Freud, *Beyond the Pleasure Principle*, trans. by James Strachey (New York, 1961), pp. 35–26; see pp. 5–6 above.

19 Ernst Jünger, *Storm of Steel*, trans. by Michael Hofmann (London, 2003), pp. 6–7.

20 Wilhelm Fraenger, "Max Beckmann: Der Traum; Ein Beitrag zur Physiognomik des Grotesken" (1924), in Fraenger, *Von Bosch bis Beckmann: Ausgewählte Schriften* (Cologne, 1985), pp. 320–22; originally in Glaser et al., *Max Beckmann*.

21 Ibid., pp. 310, 326.

22 Beckmann, *Self-Portrait*, p. 287.

23 Ibid.; emended translation based on Max Beckmann, *Die Realität der Träume in den Bildern: Schriften und Gespräche 1911 bis 1950*, ed. by Rudolf Pillep (Munich, 1990), p. 37 (original emphasis).

24 Carl Schmitt, *Political Theology: Four Chapters on the Concept of Sovereignty*, trans. by George Schwab (Chicago, 1985), p. 5.

25 Jeffrey Ashcroft, *Albrecht Dürer: Documentary Biography*, 2 vols (New Haven, CT, 2017), vol. 2, p. 873; Ernst H. Kantorowicz, "The Sovereignty of the Artist: A Note on Legal Maxims and Renaissance Theories of Art," in Millard Meiss, ed., *De Artibus opuscula XL: Essays in Honor of Erwin Panofsky*, 2 vols (New York, 1961), vol. 1, pp. 267–79.

26 Beckmann, *Self-Portrait*, pp. 287–88.

27 Max Weber, *Politik als Beruf*, 2nd edn (Munich, 1926), p. 51; on the "value vacuum," see Hermann Broch, *Hugo von Hofmannsthal and His Time*, ed. and trans. by Michael P. Steinberg (Chicago, 1984), pp. 51–58.

28 Max Kommerell, *Der Dichter als Führer in der deutschen Klassik* (Berlin, 1928); Eric Michaud, *The Cult of Art in Nazi Germany*, trans. by Janet Lloyd (Stanford, CA, 2004), pp. 2–13.

29 Beckmann, *Self-Portrait*, p. 288.

30 Ibid., p. 287.

31 Carl Schmitt, *The Crisis of Parliamentary Democracy*, trans. by Ellen Kennedy (Cambridge, MA, 1985), pp. 39–40.

32 Beckmann, *Self-Portrait*, p. 290.

33 Olaf Peters, *Vom schwarzen Seiltänzer: Max Beckmann zwischen Weimar Republik und Exil* (Berlin, 2005), pp. 99–101.

34 Beckmann, *Self-Portrait*, p. 303.

35 Friedrich Nietzsche, *Thus Spoke Zarathustra*, trans. by Walter Kaufmann (New York, 1954), p. 19.

36 Friedhelm Wilhelm Fischer, *Max Beckmann: Symbol und Weltbild* (Munich, 1972), p. 94.

37 Beckmann, *Self-Portrait*, p. 287, translation modified.

38 *Kölnische Zeitung* 129b (February 29, 1928), p. 2.

39 Stephen Lackner, *Max Beckmann* (New York, 1977), p. 98.

40 Bruno Erich Werner, "Mensch hinter Masken," *Deutsche Allgemeine Zeitung*, April 1928; cited in Roth, *Max Beckmann*, p. 105.

41 Carl Schmitt, *State, Movement, People: The Triadic Structure of the Political Unity*, ed. and trans. by Simona Draghici (Corvallis, OR, 2001), p. 48; Raphael Gross, *Carl Schmitt and the Jews*, trans. by Joel Golb (Madison, WI, 2007), pp. 32–47, 177–80.

42 Gross, *Carl Schmitt and the Jews*, p. 72.

43 Carl Schmitt, "Die deutsche Rechtswissenschaft im Kampf gegen den jüdischen Geist," *Deutsche Juristen-Zeitung*, October 14, 1936, p. 1197.

44 Ibid., p. 1198.

45 The exhibition catalogue "Große Deutsche Kunstaustellung" (1937) and Hitler's opening speech are reproduced in Peter-Klaus Schuster, ed., *Nationalsozialismus und "Entartete Kunst": Die "Kunststadt" München, 1937* (Munich, 1987), pp. 222–52.

46 John Gunther, *Inside Europe*, rev. edn (New York, 1940), p. 2.

47 Joseph Goebbels, *Michael: Ein deutsches Schicksal in Tagebuchblättern* (Munich, 1934), p. 41; cited in Michaud, *Cult of Art*, p. 1.

48 Schuster, *Nationalsozialismus*; and Stephanie Barron *"Degenerate Art": The Fate of the Avant-Garde in Nazi Germany* (Los Angeles, 1991).

49 Dirk Rupnow, *Vernichten und Erinnern: Spuren nationalsozialistischer Gedächtnispolitik* (Göttingen, 2005), pp. 99–136.

50 Adolf Ziegler, "Rede zur Eröffnung der Ausstellung 'Entartete Kunst,'" in Schuster, *Nationalsozialismus*, p. 217.

51 Mario-Andreas von Lüttichau, " 'Deutsche Kunst' und 'Entartete Kunst': Die Münchner Ausstellungen 1937," in Schuster, *Nationalsozialismus*, pp. 83–118.

52 Schuster, *Nationalsozialismus*, p. 218.

53 Ibid.

54 Christopher Isherwood, *Goodbye to Berlin* (London, 1938), p. 317.

55 Peter Guenther, "Three Days in Munich, July 1937," in Barron, *"Degenerate Art"*, p. 38; see also Lüttichau, " 'Deutsche Kunst,'" pp. 98–99.

56 Schuster, *Nationalsozialismus*, p. 217.

57 Fritz Kaiser, *Führer durch die Ausstellung Entartete Kunst* (Munich, 1937), p. 19; Barron, *"Degenerate Art"*, p. 377.

58 Paul Schultze-Naumburg, *Kunst und Rasse* (Munich, 1928), pp. 91–93.

59 Carl Schmitt, *Positionen und Begriffe im Kampf mit*

Weimar–Genf–Versailles 1923–1939 (Hamburg, 1940), p. 312.

60 Carl Schmitt, *The Concept of the Political*, trans. by George Schwab, expanded edn (Chicago, 2007), p. 35.

61 Kaiser, *Führer*, p. 20; Barron, *"Degenerate Art"*, p. 378.

62 Kaiser, *Führer* p. 18; Barron, *"Degenerate Art"*, p. 376.

63 See p. 250 above.

64 Letter of February 11, 1938 to Curt Valentin, cited in Peter Selz, *Max Beckmann* (New York, 1964), p. 61.

65 Beckmann, *Self-Portrait*, p. 287; Beckmann, *Die Realität der Träume*, p. 37.

66 Diary entry of May 7, 1940, cited in Reinhard Spieler, *Max Beckmann, 1884–1950*, trans. by Charity Scott Stokes (Cologne, 2011), p. 115.

67 Spieler, *Beckmann*, p. 116.

68 Ibid., p. 108.

69 Beckmann in conversation with Lilly von Schnitzler in 1937, in Beckmann, *Die Realität der Träume*, p. 46.

70 Beatrice von Bormann, "An 'Entartete' Artist in the Netherlands: Max Beckmann and the German Art Trade, 1937–1947," in Jonieke van Es, Henske Marsman, and Gwendolyn P. Boevé-Jones, eds, *"Come on, Now Buy a Beckmann Too!": Portraits of the Lütjens Family in Museum Boijmans van Beuningen* (Rotterdam, 2010), pp. 58–87.

71 William Kentridge, "Beckmann's *Death*," in Sean Rainbird, ed., *Max Beckmann*, (New York, 2003), p. 181.

72 Ibid., p. 183.

73 Ibid., p. 182.

74 See pp. 212–16, 311–28 below.

75 Joseph Leo Koerner, "Identity and the Museum," in Peter Nisbet, ed., *The Busch-Reisinger Museum* (Cambridge, MA, 2007), pp. 242–57.

76 https://harvardartmuseums.org/about/press-media/harvard-art-museums-announce-reopening-plans-for-september (accessed April 12, 2024).

77 Bernhard Fulda and Aya Soika, "Introduction," in Fulda, Soika, and Christian Ring, eds, *Emil Nolde: The Artist during the Third Reich* (Munich, 2019), p. 28.

78 Just as this book went to press, the Harvard Art Museums communicated their intention to return Beckmann's *Self-Portrait* to its old place on the main sightline of the galleries.

William Kentridge

1 Carolyn Christov-Bakargiev, ed., *William Kentridge* (Brussels, 1999), p. 28.

2 William Kentridge, *Six Drawing Lessons* (Cambridge, MA, 2004), p. 124; Kentridge, "Fortuna: Neither Program nor Chance in the Making of Images" (1993), in Rosalind Krauss, ed., *William Kentridge* (Cambridge, MA, 2017), pp. 25–26; and Rosalind Krauss, " 'The Rock': William Kentridge's Drawings for Projection," *October* 92 (2000), pp. 5–6.

3 Walter Benjamin, "Theses on the Philosophy of History," in Benjamin, *Illuminations*, ed. by Hannah Arendt, trans. by Harry Zohn (London, 1970), p. 257 (original emphasis); see pp. 230–31, 327–28 below.

4 Carl Schmitt, *Political Theology: Four Chapters on the Concept of Sovereignty*, trans. by George Schwab (Chicago, 1985), p. 12

5 Interview with Amanda Jephson and Nicholas Vergunst (1988), cited in Christov-Bakargiev, *William Kentridge*, p. 16.

6 *The New York Times*, June 13, 1986, p. 1.

7 William Kentridge, "Art in a State of Grace, Art in a State of Hope, Art in a State of Siege" (1986), extract in Dan Cameron, Carolyn Christov-Bakargiev, and J. M. Coetzee, *William Kentridge* (London, 1999), pp. 102–5.

8 Margaret K. Koerner, "Being Kentridge," in Margaret K. Koerner, *William Kentridge: Smoke, Ashes, Fable* (Brussels, 2017), pp. 8–61.

9 Morris Kentridge, *I Recall* (Johannesburg, 1959).

10 Quoted in Calvin Tomkins, "Lines of Resistance: William Kentridge's Rough Magic," *The New Yorker*, January 10, 2010.

11 On Kentridge's intellectual formation, see Leora Maltz-Leca, *William Kentridge: Process as Metaphor and Other Doubtful Enterprises* (Berkeley, CA, 2018), pp. 29–130.

12 Kentridge, *Six Drawing Lessons*, p. 55.

13 Bertolt Brecht, "The Modern Theater is Epic Theater" (1930), in Brecht, *Brecht on Theatre: The Development of an Aesthetic*, ed. and trans. by John Willett (New York, 1964), p. 38.

14 Bertolt Brecht, "Short Description of a New Technique of Acting" (1940), in Brecht, *Brecht on Theatre*, p. 143.

15 Bertolt Brecht, "Theatre for Pleasure or Theatre for Instruction" (ca. 1935), in Brecht, *Brecht on Theatre*, p. 70; see Fredric Jameson, *Brecht and Method* (New York, 1998), pp. 55–65.

16 William Kentridge, "Landscape in a State of Siege" (1988), in Krauss, *William Kentridge*, p. 110.

17 Tomkins, "Lines of Resistance."

18 Kentridge, "Art in a State of Siege," typescript p. 5, https://www.kentridge.studio/art-in-state-of-siege/ (accessed April 12, 2024).

19 Kentridge, "Art in a State of Grace," p. 102.

20 Ibid., pp. 102–3.

21 Cited in David Dyzenhaus, *Hard Cases in Wicked Legal Systems*, 2nd edn (Oxford, 2010), p. 148.

22 Maltz-Leca, *William Kentridge*, p. 51.

23 Kentridge, "Art in a State of Grace," p. 103.

24 Brink's first public reference to a "state of siege" was in 1979, in André Brink, *Writing in a State of Siege: Essays on Politics and Literature* (New York, 1983), pp. 172–95; also, André Brink, *States of Emergency* (New York, 1988).

25 Giorgio Agamben, *State of Exception*, trans. by Kevin Attell (Chicago, 2005), pp. 4–6.

26 Dyzenhaus, *Hard Cases*, pp. 34–44.

27 Seamus Heaney, "Whatever You Say Say Nothing," ll. 74–76, first published in Heaney, *North* (London, 1975).

28 Agamben, *State of Exception*, pp. 41, 65.

29 Aby Warburg, *Images from the Region of the Pueblo Indians of North America*, trans. by Michael Steinberg (Ithaca, NY, 1995), p. 1.

30 Benjamin, "Theses," p. 259.

31 Zbigniew Herbert, "Report from a Besieged City," ll. 4–7, trans. by Czesław Miłosz, *New York Review of Books*, August 18, 1983.

32 Sigrun Haude, "The World of the Siege in New Perspective: The Populace during the Thirty Years' War (1618–1646)", in Anke Fischer-Kattner and Jamel Ostwald, eds, *The World of the Siege: Representations of Early Modern Positional Warfare* (Leiden, 2019), pp. 27.

33 Kentridge, "Fortuna," p. 30.

34 William Kentridge, " 'Journey to the Moon' and '7 Fragments for Georges Méliès' including 'Day for Night'," in *William Kentridge*, exh. cat., Castello di Rivoli Museo d'Arte Contemporanea, Rivoli-Torino, January 10–February 29, 2004 (Milan, 2003), pp. 190–93.

35 William Kentridge, Program Statement for The Centre for the Less Good Idea, https://lessgoodidea.com/about (accessed April 12, 2024).

36 "Carolyn Christov-Bakargiev in Conversation with William Kentridge," in Cameron, Christov-Bakargiev, and Coetzee, *William Kentridge*, p. 17.

37 Tomkins, "Lines of Resistance."

38 Konstantin Stanislavski, *An Actor Prepares*, trans. by Elizabeth Reynolds Hapgood (New York, 1936), p. 191; Harmon Siegel, "Art of the Moving Drawing: Kentridge as Mime," unpublished MS, 2015.

39 Tomkins, "Lines of Resistance."

40 Lawrence Durrell, "Brassaï" (1968), in Durrell, *Lawrence Durrell's Endpapers and Inklings 1933–1988*, ed. by Richard Pine, 2 vols (Newcastle upon Tyne, 2019), vol. 1, p. 107.

41 Henry Miller, "L'oeil de Paris" (1938), in Miller and Brassaï, *Brassaï* (Paris, 1952).

42 Durrell, "Brassaï," p. 105.

43 Ibid., pp. 105–6.

44 Marcel Proust, *In Search of Lost Time*, 2: *In the Shadow of Young Girls in Flower*, trans. by C. K. Scott Moncrieff, ed. by William C. Carter (New Haven, CT,

2015), p. 490.

45 Brassaï, *Marcel Proust sous l'emprise de la photographie* (Paris, 1997).

46 Louis Aragon, *Paris Peasant*, trans. by Simon Watson Taylor (London, 1980), p. 217.

47 Marcel Proust, *In Search of Lost Time*, 1: *Swann's Way*, trans. by C. K. Scott Moncrieff, ed. by William C. Carter (New Haven, CT, 2013), p. 51.

48 Kentridge, "Art in a State of Grace," p. 103.

49 Personal communication to the author.

50 Klaus Lankheit, *Das Triptychon als Pathosformel* (Heidelberg, 1959).

51 Quoted in Christov-Bakargiev, *William Kentridge*, p. 16.

52 Joseph Leo Koerner, "Tummelplatz," in M. K. Koerner, *William Kentridge*, pp. 126–27.

53 Sigmund Freud, "Remembering, Repeating, and Working Through" (1914), trans. by John Reddick, in Adam Phillips, ed., *The Penguin Freud Reader* (London, 2006), p. 399.

54 The definitive survey of the first ten of Kentridge's "Drawings for Projection" is Matthew Kentridge, *The Soho Chronicles: 10 Films by William Kentridge* (London, 2015).

55 Kentridge, "Landscape in a State of Siege," p. 107.

56 Quoted in M. Kentridge, *Soho Chronicles*, p. 57.

57 Kentridge, *Six Drawing Lessons*, p. 128.

58 Interview with David Sylvester recorded in *Francis Bacon*, BBC/Arts Council, 1967, directed by M. Gill.

59 Thomas Hobbes, *Leviathan*, ed. by Richard Tuck, rev. edn (Cambridge, 1996), pp. 88, 89, 111, 9.

60 Personal communication to the author.

61 *Iliad* 3.451, trans. by A. T. Murray (Homer, *The Iliad* [Cambridge, MA, 1924]).

62 Joseph Bédier, *The Romance of Tristan and Iseult*, trans. by Hilaire Belloc and Paul Rosenfeld (New York, 1945), p. 65; see Tony Tanner, *Adultery and the Novel* (Baltimore, 1979), pp. 30–33.

63 See p. 231 above.

64 I am indebted to Felipe Pereda for this insight.

65 Hobbes, *Leviathan*, pp. 87, 90.

66 William Kentridge, *Sheets of Evidence* (New York, 2009); published by Dieu Donné Press in an edition of twenty; I am grateful to Susan Gosin for discussing the project and lending me a precious copy of the portfolio. I am also grateful to Trent Barnes, whose unpublished paper "From Voyeurs to Participants: Medium and Meaning in William Kentridge's *Sheets of Evidence*" (2014), written for my and Margaret Koerner's graduate seminar on the artist, inspired the present exploration of Kentridge's sheets.

67 Kentridge, *Six Drawing Lessons*, p. 20.

68 George Moore, *Impressions and Opinions* (New York, 1913), p. 252.

69 Francis Bacon, *The New Organon*, ed. by Lisa Jardine and Michael Silverthorn (Cambridge, 2000), pp. 151–52; John Locke, *An Essay Concerning Human Understanding* (Oxford, 1975 [1689]), p. 101; discussed in Caroline Fowler, *The Art of Paper: From the Holy Land to the Americas* (New Haven, CT, 2019), pp. 20, 119.

70 Giorgio Vasari, *Lives of the Most Eminent Painters, Sculptors and Architects*, trans. by Gaston du C. de Vere, 10 vols (London, 1912–15), vol. 1, p. xxvi.

71 Kentridge, *Six Drawing Lessons*, p. 19.

72 Ibid., p. 20.

73 William Kentridge and Rosalind C. Morris, *Accounts and Drawings from Underground* (Calcutta, 2015).

74 Mark Rosenthal, ed., *William Kentridge: Five Themes* (San Francisco, 2009); on this synthesis of German, Russian, and South African history, see Maria Gough, "Kentridge's Nose," *October* 134 (2010), p. 15.

75 Franz Kafka, *The Trial*, trans. by Breon Mitchell (New York, 1998), pp. 3–4.

76 "William Kentridge and Vivienne Koorland in Conversation with Tamar Garb," in Tamar Garb, ed., *William Kentridge, Vivienne Koorland: Conversations in Letters and Lines* (Edinburgh, 2015), p. 138.

77 Kentridge, *Six Drawing Lessons*, p. 28.

78 Ibid., p. 3.

79 Ibid., pp. 14–15, 13.

80 Jacques Rancière, *Dissensus: On Politics and Aesthetics*, ed. and trans. by Steven Corcoran (London, 2012), pp. 45–48.

81 Stephanie Buck, *Die niederländischen Zeichnungen des 15. Jahrhunderts im Berliner Kupferstichkabinett* (Turnhout, 2001), pp. 197–206.

82 See p. 82 above.

83 Kentridge, *Six Drawing Lessons*, p. 10.

84 Plato, *The Republic* 514a; trans. by Allan Bloom (New York, 1968), p. 193.

85 Ibid., 516a (p. 195).

86 Kentridge, *Six Drawing Lessons*, pp. 6–11, 14.

87 Plato, *Republic* 514a (p. 193).

88 Kentridge, *Six Drawing Lessons*, p. 9.

89 Ibid., p. 11.

90 Francisco de Quevedo, "Alguacil del Parnaso [...]" (1620), quoted in Helmut Heidenreich, "Hieronymus Bosch in Some Literary Contexts," *Journal of the Warburg and Courtauld Institutes* 33, no. 1 (1970), p. 182; see p. 78 above.

91 Ernst Cassirer, *An Essay on Man* (New Haven, CT, 1944), p. 41.

92 Plato, *Republic* 516a–517a (p. 195).

93 Philostratus, *Imagines* 1.14, "Semele"; Hans Blumenberg, *Höhlenausgänge* (Frankfurt am Main, 1989), p. 42.

94 Kentridge, *Six Drawing Lessons*, p. 74.

95 Ibid., p. 18.

96 Ernst H. Gombrich, *Art and Illusion* (Princeton, NJ, 1960), p. 199.

97 Freud, "Remembering," p. 398.

98 Kentridge, *Six Drawing Lessons*, pp. 124–28.

99 https://www.kentridge.studio/listening-to-the-trees/ (accessed April 12, 2024).

100 Sigmund Freud, "Screen Memories" (1899), trans. by David McLintock, in Phillips, *Penguin Freud Reader*, p. 559.

101 Aristotle's lost dialogue comes via Cicero, *De natura deorum* 2.95: Jacob Bernays, *Die Dialoge des Aristoteles in ihrem Verhältnis zu seinen übrigen Werken* (Berlin, 1863), pp. 106–7; discussed in Blumenberg, *Höhlenausgänge*, p. 203.

102 Immanuel Kant, *Critique of Judgment* (1790), trans. by Werner S. Pluhar (Indianapolis, 1987), p. 197.

103 Friedrich Schiller, *On the Aesthetic Education of Man* (1794), ed. and trans. by Elizabeth M. Wilkinson and L. A. Willoughby (Oxford, 1967), pp. 107, 145 (original emphasis).

104 Friedrich Nietzsche, *"The Birth of Tragedy"* [1872] *and "The Case of Wagner"*, trans. by Walter Kaufmann (New York, 1967), p. 83.

105 Friedrich Nietzsche, *Sämtliche Werke (KSA)*, ed. by Giorgio Colli and Mazzino Montinari, 15 vols (Berlin, 1980), vol. 7: *Nachgelassene Fragmente 1869–74*, p. 199 (fragment 7 [156]) (original emphasis); also, Martin Heidegger, *Nietzsche*, trans. by David Farrell Krell (San Francisco, 1991), p. 154.

106 Karl Heinz Bohrer, *Suddenness: On the Moment of Aesthetic Appearance*, trans. by Ruth Crowley (New York, 1994), pp. 123–31.

107 Virgil, *Aeneid* 6.1–55; Dante, *Paradiso* 33.85–87; James Joyce, *Finnegans Wake* (New York, 1958), p. 628; Joseph Leo Koerner and Margaret Koster Koerner, "Whichever Page You Open: William Kentridge in New York," in Krauss, *William Kentridge*, p. 182.

108 Plato, *Republic* 517a (p. 196).

109 Ibid., 517d (p. 196).

110 Personal communication to the author.

111 Kentridge, *Six Drawing Lessons*, pp. 71–72.

112 Plato, *Republic* 516c–d (p. 195).

113 Freud, "Screen Memories," p. 549.

114 Kentridge, *Six Drawing Lessons*, pp. 15, 106.

115 Ibid., p. 83.

116 Thomas Mann, *Der Zauberberg*, 2 vols (Berlin, 1924), vol. 2, p. 629.

117 Ernst Jünger, "Einleitung," in Ferdinand Bucholtz, ed., *Der gefährliche Augenblick: Eine Sammlung von Bildern und Berichten* (Berlin, 1931), p. 16.

118 Kentridge, *Six Drawing Lessons*, pp. 83–84.

119 William James, review in "Psychological Literature," *The Psychological Review* 1 (1894), p. 199.

120 Josef Breuer and Sigmund Freud, "On the Psy-

chical Mechanism of Hysterical Phenomena" (1893), in *The Standard Edition of the Complete Psychological Works of Sigmund Freud*, ed. and trans. by James Strachey, 24 vols (London, 1953–1974), vol. 2 (1955), p. 6.

121 Sigmund Freud, *Beyond the Pleasure Principle*, trans. by James Strachey (New York, 1961), p. 30 (original emphasis).

122 Breuer and Freud, "On the Psychical Mechanism," p. 8.

123 Kentridge, *Six Drawing Lessons*, p. 84.

124 Dyzenhaus, *Hard Cases*, pp. 34–54, 146–64, 250–57; Richard L. Abel, *Politics by Other Means: Law in the Struggle Against Apartheid, 1980–1994* (New York, 1995), pp. 1–21.

125 Sydney Kentridge, "The Pathology of a Legal System: Criminal Justice in South Africa," *University of Pennsylvania Law Review* 128, no. 3 (1980), pp. 603, 604.

126 Ibid., p. 613, citing William Blackstone's *Commentaries on the Laws of England*.

127 Abel, *Politics*, p. 13.

128 S. Kentridge, "Pathology," p. 621.

129 Kentridge, *Six Drawing Lessons*, p. 84.

130 Sydney Kentridge, "Telling the Truth About the Law," *The South African Law Journal* 99, no. 4 (1982), p. 650.

131 Ibid.

132 Kentridge, *Six Drawing Lessons*, p. 84.

133 Ibid., pp. 92–93.

134 Freud, "Remembering," p. 396.

135 Sigmund Freud, *The Interpretation of Dreams* (1900), trans. by James Strachey (London, 1955), p. 536.

136 Aimee Dawson, "William Kentridge on Turning his Drawing into Films, Being Inspired by Dreams—and Catching Covid-19," *The Art Newspaper*, October 6, 2020.

137 M. Kentridge, *Soho Chronicles*, p. 177; see also W. Kentridge, "Fortuna," pp. 29–30.

138 Sigmund Freud, *Totem and Taboo*, trans. by James Strachey (New York, 1950), p. 95.

139 Kazimir Malevich, handout for the *Last Exhibition of Futurist Painting 0.10* (1915).

140 Benjamin H. D. Buchloh, "Seven Types of Obsolescence," in M. K. Koerner, *William Kentridge*, p. 178.

141 William Kentridge, "Felix in Exile: Geography of Memory" (1994), in Christov-Bakargiev, *William Kentridge*, p. 93.

142 William Kentridge, quoted in the gallery guide for *William Kentridge: Drawings for Projection* at The Drawing Center (New York, 1998).

143 Kentridge, "Felix in Exile," p. 96.

144 Kentridge, "Landscape in a State of Siege," p. 109.

145 Ibid., pp. 111, 110.

146 Ibid., p. 110.

147 William Wordsworth, "Ode: Intimations of Immortality from Recollections of Early Childhood" (1804), ll. 51–53.

148 Bertolt Brecht, "An die Nachgeborenen" (1939), ll. 7–8.

149 Kentridge, *Six Drawing Lessons*, p. 79.

150 William Kentridge and Angela Breidbach, *William Kentridge: Thinking Aloud* (Johannesburg, 2006), p. 36.

151 Kentridge, *Six Drawing Lessons*, p. 25.

152 Kentridge, "Refuse the Hour," lecture delivered 2012, p. iv; in Peter Galison, William Kentridge, Catherine Meyburgh, and Peter Miller, *The Refusal of Time* (Paris, 2013), unbound insert.

153 Kentridge, "Felix in Exile," p. 93.

154 Bruce R. Smith, "Scene," in Henry S. Turner, ed., *Early Modern Theatricality* (Oxford, 2013), p. 98; cited in Claire M. L. Bourne, *Typographies of Performance in Early Modern England* (Oxford, 2020), p. 142. I am grateful to Clio Takas and her "Staging Siege and Heroick Romance in William Davenant's *The Siege of Rhodes*" (unpublished MS, 2020), and to Stephen Greenblatt, for referring me to Bourne and for their insights into the early modern stage.

155 Pedro Calderón de la Barca, *Life's a Dream*, trans. by Michael Kidd (Boulder, CO, 2004), p. 132 (Act II, scene 2).

156 Walter Benjamin, *Origin of the German Trauerspiel*, trans. by Howard Eiland (Cambridge, MA, 2019), pp. 57–60.

157 Samuel Weber, "Taking Exception to Decision: Walter Benjamin and Carl Schmitt," *Diacritics* 22, no. 3/4 (1992): 5–18.

158 Benjamin, *Origin*, p. 81.

159 Ibid., p. 115.

Index

Note: Page numbers in italic type indicate illustrations.

German Democratic Republic (GDR). *See* East Germany

German Expressionism: Beckmann and, 169; in the Busch-Reisinger Museum, 169; feeling as guiding principle of, 175, 246; Fraenger and, 35; Kentridge and, 13, 247; Nazi responses to, 196, 203; and "primitive" art, 7, 246–47

Germanic Museum. *See* Busch-Reisinger Museum

German Modernism. *See* Modernism

Germany after World War II, 162–64

Germany between the wars: Beckmann's work and, 169, 204; economy of the mid-1920s, 178; emergency states in, 40–44, 178, 188, 193, 222; liberal humanism in, 23; political upheaval in, 178–79, 188, 191, 251; as a Reich, 41; religious upheaval in, 40–41; Warburg and, 3, 12; war veterans in, 178–79; and Weimar constitution, 40, 43–44. *See also* Nazi Germany

Gerung, Matthias, *Satire of Indulgences*, 122–23, *123*, 147

Ghent, 96–98

Ghirlandaio, Domenico, *Birth of John the Baptist*, 10–11, *11*

Gibson, Angus, 265, 315

Giles the Cantor, 38

Gillis, Pieter, 30

Gislebertus, *Eve*, 133–35, *133*

Glaser, Curt, 186

Gleichschaltung (coordination/synchronization), 193–96

Gnosticism, 41

God: all-seeing vision of, 50, 71–73, 77, 87, 91, 115, 127, 143, 171; artists likened to, 133, 189, 292; and creation, 37–38, 76, 82, 194; judgment/sovereignty of, 73, 93, 188–89; modern secular challenges to, 41, 188–89; state sovereignty grounded in, 57, 188. *See also* idolatry

Goebbels, Joseph, 155, 196

Goes, Hugo van der, 122

Goethe, Johann Wolfgang von, *Faust*, 157

Gogh, Vincent van, *Self-Portrait*, 203

Gogol, Nikolai, 233, 284, 303

Goiris, Greta, 284

Gombrich, Ernst, 14, 54, 106, 147–48, 287, 291, 298

Gombrich Lectures, Warburg Institute, 14

Góngora, Luis de, 78

Göpel, Barbara, 161

Göpel, Erhard, 161, 205

Gordimer, Nadine, 249

Göring, Hermann, 45, 161

Gosin, Susan, 276, 282

Gossaert, Jan, *Hercules and Deianeira*, 54, *55*, 56

Goya, Francisco, 220, 222; *The Colossus*, 268; *Fight with Cudgels*, 268

Gramme, Agnes de, 103

Granvelle, Antoine Perrenot de, 61, 63–65

Great Soviet Encyclopedia, 36

Greenberg, Clement, 237

Gregory, Saint, 103

Gregory I, Pope, 119

Grosz, George: *Die Besitzkröten* (The property toads), 257, *258*; *Nutcracker*, 208

Grünewald, Matthias, 7, 169, 179; *Isenheim Altarpiece*, 28

Guevara, Diego de, 62, 72

Guevara, Felipe de, 62, 66, 72, 77

Guicciardini, Ludovico, 62

Habsburg rule, 48, 66, 73–74, 85, 91–92, 96

Hameel, Alart du, 82, 91; *War Elephant* (after Hieronymus Bosch), 100, *101*

·Hammons, David, *Phat Free*, 209

Handspring Puppet Company, 283

Hani, Chris, 215, 321

Harnack, Adolf von, 41

Harvard Art Museums, Cambridge, Massachusetts, 168, 173–74, *173*, 203, 206, 208, 246

Harvard Natural History Museum, Cambridge, Massachusetts, 207

Harvard University, 22–24

Heaney, Seamus, 230

Heckel, Erich, 7, 246–47, 249; *To the Convalescent Woman*, 208, 246–47, 250, *plate 23*

Heesch, Daan van, 125

Hegel, G.W.F., 220

Heidegger, Martin, 23, 28, 44, 155

Henry III of Nassau, 57–59, 64

Henry II of Nassau, 84–85

Henry of Selles, 38

Herbert, Zbigniew, "Report from a Besieged City," 231

heresy: in Germany between the wars, 40–41; in the Netherlands in sixteenth century, 65; Sigüenza and, 77–78, 123

Hertz, Mary, 3

Heyden, Pieter van der, engraving after Pieter Bruegel the Elder, *Big Fish Eat Little Fish*, 66, *67*

Hiemer, Ernst, *The Poison Mushroom*, 194, *195*

Hieronymites, 79

Himmler, Heinrich, 162

history: Benjamin's conception of, 19, 230–31; Fraenger's approach to, 34, 36; interpretations of Bosch in context of, 112–15, 123–25, 128; Kiefer's engagement with, 236–37; Marx's dynamic conception of, 219, 265; South Africa's reckoning with, 206, 216, 220, 224, 322; sovereignty (decisive action) in relation to, 176–77, 189; as theme and process for Kentridge, 206, 213–16, 220, 222, 224, 233, 248, 253, 255, 258, 277, 281, 296, 304, 317–19, 322–24, 327; as theme in Bosch's works, 89, 94,

99, 103, 128–29; threats to, 19–20; written by the victors, 20, 216, 220, 232. *See also* temporality

Hitler, Adolf: American antagonism toward, 207; anti-Semitism of, 23, 31, 36, 46; and art, 161, 189, 196, 203, 209, 248; and art historical scholarship, 14; politics and statecraft of, 15, 18, 19, 40–42, 44–45, 148–49, 151, 155, 162, 188, 193–94; and World War II, 16, 158–59, 207, 231

Hobbes, Thomas, 45, 65–66, 150–52, 266, 270; *Leviathan*, 260, *261*

Höch, Hannah, *Dada-Rundschau*, 191

Hogarth, William, 220

Holbein, Hans, the Elder, 122, 169

Hollanda, Francesco de, *Four Dialogues on Painting*, 99–100

Holocaust, 155, 157, 162–64

Hopi peoples. *See* Pueblo peoples

Horace, 75

humanism, 31, 292

Hus, Jan, 112

hyle (matter), 82–83, 89

hysteria, 4–5

Ibsen, Henrik, *The Master Builder*, 8

iconoclasm: artists' response to, 116, 122; Bosch associated with, 125, 127; controversy over, 120, 122; and enemy-friend distinction, 32, 117–18, 120; Malevich and, 318; meanings/motivations of, 32, 62, 118, 120; Protestant, 32, 61–62, 84, 117–22, 249. *See also* idolatry

iconography: of Bosch's *Adoration of the Magi*, 106; defined, 28; Gombrich and, 287; iconology in relation to, 23; Panofsky and, 24, 27–30; transparent, 32. *See also* symbols/symbolism

iconology: defined, 5, 23; Fraenger and, 34; Panofsky and, 23, 27, 29–32; Warburg and, 5, 23. *See also* symbols/symbolism

idolatry: art and, 115; Bosch and, 109–10, 114–15, 125, 127, 142, 144–46; Catholics and, 119, 127; criticism of, 117–18, 120, 147; iconoclasm aimed at, 61, 117–20; Israelites and, 73, 117–18; lust associated with, 119, 132, 142; Turks and, 107, 127. *See also* iconoclasm; imagining/image-making

illusion: art and, 115, 172, 220–22, 278, 297, 300; Bosch and, 114, 287; dreams and, 300, 315; idols as, 110; Kentridge and, 288, 298–99; motion pictures and, 216; in Plato's cave allegory, 295–300; political uses of, 300; reality vs., 204, 220–22, 226, 296, 300, 327; Satan's/Antichrist's trafficking in, 106, 115, 287. *See also* imagination; imagining/image-making

imagination: artists', 278, 299; viewers', 13–14, 17, 103, 147, 291, 298. *See also* illusion; imagining/image-making

imagining/image-making: Bosch and, 37, 62, 95, 127–28, 143, 145, 197; Jan van Eyck's *Ghent Altarpiece and*, 98; Kentridge and, 248, 278, 324–25; in sixteenth-century German art, 122. *See also* idolatry; illusion; imagination

IMT. *See* International Military Tribunal

indulgences, 103, 110–12, 116–17, 122

inkpot, fight over, 90

Inquisition, 38–39, 64–65, 77

insanity: art and, 8; Warburg and, 2–8

Institute for Advanced Study, Princeton University, 22, 23

Institute of Fine Arts, New York University, 23

Internal Security Act (South Africa, 1982), 256

International Military Tribunal (IMT), 47

Iron Guard, 153

Isabella I, Queen of Spain, 92

Isherwood, Christopher, 198–99

Istanbul Biennial (1999), 294

ius publicum Europaeum (European public law), 46, 47, 57, 65, 112, 152

James, William, 306

Janet, Pierre, 306

Jerome, Saint, 79–81, 114, 145, 292

Jerusalem, 14, 93–94, 102, 107

Jews and Judaism: anti-Semitism directed at, 102; Bosch and, 42, 48–50; Bosch's depiction of, 102–3, 105–6; and conversion to Christianity, 42, 44, 48; dangers of, 194–95; as enemies, 31, 32, 44–45, 50, 52, 102–3, 105–7; Nazi persecution of, 23, 31, 36–37, 44–46, 50–51, 155, 159–63, 194, 204; Kentridge and, 219; looting of art from, 161, 163; Modernism associated with, 202–3; Netherlandish persecution of, 48–49; Nolde's hatred of, 196, 209; Panofsky and, 22–23, 31–32, 51–52, 149; Schmitt's hatred of, 32, 44–46, 50–51, 149, 151, 194–95; and sieges of Jerusalem, 14, 93–94, 102; Warburg and, 3, 10, 12. *See also* Holocaust

Johannesburg, South Africa: discovery of gold in, 297, 315, 324; Kentridge's animated film on, 252–70

Johannesburg Art Museum, 218

John IV of Nassau-Siegen, 57

John the Baptist, 85

John the Evangelist, 85. *See also* Revelation, Book of

Jonas, Hans, 41

Jonson, Ben, 82

Joyce, James, *Finnegans Wake*, 301

joyous entries, 98–99

Juana of Castile, 92

jubilees, 111–12

Jud Süß (film), 37

Junction Avenue Theatre Company, Johannesburg, 222

INDEX 357

Moore, George, 274

morality/ethics: decision-making and, 127, 131, 135, 137–38, 143, 149–50, 152, 205; drawing medium and, 277; Kantian conception of, 130–31; lust and, 135; the momentary/exceptional as essence of, 144; stories/art as vehicle for expression of, 130–32, 135, 138, 140; of viewer-art relationship, 18

More, Thomas, 30

Morris, Rosalind, 280

Morrison, Toni, 22

Moses, 73, 82, 102, 111, 117–18, 125

Mozart, Wolfgang Amadeus, *The Magic Flute*, 233, 283, 284

Murray, Gilbert, 289

Museum of Modern Art, New York, 284

Mussolini, Benito, 22

Muybridge, Eadweard, 140

Napoleon, 16, 78, 229

Nationalgalerie, Berlin, 174, 193, 204, 206, 209

National Party (South Africa), 218, 227, 229, 321

National Union of Miners, 280

National Unity Government (South Africa), 321

Native Lands Act (South Africa, 1913), 218

natural history, 214, 281, 327

Nazi Germany: and art, 14, 193, 195–203, 209, 257, 287; art looted by, 163, 165; attempts at total control by, 193–96; Beckmann and, 192, 193, 203–5, 317; Benjamin and, 19; book-burning by, 44, 110, 323; Fraenger in, 36–37; Jews persecuted by, 23, 31, 36–37, 44–46, 50–51, 155, 159–63, 194, 204; Jünger and, 154–62; racial theories of, 31, 155, 194, 196, 200, 202; Schmitt and, 37, 42–47, 149, 194; as Third Reich, 41, 46, 193; Warburg and, 6; war strategy of, 158. *See also* Holocaust

Nedelkovich, Brashich, and Kuharich (attributed to), *Pyramid of Capitalist System*, 265–66, *266*

Netherlandish painting: art market for, 85; Last Judgments in, 93; Panofsky's lectures on, 24–33; scholarly study of, 78; symbolism in, 26–28

Netherlands: art's flourishing in, 24; Burgundian rule over, 48, 56–58, 91–92, 96–98, 101; Duke of Alba in, 62–65, 70; iconoclasm in, 61–62; Jews in, 48–50; Nassau counts in, 57–58; rebellion in, against Spain, 61–65, 70, 74; religious reform movement in, 79

Neumann, Israel Bar, 180

New Objectivity (*Neue Sachlichkeit*), 187

Nietzsche, Friedrich, 23, 41, 192, 300

Nijinsky, Vaslav, 6

Nolde, Emil, 169, 196, 200, 209; *Mulattin* (*Woman of Mixed Race*, formerly *The Mulatto* and *Mulatto*), 200, *202*, 208–9

Norton Lectures. *See* Charles Eliot Norton Lectures

nudity, representations of, 132–37

Nuremberg trials, 19, 46–49, 51, 65, 148–50, 152–53, 162

Office of Military Government (OMGUS) [United States], 163–64

Office of Strategic Services (OSS) [United States], 162

Office of War Information (United States), 163

ogenblick. See Augenblick ("blink of an eye")

Operation Reinhardt, 157

Oppenheimer, J. Robert, 23

Order of the Golden Fleece, 59, 65, 92

Ovid, *Metamorphoses*, 70

Pacheco, Francisco, 78

Pan-Africanist Congress, 322

Panofsky, Erwin: and Bosch, 24, 32–33, 147; Jewish heritage of, 22–23, 31–32, 51–52, 149; Norton Lectures by, 19, 22, 24–33; and phenomenology, 28–29; scholarship of, 23, 29–33, 249; student of, 106; US career of, 23–24

paper and papermaking, 276–79, 282–83

Pappenheim, Bertha, 6

Paul, Saint, 115–16

Paul II, Pope, 111

Paul V, Pope, 112

Peabody Museum of Archaeology and Ethnography, Cambridge, Massachusetts, 207

Penrose, Roger and Lionel, 68

Petrarch, 31

phenomenology, 28–29

Philip, Lotte Brand, 106

Philip II, King of Spain, 58, 62, 65, 70–75, 77, 125, 127, 147

Philip the Fair, 48, 58, 59, 85, 91–93, 96, 109

Philip the Good, 25, 58, 96–98

photography, 243–45, 251, 305–6

Piano, Renzo, 168, 173

Picabia, Francis, 243

Picasso, Pablo, 172, 246

Pierneef, Jacobus Hendrik, 255, 322

Piper, Reinhard, 35

Pisano, Andrea, 135

Plato, 82, 150; allegory of the cave in *Republic*, 295–304, 310, 318, 326, 327; *Parmenides*, 144

play. *See* aesthetic play

Pleydenwurff, Wilhelm, *God the Father and Yle* (with Michael Wolgemut), 82, *83*

Plievier, Theodor, 159

Pliny the Elder, 76

poetry. *See* art; *poiesis*

poiesis (art, creation), 22–24, 31, 56, 288, 292, 300, 304–5

Photo Credits

© Akademie der bildenden Künste / Erich Lessing / Art Resource, NY (plate 10)

© Album / Art Resource, NY (fig. 7, fig. 102)

© Author (fig. 1, fig. 8, fig. 9, fig. 10, fig. 15, fig. 16, fig. 21, fig. 22, fig. 23, fig. 25, fig. 26, fig. 27, fig. 30, fig. 33, fig. 34, fig. 37, fig. 41, fig. 55, fig. 56, fig. 60, fig. 63, fig. 78)

© Bayerische Staatsbibliothek, Munich (fig. 13)

© Bodleian Libraries (plate 17)

© bpk Bildagentur (fig. 69)

© bpk Bildagentur / Gemäldegalerie, Staatliche Museen zu Berlin / Art Resource, NY (plate 6, plate 7)

© bpk Bildagentur / Kunstammlung Nordrhein-Westfalen, Düsseldorf / Art Resource, NY (fig. 44)

© bpk Bildagentur / Kupferstichkabinett, Staatliche Museen zu Berlin / Art Resource, NY (fig. 96)

© bpk Bildagentur / Nationalgalerie, Staatliche Museen zu Berlin / Art Resource, NY (plate 21)

© bpk Bildagentur / Private Collection   Art Resource, NY (plate 19)

© bpk Bildagentur / Zentralarchiv, Staatliche Museen zu Berlin / Art Resource, NY (fig. 58, fig. 59)

© Cameraphoto Arte, Venice / Art Resource, NY (fig. 39)

© CNAC/MNAM, Dist. RMN-Grand Palais / Art Resource, NY (fig. 73)

© Daan van Heesch (fig. 29)

© DeA Picture Library / Art Resource, NY (plate 14, fig. 20)

© Erich Lessing / Art Resource, NY (fig. 14, fig. 43)

© Estate of George Grosz 2024 / Licensed by VAGA at Artists Rights Society (ARS), NY (fig. 76)

© Graphische Sammlung Albertina / HIP / Art Resource, NY (fig. 28)

© Groeningemuseum, Bruges / HIP / Art Resource, NY (plate 11)

© The Henry Barber Trust, The Barber Institute of Fine Arts, University of Birmingham / Bridgeman Images (fig. 6)

© Hessisches Landesmuseum Darmstadt / HIP / Art Resource, NY (plate 15)

© His Majesty King Charles III, 2024 / Royal Collection Trust / Bridgeman Images (fig. 11)

© Kunstmuseum Basel (fig. 54)

© The Morgan Library and Museum, New York / Art Resource, NY (fig. 36)

© Museo Lázaro Galdiano, Madrid / HIP / Art Resource, NY (plate 5)

© Museo Nacional del Prado / Art Resource, NY (plate 3, plate 13, fig. 12)

© Museo Nacional del Prado / Album / Art Resource, NY (plate 2, plate 12, plate 16, fig. 38)

© Museo Nacional del Prado / HIP / Art Resource, NY (plate 1, plate 8)

© The Museum of Modern Art / Licensed by SCALA / Art Resource, NY (plate 20, fig. 45, fig. 46, fig. 47, fig. 48, fig. 49, fig. 50, fig. 51, fig. 52)

© Museum voor Schone Kunsten, Ghent / HIP / Art Resource, NY (plate 4)

© National Gallery, London / Art Resource, NY (fig. 18)

© Nolde Stiftung Seebüll (fig. 62)

© Pond5 (fig. 61)

© President and Fellows of Harvard College (plate 18, plate 23, fig. 62)

© President and Fellows of Harvard College / Katya Kallsen (fig. 42)

© Private Collection / HIP / Art Resource (fig. 57)

© Real Monasterio de San Lorenzo de El Escorial, Madrid / HIP / Art Resource, NY (plate 9, fig. 17)

© RMN-Grand Palais / Art Resource, NY (fig. 5, fig. 92)

© Saint Louis Art Museum (fig. 53)

© Scala / Art Resource, NY (fig. 4, fig. 31, fig. 32)

© Sheldon Museum of Art, University of Nebraska-Lincoln (fig. 40)

© Staatliche Museen zu Berlin, Zentralarchiv (fig. 64)

© Städel Museum, Frankfurt am Main / HIP / Art Resource, NY (fig. 19)

© SZ Photo / Bridgeman Images (fig. 81)

© Tomasz Samek / Stadtmuseum Münster (fig. 24)

© The Trustees of the British Museum / Art Resource, NY (fig. 35)

© The Warburg Institute (fig. 2, fig. 3)

©William Kentridge Studio (plate 24, plate 25, plate 26, plate 27, plate 28, plate 29, plate 30, plate 31, plate 32, fig. 65, fig. 66, fig. 67, fig. 68, fig. 70, fig. 71, fig. 72, fig. 75, fig. 77, fig. 79, fig. 80, fig. 82, fig. 83, fig. 84, fig. 85, fig. 86, fig. 87, fig. 88, fig. 89, fig. 90, fig. 91, fig. 93, fig. 94, fig. 95, fig. 97, fig. 98, fig. 99, fig. 100, fig. 101, fig. 103)

© William Kentridge Studio and Robert Loder Collection (fig. 74)

© William Kentridge Studio and Wits Art Museum (plate 22)

E. H. Gombrich Lecture Series

Joseph Leo Koerner, *Art in a State of Siege*

K.J.P. Lowe, *Provenance and Possession: Acquisitions from the Portuguese Empire in Renaissance Italy*

Philip Hardie, *Celestial Aspirations: Classical Impulses in British Poetry and Art*

Jonathan Bate, *How the Classics Made Shakespeare*

Marjorie Curry Woods, *Weeping for Dido: The Classics in the Medieval Classroom*